THE STUDY OF ANTHROPOLOGY

THE STUDY OF ANTHROPOLOGY

David E. Hunter
Southern Connecticut State College

Phillip Whitten
Harvard University

Harper & Row, Publishers
New York   Hagerstown
San Francisco   London

THE STUDY OF ANTHROPOLOGY

Library of Congress Cataloging in Publication Data

Hunter, David E.
    The study of anthropology.

    Includes index.
    1. Anthropology.   I. Whitten, Phillip, joint
author. II. Title.
GN25.H86   301.2   75-41385
ISBN 0-06-047093-3

Produced by Ken Burke & Associates
Text and Cover designer: Christy Butterfield
Copyeditor: Sandy Craig
Illustrator: Barbara Hack
Photo researcher: Audrey Ross
Compositor: Applied Typographic Systems
Printer: Kingsport Press

Credits

Photographs

Cover photograph Raghubir Singh, Woodfin Camp & Associates

2 Cornell Capa, Magnum Photos, Inc.

3 Stanley Washburn, Anthro-Photo

4 The New York Public Library, Rare Book Division

6 The Bettmann Archive

7 Culver Pictures

8,9 The Bettmann Archive

10 Robert F. Sisson © National Geographic Society

11 The Society of Antiquaries of London

12 Courtesy of The American Museum of Natural History

15 Parekh, Magnum Photos, Inc.

16 Wide World Photos

19 Napoleon Chagnon, Anthro-Photo

22 Marc & Evelyne Bernheim, Woodfin Camp & Associates

23 Ralph Solecki

25 The Bettmann Archive; Painting by Lucas Cranach

26 Culver Pictures

27,28 The Bettmann Archive

33 Wide World Photos

35 Elliott Erwitt, Magnum Photos, Inc.

36 U.S. Department of Agriculture

40 The Peabody Museum of Natural History, Yale University

44 Left: R. Campbell, reproduced by permission of Professor P. V. Tobias, Department of Anatomy, University of Witwatesrand Medical School, Johannesburg, South Africa Right: R. G. Klomfass, reproduced by permission of Professor P. V. Tobias

46,56 Lowie Museum of Anthropology, University of California, Berkeley; photos by Audrey Ross

57 Irven DeVore, Anthro-Photo

59 Musée de l'Homme, Paris

68 Bernard Pierre Wolff, Magnum Photos, Inc.

70 The Bettmann Archive

72 Left: David E. Hunter Right: Edward O. Henry

75 George B. Schaller, Bruce Coleman, Inc.

76 Leanne T. Nash

80 Marjorie Shoslak, Anthro-Photo

81 Bill Owens

82 La Documentation Française, Paris

83 Service Info Sénégal and La Documentation Française, Paris

84 Wide World Photos

87 F. S. Vidal

89 Henri Cartier-Bresson, Magnum Photos, Inc.

91 United Press International Photo

96 J. M. Bishop, Bruce Coleman, Inc.

97 Courtesy of The American Museum of Natural History

99 Steve Gaulin, Anthro-Photo

101 Top: Harry F. Harlow, University of Wisconsin Primate Laboratory Bottom: José M. R. Delgado

103 Leanne T. Nash

104 Irven DeVore, Anthro-Photo

108 George B. Schaller, Bruce Coleman, Inc.

109 Dr. Helmut Albrecht, Bruce Coleman, Inc.

111 Irven DeVore and William Jones, Anthro-Photo

113 Wide World Photos

114 Cornell Capa, Magnum Photos, Inc.

118 a. Carl Frank b. Marc and Evelyne Bernheim, Woodfin Camp & Associates c. Jean Claude Lejeune, Stock, Boston d. Audrey Ross e. Carl Frank f. Michol Heron, Woodfin Camp & Associates

119 g. Werner Bischol, Magnum Photos, Inc.

121 Courtesy of The American Museum of Natural History

122 Irven DeVore, Anthro-Photo

125 Courtesy of The American Museum of Natural History

128 Leonard Freed, Magnum Photos, Inc.

131 Cornell Capa, Magnum Photos, Inc.

134 a. Marc Riboud, Magnum Photos, Inc. b. Ken Heyman

135 c. Cornell Capa, Magnum Photos, Inc. d. Carl Frank e. Ken Heyman f. Erich Hartman, Magnum Photos, Inc.

136 g. George Rodger, Magnum Photos, Inc. h. Ken Heyman i. Henri Cartier-Bresson, Magnum Photos, Inc. j. Ken Heyman k. Rene Burri, Magnum Photos, Inc.

138 Rene Burri, Magnum Photos, Inc.

139 Bernard Pierre Wolff, Magnum Photos, Inc.

141 Edward O. Henry

142 Ken Heyman

146 Bill Owens

147 Bill Owens

149 Napoleon Chagnon, Anthro-Photo

150 Top left: Burk Uzzle, Magnum Photos, Inc. Bottom left: Abigail Heyman, Magnum Photos, Inc. Right: Burk Uzzle, Magnum Photos, Inc.

151 Bob Adelman, Magnum Photos, Inc.

152 Richard N. Henderson

154 Ken Heyman

155 Martin Etter, Anthro-Photo

156 Ken Heyman

157 Ken Heyman

162 Marilyn Silverstone, Magnum Photos, Inc.

163 Courtesy of The National Trust for Scotland

166 Helmut Albrecht, Bruce Coleman, Inc.

169 Press Information Bureau, Government of India

173 Micha Bar-Am, Magnum Photos, Inc.

174 Richard Pipes, Nancy Palmer Agency

181 Rene Burri, Magnum Photos, Inc.

185 Charles M. Hagen, Stock, Boston

186 United Press International Photo

188 Ken Heyman

189 Irven DeVore, Anthro-Photo

191 Bill Owens

193 Photograph Courtesy of Museum of the American Indian, Heye Foundation

195 Courtesy of The American Museum of Natural History

196 Majorie Shostak, Anthro-Photo

199 Irven DeVore, Anthro-Photo

201,202 Wide World Photos

205 Rada and Neville Dyson-Hudson

208 Bill Owens

209 Lowie Museum of Anthropology, University of California, Berkeley

211 George Peter Murdock

213 Denver Public Library, Western History Department

215 The Bettmann Archive

216 Bob Fitch, Black Star

222 Rosen, Magnum Photos, Inc.

226 Marilyn Silverstone, Magnum Photos, Inc.

230 Bob Adelman, Magnum Photos, Inc.

231 Courtesy of United Nations

233 Illustration by Alberto Beltran from WORLD OF THE MAYA by Victor Von Hagen. Copyright © 1960 by Alberto Beltran. Reprinted by arrangement with The New American Library, Inc., New York, N.Y.

236 Library of Congress

239 Georg Gerster, Rapho Guillumette Pictures

242 Courtesy of United Nations

245 Irven DeVore, Anthro-Photo

250 Wide World Photos

252 Cornell Capa, Magnum Photos, Inc.

254 Elliott Erwitt, Magnum Photos, Inc.

255 Alex Webb, Magnum Photos, Inc.

257 National Museums of Canada

261 Wide World Photos

263 George Rodger, Magnum Photos, Inc.

264 United Press International Photo

267 Rene Burri, Magnum Photos, Inc.

268,270 George Rodger, Magnum Photos, Inc.

272 Alex Webb, Magnum Photos, Inc.

274 Inge Morath, Magnum Photos, Inc.

275 Irven DeVore and William James, Anthro-Photo

277 Library of Congress

279 George Rodger, Magnum Photos, Inc.

281 Leopold Pospisil

285 United Press International Photo

287 George Rodger, Magnum Photos, Inc.

290 Wide World Photos

292 Tony Howarth, Woodfin Camp & Associates

294 Ken Heyman

295 Pitt Rivers Museum, University of Oxford

297 Courtesy of Alexander Marshack

300 The Museum of Primitive Art

303 Top: Courtesy of The American Museum of Natural History   Bottom: Martie and Stewart Guthrie

305 David Maybury-Lewis, Anthro-Photo

307 Courtesy of The American Museum of Natural History

310 Marjorie Shostak, Anthro-Photo

312 Edward O. Henry

314 The Bettmann Archive

316 Sergio Larrain, Magnum Photos, Inc.

317 United Press International Photo

319 Wide World Photos

320 Fred Eggan

321 Colin Turnbull

325 Bruno Barbey, Magnum Photos, Inc.

327 Audrey Ross

328 Raghubir Singh, Woodfin Camp & Associates

331 Henri Cartier-Bresson, Magnum Photos, Inc.

333 Joshua Freiwald

334 Martie and Stewart Guthrie

338 Ian Berry, Magnum Photos, Inc.

339 John Nance/Panamin, Magnum Photos, Inc.

341 Wide World Photos

342 The Hamlyn Group Picture Library

343 Ken Heyman

345 Hiroji Kubota, Magnum Photos, Inc.

346 Wide World Photos

349 Stock, Boston

353 Ian Berry, Magnum Photos, Inc.

356 K. Gunnar, Bruce Coleman, Inc.

360 Marc Riboud, Magnum Photos, Inc.

361 Carl Frank

363 Wide World Photos

366 Donald McCullin, Magnum Photos, Inc.

369 Richard Harrington, Camera Press, Ltd., London

371,372 Richard N. Henderson

375 Bruno Barbey, Magnum Photos, Inc.

377 Top: United Press International Photo Bottom: Brian Brake, Magnum Photos, Inc.

380 Bruno Barbey, Magnum Photos, Inc.

381 Wide World Photos

385 Photograph Courtesy of Museum of the American Indian, Heye Foundation

387 Colin Turnbull

388,389 Klaus Friedrich-Koch

392 United Press International Photo

395 Wide World Photos

396 Courtesy of United Nations, T. Chen

398 Top and bottom: Napoleon Chagnon, Anthro-Photo

399,400 Napoleon Chagnon, Anthro-Photo

405 Wide World Photos

408 Ken Heyman

409 United Press International Photo

411 Ministry of Tourism, Mexico

415 Top and bottom: Nancy Geilhufe

417 Top and bottom: Shirley Fiske

420 United Press International Photo

421 Jeffrey Blankfort, BBM Associates

422 Ernest Lowe, BBM Associates

425 Louise C. Brown

448 Marc Riboud, Magnum Photos, Inc.

429 George Rodger, Magnum Photos, Inc.

435 Irving Louis Horowitz

438 Wide World Photos

439 Mrs. B. Prynn, London

441,443 George Rodger, Magnum Photos, Inc.

448–465 passim David E. Hunter

468–484 passim Richard B. Lee, Anthro-Photo

487–503 passim F. S. Vidal

506–522 passim Martie and Stewart Guthrie

524–543 passim Richard N. Henderson

546–559 passim Jeff Russell

Line Drawings

Endpapers "Languages of the World" from Spencer, Robert F. and Elden Johnson, *Atlas for Anthropology*, 2nd ed, William C. Brown Company, Publishers. Used with permission from the authors.

Figure 2-7 From Proceedings of the National Academy of Sciences.

Figure 2-8 Modified from Dr. A. L. Zihlman's drawing, 1967. Used with permission of Dr. A. L. Zihlman.

Figure 2-9 Reprinted by permission from Bernard Campbell, *Human Evolution* (Chicago, Aldine Publishing Company); Copyright © 1966, 1974 by Bernard C. Campbell.

Figure 2-18 Reprinted by permission from H. L. Movius, "The Lower Palaeolithic Cultures of Southern and Eastern Asia," *Transactions of the American Philosophical Society*, Vol. 38, Pt. 4 (1948)

Figure 7-1 From "The Origin of Speech" by Charles F. Hockett in *Scientific American*. Copyright © 1960 by Scientific American, Inc. All rights reserved. Reprinted by permission of W. H. Freeman and Company for Scientific American, Inc.

Figure 7-3 Reprinted by permission from Philip Liebeman, *On the Origins of Language* © 1975 by Macmillan Publishing Co. Inc.

Figure 10-1 From Jack R. Harlan, "Agricultural Origins: Centers and Noncenters," *Science*, Vol. 174, October 29, 1971, p. 472. Reprinted by permission.

Figure 10-2 From Harris, Marvin, *Culture, People and Nature* © 1971, 1975 by Thomas Y. Crowell Co., Inc. Reprinted with permission of the publisher.

Figure 10-3 From Hammond, Peter B., *An Introduction to Social and Cultural Anthropology* © 1971 by Macmillan Publishing Co. Reprinted by permission of the publisher.

Preface

The purpose of a liberal arts education is to inform students about the nature of the world as we know it, teach them ways of thinking about the world as we conceive it, discipline them as critical thinkers, while at the same time provide them with the intellectual equipment that will enable them to open their minds so that they can contemplate new concepts, ideas, and "facts" as these become available. In the end, this boils down to educating an enlightened citizenry.

Anthropology has a critical contribution to make in this process. Very few students who take undergraduate courses in anthropology will go on to become professional anthropologists. But quite possibly their introduction to anthropology will be a cornerstone in their liberal arts education. Many anthropologists have made this point. They argue that anthropology, specializing as it does in the study of remote and "foreign" peoples, is an ideal vehicle for showing the amazing variety of ways of life, how culturally relative world views are, how each society accepts its world view as "truth," how damaging this perspective can be in a rapidly changing world, and how liberating it feels to free oneself from the bonds of such ethnocentric thinking.

We believe, however, that anthropology has something much more subtle and, ultimately, more profound to contribute to a liberal arts education. In this respect we would argue that it is useful to conceive of anthropology not only as an academic discipline, but also as an intrinsically interesting and pragmatically useful *perspective.* The purpose, then, of an introductory course in anthropology is to provide students with an anthropological perspective that will be useful to them both in their personal lives and in their consideration of larger issues of concern to all humanity.

The Study of Anthropology is meant to be an introduction to college anthropology. It treats the four divisions of anthropology—prehistoric archaeology, physical anthropology, cultural anthropology, and linguistics—and the major topical areas within each subdiscipline, and it presents key concepts and personalities. In presenting the processes and principles of anthropology, the book has taken an eclectic approach, drawing on a wide variety of research studies and many different theoretical approaches—cultural ecology, evolutionism, historical particularism, diffusionism, functionalism, French structuralism, structural-functionalism, etc.

Features of the Text

The Study of Anthropology is the first anthropology textbook in which the entire structure—both the structure of the book as a whole and the structure of each chapter—has been carefully thought through and designed both to reflect and teach the unique anthropological perspective.

Part I consists of three introductory chapters. Chapter 1 is unique in itself in its presentation of the anthropological paradigm. Chapter 2, "Human Biological and Cultural Evolution," presents biological and cultural evolution in one chapter in an integrated form: the processes of evolution are shown to be identical in both realms (involution and general evolution) but the mechanisms, of course, are different. In Chapter 3, "The Evolution of Social Forms," the concept of adaptation is used to generate a model of the evolution of social forms, with the adaptive features of each form carefully explored and explained.

Part II, "Biology and Culture" also consists of three chapters. Chapter 6 presents an in-depth consideration of the biological and sociocultural dimensions to human sexuality that goes far beyond any such discussion in any other textbook. And, because the book is organized around the anthropological paradigm, because that paradigm is inherently evolutionary in perspective, and because the central thrust of an evolutionary perspective is a dynamic approach stressing adaptation—there is no awkward chapter trying to present the myriad of idiosyncratic taxonomic approaches to the concept of race. Rather, the issue of human variation is dealt with in the context of human adaptation, reflecting the most modern trend among human biologists to abandon the static classificatory approach in favor of a consideration of adaptive processes.

Part III, "Topics in Cultural Anthropology," consists of eight chapters covering communication, social organization, economic anthropology, political anthropology, control of behavior, belief systems and psychological anthropology. Chapter 7 integrates and conceptually unifies in a holistic manner verbal and nonverbal communication, topics usually treated in separate chapters. In all chapters dealing with sociocultural anthropology, the relevant data from physical anthropology and archaeology are introduced. Thus physical anthropology and archaeology are threads winding their way through the entire textbook—not isolated in a wasteland after having been given their due.

Part IV, "Issues in the Contemporary World," contains five chapters. Chapter 17 discusses peace and conflict as ends of a continuum of sociocultural behavior. Where most textbooks focus on warfare and treat it as a form of social pathology, this chapter explores the systematic relationships between various levels of aggression and peaceful behavior, and shows the steps that must be taken to convert the former into the latter. Chapter 19 is a full discussion of the social and political contexts in which anthropology developed as a discipline and in which it currently is active. The ethical issues that arise from these considerations are explored through the use of extended case examples at a much greater depth than is usual in introductory texts.

Finally, Part V contains five full chapter *case studies.*

The groups described in the case study chapters have been carefully selected to represent diverse levels of sociocultural evolution, especially with regard to subsistence strategies. They provide students with extended bodies of data against which they can test the theoretical materials they learn in the other sections of the book.

In creating *The Study of Anthropology* we emphasized making the book *readable*—an effective and enjoyable vehicle for learning. Thus, great attention was devoted to the book's structure, to writing style and to providing numerous case examples. The textual material was carefully coordinated with an extensive graphics program including photographs, maps, figures, models, tables, charts and diagrams which both illustrate and add to the text. Unusually long and comprehensive caption materials—frequently self-contained essays—amplify and complement text materials. Finally, each chapter ends with a summary and an annotated bibliography. The glossary, located at the back of the book, contains more than 600 definitions.

Because of the book's unique structure, *The Study of Anthropology* can easily be used in courses of various lengths; in one semester and two quarter-length courses as well as in the more usual two semester sequence.

The Study of Anthropology will be revised and updated regularly, not only in response to changes in the discipline but in response to the feedback we receive from both instructors and students who have used the book. To facilitate this feedback we have inserted a Response Card at the back of the book. Please take a few minutes to fill out the card and mail it in to Harper and Row.

Acknowledgements

As with any project of this scope, there are many people who have contributed, both directly and indirectly, to its creation. The thirteen contributors to the book, of course, must go at the top of our list for their fine work and for their patience in putting up with a demanding schedule. A debt of gratitude is also owed to the students in David Hunter's classes, who participated in the classroom testing and evaluation of all the chapters in the book, and whose criticisms helped bring about several important revisions. Anthony Leeds (Boston University), Malcolm McFee (Univ. of Oregon), Martin K. Nickels (Illinois State Univ.) and Keith Otterbein (S.U.N.Y., Buffalo) reviewed individual chapters and provided cogent insights and valuable feedback that helped greatly in improving the quality of the book. We are also indebted to Ian Robertson, whose fine scholarship and editorial skills were extremely helpful to us. We would also like to express our thanks to Adam Curle, Irving Louis Horowitz, Malcolm McFee, Jack Pierce, Leopold Pospisil, Richard L. Roe, and Edward H. Spicer—mentors, colleagues and friends.

Bill Eastman, our editor for this book and the Editorial Director of Harper & Row's College Department, deserves a special vote of thanks for his editorial assistance and wise advice during all stages of the book's preparation. Ken Burke has done his usual spectacular job in designing and producing *The Study of Anthropology*. We would also like to express our appreciation to Sandy Craig for her fine editorial work, Christy Butterfield, the designer of the book, Barbara Hack, the illustrator, and Audrey Ross our photo editor. Leslie Palmer, Bev Hower, and Ronna Greif did excellent work under severe time constraints in typing the manuscript. Finally, Gayle Johnson Whitten and Russell Whitten deserve a special mention for their patience and their understanding.

David E. Hunter
Phillip Whitten

Contents

xv

xvii

xxi

Part I

Introduction

1
The Study of Anthropology

The Historical Roots of Anthropology

Anthropology is the systematic investigation of the nature of human beings. The term derives from two Greek words: *anthropos,* meaning "man," and *logia,* meaning "to study."

The scope of anthropology is vast and ambitious, including such subjects as the supernatural beliefs of an isolated tribe in the Brazilian jungle, the eating habits of an African pigmy, the evolving shape of the human jawbone, the social behavior of our primate relatives, the grammar of an English sentence, the circumcision rites of Australian aborigines, the physical differences between Eskimos and Arabs, the position of women in modern America, the social structure of medieval society, and the taboo that inhibits us from having sexual intercourse with close relatives. In short, the subject matter of anthropology is as infinite and as fascinating as humanity itself.

The origins of anthropology can be traced back to the classical civilizations of Europe and the Middle East. Early travelers and philosophers noticed that the forms of society differed from place to place and that the body shapes and skin colors of peoples varied as well. These observations led to speculations about human origins and about the nature and development of human society and culture—concerns that can be traced from the ancient world to the anthropology of the twentieth century.

The Ancient World

Perhaps the earliest statement of the anthropological perspective was made by Xenophanes (570?–475? B.C.), a Greek who traveled widely and is credited with being the first philosopher to emphasize that society is created by human beings themselves. Rejecting a literal understanding of mythological tales, Xenophanes even argued that gods are created in human images and that religion is a social product.

The best-known early traveler and recorder of different social customs is probably Herodotus (484?–425? B.C.), whose writings describe the life-styles of

Anthropologist Irven DeVore measuring the amount of water used in a day by a group of !Kung hunters in the Kalahari desert of southern Africa. The hunters carry their water in ostrich egg shells. Standing, in shirt and shorts, is a Bantu interpreter. This kind of careful, quantitative research is becoming standard practice in anthropological fieldwork.

Early accounts of "foreign" peoples exaggerated and distorted them, comparing their physiques and life styles unfavorably to Europeans. This practice is called ethnocentrism and is well illustrated by this page from Sir Thomas Herbert's *Travalle into Afrique and Asia*. This book was published in 1634 and contains one of the earliest commentaries on the Hottentots of South Africa. Ethnocentrism is a universal practice.

some fifty different peoples he visited. His methods of analysis were crude, but his perspective was broad enough to satisfy modern standards, for he systematically described the environment in which a people lived, their physical characteristics, language, institutions, customs, laws, political organizations, military practices, and religious beliefs. Although he believed that the Greek way of life was superior to all others, he understood that all people feel a loyalty to their own society and way of life. Thus Herodotus explicitly stated one of the fundamental propositions of anthropology: All human groups are *ethnocentric*—that is, they prefer their own way of life to all others and judge other groups' life-styles (usually negatively) in terms of their own value system (Malefijt 1974:5-6).

As Greek society became transformed into city-states such as Athens, the political duties of citizens demanded that they understand the nature of society. Social thought flourished. Socrates (who was executed in 399 B.C. for the "dangerous" influence of his ideas on young people) and his student Plato (427?-347 B.C.) refined social, political, and cultural analysis to such a degree that their work can still instruct us.

The nature of human society continued to be a subject of concern throughout classical times, but anthropology did not develop as an identifiable social science for many centuries. One reason was a change in the perspective and value system of Western civilization after the fall of the Roman Empire in the West in the fifth century A.D.

Medieval Perspectives

As the Roman Empire gradually collapsed, the early optimism of the classical civilizations evaporated. By the time of Augustine (A.D. 354-430), Roman society was disintegrating, and a new view arose: that human beings are inherently alienated from divine perfection and order.

In Augustine's view, the cosmos was not at one with man. The universe was made by an omnipotent and perfect Creator, who was also inscrutable, and His work and purposes could never be fully understood by man. It was thus useless to study the universe and nature, and it was similarly superfluous to study society. . . . Coercive social institutions such as the monogamic family, laws, government and slavery were divinely instituted after sin had entered the world, both as punishments and as remedial measures to counteract man's evil will. The study of man's social life was thus useless, because the only thing that mattered was God, His commands to man, and man's relationship to the Divine. Greek ethics had been man-centered, aimed at happiness through correct social behavior. In the Christian view social behavior was to be judged not by men but by God (Malefijt 1974:25).

The period of chaos following the fall of Rome did little to promote serious social studies. Much of the wealth of knowledge and philosophy produced by the classical civilizations was lost to the wider society and survived only in small, enclosed communities of monastic scholars in remote settings on the fringes of pagan European society (Clark 1969:7–8).

Not until the twelfth century A.D. were the classical works rediscovered by large numbers of European scholars. Once more there was room for optimism. Thomas Aquinas (1225–1274) conceived of a universe in which humans were rational beings of great potential who occupied a place just below the angels. Aquinas was concerned with two opposed characteristics of humans, which gave them a dual nature. On the one hand, humans come close to the angels in their ability to acquire knowledge and apply it; on the other hand, they share with the animals a base sensuality. This paradox of the *dualistic nature* of the human species continues to occupy a central position in anthropological debate; it has been highlighted in recent years by those who attempt to explain human behavior in terms of observations of animal behavior (see chap. 4).

Although medieval scholars fixed their eyes firmly on the Creator in heaven, they nevertheless knew that they were members of human society, and they gave their social environment careful contemplation. An interest in history and especially in non-European peoples developed and was encouraged by the adventures of merchants and Christian missionaries. This age produced works describing a wide variety of foreign peoples and their customs, as well as serious attempts to account for the development of political organization, the nature of legal systems, the divinity of kings, and other social phenomena. Anthropological concerns, if not the beginnings of anthropology itself, are certainly discernible in medieval times (Malefijt 1974:30–35). These concerns are perhaps best represented by the writings of the explorer Marco Polo (1254?–1324?), who served seventeen years in the court of the Kublai Khan and described in remarkable detail Asian customs, practices, and social institutions.

The Renaissance and the Enlightenment

In 1453 the Roman Empire in the East (Byzantium) fell to Islam, and thousands of refugees fled into western Europe, bringing with them the writings of most of the classical philosophers. The invention of a printing press using movable type by Johann Gutenberg of Mainz, Germany, and the publication in 1457 of the first (surviving) dated book were of tremendous significance in this context. The treasures of classical society could now be—and in fact were—cheaply reproduced and made available to large numbers of people.

Europe became infatuated with the classical civilizations. Excavations were undertaken to retrieve classical art, Greek and Roman texts were studied, and visual arts were executed in terms of classical aesthetic notions. This preoccupation led to a reawakening of interest in studying society, since much of classical thought focused on this subject. In 1513 one of the masterpieces of political science—Niccolo Machiavelli's *The Prince* —was published, an event that marked a trend to consider society as a separate phenomenon, independent of religious and ethical assumptions (Garraty and Gay 1972:489).

This period also saw the widening of European horizons. Monarchs came to appreciate the possibilities of world trade and subsidized exploratory expeditions. Accounts of these voyages were eagerly read for their descriptions of the physical appearance, dress, customs, political systems, religions, and dietary habits of the "strange," remote peoples who were being discovered by an expanding European civilization. The information contained in these often incorrect and distorted reports was used by social theorists to compare and contrast "primitive" society with that of Europe in order to understand basic social processes.

Modern anthropological theory had its real beginnings in the period of Western civilization known as the Enlightenment—that is, the hundred years or so between the publication of John Locke's *An Essay Concerning Human Understanding* (1690) and the eruption of the French Revolution. Locke's remarkable essay contains many concepts that twentieth century students of human behavior still use. Locke proposed, among other things, that people are born with blank or empty minds, and that they learn all they know through their enculturation into groups. There are no innate ideas—all knowledge is learned as a result of personal experience. Marvin Harris emphasizes the radical implications of this position: "No social order is based upon innate truths; a change in the environment [be it the social or natural environment] results in a change in behavior" (1968:12). But Locke and his followers failed to follow their theme to its logical end. Although they understood that ideas are learned (rather than innate) and hence relative to each society, they firmly believed in moral universals and judged all societies in terms of the ethical and scientific "truths" of their own civilization.

The Enlightenment was marked by lively debate about the nature of the human species and of human societies. The arguments were far from trivial. Thomas Hobbes's (1588-1679) pessimistic assumptions about the inherent selfishness of human beings were used to defend the doctrine of despotic rule by monarchies —without which life would be "nasty, brutish, and short." On the other hand, the liberal philosophers following John Locke (1632-1704) advocated democratic institutions in the belief that the human species had a much nobler potential.

By the eighteenth century such fathers of modern social science as Montesquieu (1689-1755) and Giovanni Battista Vico (1668-1744) could attempt to describe evolutionary stages, sequences of social development, and "natural laws" governing human society without reference to divine control or order. This trend was perhaps climaxed by the works of Jean Jacques Rousseau (1712-1778), who argued in *The Social Contract* (1762) that political organization and

John Locke (1632-1704). English social philosopher. In his writings Locke proposed that people are born with blank or empty minds, and that they learn all they know through enculturation into groups. Rejecting the concept of innate ideas, Locke and his followers developed the concept of culture as the source of each person's knowledge of the world. This perspective was opposed by Thomas Hobbes (1588-1679) who argued that humans are inherently selfish. Both sides of this debate still find their adherents today, with most anthropologists lining up behind Locke while some ethologists (students of animal behavior) write in Hobbes' tradition.

Karl Heinrich Marx (1818–1883). German social philosopher, who insisted that social theory and social practice (political organizing) must constantly inform each other. Thus Marx and his collaborator Friedrich Engels issued the *Communist Manifesto*—their famous analysis of the antagonistic class relations to be found under the capitalist (industrial) economic system—in 1848 when Europe was rocked by social upheaval and revolution. They were hardly neutral bystanders. The document ends with a ringing call to action: "WORKING MEN OF ALL COUNTRIES, UNITE!"

power ultimately are based on—and responsible to—the legitimizing force of popular will. The political and social conclusions that could be drawn from this new doctrine helped lay the groundwork for revolutionary thought and practice in the American and French revolutions and the subsequent social upheavals of the nineteenth and twentieth centuries.

The Nineteenth Century

The last part of the eighteenth century and the first half of the nineteenth century were eventful times in the history of the West. The American colonies rebelled against British rule in 1776, and the French Revolution (1789–1799), inspired by the writings of Rousseau and the immediate example of America, threw Europe into convulsions of struggle. In 1848 a series of abortive revolutions occurred in France, Italy, the German states, and the Austrian Empire. The ruling classes in these countries allied to crush the revolutions, but not before social theorist Karl Marx and his colleague Friedrich Engels published *The Communist Manifesto* (1848) and propelled social science irretrievably into the political arena.

This era saw the expansion of European empires in Africa, Asia, and Latin America, coupled with an intensification of missionary activity. The subjugated peoples of the various empires were studied and described by missionaries, military personnel, and the colonizers who exploited the economic potential of these countries and their inhabitants. As in the Renaissance, Western "armchair" social philosophers used this information to explain the nature of human society.

Many scholars trace the invention of modern social science to Claude Henri de Rouvroy, Comte de Saint-Simon (1760–1825), and Auguste Comte (1798–1857). These collaborators set out to develop a "science of man" in which a "social physics" would lead to the discovery of underlying, unifying principles comparable to the principle of gravity, which had explained so much in the natural sciences. Comte believed he had discovered such a unifying principle, that social scientists were now in a position to create a new level of knowledge called *positivism*, which embodied the scientific method with its built-in tests for truth.

Franz Boas (1858–1942). German born, Boas first studied mathematics, physics, then geography. After becoming interested in the Northwest Coast Indians, he shifted to anthropology. His early training as a natural scientist made him impatient with speculative theory-building without a firm foundation in empirical fact. As a professor at Columbia University until his death, he taught many outstanding American anthropologists (including Alfred Kroeber, Robert Lowie, Paul Radin, Edward Sapir, Melville Herskovits, Ruth Benedict, Ruth Bunzel, Ruth Underhill, Ashley Montagu, and Margaret Mead) to concentrate on gathering concrete data—ethnographic, linguistic, archaeological, and biological—rather than "waste" time in constructing grand theories. Due to his influence, interest in cultural evolution, very strong in the 19th century, was for many years neglected in the United States.

When Marx and Engels put forth their analysis of the antagonisms built into the class structure of capitalist society, they were following the course charted earlier by Rousseau, Saint-Simon, and Comte. They also believed that they had discovered scientific laws governing the workings of society. They based their arguments on an analysis of contemporary European (especially English) industrial society. However, they also argued that the evolution of social forms, which they reconstructed from the information that had been collected about the "primitive" world, was added proof of their views (Engels 1884). Although their data on "primitive" societies has since been shown to be more fantasy than fact, the Marxist analysis of industrial capitalism continues to influence large numbers of social scientists, and the social movements that Marxism has inspired have had a continuing, massive impact on the modern world.

With the dramatic emergence of the theory of evolution on the European intellectual scene in 1859 (see Chap. 2), interest in the "primitive" peoples of the world increased. Anthropology came into its own as a separate professional and academic field of study in the second half of the nineteenth century as scholars sought reliable information about isolated and technologically less developed peoples. They believed that this information could be used to draw a baseline from which modern industrial society could be seen to have evolved. An era of ambitious comparative studies commenced, covering areas such as jurisprudence (for example, Sir Henry Maine's *Ancient Law*, 1861), kinship systems (for example, Lewis Henry Morgan's *Systems of Consanguinity and Affinity of The Human Family*, 1870), and religion and other elements of culture (for example, E. B. Tylor's *Primitive Culture: Researches into the Development of Mythology, Philosophy, Religion, Art and Custom*, 1871).

Two major approaches to the comparative perspective emerged in the latter half of the nineteenth century. One approach—often called the school of classical evolutionists—focused on the concept of *progress*. Followers of this approach attempted to arrange what was known about different societies in terms of *time* in the hope that a universal evolutionary sequence of social forms would be discovered. Thus

E. B. Tylor, Lewis Henry Morgan, Friedrich Engels, and other similarly inclined scholars

> assumed that cultural developments everywhere followed definite laws—unfolding uniformly from the simple to the complex and culminating in the institutions of western Europe. Individual cultures were of interest mainly insofar as they illustrated points along the path of cultural progress; once this path was fully laid out the history of culture would be complete (Eggan 1968:122).

The second major comparative trend focused on geographical *space* rather than on time. Scholars in this tradition were concerned with the appearance and distribution of cultural traits in various geographic areas. They emphasized "the importance of the natural environment in cultural development and the role of diffusion and migration in bringing about cultural similarities" (Eggan 1968:123) (see Chap. 2). The "histories" that this group of researchers reconstructed were often incompatible with those of the evolutionists. Because anthropological theory had not yet developed sufficiently to enable scholars to decide on the relative merit of these two approaches, Franz Boas (1858–1942), the "father of American anthropology," called for an indefinite halt to the building of grand theories. By emphasizing the importance of the painstaking collection of accurate ethnographic data, Boas led anthropologists from Victorian parlors to the field, and thus led anthropology into the twentieth century.

The Twentieth Century

Bridging the nineteenth and twentieth centuries was the French social scientist Émile Durkheim (1858–1917). He was interested in the ways societies maintain themselves, the manner of their *functioning*. Both modern sociology and anthropology have intellectual roots in his writings, which deal with a broad range of theoretical issues, including primitive religion, problems of social organization and group cohesion, and the difficulties that modern society poses for the individual who is struggling to find a meaningful identity.

Since the turn of the century anthropology has developed into an increasingly complex and segmented academic discipline. Less and less are theories and

Émile Durkheim (1858–1917). Both anthropologists and sociologists trace their intellectual roots through Durkheim. His theoretical writings include both 19th century evolutionary interests and a very contemporary interest in how societies "work." His major works dealt with religion, the division of labor in society (social organization), and suicide (symptomatic, often, of social disorganization).

Louis Seymore Bazett Leakey (1903–1972). British paleontologist, Leakey along with his wife and colleague Mary Leakey, was responsible for some of the most important fossil finds in the hominid line. At Olduvai Gorge in Tanzania the Leakeys found the skull of a hominid they called *Zinjanthropus* (now classified as *Australopithecus robustus*—see Chapter 2) which was dated as being what was then an incredible 1.75 million years old. With this and other subsequent finds (including their famous *Homo habilis*) the Leakeys constantly forced re-evaluation of current theories of human evolution. Their son Richard Leakey continues to do so (see Chapter 2).

trends tied to one particular scholar; few giants inhabit the field of anthropology today. However, rather than presenting a large cast of characters in this introduction, we shall introduce contemporary anthropologists in the context of their contributions to the discipline. Some anthropologists will appear repeatedly—testimony to the broad range of their interests and the versatility and usefulness of their theories. For now, we shall simply outline the four major subfields of anthropology that have emerged in the twentieth century: physical anthropology, archaeology, linguistics, and cultural anthropology.

Physical anthropology deals with human biology across space and time. It is divided into two areas: *paleontology*, the study of the fossil evidence of primate (including human) evolution, and *neontology*, the comparative biology of living primates, including population and molecular genetics, body shapes (morphology), and the extent to which behavior is biologically programed.

Archaeology is the systematic retrieval and analysis of the physical remains left behind by human beings, including both their skeletal and cultural remains.

An archaeological excavation at Maiden Castle, England. The excavation of a site forever destroys it; thus archaeologists must collect their data in such a way that they can record the exact position of each object. The vertical and horizontal spacial relationships of all the site's contents are called the *structure* of the site, and are very important variables in interpreting the remains. At this site, Sir Mortimer Wheeler, an eminent English archaeologist, carefully excavated each layer (stratum) of the site one at a time and recorded the positions of retrieved remains in reference to a carefully laid out grid. This is a standard archaeological technique known as horizontal, grid-type excavation.

Both the classical civilizations and prehistoric groups, including our prehuman ancestors, are investigated.

Linguistics is the study of language across space and time. *Historical linguistics* attempts to trace the tree of linguistic evolution and to reconstruct ancestral language forms. *Comparative* (or *structural*) *linguistics* attempts to describe formally the basic elements of languages and the rules by which they are ordered into intelligible speech.

Cultural anthropology includes many different perspectives and specialized subdisciplines but is concerned primarily with describing the forms of social organization and the cultural systems of human groups. In technical usage, *ethnography* is the description of the social and cultural systems of one particular group,

whereas *ethnology* is the comparison of such descriptions for the purpose of generalizing about the nature of all human groups.

As we mentioned before, you should know about many schools of thought and many individual theories and theorists if you are to have a basic knowledge of anthropology. However, rather than present all these theories, concepts, and personalities in the abstract, in this book we present them in the context of chapter discussions of real issues and problems. We hope that they will thus become more meaningful to you.

A Paradigm for Anthropology

What Is Science?

"Empirical science has two major objectives: to describe particular phenomena in the world of our experience and to establish general principles by means of which they can be explained and predicted" (Hempel 1952:1). What sets science apart from other belief systems is that it includes rigorous standards for testing the truth of findings (see Chap. 13). Nevertheless, it is apparent to scientists who have examined carefully how they arrive at their "truths" that the story is a bit more complicated than most people believe.

Although most of us accept that there is in fact a world "out there" that can be described, we are becoming increasingly aware that the ways in which scientists describe that world are as much a product of their approach to observing and measuring it as a reflection of what is "really" out there. The argument can even be taken one step further: The theories that one accepts can determine the nature of one's observations, which in turn can determine the nature of the data that are recorded. Thus although we often think the data of scientific research are somehow objective or neutral, this is far from true (Heisenberg 1971).

This perspective has been forcefully advanced by Thomas S. Kuhn, who in 1962 published a controversial book called *The Structure of Scientific Revolutions.* Kuhn observes that any scientist works in terms of a set of existing beliefs and practices that are specific to his or her discipline. Kuhn calls such a set of beliefs and practices a *paradigm.* A paradigm represents the

Margaret Mead (b. 1901) Among America's most famous anthropologists, Margaret Mead is respected not only for her ethnographic research in such places as Samoa and New Guinea but also with her insistence on applying her anthropological perspective to contemporary America. Especially in the area of culture and personality, her contributions to the study of sex and gender identity and the dynamics of the transmission of culture endure as guideposts for anthropological research.

underlying structure of a discipline—expressed in basic theories, laws, generalizations, methods of research and evaluation, and instruments used for measuring and observing. The paradigm defines the problems of a discipline, the appropriate research methods, the nature of the data that are gathered, and the kind of explanations that are finally produced.

The scientists who work in a particular discipline have all received much the same education, and thus have been exposed to a fairly standardized version of the paradigm; consequently, they tend to share the same basic assumptions about their subject. Kuhn says that such a shared paradigm is essential for the progress of science. Nature is too vast to reveal her secrets to random investigations, and the paradigm focuses the attention of a community of scholars on crucial problems, while providing the theories and methods for solving them.

Occasionally, however, research under a particular paradigm will generate findings that do not fit the

existing assumptions. If serious anomalies of this kind occur, the paradigm may start to crumble, and scholars must then modify it or develop a completely new one. This process, in Kuhn's language, is a scientific revolution. An example from physics was the replacement of the Newtonian paradigm by Einstein's paradigm of general relativity; now this latter paradigm is being challenged by the paradigm of quantum mechanics. Thus scientific progress in a discipline takes place through two distinct processes: the gradual accumulation and organization of knowledge under one paradigm, and the eventual replacement of each paradigm by another. In brief, the scientific method is a cultural system that can be described and analyzed like any other cultural system, making its basic structure—its paradigm—clear.

Anthropology as a Social Science

A paradigm is by no means easy to describe or identify. It is not a simple, unified statement or position. Rather, it is a perspective, or to be more precise, a set of themes or dimensions. It is also a set of practices that recur in various forms and combinations throughout the training, research, and writings of an academic discipline. These themes and practices combine to structure the world view of those within the discipline.

Anthropologists share and participate in such a paradigm (Hunter and Whitten 1975). Although each of us may choose to emphasize one aspect more than another, we nonetheless perceive our work in relationship to this paradigm's entirety; we understand how our work fits in with the work of other anthropologists, and how all anthropological research and writing contribute to the process of refining and improving this perspective.

What, then, is the anthropological perspective? Certainly it is not to be found among the various *-isms* that fragment the discipline; it is not structuralism, functionalism, evolutionism, historicism, or any other school of anthropology that you will learn about in this book. Nor can the paradigm be found on the grander level of generalizations or laws about human behavior. These generalizations are either banal (for example,

Bronislaw Kasper Malinowski (1884–1942). Polish born, Malinowski had received his Ph.D. both in physics and mathematics before he became interested in anthropology and received his training at the London School of Economics and the British Museum. Caught in his travels by the outbreak of World War I, Malinowski was interned for the duration on the Trobriand Islands off the eastern coast of New Guinea. He made good use of his time, engaging in the most extended and sophisticated piece of ethnographic field research that had ever been achieved by a trained anthropologist; to this day, his ethnography of the Trobrianders remains as a standard of excellence—both in its wealth of detail, and in the way Malinowski perceived and described the interrelations of all elements of the culture. His attempt to generalize his fieldwork methodology into a theory which he called *functionalism*—though very influential in its impact on both anthropology and sociology—had numerous weaknesses, especially his attempt to establish a one-to-one matchup between biological "needs" and cultural responses.

human beings depend more on culture and have elaborated cultural complexity more than any other creature); or obvious (for example, all cultures show tendencies to change, but at the same time also show tendencies to conserve themselves); or are controversial and far from accepted by all, or even most, anthropologists (for example, human beings are innately aggressive).

The anthropological paradigm can be seen as the intersection of five themes that recur throughout the body of anthropological work. Not all anthropologists work in terms of all five themes by any means, but all anthropologists appreciate the importance of every theme. Further, this particular combination of themes differentiates anthropology from the other social sciences and is the core that makes the study and practice of anthropology especially important in today's world. The five themes that form the anthropological paradigm are: the comparative theme, the holistic theme, the concentration on systems and processes, emphasis of the dichotomy between the folk perspective and the analytical perspective, and the emphasis on case studies.

The Comparative Theme   **Modern anthropology has its roots in the nineteenth century, as we have seen. During that colonial period, some of the colonizers, merchants, and missionaries described the "curious" ways of life they were discovering, and a great amount of ethnographic material was amassed. But only when these descriptions were analyzed and systematically compared by scholars in Europe or in the United States did anthropology begin to emerge as a distinct discipline. This comparative theme has remained an enduring characteristic of anthropology.**

Although many anthropologists devote most or all of their time to ethnography—the study of a small group, community, or archaeological site in a local context—even these individuals acknowledge that the long-term aim of anthropology is to accumulate sufficient ethnographic data to enable the discipline to arrive at meaningful, scientific laws describing the behavior of people everywhere. Such laws would have to rely on generalizations arising from the systematic analysis and comparison of data from a vast number of cultures (ethnology).

Anthropologists use two dimensions of comparison in their work: *synchronics,* **the systematic comparison of ethnographic materials across a wide range of cultures at one arbitrarily selected point in time, and** *diachronics,* **the comparative study of culture and society as they change through time in a specified geographical area. From synchronic studies we learn about the regularities of human behavior around the world at a particular time, usually the present or the recent past. From diachronic studies we learn about the evolution of human beings and their cultures.**

In the end, it is difficult to be an anthropologist without also being an evolutionist—at least to the extent that one acknowledges the importance of understanding the relationship between any particular way of life and the developments which led up to it. These developments are both historical (particular to the given case) and evolutionary (exhibiting patterns of change that also characterize similar developments at other times and places).

The Holistic Theme   Anthropology generally resists simplistic, reductionistic explanations of social phenomena, instead taking the whole context of a phenomenon into account. When anthropologists attempt to understand human behavior, they consider biological, social, cultural, psychological, economic, political, ecological, and many other factors. Anthropologists are thus sensitive to the complexity of human behavior. This holistic perspective sets anthropology

San Carlos Apaches. Anthropologists are interested in knowing the small details which add up to the unique life experiences offered by every culture. Thus much of our research consists of detailed case studies using the *participant observation* research method, in which the researcher is immersed in the ongoing daily life of the group she or he is studying. This approach to social research has made anthropologists acutely aware of the different conceptions, understandings, and points of view which separate them from the people they study. For example: the anthropologist describes the event pictured here as "A HARD LIVING. An Apache woman chips away at rocks on the San Carlos Apache Indian reservation in Arizona, in search of semiprecious perido. These green stones are found in large deposits at a mesa on the reservation, and digging for them helps a few Indians eke out their meager existence." However, only very careful and sensitive research will enable us to discover the participants' conception of the situation. The former description we call the *analytical perspective;* the latter is the *folk perspective.*

apart from sociology, which often considers only patterned social behavior and such cultural factors as norms and values. It also distinguishes anthropology from psychology, which, anthropologists believe, ignores cross-cultural, comparative data and focuses almost entirely on psychological data, with a deterministic dependence on biological information when it is available.

Systems and Processes   **Early anthropology often consisted of static, ethnographic descriptions of relatively isolated communities. Where the forces of expanding industrialism had already wrought dramatic changes in the traditional life-styles of remote groups, these bygone ways of life were recreated and presented to readers in the eternally frozen form of the "ethnographic present" (that is, as if things had never changed).**

A major current trend in anthropology is a move away from such static descriptions to a consideration of continuing processes. Anthropology approaches the study of human behavior through the systems that contribute to it: the biological system, social system, cultural system, psychological system, and environmental system. Analyzing the internal dynamics of each system and the processes of interaction among systems is one of the most important tasks of anthropology.

The Folk Perspective-Analytical Perspective Dichotomy   **Traditionally, anthropologists have studied remote peoples whose patterns of life are very different from those of Western civilization. As a result of the cross-cultural nature of so much of anthropological fieldwork, students of the profession have generally had to acquire a working knowledge of linguistics —both practical and theoretical—in order to learn the language of the peoples they study. Moreover, anthropologists are confronted with the difficulty of translating the cultural world of their subjects into the idiom of Western knowledge. For these reasons linguistics has had a great impact on anthropology.**

Because the issue of translation is such a central one—both for the fieldworker attempting to understand a new language and for the author attempting to make his or her data meaningful to other scholars —anthropologists have been forced to deal rigorously with the distinction between the world view of their

subjects and their own assumptions. In order to keep these two sets of phenomena separated, anthropologists have followed linguistics in distinguishing between *emics* and *etics*. *Emics* is the set of related categories through which the anthropologist's subjects perceive the world; in this book we refer to emics by the term *folk perspective*. *Etics* is the set of related categories used by Western social scientists to explain social phenomena; we refer to etics as the *analytical perspective*.

Keeping folk and analytical perspectives separated is a difficult task whether one is doing research or analyzing the data afterward. Because they so often face this problem, anthropologists are extremely sensitive to the relativity of cultural patterns. They attempt to appreciate the life-styles of their subjects on the subject's own terms, avoiding *ethnocentrism*—the complacent assumption that the ways of one's own society are the only correct ways—in favor of a research methodology of *cultural relativism*—a nonjudgmental approach to studying each human society.

The Emphasis on Case Studies   As anthropology developed, its research tended to focus on relatively small, isolated, foreign social groups. The research technique that anthropologists developed and relied on is called *participant observation*. In this method, anthropologists immerse themselves in their subjects' way of life and at the same time attempt to observe, describe, and analyze objectively the social behavior and culture of their subjects. This approach is often necessary because formal research tools, such as questionnaires, cannot be developed without some prior knowledge of the society and its language.

One weakness of the participant observation approach is the tendency of the researcher to become emotionally involved with the community he or she is studying, perhaps rendering the data less objective than would be desirable. Another possible consequence is that the experience of participant observation may become a crucial episode in the anthropologist's life, assuming the character of a rite of passage and influencing his or her life's work. This attachment to the fieldwork experience has an interesting effect. Few anthropologists are content solely with masses of data subjected to complex statistical analysis; rather, they look for the concrete social fact—the item of behavior,

the description of a recognizable experience—on which to anchor an understanding of social processes. In other words, although anthropologists appreciate the power of statistical analysis as much as do other social scientists, they are oriented toward the rich descriptions of setting (whether prehistoric or contemporary) and behavior which are to be found in case studies.

Some people believe that this orientation makes anthropologists too particularistic; but it prevents anthropology from embracing grand, abstract theories that bear little relationship to social life. This down-to-earth perspective might prove to be crucial in the future, helping social science to educate citizens politically and socially and contributing to the resolution of the important social questions of our day.

The Organization of This Book

The importance of learning structure as well as mastering facts and techniques has been emphasized consistently by psychologists who have studied the learning processes. In his seminal book *The Process of Education*, Jerome Bruner argues that the curriculum of a subject should be determined "by the most fundamental understanding that can be achieved of the underlying principles that give structure to that subject" (1960:31). Structure, he states, is at the center of the classic problem of the transfer of learning; unless facts and details are placed into a structured pattern, they are quickly forgotten:

There are many things that go into learning . . . [the structure of a discipline], not the least of which are supporting habits and skills that make possible the active use of the materials one has come to understand. If earlier learning is to render later learning easier, it must do so by providing a general picture in terms of which the relations between things encountered earlier and later are made as clear as possible (1960:12).

The five dimensions of the anthropological paradigm are:

1. **The comparative theme**
2. **The holistic theme**
3. **Systems and processes**

4. **Folk perspective-analytical perspective dichotomy**
5. **The emphasis on case studies**

We have organized this book (with the exception of the first three chapters, which are introductory) to reflect this basic structure. Thus, as you read the book, you will learn the processes of inquiry underlying the discipline of anthropology—in effect, you will be learning to think like an anthropologist.

Specifically, chapters 4–19 are organized consistently, expressing the imperatives of the first four dimensions of the paradigm. Each chapter has four sections: The World Context, Theory, Analysis, and Conclusions.

The World Context The purpose of this opening section is to provide descriptive data, arranged both diachronically and synchronically. Thus this section has two parts: (a) Origins and Development through Time and (b) Contemporary Examples. This part of each chapter represents the *comparative theme*.

Theory This section is also divided into two parts: (a) Systems and (b) Processes. Here we present the *holistic theme* and the *systems and processes* dimension of the paradigm. You will learn about the theoretical tools anthropologists use to analyze the materials introduced in the first section. Those biological, environmental, cultural, and social systems pertinent to the understanding of the materials presented in the chapter are introduced, and the processes that characterize the operation of those systems are explained.

Analysis This section covers the fourth element of the paradigm in two parts: (a) The Folk Perspective and (b) The Analytical Perspective. Here you will learn how anthropologists try to make sense out of social phenomena—from the subjects' point of view (folk perspective) and from the anthropologist's (analytical) perspective.

Conclusions The purposes of this section are to summarize the chapter and to expose you to the current debates about the materials of each chapter. This is accomplished in two parts: (a) Schools of Thought and (b) Author's Conclusions (these are the views of the author of each chapter, not the authors of the book). As you will learn, anthropologists are far from achieving universal agreement on many important issues.

Anthropologist Napoleon Chagnon. Dressed in the traditional feast finery of the Yanomamö, an Amazon Indian group living near the boundary between Venezuela and Brazil, Chagnon is confronted by a most difficult problem of participant observation research: how does one participate in the activities of a group whose culture one barely comprehends while maintaining a credible social role in that context and also preserving one's personal sense of self.

The Case Studies

Chapters 20–25 are each chapter-length case studies. This entire section of the book represents the fifth theme of the paradigm, the *case study approach* to social research. Consistent with our belief that people learn better when materials are presented within a predictable structure, the case studies also follow a consistent organization:

1. Introduction: **The flavor of the group and area being studied.**

2. The environment: **The important ecological features of the environment, with an emphasis on making the group's subsistence activities readily understandable.**

3. The group: **A detailed description of the people under consideration. Sufficient information is provided for you to apply many of the concepts you learned in earlier chapters to the case material. Each account of a group discusses: (a) subsistence activities, (b) social organization, and (c) culture.**

4. Problems and prospects: **A survey of the important political, ecological, health, economic, or demographic problems facing the group; the community in relationship to the wider historical processes changing the face of the world. The relationship between these problems and the industrial world is often emphasized so that you can discover connections between yourself and the community under consideration.**

The book is organized to make anthropology easy and pleasant to learn. We hope that after reading this book you will want to learn more about that inherently interesting subject, the human species.

Summary

Anthropology is the systematic investigation of the nature of human beings.

The historical roots of anthropology can be traced back to the ancient world, when travelers noted and speculated about human cultural and physical differences. Religious beliefs inhibited rational discussion of human origins and human nature in medieval times, but during the Renaissance and the Enlightenment scholars devoted increasing attention to these concerns. The colonial period brought Europeans into contact with "primitive" peoples and encouraged new interest in other cultures. By the nineteenth century, thinkers were attempting to formulate general laws and principles underlying human society and its evolution. Modern anthropology has become an increasingly complex academic discipline.

Today anthropology is divided into four main subfields: (1) *physical anthropology,* which deals with human and other primate biology; (2) *archaeology,* the study of the physical remains (both skeletal and cultural) left by human beings; (3) *linguistics,* the study of language; and (4) *cultural anthropology,* which is concerned with the social organization and cultural systems of human groups.

A science is, among other things, an organized belief system, including rigorous standards for testing its findings. A science has a paradigm, or set of beliefs and practices specific to the discipline. Such a paradigm includes basic theories, laws, generalizations, modes of research and evaluation, and instruments for measuring and observing. Scientific progress takes place through the accumulation of knowledge obtained under a paradigm and through the periodic replacement of one paradigm by another.

The anthropological paradigm consists of five basic themes.

The *comparative theme* is the systematic comparison of evidence from various cultures over space and time.

The *holistic theme* is the consideration of a wide range of factors in the attempt to gain a "whole" explanation of human behavior.

The *systems and processes theme* is the attempt to explain social phenomena dynamically in terms of processes of interaction between the various systems that contribute to human behavior.

The *folk perspective-analytical perspective* dichotomy is the distinction between the viewpoint of the people observed and the "scientific" viewpoint of the observer.

The *emphasis on case studies* is the crucial anthropological method of participant observation.

This textbook is organized to systematically reflect the basic structure of the anthropological paradigm.

Annotated Bibliography

Brew, J. O., ed. (1968)   *One Hundred Years of Anthropology.* Cambridge, Mass.: Harvard Univ. Press. A somewhat dry but useful collection of essays covering the last hundred years in the history of anthropology, this volume reflects the perspectives of some major American scholars on their own subdisciplines: Gordon R. Willey on American archaeology, Glyn Daniel on Old World prehistory, Stanley L. Washburn on biological anthropology, Fred Eggan on ethnology and social anthropology, and Floyd G. Lounsbury on anthropological linguistics.

Malefijt, Annemarie de Waal (1974)   *Images of Man.* New York: Knopf. A readable, useful history of the development of anthropology as an academic discipline. Starts with philosophers and travelers in ancient Greece and proceeds through the most contemporary developments in cognitive anthropology.

Voget, Fred W. (1975)   *A History of Ethnology.* New York: Holt. Although somewhat idiosyncratically organized, this survey of the history of ethnology is comprehensive and useful.

2
Human Biological and Cultural Evolution

The Concept of Evolution

History

As far as we know, all societies have beliefs about their own origins and often about the origin of the entire human species as well. The ancient Greeks had a number of origin myths, including the tale of Prometheus, who created people out of earth and water. The philosopher Thales (640?–546 B.C.) broke away from mythological stories and claimed that everything in the world had its ultimate origin in one substance —water. This perspective, if not the specific belief itself, was significant because it tied the origins of the material world to a material rather than mythological base (Malefijt 1974:3).

Writing in the following century, the Greek philosopher Empedocles (495?–435? B.C.) even suggested the idea of natural selection, which would become the cornerstone of Darwin's theory of evolution some 2,300 years later. Empedocles believed that the various body parts originally existed in isolation from each other and combined randomly, often forming grotesque combinations, such as the Minotaur, a mythological creature with the body of a human and the head of a bull. However, only those combinations

Skull of Neanderthal no. 1, still lying in place in Shanidar Cave. This was an adult male who died in the cave under a rockfall about 46,000 years ago. He had been a cripple (having only one arm) and evidently had been looked after by his group during his lifetime. He is one of nine Neanderthals found in Shanidar Cave located in the Zagros Mountains of Kurdistan, Iraq, by Dr. Ralph Solecki of Columbia University.

of body parts that functioned well enough to nourish and reproduce themselves ultimately survived; the human species was an outcome of this selective process.

Some ancient Greeks were also concerned about the evolution of human society. Xenophanes (570?–475? B.C.) rejected the Homeric image of the divine origins of human society. He is the earliest known Western scholar to explicitly conceive of society as an entity created solely by human beings and developing as humans accumulated knowledge (Malefijt (1974:5).

But the speculations of these classical philosophers did not lead to systematic empirical investigations into human biological and social origins. And the advent of Christianity, with its view of the universe as a static representation of God's creative drive, stifled the motivation for such research. Medieval scholars thought that their major task was to detect and formally describe the natural laws governing the universe, thus providing people with a glimpse of the Creator's awesome ingenuity and perfection. Any search for origins (which would imply development and hence change)

Some of the forms of life which did not survive the pressures of natural selection as conceived of by Empedocles (c. 495–445 B.C.).

TRITON.

A CENTAUR.

was not compatible with this world view, because if the universe was an expression of the Creator, it must be perfect. To believe it had changed significantly meant that it had either been created imperfectly or had become imperfect. This idea would lead inevitably to the conclusion that God, having created imperfect things, must therefore Himself be imperfect—a theological impossibility. Thus theories about human origins were confined to an acceptance of the biblical story of Adam and Eve (Clark 1957:26).

During the Renaissance in fifteenth century Europe, scholars devoted considerable attention to classical Greece and Rome as the origins of much of European civilization. Nonetheless, a literal interpretation of the Bible continued to inhibit historical investigation for hundreds of years. As late as the first part of the nineteenth century, most scholars uncritically accepted the calculations of Archbishop James Ussher and John Lightfoot (vice-chancellor of the University of Cambridge), who in the early 1600s had deduced from a careful study of Genesis that the earth had been created at 9 o'clock in the morning on October 23, 4004 B.C. (Daniel 1963:24–25).

However, scientific discoveries, especially in geology and biology, gradually forced scholars to reassess their traditional points of view. As more and more of the earth's geological strata were discovered, and as it was realized that the thickness of some strata (and the nature of certain minerals in them) demanded a very long developmental process, late eighteenth and early nineteenth century natural scientists faced the need to push back the date of Creation. In addition, the fossilized record of extinct forms of life accumulated, obliging scientists to produce plausible explanations for the existence and subsequent disappearance of such creatures as the woolly mammoth and the saber-toothed tiger.

In 1833 Sir Charles Lyell published the third and last volume of *Principles of Geology*, a work that tremendously influenced Charles Darwin as he worked on his theory of evolution (Daniel 1963:40). Lyell attacked such schools of thought as *diluvialism,* whose followers claimed that Noah's Flood accounted for what was known of the earth's history, and *catastrophism,* whose adherents proposed a series of natural catastrophes

The Christian doctrine that creation had been a single event became more and more troublesome in the course of the 16th century. With Vasco Nuñez de Balboa's discovery in 1513 that America was not an extension of Asia but rather a separate continent, the origin of the "Indians" became a source of heated debate. The *Monogenists* defended the doctrine of a single origin for all humans; many proposed that the "Indians" had come from Atlantis (a mythical continent which was believed to have stretched from Spain to Africa before it sank), others that they were one of the lost tribes of Israel. The *Polygenists* argued for more than one creation—but attempted to reconcile their views with the Scriptures by claiming that although God had created all people, all people were not necessarily descendants of Adam.

The Polygenist position is represented in contemporary anthropology by Carleton S. Coon, who argues in his controversial book *The Origin of Races* (1963) that the human species evolved five separate times—each time producing one of the five races which he believes continue to exist. Most anthropologists believe that this argument is wrong, that the evolution of the modern human species is the result of a widespread process in which all populations participated to an equivalent degree.

Charles Lyell (1797–1875). Even great thinkers are limited by the paradigms of their day. Lyell's insistence that uniform and ongoing processes were responsible for the creation of the different strata which constitute the earth's crust cut through many of the *ad hoc* theories which attributed the appearance of every newly identified stratum to a unique act of God. However, he was unable to transfer his vision of a gradually developing world from the inanimate to the realm of the animate—where the logical result would have been a theory of evolution, and a challenge to orthodox Christian doctrine. However, he took a keen interest in the researches of Charles Darwin, and actively encouraged him.

of which the biblical Flood was merely the latest, for failing to realize that the processes shaping the earth are continuous and uniform in nature. In promoting this *uniformitarian* position, however, Lyell was unable to free himself entirely from the doctrinaire Christian framework; he continued to believe in the divine creation of unchanging species and accounted for each species' disappearance in terms of small, localized catastrophes (Mayr 1972:985).

Some biologists did comprehend the implications of comparative anatomy and the fossil record. For instance, the French biologist the Chevalier de Lamarck (1744–1829) advanced his "developmental hypothesis," in which he arranged all known animals into a sequence based on their increasing organic complexity. He clearly implied that human beings were the highest product of a process of *organic transformation* and had been created through the same processes that had created all other creatures. However, Lamarck's imagination was also bound by theological constraints, and he did not carry his research to its logical conclusion. Rather than rely solely on material forces to shape organic transformation, he discerned an underlying, divinely ordained pattern.

Before researchers could appreciate fully the antiquity of the earth and the processes that gave rise to all species, including human beings, they had to change their perspectives, their belief systems (see Chap. 13). Scholars had to look at the evidence before them in an entirely different way and with quite different ends in mind. They had, in other words, to change the *paradigm* by which they were trying to make sense of the world (see Chap. 1). In effect, a scientific revolution was needed.

If the revolution was to overcome the ideological inertia of Christian dogma, it would have to be very convincing. It would have to be based on a unified, simple, universally applicable principle. Alfred Russel Wallace arrived at this principle more or less at the same time as Charles Darwin, who provided the general theoretical framework of evolution in *On the Origin of Species* in 1859, and his views on human evolution in *The Descent of Man* twelve years later. Wallace and Darwin had hit on the same basic mechanism to account for both the creation and extinction of living forms: *natural selection.*

General Principles

Before we begin a detailed discussion of the particular elements of evolutionary theory, let us consider some general principles underlying the concept of evolution. At its most elementary level, evolution always involves change. But although all evolution is change, all change is not necessarily evolutionary. So we must answer a basic question: What is distinctive about evolutionary change? Whether we are talking about forms of human society or forms of biological organisms, the answer is the same. *Evolutionary change is the transgenerational change that occurs when social or biological forms adapt to their environments.* Because aspects of environments—both natural and social—are always changing, it follows that evolution is a never-ending process in both the biological and social worlds.

Adaptational change can take two fundamentally different paths. On the one hand, a social or biological form can achieve a state of complexity and organization that adapts it exquisitely for a particular environment or even for a range of environments. When this happens, there is no longer any pressure on that particular form to evolve further. An example of this kind of adaptation is the so-called horseshoe crab. Although the horseshoe crab has existed for some 200,000,000 years without any significant structural changes (Simpson 1949:101), it is still quite well adapted to the environment it inhabits. This kind of specialized adaptation is called *involution* or *specific evolution.*

On the other hand, a social or biological form can respond to the demands of the environment by becoming more adaptable and flexible. In order to achieve this, the form must develop to a qualitatively new stage of structural complexity, a new stage of organization that makes it more versatile in coping with problems of survival posed by the environment. This kind of adaptation is called *general evolution* or *evolutionary progress.*

An important difference between the two adaptive modes is that involution involves specialized adaptation to a particular environment and hence is entirely *relative,* whereas evolutionary progress, involving as it does the emergence of higher forms that are inherently

Charles Darwin (1809–1882). Darwin and Alfred Russel Wallace developed the theory of evolution independently and at the same time. They built upon Lamarck's concept of transformism and his ideas regarding the selective process in the struggle for existence, but rejected his notion that traits acquired by individuals in their lifetimes could be passed on to the next generation. In 1858 Darwin and Wallace presented a joint paper on their theory of evolution to the Linnaean Society. However, it was the publication of Darwin's *On the Origin of Species by Means of Natural Selection, or the Preservation of Favored Races in the Struggle for Life* in 1859 which made the theory available to a wide reading public and changed the course of European intellectual history.

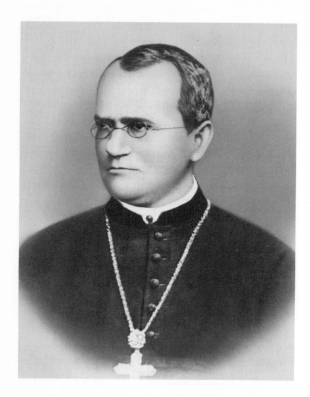

Gregor Mendel (1822–1884). While raising peas in the garden of the Moravian monastery in which he lived as a monk, Mendel experimented with their breeding under very strictly controlled conditions. His research led him to discover two crucial "laws" of genetics: (1) *The Law of Segregation:* genetically inherited features are inherited as separate, discrete units; they do not blend together. These discrete, segregating units of inheritance we now call *genes.* (2) *The Law of Independent Assortment:* genetic traits are inherited independently; chance and chance alone determines which combination of alleles will be transmitted from parents to offspring.

more complex and more adaptable than their ancestors, is intrinsically *directional.* In our discussion of human biological and cultural evolution, we shall see that both involution and evolutionary progress play significant roles. (Service, 1971)

The Dynamics of Evolution

Biological Evolution

Charles Darwin's theory of evolution described a process in which those organisms or groups of organisms that had the ability to survive and procreate in a given environment did so at the expense of those that lacked the ability. The qualities that allowed some forms to survive and procreate would thus, over the generations, become outstanding characteristics of the entire group. Darwin termed this process *natural selection.*

> The result of Darwin's inquiry was a victory for the principle of natural causation. . . . He disclosed the presence of continuity in a sphere where hitherto men had believed in supernatural interventions and interruptions, or . . . at the most, had appealed to an inner impulse towards development, which might be supposed to lead from one stage to another (Höffding 1955:440).

But although Darwin explained the process of evolution, he was not able to describe the biological mechanisms on which natural selection was based.

An Austrian monk and amateur biologist named Gregor Johann Mendel (1822–1884), by experimenting with the breeding of peas, discovered and formulated the principles of genetic inheritance that explain *how* natural selection takes place. Since Mendel's time, scientists have explored the biological processes that underlie these genetic mechanisms, and the genetic basis of inheritance and evolution is now well understood.

Human beings, like all other organisms, are composed of cells. We may think of the cells as the basic building blocks of the body. Each cell consists of: (1) a *nucleus,* in which we find (among other things) essentially all the genetic materials contained in the cell, (2) the *cytoplasm,* which consists primarily of a protein mass surrounding the nucleus, and (3) a *membrane* or wall that encloses the entire cell.

The human body consists essentially of two kinds of cells: (1) the *somatic* cells, which make up all the body parts and which are constantly dying and being replaced, and (2) the *gametes,* or sex cells, which, as sperm in males and eggs in females, combine to form a new human being as a fetus in a mother's womb.

When discussing genetics, we are primarily interested in the nucleus of the cell. Within the nucleus

Figure 2-1
Chromosomes, Genes, Alleles

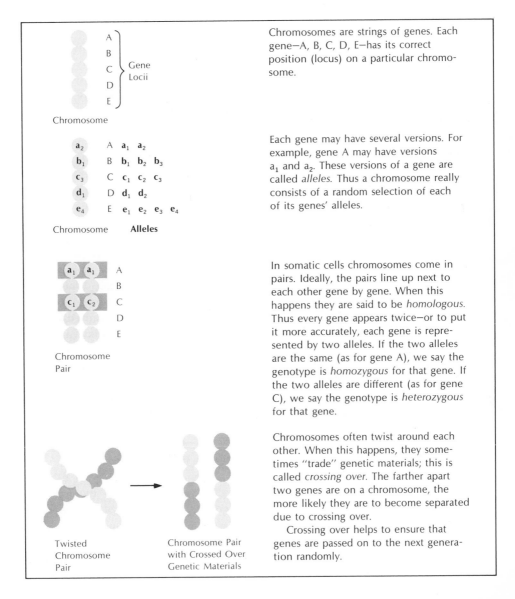

Chromosomes are strings of genes. Each gene—A, B, C, D, E—has its correct position (locus) on a particular chromosome.

Each gene may have several versions. For example, gene A may have versions a_1 and a_2. These versions of a gene are called *alleles.* Thus a chromosome really consists of a random selection of each of its genes' alleles.

In somatic cells chromosomes come in pairs. Ideally, the pairs line up next to each other gene by gene. When this happens they are said to be *homologous.* Thus every gene appears twice—or to put it more accurately, each gene is represented by two alleles. If the two alleles are the same (as for gene A), we say the genotype is *homozygous* for that gene. If the two alleles are different (as for gene C), we say the genotype is *heterozygous* for that gene.

Chromosomes often twist around each other. When this happens, they sometimes "trade" genetic materials; this is called *crossing over.* The farther apart two genes are on a chromosome, the more likely they are to become separated due to crossing over.

Crossing over helps to ensure that genes are passed on to the next generation randomly.

Figure 2-2
Cell Division: Mitosis and Meiosis

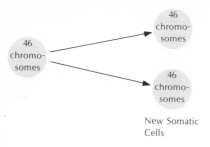

New Somatic
Cells

Mitosis: One cell with the diploid number of chromosomes (46 for humans) duplicates its chromosomes and then divides—producing *two copies,* each with the *full diploid* number of chromosomes.

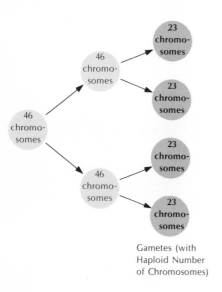

Gametes (with
Haploid Number
of Chromosomes)

Meiosis: In the production of sex cells (gametes), one cell with the diploid number of chromosomes duplicates its chromosomes and then divides—producing *two copies,* each with the *full diploid* number of chromosomes. Both of these two cells then divide *without* first duplicating their chromosomes—producing *four copies,* each with the *haploid* number of chromosomes (23 for humans).

are the *genes,* which are physical structures that determine the potential for one or more biological or behavioral characteristics of the organism. Genes are inherited as units; they do not blend with each other. Genes are located along stringlike molecules of very complicated proteins known as *chromosomes.* In somatic cells, chromosomes are normally found in pairs, each pair consisting of two chromosomes that contain the same genes. The major exception to this arrangement is the pair of chromosomes that determines sex. In females sex is determined by an equivalent pair (called X chromosomes), but in males two different kinds of chromosomes are required, a "female" X chromosome and a "male" Y chromosome.

Human beings normally have forty-six chromosomes in each somatic cell nucleus (that is, twenty-three pairs). This number, called the *diploid number,* varies from species to species. Gamete cells, on the other hand, have single rather than paired chromosomes; thus human gametes have twenty-three chromosomes. This number is called the *haploid number,* and it also varies from species to species.

All the different versions of any gene are called *alleles* of that gene. For instance, there is a gene that determines the ABO blood type of every person. This gene has three versions, or alleles: A, B, and O.

Each person inherits half of his or her genes from each parent because the gametes of each parent have half the genetic material carried in the somatic cells. Thus two gametes (one from each parent) combine and produce a new human being, each gamete bringing with it the haploid number of genes. Combining the two haploid numbers results in the diploid number—the number of chromosomes necessary for an organism to develop. With the exception of identical twins, the genetic component of each person is unique because we receive from each parent a random sample of the alleles the parent carries.

The genetic component that each person inherits is called the *genotype* of the person. The person's observable and measurable characteristics are called the *phenotype.* Some aspects of the phenotype, such as blood type or eye color, are completely determined by the genotype. Other aspects of the phenotype result from the interaction of genotype-determined bodily

Figure 2-3
Mendelian Inheritance

This figure shows the possible combinations of alleles in the children of parents who are both heterozygous for a given gene. Two alleles are shown. The combinations and the frequencies of their occurrences are:

4 ●● homozygotes
8 ●● heterozygotes
4 ●● homozygotes

Dividing by 4 to find the lowest common denominator, we find that the ratio of homozygotes to heterozygotes is:

1 ●   2 ●●   1 ●

This means that, according to probability, one-fourth of the children will be homozygous for ●
one-fourth will be homozygous for ●
and half will be heterozygous ●●

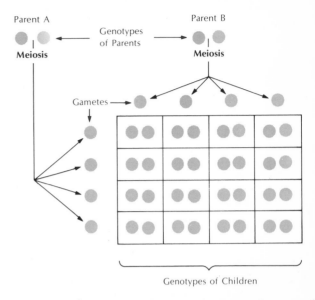

Genotypes of Children

potentials with the environment. For example, part of what determines a person's height is his or her genetic programing for limb, trunk, neck, and head length. However, the diet (clearly a part of the person's environment) of the maturing person and his or her mother during pregnancy also has a determining influence on the individual's eventual stature.

The group of individuals within which mating takes place is called a *breeding population*. If genes never changed, if all people mated randomly, if all breeding populations were extremely large, if the numbers of males and females were equal, and if all matings were equally likely to result in offspring, then the proportion of different alleles would remain constant from generation to generation within these breeding populations. This principle is called the *Hardy-Weinberg law*. To the extent that the Hardy-Weinberg law is operating, the genotype of a breeding population does not change over the generations, and no evolution takes place. In genetic terms, then, *evolution is measured in the change of allele and gene frequencies within breeding populations from generation to generation*. In practice the Hardy-Weinberg law never operates completely; allele and gene frequencies change constantly and evolution never stops.

Figure 2-4

Dominance, Recessiveness, and Codominance among Alleles as Expressed in the ABO Blood System

A **dominant** allele masks out the expression of a recessive homologous allele in the phenotype of an organism. A **recessive** allele is prevented from affecting the phenotype of an organism by a homologous dominant allele. Thus recessive alleles can affect the phenotype of an organism only if the genotype of that organism is homozygous for that recessive allele. **Codominant** alleles express themselves equally in (affect equally) the phenotype of an organism when they are homologous.

Genotype	Phenotype	Relationship Between Alleles
AO	A	A is **dominant** over O; O is **recessive** to A
BO	B	B is **dominant** over O; O is **recessive** to B
AB	AB	A and B are **codominant**
OO	O	O alleles are **recessive** to the other alleles of the **ABO** gene; the only way they can be expressed in the **phenotype** is if the **genotype** is **homozygous** for O

What causes this never-ending evolutionary process? Four mechanisms either singly or in combination constantly affect these genetic frequencies: mutation, random drift, gene flow, and natural selection.

Mutation   The delicate molecular structure of genes is continuously being affected by such factors as radiation (ranging from cosmic radiation to X rays), chemicals taken into the body, and even simple mechanical breakdowns. When the effects are permanent and result in changes in the inherited phenotypic potentials of genes, we say that a mutation has taken place. We discover a mutant gene when we notice a change in a phenotypic trait (in a population) that we know is genetically determined. As far as we know, mutations occur randomly. This means that mutations do not happen because it would be convenient or adaptively useful for a population to acquire a new trait in order to adapt to environmental changes. It is very difficult to know the frequencies of gene mutations among human breeding populations, because we usually only detect harmful mutations and have no means of knowing whether the frequencies of harmful and useful changes are similar. Present calculations range from 4×10^{-6} to 1×10^{-3} mutations per gene per generation (Buettner-Janusch 1973:352). Whatever the actual rates, *mutation is the only source of entirely new genes and alleles.*

Random Drift   A very large breeding population is necessary for the Hardy-Weinberg law to operate. When a small breeding population splits off from a larger one and becomes isolated as a result of geographical or cultural barriers, there is a good chance that it is an unrepresentative sample of the entire original gene pool and that, over the generations, it will pass on increasingly differing percentages of alleles. This random drift will eventually result in a breeding population with genetic characteristics that are quite different from the population from which it split—especially since mutation and the other forces of genetic evolution continue to operate on both populations.

Gene Flow   When two breeding populations that have been relatively isolated from each other—and thus have different gene and allele frequencies—start to interbreed, the genetic components of both popula-

These residents of Pitcairn Island go out in their small boat to meet Admiral Richard E. Byrd. The entire population of Pitcairn Island is descended from 12 British sailors who mutinied on the HMS Bounty, sailed to Tahiti, married Polynesian women, and left with their wives to find an uncharted island where they could hide from the wrath of the British Navy. Their offspring are different genetically, from either of the breeding populations (European and Polynesian) of these original settlers. The two mechanisms which are most obviously at work in the history of Pitcairn Island's population are *gene flow* and *genetic drift.* Can you explain why this is so?

tions are changed. This situation often occurs when populations migrate or when geographical features change sufficiently to allow contact between previously isolated peoples. The source of new genes for each population is the flow of genes (sometimes called *hybridization*) from the other group. The groups may eventually merge to form a new breeding population; or they may maintain their social separation sufficiently to remain relatively distinct entities. An interesting side effect of gene flow is that the new generation, which has inherited genetic materials from both groups, is generally healthier and larger than either of the parent populations—a phenomenon known as *hybrid vigor.*

Natural Selection **This mechanism of evolution is the most important and most misunderstood. Darwin saw the process by which new species are created and old species die out as the result of an unending struggle for existence in which the environment favors certain qualities in individuals. The members of the group who are better adapted to the environment are more likely to survive and reproduce. Thus these favored characteristics are more likely to be passed on from generation to generation and to eventually become outstanding features of a new form of organism.**

What troubled Darwin was how to account for the appearance of the new qualities in individual organisms that would better adapt them to the environment and thus provide the basis for natural selection. On November 25, 1859, shortly after the appearance of his *On the Origin of Species,* he acknowledged in a letter to his friend Thomas Huxley (also an eminent biologist): "You have cleverly hit on one point which has greatly troubled me; if, as I must think, external conditions produce little *direct* effect, what the devil determines each particular variation?" (quoted in Höffding 1955:445; emphasis in source).

We know now that the source of these variations is mutation, and for some breeding populations, gene flow from another group. These variations are not created in order to make a given individual or group of organisms superior or better adapted. Natural selection does not imply inherent superiority of one individual or group at the expense of another. It simply means that, given whatever environmental conditions prevail, certain *accidentally* acquired genes that produce variations in the phenotype of individuals of a particular group may give those individuals a better chance to survive and reproduce than members of another group— or members of their own group who do not have these features. Should the environmental circumstances change, what is adaptive and thus selected for in one niche might well be maladaptive and selected against in another.

Summary **Mutation, random drift, gene flow, and natural selection are the genetic mechanisms that account for biological evolution. Whereas the first three mechanisms affect the frequencies of genetic materials in populations in the statistical sense, only** natural selection gives an identifiable direction to these frequency changes. The direction, however, is not determined by mystical forces such as divine intent. Rather, it is charted by the selective pressures of the environment.

Cultural Evolution

Before we can begin to talk about cultural evolution, we must define the term *culture*—probably the most important concept in anthropology. Although scholars differ on its exact definition, most anthropologists would agree in general with the following: *Culture consists of the patterned behavior (both mental and physical) that individuals learn and are taught as members of groups.* It therefore includes subsistence activities, technology, beliefs, knowledge, values, standards, customs, traditions, language, and all other learned patterns of behavior that are passed on from generation to generation among group members. Each human group, then, has its own unique culture.

The history of human biological evolution is inseparable from the history of human cultural evolution. As the human line began to separate and differentiate itself from the evolutionary lines of our primate relatives, cultural and biological developments were (and continue to be) in a state of dynamic interaction—stimulating each other and making further development possible. However, just as we can describe the mechanisms of biological evolution without reference to culture, we can also discuss the mechanisms and processes of cultural evolution separate from biology. Although culture "has its origin and basis in the biological makeup of man, in its relation to human beings after it has come into existence and become established as a tradition, culture exists and behaves and relates to man as if it were *nonbiological in character*" (White 1959:12; emphasis in original).

Although we can measure biological evolution by monitoring gene frequencies and calibrating phenotypic features such as body shape or brain size, it is a much more complicated task to measure cultural evolution. A frequently used though narrow measuring rod is technology. Leslie White argues that "culture advances as the amount of energy harnessed per capita

The ability of our society to harness massive amounts of energy is used by some to chart our great evolutionary progress. However, if other measures (such as the amount of leisure time available to the average person or the degree to which all people are able to satisfy their wants) are used, the hunters and gatherers of 15,000 B.C. were probably better off than we are now.

per year increases, or as the efficiency or economy of the means of controlling energy is increased, or both" (1959:56). We can extend this concept, however, to encompass more of the totality of human social life. For our purposes we shall agree with Alan Lomax and Norman Berkowitz that "the progress of human culture is plainly reflected in the degree of *differential control* man brings to bear upon the whole spectrum of his activities" (1972:238; emphasis added).

Two fundamental mechanisms—invention and diffusion—enable cultures to increase their control over the activities in which they engage—that is, to evolve.

Both result in the introduction to a culture's repertoire of new knowledge or abilities (or both) that increase the culture's ability to flourish in its particular environmental and social setting.

Invention   An outstanding property of human beings is their inventiveness. This characteristic expresses itself both in the realm of ideas and in the realm of material artifacts. Cultural progress can come about through the invention of a new concept, the solution of a problem, or the discovery of a new item of knowledge. Sometimes, but not always, the invention of new ideas results directly in a change in people's

behavior or the invention of some new tool. But the relationship between an invention and improvements in adaptive behavior or technology can also be indirect. For example, the discovery that matter is composed of atoms did not lead directly to the harnessing of atomic energy. Other inventions in both knowledge and tools were necessary before this could be accomplished.

Diffusion   A fundamental element of culture is communication, both within and between cultural groups (see Chap. 7). When members of one culture learn new items of knowledge, new aptitudes, new solutions to problems, or the production and use of

Agriculture was *invented* independently at least three times and in three different places in the world. From these centers—the Middle West, East Asia, and Mesoamerica—it *diffused* outward. See Chapter 10.

new tools, or they acquire any other new (to them) element of culture from another group, we say that these elements have diffused from one culture to the other. Diffusion can take place directly, through contact between both groups. An example of this process would be the Native Americans teaching the Pilgrims how to plant corn. Or diffusion can take place indirectly, through intermediary groups. This process, called *stimulus diffusion,* involves the spread of cultural traits beyond the groups with which the originating culture had direct contact. For example, when a group of cultivators called the Danubians moved into western Europe some 7,500 years ago, they brought with them the knowledge of how to plant grains and domesticate animals. Local groups picked up these techniques from the Danubians and passed them on to other groups. Thus the domestication of plants and animals spread much farther in Europe than the Danubians themselves migrated.

All known societies increase their ability to survive through both invention and diffusion. Some adapt to their environments by becoming more and more specialized and efficient in exploiting the resources of their environments. As noted earlier, we call this involution or specific evolution. Other societies increase their ability to make use of their environments by becoming more complex and adaptable, more able to deal productively with a greater range of environments. This, as we have defined it, is general evolution or evolutionary progress.

Summary   Evolution, or the process of adaptation to environments, operates in both the biological and cultural realms. On the biological or organic level the mechanisms by which evolution occurs are mutation, random drift, gene flow, and natural selection; on the cultural level the mechanisms are invention and diffusion. On both levels these mechanisms can result in two very different evolutionary processes—involution and evolutionary progress. We can see these mechanisms and processes at work in human biological and cultural evolution.

It is important, however, to note a crucial difference between biological and cultural evolution. Whereas the former is always in response to environmental pressures and lacks any *intent,* the latter frequently—

though not always—results from deliberate behavior varying from trial-and-error experimentation to formal research on the part of individuals or groups. Thus cultural evolution can be and frequently is consciously sought and planned for. Of course, as humans extend their knowledge about genetics, it may come to pass that societies will plan to control biological evolution as well—a development of both great promise and terrifying possibilities.

The Remains of Our Ancestors

The First Hominids

Human beings belong to a group of mammals known as the order of *primates.* This order is divided into two suborders: *Prosimii,* which includes lemurs, lorises, tarsiers, and similar creatures; and *Anthropoidea,* which includes monkeys, apes, and human beings.

Figure 2-5

Taxonomy of the Order of Primates

The taxonomy, increasingly differentiated as we approach humans, shows phylogenetic (evolutionary) relationships as well as how categories are included in each other. Thus, for example, the great apes (chimpanzee, gorilla, orangutan) are our closest living relatives, with the lesser apes (gibbon, siamang) next. Humans and apes (Hominoidea) are more closely related to Old World monkeys (Cercopithecoidea) than to New World monkeys, which belong to a different infraorder, the Platyrrhini.

Suborders	Infraorders	Subfamilies	Families	Examples
Prosimii	Lemuriforms			lemurs indris sifakas
	Lorisiforms			lorises bushbabies
	Tarsiiforms			tarsiers
Anthropoidea	Platyrrhini			New World monkeys
	Catarrhini	Cercopithecoidea		Old World monkeys
		Hominoidea	Hylobatidae	lesser apes
			Pongidae	great apes
			Hominidae	humans

Figure 2-6
The Cenozoic Era
The Cenozoic era follows the Cretaceous
era and is divided into the six epochs
shown. Although the earliest primates
actually evolved late in the Cretaceous,
the first apes evolved in the Oligocene,
and the first hominids, late in the Miocene.

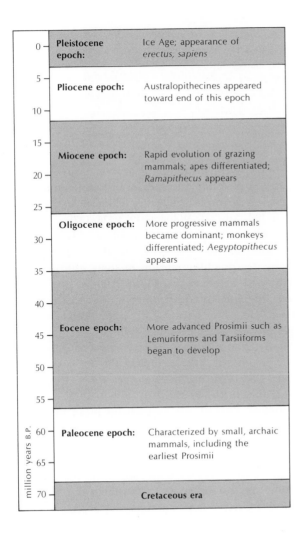

Pleistocene epoch:	Ice Age; appearance of *erectus, sapiens*	
Pliocene epoch:	Australopithecines appeared toward end of this epoch	
Miocene epoch:	Rapid evolution of grazing mammals; apes differentiated; *Ramapithecus* appears	
Oligocene epoch:	More progressive mammals became dominant; monkeys differentiated; *Aegyptopithecus* appears	
Eocene epoch:	More advanced Prosimii such as Lemuriforms and Tarsiiforms began to develop	
Paleocene epoch:	Characterized by small, archaic mammals, including the earliest Prosimii	
Cretaceous era		

million years B.P.

The suborder *Anthropoidea* is further divided into two infraorders: *Platyrrhini,* the New World monkeys (such as the spider monkey); and *Catarrhini,* the Old World monkeys, apes, and humans.

Catarrhini are divided into two superfamilies: *Cercopithecoidea,* the Old World monkeys, and *Hominoidea,* apes and human beings. There are three families of *Hominoidea: Hylobatidae,* which includes the lesser apes—the gibbon and siamang; *Pongidae,* the great apes—the gorilla, chimpanzee, and orangutan; and *Hominidae,* which refers to human beings.

To discuss human (hominid) evolution is to speculate about how and when the developmental history of our own evolutionary line broke away from the lines of development of our nearest relatives, the great apes (pongids). The search for our own origins leads us, then, to look for an ancestor common to both pongids and hominids, to identify the first of these hominid ancestors, and to explain how they came to split off from the pongid line. The most direct source of information on this subject is the fossil record of preserved pongid and hominid skeletal remains, which we can compare in terms of their morphology (shape), age, and the environmental contexts in which they are found.

Morphologically, the common ancestor of apes and human beings would have to be a connecting link between the primitive primates of the Paleocene and Eocene epochs (see fig. 2-6) and the Miocene apes of East Africa. The group of fossils that fits neatly into this role is called *Aegyptopithecus,* an Oligocene pongid some 30 million years old. By the shape of its teeth it could certainly have been ancestral to *Dryopithecus,* which appeared some 10 million years later and is the ancestor of the modern great apes. But despite its relatively long snout and small braincase, *Aegyptopithecus* exhibits characteristics (such as large eye sockets that are directed fully forward) that could easily make it ancestral to *Ramapithecus,* the first hominid.

Aegyptopithecus was found in the Fayum area of Egypt, which during the Oligocene was a wet and forested environment. From what we can discover from its remains, it seems to have been an agile, quadrupedal forest canopy dweller approximately the size of a mod-

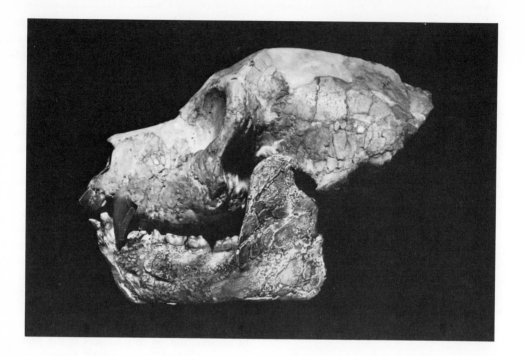

Skull of *Aegyptopithecus zeuxis*. Recent research suggests that this Oligocene pongid is the ancestor of both apes and humans.

ern gibbon, whose dentition (teeth formation) suggests that it was probably adapted to an herbivorous and possibly a frugivorous (fruit) diet (Pillbeam 1972:42–43; Simons 1972:216–221; Williams 1973:126–127).

In 1937 G. Edward Lewis completed his doctoral dissertation at Yale University. In this unpublished work he described the remains of some primate jaws that he had found in the Siwalik Hills of India. He called this primate *Ramapithecus brevirostrus* and claimed that it was ancestral to *Australopithecus* and hence also to modern human beings (see fig. 2-11). His dissertation was ignored for twenty-five years until Elwyn Simons of Yale restudied the materials and decided that Lewis had been correct in his interpretations (Pilbeam 1972:91–92).

Renewed interest was focused on these fossil remains, and additional discoveries were soon made, including some jaws found by Louis S. B. Leakey in Kenya (which he called *Kenyapithecus wickeri*). Although we have only the upper and lower jaws of this primate, very careful study of the teeth has enabled physical anthropologists to construct a picture of a late Miocene hominid with a cranial capacity of some 300 cubic centimeters (cc), living some 10 to 14 million years ago in open woodland areas from Africa (*Kenyapithecus wickeri*) to India (*Ramapithecus brevirostrus*). This primate is now referred to as *Ramapithecus.*

Taken as a whole, the evidence to be obtained from the *Ramapithecus* material points to an animal with a facial-dental complex of characteristics similar to or foreshadowing those of later hominids, both morphologically and functionally. The relative proportions of front and back teeth, as well as many other features, suggest that [*Ramapithecus*] was, or was becoming, a ground feeder eating a diet including numerous small, tough morsels (Pilbeam 1972:94).

The resemblances to *Australopithecus* pervade the whole face and dentition of *Ramapithecus.* Together these features combine to indicate increased power of the grinding cheek teeth and a decrease in the size of the front teeth, presumably as a result of a de-emphasis on the juicing and shredding function of the . . . incisors and large interlocking canines of typical apes (Simons 1972:271).

Very sophisticated research by Charles Oxnard (1969) on the effect of forms of locomotion on bone shape has been applied to what we know of *Ramapithecus.* These researches suggest to David Pilbeam that this hominid was quite possibly a creature weighing between 40 and 80 pounds, that it swung by its arms, and that it lived predominantly in trees but came to the ground for food (1972:97–98). Although *Ramapithecus* might well have been a more permanently terrestrial knuckle walker (like the modern gorilla) rather than primarily a tree dweller, it quite possibly moved bipedally (on two legs) when it ventured out into open foraging areas. Over several million years the hominid line of primates gradually adapted to bipedal locomotion through natural selection, and hominids became habitual ground-dwelling bipeds.

If we accept *Ramapithecus* as the earliest known hominid, this means that our ancestors first split off from the ancestors of apes at the edges of forests along

Figure 2-7

Reconstruction of the Face of *Ramapithecus* Derived from Mandibular and Maxillary Fossil Remains

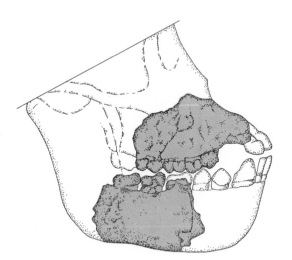

lakes and rivers, where they picked vegetable foods off the ground. The fact that *Ramapithecus* is a Miocene fossil suggests that the traditional assumption that the first hominids appeared in the Pliocene in the savannah grasslands of Africa is wrong. And since we have found no tools associated with *Ramapithecus,* theories that tie the differentiation of hominids to the use of tools (Washburn 1960) also appear to be problematical. However, *Ramapithecus* might have made and used occasional tools—as modern chimpanzees do—but left no trace of them.

A persuasive reason for accepting *Ramapithecus* as our first hominid ancestor is the fact that the human shoulder still reflects our ancestors' arm-swinging tree

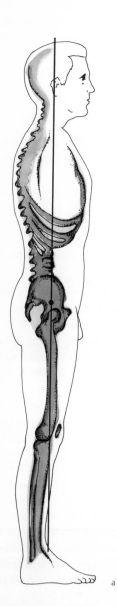

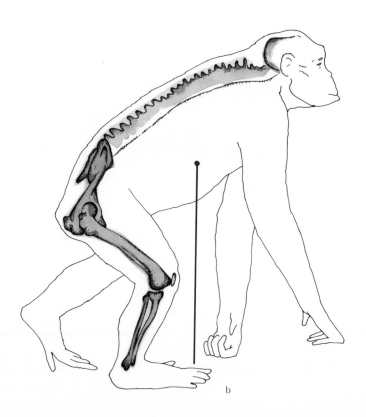

a

b

Figure 2-8
**Bipedalism Versus Knuckle Walking:
A Human Evolutionary Development**

a. Humans maintain a bipedal posture, in which the body's center of gravity is located directly behind the midpoint of the hip joint. When erect, both hip and knee are extended, thus conserving energy.
b. In knuckle-walking chimpanzees, the center of gravity of the body is located in the middle of the area bounded by the legs and arms. When a knuckle-walking ape walks bipedally, its center of gravity shifts constantly, from side to side and up and down. In humans, there is much less displacement of the center of gravity, and thus bipedal walking is much more efficient.

life. *Ramapithecus* probably had the morphology to be such a creature, yet it was clearly moving out from the forests and toward a ground-dwelling way of life. With *Ramapithecus* as our ancestor, it is easy to envision the adaptive steps that led to the fully bipedal *Australopithecus,* who had lost the tree-dwelling, arm-swinging mode of locomotion and was living in the open savannah grasslands of Africa some 3.5 million years ago.

For many years the nature of the australopithecine fossil remains has puzzled physical anthropologists, and opinions still differ over how these finds should be interpreted. We shall present one widely held interpretation, but indicate some areas where there are serious disagreements.

In 1924 in a limestone quarry at Taung in South Africa, workers discovered the fossilized remains of some skulls. The limestone blocks containing these skulls were sent to Raymond Dart at Witwatersrand University, who found that two of the skulls were of baboons, but that fragments of a braincase and face of a third skull were clearly hominid rather than pongid in nature. Although the skull belonged to a six-year-old child, enough of its features were present for Dart to conclude that this child represented a population of "ape-people"—that is, a population that had characteristics of both pongids and hominids but that was relatively clearly in the hominid line. Dart named this species *Australopithecus africanus* (Leakey and Goodall 1969:112).

Since that time a number of similar remains have been found (many by the famous team of Louis and Mary Leakey in East Africa), suggesting the following picture. Apparently two distinct lines of *Australopithecus* developed, called *robust* and *gracile* (see fig. 2-11). Robust australopithecine adults averaged close to 5 feet in height and weighed between 120 and 150 pounds. They had the limbs of fully erect bipeds and were thus well adapted to the savannah grassland environment (although their lower back and pelvic structure was not fully evolved for erect posture). Their cranial capacity was approximately 500 cc. They had massive brow ridges, no forehead, and a bony crest (the sagittal crest) running down the middle of the top of the head that served as a platform for the attachment of the muscles that worked a quite massive jaw. Their teeth were fully hominid, with relatively small incisors and canines; their premolars and molars, however, were quite large.

Two species of robust australopithecines apparently existed. *Australopithecus robustus* appeared some 3.5 million years ago, surviving until approximately 1.6 million years ago. At this time the very similar form called *Australopithecus boisei* appeared (Pilbeam 1972:156), differentiated from *Australopithecus robustus* by a less striking difference in size between the front and back teeth.

Gracile australopithecines were approximately 4 feet tall and may have weighed as little as 40 to 50 pounds or as much as 100 to 120 pounds as mature adults. Like the robust australopithecines, they were fully bipedal (although not entirely erect) and lived in open savannah country. They also had large brow ridges and lacked a forehead. However, their bone structure was much less rugged than that of their robust relatives, and they mostly lacked the sagittal crest on the top of the skull. Their dentition, like that of the robust

Robust australopithecines, side and back views of skulls. The cranium is from Olduvai and the jaw from Peninj.

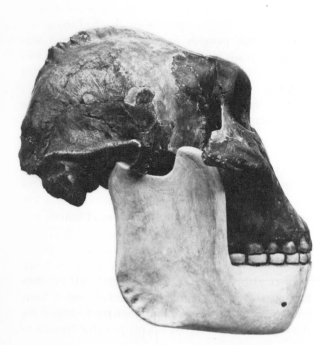
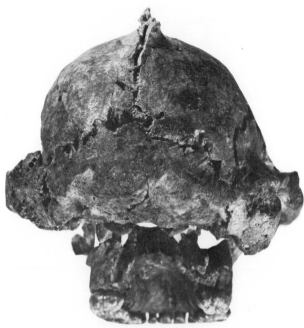

Figure 2-9
Reconstruction of the major australo-pithecene fossil forms; note the heavier build of *robustus*.

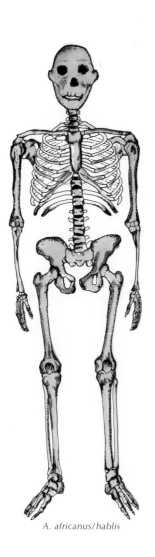

A. africanus/hablis

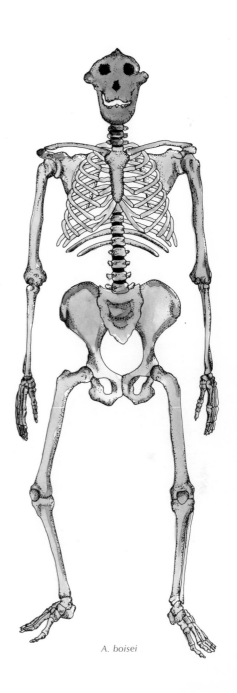

A. boisei

Figure 2-10
Geographical Distribution of the Australopithecines

Australopithecine fossil remains are con-centrated in southern, central, and east-ern Africa. However, these hominids apparently did exist outside the continent of Africa; specimens have been found in Israel and possibly in China and Java as well (although the taxonomic status of these eastern fossils is not clear).

1	South Africa
2	East Africa
3	Chad
4	Israel
5	Java
6	Southern China

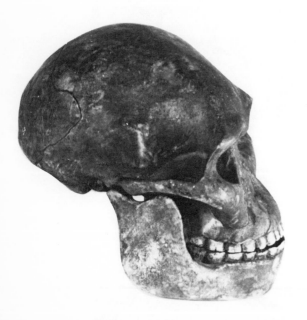

Restoration of a gracile *Australopithecus* from Makapan limeworks, Transvaal, South Africa.

line, was fully hominid in that their canines were small—as were their incisors, premolars, and molars.

After much debate, many anthropologists now agree that the gracile line of australopithecines is also represented by two species. *Australopithecus africanus* had a cranial capacity roughly the same as the robust australopithecines (about 500 cc). Remains have been discovered in both East and South Africa. The dates of the South African finds are not established, but in East Africa, *Australopithecus africanus* has been placed between 3.5 million years ago and 1.6 million years ago—making it roughly contemporaneous with *Australopithecus robustus*. Between 1.85 and 1.65 million years ago, *Australopithecus africanus* apparently evolved into a somewhat larger and more advanced form, with a cranial capacity around 600 cc. For a while its finders (Louis and Mary Leakey) called it *Homo habilis*, but most experts agree that it was a form of gracile *Australopithecus* and it is now generally referred to as *Australopithecus habilis* (Butzer 1971:413–421).

It is possible that by 2 million years ago some australopithecines had radiated out of Africa. Finds in Israel, southern China, and Java suggest that they may have moved all the way across southern Asia. However, both the southern China and Java finds are problematic. Simons believes the Chinese teeth do represent robust australopithecines, but others assign them to an entirely different genus, *Gigantopithecus* (Simons 1963). The Javanese fossils, called *Meganthropus paleojavanicus* by some, might also be robust australopithecines. However, Pilbeam believes that these specimens represent an intermediate stage between *Australopithecus habilis* and *Homo erectus,* and could with equal logic be classified as either (Pilbeam 1972:162).

Figure 2.11 indicates the various interpretations of the evolutionary lines represented by the australopithecine fossils. The author favors the following interpretation: *Ramapithecus,* the first hominid, evolved into two lines of australopithecines. The robust line is first represented some 3.5 million years ago by *Australopithecus robustus,* which evolved into *Australopithecus boisei* around 1.6 million years ago. This line eventually became extinct. The gracile line of australo-

Figure 2-11
Some Alternative Interpretations of the Phylogenetic (Evolutionary) Relationships among the Australopithecine Fossil Forms
The major author representing each interpretation is shown. The present author follows D. Pilbeam (c).

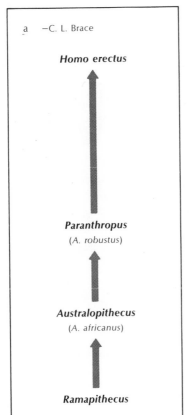

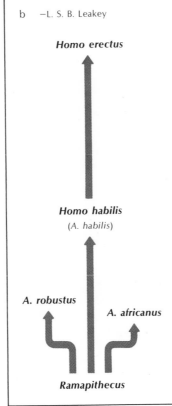

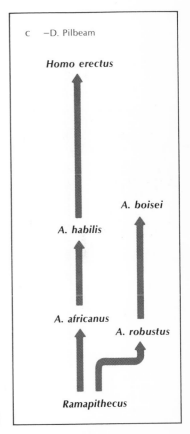

pithecines also appeared some 3.5 million years ago in the form of *Australopithecus africanus,* which evolved into *Australopithecus habilis.*

Richard and Mary Leakey have recently announced the finding of skulls with a cranial capacity of 800 cc, 30 percent larger than *Australopithecus habilis* crania found previously. These skulls probably belong to a hominid that was ancestral to *Homo erectus,* yet are over 3 million years old. But this discovery need not overly disturb our picture. Although the Leakey's believe "Skull 1470" and other recent finds near Lake Rudolf and in Laetolil region of Kenya represent a line of evolution entirely separate from the australopithecines, they may simply have found evidence that *Australopithecus habilis* evolved earlier and had a wider range of morphological features than we had previously assumed. In any event, it still seems reasonable to argue

that *Australopithecus africanus* evolved into a more advanced form, *Australopithecus habilis,* which subsequently evolved into *Homo erectus* some 1 million years ago.

The Origins of Human Culture

So far our discussion of human origins has focused on the nature of the skeletal remains of our early hominid ancestors. But the outstanding feature of modern human beings is perhaps the complexity of the cultural systems they have developed. Indeed, culture has become the major means through which human beings adapt to their environments. As the species evolved, modern *Homo sapiens* lost biological pro-

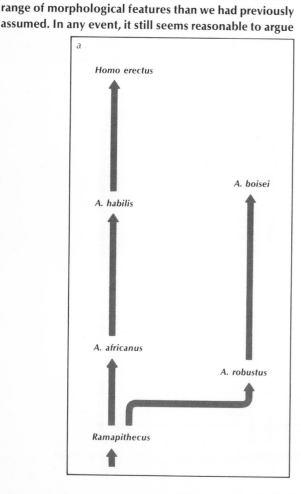

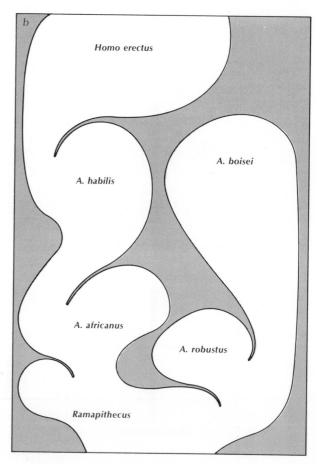

Figure 2-12
**Two Methods of Diagramming
Phylogenetic (Evolutionary) Relationships
among Fossil Populations**
Style *a* is easier to read, but it distorts
the materials by suggesting sudden beginnings and ends for the existence of
fossil populations. Style *b* is more difficult to read; however, it has the virtue
of suggesting gradual evolutionary development from one fossil population to
another. It also illustrates how one fossil
form can evolve into another yet later
coexist with the new form. This model
should be kept in mind throughout the
discussion of hominid evolution.

graming (instincts) as a source of specific instructions
on how to deal with the environment and came to
depend heavily on culturally learned behavior. Thus, in
a sense, culture itself has become one of the major
environments to which human beings have adapted:
We have evolved into culture-dependent creatures,
with a body shape, a central nervous system, and
physiological characteristics that are structured by—
and enhance—this dependence. Clifford Geertz dramatically expresses the complete interdependence of
biology and culture:

> There is no such thing as human nature indepen-
> dent of culture. Men without culture would not
> be the clever savages of Golding's *Lord of the
> Flies* thrown back upon the cruel wisdom of their
> animal instincts; nor would they be . . . intrin-
> sically talented apes who had somehow failed to
> find themselves. They would be unworkable
> monstrosities with very few useful instincts,
> fewer recognizable sentiments, and no intellect:
> mental basket cases. As our central nervous
> system . . . grew up in great part in interaction
> with culture, *it is incapable of directing our
> behavior or organizing our experience without
> the guidance provided by systems of significant
> symbols* (1966:49; emphasis added).

A reasonable question, then, is: when did human
culture evolve? Pilbeam and Simons (1965) believe that
Ramapithecus might have been a tool-using animal and
might even have had some bipedal tendencies. But no
tools have been found in association with *Ramapithecus*—nor, for that matter, with any of the australopithecines other than *Australopithecus habilis*. Many
scholars presume that the gracile australopithecines
were able to survive as relatively small, savannah-
dwelling bipeds by using items in their environment
such as sticks, bones, and unmodified stones for tools,
much as chimpanzees have been observed to do in
their natural environment (van Lawick-Goodall 1971).
But the first manufactured stone tools are found unambiguously only in the presence of *Australopithecus
habilis*.

These tools are called *pebble tools*. They consist
of pieces of flint that are somewhat larger than fist
size and that have had some six or seven flakes knocked

off them. What remains is a *core tool* (the flakes are not used), very rough and unfinished and weighing several pounds. It can be used to crush the heads of small game, to skin them, and to dissect the carcasses.

Most scholars associate these tools with the beginnings of a diet that regularly included meat—meat obtained as the result of deliberate (and possibly even organized) hunting. Although their diet was presumably still mostly vegetable in nature, *Australopithecus habilis* groups did systematically devour a wide range of small game: rodents, birds, bats, insectivores, lizards, fish, crabs, and turtles. On occasion they apparently hunted big game as well. At Olduvai Gorge in East Africa we find the remains of a primitive elephant that was apparently driven into a swamp and then beaten to death. Its bones were scattered nearby, mute testimony to our ancestors' butchering and dissecting abilities (Butzer 1971:427).

Although modern human beings are descended from this gracile line of australopithecines, which survived competition with other species for the resources of the early Pleistocene savannah, we need not draw the pessimistic conclusions that some journalists and popularizers of anthropology and ethology (the study of animal behavior) have offered. Writers such as Robert Ardrey (1961, 1966, 1970) and Konrad Lorenz (1966) argue that australopithecine hunting behavior

Figure 2-13
Oldowan Pebble Tools (or Choppers)
Two Oldowan chopping tools (front and side views) made by removing a few flakes from lava lumps to form jagged working edges, indicated by arrows (16/25 actual size).

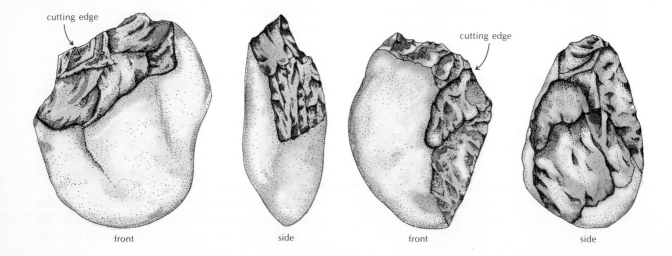

cutting edge

front   side   front   side

provided the evolutionary origin of human violence. But they fail to appreciate that the outstanding achievement at this stage of evolution was the development of patterns of *cooperation*—patterns that are fundamental to the evolution of human culture (see Chaps. 3 and 4).

The Great Expansion

By the middle Pleistocene, between 1 and 1.5 million years ago, our ancestors seem to have become widely dispersed throughout the Old World. By 700,000 years ago they had certainly spread from Africa to western Europe, and they extended across the Near East and out into the far reaches of southern Asia by 300,000–500,000 years ago. Although there is considerable regional skeletal variation, most scholars agree that the hominid line was represented by one species, *Homo erectus,* which had evolved in Africa from *Australopithecus habilis* and had begun to occupy the colder climates that were previously inhospitable to hominids.

Homo erectus was about five feet tall, with a body and limbs that were within the range of modern human variation. The only "primitive" feature of this ancestor was its head, which exhibited such features as heavy ridges of bone across the eyes; a minimal forehead that sloped back dramatically; a narrowing of the skull behind the eye orbits and a slight sagittal crest, both of which suggest heavy facial musculature; and a cranial capacity averaging around 1,000 cc, which is the lowest limit of the range for modern human beings (Williams 1973: Chap. 10).

For over 1 million years, until about 200,000–300,000 years ago, *Homo erectus* roamed across the Old World. In Africa these early humans developed a new tool, called a *hand ax,* which apparently evolved directly out of the pebble tool of the australopithecines. Hand axes, like pebble tools, are cores; they are made by chipping flakes off a flint nodule and using the remaining core as the tool rather than using the flakes. But whereas the makers of pebble tools merely trimmed away part of the stone to make a cutting edge, the producers of hand axes actually modeled the stone, trimming it all around to achieve a desired shape (Fagan 1974:84–90). This in itself suggests that culture was

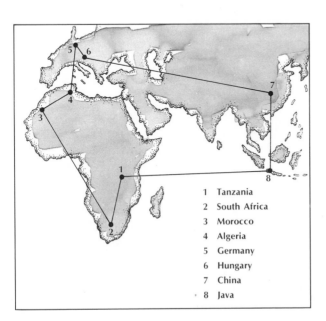

Figure 2-14
Geographical Distribution of
Homo Erectus

The more advanced culture of *Homo erectus* enabled some of these groups to inhabit far colder climates than had any previous australopithecine populations. Not surprisingly, it was *H. erectus* who first controlled fire in Europe and China.

1   Tanzania
2   South Africa
3   Morocco
4   Algeria
5   Germany
6   Hungary
7   China
8   Java

Figure 2-15
Hominid Biological and Cultural Evolution

A = *Ramapithecus* (300 cc)
B = *Australopithecus africanus* (450 cc)
C = *Australopithecus habilis* (600 cc)
D = *Homo erectus* (1,000 cc)
E = *Homo sapiens* (1,375 cc)

evolving and that technical skill—human mastery over the environment—was increasing.

All australopithecines had lived in similar climates —subtropical savannahs near streams and lakes—in which they produced only one technological tradition,

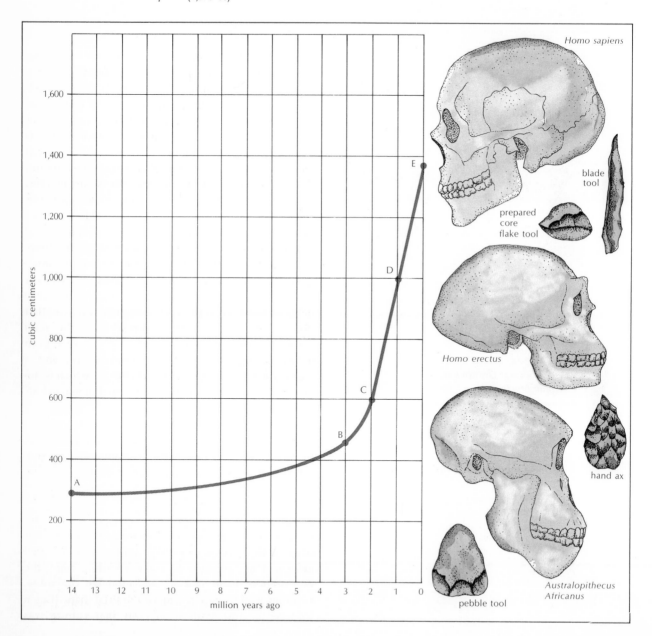

the pebble tool. *Homo erectus,* however, lived in a wider range of environmental conditions and was thus clearly more adaptable than the australopithecines were. Consequently, we can say that it represents a new stage of evolutionary progress beyond the australopithecines. But although there was biological progress in the evolution of the body and especially in the expansion of the brain, it is very significant that at this stage of evolution culture progressed as well. *Homo erectus* did not have to evolve into many different biological forms in order to adapt to the different (and especially colder) ecological zones that it occupied. Instead, *Homo erectus* adapted to the environmental challenges primarily through cultural means.

Homo erectus apparently produced three distinct technological traditions in different geographical regions of the Old World. Evidence of the earliest of these was found at Olduvai Gorge in East Africa, where the *hand ax* or *Chellean tradition* developed out of the pebble tool tradition. Our earliest dates for the hand ax culture are around 600,000 years ago. It apparently spread from East Africa to North and West Africa, southern Europe, and the Middle East. In some parts of Africa this tradition lasted until 60,000 years ago (Fagan 1974:84–90).

The hand ax tradition had two stages. The earlier stage, called the *Abbevillean* or *Chellean culture,* lasted from 600,000 to 400,000 years ago (Rouse 1973).

Figure 2-16
An Abbevillean (Chellean) Hand Ax
Front and side views of two early hand axes from Olduvai Gorge, Bed II (9/16 actual size). This tool complex is associated with the remains of *H. erectus,* dating back to 600,000 B.P. It is the first stage of the hand ax tradition.

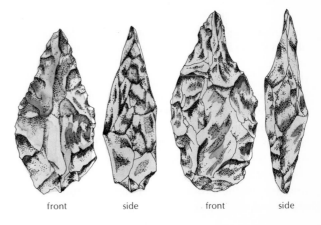

front   side   front   side

Its best-known trait is the Chellean hand ax, a core tool from which much, but not all, of the surface has been chipped away. Like the pebble tool, it was made in one continuous process of chipping away the outside layer; however, many more flakes were knocked off—about twenty to twenty-five pieces—producing a more versatile tool.

The second stage of the hand ax tradition, the *Acheulian culture,* lasted from 400,000 to about 60,000 years ago. The Acheulian hand ax was made in two stages. First, the entire outer layer of the flint nodule was flaked off, then the tool was carefully shaped into the preferred form. In Europe this form tended to be heart shaped; in Africa it was larger, with straight sides.

Another roughly contemporary cultural tradition was the east Asian *chopper tradition.* Like hand axes, choppers were also core tools, but they were merely flaked in alternate directions along one edge to produce a zigzag cutting surface. As with the Chellean hand ax, the makers did not remove the entire surface from the tool.

Although in both the hand ax and chopper traditions crude flakes were also used for cutting and scraping (Clark 1969:37), it was the third tradition, the *Clactonian culture* of the northern areas of western and central Eurasia, in which *Homo erectus* did not make hand axes or choppers at all, but rather knocked large, somewhat clumsy flakes off nodules of flint and *used the flakes* instead of the remaining core. The Clactonian culture may have begun as early as 600,000 years ago and lasted until about 60,000 years ago. Although these Clactonian flake tools were not discernibly more versatile than were hand axes, the idea that one might use flakes rather than cores ultimately became the basis for another great cultural advance—the evolution of Middle Paleolithic culture (Rouse 1973).

But before we discuss this further advance, let us fill out the picture of *Homo erectus*'s accomplishments. Along with the tools of the three major technological traditions (hand axes, choppers, and Clactonian flake tools), these early humans produced a variety of implements. The diverse flakes, produced as byproducts in the process of making core tools, were retouched and formed into scrapers, knives, cleavers, and chisels. These could be used for butchering animals, preparing hides, and carving bone, and they may also have been used to collect vegetable foods.

Both wood and bone were also widely used. The Spanish site of Torralba, some 400,000 years old, has provided evidence that the long bones and ribs of large animals were split down the middle and retouched to make knives, picks, and cleavers. Found in the same site are pieces of pine that have been cut, trimmed, or sharpened. At Lehringen, Germany, the remains of a six-foot-long wooden spear that was stuck between the ribs of an elephant some 125,000 years ago have been recovered. *Homo erectus* was also the first creature to control fire, as indicated by the remains of hearths, charcoal, charred bones, and carbon found in various European sites of 400,000 years ago or possibly even earlier (Butzer 1971:445). Similar evidence shows the use of fire by *Homo erectus* near Peking at the same time. It is not surprising that this invention was made in the northern latitudes where the environment was quite cold. Fire diffused southward gradually and may not have reached sub-Saharan Africa until late Pleistocene times (Clark 1960).

Home erectus was also apparently the first hominid to build full-fledged structures for shelter against the elements. A site about 300,000 years old at Terra Amata, near Nice, reveals the presence of huts,

> indicated by: (a) imprints of a series of stakes, each averaging about 8 cm. in diameter, that were driven into the sand to form the walls of a shelter; (b) lines of stones, paralleling the stake imprints, and occasionally stacked one on the other, apparently to brace the walls of the shelter; and (c) impressions of thick posts along the central axis of the structures (Butzer 1971: 446).

Nor were these structures small; they ranged from around twenty-five to forty-five feet in length by some thirteen to twenty feet in width. They were oval in shape, and the floors were covered with organic matter (for beds?), ashes (from fires for heat and possibly for cooking), and waste flakes from the production of tools (Butzer 1971:446).

These huts are the earliest evidence we have that hominid groups were divided into subgroups. We may conjecture that these subgroups were drawn along the lines of blood relationship and thus constitute the earliest form or forms of the family in human evolutionary history.

How did *Homo erectus* populations subsist? For the most part, they continued the hunting and foraging way of life of the advanced australopithecines, with an added emphasis on the hunting of larger game such as elephants, horses, pigs, hippopotamuses, rhinoceroses, and even wolves and lions. Many of these animals were

Figure 2-17
Acheulian Toolkit

Acheulian tools from Kalambo Falls, Zambia, front and side views (one-fourth actual size). This represents the second stage of the hand ax tradition, which evolved out of the first stage around 400,000 B.P.

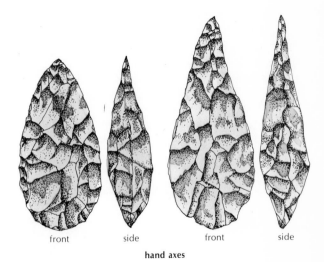

front   side   front   side

hand axes

Figure 2-18
Tools of the Asian Chopper Tradition

A crude chopping tool from Choukoutien, China, front and side views (three-eighths actual size).

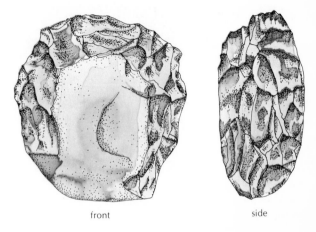

front   side

Reconstruction of a female skull and face (*Homo erectus pekinensis*) from Choukoutien.

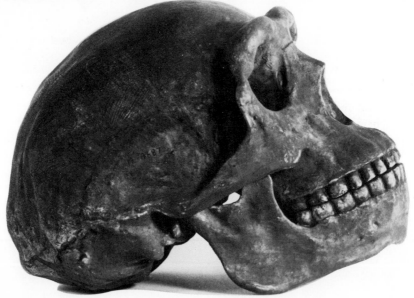

driven into swamps and bogs, possibly by setting fire to the grass. Baseball-sized round stones may have been attached to leather thongs and used in bola fashion to entangle the legs of running animals. Hunting, as opposed to the gathering of vegetable foods, probably became increasingly important as groups of these early humans migrated out of the tropical and subtropical areas and into colder temperate regions where plants were seasonally scarce (Butzer 1971:448–449).

Clearly, *Homo erectus* was both biologically and culturally more advanced than the australopithecines. What caused this evolutionary progress, this transition from *Australopithecus habilis* to *Homo erectus* around 1 million years ago in East Africa? We may never know for sure. One plausible theory has been advanced by Grover S. Krantz (1968). He points out that contemporary hunting and foraging groups with Stone Age technology (such as the southern African group discussed in Chap. 21) use what he calls *persistence hunting.*

Humans are unique in their ability to pursue game over vast distances and often for days at a time, literally driving their quarry into the ground. To persist despite fatigue, discouragement, hunger, and thirst requires a tough-minded commitment to a mental image of the final success of the hunt. The ability to maintain this

A !Kung San hunter of the Kalahari desert in South Africa bringing home a skinned porcupine which he has found and dug out of its den. Tracking and stalking the animal take skill and patience. But because they lack the technology to quickly kill large game, these hunters must often track an animal they have wounded with poisoned arrows for days on end. Both the physical ability and the psychological drive or determination to persist in this exhausting task contribute to these people's ability to survive. It is entirely possible that our early hominid ancestors evolved their upright posture in part, at least, in response to the demands made on them by this form of persistence hunting, which was the only kind available to them given their extremely primitive technology.

image for motivation requires a memory of previous successes. One of the conspicuous aspects of the transition from the australopithecine stage to the stage of *Homo erectus* is the dramatic expansion of the size of the brain and the development of the cortex. Krantz suggests that this evolutionary development helped make possible a vastly improved memory, providing a selective advantage to those individuals who were better able to keep images in their minds to motivate their hunting behavior.

Why did our ancestors adopt persistence hunting as a survival technique? A reasonable explanation is that this form of behavior helped them to compensate for the fact that although bipedalism is very useful as an adaptation to tool use (Washburn 1960), it is a slow form of locomotion. Bipedalism, then, like all adaptive specializations, solved old problems but posed new ones.

Hunting was not the only behavior facilitated by the evolution of both bipedalism and the brain; social behavior was promoted as well. Under the term *social behavior* we include the ability to communicate through spoken language (see Chap. 7), to cooperate, to organize social relations, and to pass culture on from generation to generation. These abilities certainly were selectively advantageous in that they enabled *Homo erectus* to be more flexible in solving the problems posed by the various environments these early humans occupied. Thus they represent important aspects of the process of general evolution in the history of our species.

The Arrival of Homo Sapiens

The most recent evidence suggests that as early as 300,000 years ago the hominid populations living in Africa and Eurasia were practically modern human beings.

Their brain size was well within the range of modern man and their bodies were indistinguishable from ours, though some of the early populations may have been rather more robust. Only their heads still looked strange, with long skulls and heavily built faces and jaws. Through the evolution of *Homo sapiens* during the last 300,000 years, we see the final reduction of the jaws and the appearance of man's chin. As the jaws became smaller, the whole face shrank and receded under the brain case, so that it became surmounted by a vertical forehead. This changed the balance of the head, and the long narrow skull of *Homo erectus* became the rounded skull of many modern populations (Campbell 1974:111).

The earliest remains of *Homo sapiens* are all found in Europe and date back to between 300,000 and 200,000 years ago. The fossil record for the following 100,000 years is extremely sketchy (see Campbell 1974:111; table 3.7). Only for the most recent 100,000 years do we have enough remains to reconstruct the evolutionary sequence with reasonable accuracy.

The skeletal remains indicate that *Homo sapiens* probably evolved in two stages. The earlier stage, lasting from about 300,000 until perhaps 70,000 years ago, is called the Neanderthal stage—technically known

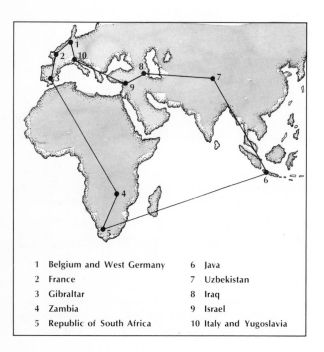

1	Belgium and West Germany	6	Java
2	France	7	Uzbekistan
3	Gibraltar	8	Iraq
4	Zambia	9	Israel
5	Republic of South Africa	10	Italy and Yugoslavia

Figure 2-19
The Geographical Distribution of *Homo Sapiens Neanderthalensis*
Neanderthal groups in Europe inhabited greater extremes of environment than had any previous hominid form, living as far north as the ice sheets of the Würm glaciation would allow, in arctic tundra environments. They were able to do this because they had developed a sufficiently complex and versatile technology.

as *Homo sapiens neanderthalensis*. Remains at this stage are found all across the Old World, from Africa through the Middle East, down into Southeast Asia, and across Europe into the north just below the continental ice sheets. We also find Neanderthal stage sites in southern Europe (Campbell 1974:111–122).

Homo sapiens neanderthalensis varied considerably in appearance; these people acquired their largest-jawed and most robust forms in the northern latitudes, which they were the first hominids to occupy. In these areas the cranial capacity of Neanderthaloid people averaged over 1,400 cc, roughly 100 cc more than that of modern human beings.

The transition from the Neanderthal stage to the modern human beings called *Homo sapiens sapiens* was very rapid in some places and gradual in others. In western Europe the transition was so abrupt around 35,000 B.C. that most scholars believe the modern human beings invaded the area, probably from the Middle East during a temporary retreat of the Würm glacial. In South Africa, *Homo sapiens neanderthalensis* and *Homo sapiens sapiens* appear to have lived side by side for a while. Only in the Middle East have we discovered a series of progressive changes, starting around 70,000 years ago, that show the evolution of smaller-jawed, smaller-skulled, slightly lighter boned modern *Homo sapiens sapiens* from the more robust *Homo sapiens neanderthalensis* (Campbell 1974:111–112).

The simplest hypothesis on the basis of the present evidence is that modern forms first appeared in western Asia or northern Africa and soon spread south, moving later to eastern Asia and finally to Europe. We might expect the big-jawed forms to have survived longer in outlying areas. We do not at present have enough evidence to determine whether the big-jawed populations were genetically swamped by the invaders, were exterminated by them, or evolved into their successors. Just one thing is certain: the genes of the big-jawed people survived longer in Southeast Asia than elsewhere, and have made a substantial contribution to the aboriginal people of Australia, who have the largest jaws and teeth among living peoples (Campbell 1974:112).

This skull of a Classic Neanderthal Male, Circeo I, shows limey concretions deposited by water in the burial site.

Although on a biological level the evolutionary step from the stage of *Homo erectus* to the stage of *Homo sapiens neanderthalensis* was taken some 300,000 years ago, no significant cultural change took place until approximately 70,000 years ago, at the onset of the Würm glaciation in Europe. The Clactonian, chopper, and hand ax traditions (which, with the australopithecine pebble tool tradition, are collectively called Lower Paleolithic culture) continued essentially unchanged in their respective areas of the world, even though our ancestors were evolving biologically.

In Europe, however, a new form of stone tool technology eventually evolved out of the local Acheulian and Clactonian cultures. The Neanderthal groups living in this northern and increasingly colder environment developed a way of producing versatile, multipurpose tools consisting of flakes rather than cores. But these were not the relatively unformed and coarse flakes of

Figure 2-20
The Technique of Prepared-Core Flake Tool Production

The making of a Levallois flake tool: (1) the sides of a stone are trimmed; (2) the top is then trimmed; (3) a small straight edge is trimmed on the side to make a striking platform, the point where the flake will originate; (4) a flake whose shape is thus pre-formed is struck from the core. Prepared cores were designed to enable the toolmaker to produce large flakes or predetermined shapes.

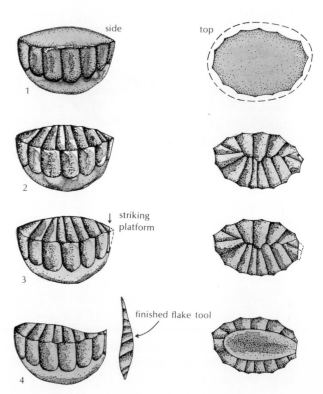

the Clactonian culture. Rather, these people first carefully preshaped flint cores and then knocked off the flakes, which thus had predetermined shapes. These preshaped flakes were further modified into a vast array of specialized tools, including knives, various kinds of scrapers, and spear points that were fastened onto shafts (Fagan 1974:109–111). This process of producing preshaped flakes often produced flake tools with backs that look like turtle shells; for this reason they are often called *tortoise-back* flake tools, as well as *prepared-core* flake tools. This type of tool is typical of the Middle Paleolithic stage of cultural development.

Because people had greater control over the shapes of these tools, they could make much more specialized implements that were well adapted to their particular ecological niches. Thus during the Middle Paleolithic we find a great deal of regional differentiation in technology.

In the northern areas of Eurasia the Middle Paleolithic *Mousterian culture* developed, with a great emphasis on projectile points and scrapers—tools that were used for hunting, woodworking, and the preparation of skins. These northern Neanderthal people migrated seasonally, following the large herds of mammoths, reindeer, and horses into the subarctic tundra areas during the summers, and retreating in the face of the winter cold to more temperate European environments (Fagan 1974:110–111).

In the warmer parts of Europe near the Mediterranean Sea, Middle Paleolithic Neanderthaloid peoples produced less finely made tools than their Mousterian neighbors. Although similar in form, these *Levalloisian* tools were larger and less specialized than their Mousterian counterparts and probably reflected a less demanding environment. These people lived in caves and rock shelters and probably stayed at their home bases all year, gathering vegetable foods and hunting the plentiful game as needed.

Technologically, Middle Paleolithic culture clearly represents evolutionary progress over Lower Paleolithic tools. A typical prepared-core flake tool is produced in four distinct stages—trimming the surface off the nodule, preparing the core, knocking off the flake, and retouching the flake with fine pressure flaking—a far more complex process than the two stages necessary to

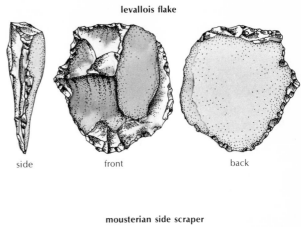

levallois flake

side   front   back

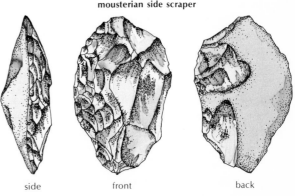

mousterian side scraper

side   front   back

Figure 2-21
Levalloisian and Mousterian Prepared-Core Flake Tools

Pretrimming the core and secondary retouching of the flake tools enabled Middle Paleolithic people to produce a large variety of tools.

produce advanced hand axes. With this new level of technology, human beings were able to penetrate into northern latitudes never before inhabited by hominids and survive there for many thousands of years. These tools were more *adaptable* than their predecessors and were carefully *adapted* by their users to the particular demands of the specific environment each group occupied.

Yet Middle Paleolithic culture represents far more than mere technological progress. In Chapter 13 we show that a whole new form of thinking emerged at this time, a form that we call *transcendental beliefs.* We have evidence that *Homo sapiens neanderthalensis* had developed beliefs about the nature of things far beyond the immediate reach of the senses; specifically, they had apparently developed religious beliefs. For the first time in the unfolding of human evolutionary history we find evidence of systematic burial of the dead.

Wherever we find Neanderthaloid remains—from the Siberian steppes through western Europe and especially in the Middle East—we find carefully buried human remains. Some have been tied in fetal positions, others surrounded with hunting trophies, others provided with morsels of food, and many sprinkled with red powder made by grinding colored soils. In Shanidar Cave in northern Iraq, Ralph Solecki even discovered evidence that some corpses had been covered with flower petals (1972).

Middle Paleolithic Neanderthal people, then, achieved a level of technological and cultural development that represented a new evolutionary stage. Complex, subtle, and highly adaptable, Neanderthal culture provided the basis for the evolution of the infinitely varied, highly complex, ecologically flexible cultures of modern human beings (Fagan 1974:115–116). Middle Paleolithic culture flourished across vast reaches of the Old World from Europe to Asia and Africa for some 40,000 to 50,000 years. Then around 35,000 B.C. a radically new form of culture emerged. This new culture is called the Upper Paleolithic, and the people who produced it were modern *Homo sapiens sapiens.*

Exactly where modern human beings evolved is still a mystery. As we mentioned earlier, the only area where we have found a sequence of skeletal remains changing from Neanderthaloid to modern humans is the Middle East, and many scholars believe that *Homo sapiens sapiens* evolved there. Others expand the area to include East Africa, western Asia, Arabia, and India (Brothwell 1963), but the evolutionary step might well have taken place over even broader areas at differential rates. The question must remain open until more remains have been found (Fagan 1974:120–121).

Upper Paleolithic culture is customarily defined by the invention of stone blade tools. However, we should note that blades in cruder forms had been around for a long time, even as far back as the Acheulian culture. Upper Paleolithic peoples—especially in Europe—produced sophisticated blade and modified blade tools that represent the ultimate technical refinement in stone tool making. The blade is essentially a long and narrow flake that is knocked off a carefully prepared core. Upper Paleolithic peoples became superbly adept at controlling the sizes and shapes of their blades. They developed precise methods of applying pressure to blade surfaces, chipping off minute flakes, and fashioning intricate and delicate blade tools, varying from chisels (known as *burins* or *gravers*) for bone and wood carving to delicate projectile points, knives, scrapers, and drills. But impressive as these tools are, the outstanding characteristic of Upper Paleolithic culture is its versatility and the accelerated rate of cultural change that enabled local groups to adapt to their particular environments and exploit them efficiently (Chard 1969:126–129).

Upper Paleolithic people conquered most of the world's remaining frontiers. They crossed over the Bering Strait and populated the New World, probably between 20,000 and 45,000 years ago. Those living on the seashores developed sophisticated fishing techniques, including bone fishhooks, nets with floats, and harpoons for hunting seals and possibly even whales (Clark 1952: chap. 3). Inland groups had similarly advanced toolkits and produced ingenious new inventions, such as the spear thrower. From the evidence of the sharp bone needles they produced, we conclude that many of these peoples apparently tailored their leather clothing.

However, the culture trait for which European Upper Paleolithic cultures are most famous is their

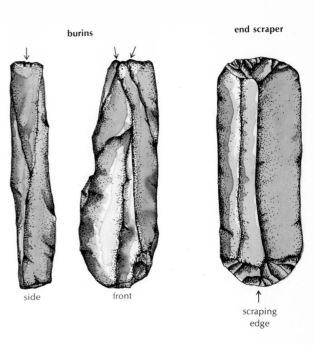

Figure 2-22
Upper Paleolithic Stone Tools
Burins and scrapers, made from blades, are typical Upper Paleolithic artifacts. Burins were used for carving wood, bone, and antlers, which were used to fashion spear and harpoon points. Arrows indicate the chisel ends of a burin formed by striking tiny flakes off the end of a blade. End scrapers were used to shape bone and wood. Whereas burins were used for fine line engraving and delicate carving, end scrapers were used for larger (less delicate) tasks.

magnificent artwork. Found principally in the caves of southwestern France and northern Spain, this artwork evolved rapidly from the Aurignacian phase between 30,000 and 27,000 B.C. to a climax in the Solutrean (18,000–15,000 B.C.) and Magdalenian (15,000–8,500 B.C.) phases (Leroi-Gourhan 1968). This magnificent cave art included extremely naturalistic drawings and sculptures of many wild animals, created with increasing realism and dynamism. Although the techniques were at first limited to crude sketching and rough engraving, artists gradually achieved greater control over their materials. At its peak, Upper Paleolithic cave art was carefully carved and engraved, and earth pigments and grease were used to apply bright colors to cave walls.

It is even possible that these people invented a form of lunar calendar. Alexander Marshack has proposed a controversial interpretation of the tiny engraved dots on a piece of reindeer antler (1972). Using computer analysis, he discovered that 69 dots that are aligned in a curved band on the antler correspond in a statistically significant manner to phases of the moon. If this theory is correct, human beings in the Dordogne region of France were making written notations more than 30,000 years ago.

Perspective

Since the Upper Paleolithic, which ended some 10,000 years ago with the gradual warming of the earth's climate, human evolution has moved at an almost dizzying pace. Although these changes have been primarily in the cultural rather than in the biological domain, evolution has nevertheless continued on both levels. Each of the succeeding chapters will provide its own part of the story—from the evolution of social forms (Chap. 3), through the development of systems of communication (Chap. 7), new subsistence activities (Chap. 10), political systems (Chap. 11), belief systems (Chap. 13), and so forth. What remains for us to do is to put the materials of this chapter into perspective. What does it all mean? The following points seem crucial for understanding human evolutionary development.

Since the early differentiation of the hominid line, cultural and biological evolution have been in a dynamic relationship. Over all, hominids became biologically less and less specialized, except in the areas—such as erect bipedalism and the expansion of the human brain—that facilitated cultural behavior.

Increasingly, the hominid line used cultural rather than biological means to adapt to the ever-increasing range of environments that were being occupied.

date (B.P.)	CULTURAL EVOLUTION		BIOLOGICAL EVOLUTION	
	Technology	Economy	Brain Developments	Body Developments
10,000	bow and arrow	food production		
20,000	art	broad spectrum hunting and gathering		modern skull shape
40,000	blade technology		modern brain	
	mounted tools	specialized hunting and gathering		
	prepared-core flake tools			relative reduction of facial skeleton
200,000				
	fire in use			
500,000		big game hunting	rapid brain expansion	modern post-cranial skeleton
	hand axes			
				bipedalism perfected
2,000,000	pebble tools	hunting and gathering	reorganization of brain and slow expansion	
		terrestrial gathering		bipedalism begins (?)
10,000,000				

Figure 2-23
Elements of Human Cultural and Biological Evolution

The aspects of human cultural and biological evolution that appear on this table originated at the period indicated by their placement and are assumed to continue until they are either replaced or refined.

There is a significant difference between biological and cultural evolution. Genetic novelties (mutations) occur randomly, and thus there is no internally operating direction to biological evolution. Cultural novelties such as inventions or the adoption of elements from other cultures, however, are often the result of conscious deliberation. They are attempts to solve problems posed by the environment. Because the course of cultural evolution is in some respects a product of the intentions of cultural innovators, it is an active process, whereas biological evolution is inherently passive.

However, the same principles of evolutionary change—involution and evolutionary progress—operate in both the biological and cultural spheres. The australopithecine materials provide us with examples of both these principles at work. The robust line represented an advance over *Ramapithecus,* but it apparently became so specialized in its vegetarian diet and its large, heavily muscled body that it could survive only as long as its environment did not change too much. This is involution. Evolutionary progress took place in the gracile line of *Australopithecus.* Here the body shape remained less specialized, and thus was changeable enough so that through natural selection it could become the culture-carrying form that ultimately evolved into *Homo erectus.*

Similar circumstances account for the fate of the European Neanderthal people. At least partially cut off from other Neanderthaloids by the ice sheets of the Würm glacial, these groups became biologically involuted through natural selection and random drift. At the same time, they were isolated from the cultural evolution occurring in the Middle East, where Middle Paleolithic culture was evolving into Upper Paleolithic culture. Thus they apparently were unable to maintain their separate existence when, 35,000 B.C., the ice sheets retreated somewhat and Middle Eastern groups—of the modern human biological type and carrying a more advanced (Upper Paleolithic) level of culture—moved into western Europe and abruptly replaced the Neanderthal people and their culture.

This leads to an interesting proposition. We may regard the contemporary industrial states as highly involuted societal forms that are extremely well adapted to the social and environmental world in which they developed. But should either the social conditions or the natural conditions (such as the availability of energy resources) upon which these societies are predicated change, they may be too involuted to provide the basis for the evolution of new social forms. This proposition suggests that the future of the world may lie with the less complex, less differentiated societies of the Third World. As they assimilate the technological expertise of the temporarily more advanced societies, they will have the potential adaptive flexibility to create new social orders, to set more socially productive priorities, to assimilate the best that industrial civilization has to offer and leave the fossilized, rigid structural elements behind. To these societies, it appears, belongs the potential for the next step of evolutionary progress (see Service 1971).

Summary

Speculations about human origins have taken place throughout history, but the core concepts of evolution—natural selection—was discovered only in the mid-nineteenth century by Alfred Russel Wallace and Charles Darwin.

Evolution is the change that occurs over generations when social or biological forms adapt to their environments. Adaptational change may be specialized (involuted), or it may involve development to a new level of structural complexity (evolutionary progress).

Biological evolution is the product of changes in gene frequencies within a given population (genes are inherited and determine the potential for biological or behavioral characteristics). Four mechanisms constantly affect genetic frequencies: (1) *mutation*, resulting from a change in the chemical structure of genes; (2) *random drift*, resulting from the isolation of a small breeding population from a larger one; (3) *gene flow*, resulting from the interbreeding of previously isolated populations; and (4) *natural selection*, resulting from environmental pressures that favor some characteristics more than others.

Culture consists of the patterned behavior that individuals learn and are taught as members of groups. Cultural and biological evolution are in a state of continual interaction. Cultural evolution occurs through two main mechanisms: (1) the invention of new concepts or the discovery of new knowledge, and (2) the diffusion of knowledge and concepts from one culture to another.

Human biological evolution may be traced, on the basis of fossil evidence, from the point at which the human (hominid) and ape (pongid) lines separated. The evolutionary sequence is still a matter of debate, but it seems likely that modern humans have descended from *Ramapithecus*, which lived some 10 to 14 million years ago, through various australopithecine forms to *Homo erectus*, and then to modern *Homo sapiens sapiens*.

Archaeological evidence points to a cultural tradition among hominids at the end of the australopithecine line. This evidence takes the form of tools, which evolved from simple pebbles to hand axes and eventually to finely shaped and specialized implements. By the time of *Homo erectus*, we find evidence of dwellings, fire, and some forms of social organization. Earlier forms of *Homo sapiens* appear to have had transcendental belief systems, and the more recent Upper Paleolithic peoples developed a relatively sophisticated technology and complex cultural (especially artistic) forms.

Annotated Bibliography

Ardrey, Robert (1961) *African Genesis.* New York: Atheneum.

(1966) *The Territorial Imperative.* New York: Atheneum.

(1970) *The Social Contract.* New York: Dell.

These books present a popularized account of the origins of human society. The presentation is entertaining reading by a professional journalist, but bad science. Both human society and its shortcomings (especially violence and aggression) are interpreted as an expression of unchangeable biological characteristics of the human line of evolution, starting with the australopithecines, who according to Ardrey, fell from grace when they gave up the quiet, vegetarian, contemplative way of life and took up hunting, the eating of meat, and thus an aggressive, violence-prone life-style.

Geertz, Clifford (1973) *The Interpretation of Cultures.* New York: Basic Books. A fascinating collection of essays by one of America's most provocative, intellectually stimulating anthropologists. Especially pertinent are his essays "Thick Description: Toward an Interpretive Theory of Culture," "The Impact of the Concept of Culture on the Concept of Man," and "The Growth of Culture and the Evolution of Mind."

Greene, John C. (1959) *The Death of Adam.* New York: Mentor. A philosophical and historical investigation of the intellectual roots of the concept of evolution.

Service, Elman R. (1971) *Cultural Evolutionism: Theory in Practice.* New York: Holt. A collection of essays (some not previously published) that presents a clear and readable approach to evolutionary theory. The concept of evolution is applied to both biological and sociocultural forms, developing many of the concepts used in this chapter.

3
The Evolution
of Social Forms

Human Social Origins: Myth and Science

All human cultures seem to share a certain impatience with the unknown, and thus all cultures seek to solve the intriguing mystery of how the human species and human societies evolved to their present forms. The explanations vary from one culture to the next, but within each culture they are deeply held and transmitted as indisputable fact from generation to generation. All human beings are provided by their culture with a creation myth in which their ancestors are separated from the rest of the animal kingdom and in which their biological and social development is explained. These myths always have a moral dimension— that is, they reveal to human beings why, for example, males and females act differently, why certain types of social behavior are supernaturally approved or sanctioned, and why the traditions, values, and beliefs of one's own culture are naturally superior to all others. In Judeo-Christian mythology, for instance, Adam and Eve are not merely the propagators of the species but the personification of male-female behaviors, lust and temptation, good and evil. Such folk mores and values become indelibly fixed in the consciousness of individuals everywhere, whether they are Eskimo fishermen, African kings, Peruvian peasants, or American scholars.

In an important sense, Western science is simply a cultural elaboration of this seemingly fundamental human obsession with the unknown. And because our science grew out of a single cultural tradition, its perception of the world is necessarily skewed by this heritage. Anthropologists, like other scientists, must eliminate from their discipline mystical associations specific to their own culture. But the maintenance of total objectivity is especially difficult when one's subject matter is the full range of human cultures and behaviors, some of which may appear strange to the outsider. For example, why do people in some societies hunt heads, have multiple husbands or wives simultaneously, kill their infants at birth, or abandon their elderly and helpless parents to carnivores? Only through a conscious effort to place herself or himself in another perceptual framework can the investigator understand how such customs may promote the survival of a population in a particular environment.

Cultural bias, or what anthropologists call *ethnocentrism,* is perhaps an even greater danger when the theorist attempts to reconstruct extinct societies that can no longer be directly observed. For example, were Paleolithic hand axes really used for hunting, or were they primarily tools for pulverizing vegetable matter? Did *Homo erectus* males and females marry and form conjugal families, or is this domestic portrait a projection of our own preconceptions?

This is the problem in this chapter. If we are to propose a scientific theory about human social origins and the evolution of human society over the past few million years, where shall we look for clues? To rely solely on intuition would be to lapse into mythological explanations. And to use ourselves or peoples from simpler societies as models for ancient human or hominid behavior may be very misleading.

To avoid this apparent dilemma, anthropologists typically have attempted to use data from three areas: (1) contemporary primate behavior, (2) ancient cultures, and (3) modern human societies of varying com-

plexity. The rationale for studying the first area is the assumption that all primates share a common heritage, and that by observing their social behaviors we can learn more about the biological roots of human nature. The reason for investigating the second area is that because the artifacts of modern societies are so similar to those found in ancient cultural deposits, anthropologists believe that they can reach valid conclusions about these extinct societies. Underlying the study of the third area is the assumption that the tremendous range in the technological and organizational complexity of contemporary societies throughout the world roughly approximates stages in the evolution of culture—that these existing societies represent, at least in outline, survivals of ancient cultural traditions whose remnants are found in archaeological sites.

Most anthropologists agree on the data that are relevant to the problem of reconstructing human social and cultural evolution, but their interpretations of these data often differ. However, two basic approaches typify much anthropological thought over the past century: the *classificatory* and *adaptational* approaches.

The Classificatory Approach

The classificatory approach may be defined as the identification of structural regularities among the world's cultures, and the subsequent construction of a limited number of types that are arranged in a progressive sequence. In other words, the investigator surveys a large sample of contemporary societies and chooses a feature, such as the nature of technology, that appears in all of them but that has a different form in almost every society. On the basis of the variations found in this feature, a number of types or categories are created into which, ideally, any known society can be fitted. These types are then ranked in order according to their relative complexity, on the general assumption that cultures have evolved from simple to complex.

This classificatory or typological approach was popular among Victorian scholars and still finds adherents today. Elman Service, for example, outlines general stages in the evolution of culture based on the nature of social and political life (1962, 1963), and he proposes five levels (the band, tribe, chiefdom, primitive state, and archaic civilization) of increasingly complex social organization. The result is a useful scheme for categorizing contemporary peoples and for drawing evolutionary parallels with ancient peoples whose cultural remains suggest similar forms of social organization.

A weakness of this approach to social and cultural evolution is that because of the concern with the creation of typologies that can locate the entire range of diverse ancient and modern cultures along a single dimension, little effort is expended on how or why cultures evolve from one hypothetical stage to the next.

An Apache Chief with his family. Although we are used to calling people like this Apache "chiefs," the use of this term distorts the nature of their society, which falls into the category of social organization that Service labels *tribe*. Such societies are egalitarian, with no centralized hierarchy. They hunt and forage for food and do not produce a surplus which a central authority could collect and redistribute. Thus leaders have no economic and no formal political power. Rather, they are able to lead by living exemplary lives themselves and using moral persuasion to induce others to follow their suggestions.

The Adaptational Approach

Theorists using the adaptational approach are primarily concerned with what causes change and how change occurs. They identify the regularities of cultural change by analyzing the dynamic interactions between human populations and their environments—the *ecology* of a culture. The underlying assumption is that, in order to survive, human beings must organize themselves into social, economic, and political groups that somehow fit in with the resources and challenges of a particular environment. If an organization promotes the survival of the population (for example, the organization of men into cooperative hunting groups), then it is said to be *adaptive*. An important implication is that if any feature of the environment changes, corresponding changes must occur in the population's organization if it is to maintain or improve its chances of survival.

The concept of adaptation thus offers a means of predicting which types of social organization we can expect to find under given environmental conditions. The concept also provides a tool for understanding how and why societies pass from one type of organization into another. With these techniques, then, we not only can identify stages in the evolution of human culture but can also offer hypotheses to explain this progression of social forms.

The adaptational approach is certainly not new, although it seems to have been rediscovered by anthropologists only recently. Karl Marx and Friedrich Engels first applied it to cultural phenomena in the nineteenth century (for example, see Engels 1972, orig. 1884). They believed that the nature of economic institutions (how people produce and distribute wealth) largely determines the nature of their social, political, and ideological systems.

The more contemporary evolutionary model of Leslie White (1943, 1949, 1959) is in many ways similar to that of Marx and Engels. White sees human culture as consisting of three basic systems: technoeconomic, social, and ideological. He strongly emphasizes the importance of the technoeconomic aspects of societies, as measured by the ability of a given culture to harness and produce "energy." White argues that throughout

Two artisans at work. On the left, a full time carpenter, wagonmaker, and wheelwright in a community of Swiss peasants of the Alpine foothills region forms the handle of a cart he is crafting for a local farming household. At right, a man of the *Lohar* ("blacksmith-carpenter") caste in a North Indian village fashions a steel-tipped plow for one of his patrons.

Both artisans are producing basic implements needed by the agricultural groups they serve. One uses only his hands and hand-held tools; the other has a band saw and other power tools at his disposal. In Leslie White's terms the technology of the Swiss craftsman is more evolved than that of the Indian craftsman because he controls much more energy while executing his work.

the development of human culture, increasing technological sophistication—as represented in the agricultural, industrial, and nuclear revolutions—has made available greater and greater energy supplies. The amount of energy captured by a population, he believes, plays a major role in structuring the social and ideological aspects of culture.

In this chapter we will attempt to outline general stages in cultural evolution and identify the dynamics of this evolutionary process. Our general assumption will be that *the requirements of survival in a given environment shape a population's economic, social, and political organization in predictable ways.* We will first examine nonhuman primates, noting the possible differences in activities relating to survival that separate them from our own fossil ancestors. We will then consider in detail the distinctively human mechanisms for survival—cooperative subsistence groups and cooperative offensive-defensive groups—in four basic economic adaptations: (1) hunting, fishing, and gathering, or *foraging,* (2) hoe cultivation, or *horticulture,* (3) intensive farming, or *agriculture,* and (4) *industrialism.* Our hypothesis will be that *social groups and*

social organization are shaped in a consistent manner by the nature of the ecology, and that the evolution of social forms has always been precipitated by a fundamental change in the economic orientation of societies.

Survival, Labor, and Societal Origins

All species have certain built-in mechanisms for survival. Young mammals experience an initial period of dependency during which they learn the more complex behaviors required to sustain life independently. Some mammals, such as the mountain lion, then go on to live alone, interrupting their solitude only to reproduce. Other mammals, such as wolves, horses, baboons, and humans, learn to depend extensively on the com-

Figure 3-1

A Schematic Representation of the Relationship between Forms of Social Organization, the Natural Environment, and Technology

Read any capitalized label and follow any arrow leaving that label. Read the text along that arrow and continue to another capitalized label. This will result in a complete sentence. Each of the sentences you will discover in this manner expresses one aspect of the interaction of social organization, technology, and the environment. (For a more inclusive model of cultural and biological adaptation to the natural environment, see fig. 5-1.)

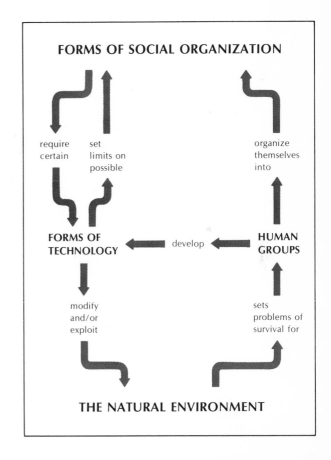

FORMS OF SOCIAL ORGANIZATION

require certain   set limits on possible

organize themselves into

FORMS OF TECHNOLOGY   ◀ develop ◀   HUMAN GROUPS

modify and/or exploit

sets problems of survival for

THE NATURAL ENVIRONMENT

pany of others. All gregarious species seem to be genetically predisposed toward cooperative activities relating to mutual defense and shared territory, which ensure their survival. Because living in groups requires at least some sort of conformity to expected behaviors as well as patterned relationships among individual group members, gregarious animals are generally acknowledged as having a form of society.

The social life of gregarious mammals appears to be the most highly developed among monkeys, apes, and humans. In comparison with other animals of comparable size and weight, these primates have considerably longer lifespans, larger brains, and more extended periods of infant dependency. In all primates, learned behaviors are particularly important for survival. Primates are distinguished from other groups of mammals by their intelligence, ingenuity, and complex social relationships. Since this heritage is shared by all living higher primates, we can assume that it represents a very ancient pattern that gave adaptive advantages to our common ancestors millions of years ago.

But what distinguishes human social life from that of monkeys and apes? At what point in the succession of ancient hominoid fossils can we see the origins and development of society that is fully human? To answer these questions, we must examine the ways in which human and nonhuman primates relate socially for survival.

Labor Specialization and Nonhuman Primate Society

The survival mechanisms of monkeys and apes share many features with lower-order gregarious species. Nonhuman primates living in exposed, somewhat dangerous conditions on the open plains, such as the savannah baboons, have learned to improve their bid for survival against predators by developing *symbiotic* relationships with herd animals of other species. For example, the zebra's highly developed sense of smell complements the baboon's keen vision; hence both groups of animals benefit from the association. Such cross-species alliances are commonplace and require only minimal social interaction based on the recognition of mutual danger signals.

But we need only introduce a hungry predator to this tranquil scene of baboons and zebra to observe the social features that distinguish primates from lower animals. Whereas zebra rely solely on the mechanism of flight for survival, baboons combine a scurry for the safety of trees with a critical division of responsibility among troop members. Under attack, the strongest, most able males take up the task of repulsing the intruder. They also play a protective role when the troop moves as a unit. Females with young always move in the center of the formation, and if they fall behind, they are escorted individually by the stronger males. Males also seem to assume general policing duties within the troop. In contrast, female baboons promote the survival of the troop through nurturant rather than aggressive behaviors. They not only bear the young but also play the major role in their early socialization. There is every indication that the sexes have even developed expectations of these complementary behaviors. For example, in situations of threat females have been observed pulling the tails of their male protectors, fast asleep in nearby trees, to awaken them to their duties.

The males' responsibilities for the troop's survival are patterned from a young age. By the time a male baboon has reached adolescence, he has already established his positions of relative dominance and subordination among his peers and elders. The continual vying in the dominance hierarchy among exposed savannah baboons that takes place throughout life helps to ensure that only the ablest males will confront intruders, and that the most fit will make greater genetic contributions to the next generation through the special sexual privileges that go with dominance. Similarly, juvenile females prepare themselves for future reproductive and socialization functions in the troop through nurturant behavior toward infants and younger siblings.

Among this highly specialized group of primates, then, the challenges of the savannah ecology have been met by the formation of troops, within which a primitive form of labor division on the basis of sex and age has developed. Males are dominant over females, and adult males over adolescents. So adaptive have these patterns been in the evolutionary develop-

A gorilla band in its habitat. For all the higher primates, learning plays a great role in their social behavior. However, it is also true that we share with the other higher primates an evolutionary history and a biological substratum which inevitably has some consequences in human behavior. Ethologists, physical anthropologists, and cultural anthropologists are attempting to discover the extent to which our understanding of the entire order of primates will tell us about human nature as well.

ment of baboons that they have selected for actual structural differences between the sexes as well. Sexual *dimorphism*—that is, a significant difference in female and male body shape—among baboons is very pronounced: Adult males are nearly twice the size of females.

In the past, anthropologists often pointed to savannah baboons as models of ancient hominid society. Their sex roles seem to fit amazingly well with Western folk conceptions of human nature, and their social behavior has even been taken as evidence that human aggression and male dominance are genetically based (see Morris 1967; Ardrey 1961, 1966; Tiger 1969, 1970). However, recent observations of baboons and apes in a variety of environments have indicated a much greater plasticity and variation in behavior than had previously been reckoned. Chimpanzees occupying a forest environment, for example, are characterized

This male baboon is displaying a dramatic aspect of sexual dimorphism among his species: the canine teeth of males are considerably larger than those of females; not surprisingly, male baboons often open their mouths to display their impressive weaponry when making hostile gestures.

generally by noncompetitive, nonaggressive relationships. Although an informal male ranking system exists, it is not called into play in situations of threat or sexual access. Forest chimps rely on the protection of trees on an individual basis to avoid danger and do not use a sex-based division of labor for defense. Interestingly, physical dimorphism among male and female chimpanzees is also much less pronounced.

Much evidence indicates that these contrasts in baboon and chimpanzee behaviors do not stem solely from the fact that they are different species but from the social effects of survival pressures in specific environments as well. Among baboons living on the more protected fringes of forested areas, for example, the male dominance hierarchy is less well defined and the frequency of aggression is much less than among baboons living in savannahs. Moreover, male chimpanzees living in savannah fringes show more aggression than forest-dwelling chimps, and *both* sexes tend to jointly attack an intruding predator. Higher primates have the ability to adjust their social behaviors to meet the survival requirements of different environments. The basis of this ability is the fact that much of the social behavior of monkeys and apes is learned, and not simply the result of genetic programing.

To sum up, the picture of nonhuman primate social life that emerges is a variable blend of mammalian biological characteristics and primate ingenuity. As mammals, primate males and females have different reproductive commitments and hence potentially different social spheres. The extent to which their behaviors actually do become different seems to relate directly to the nature of the ecological niches they occupy. If competition with other species in the same niche is high, we find rigidly structured relationships among males and increased levels of aggression. In contrast, noncompetitive environments seem to encourage more convergent male and female behaviors and less ferment among community members.

What distinguishes monkeys and apes from other mammals is the potential for learning labor specialization along sex and age lines to meet the diverse challenges of different environments. Among nonhuman primates, this ability seems to have always been limited to cooperative activities relating to defense. But among early humans, labor specialization for the purpose of survival took on an expanded and revolutionary dimension.

Labor Specialization and Early Human Society

Most animals experience two immediate threats to survival—the lack of adequate food and the danger of becoming food for others. As we have seen, nonhuman primates such as baboons strike a balance with other species in their environment and develop specialized mechanisms for defense within their own communities. When resources are adequate, food-getting activities may be successfully carried on by individuals under the general protection of the troop. But if the resources of such a primate community were suddenly to become inadequate for survival due to a rapid environmental change, this might throw a number of species into vigorous competition for the same food resources. Under such conditions, extinction would be the fate of species that could not exert dominance or that could not rapidly adapt themselves to alternative resources.

The fossil record shows that at some point in hominid evolution, probably at the *Homo erectus* stage (see Chap. 2), one or more species of ancient primates achieved just such a reorientation. The result was the origin of human society. Exactly why and how this transition took place we can only guess, but observations of nonhuman primates provide us with some vital clues. In a situation of extreme stress, we would expect males in ancient hominid communities to be highly organized for defense and to engage in cooperative aggressive activities. They may have undertaken these activities not only against their natural predators but also against those species competing for the same limited food resources. The systematic killing and consumption of other animals may have evolved out of a heightened struggle for survival.

All human societies are characterized by at least two elements: a division of labor by sex, and the sharing of food. The same characteristics seem to have been present in our hominid ancestors. The material artifacts of *Homo erectus, Homo sapiens neanderthalensis,* and early *Homo sapiens sapiens* (see Chap. 2) tell us

little about the regulation of sexuality or the presence, absence, or nature of marriage. However, they do indicate something about patterns of economic cooperation and community structure.

Archaeological remains (see Chap. 2) indicate that by the *Homo erectus* stage, ancient hominids were living in small groups of economically cooperating individuals of both sexes. Moreover, their communal dwellings or shelters show evidence of compartmentalization. These compartments suggest to us that the community was divided into food-sharing units which —if the social organization of modern foragers is in any way comparable—may have been based on common kinship. We would expect the size and structure of such groups to vary according to the nature of the resources in an environment. Some groups appear to have depended primarily on hunting by males or by the entire community (such as in the driving of herds into ambush), whereas others undoubtedly depended heavily on the vegetable products collected by females. Once this very adaptive organization of humans into communal production and distribution groups was achieved, there appears to have been little elaboration in social forms throughout the Paleolithic era.

Throughout the discussion of primates we have been concerned with the varying abilities of these related species to mold their social behaviors and social groups to changing environments to survive. Nonhuman primates have achieved a more complex and flexible social organization than most lower-order mammals; they are able to pattern roles among community members on the basis of age and sex. However, the ecological niches of modern baboons, chimpanzees, and gorillas have remained stable enough to allow their survival without further social advance. This could not have been the case for our ancestors, who successfully expanded their cooperative social mechanisms for survival to a new field: the acquisition and distribution of food. From that moment, predatory and defensive aggression became permanently linked to the economic considerations of territory, resources, and wealth. Humans soon found that their own species contained their greatest competitors and their deadliest predators. It was through ingenuity rather than highly developed sexual dimorphism, through learning rather than innate responses that hominid species radiated throughout much of Africa, Asia, and Europe and successfully matched their ability to create adaptive behaviors against the fluctuating challenges of Paleolithic environments.

Economic Adaptations and Social Forms

Some gregarious species, such as ants, seem merely to be acting out genetically based blueprints for behavior. In mammals, however, innate behaviors are combined with a potential for learning. The greater this potential is, the more malleable a species' social behavior and adaptive ability becomes. Our ancient human forebears, with their progressively superior learning capacities, were able to extend their cooperative activities from defense to hunting and collecting, from individual food gathering to food sharing; and eventually they were able to form permanent, special-purpose groups for political and economic ventures.

The first human social groups appear to have been kin groups, which are based on an extension of sex criteria. All-purpose kinship groups (formed around a cluster of related males and their mates or, alternatively, around a cluster of related females and their mates) are characteristic of preindustrial human societies the world over (see Chap. 9).

In the rest of this chapter we will focus on the unique human capacity to adapt socially to a variety of ecological niches. We will find that human adaptation is often a two-way street: We have prospered through our ability not only to adjust to environmental conditions but also to adjust the environment to human needs. Purely cultural inventions, such as technological innovation and increasingly efficient division of labor, have enabled humans to overcome enormous obstacles to survival. The archaeological record of the past 2 million years reveals, however, that humans have developed only a limited number of basic subsistence strategies: those based on foraging, on domesticated plants and animals, and on industrial production. Our initial assumption—that the social organization of animals is shaped by their ecological niche—is supported by the fact that humans have developed only a

Figure 3-2
Subsistence Strategies and Social Forms
This chart is a summary of major trends. It oversimplifies the actual complexity of the materials and makes them look much more static and unchanging than they in fact are.

Subsistence Strategy			Marriage Form	♀ / ♂ Dominance	Social Organization	Degree of Competition for Resources	Political Form	Work Tasks	
								♀	♂
hunting and gathering			primarily monogamy	social equality	♂ centered kin groups in small bands*	variable	amorphous*	foraging for vegetable foods and small game; nurturance (child care)	fishing and hunting large animals; community protection
horticulture	subsistence farmers	poor environment	frequent polygyny	♂ dominance	♂ centered kin groups	high	variable centralization	primary producers: planters, tenders, and harvesters of crops; nurturance	heavy tasks such as land clearing; community protection
		rich environment	primarily monogamy	social equality	♀ centered kin groups	low			
	surplus farmers		frequent polygyny	♂ dominance	♂ centered kin groups	high	partiarchal centralization and incipient development of state		
pastoralism			monogamy and polygyny	♂ dominance	♂ centered kin groups	high	patriarchal clan organiza- tion; uncen- tralized except where under political or economic pressure from neighboring states	some dairying; nurturance	limited cultivation; herding; community protection
agriculture			primarily monogamy	♂ dominance	differentiation of non-kin groups	high	state bureaucracy of a feudal nature	processing of raw produce and manufac- turing; nuturance	predominate in agricultural sphere; urban wage labor; community protection
industrialism			monogamy and serial monogamy	♂ dominance with increasing androgeny	kin groups lose social impor- tance to industrial corporate structures and state insti- tutions	high	state bureaucracy of a bourgeois or workers' state nature	increasing participation in labor force; nurturance	predominate in labor force; community defense

* The social forms of contemporary hunters and gatherers have been greatly simplified by culture contact. It is likely that they formerly exhibited the same social forms as do subsistence horticulturalists, varying according to ecological niche.

limited variety of social forms as well. Our task is to relate the evolution of these social forms to the parallel development of increasingly efficient subsistence strategies.

Foraging Societies

The simplest known human societies are those whose economies are based solely on the collection of wild plant foods and the hunting of animals or fishing, or both. Modern representatives of this Stone Age tradition were distributed widely throughout the world before the assault of European colonialism, occupying much of what is now Canada; the coastal regions, Great Basin, and Great Plains of the United States; the southern archipelago and plains of South America; Australia; parts of the Philippines, Japan, and Southeast Asia; the Eurasian Arctic; and the Congo basin and Kalahari Desert of Africa. The majority of these peoples are now extinct, and the life-styles of those that survive have been greatly changed by depopulation and the influence of foreign ideas and foreign economies. We cannot, therefore, take modern foragers as perfect living models of Paleolithic social life. But they do provide us with an important glimpse of how humans, with only stone tools and no knowledge of cultivation, may have organized themselves for survival.

Similarities among Foraging Groups   The data on a large number of foraging societies living in the interior and coastal regions of five continents reveals a number of consistent features. As among higher primates, males are charged with the duties of community protection and offensive maneuvers, while females share responsibilities for the nurturance and socialization of new community members. Men everywhere assume the task of hunting large animals, whereas women involve themselves primarily with food gathering, although joint hunting by men and women and the hunting of smaller animals by women are not uncommon. The division of labor by sex and the sharing of food in domestic households are universal, as is some form of marriage. Monogamy prevails, but in contrast to our own culture, food-sharing units may be made up of

(bottom left)
!Kung San women in the Kalahari Desert of South Africa carrying home *mongongo* nuts, one of their staple foods. As in all human societies, work among these hunters and gatherers is divided (in this case principally along male/female lines—see Chapter 21). In fact, the ability of human beings to cooperate in groups and divide their labor while sharing the fruits of all group members' work is an outstanding feature of the evolution of our species.

(below)
Sharing food. Systematic and organized food sharing is a feature of human social organization which sets us off from our close relatives. Among other primate groups, each adult generally forages for its own food.

more than one couple and their offspring. Foragers always organize themselves into communities of individuals who share a common ancestor or living blood relative, although the number of people who remain together throughout the entire year is usually small (less than fifty among modern foragers) because food becomes too scarce to support larger groups during lean seasons.

Differences among Foraging Societies   Given the tremendously wide range of environments that modern foragers occupy, however, we would expect considerable variation in their social forms (Martin 1974). For example, although men are typically the hunters in these societies, they do not always assume the role of provider to domestic units. Contrary to our "cave man" folk images—and indeed to some scientific theories—women are the primary suppliers of food among most foragers in all but the coldest latitudes, where few wild plants grow. This central productive role for women may account for the high degree of social equality between men and women among hunters and gatherers.

No universal pattern of male-centered social groups exists among foraging peoples. Instead, we find several ways of structuring society, including groups of female kin and their respective husbands, and mixed groups of related men and women and their spouses. We would expect this variation to be related to differences in economic strategies, but unfortunately the colonial obliteration of aboriginal adaptations prevents valid testing of this hypothesis.

Because of their low economic productivity, foraging societies are typically small, with simple political structures. However, groups with access to plentiful seasonal resources often congregate into sizable communities under a common advisory official, war leader, or council of representatives. These larger groups then disperse into smaller segments during the leanest season. In some environments, such as the northwest coast of America, some foragers were even able to congregate into permanent sedentary villages with considerable political complexity. This was made possible by the production of *food surpluses* through the storage of fish caught in the annual salmon runs.

Horticultural Societies

For approximately three-fourths of human history, foraging was the only technology known. It undoubtedly provided an adequate or even comfortable existence in environments with abundant wild vegetables, fruits, nuts, game, and fish. Approximately 10,000–15,000 years ago, however, some of the more favorable habitats in the Old World began to change radically. Coinciding with the retreat of the last glaciation, a sharp reduction in rainfall started the development of the great Saharan, Arabian, and Mesopotamian deserts. These arid regions are still expanding, and the changing environment causes a great deal of suffering among the people who attempt to live there. Like modern African and Asian peoples affected by severe drought, ancient populations were forced to migrate to other areas and to seek new, more reliable sources of food. Some followed the game to more favorable settings where their old traditions could be resumed much as before. Others began to experiment with techniques that were to revolutionize

(left)
A hunting and gathering group. These pygmies in the Congo rain forest have developed an interpersonally warm, non-aggressive way of life (see Chapter 17).

(below)
Senegalese hoe horticulturalists. Horti-culture refers to plant food production with a technology limited to the use of a digging stick or hoe to turn the topsoil. Thus a major source of work energy is human muscle power only minimally amplified by tools.

human subsistence—the controlled breeding and exploitation of plants and animals.

At this stage of our knowledge, we cannot point with certainty to a particular population or area of the Old World for the first achievement of domestication. Not long ago, many theorists saw the Middle East as the center of innovation. In Israel and Jordan some 10,000 years ago, villages of foragers were reaping plants with primitive sickles and supplementing their diets with wild wheat and barley seeds. More developed tradi-tions of cultivation appeared approximately 1,000 years later in northern Iraq and at the sophisticated town of Catal Hüyük in Turkey. However, recent evidence indicates that plant domestication occurred simul-taneously in several areas of the Old World (Wendorf 1968). In the Far East, domesticated plants appear at an extremely early date that may prove to precede the dates of Middle Eastern traditions (Chang 1970). In America, cultivation was independently invented in the Valley of Mexico at a somewhat later date, perhaps 6,000–7,000 years ago (MacNeish 1964).

At least until the colonial era, the great majority of the world's cultivators employed hand tools similar to those found in these ancient societies and had only limited knowledge of techniques for soil maintenance or water control. Hoe farmers exhausted the fertility of their plots and fields and periodically moved on to virgin land, leaving the old tracts to fallow. Horticulture is consequently a wasteful type of farming in terms of land use,* and it does not generally permit a fully sedentary way of life. However, the population density and organizational complexity of horticultural groups is far greater than that of foragers in comparable environments. Today horticulturalists are confined largely to remote rural regions, especially in the tropics.

Two basic types of horticulturalists may be distin-guished: subsistence farmers and surplus farmers. *Subsistence farmers* are those whose efforts, regardless of their aspirations, yield only enough food to sustain life on a comfortable level. In contrast, *surplus farmers* live in more favorable environments and produce more

---

* *However, recent research shows that slash-and-burn hor-ticulture is much more efficient than had previously been believed (see Chap. 5).*

than they can consume. All surplus farmers are pre-occupied with the accumulation and exchange of wealth. These differing economic strategies seem to have an important influence on the social forms of horticultural society.

Subsistence Farmers   These farmers are found in habitats containing major obstacles to successful cultivation. Most live in tropical forest settings where they must expend considerable effort in clearing plots and in keeping them unmolested by animals and competing vegetation. Competition among neighboring communities is high, and endemic warfare is not uncommon. In this situation, political units are always small and are typically composed of a number of related men and their families. In essence, each local group consists of a small army of male kinsmen who stand ready to protect their own fields or to pillage those of others.

Subsistence farmers in more favorable environments produce adequate food supplies with considerably less effort and with only minimal competition with other societies in the same niche. These farmers are able to produce surpluses, but the accumulation and exchange of wealth are simply not culturally valued. This type of economic strategy, in which human populations strike an essentially noncompetitive balance with one another and with nature, seems to have been systematically eliminated in both ancient and modern times by more productive, expansive economies. Those groups that have survived display social forms distinct from those of subsistence farmers in more challenging environments. Because resources are abundant, social organization encourages cooperation rather than competition among groups of people who produce and share food. Such societies often favor kinship groups that are formed around clusters of related women rather than related men (Martin and Voorhies 1975: 220-229).

The usefulness of this type of arrangement seems to lie in two basic social facts: Men are the warriors in most societies, and hostilities such as feuding and warfare usually occur between groups of kinsmen.

These two Hopi elder councilmen show a customary restraint at a Senate Interior Committee hearing in Washington in 1974. The Hopi are well known for their nonaggressive behavior and a world view which teaches the importance of interacting harmoniously. The author of this chapter suggests that there is a meaningful connection between Hopi emotional and cultural orientation, and their matrilineal, matrilocal social organization —in the context of their subsistence farming technology.

Cross-cultural studies have shown that societies organizing their local communities around related men have a significantly higher incidence of armed combat than those who orient them around related women (Otterbein and Otterbein 1965). Accordingly, if related men are required to join the social groups of their respective wives at marriage and spend their entire lives working and sharing food with people who are *not* their immediate kinsmen, they are much less likely to come together for common aggressive activities. Subsistence farmers in favorable habitats have, in fact, a very low incidence of feuding.

Among horticulturalists who produce only what they consume, then, we see two blueprints for human social relations. Where competition for resources is great, males are more likely to form the locus of social and economic groups. In situations that produce less competition for resources, the opposite occurs, and relationships among males are less structured. This pattern shows an uncanny similarity to the labor specialization on the basis of sex noted earlier for nonhuman primates and may be an extension of this adaptive primate pattern into human social forms.

Surplus Farmers **Surplus horticulturalists are always found in relatively favorable environments and seem to be the direct descendants of noncompetitive subsistence farmers in these same regions. Why the latter communities at some point shifted their economic strategy to *over*production (the deliberate creation of surpluses) is a question about which we can only speculate. Perhaps the critical factor was some ecological change resulting in increased competition for available resources, such as the population explosion that accompanied the farming revolution.**

All surplus horticulturalist groups have relatively dense populations, highly developed internal and external markets, more sophisticated political forms, and a tendency toward military expansion. They are geared not only toward the production of adequate food but also toward the acquisition of new land, new labor supplies, and new wealth outside their own territorial boundaries. Surplus farmers, with their strong competitive orientation, generally organize themselves into social groups of related males that can reach colossal proportions: Thousands of individuals may

claim descent through a common ancestor. The surplus wealth is unevenly distributed among the population, giving rise to social classes and, in many cases, to a distinction between the slaves and the free. The primitive *state*—in which a person or body of individuals exerts control over the production and distribution of goods and a monopoly over the threat or use of force—makes its debut.

However, in all horticultural societies, women continue to be the primary producers. In the vast majority of cases, they plant, tend, and harvest crops (Murdock 1937; D'Andrade 1966). Where they participate, the men always engage in the heaviest tasks, such as land clearing. (For a comparison of horticultural and agricultural patterns of sexual labor division, see fig. 3-3.) Interestingly, this basic division of labor by sex is influenced by the horticulturalists' economic needs. Groups that are geared toward maximum production favor the accumulation by men of multiple wives. This form of marriage increases the number of laborers, and hence the quantity of produce, for individual male household heads. In contrast, groups that are geared only toward subsistence production prefer monogamy. In this situation, fields are often cultivated jointly by a number of related women, and the resulting produce is shared among their respective husbands and children.

Pastoralist Societies

In environments where aridity or extremes of temperature seriously inhibit successful cultivation, domesticated animals often replace plants as the primary source of food. Societies that depend on the meat and dairy products of herd animals for the greater part of their diets are termed *pastoralist*. Such societies are found today in the extreme northern, central, and southwestern regions of Asia, and in the northern, central Saharan, Sudanic, and eastern areas of Africa.

All herd animals—reindeer, sheep, goats, horses, camels, or cattle—require a constant supply of water and fresh pasturage. For this reason, herding societies are highly mobile and rarely cluster into sizable, sedentary communities. The frequent harshness of their environments encourages heightened competition

Figure 3-3
Sexual Labor Division
A comparison of sexual labor division in cultivation between a sample of 104 horticultural and 93 agricultural societies. Equivalent participation indicates the clearing of land by males, and tending and harvesting by females (see Fig. 3-2).

Cultivation Type	SEXUAL PRIMACY AS FOOD PRODUCERS					
	Females Primary		Males Primary		Both Sexes Equivalent	
	N	%	N	%	N	%
Horticulture	52	50	17	17	35	33
Agriculture	15	16	75	81	3	3

A Mutayr Bedouin encampment. The Mutayr are a nomadic pastoralist group whose way of life is described in detail in Chapter 22. Their society is organized around male-centered kinship groups. Among the Arab Bedouin nomads the great concentrations of livestock and people occur during the hot dry season— unlike, for instance, among the Fulani nomads of Africa, where cattle and people concentrate during the cool wet season. Bedouin summer camps are located near permanent wells. The camels are brought to camp in the afternoon, watered (about 35 gals. per adult camel), then taken to the edge of the camp to rest for the night. They are watered again in the morning (about 15 gals.), then led to pasture. At the height of the summer this process is repeated every third or fourth day. This picture shows the edge of a Mutayr summer camp. Their black tents are in the background; in the foreground a Mutayr tribesman is coaxing his camels to settle down for the evening.

among neighboring groups for rather limited resources. Indeed, the vast majority of pastoralists have male-centered economic and kinship groups and are notorious for their militarism. Although animal products form the major portion of their diets, herding societies continue to cultivate crops or to acquire cultivated foods from others through trade or plunder. It is likely that pastoralism represents a specialized adaptation of formerly sedentary peoples to marginal habitats rather than an independent stage in social evolution.

Societies that have domesticated plants and animals, then, vary greatly in their subsistence strategies and productive success and hence in their social forms and organizational complexity. As the idea of cultivation and herding diffused from the centers of innovation, each culture imparted its distinctive patterns and each new environment its unique limitations on the new technology. The transition from food foraging to food production marked a qualitative advance in the human ability to survive, to perpetuate the species, and to apply creative intelligence to the manipulation of the physical and social environment. It was truly a point of no return.

Agricultural Societies

Once they had been developed as a food source, domesticated plants spread throughout the world in the short span of about 8,000 years. In the original centers of development, more sophisticated farming techniques greatly increased crop yields and resulted in the production of massive surpluses. Despite the great distances between Egypt and the Orient, Mesopotamia and the Valley of Mexico, the Indus Valley and Peruvian Andes, these advanced technologies showed striking consistencies in both form and consequence. Water was systematically controlled through aqueducts, reservoirs, and irrigation ditches. In the Old World, organic fertilizers were used, and domesticated animals were attached to the plow. These technological innovations signaled the genesis of urban civilization.

The technology of irrigation was developed in the Old World around 6,000 years ago and in the New World about 3,000 years ago by surplus-oriented peoples with a tradition of primitive statehood. The scale of these early states was small, and their rulers were usually hereditans. Monarchs, royal families, religious and military officials, and bureaucrats enjoyed the support of their citizenry through taxation and conscripted labor. However, something about intensive agriculture permanently altered the nature of the state as well as the quality of human life.

Irrigation agriculture created unprecedented surpluses and presented new challenges for political organization. The diversion of water from distant rivers and its dispersal over hundreds or even thousands of square miles required the construction and maintenance of a complex network of canals and reservoirs and therefore demanded a high degree of centralized control. Thus was born an administrative elite that successfully monopolized the new technology and exacted tribute, labor, and allegiance from commoners in exchange for material, military, and religious security. Writing systems evolved independently in both Old and New World civilizations, apparently in response to the need for accurate records of commercial transactions, census statistics, taxes, and other state business.

The development of cities was a direct consequence of the greater productivity brought by irrigation and plow cultivation. In the earlier primitive state, monarchs frequently resided in a capital town surrounded by numerous personal retainers, bureaucrats, religious and military officials, merchants, and noblemen, but these full-time specialists represented only a small fraction of the total population. When agricultural yields began to rise dramatically, a significant proportion of the citizenry was able to migrate permanently to the towns and to engage in nonagricultural tasks, creating subcultural differences between sophisticated urbanites and the more traditional peasant farmers of the countryside.

The development of crafts, trades, professions, and other forms of specialized labor depended on the liberation of large numbers of people from the soil and also on the presence of internal and external markets for their goods and services. In their earliest stages of development, the great agricultural civilizations were what we might call socialist theocracies. That is, their power structures were legitimated by religion, and the state acted as the sole distributor of surplus wealth. In their more developed forms, these civilizations became increasingly militaristic and were oriented primarily toward expansion and conquest, the control of foreign markets, and the creation of domestic ones. Those in power ruled more and more by coercion than by consent, as conquered populations with different languages, life-styles, and gods were added to their growing empires. Warfare was so pronounced that the development of metallurgy, like many modern technological advances, is usually attributed to the need for improved weapons.

These changes in the economic and political aspects of culture were accompanied by changes in human social forms. With the advent of irrigation and the plow, men replaced women as the primary cultivators. (This rather dramatic shift in the division of labor by sex is illustrated by the cross-cultural data presented in fig. 3-3.) The agricultural revolution thus marked the first departure of females from the mainstream of production and a corresponding trend toward their domestic isolation. Since multiple wives were now economic liabilities rather than assets, monogamy regained a position of dominance. In the cities the insecurities of wage labor led to a reduction in kin

Terraced rice agriculture in Java. Very often agricultural food production requires large scale irrigation, terracing, or drainage. These projects are frequently beyond the capacity of any one household to achieve; hence they necessitate some form of centralized planning, as well as a centrally organized work force to execute the plans. It is hardly surprising, then, that it is with the advent of agriculture that the state emerged.

group size, giving rise to the family much as we now know it. For perhaps the first time in human history, the groups in which one lived, socialized, worshiped, and fought were composed of strangers. The urban revolution shattered large kinship groups and led to the emergence of new social institutions designed to regulate city life.

Agricultural civilization spread over much of the world. However, the ancient empires periodically fell to barbarian invasion or, ironically, to the new civilizations that they themselves had spawned. One con-

tinent in particular, Europe, had remained peripheral to cultural evolutionary developments until advanced ideas from Africa and the Near East initiated the Minoan and Greek civilizations. Over the next 2,000 years, Europeans successfully captured foreign markets, foreign resources, and foreign labor and maintained an ardent quest for surplus production that eventually led them to the conquest of every known major ancient center of civilization.

Industrial Societies

The outstanding achievements of European cultures in historic times are not attributable to a biological variation in talent any more than are the previous achievements of Africans, Asians, and New World Indians. Europeans initially found themselves at the receiving end of advanced ideas in science, technology, political and military organization, writing systems, and so forth. It was thus possible for their civilizations to develop rapidly, skipping over the rudimentary stages of development through which other societies had evolved. The first major European civilizations, those of Greece and Rome, became in their turn tremendously influential throughout the Mediterranean region and laid the foundation for Christian mythology and European cultural traditions.

Shortly after A.D. 1000, smaller states began to evolve in the ruins of the Roman empires. Most were feudal in structure. Feudalism divided the entire population into three broad categories on the basis of their rights to land: the nobility, who owned the land; the yeomanry, who were granted special privileges in land and produce in exchange for military and other allegiances to the lord; and the serfs, who had rights to cultivate land and to a portion of its produce in exchange for the protection of the lord. This division of society into *estates* also occurred simultaneously in the empires of the West African Sudan. States in both these areas shared an orientation toward surplus production, profitable long-range trade, and, in their cities, universities, craft and trade unions, and a growing class of merchants. One might well wonder, then, why Europe developed industrial production in the next few centuries and Africa did not.

The answer seems to lie in their changing positions in world trade. Geographically, Europe had been isolated not only from cultural advances elsewhere but also from crucial raw materials. One of the keys to the success of the Roman Empire had been its direct control of resources abroad. During the centuries after its fall, European states continued to depend on this flow of raw materials, but because they dealt through a long series of middlemen, the states had little control over their sources of supply or the cost of the materials. The desire to gain direct access to foreign markets inspired the development of merchant fleets and improved maritime navigational devices. The control of resources and markets abroad, first in Africa and Asia and then in the New World, brought immediate prosperity to European mercantilist nations and signaled the development of a system of production that could keep pace with the new found abundance of raw materials. The steam engine was the first effective replacement for human muscle power since the domestication of draft animals thousands of years earlier. With its invention, productive efficiency leaped ahead.

The social consequences of industrial development may be viewed from two perspectives: the restructuring into new productive groups of society as a whole and the restructuring of the family and domestic groups that were drawn into the emergent market economy. After the invention of the steam engine, factories became a permanent part of the human landscape. With them came demands for the recruitment of huge labor forces from rural areas. Discriminatory tax laws were instituted that ultimately forced peasants to sell their labor for money, and medieval cities swelled with unskilled rural workers, whose migration from the countryside undermined the older feudal economy.

New social distinctions began to take shape. Descendants of the feudal nobility, the *aristocracy*, maintained their ownership of large tracts of land for many decades and stood at the pinnacle of high society, living off the accumulated wealth of their ancestors as well as the efforts of the remaining tenant farmers. In the cities, those who had made their fortunes through mercantilism turned their attention to domestic mass production. A class of factory owners and businessmen, known collectively as the *bour-*

A commune in Shantung Province of the People's Republic of China. The Chinese have launched an immense social experiment: restructuring their social organization in adapting to their newly created forms of economic organization.

geoisie, emerged as the dominant force in all capitalist states. The broad mass of the people, the *proletariat* or workers, was composed of men, women, and children who sold their labor in the shops and factories and who had no access to the means of production or voice in the political decisions of the larger society.

This polarization of wealth and power led to numerous revolutions in the middle of the nineteenth century and to the famous 1917 revolution in the Soviet Union. Major goals of these revolutionary movements were the elimination of private property and free enterprise, and a fairer distribution of wealth. In Western Europe and in America, however, colonialism and the monopolization of world trade brought such incredible prosperity that even the proletariat shared in the general affluence. This factor has made socialist revolution less likely in the Western capitalist, industrialized world.

Social changes in the domestic economy varied among social classes. Those who had the greatest stake in the past, aristocratic families, tried to preserve their titles and wealth through the maintenance of extended kinship groups and elaborate genealogies. Their class felt itself unsuited to physical labor, and so idleness was highly valued for both sexes, even in the face of vanishing economic resources. Members of the bourgeoisie tried to imitate the aristocratic life-style, but they measured their worth through the economic aggressiveness of their men and the adornment and idleness of their women rather than through heredity. Financial success and manhood became closely identified, as did dependency and femininity. Among working-class families, however, a significant deviation from older agricultural labor divisions arose. In order for the family to survive, *all* family members had to work. Women thus returned to production on a massive scale and figured importantly in the development of industrialism. Cooperation among related families was not of particular adaptive value in the cities and vanished rapidly. The matricentric family, created by the death or desertion of a husband, emerged as a frequent accompaniment to urban poverty.

As noted previously, the horror of early industrialism for the working classes of Europe and America was soon diminished, either through revolution or prosperity. The socialist and capitalist experiments of the modern world, although differing in their philosophies of economic distribution, have shown similar evolutionary trends. One is the continued development of mechanized aids to production and the development of new sources of energy. (Ironically, industrial populations have become so proficient in their bid for survival that they now face the secondary problems of overpopulation and overexploitation of their environments.) A second trend has been the organization of humans into a large number of complex institutions that cut across the family structure and have largely replaced the functions of basic kinship groups. For example, specialized institutions have come to monopolize the care and socialization of children and youth. The primate potential for sex-role differentiation has lost much of its utility as a basis for labor division, and more than ever before, the creative talents of both sexes are needed to meet the special challenges of survival for our species—a species that has developed not only a knowledge of its own evolution but the awesome power of its own extinction as well.

Summary

This chapter could have been written in several different ways. For although we can trace human biological evolution through fossils, and the development of human technological sophistication through tools and other artifacts, human social life is nonmaterial. Its reconstruction through time is therefore highly conjectural and subject to many interpretations.

The major theme in this chapter is that the ways in which both nonhuman and human primates relate socially is a mechanism of *survival*. Although primitive, the malleable forms of social interaction present among monkeys and apes foreshadow the division of bounded communities into specialized units of individuals with discrete structures and functions. This specialization of labor is specifically designed to promote the survival of the group. Nonhuman primates use age and sex distinctions to ensure reproductive success and community defense. Early humans also embraced this seemingly basic primate pattern, but they extended labor specialization on the same criteria to the pursuit and sharing of food as well. Their social forms were thus infinitely more complex and diversified and required a greater reliance on learning and on refined systems of communication and interpersonal bonding.

The primitive family group, so essential for the expanding requirements of socialization among evolving humans—with their slower maturation rates and increasing brain size—became more permanent in its membership and also became the center of food-sharing activities. Kinship groups of certain forms increased in size with the perfection of techniques for food getting, and they formed the center of all social, economic, political, and religious activity.

With the achievement of surplus production came increased populations, political centralization, the stratification of society into segments with variable access to wealth and power, and the gradual erosion of kinship groups by more efficient corporate institutions.

Annotated Bibliography

Alland, Alexander, Jr. (1972) *The Human Imperative.* New York: Columbia Univ. Press. A well-reasoned critique of the hypotheses of Konrad Lorenz, Robert Ardrey, and Desmond Morris that territoriality and aggressiveness are innate among humans.

Braidwood, Robert J. (1967) *Prehistoric Men.* 7th ed. Glenview, Ill.: Scott, Foresman. A general introduction to prehistory and toolmaking through the Neolithic period.

Childe, V. Gordon (1951) *Man Makes Himself.* New York: American Library. A classic study of the development of civilization in the Middle East.

Dalton, George, ed. (1967) *Tribal and Peasant Economies.* Garden City, N.Y.: Natural History Press. A general collection of readings on systems of production and distribution in non-Western societies.

Lee, Richard B., and De Vore, Irven, eds. (1968) *Man the Hunter.* Chicago: Aldine. A collection of papers from an international conference of scholars that examine the institutional structures of modern foragers. Also contains several papers that romanticize the importance of hunting in human biocultural evolution.

Martin, M. Kay, and Voorhies, Barbara (1975) *The Female of the Species.* New York: Columbia Univ. Press. A comprehensive anthropological approach to the origin and significance of human sex roles. Contains an extensive cross-cultural analysis of the relationship between social organization and ecological niche.

Sahlins, Marshall D. (1968) *Tribesmen.* Englewood Cliffs, N.J.: Prentice-Hall. A comparative study of tribal societies with an emphasis on social organization.

Sahlins, Marshall D., and Service, Elman R. (1960) *Evolution and Culture.* Ann Arbor: Univ. of Michigan Press. An important discussion of cultural evolutionary processes that attempts to integrate the disparate perspectives of Julian Steward and Leslie White.

Service, Elman R. (1966) *The Hunters.* Englewood Cliffs, N.J.: Prentice-Hall. A general survey of contemporary foragers and their classification into two ideal types: patrilocal and composite bands.

(1971) *Primitive Social Organization: An Evolutionary Perspective.* 2d ed. New York: Random House. Traces the general evolutionary development of culture from simple bands to the primitive state through the definition of levels of sociocultural integration and the creation of ideal types.

Tiger, Lionel (1969) *Men in Groups.* New York: Random House. A highly controversial work that argues for an innate basis for social bonding relationships among human males and corresponding absence of such a basis among human females.

White, Leslie (1959) *The Evolution of Culture: The Development of Civilization to the Fall of Rome.* New York: McGraw-Hill. A classic in modern anthropology; correlates the general evolution of culture with the increasing capture of energy.

Wolf, Eric R. (1966) *Peasants.* Englewood Cliffs, N.J.: Prentice-Hall. A cross-cultural investigation of peasant societies.

Part II

Biology and Culture

4
Primatology and Human Nature

The World Context

Origins and Development through Time

Throughout history, human beings have demonstrated a characteristic that is apparently unique in the animal kingdom—a curiosity about themselves. This curiosity is manifested in innumerable theories about human origins—theories whose sources range from ancient myths to the molecular genetics of the 1970s, from weighty philosophical tomes to the careful excavations of paleontologists. In this search for our "true nature," the nonhuman primates have always particularly fascinated us. Many people see monkeys and apes as living repositories of our ancestral nature, unobscured by the veneer of "culture" and "civilization." This nature has been vaguely envisaged as various combinations of deep-seated needs, desires, passions, and fears—all of them inevitable results of our belonging to the species *Homo sapiens*. The search has aimed at discovering inherited forces or instincts that govern much of our behavior; indeed, some people dismiss learning and culture as largely an illusion, and see our species as driven by deeper and darker forces.

Orangutan male about five years old. Reclusive and quiet, orangutans are very difficult to find and observe. However, since orangutans, chimpanzees, and gorillas are our closest living relatives, the more we learn about their behavior in their natural habitats the better we shall be able to understand how much of our own behavior represents ancient primate patterns.

In the West, descriptions of apes and monkeys have gradually amassed since adventurers began to explore the tropics and survive to tell the tale. As early as 1295, Marco Polo reported on great apes in Asia, apparently orangutans. By the sixteenth century we find the first reference to the lemurs of Madagascar, one of the most primitive groups of primates: Sieur Etienne de Flacourt concluded: "All in all, they are idle, dull, and stupid creatures" (1661). However, not until the eighteenth century did such reports make a significant impact on Western thought. The sudden increase in interest was largely due to a young chimpanzee that was caught in Angola and brought to live in England. Edward Tyson, an English anatomist, described this animal's anatomy in a book that also included a survey of the ancients' knowledge and beliefs about apes and monkeys. Tyson's work was widely praised, and the extraordinary likeness of the chimp to human beings impressed the public (Taylor 1973:6).

Since the appearance of that eighteenth century chimpanzee upon the English scene, the attitude of thinkers and scientists toward our primate relatives seems to have been more often determined by wishful thinking than by scientific observation. As John E. Pfeiffer says: "Depending on whom you read, animals are cute, charming, and a bit bumbling and foolish (the Br'er Rabbit or Disney approach); noble, wise and pure; brutes and innate killers" (1969:246). Non-human primates have been paraded both as models of peace (in contrast to their "fallen" human cousins) and as living examples of the unavoidable viciousness of all primate life, whether human or nonhuman (the "King Kong" approach). Not even Darwin avoided these tempting comparisons. In *The Descent of Man* he comments:

> For my own part, I would as soon be descended from that heroic little monkey, who braved his dreaded enemy in order to save the life of his keeper; or from that old baboon, who descending from the mountains carried away in triumph his young comrade from a crowd of astonished dogs—as from a savage who delights to torture his enemies, offers up bloody sacrifices, practices infanticide without remorse, treats his wives like slaves, knows no decency and is haunted by the grossest superstitions (1871:387).

But Darwin's message contained one clear principle: animal species either adapt to their wild environment or die out. Logically, therefore, they should be studied in that environment. Biologists in the latter part of the nineteenth century and early part of the twentieth century ignored this dictum; instead, they studied monkeys and apes living behind bars in laboratories and zoos (Pfeiffer 1969:247). Just as human beings show signs of stress and abnormal behavior when kept in captivity (Goffman 1961:11), so these animals often responded to crowded, confined conditions by exhibiting highly aggressive and sometimes pathological behavior. But many biologists assumed that the behavior of these imprisoned, neurotic creatures was the same as it would be under natural conditions. Perhaps even more startling was their further assumption that their research findings could be applied directly to people. The chain of reasoning was complete: Because primates (in cages) are often violent, we know that they are violent "by nature"; since we are the closest relatives of these primates, it follows that we must share in this common heritage of violence.

False, inferential arguments of this sort are still advanced. However, the mainstream of serious primatological research has progressed far beyond these naive efforts. Modern research has been directed into two primary channels: the study of the behavior of animals living under conditions in the wild, and the study of specific aspects of the behavior of animals living in carefully controlled captive conditions.

Let us first consider the recent history of field research. The forerunners of the field study were, as we have seen, the anecdotal reports of early explorers. However, the pioneers of modern research in the wild were H. W. Nissen, who studied the chimpanzee (1931); H. C. Bingham, who studied the gorilla (1932); and Clarence Ray Carpenter, who studied the howler monkey (1934). Of the three, only Carpenter hit upon favorable conditions of observation and was successful in his field research on the howler monkey (*Alouatta palliata*)—a large, black, rather clumsy animal living in the forests of Central and South America. When Carpenter published the results of his investigations, he emphasized the problems and shortcomings inherent in the work he had done and concluded: "Field studies

of primates require special combinations of broad and advanced scientific training, special observational abilities and skills, intellectual curiosity and honesty, and the endurance and patience of a pack mule" (1965:257).

Many of Carpenter's reflections have become elementary truths of primatology today, but in the 1930s they were a major milestone in the development of primatology, and his methods were closely followed by field observers for the next thirty years. Carpenter systematically collected specific types of information. First, he classified the animals he was watching into *age-sex categories*. Using these classifications, he took censuses of groups living in the area, noting the number, age, and sex of animals in each group. He estimated the size of the geographical area, or *range*, that these groups habitually used, and noted that the animals behaved differently in familiar parts of the range than in less familiar, peripheral areas. Carpenter also discussed the relationship between neighboring groups, hypothesizing that the loud roar vocalization of the howler monkey acts as a *spacing mechanism*, helping groups to remain at some distance from each other. Turning to relationships between animals within the group, he made *interactional analyses* of the behavior of paired classes of animals of different sexes and ages in order to identify characteristic patterns of interaction between these classes. Finally, he looked at *postures* and *locomotion;* at *feeding* and *drinking* behavior; and at the *activity cycles*, or daily "schedule," followed by each group. He set all these observations within an *ecological context* by measuring rainfall and temperature patterns, describing the plants and other animals of the island, and assessing the distribution of the monkeys' preferred foods.

The Second World War brought a temporary halt to field research, and the modern period of primate studies, with its emphasis on long-term, systematic observation, began only in the 1950s. This modern research included the establishment of the Japan Monkey Center at Kyoto University, and Stuart A. Altmann's influential two-year study of the rhesus monkey colony on Cayo Santiago, a forty-acre islet off the east coast of Puerto Rico (1962). Since then a proliferation of primate "ethnographies" has appeared although over one-third of the world's primate species have yet to be studied.

Another important feature of primatology over the past fifty years has been the emergence of laboratory studies. Wolfgang Köhler and Robert Yerkes pioneered research on the thought processes and abilities of primates kept in captivity. During the First World War, Köhler conducted a series of experiments on chimpanzees in an attempt to investigate the *Gestalt* or insight theory of learning. According to this theory, understanding occurs when a whole idea or pattern is suddenly comprehended. This "whole" (Gestalt) is considered to be greater than its parts; in other words, putting together the parts randomly would not in itself make up the whole, the new insight. For example, in one experiment, chimpanzees learned to construct a long pole from a series of sticks left lying in their cages in order to hook in a bundle of bananas left just beyond arm's reach outside the cage. This, argued Köhler (1927), indicated that the chimpanzees perceived the sticks as more than just a collection of sticks; in a sudden insight, they saw the potential use of these sticks to create a new and extremely useful implement.

Robert Yerkes' great contribution to early primate studies was a sweeping survey of all that was known about the great apes in a book entitled simply *The Great Apes* (1929). This book revealed the vast lack of systematic research into the abilities and behavior of any of the great apes and thus challenged psychologists, zoologists, and anthropologists. In a sense, much of the research carried out in recent years can be seen as a response to this newly awakened awareness of our ignorance.

Contemporary Examples

Let us first look at the species and parts of the world on which modern research has focused, for not all the primates have been studied in equal detail, and some have not been observed at all. The most studied primates are probably the chimpanzees of Gombe Stream in East Africa (for example, van Lawick-Goodall 1968) and the macaque monkeys living on the islands of Japan (for example, Miyadi 1967; Mizuhara 1964). In both cases, the animals have been under more or less

Howler monkey using his prehensile tail. These primates were the first to be studied successfully in their natural habitat. From this research, Clarence Ray Carpenter was able to isolate what he called a "primatological blueprint" which continues to be used as a practical guide to field observations of primates, even now when longer, more systematic research is forcing us to reevaluate some of Carpenter's postulations.

continuous observation for at least ten years. The baboons living in the savannahs of East Africa are perhaps our next best-known relatives. In the last ten years, researchers have also finally sought out the elusive occupants of the African forests, although the problems of studying a small, fast-moving, and probably timid animal 150 feet up a tree in the pouring rain are overwhelming! Despite the inevitable setbacks, however, a picture of these forest dwellers is now emerging as well. Similar efforts are underway in Madagascar (the Malagasy Republic) and Southeast Asia. The biggest question mark now hangs over South America; although no primates are found on the open lands south of the Amazon river basin, the rain forests in the region of the Amazon and further to the north are teeming with unstudied species.

Recent field studies have relied on many new methods of recording information, and the largely descriptive approach used by Carpenter is giving way to more rigorous methods of measurement (for example, Struhsaker 1967). Research tends to focus on a specific problem; then a series of questions that may shed light on it are carefully formulated. For example, in addressing the problem of how animals use their environment, we might ask: How much time does the group spend in each part of its range? Do animals perform different activities in different parts of the range? What percentage of the animals' diet consists of leaves, and what of fruit and flowers? How much time do animals spend at different levels (such as ground, low branches, high canopy) in the forest? Such questions are answered by sampling the relevant behaviors and factors involved at timed intervals during set observation periods. Throughout the study, observers try to pay close attention to the possible distortions of behavior introduced by their own presence. They must also take into account the fact that some behaviors occur in more visible settings than others. Thus the observer must assess to what extent he or she is recording a large amount of feeding behavior, for example, simply because the animals are easier to see when feeding than when doing anything else.

Many other aspects of primate life are currently being investigated through the same general approach. In Japan, the spread of new behaviors in a provisioned group of macaques is being studied (Miyadi 1967). It appears that juveniles and infants are almost always responsible for introducing a new behavior, such as washing sand-covered potatoes before eating them. From them the behavior spreads to closely related females, and from these to other females and consort males; only the older males of the troop remain obstinately impervious to such untraditional habits and stick to eating sandy potatoes! In East Africa, Michael Rose has been studying the different postures used by monkeys and the time spent in each posture type. He found that in a 24-hour period, an animal spends nearly 90 percent of its time simply sitting (1974:203).

Just as field studies have become more topic oriented, so studies of primates in captivity have also diversified and become more specialized, calling upon the skills of psychologists, neurophysiologists, and endocrinologists as well as upon zoologists and anthropologists. Some researchers are investigating the nature of mothering, including the ways in which the relationship between the mother and her infant develops, and the long-term effects on the infant's social development of isolation from its mother or peer group or both (examples are: Harlow, Schitz, and Harlow 1969; Hinde and Spencer-Booth 1967; Rowell 1968). Others are attempting to identify the functions of various parts of the brain. Researchers implant tiny electrodes in the brain of a monkey—usually the rhesus monkey, *Macaca mulatta*—and apply a mild electric current to specific brain regions, causing the animal to exhibit a fairly predictable behavior, such as aggression or a particular physical activity (Delgado 1966). Endocrinologists and physiologists are attempting to unravel the interaction between the behavior of a monkey and the type and amount of hormones present in its blood. It has been shown, for instance, that female rhesus monkeys' attractiveness to the male depends heavily on vaginal odor, which is stimulated by the hormone estrogen and blocked by the hormone progesterone. However, it has also been found that external social stress can influence female hormonal levels and can increase the length of the menstrual cycle (Michael and Keverne 1968).

One interesting example of the highly specific work being done with captive primates is the research into

chimpanzee communication systems. Early attempts (Kellogg 1968) to teach a chimp to pronounce words met with little success; it now appears that chimpanzees simply do not have an adequate vocal apparatus to enunciate the sounds of human language (Lieberman, Crelin, and Klatt 1972). For this reason, two researchers, Beatrice and Allen Gardner, decided to teach sign language to a chimpanzee (1969). In the course of her training, the chimp, named Washoe, learned over 130 different signs and even combined them into two-word and three-word phrases (see also Chap. 7).

David Premack has taken quite a different and in some ways more interesting approach with a young chimpanzee named Sarah (1970). He is not as concerned with discovering the possible size of a chimpanzee's vocabulary as with the grammatical complexity the chimp is able to handle. To this end, Premack has taught Sarah to place pieces of plastic of assorted shapes, sizes, and colors on a magnetized board. Each plastic piece represents a word, and strings or sequences of pieces represent phrases. In order to be sure that she is really using the plastic pieces as sym-

A young rhesus monkey clings to its "pseudomother" in the famous laboratory research of Harry Harlow and his colleagues. They concluded that their monkey subjects needed warm body contact—even if it were a terrycloth-covered pseudomother heated from within by a lightbulb—in order to achieve normal maturation.

By stimulating the various sections of the brain with electrodes and observing the resulting behavior, researchers are attempting to isolate areas of the brain which control specific behaviors.

bols, Premack asks questions such as "Apple same as——?" The plastic symbol for an apple is a blue triangle, but when she is asked this question, Sarah responds that it is red and round, with a stem, and not as good as grapes! In fact, Sarah's aptitude has proved so great that Premack has commented: "To cynics who doubt that Sarah understands language, we can say only that she understands well enough to teach her teachers" (1970:58).

In what ways is the information gained from these studies being used to help—or hinder—our understanding of ourselves? Unfortunately, we have not lost our primate fantasy, and several recent books have popularized dubious theories and evidence about human nature and primate nature (for example, Ardrey 1967; Lorenz 1966; Morgan 1972; Morris 1967; Tiger 1972). Primatologists and anthropologists criticize these books on the grounds that either the theories bear little relationship to the data emerging from primate studies today, or the authors select their facts to fit their particular case and disregard information that does not support their arguments.

Most of these writers contend primarily that we are animals; that we can trace our behavioral evolution through the primates living today; and that most of the less likable aspects of our behavior (such as warfare and status seeking) result from our primate heritage. This heritage is alleged to be genetically based, but when genetic theory fails to account for the facts, less defined, more mystical ideas are invoked. Robert Ardrey in particular adopts this approach: "Not in innocence and not in Asia was mankind born. The home of our fathers was . . . a sky-swept savannah glowing with menace" (1961:9). Although Desmond Morris' prose is less purple, he too stumbles into misstatements and hypotheses stated as fact. To take but one example: "The forest ape . . . became a hunting ape; . . . we are vegetarians turned carnivores" (1967:21). Yet recent studies show that the diet of the !Kung San, a hunting and gathering people living in the Kalahari Desert (see Chap. 21), is only 37 percent meat; the rest is made up of various vegetable foods (Lee 1968).

One of the most commonly aired as-in-primates-so-in-people arguments centers around baboon social structure; it illustrates well the misuse of selective and often inaccurate information. Let us look first at the information derived from the early baboon studies (for example, Washburn and DeVore 1961)—information commonly used to "shed light" on human nature. Then we shall look at the data emerging from more recent, systematic studies (for instance, Altmann and Altmann 1970; Rowell 1966); these data are invariably ignored by those who would enlighten us.

Most of the early studies were made of baboons living within national parks in East Africa, where they were accustomed to the presence of people and thus were easy to watch. These studies typically reported that baboons are highly sociable animals, living in stable groups of thirty to fifty animals. Most baboons forage alone and rarely share food. Males are twice the size of females and sport huge canine teeth. The role of these big, fierce-looking males is to drive off predators, to police the group itself, and to fight among themselves for precedence in the dominance hierarchy, or order of social rank. The alpha, or top, male gets first choice of food and females, and because he is the most aggressive male, he wins all the fights. The other males in the group are duly ranked according to their performance with respect to food, females, and fights. Females, on the other hand, are little more than perpetual baby producers, protected and kept in line by the males of their troop. The males' dominance hierarchy controls the frequency of aggression because through it each male knows his place in the social order. When neighboring groups meet, they generally threaten each other and sometimes actually fight. When the group moves, males surround the females and young, and if the group is attacked, they rush into the breach as the females and young flee to safety.

In a nutshell, here is a picture of an aggressive, rigidly structured society dominated by status-conscious males who lord it over small, put-upon females. Time and time again this picture has been put forward as a model of the social life of our ancestors on the African savannah (for example, Service 1966:29).

However, as David Pilbeam has observed (1972), even a cursory examination of this model of prehistoric strife is enough to demonstrate its improbability. First, the baboons on which the model is based were almost certainly subject to considerable stress, their high-

A female baboon, with her baby clinging to her stomach, "presents" herself to a dominant male. Although the position is that which is used for sexual intercourse, in this case it is being used to signal social submissiveness within the group hierarchy. Many of our current conceptions about baboon society, however, are based on observations such as this one which were made in game parks or in crowded conditions which might well distort baboon behavioral patterns. Thus contemporary research is emphasizing the study of baboons and other primates in their uncrowded, natural habitats—far from contact with human beings.

density population in a game park making them an easy target for predators and subjecting them to harassment by streams of tourists. Second, Pilbeam notes that more recent studies of baboons living outside a game park, or in a forest habitat, have told a very different story. The membership of groups living under these conditions is not closed; animals, especially males, change groups quite frequently and are apparently admitted to new groups without hostility. Fights are infrequent, and the much-vaunted male dominance hierarchy is almost undetectable. Intertroop encounters are rare and are neutral when they do occur. The presence of any kind of threat tends to cause a precipitous flight—with the bigger and stronger males leading it. It is not clear whether troop movements are determined by males or females—perhaps by a combination. And positioning of animals in the troop during travel varies much more than the early studies indicated.

The significance of the differences between these studies becomes clearer in the light of an experiment carried out with peaceable, forest-living baboons in Uganda (Rowell 1967). A troop of these baboons was captured and caged so that they were forced to live in crowded, confined conditions. The result? Fights and aggression became common, and a rigid dominance hierarchy emerged. Thus, as Pilbeam says, the baboons that were first used as models for early hominid society "probably were under stress, in a relatively impoverished environment, pestered by humans of various sorts. The high degree of aggression, the hierarchies, the rigid sex-role differences, were abnormalities" (1972:66).

We cannot, then, make rash extrapolations from the behavior of other primates to our own species. But cautious, speculative inferences can be and have been made about certain aspects of our behavior, if not our nature. These inferences are merely hypotheses, and they involve both the possible nature of early human societies and the psychological underpinnings of all contemporary primate societies—human and non-human (Crook 1973; Pilbeam 1972; Reynolds 1966). The hypotheses draw upon much of the more recent and reliable evidence about living primates rather than highlighting a few—probably abnormal—cases. They also take into account the potential effects of the envi-

A lioness has driven a troop of baboons into a tree. Baboons usually attack and chase large cats, but run wildly from humans. However, lions are too formidable; generally they will flee to the trees when one approaches.

ronment upon our way of life and use a number of recent studies that attempt to relate ecological factors to different types of social structure (for example, Crook and Gartlan 1966). In these studies, specific questions are asked: During how many months of the year is fruit available in the area? Where and how big are the fruit trees? Where and how many safe sleeping trees are there? The answers to these kinds of questions may help explain the form that the social organization of a group of primates takes. For example, if there are only two safe sleeping trees in an area of thirty miles, baboons in that area could hardly live in small, mutually intolerant territorial groups. If they did, only two lucky groups would survive! Thus, if we know the type of environment in which a species lives, we can begin to make educated guesses about at least some aspects of that species' way of life—and this is true of our own species as well as for the nonhuman primates.

When this broadly based, ecology-oriented approach is taken, the resulting picture is very different from that of the killer-ape doomsday watchers: "The closest we can come to a concept of 'natural man' would indicate that our ancestors were, like other primates, capable of being aggressive, but they would have been socialized culturally in such a way as to reduce as far as possible the manifestation of aggression" (Pilbeam 1972:69).

Theory

Systems

Let us consider the theoretical pigeonholes into which the various aspects of nonhuman primate social life are sorted. Imagine a group of monkeys sitting in a tree in a forest. The first factor the primatologist must take into account is the range of *environmental influences* affecting the group. These include climate, the physical structure of the forest, the distribution and availability of food and water, the presence of other animal species in the forest that may compete with our group for the available resources, and last but not least, the potential danger from snakes, predatory birds, or wild cats. All these features must be assessed not once but regularly, for all can vary seasonally, and as they change, so must the animals' tactics change.

The primatologist's next preoccupation is with the *composition of the group.* How many adult males and females are there? How many subadults, juveniles, and infants? Armed with this information, the researcher can classify the group into one of the five general categories describing the range of primate group structures (Crook and Gartlan 1966): (1) solitary animals, (2) family groups, (3) small- to medium-sized multimale groups, (4) medium- to large-sized multimale groups, and (5) one-male groups.

The first category, *solitary animals,* is perhaps misleading, for although these animals usually forage alone, neighboring individuals form a loose community in which members often sleep together and are more tolerant of each other than of strangers. Each "solitary" female occupies a range that she shares with her immature offspring, and she is regularly visited by "solitary" males, for males travel over a larger area that includes the ranges of a number of females with whom they interact socially. The second category, *family groups,* describes groups composed of one adult male, one adult female, and their immature offspring. (That the family group describes only a monogamous situation is perhaps a reflection of the ethnocentricity of primatologists.) The third and fourth categories, *multimale groups,* both refer to groups containing more than one male and more than one female and each female's offspring. Finally, the *one-male group* category describes a group structure in which there is one male, two or more females, and all their immature offspring.

Each primate species usually has a characteristic group structure that falls more or less into one of these categories. However, occasional exceptions exist, such as the Indian langur, which lives in multimale groups in one part of its range and in one-male groups in another area of its range (Yoshiba 1968).

Once the nature of the environment and the composition and structure of the group have been established, the observer can see how the group shares the forest with other groups of the same species. We know of no nomadic primate. Every species that has been studied has a *home range,* an area through which it habitually moves in the course of its daily activities (Burt 1943). The home ranges of neighboring groups

usually overlap somewhat. Such groups may avoid meeting each other in the overlap area—by giving loud calls to signal their approach, for example—or they may meet and interact aggressively before going their separate ways, or they may simply move apart as soon as they catch sight of each other.

A few primate species allow little or no overlap between the home ranges of neighboring groups, and each group appears to defend its range against intruders. These species are said to occupy *territories* (Burt 1943; Jewell 1966). It is easy to confuse true *territorial behavior,* or defense of a geographical area, with the *hostile interaction* that may occur when neighboring groups of nonterritorial species meet each other. Such hostile interactions occur whenever and wherever the groups may meet, so the groups cannot be said to be defending or delineating any boundary. These interactions serve to defend the space occupied by the group at the time of the interaction rather than a territory, an area that is fixed in space and time.

Primatologists use special concepts and terms to analyze relationships within the group. Behavior is commonly categorized into four general realms: maintenance; agonistic, or aggressive, interactions; nonagonistic interactions; and sexual relations. *Maintenance behavior* refers to such activities as resting, feeding, moving, and self-grooming, although even these socially neutral activities often contain an agonistic or nonagonistic component. *Nonagonistic interactions* include the relationship of mothers and infants, play, greeting, or grooming of another animal. The *sexual relations* category refers to behaviors leading up to and including mating.

The category *agonistic interactions* requires the most discussion. The term is used to describe behavior that is aggressive or unfriendly, including the behavior of both the initiator and the recipient of aggression. In the past, the concept of the dominance hierarchy was central to most discussions of agonistic behavior. The dominance hierarchy is a ranking order that is supposedly present in most or all primate species, particularly among the males, who establish their status partly through their own physical strength, partly through the rank of their mother, and partly through their ability to enlist the support of their peers. The high-ranking male has priority of access to limited resources, whether they are food or females. The crucial function of the hierarchy is to minimize aggression by teaching every animal his or her place in the social order.

However, recent studies of primates in the wild are beginning to suggest that dominance hierarchies may be a figment of the observer's imagination, and new studies are now under way to evaluate both agonistic and nonagonistic behavior in terms of a social network of roles: If the group is to survive and prosper, each animal must play its role in fulfilling various necessary functions (Gartlan 1968; Stoltz and Saayman 1970). For example, the group must be led, fights must be stopped, a watch must be kept for predators, and infants must be taken care of and integrated into the social life of the group. Viewed in these terms, primate societies emerge as a series of complex and interesting relationships, whereas the traditional theory of dominance, which analyzes all behavior solely in terms of motivation, tends to reduce them to a single, unending struggle to climb the social totem pole.

Processes

A number of efforts have been made to integrate the various concepts described previously into a total theory explaining the underpinnings of primate social systems. These theories postulate a close relationship between environment and society and attempt to identify the causal links unifying the elements of the society in its environment (see Chap. 3).

The first and still the most influential of these models was published in 1966 by two British fieldworkers, John Crook and Steven Gartlan. Although their design does not fit some primate societies now known, and although there are many obvious oversimplifications and generalizations in their system of classification, it remains an interesting and innovative approach that has not yet been superseded by anything substantially better. Crook and Gartlan propose five *adaptive grades* of primate social organization. Each grade represents a particular complex of behavioral features that are adapted to those aspects of the environment that form major selection pressures. Each grade is a level of adaptation in the forest, tree savannah, grassland, and arid environments. This progression, Crook and Gartlan argue, reflects not only a description of contemporary primates but also an evolutionary trend from forest-dwelling insectivorous animals to larger, open-country animals with a predominantly vegetarian diet (see Chap. 2).

Grade I comprises the forest-dwelling, nocturnal primates. Their diet consists mainly of insects, and they have a generally solitary form of social organization. As we have seen, *solitary* is a relative term, but in this context it means that when stalking their insect prey, animals are unlikely to have either their intended meal or their own concentration disturbed by a close neighbor's untimely stepping on a dry leaf. It is thought that the earliest primates lived similar lives 50 million years ago or more.

Animals in *Grades II and III* are frugivorous and leaf-eating forest dwellers. This dietary switch is associated with diurnal, or daytime, activity and the formation of larger social groups. With a diet consisting of fruit and leaves, group living is advantageous, for food sources are frequently concentrated in a small area—as when a single tree is loaded down with hundreds of berries—and the development of social tolerance means that animals can feed together at these sources. Grade II contains species grouped into small family parties; Grade III species are grouped into small to occasionally large parties that may contain more than one adult male. Groups from both these grades often exhibit marked territorial behavior, and Crook and Gartlan attribute both the smallness of their groups and their territoriality to the nature of the food supply in a rain forest: "A non-seasonal climate with a moderately constant availability of various fruits presumably allows increase in numbers to a ceiling imposed by periodic food shortages due to local food crop failures. . . . The 'territorial' behavior of forest groups may be interpreted as ensuring an adequate provisioning area for the individuals comprising them" (Crook and Gartlan 1966: 1201).

Species included in *Grades IV* and *V* occupy forest fringes, tree savannah, and grassland or arid savannah. Grade IV species characteristically form medium to large groups containing several males, and the species show marked sexual dimorphism (differences in body shape and size according to sex). The species live in home ranges—and either avoid or fight with other groups. In contrast, Grade V species live in medium to large groups, but they frequently fragment, and the basic social unit is the one-male group. Crook and Gartlan see the larger groups found in open-country primates partly as a response to the threat of being hunted and eaten by other animals: Small groups would be easy prey to the carnivores of the savannah, whereas there is safety in numbers. Fluctuations in the availability of food—seasonal shortages followed by a local superabundance—encourage the formation of large, cohesive groups to exploit temporary concentrations of food. The size and aggressiveness of males is seen as a result of intrasexual selection over which males shall have access to females in estrus, which in turn leads to more pronounced structuring within the group. The difference between Grade IV and Grade V groups is attributed to less abundant food supplies in Grade V habitats: Animals need to be able to fragment into small, dispersed groups in order to exploit sparse and widely scattered foods.

Each category, then, contains a society type together with the ecological features believed to determine that type. But although this approach provides a valuable tool and a basis for future research, it should be treated with reservation. A number of primate societies do not fit into any single category, for the classification system oversimplifies the complex nature of the interaction between animals and their environment.

Analysis

Until we have greatly improved our ability to communicate with other primates, a presentation of a nonhuman primate folk perspective is impossible. In this

Chimpanzees in their natural habitat.

Chest-thumping adult male gorilla. For years used to stereotype gorilla behavior, this act is now seen to be part of a whole behavioral sequence of distinct acts performed by silverbacked males. First he will sit, tip head side to side and emit some soft "hoops." These hoops become more rapid, fusing into a "growl." Sometimes this early sequence is interrupted when the actor stops, daintily picks one leaf from a nearby tree, and places it between his lips before resuming. Just before the climax of the sequence he rises, rips up some vegetation and throws it in the air. Then he will beat his chest with cupped hands, although sometimes he will slap his belly, a nearby tree, or even the back of another gorilla. During or at the end of the beating, the gorilla will step sidewards a few paces on his hind legs; and finally, he will dash away on all fours, bowling over anything in his path. Such displays are very infrequent and cause great excitement among onlooking gorillas.

section, therefore, we shall simply review data collected and tabulated by an observer who obviously is not in a position to interview her or his subjects. We shall then proceed to show some of the ways in which these materials have been analyzed.

One of the best-known serious attempts to use a primate model to shed light on the social life of early *Homo sapiens*—and thereby on human nature—was made by a British primatologist, Vernon Reynolds (1966). He used behavioral data on three of the great apes, or Pongidae, to make inferences about possible early human behavior. The three apes he chose for his discussion are the chimpanzee (*Pan troglodytes*), the orangutan (*Pongo pygmaeus*), and the gorilla (*Gorilla gorilla*). We must bear in mind, though, that our knowledge of these apes has increased significantly since this paper was published in 1966 (for example, van Lawick-Goodall 1968; McKinnon 1974), and our ideas about their social organization have been modified. After describing the social organization of these apes as reported by Reynolds, we shall see how he used the available information to build a hypothetical model that he believes tells us about the social life of our own ancestors. The author's opinions on the value of this model are presented in the conclusion.

Reynolds lists five features that he believes are "common to the societies of gorillas, chimpanzees and orangs, and are not often found in those of Old World Monkeys" (1966:444): (1) nomadism, (2) open groups and a sense of community, (3) individual choice in sexual relationships, (4) exploratory behavior of adult males, and (5) unique behavior patterns. We shall briefly discuss these features in order.

First, recent research has demonstrated that the great apes are not truly nomadic. However, they do roam through home ranges that are often very large.

Second, Reynolds contrasts the open groups and sense of community of the great apes with the closed groups common among monkeys. In a closed group system, an animal either is or is not a member of a particular group. The group maintains itself in a stable manner through time and space, and in fact an animal will often spend his or her whole life in the same group. In contrast, the societies of the great apes seem to be based on far wider and looser social ties that constitute something approaching a sense of community. According to Reynolds, all three species appear to recognize relationships and bonds outside the immediate confines of the group.

The data do tend to support Reynolds' third point, that individuals do not mate randomly. Rather, both females and males show preferences for individual members of the opposite sex in their mating activities.

The fourth feature, the exploratory behavior of adult males, is also described by Reynolds as an "innate urge to roam and explore" (1966:445). Male gorillas do not attach themselves to any one group, but prefer to roam the forest. Similarly, adult male chimpanzees tend to form small, highly mobile bands that cover considerable distances in short periods of time. On the other hand, females of both species are much less adventurous; they are almost always found in groups, together with a few males. In some cases these males are old animals who appear to have retired from the wanderings of their youth; in other cases they are simply individuals who apparently prefer to stay at home.

The last feature of pongid society that Reynolds considers unique is a constellation of activities that "are evidence of great behavioral plasticity and inventiveness" (1966:445). Included in these activities are the use of tools and weapons, drumming and dancing, and the making of beds. Reynolds cites instances of both chimps and gorillas in captivity using large objects such as rocks and chairs as weapons in a direct clubbing attack or an airborne projectile one. There is no evidence that gorillas in the wild use tools, but in captivity they have been taught to paint and draw. Chimps, however, are well known for their termite-fishing abilities: They pick a thin branch from a bush or sapling, strip it down until one slender stem remains, and poke it down holes into termite mounds. They pause a moment, pull the stem out, and eat the termites that crawled onto their stem while it was inside the mound.

Reynolds argues that the features characteristic of and unique to present-day large apes were probably present in the common ancestor of apes and *Homo sapiens,* and that these "genetically programmed behavior patterns" determined the social evolution of our early ancestors when they took to life on the open grasslands (1966:446). Forerunners of modern apes were probably living in the African forests about 30 million years ago (see Chap. 2). From them, says Reynolds, evolved a species that colonized the forest fringe, where savannah and forest mingle to form a wooded grassland.

Reynolds envisages this species as becoming more and more specialized in its social organization. Males began acting cooperatively as they improved their skill with tools and weapons. Females and their offspring remained in groups on the edge of the forest and foraged for fruit and plant foods, accompanied by a few older males or simply males who stayed at home. The other males returned from their hunting forays in the savannah to sleep with the rest of the community in tree nests on the edge of the forest. Whenever the males found a large source of meat out on the savannah, they drummed and shouted until other groups joined them, and the females and young left the safety of the forest edge to join the feast. As juvenile males grew up, they began tagging along with the adult males. But the family ties remained, and they periodically returned to visit their mothers and siblings.

Reynolds suggests that these communities may have contained about fifty individuals. At some times of the year they would be widely scattered; at others, they would be clustered around a large local food source. Although each community had its own sense of identity, groups were far from being closed circles; bands of males would frequently visit neighboring communities, sometimes accompanied by young females.

According to Reynolds, this transitory phase ended around 15 million years ago, when during the Pliocene period the tropical rain forests began to shrink, leaving in their wake an early hominid who was perforce a savannah dweller. Mothers and their offspring now partially depended on meat provided by males; food and water were more widely spaced, and population density declined. Such conditions must have favored the development of more permanent groupings. These female-centered groups would cluster near water holes, with temporary shelters constructed in clumps of trees or among rocks and caves. Members of the group would have to spend much of their day foraging for vegetable foods.

During the past few million years, the selective pressure exerted by the savannah habitat further molded existing behavioral patterns. For example, an environment where there was a premium on successful hunting and scavenging would favor an improvement in communication (see Chap. 7). Similarly, the development of weapons or cutting tools was favored, with a concomitant increase in that nebulous attribute, intelligence (see Chap. 2). It was clearly an advantage to be able to learn and predict the habits of other carnivores and of prey species such as gazelles, or to remember directions and places previously visited. The wide network of social relationships within and between communities enhanced the formation of large cooperative male bands for mass hunts and led to a rapid spread of any technological advance. "Already two typically hominid social institutions were clearly in operation: the sexual division of labor, and the basis of the family and tribal systems" (Reynolds 1966:448) (see also Chap. 3).

Reynolds' overview of early hominid society, based on this kind of extrapolation from our "ape-like behavioral inheritance" (1966:449) and the probable ecological pressures affecting our ancestors, can be summarized as follows: The early hominid family was built around the mother and her offspring, often in

Adult male baboon eating infant Thomson's Gazelle which he found in the tall grass during the gazelles' birth season. This unusual photograph documents that—contrary to popular belief—human beings are not the only meat-eating primates.

association with other friendly or related females. This was a bond of female friendship rather than common subservience to a male overlord, as has often been postulated. Although males may have attached themselves intermittently to these groups, their role as exclusive sexual partners probably developed later. Human tribal systems came into existence when communication became sufficiently sophisticated to denote concepts of family, friend, group, tribe, other friendly tribes, and not so friendly tribes, thereby permitting a system of social interaction among large numbers of people.

Conclusions

Schools of Thought

Writers who attempt to illuminate human nature through the study of primate behavior can be roughly divided into two camps: those who draw strong and on the whole pessimistic conclusions, and those who make tentative and generally less pessimistic suggestions.

Within the field of ethological studies, Konrad Lorenz (1966) is probably the chief exponent of the first viewpoint, although Robert Ardrey (1967) is undoubtedly its most widely read advocate. The arguments of this camp are united by three fundamental assertions. First, these writers contend that Man (and they invariably talk about "Man"), like many other primates, has an inborn territorial or aggressive drive that needs to be expressed and unavoidably *is* expressed at periodic intervals. Second, the writers undertake limited surveys of a number of primate societies and conclude that there is a variety of patterns of territoriality and of social organization to which simple survival values can be attributed. These survival values are presented in terms of optimum use of resources, selective elimination of the least fit, security, and the "good life" for the survivors. Third, the writers assert that man is defective in the control of his aggression because his recent rapid technological development has not been accompanied by the evolution of built-in (genetically programed) restraints. The writers tend to ignore human culture and the vast array of possible behaviors that are learned through cultural transmission. Believing as they do in

innate human aggressive drives, their only suggestion for saving our species is to channel these instinctive passions into harmless competitive conflicts such as the Olympic Games instead of war.

Exponents of the second viewpoint, on the other hand, acknowledge the common heritage of human beings and our nonhuman relatives but reject the view that early or modern members of our species are irrevocably violent, status-seeking animals. In the words of Pilbeam: "To be sure, we are not born empty slates upon which anything can be written; but to believe in the 'inevitability of beastliness' is to deny our humanity as well as our primate heritage—and, incidentally, does a grave injustice to the 'beasts'" (1972:70).

John Crook takes a similar position (1973). The ethnological literature, he argues, shows that aggression is not an innate drive demanding regular expression; it is, rather, a response to particular circumstances, and it ceases when those circumstances change (see Chap. 3). Crook attributes the widespread aggression in the world today to "features in the complex, overcrowded, overcompetitive, overstratified social world in which [people] live rather than to some unsatisfied vital urge. . . . The manifestation of aggression in human society is thus largely a cultural attribute" (1973:215). He and Pilbeam both emphasize that the nonhuman primates are singularly lacking in simple territorial behavior—or, for that matter, in many of the somewhat derogatory characteristics attributed to them by Ardrey and others. They contend that the primatological premises from which many writers argue are more often than not a distorted and outdated version of what is known about the social life of the primates.

Other writers reject both these viewpoints. They might be termed the *nurturalists,* and their case is most strongly argued by Ashley Montagu: "Whatever man is he learns to be" (1973:16). According to Montagu, "What we are unwilling to acknowledge as essentially of our own making, the consequence of our own disordering in the man-made environment, we saddle upon 'Nature', upon 'phylogenetically programmed' or 'innate' factors" (1973:16). In reality, Montagu believes, *Homo sapiens* are cultural beings products of their environment, of the attitudes to which they have been exposed. Montagu agrees with Pilbeam, Crook, and

Human warfare. Although some ethologists account for the presence of human aggression by pointing to the hypothetical presence of aggressive instincts, the author of this chapter rejects such reductionism and concludes that human social behavior is explicable as learned and adaptive to social and environmental contexts.

others that primates are not inherently violent, aggressive creatures, but unlike them, he is unwilling to admit that the nonhuman primates can tell us anything at all about ourselves.

Author's Conclusions

After this submersion in a sea of inferential arguments, I resurface torn between dismay, total exasperation, and vague thoughts of babies and bathwater. Let us begin with the dismay. Most of the popular attempts to interpret the behavior of *Homo sapiens* through (distorted) accounts of (frequently aberrant) behavior in (carefully selected) primates would be simply laughable were they not so superficially acceptable. I cannot help finding some comments faintly comical, such as Lorenz's "Peking Man, the Prometheus who learned to preserve fire, used it to roast his brothers" (1966:239)—with mustard or without, I wonder. However, beneath the surface of the flowing prose lies a potentially destructive phenomenon. For these writers are proclaiming a dangerous philosophy; they claim to demonstrate the inherent beastliness of our species, and in doing so, they implicitly deny our self-awareness, our evident control over many of our actions—in short, our humanity.

This attitude is not new. Thomas Hobbes, for one, was busy in the eighteenth century describing our ancestors' lives as "nasty, brutish, and short." What is new is that today these writers unleash their arguments on a huge and unsuspecting public with all the confidence and authority of bona fide scientists. They invoke the name of science as if it were a rubber stamp of truth, when in reality, the scientific facts in question are highly controversial, if not actually wrong. We live in uncertain and anxious times, and these writers pander to our fears, rationalizing them, justifying them, making our wildest nightmares seem like inevitabilities. I am appalled by the mass marketing of fatalistic pessimism dressed up in a pseudoscientific garb at a time when what is needed is careful, systematic research.

And so I turn to the nurturalists in search of support for my case, only to be exasperated. Their arguments seem to be little more powerful, although perhaps much less dangerous. For while I agree with their emphasis on the importance of learning for human beings, they in turn dismiss the idea of *Homo sapiens* as a biological species. One looks in vain through the writings of Ashley Montagu for a well-reasoned refutation of Ardrey's and Lorenz's views of human nature. He does not counter bad arguments with better ones, but simply discounts them as "myths" and "erroneous interpretations"—without ever stating *why*.

It seems to me that the only writers on the subject of primatology and human nature who manage to empty the bathtub and leave the baby alive and well—and fascinating—are those who restrict themselves to tentative suggestions based on the whole spectrum of primate adaptations. Crook and Pilbeam are examples, as is Reynolds, although to a lesser extent. I quarrel with the latter because he bases his picture of early human society on information that has since proved to be inaccurate in some instances and in others plain wrong. For example, we now know that chimpanzees are not nomadic in the true sense of the word, although they do roam through large areas (Suzuki 1969). Reynolds deserves credit for the caution with which he puts his case and for his willingness to base it on *all* the data available at that time. His mistake was perhaps to put too much faith in one or two fairly short studies of what is clearly an extremely complex animal who is by no means totally understood, and also to concentrate on one nonhuman primate species. Pilbeam and Crook's approach is interesting because it does not indulge in axioms and hypotheses stated as fact, but rather sees the nonhuman primates as a source of ideas about primate behavior in general—ideas that may be relevant to ourselves in particular. Theirs is the art of suggestion rather than prescription.

In conclusion, I believe that the careful study of our nonhuman primate relatives, whether they are chimpanzees or the smallest of all the primates, the mouse lemur, can give us insight into some of the many possible explanations for the ways in which we behave. It *cannot* tell us why we behave as we do, but it *can* indicate some possibilities, and from that point on, the study of human nature should concern itself with human beings and human beings only.

Summary

The development of the study of primates has been hindered by the assumption that information from captive animals can legitimately be extrapolated to all members of a species—and even to other primate species as well, including humans. Modern research, however, focuses on the behavior of animals under natural conditions. Primatologists study a wide range of primate species and an immense variety of specific primate behaviors.

Some writers, such as Konrad Lorenz and Robert Ardrey, have attempted to use evidence from studies of other primates (and even nonprimates) to draw conclusions about human nature. However, much of their information is inaccurate or is based on studies of primates in specific ecological conditions from which no valid general inferences can be drawn.

Environmental influences affect the composition of primate groups, the area of their home range, the degree to which their behavior is territorial, and the nature of the relationships within the group.

The degree of sexual dimorphism within a species appears to be correlated to its habitat; the most marked dimorphism occurs in ground-dwelling species or partially ground-dwelling species living in forest fringes or savannah.

The selective pressures of the savannah habitat provided a direction to hominid evolution: Males tended to act cooperatively, whereas females tended to stay at "home" and to engage in foraging activities more or less or their own. The environment favored the development of tools and weapons, with a concomitant increase in "intelligence" and the development of a network of social relationships. Two distinctive hominid characteristics thus emerged: a *sex-based division of labor* and the *basis of family and tribal systems*.

Considerable disagreement in the field of ethological studies arises between those who use evidence about other primates to draw strong and usually pessimistic conclusions about human nature and those who use these studies to draw cautious and generally more optimistic conclusions. The author considers that reckless assertions about human behavior on the basis of animal studies are not justified.

Annotated Bibliography

Crook, J. H. (1973) "The Nature and Function of Territorial Aggression." In *Man and Aggression,* ed. Ashley Montagu. London: Oxford Univ. Press. Crook first summarizes the views of Robert Ardrey and Konrad Lorenz on the inevitability of aggressive behavior in our species. He then uses examples from primate literature to demolish their case with his own carefully reasoned, well-substantiated arguments.

Morgan, Elaine (1972) *The Descent of Woman.* New York: Stein and Day. This book gives the student a feel for the style and attitudes adopted by popular writers on human evolution and human nature. Unlike the work of Lorenz and Ardrey, however, the author's emphasis is not on aggression but on the biological and cultural roles of men and women. The book should be read critically; although it is full of interesting ideas, their scientific validity is often questionable.

Van Lawick-Goodall, Jane (1971) *In the Shadow of Man.* Boston: Houghton Mifflin. Provides an interesting description of many aspects of the behavior and personalities of the chimpanzees studies; also gives a picture of the lifestyle—including the problems and highlights—of a field researcher. Although the book is no masterpiece of scientific endeavor—nor presumably was it intended as such—it is a fascinating and informative introduction to primate fieldwork.

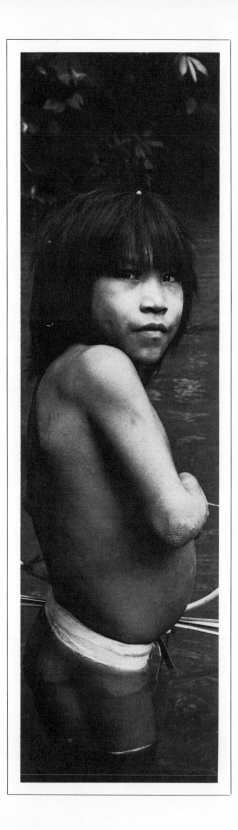

5
Human Adaptation:
Biological and Cultural

The World Context

Origins and Development through Time

It is an unfortunate fact that physical and cultural anthropology developed as two separate disciplines. Historically, physical anthropology, the biological study of our species through time and space, has its its roots in the sciences, particularly in zoology and medicine. Cultural anthropology, on the other hand, emerged from the humanities and social sciences. The two branches of anthropology have diverged to such an extent that "a specialist in one of these disciplines, in most cases, could not unfairly be described as one who agreed not to know what was going on in the other" (Montagu 1970:viii). Only over the past few years have scholars realized that the human species incorporates a biological and a cultural self and that the two are inextricably interwoven.

Early beliefs about the origins and nature of life were based on the notion of a ladder of existence, the *scala naturae*. People believed that all forms of life were ranked on this ladder in a rigid hierarchy. In Christian doctrine, the hierarchy was an expression of God's infinite abilities and of the eternal stability of the world He had created. The biologist Carolus

Linnaeus (1707-78) captured the essence of this view of the world in his famous aphorism: "Just so many species are to be reckoned as there were forms created at the beginning." In other words, there was no room for the evolution of new life forms. These beliefs held sway until the middle of the nineteenth century, when Darwinism caused profound changes in attitudes and methods of study.

Physical Anthropology   **Physical anthropology** is necessarily post-Darwinian, for it focuses on the evolution of the human species and on the biological variation found in that species today. Both these problems are closely tied to the process of natural selection. Through natural selection, we have evolved into the species that we are; and it is largely through natural selection that our species displays such a variety of complexions, hair types, body builds, and so forth.

However, the work of physical anthropologists at the turn of the century shows little evidence of Darwin's influence. The founding fathers of the discipline viewed human variation as a series of types and constructed sets of "racial" classifications that represent little more than those earlier historical conceptions of the ladder of existence, with its unchanging categories. A book entitled *Up from the Ape* is a classic example of the viewpoint of typological anthropologists on the subject of human variation. Published in 1931 and written by Earnest Albert Hooton, then professor of anthropology at Harvard University, this book argues that human variation has little to do with adaptation and natural selection. Hooton writes that

the inherited characters which we select as criteria of race are, for the most part, nonadaptive features of slight functional importance and of little selectional value. They are variations which, having once originated in one way or another, are likely to be perpetuated and exaggerated by the sheer inertia of heredity, since they are largely immaterial and indifferent. (1931:572)

Among the supposedly "immaterial and indifferent" variations that Hooton selected as criteria by which to divide up the human species into "races" were head form, face form, eyes, nose, ears, lips, hair, skin color, hair color, eye color, stature, weight, and body propor-

tions. These are all *phenotypic* characters—that is, they are characteristics of the individual's appearance. As such, they are products not only of the individual's genetic constitution, or *genotype*, but also of the environment with which he or she has interacted.

To the early physical anthropologist, armed only with a set of calipers and a penchant for measuring, these phenotypic characteristics were the easiest features of the human physique to assess and compare. Take the nose, for example. Using a nasal index computed from the ratio of nose breadth to nose height, Hooton and his colleagues divided up the human species by its noses: the leptorrhine, or narrow-nosed, with an index under 47; the mesorrhine, or intermediate-nosed, with an index between 47 and 51; and the platyrrhine, or broad-nosed, with an index over 51. Skin color was harder to categorize, but Hooton nonetheless differentiated between brunet white, swarthy white, pale white, white—ruddy, and white—freckled. You might try to decide in which category the people around you belong; the difficulty of so characterizing an entire "race" will soon become apparent!

Undaunted by such problems, Hooton went on to classify *Homo sapiens* into "four great groups": the Negroids, the Mongoloids, the Whites, and the Composites. These he subdivided into a number of "natural physical groups," or "races." The Negroids, for example, were made up of Negroes, Melanesians, and Negritoes, with the Nilotics and Tasmanians thrown in as "subraces." These divisions and subdivisions may seem fanciful and farfetched, but in comparison with some of the other attempts at a typological classification of people into "races," Hooton's range of categories was quite limited. Joseph B. Birdsell, in a discussion of supposed racial subdivisions, notes that "a final record was set by a man named Burk whose sole distinction is that he labeled 63 subraces" (1972:491).

One of the many shortcomings of these early typological classifications was that they said almost nothing about the frequencies, within the different groups, of the genes associated with physical characters. Since, as we have said, major physical characters result from an interaction between an individual's genes and the environment, observable physical characters (the phe-

Mosaic of the human species. What is the
meaning of physical variation?
(a) Republic of Niger
(b) Ivory Coast
(c) Mexico
(d) U.S.A.
(e) San Blas Indian of Panama
(f) Sioux girl, U.S.A.
(g) Japan

(a)

(b)

(c)

(d)

(e)

(f)

notype) cannot be used to make direct statements about the genetic makeup (the genotype) of the individual. Head form, for example, depends on the interactions of many genes with aspects of the physical environment, such as nutrition resources, and with aspects of the cultural environment, such as the custom of head flattening (Dunn 1970:94).

Such considerations have led to a shift of emphasis in investigations of human variability; general measurements of body form and so forth have gradually given way to records of characters that do reveal gene frequencies. An example of such a set of characters is the blood-group systems. Of the tens of thousands of genes in human chromosomes, those involving allelic differences (see chap. 2) in the hereditary characteristics of various blood components are the best known. The method of using blood-group gene frequencies to distinguish between different groups of peoples was first undertaken by the Hirzfelds, two Polish physicians. During the First World War, they noted that there were wide and consistent variations in the proportions of the ABO blood groups among different nationalities in the Allied Forces assembled near Salonika, Greece. Since then, more sensitive analytic techniques have been developed, and with their use further blood-group systems have been discovered. Other genes have also been identified, such as those for sickle cell anemia, thalassemia, taste blindness, and color blindness.

However, this slow change in physical anthropologists' approaches to human variability is but half the story. It went hand in hand with an equally gradual but radical change in the interpretation of this variability. One reason for the change was that the various classification systems devised by physical anthropologists differed so widely in the number of "races" they recognized. Also, there was minimal agreement on which people belonged to which "race." Something had to be wrong with the whole approach when disagreement was so unanimous! The real message of Darwinism finally began to restructure the anthropological perspective: Natural selection and the closely related notion of adaptation became genuinely incorporated into the anthropological paradigm at last. Thus, instead of looking at physical characters

(g)

in order to set up a typological system of "racial" classification, physical anthropologists turned to the study of the adaptive significance of those physical characters, and to variation in the frequencies of genes in different populations. In short, their interest turned from the fruitless classification of "races" to an attempt at understanding the variety of ways in which groups of our species are specially adapted, or fitted, to their surroundings.

Cultural Anthropology   Let us now look at the development of ideas concerning cultural adaptation. If we look back once more to the dawn of evolutionary theory a century ago, we find that the cultural anthropologists readily adopted the concept of evolution. But they were not influenced primarily by the ideas of Charles Darwin and Alfred Wallace; instead, they tended toward the attitudes of the third great evolutionist of the nineteenth century, Herbert Spencer (1820–1903). Darwin and Wallace saw evolution as the product of random variation in organisms, with natural selection operating on this variation through environmental factors. In contrast, Spencer saw evolution as an inevitable process, inherent in the very nature of things: "All matter shall proceed in time from the simple to the complex, from the unordered to the highly ordered" (Alland and McCay 1973:157). Such a conception of evolution dismissed environmental factors as unimportant or irrelevant and gave rise to an evolutionist school that adhered to Émile Durkheim's golden rule: Social facts can be derived only from social facts. In other words, culture can be explained only by culture. But as Alex Alland and B. McCay comment, "Such a view has until recently inhibited a true ecological approach to human behavior" (1973:158).

One of the first anthropologosts to seriously examine the relationship between environment and culture was Alfred Kroeber (1939). He envisioned the environment as a conservative force as far as culture is concerned. Certain aspects of culture must be adapted to the environment, and assuming that the environment remains stable, there will be little cultural variation. Kroeber also discussed the possible influence of specific environmental features on culture, but on the whole he viewed the environment as a limiting rather than a positive selectional force.

A truly ecological approach to the analysis of culture has only recently emerged, and it is based largely in the United States. Several anthropologists have related specific aspects of the environment to particular aspects of a population's behavior and culture. They try to show that certain social and cultural phenomena have evolved in response to selective pressures exerted by the environment and that the population has adapted to that environment (for example, Harris 1974).

Summary   Early physical anthropology was characterized by a typological approach. More recent studies, however, have concentrated on the adaptive significance of physical traits—that is, on the ways in which physical characteristics function to promote survival. Studies have also been aimed at estimating variation in the frequencies of genes among different populations and at investigating the meaning of this variation. Early cultural anthropology, on the other hand, quickly included evolutionary ideas into anthropological theory: The evolutionist school saw cultures as evolving, but doing so without reference to the environment. In the late 1930s, the idea that the environment might influence culture was seriously entertained for the first time, and a truly ecological approach to the analysis of culture has taken shape only in the last few years.

Contemporary Examples

All the primates show great biological and behavioral flexibility, but this flexibility is most developed in *Homo sapiens*. A number of our body characteristics increase our chances of surviving in a wide variety of environments. These characteristics include the regulation of body temperature, the capacity for prolonged physical labor, protection against ultraviolet radiation from the sun, immunological (defensive) responses to infectious disease, and nutritional and metabolic flexibility. (When food is digested, it is changed by a series of chemical processes—referred to collectively as *metabolism*—into simpler compounds. This process releases energy for many activities. A further metabolic process builds up these simple compounds into new, more complex substances that are used to maintain or develop the body's structure.)

Let us look more closely at some of these characteristics. We have the ability to maintain a constant body heat even when exposed to wide range of environmental temperatures. This capacity deserves closer scrutiny, for it may have played an important role in allowing early hominids to expand from the tropics into colder regions of the world. Our relative hairlessness, in which we differ strikingly from the great apes and monkeys, is one feature of our body that contributes to temperature regulation (Harrison et al. 1964:442). We have about 60 hairs per square centimeter, compared with the 1,000 or so on animals such as sheep (Weiner 1971:124). This relative hairlessness enables us to lose heat rapidly during, for example, strenuous and prolonged activity on hot days. On such occasions, the body temperature is reduced primarily through the sweat glands under the skin, which produce a secretion that uses up some of the body's heat as it evaporates. J. S. Weiner points out that "if this evaporative heat loss is to be maximally effective, it is of great advantage that hair should be absent or sparse. A hairy pelt with a layer of trapped still air will greatly reduce evaporation" (1971:124).

In fact, the human body is covered with almost 2 million special sweat glands that are far more efficient than the type of skin gland found in nearly all other mammals. In addition to providing the body with a year-round thermostat, our sweat glands can be "trained" to improve their output and the speed with which they respond to an increase in body temperature. This process, known as *acclimatization*, is experienced by anyone going to the tropics after a spell in a cooler climate. For the first few days one feels hot, tired, and thirsty, but within a week or so the body's sweat glands and associated mechanisms have adjusted to the new conditions, and the individual becomes as active as before (Harrison et al. 1964:446).

Turning to the other end of the thermometer, human tolerance to cold is based on body processes found in most mammals, but limited in ways characteristic of tropical animals (Weiner 1971:128). Exposure to cold leads to a constriction of those blood vessels that carry the blood close to the surface of the skin, reducing heat loss from the body. In humans—the "naked apes"—insulation cannot be increased by the

Cape Fuller Eskimos inside their snow dwelling (igloo). The Eskimos have adapted to their arctic habitat both physically and culturally. Their body shape is stocky with short limbs, a heat-preserving feature described by Bergmann's rule. However, they could not survive in this extreme environment without their elaborate cultural "toolkit" which includes not only the ingenious snow shelter, but their use of skins, their hunting and fishing technology, and even their patterns of gathering and dispersing according to the season.

erection of a wooly barrier of fur, a response found in many cold-climate creatures. All we can muster is the fairly futile gesture of coming out in goose flesh. Another common response to the cold is shivering, which increases body heat by speeding up the metabolic rate through the muscular effort involved in the very act of shivering (Buskirk and Bass 1960).

The Eskimos live farther north than any other group in the world, and they show some special physiological adaptations to the cold. For example, their hands seem to be toughened up by repeated, prolonged exposure to cold air and cold water. Compared with visitors to Arctic areas, their hands are warmer, the blood flow is greater, and their capacity for doing delicate tasks with their hands is superior (Hammel 1964; Hildes 1966). This difference is due not to a basic genetic pattern unique to the Eskimos but rather to the flexibility of our species as a whole: The same adaptation is also found in Newfoundland fishermen (Weiner 1971:129).

Three elements make up the color properties of the skin: the brown pigment melanin, the red pigment hemoglobin, and a yellowish pigment called carotene. Melanin pigmentation protects against the damaging effects of ultraviolet radiation, which burns the skin and can induce cancer (Blum 1961). People differ genetically in the amount of melanin their bodies produce, but all (except albinos) react similarly when exposed to sunshine (and hence solar radiation): their bodies increase the production of melanin. Sunbathing thus takes on a new perspective: A suntan is caused by an increase in melanization as the body improves its protection against the increased exposure to ultraviolet radiation. Geographical variations in skin color are probably related to varying intensities of ultraviolet radiation; the skin is darker or lighter, depending on the amount of melanin pigmentation necessary to protect it from the sun's rays.

Clearly good reasons exist for having a heavily pigmented skin in sunny areas. But is there any advantage in having a less pigmented skin in colder, cloudier regions? Nobody knows for sure. One advantage that has been suggested is that the loss of melanin pigment facilitates the production of vitamin D (Loomis 1967). Vitamin D is crucial for healthy bone development,

A !Kung San baby being carried by his older sister (see chapter 21). It is commonplace for Westerners to ask: "Why are other peoples so dark?" As we learn more about human evolution and the processes of adaptation, it becomes apparent that this is a very ethnocentric question. Since early hominids were probably darkskinned, the question might well be turned around: "Why are Europeans so light?" Actually, the best way to put the question is in the more general form: "What are the adaptive properties of skin color?" and "What relationships can we establish between populations' skin color and their natural and cultural environments?"

and ultraviolet light is necessary to the process of "manufacturing" it. If the amount of melanin in the skin is reduced, the amount of ultraviolet radiation that can pass into the skin is increased, and, presumably, the rate of vitamin D production goes up as a result. This might be crucial for the survival and growth of small children in areas where the dietary supply of vitamin D is low.

Body size and shape, or *physique*, varies considerably throughout the world. Probably this variation originally represented a series of local adaptations by different groups to local climates and food supplies. Even today, a reasonably close association exists between the physique of a people and the climate they live in. C. Bergmann (1847) and J. A. Allen (1877) formulated this relationship into two ecological rules: (1) Within a warm-blooded species, the body size of any subspecies usually increases with decreasing temperature of its habitat; (2) in warm-blooded species, the relative size of protruding organs, such as the ears and tail, tends to increase with the temperature of the habitat. Statistical comparisons of the weights, heights, and limb and trunk proportions of living populations tend to confirm these rules (Newman and Munro 1955; Roberts 1953). What is the adaptive significance of this variation? Weiner advances this argument for being small in a hot country:

> Where heat is gained from the environment, this gain per unit area of skin is at the same rate for individuals of different physique. The heat produced by metabolism is the same per kg. body weight, but the smaller individual has a greater surface area per kg. body weight available for heat dissipation. The smaller man thus loses heat by sweating more efficiently. (1971:134)

Let us turn from the biological sphere and look briefly at some of the research in progress on the adaptive importance of culture. A theory that has strongly influenced current ideas about the relationship between culture and the environment was proposed by Fredrik Barth (1956). He borrows from animal ecology the concept of the *ecological niche*. This term encompasses all the environmental factors affecting any given organism and the way in which an organism uses this environment (Boughey 1971:150). Barth

then examines the ways in which three different ethnic groups in Pakistan divide a single geographical area among them, each group occupying segments, or niches, of the environment. Barth's most significant claim is that the culture of each of these groups is specially adapted to its particular niche; he sees the environment as a controlling, rather than limiting, factor in change. Adaptation, for Barth, is the result of a continual interaction between culture, which produces variation, and the pressures of the environment, which select from this variation.

Michael Coe and Kent Flannery, two New World archaeologists, have also used an ecological approach and the concept of the niche to gain insight into the development of settled village life in the past. In a paper focusing on the way of life of early Mesoamericans (those aboriginal peoples living in southern Mexico, Guatemala, and the isthmus connecting North and South America), they ask three questions: (1) What factors favored the early development of food production in Mesoamerica as compared with other regions of the hemisphere? (2) What was the mode of life of the earlier hunting and collecting peoples in Mesoamerica, and in exactly what ways was it changed by the addition of cultivated food plants? (3) When, where, and how did food production make it possible for the first truly sedentary villages to be established in Mesoamerica (1966:348)? However, while Barth concentrated on three niches, each used by a different group, Coe and Flannery concern themselves with the multiple use of a range of niches, or *multiniches*, occupied by two closely related groups living in two very different areas, one in Mexico and the other in Guatemala.

A number of cultural anthropologists emphasize *population pressure* as a critical factor in the adaptive process. Instead of looking to external factors such as the distribution and availability of potential food resources as molders of culture, they pinpoint increasing population density as the mechanism that causes the cultural changes necessary for continued survival. Robert Carneiro, for example, states: "The thesis advanced here is not that societies become more complex only by growing larger, or that as they grow larger they invariably become more complex. Rather the contention is that if a society does increase significantly in size, and if at the same time it remains unified and integrated, it must elaborate its organization" (1967:239).

Ester Boserup is also concerned with population pressure as a dynamic force. She argues that agricultural techniques develop and become more productive in response to increases in the size of the population that has to be fed (1965). In other words, she does not believe that the environment sets a limit on the possible number of people who can be supported in a given area, but rather that population size is self-limited by the existing techniques of food production. We are limited only insofar as we limit ourselves, she insists, and increases in population almost automatically improve subsistence techniques and increase productivity.

Discussions of the effects of increasing population density are mainly concerned with the forces underlying cultural change, or evolution. Another group of anthropologists is more interested in the study of stable ecological systems—systems in which the population is neither increasing nor decreasing in size. The work of Roy Rappaport in New Guinea is a good illustration of this approach. In *Pigs for the Ancestors* (1968), he argues that the ritual cycle of pig slaughter by New Guinea tribes can be related to changes in the size of both the pig and the human populations. Rappaport suggests that these ritual slaughters are far from being the exclusively "cultural" affairs they are generally supposed to be. Rather, they are of central importance in the process of ecological adjustment between the population and its resources. In other words, ritual practices are used to regulate both the nature of the diet of these people and the size of their herds.

Marvin Harris is one of the firmest believers in the ultimately ecological and adaptive significance of cultural practices. He sees the wide, complex range of habitats occupied by the human species as one of the most important causes of the great variety of cultures we find in the world: "any item of technology must interact with a specific natural environment. Hence, similar kinds of technologies in different environments may entail very different levels of output and amount

and quality of labor, which may in turn affect the social structure and system of economic management" (1971:200).

He illustrates this argument by referring to a number of technologically simple but diverse societies. In the tropics, where vast areas of forest can be cut down and the cleared land planted with crops until the soil becomes impoverished a few years later, small, temporary villages of closely related kinspeople tend to be the rule. When the technology of farmers includes irrigation, larger and more permanent settlements will probably be formed, although the precise nature of these settlements is affected by the "form of irrigation, which in turn varies according to the size and dependability of the water supply, the availability of flat terrain, the amount of minerals in the water (1971:201).

Similarly, Harris attributes the small size of the !Kung San (Bushman) band (see chap. 21) to the amount of water in the permanent water holes available to these people: "although in average years there is probably sufficient water for more that 30 people, the decisive barriers to greater nucleation are the years of maximal drought" (1971:208). Contrary to common belief, even the technologically more complex industrial societies are far from liberated from the influence of the environment, according to Harris. The natural resources vital for any kind of industrial production are limited, which imposes restraints on production and hence on many aspects of the social structure.

Theory

Systems

Up to this point, the term *adaptation* has been used in a general sense and in several different contexts to describe the ways in which people are fitted—physically or culturally—to particular environments. We now need to more carefully define what we mean by adaptation. In addition, the concept has been criticized as being *tautological*—that is, circular in its reasoning—and we should examine that accusation. It is also well to remember that although we are primarily concerned with adaptations made by the human species to a variety of habitats, adaptation is actually a two-way process: People make changes in their physiological and social mechanisms to cope successfully with the environment, but these mechanisms in turn affect the environment. (The term *environment* here includes every aspect of the surroundings in which an individual or group finds itself, from the geology, topography, and climate of the area to its vegetational cover and insect, bird, and animal life.)

Let us first consider an example of the circularity of which the concept of adaptation has been accused: "organisms are surviving because they are adapted, and they are adapted because they are surviving" (Burnett and Eisner 1964, quoted in Alland and McCay 1973:145). All too often, the assumption has been made that if a structure or behavior exists, then it must be adaptive; no further proof is considered necessary. However, Alland and McCay point out that circularity *can* be avoided and that more recent considerations of the concept do indeed avoid it: "If . . . a distinction is maintained between an operational definition of adaptation, such as population survival, and the theoretical meaning of the concept, then no such tautology exists" (1973:145).

Pig slaughter festival in Meganum, New Guinea.

The problem thus becomes the operational one of translating the original Darwinian idea of adaptation as a "good fit" into some more measurable phenomenon. This search for a precise measure has led anthropologists to emphasize reproductive success as an index of adaptation. In 1942 Theodosius Dobzhansky wrote that organisms are adapted to their environments when they are constructed and act in such a way that they not only survive as individuals but they also produce offspring. Through the study of population genetics, which has emerged as a field during the last thirty years or so, scholars have now determined that *differential reproductive success* is the actual process of adaptation. Differential reproduction leads to "a change, within a population, of the proportions of individuals exhibiting some advantageous trait under a given environment" (Wallace and Srb 1964). Under this operational definition, adaptation can be seen as "heritable variation in different directions . . . followed by differential survival and multiplication of the variants" (Muller 1949).

Having thus pinned down the concept of adaptation as a measurable phenomenon, it remains to be said that, at least in the biological world, the concept is also used in a much narrower sense. Alland and McCay (1973), for example, distinguish between (a) the process of adaptation that occurs continuously in the individual throughout his or her life, and (b) the process of adaptation that takes place in a group of individuals throughout that group's history. The time span in the latter will probably be more than one lifetime and may be hundreds, thousands, or even millions of years.

Adaptations by individuals are generally *physiological* in nature—they relate to the functioning of the body. These adaptations are also generally homeostatic responses to short-term variations in the environment, such as changes in temperature or cloud cover. *Homeostasis* is the process by which the body buffers the effects of the environment. For example, on a 100-degree day our body temperature remains at or close to normal—98.6 degrees Fahrenheit—because the body can make a homeostatic, self-regulating response (in this case sweating) to the environmental variation.

But such adaptive capacities also evolve through successive generations. Natural selection will favor individuals who respond more rapidly or efficiently to changes in the environment. In this way whole populations will become adapted to local conditions in the course of time. For example, populations living in very dry or cold environments tend to have narrow noses so that the air is moistened and warmed in the narrow nasal passage before it enters the lungs. Thus the short-term adaptability of the individual becomes, in the long term, an adaptation characteristic of a whole population or species. The two phenomena are distinct but inseparable.

To sum up, early assumptions that if a behavior exists, it is by definition adaptive have been replaced by a more quantitative approach. Differential reproductive success is now generally accepted as the process by which populations adapt to their environment, and the adaptation of a population is measured by its reproductive success. Anthropologists distinguish between the phenotypic, usually physiological, adaptations made by individuals during their lives, and the genotypic adaptation of a whole population that occurs over a number of generations. The two phenomena are nevertheless closely linked: Natural selection favors the phenotype best suited to the environment. Through differential reproductive success, the genotype underlying this phenotype is selected for, and thus gene frequencies in the population will change through time.

Processes

Like most other species, *Homo sapiens* is not randomly scattered over the surface of the earth, but rather is grouped into clusters or *populations*. Usually populations are structured—that is, they have an internal social organization—and are defined in spatial—or geographical—terms. It should be reemphasized that this approach differs radically from the typological approach: A population is a collection of individuals who have features in common, whereas the typological approach delineates a "type" that all members of the group supposedly resemble.

The nature of the population units that are studied varies according to the problem the anthropologist is investigating. In fact, on some occasions populations

Figure 5-1
Biological and Cultural Adaptation
This model is intended to illustrate how forms of technology act as an adaptive buffer between human groups and their natural environment—but with both biological and cultural consequences. Changes in any of the elements can affect the other elements either directly or indirectly.

Read any capitalized label; then follow an arrow leaving that label and read the text along the arrow; finally, read the capitalized label to which that arrow leads. Each time you do this you will find a sentence that expresses one of the relationships or processes operating in the interactions between human groups and their environment.

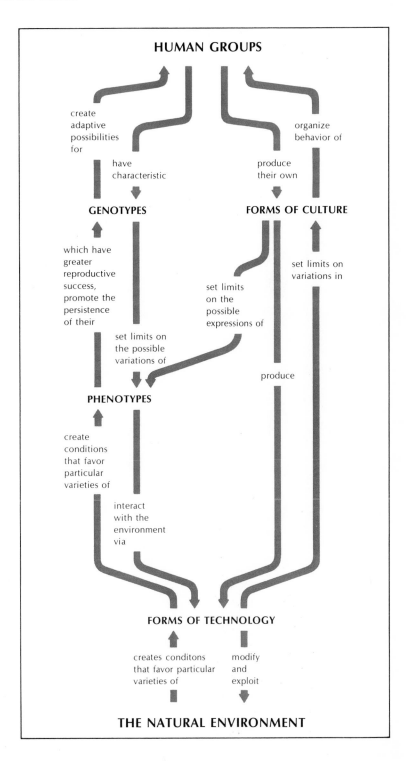

are defined without reference to geography. For example, individuals sharing common religious beliefs belong, in that sense, to a single population no matter where they live. The concept of a population may also involve a hierarchical classification; the world population of *Homo sapiens* comprises the populations of continents, nations, states, districts, cities, towns, villages, and so forth.

The term *population* can thus refer to many different units of varying size and structure within the species. For practical purposes, populations are recognized by the component that is under study. Contemporary students of human biological and cultural adaptation focus on populations defined by four major areas of interest: demography, genetics, society or social structure, and ecology.

Demographic Studies   Studies of demographic data—that is, the statistics of human populations—are primarily concerned with analyses of fertility, mortality, and migration. Such analyses provide estimates of

Hassidim, a very traditionally oriented, conservative group of Jews. Even those who live in America (pictured here in New York) resist speaking any languages other than Hebrew and Yiddish. Such strong cultural boundary marking (also exhibited in their clothing and hair style) leads to breeding population boundaries as well, since marriage is strictly confined within the group.

the reproductive success of a demographic population, and thus they contribute directly to the study of adaptation. The definition of a demographic population for these purposes can be entirely arbitrary: "It need be no more than a group of individuals in which a demographer is interested, and whilst such a group often corresponds more or less to a genetic, social or ecological population, it may have no real structural coherence" (Harrison and Boyce 1972:3).

Genetic Studies   Genetic populations, on the other hand, consist of individuals who share a common gene pool—that is, groups of more or less biologically related individuals. The smallest such group is the family, and the largest is the whole species. (A species, by definition, potentially if not actually shares a common gene pool. In contrast, different species can never share a common gene pool because they are reproductively isolated from each other.) Between the family and the species are many intermediate population categories of persons who are biologically related in different degrees. Knowledge of the genetic structures and relationships of all these categories in the population hierarchy is vital if the nature of human variability is to be understood.

Social Studies   In some respects, the population unit studied by the social anthropologist depends simply on his or her interests and the problem that he or she is addressing. However, G. A. Harrison and A. J. Boyce point out: "there is certainly a social parallel to the genetic concept of population with people sharing to varying degrees common cultural heritages" (1972:4). The social population is based on degrees of social affiliation, such as the band, clan, tribe, occupation, or caste, rather than on degrees of biological relationship. Sometimes these social populations correspond to genetic populations.

Ecological Studies   From an ecological perspective, populations can be defined by the extent to which people share and exploit a common set of environmental resources. The individuals in the population interact among themselves, generally in some cooperative manner, by virtue of this sharing. Like the other populations, an ecological population is difficult to define. Habitats blend into one another, and there are varying degrees of interaction between "populations" living in different habitats. Thus the choice of the population to be studied in this case is also somewhat arbitrary.

Summary   The study of human biological and cultural adaptations, then, is accompanied by the inherent problem of how to define populations. A definition can be based on demographic, genetic, social, or ecological criteria. In some cases a single population may fit all four criteria, but this need not be so. Each definition is necessarily somewhat imprecise and arbitrary; the researcher simply defines the population in the way that will provide the most appropriate answers to the questions being asked.

Analysis

The Folk Perspective

The Hanunóo occupy part of the island of Mindoro, the seventh largest island in the Philippines. Between 1952 and 1954 Harold Conklin lived on this island and studied the relationship between this people's culture and their natural environment. In this section we shall consider the attitudes and techniques—that is, the folk perspective—of the Hanunóo with regard to farming as related by Conklin (1957). In the next section we shall look briefly at the analysis that Conklin makes.

The Hanunóo grow their food by a system of shifting cultivation, or swidden farming—"the impermanent agricultural use of plots produced by the cutting back and burning off of vegetative cover" (Conklin 1969:222). The people have no general term for this production system. Instead, they have a series of terms, each of which describes a different phase in the development of a piece of land from the time clearing begins, through the period when the land is actually used, until the time when it is at least temporarily abandoned.

Rather than basing the timing of agricultural activities on an absolute calendar system, people estimate the best time for planting, harvesting, and performing the other activities in the agricultural schedule by taking cues from the environment. The Hanunóo have extremely detailed knowledge of the growth stages of

The Amahuaca, a Panoan people of Peru and Brazil, also practice slash and burn agriculture. Each Amahuaca male clears 5–10 acres of jungle each year. Only one major crop is harvested before the jungle reclaims the cleared land.

wild and domesticated plants, of seasonal changes in the weather, and of the positions of the stars. They recognize four nonbiological components of the environment: *daga?*, "ground, soil, earth"; *batu*, "rock, stone"; *danum*, "water, liquid"; and *lānit*, "sky." The constituents of the last category are factors we generally think of as relating to the weather: sun, moon, constellations, stars, and winds, which are considered to be causally related to clouds, rain, and thunderstorms. The Hanunóo believe that the winds start at the six cardinal points and in fact name the winds after these points; at the same time, however, they thoroughly understand the relationship between these six winds and seasonal changes in weather: "Winds bring such agricultural needs as rain, and such destructive forces as typhoons. Hence, wind direction and duration like phases of the moon, tides, . . . and especially various stages of plant growth, . . . are 'calendric' signs and weather signals known to all Hanunóo (Conklin 1957:35).

The most important factor to the Hanunóo in their farming is the plant life of their environment. They have an extremely complex system of classifying the plant species around them. Most of the plant types they recognize are placed in three general categories related to different types of stem growth: "ligeneous vs. herbaceous vs. vineline" (Conklin 1957:44). At the most detailed level, however, the Hanunóo distinguish over 1,600 plant species, each one named differently. And even this level is subdivided: Plants are further classified according to "leaf shape, color, habitat, size, sex habit, host, length of growing period, taste and smell" (Conklin 1957:44). Nearly all of these plant types have well-defined uses as foods or in medicines, rituals, and other aspects of life.

The Analytical Perspective

Anthropologists have tended to think of swidden agriculture as "primitive, wasteful, . . . with little or no regard for such pertinent local variables as population density, available land area, climate, or native agricultural knowledge" (Conklin 1969:221). However, Conklin's study shows that swidden farmers some-

times know much more about the relationship of local cultural practices to natural phenomena than they have been credited with. The farmers' terminology differs from that of Western ecologists, of course, but their understanding of on-the-ground methods of cultivation is often just as complete.

For example, a study of the Hanunóo system of soil classification revealed a close correlation to the results of a chemical analysis of soil samples. Their ideas of which crops are suited to which soils are also soundly based when analyzed from a Western point of view: "While the farmer may not know of the minute degree of lime disintegration and low pH value of *nāpunāpu?* (a light colored sandy clay), . . . he does know that certain beans and sugar cane (considered "high lime" crops, technically) will not thrive in such soil as they will in *barag?an* (which has a higher lime content and pH value)" (Conklin 1969:229). Similarly, the effects on different soil types of erosion, exposure, and overuse are well understood, and preventive measures are often taken.

As we noted previously, the Hanunóo farmers' greatest concern is with the living world. They recognize some 1,600 plant species (including 92 different strains of one species of rice and the properties of each), and they can identify 450 types of animals. They have consciously domesticated and selectively bred some 430 "useful" plant types. Conklin suggests that, partly as a result of their detailed knowledge of tiny differences in plant structures, "Hanunóo plant categories outnumber, by more than 400 types, the taxonomic species into which the same local flora is grouped by systematic botanists" (1969:230).

In more general terms, Conklin argues that many early assessments of swidden agriculture are inaccurate and often simply false:

1. Far from being a random, haphazard affair, swidden farming follows a systematic pattern and requires constant attention and effort most of the year.

2. Swidden farmers do not cause the destruction of large areas of virgin forest; they tend to select areas of secondary forest for clearing.

3. Forests are more often destroyed by burning when fire is used in hunting than when it is used to

clear a field; in clearing, the firebreak is usually an effective barrier.

4. Swidden farming techniques—though perhaps simple—are not uniform; they are finely adjusted to local environmental conditions.

5. Swiddens are planted with several crops, so estimates of productivity based only on the main crop yield do not accurately portray the efficiency of the system.

6. Swiddens are *not* abandoned once the main crop is harvested; plantings and harvest may overlap and continue for a number of years.

7. Contrary to common belief, these swidden farmers practice a type of crop rotation in addition to the cyclical period during which the whole plot is allowed to lie fallow, or unused.

8. Anthropologists have tried to establish a universally applicable minimum fallow period between plantings that must be observed so the soil does not become impoverished. In fact, the optimal duration of this period is determined by ecological factors and may vary from eight to fifteen years. Swidden farmers usually know how long the fallow period should be.

Conclusions

Schools of Thought

This chapter has presented primarily the ideas of physical and cultural anthropologists who believe that evolutionary change results in a higher degree of adaptation. Only two exceptions have been discussed. In the field of physical anthropology, Earnest Hooton believed that much of the biological variation in our species was nonadaptive, fundamentally random in origin, and "exaggerated by the sheer inertia of heredity." Today, however, this viewpoint has been abandoned in favor of the more functional approach of such people as Harrison and Weiner. In the field of social anthropology, we looked briefly at the theories of the evolutionist school, which held that culture constantly evolves toward higher levels of complexity without any immediate or necessary relationship to the physical world. In contrast, modern theorists generally accept the concept that culture evolves through an adaptive interaction with the environment.

A balanced overview of human adaptation would not be complete without reference to a new school of geneticists, the neoclassicists. Their ideas have so far been applied only to problems in genetics, but their influence will probably pervade studies of the human species at all levels. For many years anthropologists have argued that natural selection operates in two ways: it reduces the variation that occurs naturally, and it gives shape and meaning to that variation through directional selection. At the same time, natural selection can, via other mechanisms, preserve and even increase heritable variation. Both phenomena, the maintenance of variation and the reduction of variation, have been seen as results of the same selective forces: "Because the alleles that are segregating in a population are maintained in equilibrium by natural selection, they are the very alleles that will form the basis of adaptive phyletic change or speciation" (Lewontin 1974:196).

In contrast, Richard Lewontin and his colleagues propose that "most, if not all, of the molecular variation in natural populations is selectively neutral" (Lewontin 1974:197). In other words, they claim that while the variation may be detectable by the researcher in the laboratory, it usually makes no difference to the organism whether it has one molecule or the other. Such variations are "genetic junk," revealed by the superior technology of the laboratory but insignificant physiologically. From the standpoint of natural selection they are neutral mutations" (Lewontin 1974:197).

However, Lewontin refutes the label "neutralists," saying they do not claim either that most mutations are neutral or that evolution is a process in which haphazard mutations spread randomly through populations for no apparent reason. Rather, they argue that selection does operate on most mutations, but against rather than for them. In other words, many mutations are harmful and are removed from the population by natural selection. Also, there is another commonly occurring category of mutations that has no effect on the physiology of the organism; these mutations are selectively neutral. Finally, in addition to the harmful and the neutral mutations, occasional advantageous mutations occur, and their frequency will increase as a result of natural selection "since after all adaptive evolution does occur" (Lewontin 1974:198).

Author's Conclusions

Two fundamental conclusions should be drawn from this necessarily brief survey of an enormously broad field of research. First, while past and present research generally concentrates on either biological adaptation or cultural adaptation, people function as integrated wholes. Thus in the future we should concentrate on developing an integrated view of our species. We can understand our adaptations—and the reasons for our success in a wide variety of environments—only through an interdisciplinary approach. To give but one example, it is certainly of some interest that, as we noted earlier, Eskimos' hands seem to be toughened up so that they tolerate exposure to the cold better than visitors to the Arctic. But the answer to the significant question, How do Eskimos survive and flourish in the subzero temperatures of the Polar Circle? requires a study of the history of the group as well as the contributions made by their physiological and cultural adaptations. The fur clothing of the Eskimos is an extremely efficient adaptation to the cold. It provides insulation equivalent to that of eight to ten light suits, and in addition to its thermal properties, it is waterproof and difficult to crush (Weiner 1971:129). Thus consideration of the biological without reference to the cultural, or vice versa, gives us only half the picture and will never provide us with much insight into the reasons for *Homo sapiens* being the widely spread, highly successful species that it is.

Second, I would like to introduce a cautionary note on the whole subject of adaptation. The findings of Lewontin and his colleagues have led them to question the fundamental assumption that all observable instances of variation have some adaptive meaning. Similarly, it sometimes seems to me more realistic to abandon the search for the adaptive significance of certain cultural and biological features than to offer

The human mosaic becomes meaningful only when seen in its natural and cultural environmental context.
(a) Nigeria
(b) Mexico
(c) Peru
(d) Tanzenia
(e) India
(f) Argentina

(a)

(b)

(c)

(d)

(e)

(f)

(g)

(h)

(i)

(j)

(k)

(g) Sudan
(h) Japan
(i) Sweden
(j) Navajo family, U.S.A.
(k) Mexico

weak, unsubstantiated arguments. The belief that every facet of culture can ultimately be related to the environment has led to a number of misguided interpretations. The study of human adaptations is worthwhile and meaningful as long as it increases our understanding of the ways in which we function; when the search for adaptations becomes so overriding that it distorts our vision and blinds us to other possibilities, it is time to draw back and think again.

and their method of subsistence is not nearly as wasteful of energy and land as anthropologists tended to assume in the past.

An important area of controversy in physical anthropology derives from the view of the "neoclassicists" that most of the natural genetic variations in populations are selectively neutral rather than either positive or negative. Not every observable instance of variation, they argue, has adaptive significance.

Summary

Physical anthropology focuses on the evolution of the human species and the biological variations found in that species today. Physical anthropology is thus a post-Darwinian discipline, although it was some time before the lessons of natural selection were fully incorporated into the study.

In particular, anthropologists for a long time fruitlessly attempted to divide the human species into "races"—a concept that is not recognized as scientifically useful by many modern anthropologists—and frequently confused genotypic and phenotypic characteristics. Early physical anthropology concentrated on seeking human "types," but modern anthropologists are more concerned with discovering the adaptive significance of different physical traits.

Contemporary anthropologists often take an ecological approach to human cultural variability. Each culture exists in an ecological niche, which consists of all the environmental factors surrounding the group and the ways in which the group exploits this environment. The necessity of adapting to some ecological niche provides direction to both physical and cultural evolution.

The Hanunóo, a people living in the Philippines, are an example of the relationship between culture and environment. Their subsistence technology is one of slash-and-burn (swidden) horticulture, and they have complex beliefs about their material environment that—though they are different from those of Western scientists—are highly adaptive. These beliefs enable them to make maximum use of their environment,

Annotated Bibliography

Alland, Alexander, Jr., and McCay, B. (1973) "The Concept of Adaptation in Biological and Cultural Evolution." In *Handbook of Social and Cultural Anthropology,* ed. J. J. Honigmann. Chicago: Rand McNally. A comprehensive, up-to-date review of the concept of adaptation. Includes both a history of the ways in which the term has been used in the past and illustrations of the senses in which it is used in biological and cultural research today.

Montagu, Ashley, ed. (1970) *Culture and the Evolution of Man.* New York: Oxford Univ. Press. A useful compendium of papers about various aspects of both cultural *and* biological evolution—the title notwithstanding; an interesting and representative cross section of current issues. All the authors are prominent thinkers in the field.

Weiner, J. S. (1971) *The Natural History of Man.* New York: Universe. A clearly written introductory text on human evolution and biological adaptations, simple to understand but not simplistic. It should certainly be read by students with minimal training in biology before they begin studying more advanced texts.

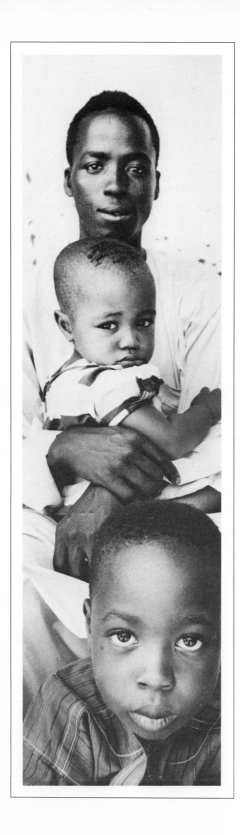

6
Human Sexes:
Biological Bases and Cultural Frameworks

The World Context

Origins and Development through Time

The study of human sexes is a vast, complex topic that extends far beyond the reproductive roles of males and females into almost every aspect of human life. The reason, as Margaret Mead has emphasized, is that societies always infuse anatomical sex with profound social meaning:

All known human societies recognize the anatomic and functional differences between males and females in intricate and complex ways; through insistence on small nuances of behavior in posture, stance, gait, through language, ornamentation and dress, division of labor, legal social status, religious role, etc. In all known societies sexual dimorphism is treated as a major differentiating factor of any human being, of the same order as difference in age, the other universal of the same kind (1961:1451).

Sex pervades human social life. Every society has a system for the communication of sex identity that usually includes nonverbal as well as verbal signals. In contemporary America, for example, sex differences are expressed through dress, hair styles, earning power, body carriage, the manner in which people greet each other, the way they laugh, the way they walk, their relative positions when entering doorways or walking along sidewalks, and many other traits. Sex identity is fundamental to the daily behavior of the average American even though sexual activity may take up only a small portion of a person's time.

Behaviors that are typically manifested by persons of one sex and rarely by persons of the opposite sex are called *gender roles.* These gender roles are the social expression of a person's sex identity. They are universal in that they occur in every society, but their specific content is unique to each society. (Much the same is true of language: All human societies have a system of verbal communication, but each society has a unique language.)

Sex identity is important in human social life because each of the sexes performs distinct economic

U.S.A. males and females. What are the signs of gender identity that they display?

functions (see chap. 3). It is not difficult to understand why a sex-based division of labor is universal in human societies. Males and females have some biological characteristics that make them suited for different roles. Moreover, it is often socially and economically useful for people to specialize in particular activities, and specialization by sex is a simple, workable way to accomplish this result. Because a person's sex is recognizable at birth and does not change thereafter, the individual can begin at infancy to acquire the vast number of qualities and skills that will be useful in adult life. Although a sex-based division of labor is not restricted to humans, because of our highly elaborated dependence on culture for our behavioral repertoire, we have elaborated the sex-based division of labor far more than have other animals.

Sexual Dimorphism In nonhuman animals, social and anatomical dimorphism takes a wide variety of forms. For our purposes, the most illuminating examples are those of our primate relatives.

In the primates, we find close relationships between the environment of populations and the amount of sexual dimorphism they exhibit. Arboreal (tree-dwelling) primates generally show the least difference between the sexes in both physical appearance and social behavior. Males and females look much alike and live independent but similar lives. Cooperative activities between male and female adults are conducted on the basis of relative equality.

In contrast, primates that live mainly on the ground show differences in appearance and behavior according to sex. In some species, the males are almost twice the size of the females, and they may have other visible distinguishing characteristics as well. In behavior, females usually assume a disproportionate share of parental responsibility compared with males, and males often assume a larger share of responsibility for defense than females. (These behavior differences do not extend to economic divisions of labor, because nonhuman primates do not share food as humans do.) The development of different but complementary behaviors for males and females thus serves important survival functions. These tendencies among nonhuman primates are accentuated in populations that live in unsafe savannah habitats, as compared to populations of the same species that live in relatively safe forest environments. Sexual dimorphism and behavior differences thus appear to be adaptive.

There is also evidence that sexual differences in human social behavior are related to economic adaptations (Martin and Voorhies 1975). Hunting and gathering societies, in which women usually perform an important economic function, display relatively little gender distinction. Rather more distinction between the sex roles is typically exhibited in horticultural societies, while agricultural and pastoral societies show a high degree of gender dimorphism (see chap. 3). In modern urban industrial societies, in which women play an increasingly important economic role outside the home and in which the daily economic activities of the sexes bear little relationship to the physical differences between them, gender role distinctions appear to be diminishing.

Contemporary Examples

Let us first compare some aspects of American and Tchambuli society to see cross-cultural variations in the content of gender roles.

The Tchambuli The Tchambuli of New Guinea were studied by Margaret Mead (1963), who found that their beliefs about the ideal personalities of the sexes are almost the opposite of American ideals. According to Mead, Tchambuli women are characterized by independence, industriousness, and high energy levels, while Tchambuli men are emotional and passive.

The differences between American and Tchambuli gender roles are not restricted to personality traits. Among the Tchambuli, the women are the major economic providers—they do most of the fishing, farming, and trade item manufacturing, and they also have the dominant parental role and exclusive responsibility for the maintenance of the residences in which they live with their children. In short, the women appear to bear most of the formal responsibility for running Tchambuli society.

Tchambuli men are in many ways socially disenfranchised. They make relatively minor contributions to the economic well-being of the society, and concentrate instead on the creation of the society's art. They

Villagers of the Brahman caste in a North Indian village. Mothers often "beautify" their daughters, who thus learn how to make themselves beautiful. Later, when they are adults, it will seem perfectly "natural" for them to line their eyes, wear *saris,* and in general behave the way a woman "should." (Black design on the child's forehead is to avert the "evil eye.")

live together, apart from the women and children, in ceremonial clan houses. Mead describes the men as mutually suspicious, competitive, and susceptible to sudden eruptions of petty jealousies. Interpersonal alliances and friendships between them tend to be intense but brief. Tchambuli men depend on their female kin "for support, for food, [and] for affection" (Mead 1963:251). In contrast, the women treat the men "with kindly tolerance and appreciation" (Mead 1963:255).

Significantly, in both American and Tchambuli societies, the sex that bears the primary economic re-

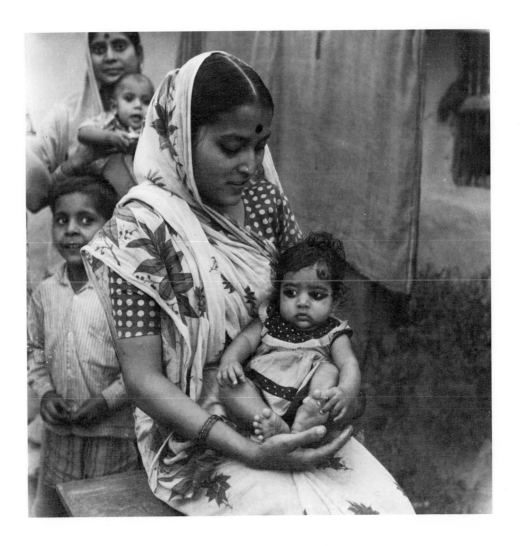

sponsibility also tends to be energetic, independent, and emotionally stable. The opposite sex (American women and Tchambuli men) tends to exhibit opposite qualities.

Carol Tavris asked a sample of Americans whether particular personality traits were characteristic of men, women, or neither sex (1972). Eighty percent of the respondents said that aggressiveness, independence, objectivity, and mathematical reasoning were typically male; nurturance, empathy, monogamy, and emotionality were said to be typically female.

These two societies indicate the possible range in the content of gender roles. However, the gender roles of all known societies exhibit some central tendencies. Nurturance is usually a characteristic of the feminine gender role, and aggressiveness is a typically masculine characteristic. Women consistently have greater child-rearing responsibilities, and men, greater defensive

responsibilities (see chap. 3). For example, George Murdock (1937) found in a comparative study that weapon making was almost always the exclusive activity of men.

Not only does the content of gender roles vary across cultures, but the degree to which gender roles are polarized varies as well. We can illustrate this by examining three societies that show relatively slight distinctions in gender roles compared with the Tchambuli and ourselves. Two of these, the Mountain Arapesh and the Mundugumor, are situated in the same general region of New Guinea as the Tchambuli. Like the Tchambuli, both of these peoples are horticulturalists, using simple, hand-held tools. Mead (1963) examined the most prevalent personality types of men and women in these two societies and found that in both cases only slight polarization existed between the typical personalities of the sexes.

Laboriously constructed hairdos worn by males of Kenya. To preserve their intricate designs, men often sleep with their heads raised off the ground on neckrests. "Primping," like all behaviors we associate with gender, is learned as we become enculturated.

The Mountain Arapesh   **Arapesh men and women both tend to be cooperative, unaggressive, responsible, and responsive to the needs of others. They perceive the major human task to be the promotion of growth in living things, especially yams, pigs, and children. These people exhibit some differences in their total gender roles, but by American standards, both sexes manifest personalities that are more typical of women than men. "We found the Arapesh—both men and women—displaying a personality that, out of our historical preoccupations, we would call maternal in its parental aspects, and feminine in its sexual aspects" (Mead 1963:279).**

The Mundugumor   **Mead found the Mundugumor to be strikingly different from the gentle Arapesh. Rugged individualism, self-assertion, passionate sexuality, and physical aggression are admired in both men and women. The Mundugumor consider women to be just as innately violent and jealous as men. Once again, distinctions in gender roles exist, but they are not highly developed (Mead 1963:210).**

The Balinese   **The Balinese people live in a larger, more complex society than the New Guinea groups. The typical personalities of the sexes are similar, as are the preferred body types. The Balinese dislike pronounced secondary sex characteristics: Neither large breasts in women nor hairiness in men is admired. Rather, they admire soft contours, narrow hips, and small breasts (that by American standards are underdeveloped for females and overdeveloped for males) (Mead 1961:1454).**

Theory

Systems

Thus far we have discussed some aspects of the differences between the sexes in human societies. The origins of these gender role distinctions are complex and involve an inseparable combination of biological and cultural systems.

Studies carried out at Johns Hopkins University under the direction of John Money (Money and Ehrhardt 1972) have helped us understand the development of gender roles. Money and his colleagues are

Variables of Biological Sex	EXPRESSION OF VARIABLES BY SEX	
	Female	Male
Chromosomal Sex	XX chromosomes	XY chromosomes
Gonadal Sex	ovaries	testes
Hormonal Sex	more estrogens	more androgens
Morphological Sex	vagina, clitoris, breasts, plus secondary sex characteristics	penis, testicles, plus secondary sex characteristics

Figure 6-1
The Expression of Biological Sex in Terms of Chromosomes, Gonads, Hormones, and Genital Morphology

Figure 6-2
Gender Identity Development
The acquisition of an adult gender identity is a long process that starts at conception with the determination of chromosomal sex and proceeds through gonadal and hormonal developments, social identification and reinforcement of a sexual identity, and finally, in adulthood, to the interaction among the person's sexual self-identification, body image, and erotic orientation(s).

probing into the origins of abnormalities in sexual development, but in the process they have learned much about normal sexual development. They distinguish four variables of biological sex: chromosomal sex, gonadal sex, hormonal sex, and morphological sex.

Chromosomal sex is determined by the chromosomes, threadlike materials found in cell nuclei that contain coded messages responsible for the determination and transmission of hereditary characteristics (see Chap. 2). In the reproduction cycle, each parent contributes a chromosome with a coded message concerning the sex identity of the offspring. When two X chromosomes are combined, the chromosomal sex is female; an X and a Y chromosome constitute male chromosomal sex.

Gonadal sex refers to the form, structure, and the position of the hormone-producing gonads. Female gonads, called *ovaries,* are located within the pelvic cavity; male gonads, called *testes,* are suspended outside the body cavity in the scrotum.

Hormonal sex refers to the type of hormone mix produced by the gonads. Although ovaries and testes produce the same hormones, ovaries produce relatively larger quantities of *estrogens,* and testes produce relatively larger quantities of *androgens.* These hormones are responsible for the development of the *secondary sex characteristics*—body hair, breasts, voice changes—that appear at puberty.

Morphological sex refers to the physical appearance, or form, of a person's genitals and secondary sex characteristics.

Money has also distinguished a concept that he labels *psychological sex,* by which he means the self-image that a person holds about his or her own sex identity. Psychological sex usually conforms to a person's (socially defined) morphological sex. When it does not, the individual may experience great emotional stress, which in our society is sometimes relieved by sex change operations.

In addition, Money studies the cultural aspects of sex determination. An individual's sex assignment at birth largely determines his or her subsequent rearing. The family, the primary socializing unit in all societies, bears the initial responsibility for transmitting cultural standards of gender behavior to a child. Later, other adults, such as teachers, contribute to the child's socialization. A great deal of this information about gender behavior is transmitted unintentionally by adults. The transmission of behavior patterns maintains the social system and ensures the individual's acceptance by the society. It is important to recognize that the behavior of a man or a woman is inextricably related to the cultural environment of the developing individual.

Processes

As we have discussed, an individual's gender identity derives from the interaction of the biological and cultural systems. Like most aspects of biological growth and cultural learning, the process is accelerated during early life. However, sex identity formation is a lifelong process: The first step in the development of a person's

STAGES OF DEVELOPMENT				
Conception	Fetal Development	Juvenile Development	Pubertal Transition	Adult Gender Identity
typical chromosomal sex XX = ♀ XY = ♂	gonadal development	genital morphology can be ♂ or ♀	pubertal hormonal sex	sexual self-identification (♂ or ♀)
atypical chromosomal sex XO, XXY, XYY, etc.	hormones external genitals neural pathways	or ambiguous behavior of others reinforces ♂ or ♀ image individual cognitive development regarding own body image (♂ or ♀) juvenile gender identity differentiates as ♂, ♀, or ambivalent	secondary sexual characteristics erotic orientation toward ♂ or ♀ psychological or cognitive self identification as ♂ or ♀	person's image of own body (♂ or ♀) erotic orientation toward ♂ or ♀ or both

gender role occurs at conception, and the last may well occur at the approach of death.

A person's chromosomal sex is established at conception when the sex chromosomes, one from each parent, combine. These chromosomes carry the genetic code responsible for the development of the sex organs in the fetus. By the second month, the human fetus has developed a rudimentary reproductive system that can become either female or male; the gonads develop into either ovaries or testes, depending on the chromosomal message that is received. The gonads begin to produce the sex hormones, which diffuse to various parts of the body, where they continue to modify the development of the individual's reproductive system.

External morphological sex differences begin to develop during the second to third month of fetal life. The genital region is identical in developing males and females until the third month, when these structures are rearranged into male and female forms. One structure becomes either a penis (male) or a clitoris (female); the genital groove becomes either the seam along the scrotum or the vaginal opening.

When a child is born, members of its society promptly identify its sex on the basis of genital morphology, triggering the social and cultural processes that develop gender identity. A newborn's sex determines the type of interaction that will take place between the child and other members of the society.

The ways in which we express our gender identity are culturally prescribed. They are a major element of our enculturation. In the United States, much of our enculturation is through the mass media. It has been estimated that by the time a child graduates from high school she or he will have spent some 22,000 hours watching television (about 7,000 hours more than were spent attending class).

Because of this, societies ensure the recognition of an infant's sex by various means.

For example, an eight-day-old girl in the Mesoamerican Indian village of San Pedro de Laguna is washed, has her ears pierced, and is dressed in the typical woman's blouse and skirt. The sticks of a loom are placed over the child's head so that she will be industrious in the tasks appropriate to her sex (Paul 1974:284). Eight-day-old boys are also bathed and are dressed in miniature male clothes. A small machete, a men's carrying bag, and tumpline (sling) are kept over each infant's sleeping hammock to symbolize his future tasks in adulthood.* In the United States a system of color coding helps strangers recognize the sex of a bundled and thus neuter-looking infant: Pink clothing indicates the child is female; blue signals a male. Confusingly for American travelers, the reverse—blue for girls, pink for boys—is customary in Switzerland.

Louis Paul 1975: personal communication.

The sex of a newborn infant may evoke powerful responses from its family. In societies of limited technology, family size must be carefully managed. For example, Mountain Arapesh parents space out their children by avoiding intercourse after the birth of each child until the child is able to walk. The newborn's sex may even determine whether the infant lives or dies. Infanticide, especially of females, is practiced in a number of societies. Arapesh families believe they must avoid having several young girls in their homes in order to avoid too great a strain on the mother and other children (Mead 1961:1440). Girls are less desirable than boys because they leave the household at the time of marriage, whereas boys bring in wives and thus contribute to the family economy. If successive children are female, the parents may decide to allow an infant girl to die. The father signals his decision when he learns of his child's sex by saying,

"Wash it" or "Do not wash it" (allow it to die). It is the responsibility of the mother to carry out the decision.

The way in which the typical family accomplishes the transmission of gender roles to the younger generation differs in every society. In some societies the most influential socializing agents are women. Nancy Tanner refers to one such form as a *matrifocal family*—"one in which the mother is central in terms of cultural values, family finances and patterns of decision making, [and] affective ties" (1974:152). In matrifocal families the mother may be assisted by other women of the household, or she may reside alone with her children.

In the contemporary urban United States, the primary responsibility for socializing preschoolers rests on a single individual, the child's mother. In lower-class black families the mother may also shoulder most of the economic responsibilities for raising her chil-

A group of Yanomamö Amazonian Indians line up as they prepare to depart to raid a neighboring village. Renowned for their fierce aggressiveness, the Yanomamö place much more social value on males than on females and frequently kill their female infants (see Chapter 17).

dren. The result is a strong matrifocal family in which the mother is the central figure. The matrifocal family is not typical among middle-class whites. Instead, the father assumes the primary economic responsibility, although the mother retains the main responsibility for transmitting cultural values. After the age of five or six, much of the American child's socialization is taken over by major institutions such as the state (through compulsory education), the church (through participation in programs of religious education), and the mass media (through exposure to television, movies, radio, records, and reading material).

In other societies, such as the Mountain Arapesh, both parents participate in child rearing from the time of a child's birth (Mead 1961:1438–1441). The Arapesh consider the father's involvement with his children essential to their healthy development. The paternal responsibility begins as soon as a wife realizes she is pregnant; the couple must have frequent intercourse to strengthen the fetus. After the child's birth, the father must sleep with his wife and child (and not with any of his other wives) and abstain from intercourse with all of his wives until the child has been weaned. An Arapesh father frequently tends his children, thus allowing his wife to pursue her household and economic tasks.

In a cross-cultural perspective, then, it seems that in all societies a child's gender role socialization begins within the child's family, but the degree of involvement of parents and other individuals varies greatly.

In a study of socialization practices in many societies, H. A. Barry, M. K. Bacon, and I. L. Child found that boys and girls are almost always reared differently in preparation for different gender roles in their adult lives (1957). Girls are usually socialized to be nurturant, responsible, and obedient, whereas boys are generally socialized to be achievement oriented and self-reliant. These practices, of course, tell us much more about the social structures of the societies than about inherent personality characteristics of the sexes. It seems that under certain conditions, social life is facilitated when half the population have nurturant, responsible, and obedient personalities, while the other half are achievement oriented and self-reliant. As we have seen (Chap. 3), agricultural production tends to generate this type of social division, which might explain the consistency of the data: Most contemporary societies are agricultural. Let us trace the dynamics of sex role socialization in a specific society, the Ibo of Nigeria, to see these processes at work.

The Ibo   This account is based on a study by two anthropologists, Helen and Richard Henderson (1966; see also Chap. 24). The Ibo are strongly individualistic, competitive, and aggressive; however, the men tend to exhibit these traits more markedly than the women. Men do the heavy farming, while women cultivate household gardens and sell their products in local or regional markets. The entrepreneurial status of these women allows them to become significant economic forces in their communities. The Ibo are organized into patrilineages whose perpetuation depends on the active participation of female as well as male members (see Chaps. 8 and 9).

The first two years of life are much the same for boys and girls. Infants are always physically close to their mothers, are breast-fed on demand, and are generally treated with a great deal of affection and respect. Ibo believe that the spirits of young children are difficult to please and may depart to the supernatural realm on almost any pretext; considerable effort must be exerted by the parents to entice them to stay.

As a child matures, he or she is usually replaced at the mother's side by a newborn brother or sister. The toddler receives much credit for the arrival of the new

infant—Ibo believe that the toddler's spirit transmits its contentment with the household to other spirits not yet born. The next oldest child is encouraged to fondle and play with the youngest family member, a pattern that establishes tight bonds between siblings.

Several people besides the mother participate in the child's upbringing by the time it is able to walk. Particularly important are the older siblings and the father—the latter especially if the child is male. Fathers include young sons in some of their exclusively masculine activities. A boy may also have his own yam garden; his mother purchases the seed yams, and his father tends the plot. When the plot has been harvested, the boy, who may be only two years old, is responsible for deciding what portion of the harvest should go into his mother's larder and what portion should be contributed to the communal storehouse of the compound. If the boy is the first-born male, he will be expected to assist his father in the transmission of male lore to his younger brothers.

Girls are instructed in the womanly traits by their mothers and older sisters. They are given stricter obedience training than boys and are taught to perform all female tasks with grace and efficiency. They are warned against exposing their genitals and are expected to be modest at an earlier age than boys.

Both boys and girls participate in formal associations of children of the same sex and of approximately the same age. Village boys between the ages of five and seven are organized by their fathers into groups that mimic the masquerade societies to which all adult men belong. Later the boys are initiated into the masquerade societies themselves. They are also members of informal play associations that practice hunting skills.

Girls are organized into dancing clubs. Each club has a core of girls aged nine to ten, but girls between the ages of five and six may join. Two sponsors, a young man and one of the girl's mothers, guide each club. As the girls mature, they perform dances at funerals and, later, at the homes of their future husbands' relatives. These clubs are the prototypes of the women's organizations that visit other villages to dance and to establish trade contacts.

In general, each parent is more tolerant of the behavior of children of the opposite sex than of those

Innocent toys . . . are shapers of the mind.

The daughters of an Onitsha (Ibo) patrilineage perform a crucial ritual in
the funeral of one of their elders by
cleaning the feet of the descent group's
men with white clay. The two senior
sisters hold leaves in their mouths to
signify their ritual condition. This
reflects part of the complex training the
women have received in their initiation
into womanhood.

of the same sex. Fathers indulge their daughters but
expect them to be obedient; daughters try to please
their fathers by obeying instructions and running
errands. Mothers believe boys are less controllable
than girls, and they are thus more tolerant of their
sons' transgressions than their daughters'. Boys who
have become members of formal associations frequently challenge the authority of their mothers.
Mothers feel that only flogging can correct such behavior, but the boys often laughingly escape.

The Ibo thus raise their children in a way that ensures the continuation of their society. Men and
women are expected to be capable and autonomous
in their respective spheres of activity. Independence
and autonomy are learned within the peer group organizations, which are relatively free from parental
controls. Women are also expected to be obedient
and faithful to their husbands—a trait learned early
by girls as they try to please their parents. Men are
expected to be aggressive and to manifest rugged
individualism, qualities they also learn during early life.

Analysis

The Folk Perspective

There are two aspects to an emic analysis of human
sex: the subjects' view of the relationship between
biological sex and gender role, and their view of morphological sex. In some societies genital morphology
is viewed as the determinant of gender roles; in other
societies the relationship between physiology and
gender role is less deterministic. In at least one society,
as we shall see, people recognized three categories of
genital morphology: male, female, and an intermediate
form. In order to understand this view, it is necessary
to recognize the existence of intersexes.

In fetal development the sex hormone mixture is
occasionally neither typically female nor typically
male. This can be caused by a malfunction of the fetus's
gonads or by the presence of other hormones from an
external source, perhaps through interconnection with
the bloodstream of a twin of the opposite sex. In such
cases the genital development is altered, and the result
can be a person who is *intersexual* in genital morphol-

ogy—that is, the genitals are neither clearly male nor female (Katchadourian and Lunde 1972; Money and Ehrhardt 1974).

Societies respond very differently to the birth of intersexes. The Pokot of Kenya view intersexes as grossly malformed (Edgerton 1964). Such infants are often killed, as are infants with deformities of other types. When Pokot intersexes are allowed to live, they have the marginal status of physical deviants—an inevitable categorization, because the Pokot emphasize love conquests and beauty for both sexes. Moreover, adult status for both males and females depends on circumcision. With their unusually developed genitals, intersexes cannot be circumcised and therefore are never socially identified as either gender. In Pokot society, then, morphological sex is considered as bipartite (either male or female), and a person's gender is invariably determined by genital sex.

The Navajo of the United States treated intersexes very differently (Hill 1935). Instead of being regarded as deviants, they were considered to be exceptional people whose existence brought the community well-being and prosperity. The Navajo called intersexes *nadle* and apparently thought of them as a third sex, according them a gender status distinct from that of males and females. The *nadle* were identified as such at birth, and they generally had more role options than males or females. They could perform any economic task and could wear men's or women's clothing or both in combination.

The relationship between morphological sex and gender identity among the Navajo was not rigidly fixed: In addition to intersexes, some men and women with normal genitals attained the status of *nadle*. These people decided to adopt this social identity later in life, perhaps because of the greater flexibility of life-style the *nadle* status offered.

The three Navajo gender statuses were founded in the Navajo view of three types of physical, or morphological, sex. Other societies, although recognizing only two types of morphological sex, may nonetheless recognize more than two gender statuses and may allow a person to assume a gender role that approximates but is not identical to that of the opposite sex. In these societies a person's gender identity is apparently not viewed as being strictly determined by genital morphology.

The Mohave Indians of the American Southwest allowed both males and females to adopt gender roles that were not congruent with their physical sex identity (Devereux 1937). Women who gained social and legal status very much like that of men were called *hwame·* The *hwame·* hunted and did other work that was ordinarily reserved for males. They also married women and were the socially recognized fathers of any children born to their wives. The social position of *hwame·* was not identical to that of men, however: They were not permitted to hold positions of authority within their community because these were reserved for the men.

Men who adopted female roles were called *alyha··*. *Alyha·* adopted most of the behaviors, rights, and duties typical of Mohave women. They married men and observed the Mohave women's custom of ritually celebrating the onset of menstruation, which in their case was fictitiously acted out. *Alyha·* also simulated pregnancy and childbirth and had full rights as mothers over the family's children.

Hwame· and *alyha·* statuses were formally assumed at an initiation ceremony at which a child adopted a name and the style of body decoration of the opposite gender. These trappings thereafter signaled the person's gender identity to the community.

Another interesting example of incongruence between genital morphology and gender role is the institution of female husbands in some African societies. Female husbands are women who assume the role of husbands within a socially recognized marriage. In a cross-cultural study of female husbands, Denise O'Brien found that in some societies female husbands are social substitutes for male kinsmen (1972). For instance, if a man dies and has not produced male heirs, a kinswoman might become a female husband, marrying a woman in the name of her deceased relative. Any children born to the wife (who is impregnated either by a man or her choice or by one chosen by the female husband's family) are identified with the female husband's patrilineage.

O'Brien also found that in some West African societies female husbands take wives on their own behalf rather than as surrogates for men (1972). Most of these female husbands are entrepreneurs, which allows them to become wealthy and requires that they spend much time away from home—in short, they lead lives similar to those of successful American businessmen.

The Analytical Perspective

Clearly, the relationship between biological sex and gender identity is by no means inevitable. Gender roles may depend more on social definitions of role-appropriate behavior than on the biological characteristics of the sexes.

Among the Pokot, morphological sex strictly determines a person's gender. Among the Navajo, this is usually the case, but two kinds of variation occur: The Navajo view genital sex as tripartite, and morphological

sex is not always congruent with gender role—some people who are physiologically male or female adopt the *nadle* role. The flexible gender roles of the Mohave and the institution of female husbands in some African societies illustrate how roles that are usually thought to be bound to biological sex can transcend anatomy and physiology.

In most human societies the social behavior of each sex is explained by folk wisdom as the natural and innate concomitant of biological sex. People tend to believe that manly or womanly behavior (as their society defines them) are inherent within persons of each sex. This belief carries the implication that these behaviors are unchangeable. However, the cross-cultural perspective of anthropologists permits them to see that males and females in one society may behave

very differently from males and females in other societies—an observation that undermines the popular
assumption of biological determinism.

In our own society people frequently express their
view of the inevitability of sex-appropriate behavior by
such sayings as "Boys will be boys." This adage implies
that it is difficult, if not impossible, to transform significantly the behavior that is believed to be characteristic of boyhood. Yet boys and girls in other societies do
not behave at all like their American counterparts.

Some of the most interesting research on gender
roles concerns children who have been mistakenly
assigned to the "wrong" sex at birth, usually because of
some confusion over their genital morphology. Money
and his associates have established that if a child is
reared as a member of the opposite sex, it readily

(right)
Initiation to "womanhood" upon a
female's first menstruation among the
San Carlos Apache of Arizona. Social
and cultural meaning is thus attached
to a biological phenomenon.

(left)
The filing of teeth, after a girl or boy
reaches puberty, is a custom that has
deep significance among the Balinese.
The essential meaning is to ward off
evil qualities of human nature, including
sensual pleasure (Raga) and love of
material things (Tresna). This illustrates
that even what our society considers
"basic" emotions are culturally
conditioned.

adopts the gender role expected of it. If the mistake is discovered by the age of three or four, it is possible to resocialize the child into the "correct" gender role, but beyond that point the child strongly resists such attempts and clings to its existing role identification. On the basis of these studies, Money has concluded that the human species is psychosexually neuter at birth (Money and Ehrhardt 1972).

Conclusions

Schools of Thought

In the past most social scientists viewed sex and gender as relatively fixed entities. George L. Trager expresses this view:

I hold, with many other present-day anthropological theorists, that culture is firmly rooted in the biological nature of man. And I believe that this biological nature is in essence the fact that man is a mammal and, like nearly all other living things on our earth, is of two sexes. This means that the examination of human biology must be *in terms always of the two sexes,* that it is through and by virtue of sex that man expresses his biological nature. (1962:115; emphasis added)

Trager's view of human sex has two important implications: A person's sex identity is static rather than dynamic, and every society responds to the bipartite nature of human sex in the same way. This biologically deterministic approach to the study of sex has characterized most social science studies until recently.

A similarly limited view has sometimes (but less often) been extended to gender roles. Psychologists, for example, have devised techniques to assess femininity or masculinity and have applied them to many cultures. But when these tests have been developed and standardized in reference to *one* cultural group—for example, white, middle-class Americans—they are invalid when applied to other social groups. Under

these circumstances the researcher is actually measuring how people fit the standards of the test group society. In itself, this might be desirable information—but it should not be confused with the delineation of gender roles and their meanings, which are always specific to each culture.

The contrary view, that gender roles are almost entirely the product of cultural forces, stated by Margaret Mead as long ago as 1935, has not yet won widespread acceptance:

> If those temperamental attitudes which we have traditionally regarded as feminine—such as passivity, responsiveness, and a willingness to cherish children—can so easily be set up as the masculine pattern in one tribe and in another be outlawed for the majority of men, we no longer have any basis for regarding such aspects of behavior as sex-linked.

We are forced to conclude that human nature is almost unbelievably malleable, responding

left
In a rural Mexican village a young girl learns how to be a woman by seeing her mother's behavior and helping her perform women's work (in this instance, washing clothes).

No matter whether in the midwestern U.S.A. (above) or among the Chinese in Hong Kong (right) cultural form determines the mode in which emotion is expressed and biological relationships are acknowledged.

accurately and contrastingly to contrasting cultural conditions. . . . Standardized personality differences between the sexes are . . . cultural creations to which each generation, male or female, is trained to conform. (1935:190–191)

Author's Conclusions

I believe that human sex and gender must be viewed as part of a single biocultural process. The simple, dichotomous explanations expressed by many previous scholars do not accurately reflect what is known about the development of human sexual identity. The different functions of females and males in the reproductive cycle establish the base for the study of human sex, and these roles are the same throughout the species. However, the ways in which these reproductive roles are carried out—through courtship behaviors, positions in sexual intercourse, marriage forms, and birth practices—acquire their meaning for the people who enact them only in the context of the world view and value system of their particular culture.

I also think that a society's beliefs about the nature of sex and gender strongly affects social behavior. Accordingly, the traditional American view that biological factors are the primary determinants of gender differences, as well as the popularity among scholars of the scientific expression of this idea, must influence the way men and women act. What is this effect? Carol Tavris found a correlation between a person's attitudes about the origins of sex differences and his or her endorsement of particular role changes for American women (1972:83). People who believe that sex differences are primarily biological in origin tend to resist role changes more vigorously than people who believe those differences are primarily cultural. This finding suggests that the deterministic view of sex and gender reinforces dichotomized gender roles.

Anthropologists have often viewed sex and gender strictly in terms of their own cultural definitions. It is extremely difficult to avoid doing so because beliefs about the biological origin of sex differences are so firmly rooted in each person's cultural tradition. The result has been that sex and gender frequently have

not been sharply distinguished by researchers; nor have the variations in human expression of these traits been carefully analyzed.

In contrast to Trager's opinion that the biological nature of humans is expressed through sex, I believe that the biological nature of sex is expressed through culture.

Summary

All societies attach great social significance to the physical differences between the sexes; thus the study of human sexes involves the consideration of both biological and cultural factors. In particular, each society constructs a gender role for each sex, and people readily come to regard the gender role—a cultural product—as being somehow "natural" (biologically determined).

The physical dimorphism of the sexes is an evolutionary product of the environmental and social pressures exerted on our hominid predecessors. In human societies, this physical dimorphism has been used as the basis for an elaborate gender-role dimorphism, especially in the division of labor. However, the content of gender roles displays considerable cross-cultural differences, as examples from the United States and various New Guinea peoples suggest. Gender roles do show some central tendencies—for example, men are usually more aggressive, and women are generally more nurturant.

At least four variables of biological sex can be identified: *chromosomal, gonadal, hormonal,* and *morphological.* An additional category, psychological sex, need not correspond to the biological variables. Individuals may be socialized into and accept a gender role that is at variance with their biological sex. Some societies, in fact, recognize and institutionalize such intersexual roles.

Some scholars hold that gender roles are to a greater or lesser extent the product of biologically inherited factors, but most anthropologists, including the author, take the view that the content of these roles is almost entirely the product of cultural forces.

Annotated Bibliography

Bird, Carolyn (1970)   *Born Female.* New York: McKay. An analysis of women's position in American economic production. A powerful argument for economic equality between the sexes.

Chiñas, Beverly L. (1973)   *The Isthmus Zapotecs: Women's Roles in Cultural Context.* New York: Holt. A discussion of the role of women among the farmer-trader Zapotecs of the Isthmus of Tehuantepec, Mexico. The author distinguishes between formalized and nonformalized roles in her analysis.

Fernea, Elizabeth Warnock (1965)   *Guests of the Sheik.* New York: Doubleday. A personal view of women's life in a small village in southern Iraq written by the wife of an anthropologist while her husband studied this community.

Ford, Clellan S., and Beach, Frank A. (1951)   *Patterns of Sexual Behavior.* New York: Harper. A cross-cultural anthropological study of sexual activity; strong on data, weak on interpretations.

Goodale, Jane C. (1971)   *Tiwi Wives: A Study of the Women of Melville Island, North Australia.* American Ethnological Society Monograph no. 51. Seattle: Univ. of Washington Press. The role of women among the foraging Tiwi; their role contradicts the prevailing stereotype of females as nonhunters.

Gordon, Chad, and Johnson, Gayle, eds. (1976)   *Human Sexuality: Contemporary Perspectives.* New York: Harper. A well-organized, highly readable collection of more than sixty articles on various aspects of human sexuality.

Katchadourian, Herant A., and Lunde, Donald T. (1972)   *Fundamentals of Human Sexuality.* New York: Holt. A readable, informative account of human sexuality.

Martin, M. Kay, and Voorhies, Barbara (1975)   *The Female of the Species.* New York: Columbia Univ. Press. An anthropological view of human sex and gender. Stresses the variations in gender that are correlative with ecological adaptations.

Mead, Margaret (1963)   *Sex and Temperament in Three Primitive Societies.* New York: Morrow. A classic discussion of gender roles in three societies of New Guinea, where American gender role stereotypes are contradicted.

Money, John, and Ehrhardt, Anke A. (1972)   *Man and Woman, Boy and Girl: Differentiation and Dimorphism of Gender.* Baltimore, Md.: Johns Hopkins Univ. Press. An incisive summary of the elegant research that has been carried out at Johns Hopkins University on sex anomalies.

Murphy, Yolanda, and Murphy, Robert (1974)   *Women of the Forest.* New York: Columbia Univ. Press. A beautiful anthropological account of women who live in the male-dominated society of Mundurucu, horticulturalists and foragers in Amazonian Brazil. The study considers the historical, ecological, and cultural setting in which the Mundurucu live, the mythology and ideology concerning women, the working and household life of the female, marriage and child rearing and the impact of social change on the female role.

Newton, Esther (1972)   *Mother Camp: Female Impersonators in America.* Englewood Cliffs, N.J.: Prentice-Hall. An anthropological study of "drag queens" that investigates one aspect of gender transformation in America. Raises many interesting points about male and female stereotypes.

Rosenberg, B. G., and Sutton-Smith, Brian (1972)   *Sex and Identity.* New York: Holt. A compact summary of the contributions made by comparative psychology, physiological psychology, psychoanalysis, social learning, sociology, and anthropology to the study of the human sexes. A good introduction to the subject, but the authors fail to emphasize the economic significance of gender roles.

Schaller, George (1963)   *The Mountain Gorilla: Ecology and Behavior.* Chicago: Univ. of Chicago Press. A readable account of the behavior of wild gorillas, a species that is closely related to humans and that provides a possible simian model for early human sex roles.

Van Lawick-Goodall, Jane (1968)   "The Behavior of Free-Living Chimpanzees in the Gombé Stream Reserve." *Animal Behavior Monographs* 1:165–311.

(1971)   *In the Shadow of Man.* Boston: Houghton Mifflin. A scholarly monograph and a popular book on wild chimpanzees, whose sex roles provide a possible simian model for early human sex differences.

Part III

Topics in Cultural Anthropology

7
Communication:
Verbal and Nonverbal

The World Context

Origins and Development through Time

By reading of this sentence, you are participating in a process of communication. Communication, particularly through language, is an essential part of our daily lives and a central feature of our humanity. Without our ability to communicate with one another, no individual could participate in society, and culture would be impossible. One noted anthropologist has stated flatly that "culture is communication" (Hall 1959:Chap. 5).

In its broadest sense, communication refers to the exchange of information between two or more beings. Communication, then, is by no means restricted to the human species. Most, if not all, members of the animal kingdom communicate to some extent, and it is even possible to regard electronic computers as communicating with one another and with human beings. The communication systems of other animals can be extraordinarily complex, as careful studies of different species in their natural environments have shown. But human beings engage in some of the richest, subtlest, and most complex forms of communication in the animal world.

The importance of communication to human groups is attested to by the many ingenious methods they have devised to accomplish it. The inhabitants of St. Kilda, one of the most remote of the New Hebrides Islands which lie off the northwest coast of Scotland, communicated with their neighboring islands by placing messages into a container which was in turn put into a sheep's bladder and attached to a piece of wood. This was then tossed into the sea with the hope that it would wash up on the shore of one of the nearby islands; many, however, were lost.

Anthropologists usually divide human communication into two distinct categories: nonverbal communication and verbal communication. *Nonverbal communication,* a type of information exchange that we share with myriads of other creatures, does not employ voices; rather, such means as gesturing, making faces, or manipulating the distance between ourselves and others expresses the message. *Verbal communication* is vocal gestures. Its most specialized form is language—a phenomenon that seems to be uniquely human and that is crucial to our socialization and daily existence.

Language   Why is language unique to the human species? Before we can answer this question, we have to know exactly what language is—what its *design features* are. The anthropological linguist Charles F. Hockett provides a useful list of thirteen such design features (1958, 1960):

1. Vocal-auditory channel: **Language is produced through the mouth (and nose); it is heard (received) through the ears.**

2. Broadcast transmission and directional reception: **When people speak, they can be heard in all directions. However, receivers (hearers) can perceive the direction from which the speaker's voice is coming. This makes language a very efficient system for communicating danger: The warning will be heard by all group members no matter where they stand in relationship to the speaker; also, those who hear the message will know where it is coming from and thus will have a better chance of avoiding the danger.**

3. Rapid fading: **The actual "signs" of speech are sound sequences that last only a short time before dissipating. This puts pressure on the receiver to "decode" the message efficiently and correctly the first time. It also explains why information is encoded at least two different ways in speech: in the words and in the patterns in which the words are arranged. This reduces the chances of mistakes in decoding messages.**

4. Interchangeability: **Every speaker can reproduce the signals he or she has heard. Every speaker is a hearer, every hearer a speaker. The entire community engages in useful, reciprocal communication. In this respect language is unlike the communication systems of other animals. For example, differences often exist in what the two sexes of a species can communicate.**

5. Total feedback: **Every (normal) speaker can monitor his or her output. This enables people to correct themselves when they make mistakes even before they receive responses from their listeners.**

6. Specialization: **Language is highly specialized: Speaking serves no other purpose than communicating. One useful consequence of this specialization is that we can do a great many other things while talking and listening. In other species, elaborate communication rituals may require the full attention of the communicators.**

7. Semanticity: **Spoken messages mean something—that is, conventionally agreed upon and quite regular associations between message elements (words) and recurring features of the natural and sociocultural environment exist.**

8. Arbitrariness: **The connections between language signs (such as words) and what they refer to (mean) is entirely arbitrary, a matter of convention. This means they have to be learned, but it also means that people can communicate about anything once they agree on these connections.**

9. Discreteness: **Although the range of sounds that can be produced by the human vocal tract is vast, every language uses only a small, sharply limited (discrete) set of such sounds to produce all its spoken utterances, to communicate its entire semantic range. The advantage is that every speaker of a language must learn only a very small sound repertoire. However, if a speaker deviates from this limited set of sounds, his or her attempts at communication will quickly become incomprehensible.**

10. Displacement: **We can talk about anything. The objects of our conversation need not be physically present: We can talk about things in another room, in another country, on another continent. We can talk about the past, the future, and things that are beyond the reach of our senses. We can talk about things that have never existed and probably never will, such as mermaids. Nonhuman communication systems, by contrast, seem to be bound for the most part to messages about the immediate context of events. The fact that language enables us to communicate about things beyond the situational context (that is, *displaced* from it) makes language a superbly useful device for the exchange of an enormous range of information.**

11. Productivity: **Rarely, if ever, is the same sentence repeated in an identical manner. Each sentence is "new," yet as long as it conforms to rules of usage, it will be understood. The feature of productivity of language is fundamental to a vital aspect of human experience: our ability to learn and transmit learning, to pass on culture from one generation to the next.**

12. Traditional transmission: **Although the human capacity to learn language is apparently genetically encoded and inherited, every individual acquires his or her language competence through the process of enculturation. In other words, we learn and are taught the language we speak; we acquire a language in the process of learning a culture. In many species, competence to communicate is acquired by genetic inheritance. But inevitably these systems—such as those used by ants—are extremely rigid. Because language is handed down from one generation to the next as a part of the transmission of culture, the older generation can choose what it wishes to teach, ignoring the irrelevant and modifying the content of the language in the light of changing circumstances. Being culturally rather than genetically transmitted, language is uniquely adaptable.**

13. Duality of patterning: **Two levels of patterning compose every utterance. On the phonological level, every utterance is a patterned sequence of sound segments that in themselves are meaningless; these sound segments are called *phonemes*. On the grammatical level, every utterance is a patterned sequence of units of meaning; these units are called *morphemes*. Morphemes are *represented* by specific sound sequences. Because the number of sounds a language uses is very limited (the feature of discreteness), duality of patterning means that an enormous (virtually unlimited) number of units of meaning (morphemes) can be represented by a small number of sounds—a very efficient communication device.**

In figure 7-1 the communication systems of other species are compared to language in terms of these thirteen design features. The uniqueness of language and its superiority as a flexible, adaptable system are evident. Clearly, human communication is significantly different from the methods of other animal species. But how and when did human communication in general and language in particular develop?

Figure 7-1
**Language Compared to Other
Communication Systems**
Although the communication systems
of other species have some of the design
features of language, none has *all* the
design features that, in combination,
characterize language. (Adapted from
Hockett 1960:8–9.)

Our complex communicative abilities are deeply
embedded in our animal past. The mutual ancestors
of apes and humans some 30 to 35 million years ago
probably communicated with each other through gestures. All our close living relatives, the apes and the
monkeys, have complex gestural communication systems. For example, chimpanzees reassure anxious group
members with hand gestures. Baboons acknowledge
social rank through ritual displays of dominance and

Design Features	Bee Dancing	Stickleback Fish Courtship	Gibbon Calls	Language
Vocal-Auditory Channel	no	no	yes	yes
Broadcast Transmission and Directional Reception	yes	yes	yes	yes
Rapid Fading	?	?	yes	yes
Interchange-ability	limited	no	yes	yes
Total Feedback	?	no	yes	yes
Specialization	?	in part	yes	yes
Semanticity	yes	no	yes	yes
Arbitrariness	no	?	yes	yes
Discreteness	no	?	yes	yes
Displacement	yes	?	no	yes
Productivity	yes	no	no	yes
Traditional Transmission	somewhat	no?	?	yes
Duality of Patterning	no	?	no	yes

submission, in which subordinate individuals assume passive sexual stances toward dominant baboons or move out of their way. But the communication between these primates is primarily nonverbal. Recent research has shown that chimpanzees are capable of very complex communication. They can ask questions, compose sentences, and manipulate symbols grammatically—but only by using hand gestures or physical objects that serve as signs (Gardner and Gardner 1971; Premack 1971). Nonhuman primates cannot be taught to speak, as one couple discovered when they tried to rear a chimpanzee in a manner identical to that of their own baby girl (Kellogg and Kellogg 1933).

The difficulties in discovering how and when language evolved are immense. What remains could signify the presence of language and survive for the millions of years that have elapsed since the hominid line differentiated from the pongids (see Chap. 2)? How can we reconstruct the sequence of events that constitute the evolution of language? Inevitably, our answers must be partial, our data circumstantial, our conjectures tentative. We have to rely on two kinds of information: the *cultural* remains our ancestors left behind, which tell us about the complexity of their social interactions, and the *biological* basis of speech in the evolving human brain.

Let us examine the cultural data first. In Chapter 2 we found that the first hominid remains associated with cultural artifacts occur at the australopithecine stage of hominid evolution more than two million years ago. We know that these early hominids engaged in occasional big-game hunting, a highly coordinated activity that suggests at least some degree of social organization. But contemporary nonhuman primates such as baboons also have a socially organized group life that is complex enough to accomplish such tasks—yet they do not have language. Moreover, the level of stone tool technology that some australopithecines

Chimpanzees: our closest living relatives. Like humans, chimpanzees communicate with each other frequently—touching, grooming, caressing. Their gestural systems are just now being investigated, since recent research has shown that although not biologically suited to learn human verbal languages, they can learn both a large number of vocabulary items and grammatical rules for using them when the medium is nonverbal, such as plastic symbols or sign language.

left behind—the so-called pebble tools—is hardly advanced enough to warrant the assumption that they must have had a fully developed language.

However, the remains left by *Homo erectus* nearly a million years ago suggest that these creatures may well have developed language. At Terra Amata, a 300,000-year-old site on the Riviera near Nice, archaeologists have found evidence of oval huts that once housed subgroups of ten to twenty individuals each (Butzer 1971:446). As we mentioned in Chapter 2, these remains are the earliest evidence we have of social groups being divided into concrete, bonded subgroups. It is reasonable to conjecture that the basis for these subgroups was some kind of blood relationship, possibly indicating that these groups were the first example of family organization.

At the nearby site of Torralba, Spain, which dates back some 400,000 years, we find the earliest evidence of the use of fire (Howell 1966). Many similar sites of the same period are divided into butchering and work areas that are separate from the living areas (Butzer 1971:450). Numerous stone tools were produced in the work areas, including the hand axes that are typical of most *Homo erectus* remains. These tools are much more complex, refined, and efficient than the pebble tools of the australopithecines. In Tanzania, at a site called Isimilia, Clark Howell found a workshop area where tools were roughed out before being brought back to the living area for finishing. These and similar finds, together with the evidence of *Homo erectus*'s highly organized hunting of big game, suggest that they had attained a level of social complexity that would be difficult to imagine unless they had developed a flexible, productive communication system such as language.*

* *Very recently, Alexander Marshack of Harvard University has indicated that computer analysis of small scratches made by* Homo erectus *on bones some 300,000 years ago suggests that these markings were a notationsl system. If so, some language-like communication system is suggested, because agreement among users of the notational system with regard to its arbitrary meanings would have to be established and shared.*

Figure 7-2
Special Areas of the Human Brain

(a) Speech areas found on the surface of one side of the brain. (b) The arcuate fasciculus, a bundle of nerves below the surface, connects Broca's and Wernicke's areas. (c) The limbic system (nonverbal communication) is found deep inside both brain halves.

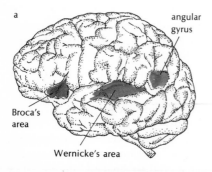

a

angular gyrus

Broca's area

Wernicke's area

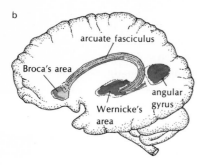

b

arcuate fasciculus

Broca's area

angular gyrus

Wernicke's area

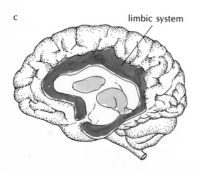

c

limbic system

What of the biological evidence? Three areas of the brain appear to be crucial for the human linguistic ability. *Broca's area,* located toward the front of the dominant side of the brain, activates, among other things, the muscles of the jaw, lips, tongue, and larynx. *Wernicke's area,* which is in the temporal lobe of the dominant hemisphere, is connected to Broca's area by a large bundle of nerve fibers (called the *arcuate fasciculus*) and is the brain site where verbal comprehension takes place. The *angular gyrus,* which is situated adjacent to Wernicke's area, serves as a link between the parts of the brain that receive stimuli from our sense organs of sight, hearing, and touch (see fig. 7-2).

The significance of these brain areas is profound: We could not possibly speak without them. Their location is also important—they are all situated in the "new" brain, the cortex, which is much more developed in humans than in any other animal. The fact that the areas are located in the cortex allows sensory inputs and verbal representations to be connected with each other without having to go through the "old" brain—especially the limbic system, which activates such basic responses as aggression, fear, hunger, and sexual arousal. Human beings consequently can think, talk, and experience the world without involving these gut level states. Other animals, including our closest primate relatives, have not developed these three brain areas to any significant degree and thus do not seem to have the brain structure necessary for the development of speech.

Our australopithecine ancestors had brains roughly equivalent in size to those of modern chimpanzees. From that time on a tremendous evolutionary expansion of the brain occurred; by the next stage of evolution, that of *Homo erectus,* we find a cranial capacity of some 1,100 cc, which is already at the lower boundary of the range for modern *Homo sapiens.* This expansion of the brain entailed the evolution of the cortex, so we may reasonably assume that *Homo erectus* had major elements of the brain structures that characterize modern human beings and are fundamental to our capacity for speech.

Apparently, then, language did not develop until the *Homo erectus* level of hominid evolution. But even at this level our ancestors were not fully adept at lan-

Ladakhi baby, India. Every normal infant human being apparently is born biologically programmed to learn language, and capable of learning any human language. The culture of the group into which he or she is born sets limits on what the child will learn (including which language), but within those limits makes possible a full range of creative and expressive behaviors.

guage. The brain of *Homo erectus* was not as advanced as our own. Moreover, recent research indicates that the shape of *Homo erectus*'s nasal cavity, palate, and tongue was long and flat compared to those of modern humans, while their larynx sat much higher in their throat than ours (see fig. 7-3). From this evidence, it seems likely that the mouth and throat of *Homo erectus* could not produce the range of sounds of a contemporary adult, and their speech was probably slower and clumsier (Lieberman et al. 1972).

Incomplete linguistic abilities may account for the otherwise puzzling question of why the culture of *Homo erectus* remained relatively unchanged for over half a million years (see chap. 2). The level of evolution of their brains necessitated a much longer period for the acquisition of language than a child requires today. Since life expectancy was much shorter, there

Figure 7-3
Comparison of Speech Apparatus

Homo sapiens. When we compare the vocal apparatus and brain power of a modern baby and adult with reconstructions of early men, we can assess the speaking ability of *Homo sapiens neanderthalensis.* Like *Homo sapiens* he had a larynx to generate sounds, but to form words with these sounds he would have had to modulate them with spaces above the larynx. In modern man, the nasal cavity, mouth, and pharynx are used for this purpose. In the mouth and pharynx the tongue movements vary the size and shape of these spaces to produce the sounds needed for modern speech.

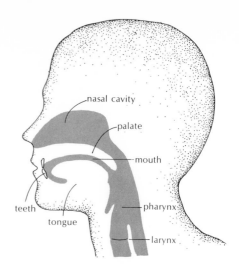

Homo sapiens neanderthalensis. H.S.N. is believed to have possessed a vocal tract similar to the one shown here. The larynx sits higher up in the throat, thus limiting the size of the pharynx. The tongue was relatively long and rested almost entirely in the mouth rather than in the throat. Therefore, it could be used only to vary the size and shape of the mouth alone, and not the pharynx. This single-cavity system restricted *H.S.N.* to slow, clumsy speech. Note the right angle formed in the modern adult's tract, the short, round tongue and mouth cavity versus *H.S.N*'s oblique angle and long, flat tongue and mouth cavity.

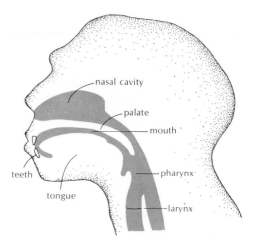

Modern baby. The fact that the vocal tract of a newborn modern baby resembles that of *H.S.N.* has caused many to assume that the sounds the baby is capable of making resemble those that *H.S.N.* could make. Although the baby's sounds are limited, they could have been formed into words by an adult brain.

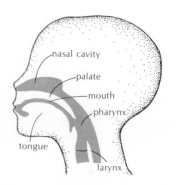

must have been a relatively brief adulthood in which individual innovative acts could take place.

After these developments at the *Homo erectus* stage, the evolution of culture and presumably of language accelerated rapidly. However, even as recently as the Neanderthal stage of human evolution some 70,000 years ago, the production of speech sounds was still limited to a much smaller range than among modern humans, and the rate of speech probably was one tenth as rapid (Lieberman 1975: 171–180). We do not know the precise mechanisms through which language evolved: Many theories exist, but all are conjecture. However, we do know that the evolution of culture, the evolution of language, and the evolution of the human body and brain are all dynamically interrelated. The vast number of contemporary languages and cultures that cover the globe in a mosaic of amazing variety is among the results of this evolutionary process.

Contemporary Examples

Depending on the instruments used for investigating, the human vocal tract can produce well over a thousand identifiable sounds. As Ray Birdwhistell has pointed out, the number of theoretically possible combinations of these sounds exceeds the number of atoms postulated for the entire universe (1970:8). In addition, an enormous number of languages is spoken around the world. The exact number is difficult to ascertain and depends on the classification system used. The *Atlas for Anthropology* (Spencer and Johnson 1968) lists 47 language families—that is, evolutionarily related groups of currently spoken languages. Figure 7-4 shows 156 major languages that are spoken in the world today, and hundreds more minor languages are spoken by small, relatively isolated groups of people. In addition, many languages are split into dialects, some of which are so different from one another that they may be mutually incomprehensible. For example, a German speaker from the Swiss capital of Bern has difficulty understanding a German-speaking Swiss from the mountain villages of Uri, a scant sixty miles away.

All around the globe, then, billions of people talk to each other every day in their own *speech communities*,

using their particular dialect to communicate, to discuss the world around them. Each group takes its own speech form for granted, accepting its sounds as natural, the categories it employs as logical, its grammatical structure as correct, the world view it provides as inherent in the nature of the universe. Other languages or dialects are regarded as comical, limited, or strange. No universal words or phrases that mean the same thing wherever they are spoken exist. Even though it is possible to analyze language in the quiet of the linguistics laboratory, we can only make sense of how a language is used by its speakers if we go to the speech community and observe the people in their everyday lives. Language is deeply rooted in culture; only in the cultural context does speech acquire its meaning.

Consider the concept of time. The passage of time affects every human being. We even have a system for calibrating time—seconds, minutes, hours, days, and so forth—that is becoming universal as industrial civilization spreads across the earth. But as any experienced, sensitive traveler knows, people from different cultures have very different concepts of time, even when they speak to one another in the same language (the native language of one of them, perhaps, or a mutually understood third language).

For example, middle-class Americans tend to think of time almost like a road along which we pass. We compartmentalize time, performing whatever tasks we consider appropriate to each section of the road. We schedule our time precisely and live with a constant orientation toward the future, toward what we are going to do next.

Time with us is handled much like a material; we earn it, spend it, save it, waste it. To us it is somewhat immoral to have two things going on at the same time. In Latin America it is not uncommon for one man to have a number of simultaneous jobs which he either carries on from one desk or which he moves between, spending a small amount of time on each.

While we look to the future, our view of it is limited. The future to us is the foreseeable future, not the future of the South Asian that may involve centuries. Indeed, our perspective is so short as to inhibit the operation of a good many practical

THE PRINCIPAL LANGUAGES OF THE WORLD

	Millions		Millions		Millions		Millions
Afrikaans (S. Africa)	5	Georgian (USSR)	3	Luri (Iran)	1	Santali (India)	4
Albanian	3	German	120	Macedonian (Yugoslavia)	1	Sepedi (see Sotho, Northern)	
Amharic (Ethiopia)	9	Gilaki (Iran)	1	Madurese (Indonesia)	7	Serbo-Croatian (Yugoslavia)	18
Annamese (see Vietnamese)		Gondi (India)	2	Makua (S.E. Africa)	2	Shan (Burma)	1
Arabic	125	Greek	10	Malagasy (Madagascar)	8	Shona (S.E. Africa)	4
Armenian	4	Guarani (mainly Paraguay)	3	Malay-Indonesian	95	Siamese (see Thai)	
Assamese (1) (India)	13	Gujarati (1) (India)	30	Malayalam (1) (India)	24	Sindhi (India; Pakistan)	9
Azerbaijani (USSR; Iran)	8	Hakka (China)	21	Malinke-Bambara-Dyula (Africa)	5	Sinhalese (Sri Lanka)	10
Bahase (See Malay-Indonesian)		Hausa (W. and Central Africa)	18	Mandarin (China)	650	Slovak	4
Balinese	3	Hebrew	3	Mazandarani (Iran)	1	Slovene (Yugoslavia)	2
Baluchi (Pakistan; Iran)	3	Hindi (1) (4)	209	Marathi (1) (India)	51	Somali (E. Africa)	4
Bashkir (USSR)	1	Hindustani (4)		Mbundu (Umbundu group)		Sotho, Northern (S. Africa)	2
Batak (Indonesia)	2	Hungarian (or Magyar)	13	(S. Angola)	2	Sotho, Southern (S. Africa)	2
Bemba (S. Central Africa)	1	Ibibio (see Efik)		Mbundu (Kimbundu group)		Spanish	213
Bengali (1) (Bangladesh; India)	123	Ibo (or Igbo) (W. Africa)	10	(Angola)	1	Sudanese (Indonesia)	15
Berber (2) (N. Africa)		Ijaw (W. Africa)	1	Mende (Sierra Leone)	1	Swahili (E. Africa)	20
Bhili (India)	4	Ilocano (Philippines)	4	Min (China)	39	Swedish	10
Bihari (India)	22	Iloko (see Ilocano)		Moldavian (ind. w/Rumanian)	.....	Tagalog (Philippines)	21
Bikol (Philippines)	2	Indonesian		Mongolian (see Khalkha)		Tajiki (USSR)	3
Bisaya (see Cebuano, Panay-		(see Malay-Indonesian)		Mordvin (USSR)	1	Tamil (1) (India; Sri Lanka)	53
Hiligaynon, and Samar-Leyte)		Italian	60	More (see Mossi)		Tatar (or Kazan-Turkic) (USSR)	6
Bugi (Indonesia)	2	Japanese	110	Mossi (W. Africa)	3	Telugu (1) (India)	53
Bulgarian	9	Javanese	44	Ndongo (see Mbundu-Kimbundu)		Thai (5)	30
Burmese	23	Kamba (E. Africa)	1	Nepali (Nepal; India)	10	Tibetan	7
Byelorussian (mainly USSR)	10	Kanarese (see Kannada)		Netherlandish (Dutch and Flem.)	20	Tigrinya (Ethiopia)	4
Cambodian (Cambodia, Asia)	7	Kannada (1) (India)	28	Ngala (or Lingala) (Africa)	2	Tiv (E. Central Nigeria)	1
Canarese (see Kannada)		Kanuri (W. and Cent. Africa)	2	Norwegian	4	Tswana (S. Africa)	2
Cantonese (China)	47	Kashmiri (1)	3	Nyamwezi-Sukuma (S.E. Africa)	1	Tulu (India)	1
Catalan (Spain; France; Andorra)	6	Kazakh (USSR)	5	Nyanja (S.E. Africa)	2	Turkish	39
Cebuano (Philippines)	8	Khalkha (Mongolia)	1	Oraon (see Kurukh)		Turkoman (USSR)	2
Chinese (3)		Kikongo (see Kongo)		Oriya (1) (India)	23	Twi-Fante (or Akan) (W. Africa)	4
Chuang (7) (China)		Kikuyu (or Gekoyo) (Kenya)	2	Panay-Hiligaynon (Philippines)	4	Uighur-(Sinkiang, China)	4
Czech	11	Kimbundu (see Mbundu-Kim.)		Panjabi (see Punjabi)		Ukrainian (mainly USSR)	42
Danish	5	Kirghiz (USSR)	2	Pashto (see Pushtu)		Umbundu	
Dayak (Borneo)	1	Kituba (Congo River)	2	Pedi (see Sotho, Northern)		(see Mbundu-Umbundu)	
Dutch (see Netherlandish)		Kongo (Congo River)	1	Persian	24	Urdu (1) (Pakistan; India)	57
Edo (W. Africa)	1	Konkani (India)	2	Polish	35	Uzbek (USSR)	9
Efik	2	Korean	52	Portugese	124	Vietnamese	37
English	358	Kumauni (India)	1	Provencal (Southern France)	6	Visayan (see Cebuano, Panay-	
Esperanto	1	Kurdish (S. W. of Caspian Sea)	7	Punjabi (1) (India; Pakistan)	55	Hiligaynon, and Samar-Leyte	
Estonian	1	Kurukh (or Oraon) (India)	1	Pushto (mainly Afghanistan)	15	White Russian (see Byelorussian)	
Ewe (W. Africa)	2	Lao (5) (Laos, Asia)	3	Quechua (S. America)	6	Wolof (W. Africa)	2
Finnish	5	Latvian (or Lettish)	2	Rajasthani (India)	21	Wu (China)	42
Flemish (see Netherlandish)		Lingala (see Ngala)		Romanian	22	Xhosa (S. Africa)	4
French	90	Lithuanian	3	Rundi (S. Central Africa)	3	Yi (China)	3
Fula (W. Africa)	7	Luba-Lulua (Zaire)	3	Russian (Great Russian only)	233	Yiddish (6)	
Galician (Spain)	2	Luganda (see Ganda)		Rwanda (S. Central Africa)	6	Yoruba (W. Africa)	12
Galla (Ethiopia)	7	Luhya (or Luhia) (Kenya)	1	Samar-Leyte (Philippines)	1	Zhuang (7) (China)	
Ganda (or Luganda) (E. Africa)	3	Luo (Kenya)	1	Sango (Central Africa)	1	Zulu (S. Africa)	4

(1.) One of the fourteen languages of the Constitution of India. (2.) Here considered a group of dialects. (3.) See Mandarin, Cantonese, Wu, Min, and Hakka. The "national language" (Guoyu) is a standardized form of Mandarin as spoken in the area of Peking. (4.) Hindi and Urdu are essentially the same language, Hindustani. As the official language of India it is written in the Devanagari script and called Hindi. As the official language of Pakistan it is written in a modified Arabic script and called Urdu. (5.) Thai includes Central, Southwestern, Northern and Northeastern Thai. The distinction between Northeastern Thai and Lao is political rather than linguistic. (6.) Yiddish is usually considered a variant of German, though it has its own standard grammer, dictionaries, a highly developed literature, and is written in Hebrew characters. Speakers number about 3,000,000. (7.) A group of Thai-like dialects with about 9 million speakers.

Figure 7-4
The Principal Languages of the World
Total number of speakers of languages spoken by at least one million persons (midyear 1975); Parenthesized numbers after names of languages refer to notes below table. (Source: Sidney S. Culbert, Assoc. Professor of Psychology, University of Washington)

projects, such as sixty- and one-hundred-year conservation projects requiring public support and public funds (Hall 1959:20).

Middle-class Americans find it difficult to adjust to other people's concepts of time. When we make a firm appointment, we expect at most a ten- to fifteen-minute margin of error. In Latin American countries, however, arriving forty minutes "late" (in our language) is to arrive "on time" (in theirs).

Nonverbal Communication **But language is only part of the story of human communication. We also use many means of nonverbal communication. In his pioneering and meticulous studies, Birdwhistell has discovered that the human face alone is capable of**

All societies mark the passage of time, though each in its own manner. Moslems pause five times during each day to pray, when they are called to prayer from the Minaret. The units of time a society marks, and the significance they attach to the passing of time sequences, is a major cultural mechanism for organizing people's perception of the world and society in which they participate. Different cultural conceptions of time are among the many factors which make it difficult for people from different societies to understand and cooperate with each other.

making some 250,000 different expressions (1970:8)! And people use not only their faces for nonverbal communication but also their fingers, hands, arms, shoulders, heads, trunks, hips, and legs—and in multiple combinations. They can also communicate through the sense of smell, by manipulating objects, and by altering the space between themselves and others. In fact, if we placed two persons in a box and completely recorded all their behavior down to microscopic levels, we could isolate the generation of between 2,500 and 5,000 bits of information per second (Birdwhistell 1970:3).

John F. Kennedy and Lyndon B. Johnson were successively presidents of the United States. However, their styles of communicating, both verbally and nonverbally, were quite different, a fact which at times made it difficult for them to get along with each other.

Nobody suggests that this awesome barrage of messages is part of the conscious experience of human beings. The study of communication is still in its infancy, and it would be presumptuous to claim that we are aware of all the ways in which we transmit and receive nonverbal signals. We do know, however, that human beings constantly communicate by nonverbal methods, that these communication systems are numerous and complex, and that they vary from culture to culture.

To the anthropologist who scans the nonverbal communication behavior of the various cultures of the world, it seems an almost hopeless task to complete even a simple inventory of gestures and their meanings. Take American society as an example. Through the simple act of shaking hands, an American can communicate enthusiasm, affection, concern, disinterest, boredom, icy tactfulness, sexual excitement, and probably a host of other responses as well. Raising one's eyebrows can suggest a questioning attitude, lack of comprehension, querulousness, thoughtfulness, or a sense of the ironic. Even such a presumably standardized gesture as the military salute may communicate a vast array of messages:

> By shifts in stance, facial expression, the velocity or duration of the movement of salutation, and even in the selection of inappropriate contexts for the act, the soldier could dignify, ridicule, demean, seduce, insult, or promote the recipient of the salute. By often almost imperceptible variations in the performance of the act, he could comment upon the bravery or cowardice of his enemy or ally, could signal his attitude toward army life or give a brief history of the virtuosity of a lady from whom he had recently arisen (Birdwhistell 1970:78–80).

Gestures also have very different meanings in different cultural contexts. Among middle-class Americans, for example, the pursing of the lips can communicate hesitancy or thoughtfulness, but among the Hanunóo of the Philippines, the degree of lip pursing is used to indicate the distance between the gesturer and what he or she is talking about. We whistle to express our enthusiasm over the performance of a sports team, but in Europe such whistling is a gesture of severe disapproval. We expect visitors to our home to wait until they are asked to sit down unless they are very close friends. In Samoa, a visitor signifies his or her friendly intentions by walking into one's home and sitting down directly, without waiting to be asked.

Conversely, the same message may be expressed quite differently from culture to culture. The intimate affection we express with a kiss is communicated by rubbing noses among Eskimos and inhabitants of parts of Polynesia. In America we nod our heads forward in assent, but this sentiment is expressed in different ways by other peoples:

> A Bengali servant in Calcutta rocks his head rapidly from shoulder to shoulder, usually four times, in assent; in Delhi a Moslem boy throws his head diagonally backward with a slight turning of the neck for the same purpose; and the Kandyan Singhalese bends the head diagonally forward to the right with an incredibly graceful turning of the chin, often accompanying this with a cross-legged curtsey, arms partly crossed, palms upward (LaBarre 1947:50–51).

The list of such examples is apparently endless. Just as no universal words or phrases exist, clearly there is no such thing as a truly universal gesture whose meaning remains constant throughout the world. Like language, nonverbal communications systems make sense only in their own cultural contexts; and like language, they are learned as part of the process by which each child is enculturated.

Theory

Systems

Before anthropologists could make significant headway in their attempts to understand the nature of human communication, they needed a conceptual scheme to organize their thoughts and eventually their research. This scheme was provided by the linguistic philosopher Charles Morris in a short but influential pamphlet, *Foundations of the Theory of Signs* (1938), in which he introduced the science of *semiotic*, the systematic study of signs.

It is often useful to regard all communication as the operation of signs in systems—that is, to study entire communications systems rather than a series of isolated examples such as those presented in the previous section. A communications system, which is simply an organization of related signs, has three main aspects: semantics, syntax, and pragmatics. *Semantics* is the relationship between signs and what they represent; the study of semantics is essentially the study of meaning. *Syntax* is the relationship between the signs themselves; the study of syntax is the study of the rules of sequence and combination of the signs, often called *grammar* by lay persons. *Pragmatics* is the relationship between signs and their users; the study of pragmatics is the study of how communication affects people.

Students of language—usually known as linguists—have traditionally studied one of two major areas: historical linguistics or descriptive linguistics. *Historical linguistics* deals with such questions as how, where, and when the languages of the world originated, what extinct languages were like, and how contemporary languages are related to one another. *Descriptive linguistics* entails the careful recording,

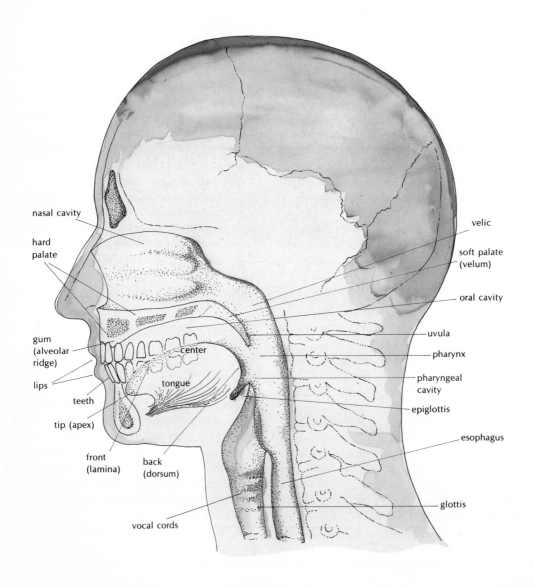

Figure 7-5

The Human Articulatory Apparatus

The positioning of the tongue in the mouth in relation to the points of articulation shown here helps form the sounds of speech: contoids (consonant sounds) and vocoids (vowel sounds) (see figs. 7-6 and 7-7).

Figure 7-6

Modified International Phonetic Alphabet Symbols of Vocoids

In each box the I.P.A. symbol is indicated above an English word, the vowel sign of which is the sound the symbol stands for.

		Points of articulation in mouth: front to back		
		front	central	back
Relative height of tongue in mouth	high	i (beat)	ɨ (bit)	u (boot)
	mid	e (bet)	ə (but)	o (boat)
	low	æ (bat)	a (bottle)	ɔ (bought)

description, and analysis of existing languages. In their historical or descriptive studies, linguists use some carefully refined concepts—concepts that are not difficult to grasp, although the terminology may seem unfamiliar.

At the most basic level, human speech consists of utterances—series of sounds produced by the mouth, larynx, and related areas of the vocal system. The human adult can produce an enormous number of vocal sounds, and linguists can determine how each sound is produced by the position of the tongue, the hardness of breath, the shape of the lips, the use of the voice, and so on. Figure 7-5 shows a cross section of a head and throat illustrating the points at which these sounds are articulated. Figures 7-6 and 7-7 demonstrate how all the sounds available to speakers of English are formed by combining these features of articulation. (*Contoids* are consonant sounds; *vocoids* are vowel sounds.)

Utterances are clearly not heard simply as undifferentiated sounds, but are perceived as a sequence of sound units, or *phonemes*. We hear the word *p i g* as a series of three sounds, and even though each phoneme is meaningless in itself, their particular nature and arrangement enable us to distinguish *p i g* from other words such as *d i g*, *p e g*, or *p i ck*. (By the way, it is important not to confuse letters with phonemes; letters are merely written symbols which more or less represent spoken sounds.)

Speech consists not only of perceived units of sound but also of units of meaning, or *morphemes*. *P i g* not only sounds different from *p e g*, *p i ck*, or *b i g*; it also means something different. Some morphemes, such as *p i g*, can stand alone and are called *free morphemes*. Others, such as the morpheme *plurality* in English, can only occur when attached to another morpheme; these are called *bound morphemes*. *P i g s*, for example, consists of the free morpheme *p i g* and the bound morpheme *plural*, in this case represented by the sound *s*. The morpheme *plural* may be represented in other ways, of course, as in the bound morpheme *r e n* attached to the end of the free morpheme *c h i l d* to yield the plural *c h i l d r e n*. All the different versions of the same morpheme are called *allomorphs*. Look at the list of words

Figure 7-7
Modified International Phonetic Alphabet Symbols for Contoids

The points of articulation shown in fig. 7-5 are indicated along the top of this diagram. Along the left-hand side the categories of action performed by the articulatory apparatus are indicated.

Stops—stopping the air flow at the point of articulation. *Plain* stops are unmodified. *Aspirated* stops (h) allow air to escape forcefully after the release of the stopped air flow. *Affricated* stops (s, z) allow air to escape forcefully through the narrow slit made between the tongue and point of articulation after the release of the stopped air flow. *Glottalized* stops (') involve closing off the pharynx simultaneously with stopping the air flow at the point of articulation. *Labialized* stops involve "puckering" or rounding the lips as the air flow is released after the stop.

Fricatives—confining the channel of air flow and thus producing a "rushing" sound due to air friction against the passage walls at the point of articulation. *Slit* fricatives are formed in a tight, horizontal slit between the tongue and the point of articulation (the tongue is kept quite flat). *Grooved* fricatives are formed by pushing up the edges of the tongue (pulling down the center line of the tongue) and forcing air through the groove that results at the point of articulation.

Laterals—articulating with the center of the tongue, directing the air flow laterally around the edges.

Nasals—closing off the mouth with the tongue and directing the air flow through the nasal passage exclusively.

Retroflex-articulating with the curled back tip of the tongue.

Flap-in a retroflex position, allowing the tip of the tongue to "slap" against the point of articulation.

Trills—allowing the tongue to vibrate as the air flow passes between it and the point of articulation.

All contoids may be either *voiced* (vd.) or *voiceless* (vl.)

			Bilabial	Labiodental	Dental	Alveolar	Alveopalatal	Dorsovelar	Uvular	Glottal
STOPS	Plain	vl.	p			t	tʸ	k	q	ʔ
		vd.	b			d	dʸ	g		
	Aspirated	vl.	pʰ			tʰ		kʰ		
		vd.								
	Affricated	vl.				tˢ	tˢ̌			
		vd.				dᶻ	dᶽ			
	Laterally affricated	vl.				tˡ				
		vd.				dˡ				
	Glottalized	vl.	p'		.	t'		k'		
		vd.								
	Labialized	vl.	pʷ			tʷ		kʷ		
		vd.	bʷ			dʷ		gʷ		
FRICATIVES	Slit	vl.		f	θ			x		h
		vd.		v	δ			γ		
	Grooved	vl.				s	š			
		vd.				z	ž			
LATERALS		vl.				ḷ				
		vd.				l				
NASALS		vl.	m̥			n̥	ñ̥	η		
		vd.	m			n	ñ	η		
RETROFLEX		vl.								
		vd.				ɼ				
FLAP		vl.								
		vd.				ř				
TRILLS		vl.				r̥				
		vd.				r̃			R	

in figure 7-8 and see if you can discover all the allo-morphs of the English morpheme *plural.*

Just as phonemes should not be confused with letters, so morphemes should not be confused with words. *P i g s* is one word composed of two mor-phemes. Obviously, every word boundary must neces-sarily be a morpheme boundary as well, but not all morpheme boundaries are word boundaries, since some morpheme boundaries occur within words. An example is the boundary occurring between the *d* sound and the *r* sound in the word *c h i l d r e n.*

Those who study nonverbal communication have not yet developed conceptual tools comparable to those developed by linguists. The study of body move-ment, or *kinesics,* and the study of the manipulation of space, *proxemics,* are still too new to have devel-oped anything resembling the standardized technical vocabulary of linguistics. However, students of these areas have discovered that nonverbal communication shares several features with language: It is segmented into indivisible units, meaningless in themselves; there are syntactic rules for combining these units into meaningful gestures; and the meanings of the gestures can only be ascertained when the entire context of the communicated message is considered.

Processes

American culture strongly emphasizes linear models. Because we read from left to right, it is easy to imagine ourselves as hearing speech in a linear, "left-to-right" manner. Nothing could be farther from the truth.

Let us return again to the word *p i g.* Obviously the phoneme *p* consists of a whole bundle of features of articulation: It is a nonvocalized, bilabial, aspirated stop. But when we hear the *p,* we do not perceive these individual features (unless we are studying linguistics); we perceive the whole unit of sound, the phoneme. The same is true of the whole word; although we know that *p i g* is a word consisting of three phonemes, we rarely perceive it that way. Even though we represent it as a sequence, we perceive it as a whole bundle of phonemes unless we are asked to break it down into its individual sound units. In fact, our perception that the word *pig* is a whole is closer to the truth than the

Figure 7-8
Singular and Plural Forms of Selected English Words

Do not confuse the way words are written with the way they *sound.* Say these words out loud. Listen. *Hear* how they change from singular to plural. Now try listing the different "sounds" of the *plurality morpheme* in English. Can you write out the singular and plural forms of these words using the I.P.A. notation system? Can you write out a list of the allomorphs of plurality using the I.P.A. notation system?

Singular	Plural
girl	girls
man	men
sock	socks
fish	fish
ox	oxen
ax	axes
pill	pills
sheep	sheep
plate	plates
woman	women*
child	children
half	halves*
loaf	loaves*
kid	kids

* *These are a bit tricky:* listen *to the words.*

notion that it is a sequence of phonemes. The signal we hear as *pig* cannot be electronically broken down into a succession of constituent phonemes: *Physically, the three phonemes are spread out along the entire length of the word* (Denes and Pinson 1963).

Much the same is true of words: We perceive them as whole bundles of meaning rather than as a sequence of meaningful morphemes. Following the lead of Floyd Lounsbury (1956) and Ward Goodenough (1956), anthropological linguists have studied semantics in terms of these bundles of meaning. A school of anthropological linguistics known as componential analysis has arisen, and the efforts of these scholars leave no doubt: The meaning of words is not a matter of units but rather, again, of feature bundles. Thus, for example, no single unit of meaning exists for *father*. The word refers to a bundle of features that includes (a) male, (b) first ascending generation, (c) noncollateral (lineal), (d) consanguineal, and (e) relative (see chaps. 8 and 9).

The same is true for phrases and sentences. Although we obviously hear the beginning of a sentence before the end, research is revealing that we understand or decode sentences as whole bundles of features rather than as sequences of morphemes.

This interpretation of how we understand sentences was introduced into modern linguistics by Noam Chomsky, who in 1957 published a small book called *Syntactic Structures*. In this work he criticized those linguists who, following in the tradition of Leonard Bloomfield (1933), divided sentences into their *Immediate Constituents*—basic units that were supposed to be perceived sequentially. Chomsky showed that Immediate Constituent analysis could not account for many of our linguistic capacities, such as the ability to create an infinite number of sentences, to understand sentences that we have never heard before, to know whether nonsense sentences (such as *The fragile pink whale flew gorgeously*) are grammatically correct or not, and to understand unambiguously the (at least) two meanings of the sentence *They talked about the shooting of the hunters* (either the hunters are shooting or they are getting shot). Our ability to perform these tasks, Chomsky argued, derives from the fact that we understand sentences as wholes, not as strings of isolated units (Immediate Constituents).

In order to explain our capacity to create and understand whole sentences, Chomsky introduced the concept of two structures in language. *Surface structure* is the arrangement of the units in an uttered sentence. *Deep structure* is the structure underlying the relationships among the units of the sentence. The deep structure precedes the surface structure, both logically (in a linguistic analysis of the sentence) and operationally (in the way human beings create and understand the sentence). This means that in both the generating and the perception of a sentence, the deep structure determines the "reading" of the surface structure.

To summarize, we have been developing the idea that, for the sake of analysis, we can break language down into different levels of units, but that in the actual process of speech communication, these units are bundled together in various ways. The same holds true for nonverbal communication. We can analyze the facial movements that constitute a smile, but much more goes into smiling than a description of the mechanics would suggest. The movement of the lips is merely part of a gesture that includes cheek, eyelid, and even eyebrow and forehead movements—and even then the smile is fully comprehensible only in the context in which it occurs.

The process of human communication, it becomes apparent, is extremely complex. Anthropologists are gradually refining their theoretical models, isolating significant units of communication, and learning how these units operate within the systems of which they are parts. So far, we have made more progress in delineating the units of these systems than in understanding their dynamic processes. But even with this limitation, students of communication can engage in some very sophisticated analyses of communicative behavior.

Analysis

Folk Perspective

The material presented so far has been quite abstract except for several examples. Now we shall present some case material and indicate the procedures by which anthropological analyses are made. As we have emphasized several times, when analyzing case

Two Japanese Zen Buddhist priests are greeting each other. Their mode of communicating is nonverbal. Their body gestures (bowing) are *kinesic* behavior, their careful distancing (use of space) *proxemic* behavior.

materials it is crucial to keep in mind that one group of people—the researchers—is trying to "explain" the behavior of another group of people—the subjects. Naturally both subjects and researchers will have points of view about this behavior and they may be quite different, since each will reflect the assumptions, categories, beliefs, and values of the people who hold them. And although the points of view are equal in that both are "true," they are not equivalent; they represent qualitatively different perspectives.

Let us begin with a description of some nonverbal behavior that was filmed by Birdwhistell and others, an excerpt from a sequence in which a mother is changing the diaper of a baby standing on her lap. The entire segment of behavior described takes place in one and three-fourths seconds (see fig. 7-9).

The onset of the film shows the mother with her left arm supporting and balancing the baby's weight. The mother's left hand assists her right hand in the removal of the diaper. It is to be noted that the mother's right hand, at the wrist, is pressed against the extended right arm of the baby. Simultaneously, the lateral aspects of the thumb side of the mother's right hand press against the baby's body in the lateral abdominal region.

In the next pictograph we see that the baby's hand has started to move down. Mother continues her pressure on the baby's upper arm, but she moves the thumb aspect of her right hand away from the baby's body and directs it in the removal of the diaper.

The third pictograph is a continued movement on the part of both which extends into the next picture.

In the fifth pictograph, as the infant's hand makes contact with the curtain, mother presses against the body of the infant with her right wrist, an action which she continues in the sixth picture.

In the seventh pictograph the baby relinquishes its hold on the curtain and begins to move its hand down. At the same time, the mother moves her hand away from the child's body and turns her attention completely to the task of removing the diaper.

In the eighth, ninth, and tenth pictographs we see the continued progress of the infant's hand down while mother continues to busy herself with the diaper.

In the eleventh pictograph, mother presses against the upper arm of the infant and reverses the movement of the infant's arm.

By the twelfth pictograph we see something entirely different. Now she pushes not only up but toward the baby's body (Birdwhistell 1970:21-22).

It should be noted that although the film of this behavior may be considered as close to raw—that is, untampered with—data as we can get, Birdwhistell's description of the data is already an abstraction that reflects his point of view (etics). His viewpoint is especially evident in his description of the twelfth pictograph, where he tells us we are seeing "something entirely different." It is also important that the raw data should not be confused with the participants' views of the data. The mother's conception of what was happening—her folk perspective (emics)—was merely that she was changing the child's diaper. It is unlikely that she perceived her behavior in the microscopic detail

Figure 7-9
Nonverbal Behavior
Birdwhistell's pictograph sequence of a mother changing the diaper of a baby standing on her lap.

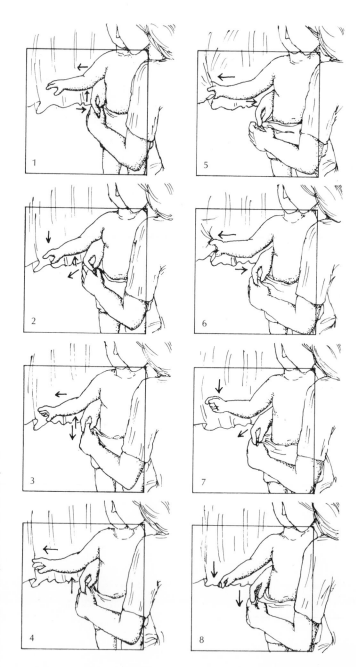

in which it was recorded and described. If we are to improve our understanding of human behavior, these three levels of phenomena—raw data, emics, and etics—must be kept rigorously separated.

The Analytical Perspective

Analyzing data takes much more time and work than collecting data. Birdwhistell and his colleagues spend about an hour analyzing a second's worth of film; and it may take months for a linguist to analyze a recorded text. Let us see the kind of analysis that can be performed on data such as the example just presented.

For the sequence of nonverbal behavior involving the changing of a child's diaper, Birdwhistell provides the following analysis:

> To review, in the first series, she pushed upward to extend the baby's arm, she pushed against the body to push it down. In the second instance the pressure against the baby's body indicated that the hand should come down and toward the body either of the mother or of the child. Pictures twelve and thirteen are critical. She now sends both messages at once, seemingly emphasizing one of the messages somewhat more strongly than the other. This time she uses not only the wrist but she curls her thumb against the baby's body. At the same time, she thrusts her wrist against the child's upper arm. Thus, the child is in what Gregory Bateson has called the double-bind—neither of the messages can be obeyed without disobeying the other. (1970: 22-23)

The analyst perceives message units in the mother's behavior, gestures that instruct the child to raise or lower its arm. He also sees what looks like destructive communication when the mother simultaneously "tells" the child to lower and raise its arm—putting the child into a double bind. He goes on to emphasize that this event took only one and three-fourths seconds, indicating that the mother could put her child into hundreds of such double binds every day. This fact is significant because the mother involved has a schizophrenic child. A growing body of evidence suggests that what has been called mental illness—especially schizophrenia—may be individuals' respon-

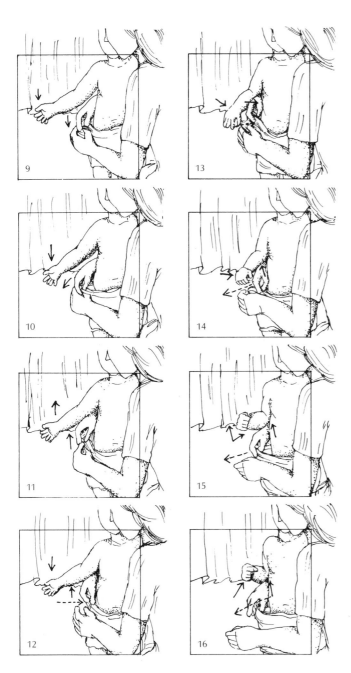

ses to family communication networks in which they are constantly placed in double binds and other damaging communication situations (see, for example, Bateson et al. 1956).

On the other hand, caution must be exercised. Bird-whistell knew the mother's case history before he analyzed her behavior. We must ask: To what extent did his knowledge of the situation precondition him to find such pathogenic behavior? If he had such expectations, did they affect his analysis? We are not criticizing, merely emphasizing the subjective as well as objective difficulties the analysis of human behavior presents. For these reasons it is important that anthropologists emphasize the separation of emics and etics—the folk and analytical perspectives, respectively—in their analytical procedures. If we can accomplish this, we will have more confidence in the validity of our analyses.

Conclusions

Schools of Thought

All students of human communication agree that it consists of many kinds of units and that these units are related to each other and to what they represent in patterned, regulated ways. Agreement even exists on the nature of these verbal and nonverbal units. Most disagreement centers on the larger models constructed by various scholars to represent the total workings of human verbal or nonverbal communication systems.

Before the publication of Chomsky's *Syntactic Structures* (1957), most linguists saw language as various *units* (phonemes, morphemes, and so on) arranged *in ordered sequences* according to grammatical rules. This school of thought, known variously as the Bloomfieldian (Bloomfield 1933), Item and Arrangement, Immediate Constituent, or Taxonomic School, has gradually given way to the Chomskian (1957) and post-Chomskian onslaught (see, for example, Chafe 1970). Most linguists now regard language as a system that consists of basic *units and processes* (rules) by which these units are arranged in sequences. This point of view has come to be called the Item and Process or Transformational School. Thus the static perspective emphasizing *arrangements* has given way to a more dynamic orientation stressing *processes*.

One major contribution of Chomsky and his followers was their insistence that every description of a language must, in effect, be a *theory* regarding that language's processes. Thus a general linguistic model should be a *theory of what language is*. We will know what language is when we have analyzed all the world's languages and come to understand their common structural and dynamic features.

Such formulations have led Chomsky into the area where linguistics and psychology intersect, and his theories have stimulated new, exciting psycholinguistic research. Chomsky has led a frontal attack on behaviorist psychology, which for many decades has reigned supreme in American psychology. B. F. Skinner's writings on language in particular and on human nature in general have come under persuasive assault (Chomsky 1959, 1971). Chomsky's most radical conclusion is that human beings are not born with blank minds, totally empty vessels ready to learn a culture and a language in a passive, stimulus-response manner. He and his followers argue instead that it is impossible to account for the quick, efficient manner in which human beings learn their native language (especially the deep structure) unless they are biologically programed to be language learners through certain structural features present in the brain at birth (Chomsky 1968). This innate capacity is seen as the result of the evolutionary development that has differentiated human beings from apes and other animals.

Chomsky's Transformational School has itself come under attack, largely for its initial insistence on rigidly separating syntax and semantics. In response to such cirticism, Chomsky revised his model of a transformational grammar considerably (1965). Now both semantics and syntax are crucial elements of a grammar, which consists of four fundamental components:

1. Base component: Sometimes called the phrase structure component, the base component generates the deep structures of sentences and feeds into two components: the transformational component and the semantic component.

2. Transformational component: This component consists of a set of rules, called transformational rules, that rearrange, add to, and delete elements of the deep structure of sentences; they then generate ac-

Noam Chomsky, America's most influential linguist, who developed the approach to linguistics known as transformational grammar (or transformational linguistics). Rejecting previous practice which viewed language as items (units) in arrangements, Chomsky proposed that it is the *process* through which these arrangements are formed that is crucial. To account for this process he proposed that a "deep structure" underlies the "surface structure" of language, and that human beings are born genetically pre-programmed to master the process of generating deep and surface structures. His work has made a major impact on psycholinguistics and the study of language acquisition.

ceptably arranged strings of words and morphemes—the so-called derived surface structure of sentences.

3. Semantic component: **This component also consists of a set of rules, called rules of semantic interpretation, which operate on the deep structures generated by the base component; in so doing these rules generate the meanings of sentences.**

4. Phonological component: **This set of rules operates on the surface structures generated by the transformational component and converts them to their representation as sequences of phonemes, then operates on the phonemes, converting them to actual sounds. The result is the actual spoken sentences we hear.**

Despite this remodeling, criticism continues. Wallace Chafe argues that what the transformationalists call deep structure is, in fact, nothing more than semantic structure (1970).

The study of nonverbal communication—kinesics and proxemics—is too new to have generated such high-level theoretical disputes. However, the major portion of the work being done in this area has been influenced by Chomsky's vision of the nature of language. Erving Goffman, who writes about the structure of relations in public (1971); Paul Watzlawick, Janet Beavin, and Don Jackson, who discuss the pragmatics of human communication (1967); Edward T. Hall, who analyzes the use of space (1966) and time (1959) in human communication; and Ray Birdwhistell, who presents what he has learned about kinesics and context in communicative behavior (1970)—they all share a view of *communication as process* rather than as simply a series of items in prescribed arrangements.

Author's Conclusions

I believe that the ultimate concern in studying human communication must be to account for the connection(s) between signals—sounds and nonverbal gestures—and meaning. How are human signals linked to their meanings? How do these signals affect human beings? These are the questions we must answer. Stated in the terminology of semiotic, I contend that the most important questions lie in the areas of semantics and pragmatics.

It is becoming increasingly clear that these questions will resist investigation as long as we arbitrarily

Human communication. A soldier comforts his grief-stricken comrade whose friend has just been killed in combat. The act is a whole, a complex unity far greater than the sum of its verbal and nonverbal components.

limit our inquiries along historically structured lines. For example, although it is apparent to everyone that in actual speech meaning is often communicated by the way words are *intoned*, this phenomenon is ignored by most linguists and assigned a separate label—*paralinguistics*. The same is true of speaking and gesturing:

> The more acute observers will note that when one speaks, he is not simply presenting data which linguists term phonetics or phonemics or morphology or simple syntax. When these linguistic particles are put together in a communicational frame, in actual speech one does a series of things with one's body. In speaking these sentences, I do not have very much choice about which movements I make. Each one of these sentences, within its context, requires a very special set of movements. (Birdwhistell 1970:17)

Indeed, when human beings communicate, they constantly underline, deny, render ironic, satirize, emphasize, and in many other ways comment upon what they are "saying" with diverse and highly conventionalized (culturally prescribed) paralinguistic and nonverbal gestures. It is this total communicational whole from which we extract meaning and to which we respond with actions, feelings, and fantasies. We may now be forced by our inadequate models and investigative tools to separate linguistic, paralinguistic, and nonverbal communication behavior for analysis. But in the end, we must develop an inclusive model that enables us to understand not only the rules that govern the processes of these individual systems but also the rules that relate these systems to each other and produce a communication whole that is more than the sum of its parts.

Summary

Communication is fundamental to human culture. It takes two basic forms: verbal and nonverbal. Language, the most important form of verbal communication, is a phenomenon that seems to be uniquely human.

All languages have thirteen basic design features: a vocal-auditory channel; broadcast transmission and directional reception; rapid fading; total feedback; discreteness—the very limited number of sounds each language uses; duality of patterning into units of sound and units of meaning; unlimited productivity; semanticity—the fact that utterances have meaning; arbitrariness—the arbitrary association of sounds with meanings; interchangeability—any normal human can utter and hear anything another human can; specialization—language is a specialized form of communication and can directly accomplish little else; displacement—the capacity to refer to distant or even nonexistent objects or concepts; and cultural transmission—the fact that language is learned in human culture and not acquired by genetic inheritance.

Since many thousands of languages and dialects are spoken in the world today, the reconstruction of the evolution of language is a difficult task. On the basis of the available evidence, it seems likely that speech first emerged at the *Homo erectus* stage of human evolution. The control centers of language in the human brain are mainly located in the cerebral cortex, which is responsible for the higher intellectual functions.

Nonverbal communication involves a wide variety of facial expressions, body movements, gestures, and other stimuli, many of which are unconsciously transmitted and perceived. The work of Ray Birdwhistell reveals the astonishing complexity of human nonverbal communication.

It is useful to study communication from the perspective of semiotic, the systematic study of signs. In this approach, semantics is the study of meaning, syntax is the study of the relationships (of sequence and hierarchy) between the signs themselves, and pragmatics is the study of how signs affect people.

All languages consist of phonemes, or units of sound, and morphemes, units of meaning. Most modern linguists accept the view of Noam Chomsky that all natural languages are generated dynamically by an underlying set of elements and processes (a generative grammar) for their organization and representation. Humans are biologically programed by structural features present in the brain at birth to learn language through their innate competence in mastering linguistic structures. The science of linguistics is still in its infancy, however, and Chomsky's work has sparked a number of theoretical disputes.

It will be impossible to understand the nature of human communication fully until explanatory models can deal with the whole of human communication acts—that is, both verbal and nonverbal messages simultaneously.

Annotated Bibliography

Bateson, Gregory; Jackson, Donald J.; Haley, Jay; and Weakland, John (1956)   "Toward a Theory of Schizophrenia." *Behavioral Science* 1:251–54, reprinted in Allman, Lawrence R. and Jaffe, Dennis T., eds. (1976) *Readings in Abnormal Psychology: Contemporary Perspectives.* New York: Harper. One of the most important (though very brief) seminal papers using research on communication to redefine basic notions about the nature and genesis of "mental illness." This is the origin of the popularly used concept of the double bind as applied to unhealthy communication.

Chomsky, Noam (1968)   *Language and Mind.* New York: Harcourt. A simply written, short, readable work that explains the state of linguistics before the conception of generative grammar, and the implications of generative grammar with regard to our conceptualization of the mind and brain.

Denes, Peter B., and Pinson, Elliot N. (1973)   *The Speech Chain: The Physics and Biology of Spoken Language.* Garden City, N.Y.: Doubleday. Short, clear presentation of exactly what the title specifies.

Goffman, Erving (1971)   *Relations in Public.* New York: Harper Colophon. A clear, lively discussion of the rules that govern verbal and nonverbal behavior in public places.

Hall, Edward T. (1959)   *The Silent Language.* Garden City, N.Y.: Doubleday. Written originally as a guide for cross-cultural courtesy to be used by American diplomats, this gem has become a small classic. It is principally concerned with the nature of nonverbal communication.

(1966)   *The Hidden Dimension.* Garden City, N.Y.: Doubleday. Another classic, reporting on Hall's continuing research on the use of space by humans and other members of the animal kingdom.

Watzlawick, Paul; Beavin, Janet H.; and Jackson, Don D. (1967)   *The Pragmatics of Communication.* New York: Norton. Readable synthesis of communication theory, kinesics, proxemics, and psychology—with an emphasis on the personal consequences of unhealthy communication practices.

8
Social
Organization I:
Marriage and the Family

The World Context

Origins and Development through Time

Marriage and the family are universal features of human society. But how did they develop, why do they take such a variety of forms, and why do they take the particular forms that they do? Human beings have long speculated about the origins and development of marriage and the family, and, indeed, these speculations contributed to the emergence of anthropology as a distinct field of study. The theories of early scholars gave later investigators many topics to argue about and many subjects for intensive research.

One early view of marriage and the family was that proposed by J. J. Bachofen (1861). Early humans, he contended, lived in sexual promiscuity: There were no rules to the game. For some reason, women found this situation inconvenient and so invented marriage and established families by asserting their "motherright" (they knew their own children even if fathers did not). When marriage was institutionalized, fathers also became more certain about which children were theirs, and so began to assume the "fatherright" in order to

A !Kung San family group. Father smokes a cartridge shell pipe, baby romps, and mother grooms a young woman's hair for lice. Unlike many of the nonliterate societies discussed in this chapter, the !Kung do not have rigid postmarital residence rules. Rather, each group is composed of a core of male and female siblings along with their spouses and children. See Chapter 21.

assert their authority. Descent, family affiliation, and power had previously been traced through a line of related women, but it was now transmitted through males. In short, the evolutionary process was one in which patriarchy replaced matriarchy.

In the same year, Henry Maine, a British jurist, theorized that marriage and the family originated in primitive hordes in which people limited sexual relations at least to recognized pairs (1861). In Maine's scheme, male dominance characterized the earliest form of marriage and the family, so that patriarchy, not matriarchy, was the most primitve form of family and social organization. A controversy was in the making.

A Scottish lawyer, John McLennan, proposed that the family originated in early hordes that lived in dangerous circumstances (1865, 1867). As hunters and defenders, males were the more important sex. Females were less highly regarded, and infanticide of female offspring was practiced to reduce the number of mouths that had to be fed. The result was a shortage of women, and, in consequence, several males commonly shared one female. The continuing shortage of women encouraged the men to raid neighboring groups for mates. A captured female became a man's own property, and thus marriage was born. Also, since a man could capture more than one woman, the preferred marriage pattern became one of multiple wives rather than the previous custom of several men sharing one woman. The practice of capturing women made it necessary for men to devote their efforts toward getting wives from groups other than their own. Thus exogamy, the practice of marrying out of one's own group, was invented. In the past, a child could know its mother but not its father, and the family had been defined through women. But now that a man knew his children, they became his family. Like Bachofen, McLennan believed that matriarchy preceded patriarchy in the development of the family system.

Yet another lawyer, the American Lewis Henry Morgan, challenged this scheme in his complicated reconstruction of the origin and evolution of society (1870). Morgan based his reasoning about family forms on the kinship terminology information that he had gathered (See Chapter 9). He believed that the most primitive societies define families through relationships to females, while more advanced societies define them through relationships to males. Morgan thus also sided with Bachofen in plotting the course of family evolution from sexual anarchy through matrilineality to patrilineality with multiple spouses. Further progress led to the ultimate form of monogamous marriage, with equal recognition of both sides of the family—the form found, of course, in our own civilization.

Human imagination combined with a shortage of hard data to keep these fruitless arguments going. Edward Westermarck disputed the idea that the family originated in sexual promiscuity or horde living (1891). He based his analysis on the fact that humans tend to pair, and he posited a biologically based instinct against incest that promoted marriage out of the family. He also emphasized the biological needs of a helpless, unspecialized human infant, whose protection and nurture, he argued, required marriage and family. For Westermarck, the primary family of a man, a woman, and their children was a fact of human life and could be found at the core of all family forms.

These theorists and others of their time were working with sparse evidence. They wrote in an intellectual climate in which scholars were arguing about whether

The mobile American family. "We're home three weekends a year. Our camper is our real home." One should not confuse mobility with "freedom." For instance, one could speculate that the children of this family are far from free to form meaningful ties with friends and relatives; rather, the extreme mobility of their parents (in which they are apparently included, as evidenced by their travel patches) must tie the family group very tightly together, reducing extrafamilial ties.

the course of early human social evolution had been one of degeneration or progress. The early anthropological thinkers chose and marked out stages of development from primitive beginnings to the glories of Western civilization. They took the view that their primitive contemporaries must still be in the early evolutionary stages represented by subsistence technologies, and that other aspects of primitive culture, including marriage and family systems, must parallel those of ancient peoples at similar evolutionary stages.

The literature grew, and the early theories collapsed as the evidence accumulated. It became clear that the origins of marriage and the family were not going to be reconstructed easily. Contemporary marriage and family patterns varied even among people with similar technologies. Much more work needed to be done before anthropologists could even begin to comprehend the relations between family forms and subsistence technology.

Not all the previous work had been in vain, however. Specific variations in family form and kinship were recognized and studied. Anthropologists came to appreciate that this variation was limited, not infinite. A terminology to deal with the variation was developed, elaborated, and refined. Grand theories were reduced to less ambitious but more useful hypotheses that could be tested against increasingly better evidence.

Anthropologists in the early twentieth century gradually turned their attention away from the speculative search for origins to the more pragmatic gathering of data. What were the marriage patterns of other peoples? What forms of family were to be found? How did ecological factors influence the forms of social organization? Some investigators were interested in the specific histories of marriage and family within a culture. Others, such as Bronislaw Malinowski, were concerned with how aspects of culture such as marriage and family function to satisfy human biological and social needs (1931). Such investigators as A. R. Radcliffe-Brown were interested in how these cultural forms maintain a social structure in equilibrium with its environment (1935). Ruth Benedict focused on how each form contributes to a distinctive pattern of configuration of total culture that distinguishes one society from another (1934). The emphasis was on gathering data by going into the field, by learning at first hand what the practices of various peoples were. Anthropologists sought better descriptions of cultural diversity and used them to refute the early theories and to develop new ones.

In this chapter, we argue that some form of continuing association of men and women is necessary to care for and educate children. Many forms of grouping could serve the purpose, but marriage and the family appear to be ancient, enduring, and almost universal responses to this need. The need and the institutions that have developed around it seem to be based in both human biology and environmental challenges (see Chap. 3).

Human beings are born relatively undeveloped. The infant has much to learn, the capacity to learn much, and the need for a long period of learning before it can fend for itself. The woman bears the child and provides the initial care and nurture, and she thus fits easily into the role we call *mother*. The mother needs support and protection during the nurturing period. Humans have long divided labor on the basis of sex, and many of the needs of mother and offspring are most conveniently supplied by men. So a man takes the role of provider, the role we call *father*. More mating and more children continue the need of nurture and protection and tend to perpetuate the association.

When women, children, and supporting men live in common residence or proximity, the conditions are present for a *family*. The family is defined by a *social* assignment of rights and privileges and a *social* determination of the roles of spouse, parents, child, and siblings. Public recognition and acceptance of the relationship between men and women constitutes *marriage*. This family may take one of a number of forms that have evolved in response to basic biological needs, although the origins and development in any particular sequence may remain in doubt.

Contemporary Examples

A look at a few of the many varieties of marriage and family will show what the arguments were about.

Greece   In the rural Greek village of Vasilika, marriages with third cousins or closer relatives are forbidden (Friedl 1962). Traditional marriages are negotiated by the fathers of the couple, who might themselves be strangers to each other. The fathers work out a contract in which the girl's family agrees to give a stated amount of money and land to the groom. Once the contract is agreed to, the couple is considered to be engaged, and they then begin a long period of getting acquainted, visiting one another, and courtship. They are married in a formal religious ceremony followed by feasting and dancing at the home of the bride's father, after which they go to live in the groom's father's house.

Alaska: The Tlingit   Among the Tlingit of southwest Alaska, the preferred marriage is between a man and his father's sister, his mother's sister, his father's sister's daughter, or—most commonly in practice—the daughter of his mother's brother (Krause 1956; Oberg 1973). Not all kin who are what we would call cousins qualify. A marriage with father's sister's or mother's brother's children is considered to be an excellent one. A marriage with a paternal uncle's or a maternal aunt's child, however, is forbidden; such kin are considered to be one's siblings, and sexual relations with them fall under the incest taboo.

Rank and wealth are important to the Tlingit, and while a young man might have some say in choosing a bride, the actual choice is in the hands of his oldest maternal uncle, who can act or choose another to act for him as a go-between in arranging the marriage. The maternal uncle helps his nephew accumulate the property that serves as a gift to the bride's family.

A traditional marriage ceremony begins with a feast sponsored by the bride's father for the relatives of both sides (Krause 1956:153–155; Oberg 1973:34–37, 129). The couple observe but do not participate in the dancing and feasting of the guests. After the feast, the couple stay together and fast for four days, then go to live either in or near the house of the groom's maternal uncle. As they leave, the girl's parents give to the groom presents of the approximate value of those he has given them. The couple is considered to be married after four weeks have passed.

The Tlingit family system provides for a wealthy man to have more than one wife. A younger brother is expected to marry the wives of a deceased older brother.

United States: The Blackfeet   The Blackfeet of the northern plains of the United States married with little ceremony (Wissler 1911). Courtship was expected to precede marriage. Premarital sex experience was expected and praised in boys but was guarded against and condemned in girls. First cousins fell under the incest rules and were not regarded as potential marriage partners.

Marriages could develop from courtship, but they tended to be arranged by the fathers of the couple. The two families exchanged gifts of horses and other property, with the most substantial presents being given by the groom and his family to the family of the bride. After the bride had been lectured by her

A Blood Indian and his pony. Like the Blackfeet, traditional marriage form and post marriage residence practices as described in this chapter were intimately tied in with their hunting and gathering subsistence mode. The assault on their way of life which Anglo-American society precipitated has reduced many to poverty and introduced marriage practices of the wider society, which they now practice. The result has sometimes been tension and confusion regarding the extent to which traditional forms can and/or should be adhered to.

parents on proper behavior and the dangers of adultery, the couple set up housekeeping in their own tepee near one or the other of the couple's parents. This act signaled their marriage.

A successful man was expected to have more than one wife, and he often married sisters of his first wife. As potential wives, sisters-in-law were people a man could joke with, even licentiously—a privilege allowed with few other people. A man and his mother-in-law were supposed to keep out of each other's way and above all, were required not to speak to each other.

Africa: The Swazi   The Swazi of southeast Africa are most concerned that marriages be arranged to unite two kin groups and produce children (Kuper 1963:16–28). Young people often form sexual alliances within the boundaries of incest rules resembling those of the Tlingit. Some of these love affairs can lead to marriage if the parents agree to the couple's request that arrangements be made. All marriages are arranged by representatives of the families involved, who negotiate an agreement about how many cattle the groom's family will give the family of the bride. The marriage ceremony is conducted, and the couple proceed to live together, but the marriage is not final until these cattle have been delivered.

At the time for the ceremony the girl leaves her family home in a ritual departure, displaying an expected reluctance to leave. She pleads with her brothers to stop her from going, but then submits and goes with gifts to the compound of the groom's family. She then moves into her own hut in the family compound, but in household matters she is under the authority of her mother-in-law. She and her father-in-law are required to avoid each other, just as the groom and his mother-in-law practice avoidance whenever he visits his wife's natal village.

A man can have several wives, and he is required to provide a separate hut in the compound for each of them and their children. He can then spend his nights with each wife in turn.

India: The Nayar   Each of these cases represents practices that are fairly widespread, but a number of exceptional cases have been reported. The Nayar of the Malabar Coast of India periodically marry all girls approaching puberty to appropriately ranked hus-

bands in a common ceremony (Gough 1961:357–363). The couples stay together for three nights, after which the husbands are dismissed and the girls remain in their family homes, where they are free to accept other men of the same subcaste as the men they married. These men can accept the culturally recognized role of "visiting husbands," and one or more of them is expected to acknowledge the children the woman bears. Thus premarital virginity is ensured, and the social legitimization of the children is accomplished.

Australia: The Tiwi   The Tiwi of northern Australia require that all girls be married before or at birth—a practice that takes care of problems of premarital sex but encourages later problems of adultery (Hart and Pilling 1960). Men promise their yet-to-be-born and often their yet-to-be-conceived daughters to other men for economic and political gain. Girls are often sent to their promised spouses in infancy, and they grow up in their husbands' camps without having attended their own wedding ceremonies—the negotiated conferences that were held before they were born.

Comparison and Summary   Each couple in the marriages described join an existing family after their marriage or establish their own family and probably begin to have children. Differing practices of residence after marriage can produce families of markedly differing composition.

The Greek couple move into the groom's father's village—more often than not into the father's home—and thus add to the membership of an existing family group. The groom in this case becomes an independent authority only upon his father's death.

The Tlingit couple move into the multifamily longhouse owned by the groom's maternal family, which is headed by his oldest maternal uncle. The couple and their children have their own compartment in the dwelling, as will each additional wife the man marries. The husband is not the head of the house, although he will have an increasing say in consultations with the old uncle. The husband is an authority figure to his sister's children, for whose guidance and protection he is responsible, rather than to his own children. His nephews will probably join his household, just as he went as a boy to live with his maternal uncle.

An Australian Aborigine family grouping. In this society the family is embedded in a very large and complicated kinship network, which is utilized by men to organize political allegiances through the mechanism of marrying off their daughters before or at their birth, in return for political and economic indebtedness on the parts of their new brothers-in-law. Successful manipulation of the "marriage market" leads to social prominence.

The Blackfoot newlyweds usually, but not always, pitched their tepee near that of the young man's father, but they did have their own separate residence within which the husband had authority over his wives and children.

The Swazi couple reside in the compound of the groom's father, where he is subject to the authority of his parents and his wife is subject to that of her mother-in-law. The wife has her separate hut, as will each succeeding wife, where she and her children have some independence. The husband spends his days outside or at his mother's house, spending the nights with each of his wives in turn. In old age the couple assume greater authority and direct the lives of their sons and daughters-in-law.

Nayar families collect around women and their children, with a series of visiting husbands dropping in.

There are other significant variations. The Pawnee of the southern United States plains allowed married women living with their husbands to have lovers; the only requirement was that any man who impregnated a woman should claim social responsibility for the resulting child. Here the family would be a man, his wife or wives, their children, and perhaps other men's children.

Among the Hopi of the southwestern United States the groom moved into the house where his wife lived with her mother. Domestic life was dominated by women. Men had little to say in the house and spent much of their time in the fields, attending to ritual matters or socializing in the underground *kiva* (ceremonial chamber). The men were nonetheless responsible for providing food for their families, and they served as advisers and companions for their children. They also had authority over their sisters' children.

These few cases indicate the variety of processes and forms that anthropologists try to describe through the familiar terms *marriage* and *family*. These concepts clearly need qualification and refinement if they are to communicate accurately the conditions they seek to describe. And in fact, anthropologists have developed a complex terminology to handle this immense variety.

Theory

Systems

Anthropologists have clustered the various forms of marriage into a few frequently occurring types. In the examples introduced above, the Greek case is representative of the use of *dowry*, in which the bride brings more gifts to the marriage than does the groom. The Tlingit *gift exchange* gives a slight advantage to the bride's family, which receives the more substantial gift. This tendency is fully developed among the Blackfeet and the Swazi, where the groom or his family gives a *bride price* to the bride's family. (The notion that this practice amounts to the purchase of a bride is not justified; the custom may be interpreted as a recompense to the girl's family for the loss of her services and of the children she is expected to produce.)

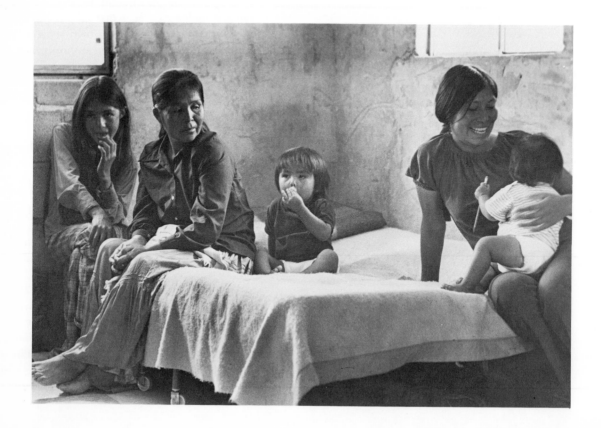

Three generations of a Navajo Indian family on the Navajo reservation in the Southwest. Like their immediate neighbors the Hopi, the Navajo still retain many of their traditional marriage practices, including matrilocal postmarital residence, which is tied to their matrilineal form of social organization.

The Tlingit case is an example of a *cross-cousin marriage*, in which the cousin is related to the individual in question through his or her parent's siblings of the opposite sex—for example, the mother's brother's children or the father's sister's children. The mother's sister's children or father's brother's children are called *parallel cousins*, and they are usually considered as siblings in societies where these distinctions count. In a few societies, parallel cousins are the preferred marriage partners.

Exchange marriage, in which two men marry each other's sister, is often found. The term is also sometimes used for more complicated patterns in which groups exchange women to provide wives for the men.

The Greek marriage was *monogamous*—men and women were allowed only one spouse at a time. Many societies, however, practice differing kinds of *polygamy*, or multiple marriages. The most frequent form of multiple marriage is *polygyny*, in which one man takes several wives. A much rarer form of multiple marriage is *polyandry*, in which a woman has more than one husband. George Murdock lists only the Toda of India, the Sherpa of Nepal, and the Polynesian Marquesans as practicing polyandry (1967:63–125).

In some societies a man is expected to marry the wife or wives of a deceased brother; this practice is known as the *levirate*. Correspondingly, the *sororate* is the practice by which women are expected to marry the husband of a deceased sister. If the marriage involves two or more sisters as wives at the same time, it is called *sororal polygyny*.

The family groupings formed by various kinds of marriage are influenced by where the marriage partners reside after the event. When the young couple move into the residence of the groom's *father*, as in the Greek case, they take *virilocal* residence. This is distinguished from *patrilocal* residence (Murdock 1967:48) as practiced by the Swazi, where the young couple move in with the groom's *father's extended kin groups*. A similar kind of distinction is made when the couple move into residence with the bride's family: Their residence is *uxorilocal* if no other members of the mother's family live there, but *matrilocal* when the mother's kin group is also in residence.

When—as among the Tlingit a youth has been living with his maternal uncle and brings his bride to this
home upon marriage, the practice is called *avunculocal*
residence. Occasionally the residence rule is *bilocal*—
the couple have a choice but must reside with one set

Figure 8-1
Forms of the Family

NUCLEAR FORM

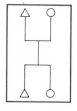

nuclear
family:
the building
block of
all family
forms

Key: △ = male
         ○ = female
         ⌐⌐ = marriage
         ⌐⌐ = sibling tie
         | = descent

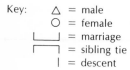

COMPOSITE FORMS

I Polygamy

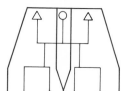

a. polyandry

female with
multiple
husbands

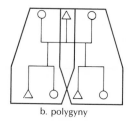

b. polygyny

male with
multiple
wives

**II Extended
Families**

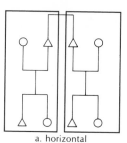

a. horizontal

joining of
two or more
siblings'
families

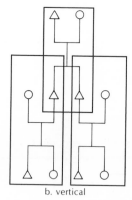

b. vertical

vertical
joining
of three
generations:
parents and
the families of
some of their
children

of parents or the other. In many other cases, among groups as diverse as certain Eskimo groups and contemporary Americans, the couple is expected to establish its own new and independent, or *neolocal,* residence.

The marriage forms, the residence rules, and the advent of children combine to produce differing kinds of family groupings. Where the marriages are monogamous and the residence neolocal, the *nuclear family* of two parents and their children is formed. Where the nuclear family or parts of it join other families (for economic reasons or on the death of a parent, for example), where multiple marriages are practiced, or where the residence rules require a couple to reside with parents, *composite families* are formed.

A composite family may be one of several types, depending on the marriage form and residence custom practiced. Where a man has several wives, they will form a *polygynous family*; a woman with more than one husband will form a *polyandrous family*. A family grouping of two or more married couples and their children is termed an *extended family*. The *horizontal extended family*, or *joint family*, is a household of two siblings and their respective spouses and children. The *vertical extended family* is one in which parents, some of their married children, and some of their grandchildren are in residence together.

Processes

The concepts that we have defined not only describe practices found in various societies but also signal dynamic processes of group formation, maintenance, and extension.

The bonds of marriage (*affinity*) and the common interest and affection created by the children of this marriage provide channels for emotional, social, political, and economic cooperation that help to organize a larger community. Let us look at various marriage forms to see how these processes operate.

Rules of *exogamy* require people to marry outside their own group, to establish ties with other groups, and to extend rights and responsibilities to them. Rules of *endogamy* require people to marry within a defined group and reinforce, reactivate, or maintain group ties.

A polygynous Kikuyu family in Kenya. Shown here are, from left to right: grandmother, second wife and her baby, second son of first wife, patriarch, first son of first wife.

Similarly, the forms of marriage that permit greater personal choice of spouse often bring people together in ways that reinforce existing ties rather than form new ties.

Cousin marriages maintain the relationship between two groups through time and can keep economic, social, and political privileges within the control of the two intermarrying families.

Polygynous marriages produce families of women and children under the direction of one man—an arrangement that often gives an economic advantage, adds to the family prestige, and is highly efficient for procreation, since one man can keep several wives pregnant. Polyandry, on the other hand, seems better designed for recreation—a woman can only become pregnant periodically, no matter how many husbands she has.

The sororate and levirate maintain existing links, whereas multiple marriages that draw wives from different families create wider ties within a community by extending the reciprocal relations among groups.

Monogamy is the most common form of marriage in the world because only a few men can afford more than one wife even in societies where polygyny is the cultural ideal. Monogamous marriages serve the group by making more marriages possible. Several daughters can marry men from the same family, thus reinforcing an existing relationship; or they can marry men of different families, and so extend affinal ties.

As we have seen, the various residence rules create differing types of family groups. In the virilocal/patrilocal forms, men remain on familiar ground, while women leave home to reside as relative strangers with their husband's kin. In the uxorilocal/matrilocal pattern, the situation is reversed. The man is the stranger in the woman's home territory. In such households, because the women and children are on familiar ground, they have an advantage that can be a source of conflict even when the man traditionally has authority over his household. Avunculocal residence, as among the Tlingit, is less stressful. The household, focused around a group of men related to each other through women, contains a man, his brothers, the sons of the sisters of these men, unmarried daughters, and the wives brought in from other households. The man probably continues to reside with the maternal uncle,

who raised him and from whom he will inherit. He is still at home, whereas his bride had to leave her childhood home, even though it had been "just across the street."

Bilocal residence seems to allow a mix of the strengths and weaknesses of the other forms. People apparently may choose to go to the home where they expect better treatment or an economic advantage. Neolocal residence offers independence to the couple, which can mean freedom from interference by others, but which also means that the couple cannot rely on help from immediate family in raising children and solving problems. The neolocal monogamous family is small and flexible, characteristics that allow relatively easy adaptation to changing conditions, whether that means following game or hunting jobs. Polygynous neolocal families seem to have the same advantages, plus the benefit of more women to share the work. However, the man usually must expend more effort to support his extra wives and children. Other types of composite families offer the sharing of residence, work, produce, and child care and training.

Families change over time. An additional spouse may be added to what had been a nuclear family. Parents, together or singly, may move in with a younger couple, or the younger family may join the family of one of the parents. As in the example of the Greek village, a son may join his father to form an extended family that becomes a nuclear family when the parent dies. The divorce of the partners or the death of one may leave a single-parent family that remains independent. In cases where one parent fills both parental roles, it is sometimes useful to distinguish between matricentered and patricentered families. Matricentered families are also found where men move in and out of households, contributing children but little or no family support.

Analysis

The Folk Perspective

For an English-speaking audience, a good description of marriage and family in another culture from the folk perspective would be one in which foreign practices were least distorted by translation into English words and familiar analogies. Such a description would require attention to the context within which marriage practices and family organization occur and of which they are an integral part. We shall describe briefly a single system to give some feel for the problem.

The traditional Greek farm village wedding represents the ideal that the people of Vasilika hold of a good wedding, but the actual ceremonies vary in the degree to which they approximate this ideal. Many daughters marry townsmen, and many sons move out to city jobs. While their wedding ceremonies might be traditional, the resulting residence and family patterns differ somewhat from those of the young people who remain on the farm.

Vasilika and villages like it house people who farm the neighboring lands. All members of the family participate in some of the farming activities, calling on hired labor only when the demands of the crops exceed the family's resources. Financial success is important to the villagers. Urban ways are considered desirable and are emulated, and people value good houses with some modern amenities.

The villagers measure prestige and honor by the degree to which a family succeeds in fulfilling its obligations. . . . The essential obligation

In Vasilika, as among many peasant groups, the household is not only the basic residence unit but the primary unit of food production as well.

is to maintain a ratio between property and children such as to enable each child, when the property is divided in equal shares among all the children, to maintain in turn, a decent standard of living. . . . The ability to transmit wealth is especially important. The villagers consider a man who is rich in lands but has no children an object of pity; the man's wife is considered even more unfortunate. This is because the contemplation of the success of their children gives the life of a married couple a large part of its meaning. (Friedl 1962:18)

Success is not measured solely by achievements in farming. Education is also valued. Not all sons can be farmers, so many are encouraged to get an education and seek urban jobs. Not all girls can marry farmers, so many take jobs in the city and become betrothed to promising urban youths.

The daughter's dowry is very important, for it represents her share in the estate of the parents, paid in advance of their death.

In short, the bride's father wants to insure, insofar as he is able, the future well-being of his daughter and of her children. He also wants the emotional satisfaction of having been successful at making a good arrangement for her. One village farmer pointed to a field we were passing and explained that he had given it to his daughter as part of her *prika* (dowry), so that all the cotton from the field was for his grandson. He then went on to say that he had married his daughter well and said of his three-year-old grandson, "Who knows, one day he might become a lawyer or a doctor. He has a brain, the little one" (Friedl 1962:53).

It is in this context that families choose marriage partners for their children, agree on the dowry the daughter will bring, and support the courtship of the couple once the agreement is reached.

In the traditional ceremony between children of farmers, the dowry is carried by young male relatives of the groom from her house to his. The next day, according to Ernestine Friedl's description (which she cautions is incomplete):

A family of Greek peasants. The fact that the woman brings a valuable dowry of land into her husband's family when she marries, gives her a source of power to assert herself within that group, since there is always the implied threat that if she becomes sufficiently alienated she might terminate the marriage, and thus her family would be able to reclaim the land.

The groom's party, including his marriage sponsor (*kumbaros*), arrive at the house of the bride. The *kumbaros* leads the group to the house, only to find the door closed and locked. He begs that the door be opened. The girls inside giggle and demand 1,000 drachmas to open the door. After some bargaining, the *kumbaros* gives a five-drachma piece and the party comes in. It is the *kumbaros* who rents the bride's white wedding gown, provides the wedding crowns, the large white candles which are held at the ceremony, and the *kufeta*, the sugar-covered almonds arranged in small packages of white netting, tied with a white ribbon, which he distributes to each of the guests after the ceremony. After the wedding feast, for which musicians are hired so that the guests can sing and dance, the bride is accompanied to the groom's home by her brothers and sometimes a sister. The women, including the bride, all cry as they leave the girl with her new husband (Friedl 1962:58).

The difficulty of presenting a description of the situation as the villagers see it is apparent: Even in a more extensive description an observer might miss certain aspects. Here Friedl has mentioned values expressed by the villagers to support her selection.

The Analytic Perspective

An analytical treatment of Vasilikan marriage and family begins with the classification of these practices. The evidence shows village exogamy, monogamous marriage, the use of a dowry, and a religious ceremony. For the young couple who will inherit the groom's family land and farm it, residence is patrilocal, and the initial family is an extended family of the vertical type. After the death of the parents, the family will be classed as a nuclear family; the previously dependent son will become the family head. In time, the family might again become extended if an inheriting son marries, and the new couple take their place as dependents of his father.

The Vasilikan practices could be described in a few words by use of these concepts, and comparative analysis might show that these are the categories that identify *Greek* practices in general (Murdock 1967:82).

The Greek pattern as a whole could then be compared to patterns of other societies that had been assessed in the same way. For instance, the Basques of Spain, the French-Canadians, the Tigrinya of Africa, the Shantung of China, the Sherpa of Tibet, and the Tamil of India all use the dowry, but their family organization and residence rules vary. The Greeks, French-Canadians, and the Tigrinya all use the dowry and form monogamous nuclear families, but their residence preferences differ. What do these similarities and differences mean? How do the various practices relate to each other and to other aspects of culture? Such questions are not easily answered, but they do call for hypotheses and attempts at explanation. The treatment of these problems often depends, however, on the analytical viewpoint of the investigator.

One frequent generalization offered by anthropologists is that marriages are more often established between groups for economic reasons than between individuals for love. The Greek marriage and family forms can be seen from this perspective as responses to economic pressures. Land is scarce and cannot be continually subdivided to provide cultivatable plots for all offspring. Yet a man needs sufficient children to help with the farm work if he is to avoid excessive costs for hired labor. The dilemma is resolved by educating children and encouraging surplus offspring to seek wage jobs or professions in the city, while keeping one son at home to inherit the farm and marry a bride who will bring a good dowry. Conversely, a man is anxious to provide a dowry for his daughters so that they will make good marriages, provide for his grandchildren, and enhance or maintain his prestige.

In this model, then, the marriages become economic moves to preserve and incorporate land holdings, to work the holdings efficiently to provide cash shares for children who leave, and to build capital for the next generation of farmers. By focusing on the social values and practices related to the tenure, use, and transmission of land, we can develop a comprehensive picture in which marriage and family are two of several strategies serving these goals. The Tlingit and Swazi cases could also be used to support such a thesis.

Another common analytical perspective focuses on the functions performed by marriage and family forms.

Some of the functions, called *manifest functions,* might be recognized by the villagers themselves. Others, *latent functions,* are recognized by the observer but are unintended and unnoticed by the participants. The marriage, for instance, establishes ties of affinity between families, but it may also channel affection, sociability, economic rights and responsibilities, and loyalties beyond the range of the families concerned. The ceremony symbolizes the unity of Greeks and the unity of the village in the shared religion, awakens the sense of family, and celebrates the values of children, enterprise, and success. The rules of exogamy and the prohibition of marriage within the range of third cousins maintain open ties with many families. The residence pattern for successive farming sons keeps them on their fathers' land and provides continuity in a community of people who know each other well, familiar people whom one can befriend or quarrel with. Marriage and family function with other aspects of the society to reassert Greek values, to maintain the community, and to satisfy felt needs of the people.

Conclusions

Schools of Thought

The current dicussions of marriage and family in anthropological literature seem to be concerned with two main problems: the definition of concepts, and whether marriages are best viewed in the perspective of descent or the perspective of affiliation.

Definitions of marriage range from the simple statement that "marriage is the socially recognized union of a man and a woman established to legitimize and raise children" to more complex attempts to capture all possible results of a recognized ceremony between persons. But none of them seems to satisfy the requirement of the sharp definition that we require as an index for comparative studies.

Definitions of family are also much debated. Murdock defined the various family forms: "the family is a social group characterized by common residence, economic cooperation, and reproduction" (1949:1). However, he found the concept ambiguous unless attention was paid to the different forms that occurred.

Among many nonliterate peoples, marriage represents much more than the creation of a new family; the importance of a marriage, rather, is the link it creates between two kinship groups. Thus, in such societies, marriages are often arranged, rather than developing out of "romantic love" between bride and groom. The Karamajong of Kenya and Uganda enact a dramatic ritual to express the fact that marriage is social rather than merely personal. Here the protesting bride is dragged by her brothers from the hut where she has been hiding. Athough the sequence of behavior is prescribed and staged as a recognized part of the larger marriage ritual, it expresses the reality that the particular wishes of the woman are subordinated to the interests of the two kinship groups.

Murdock did stress that the universality of the nuclear family made it the core around which other forms were assembled. This formulation would provide a firm standard for comparative work if everybody would agree on the underlying assumption; unfortunately, they do not.

The debate over the best way to view marriage is divided into two groups: those who follow alliance theories and those who accept descent theories.

Alliance theorists focus on marriage as a mechanism for linking two or more groups, thus forming an alliance that is maintained by successive intermarriages. Some societies apparently do view marriages in this way, and alliance for economic or political purposes

has been examined in these terms for many years. The newer approach to alliance is that of Claude Lévi-Strauss and his followers, who build on the idea that the invention of exogamy required groups, friendly or not, to trade women for wives (1969). The need for wives and the resulting marriages create alliances. The form of marriage determines the nature of the alliance, and the alliance determines and maintains the *structured* relations among the groups that exchange wives.

Those who accept *descent* theories view marriage as a mechanism by which groups provide women to bear the children who become new members of this group. Descent theorists take an inside view of the structure of the group and examine how marriage

functions to perpetuate it. In this context, marriage is a recruitment device that ensures the maintenance of the family, the preparation of children for adult roles, and descent to the proper heirs of rights and responsibilities.

To summarize, alliance theorists look from the outside with an analytical model of the overall social structure resulting from marriages. Descent theorists, on the other hand, take an inside view of the structure of the group and see how marriage and family function to perpetuate it.

Author's Conclusions

We can resolve the problems of definition if we accept the fact that we are arguing over details: We understand the general concepts well. The familiar, general definitions enable the ethnographer to translate foreign practices into language we can all understand. By adding detailed descriptions of particular forms of marriage and family, the ethnographer conveys to us the differences among various cultures. If the ethnographer presents in addition what the people under study say about what they do, we can gain an even fuller understanding.

Opting for the general definition does not solve the problem of those who wish to make comparisons, however. Unless the entities one wishes to compare are expressed in detailed, specific terms, one cannot know if they are indeed comparable. Families have often been defined in terms of the functions they perform, but all families may not perform all functions. How then can one compare, say, the basic economic units of two societies by using families as the units? The most fruitful mode of attack would seem to be to examine each society to find what you are looking for—the basic economic group, or the basic socializing group, or the minimal autonomous political group—and compare these without worrying about whether they are also families, households, or anything else not specifically relevant to your problem.

As far as the debate between alliance and descent theories is concerned, I see no reason to engage in an out-of-context argument over which is or is not the best perspective to take on marriage and the family.

The perspective to take, the analytic tool to use, is the one that best answers the questions you choose to ask. You do not tackle a haystack with a scalpel or do brain surgery with a pitchfork. Alliance theories deal with social structure: how parts of a system are shaped and perpetuated by links of reciprocal marriages, or how marriages are used to link potentially hostile groups into a more or less stable political structure. This is a view from outside a social system; it is little concerned with how people learn and play their roles or with how descent and affiliation are handled. These phenomena are taken as given, for it is the maintenance of the structural aspects of the system that is under consideration. For many purposes this perspective is useful.

Descent theories developed around different questions, and their models would be more useful if you wanted to examine how marriages provide heirs, recruit new members, provide for the socialization of children, or transmit property, rights, and responsibilities to the next generation. As already indicated, this is an inside view, more concerned with how people play their parts, act toward their relatives, or rear their children. Descent theories are particularly useful in answering questions about descent groups in societies organized on a kinship basis.

Summary

The institutions of marriage and family are found in some form in all societies. The origins of these institutions were a major concern of early anthropologists. However, the focus of anthropological attention has since shifted to the study of variations in contemporary marriage patterns around the world through the collection of first-hand data on the actual marriage and family patterns of other cultures.

Although many marriage and family forms exist, the variety is not infinite. Examples from rural Greece, the Tlingit of Alaska, the Blackfoot Indians, the Swazi of Africa, and the Tiwi of Australia are used to reveal some of the forms these institutions take and the practices that are associated with them.

Anthropologists analyze marriage patterns along several dimensions: Is there a brideprice, dowry, or gift exchange? Is the system monogamous or polygamous? Where do the marital partners live after the marriage? Is the family nuclear or extended? Are people required to marry within or outside their own group? Are specified people, such as cross-cousins, regarded as preferred marital partners?

The precise definitions of marriage and family remain a matter of debate in anthropology. Controversy also arises over how best to view marriage. Some theorists regard it as a means of creating alliances between different groups; others see it as a mechanism for preserving the structure of the group by stabilizing the process of reproduction and child rearing; and still often stress that marriage most importantly functions to legitimize children as members of a society.

Annotated Bibliography

Bohannan, Paul, and Middleton, John, eds. (1968)   *Marriage, Family, and Residence.* Garden City, N.Y.: Natural History Press. Each paper in this collection makes a theoretical statement about incest, marriage, family, residence, and household, based in most cases on specific examples of the different types. A sample of the kinds of discussions on marriage and family engaged in by anthropologists for a professional audience.

Keesing, Roger M. (1975)   *Kin Groups and Social Structure.* New York: Holt. The most recent and cogent review of the work on kinship, marriage, descent, alliance, kin terms, and current theories and methods for their study. A useful book for the instructor for both the discussion and the bibliography.

Stevens, William N. (1963)   *The Family in Cross-Cultural Perspective.* New York: Holt. A rich, comparative sampling of the variety of types of families in the world. Includes examples of each type of marriage, residence, and family pattern, with statements of their frequency of occurrence and distribution; a discussion of family roles and relationships and child training practices; and a discussion of the interrelations among the forms, with statements of the statistical correlations among them.

9
Social
Organization II:
Kinship

The World Context

Origins and Development through Time

Kinship—the ties of loyalty, responsibility, and privilege to people who are considered relatives—is a powerful organizer of human interaction. Other ties are important too—we rarely find human groups united by one tie alone. But although loyalties may also be based on common territory, similar age, the same sex, or shared social activity, political beliefs, or economic conditions, in all societies the kin group is a fundamental basis of social organization. The significance of kinship varies. In small societies almost all social interaction is handled in a kinship framework—even the visiting anthropologist is adopted into a family to make dealing with her or him easier. In large nations such as the United States, other principles often override kin ties. Yet kinship still counts in the United States. For example, if you are having a dispute with a neighbor, you might agree if he suggests going to see the judge. However, if he should say, "Let's take this matter up with my uncle, the judge," you might prefer to go on arguing.

Because kinship is so widely used as an organizer of social life, anthropologists have devoted a great deal

Alfred Louis Kroeber (1876–1960), the first of Franz Boas' students to receive his doctorate at Columbia, and the "dean" of American anthropology upon Boas' death. His interests were encyclopedically broad. In the area of kinship, he for a long time maintained the position that kin terms refer exclusively to perceived connections (of a genealogical nature) between people, not to categories of individuals or social groups. Kinship is a matter of psychology, he argued, not sociology. In his debate on this topic with W. H. R. Rivers, he hardened this position: a rigidity of thinking that he later came to regret.

of attention to the institution. Marriage and family are at the heart of kinship systems, so we have already sketched in some of the background in the previous chapter. As in the case of marriage and family, the researcher faces the double task of interpreting the "foreign" into familiar terms and identifying units that can be used for accurate comparison.

Anthropological interest in kinship developed within the intellectual contexts reviewed in chapter 8 and generated as many hypotheses, speculations, arguments, descriptive concepts, and theories as did marriage and the family. J. J. Bachofen, John McLennan, Edward Westermarck, and others we mentioned dealt not only with marriage and family but also with larger groups and categories of kin. These theorists noted that kinship forms such as clans and matrillineal or patrilineal descent groups persisted through time and regulated the affairs of their individual members. They speculated on the order in which these forms might have evolved, but they did little investigation into the actual workings of the systems.

However, Lewis Henry Morgan stimulated interest in the concentrated study of kinship systems by his observation that the Iroquois, whom he had studied at first hand, referred to all their maternal aunts by the same word that they used for their mothers, used the same word for their father and his brothers, and often grouped people of different generations under one word. "As far back as the year 1846, while collecting materials illustrative of the Iroquois, I found among them, in daily use, a system of relationship for the designation and classification of kindred both unique and extraordinary in its character and wholly unlike any with which we are familiar" (Morgan 1871:3).

Morgan began to investigate the kin terminology of neighboring groups and sent out questionnaires to missionaries and government officials around the world asking for lists of kin terms used by the people among whom they worked. By fieldwork and correspondence, he amassed a wealth of terminologies to study and compare. He noted that whereas we tend to use *descriptive* terms that apply to one individual only, many other peoples use *classificatory* terms that group many relatives under a single word. Morgan assumed that these differences could be fitted into his grand scheme of cultural evolution on the basis that the classificatory terms found in simpler societies preceded the use of descriptive terms. Morgan's more lasting contributions, however, were his accumulation of first-hand information, his demonstration that people organized their kinship universes differently by the words they used, and his conjecture that a relationship existed between a people's social organization and their kinship terminology.

Anthropologists argued over most of Morgan's conclusions, but kinship-based social organizations rapidly became central topics in anthropological research. For instance, Alfred L. Kroeber rejected the proposed relationship between kinship terms and group organization and asserted instead that the terms were merely words and hence were linguistic rather than social phenomena (1909). W. H. R. Rivers established the genealogical method of studying social organization (1900, 1914). It has since become almost the standard first task of fieldworkers to collect the kin terms of the community they are studying and to work out the genealogies of the members of the community. This method provides a framework for observing and analyzing the ways people act toward each other and for discovering the social rules that operate in kin-organized societies.

The early theorists sought the origins of kinship systems and tried to build grand evolutionary schemes on the limited information that was available to them. Those who came after Morgan rejected the grand schemes and instead turned their attention to the collection of empirical data. They found far more variety in kinship types than Morgan had suspected, yet a few basic patterns seemed to recur and were named. The relationship between kinship terminology and social organization remains unresolved, but we now have about a dozen basic types of terminology, and we expect that where we identify one of these types, we can get some preliminary clues about such things as whether kin affiliation is traced through males or females or both.

Through the 1930s, anthropologists became less interested in terminologies and more concerned with the actual workings of kin groups in social organization. Bronislaw Malinowski saw the ties of kinship as

extensions of emotional bonds from the nuclear family to other kin, in widening ties of loyalties, sentiments, and cooperation. A. R. Radcliffe-Brown analyzed kin as a system of structural relationships of rights and duties: Kin terms signaled reciprocal roles, such as father-son or husband-wife, and these basic nuclear family roles were extended by analogy to other kin. In his search for comparative regularities, Radcliffe-Brown offered the principle of the equivalence of brothers to identify the extension of rights and duties expected between brothers to other relatives who are called by the male sibling term. Students of these scholars extensively studied how kin groups function in the working of a society, such as the part they play in economic distribution and politics. Later, under the influence of Meyer Fortes, scholars began to examine the internal workings of the groups—how new members were recruited, how they were brought into adult roles, the contribution of significant social relationships to the maintenance and effectiveness of the groups.

In the United States some scholars revived the question of the relationship of terminological systems to forms of social organization. These investigations culminated in an important book by George P. Murdock that provided a sophisticated analysis of kin groups and terminology (1949). He not only attempted to demonstrate the determinants of particular terminologies but also tackled the problems of how terminologies change in response to changing life conditions. Murdock found that the changes in terminology are orderly and quite predictable in terms of the possibilities and limitations of the antecedent kinship structure.

One strong vein in American kinship studies that has stemmed from Murdock's work is best exemplified by Fred Eggan's reconstruction of how the social organization of some Native American groups was modified in response to historically documented changes (1966). Other American anthropologists have followed Murdock's interest in terminological systems and have developed intricate logical and mathematical methods of uncovering the structural principles and internal consistencies of individual systems.

We will assume that the various kin terms are verbal means to signify the wide expanse of possible mean-

George Peter Murdock (1897–   ),
American anthropologist. He led one
wing of the attack on Boasian particularism by reintroducing the comparative
perspective (the other wing of the attack
was the neo-evolutionism of Leslie White
and Julian Stweard). While teaching at
Yale University he helped set up what
eventually became the Human Relations
Area Files, the most massive collection of
cross-indexed ethnographic materials ever
assembled. In 1949 he published his
classic work *Social Structure,* which made
use of statistical methods and Hullian
(behaviorist) psychology to attempt a
cross-cultural comparison and systematic
classification of the known kinship
systems of the world.

ingful relations a person might have with kin. An
individual will not know personally or interact frequently with all possible kin he or she might have.
According to social custom, some kin will be more
important than others. The patterned kinship terminology identifies who is one of "us" and who is an
"other." The kin terms also give the anthropologist
clues to some of the expectations people have of the
appropriate relations between the persons identified
by the various terms.

The study of kinship provides an important perspective on social organization. The major kinship
patterns and the models of these that anthropologists
have worked out are useful devices to analyze and
describe existing societies. As we have said, kinship
terminology seems to reflect social forms: Analysts
have been able to show a fair degree of conformity
between the terminological system and the behavior
system, although many problems remain unresolved.
Murdock, Eggan, and others have demonstrated that
terminological systems change over time in response
to, but lag behind, changes in other aspects of the
cultural and natural environment. The lag allows investigators to reconstruct earlier forms from the current
terminology.

The time lag may also explain some of the anomalies that worry us when the terminology and aspects
of social organization of the people we study seem to
be at odds with one of our models. People often have
some options in designating kin, and changing conditions probably introduce other options. People also
make pragmatic choices when the actual rules of descent and marriage cannot be fulfilled. In practice, a
one-to-one fit of terminology with social organization
is rare, but this does not mean that no relationship
exists. The variations around the measuring device, the
model, can be explained; and the explanations of the
irregularities are often more intellectually rewarding
than the mere recognition of the kinship type itself.

It must be remembered that, like marriage and the
family, kinship is a social phenomenon resting on a
biological base. Men and women must mate so that
children can be born into existing groups. But the
assignment of membership into a particular group and
the definition of the obligations, duties, rights, and

privileges of the child and its relatives are done according to customs that depart considerably from a purely genetic model of transmission down the generations.

Contemporary Examples

In the Greek village of Vasilika, as we discussed in chapter 8, the nuclear family that frequently is extended for part of its developmental cycle is the basic social and economic unit. The father heads his family and has authority over the son who marries and comes to live with him. When the old man dies, his family comes to an end; his son's family is now owner and occupant of the home and land. Each person remembers, meets with, comes to the aid of, and designates as kin a wider circle of relatives, but the range of this circle differs for each person. The father's relatives include some of his grandparents, aunts, and uncles whom the son has never met and whom he knows only through stories. The son includes as his relatives those of his wife and, later on, the grandchildren his father could not know. Beyond the realm of memory, the Greek villagers have no long-continuing group of relatives larger than the extended family and each person's kinship circle.

A Blackfoot child was born into an extended family, but like that of the Greeks, it was a family that had little continuity over time. One knew, talked about, and interacted with both one's mother's people and one's father's people. Each person tended to live and travel with relatives, but he or she could join another group at marriage or when it seemed advantageous to do so. Family was important and each person had a kinship circle, but friendship was important too.

The Tlingit saw their universe of kin differently. At birth a person automatically became a member of a series of named groups to which the mother belonged, because her mother, and her mother's mother, and her mother's mother's mother, and so on back into the legendary past had been of these groups. The child was first either a Wolf or a Raven—everybody had to be one or the other. If the child was a Wolf, it would also belong to the Teqwedi, Kagwantan, or other divisions of the Wolf category. The divisions and subgroups competed with each other much of the time, but united in a Wolf versus Raven argument. Yet people of the Raven and Wolf divisions played important parts in the life crises of one another.

Each of the divisions of Raven or Wolf, down to the family unit occupying one section of the long plank house, was ranked in order of its prestige. Each group had "ownership" of names, social positions, objects, songs, and rituals that symbolized their social position. In many ways, a person was what his or her position within the kin groups was. If a low-ranking person should kill a person of high rank and the victim's people should call for revenge, someone's life must be forfeited. But the murderer would not die: A kinsman of equal rank to the murdered man must allow himself to be killed in mock battle to right the wrong (deLaguna 1972:462).

Among the Swazi of southern Africa, the first thing an individual is apt to ask upon meeting another for the first time is, "What is your *sibono?*" The name of the *sibono* (patrilineage) establishes the major social identity; it tells the other that here is a person who has been born into a long line of people to which the father and his father's father before him belonged. The response, "My *sibono* is ———," tells the questioner something about the social position, the political clout, and if the two are of opposite sex, the marriageability of the respondent. There are many *sibono*, and when the chips are down, it is some subdivision of these categories that counts: The group of people related to some recently deceased ancestor and over whom the grandfather has authority is the group that has the most to say about the future of a child. These people help one marry, see to one's education, and establish one in the world. This is the important "we" group of true kin, and because of the rules of marriage, neither one's mother nor one's wife belongs to it (Kuper 1963:16).

Children on the island of Rapa in French Polynesia call their father and all male relatives of his generation *metua tane,* and their mother and female relatives of her generation *metua vahine.* One's own children and the children of one's siblings and cousins are all called *tamaiti* (boys) or *tamahine* (girls). One's own siblings and cousins are all either *tu'ane* if they are males, or

Blackfoot life was organized both through kinship relations and groupings of individuals who happened to like one another. Even though we have emphasized that in technologically less developed societies kinship is the major form or vehicle of social organization, this should not be understood to mean that kinship was the only device by which social life was structured. This painting by an unknown artist shows a Blackfoot encampment near Fort MacKenzie.

tuahine if they are females (Hanson 1970). This is the kind of usage that startled Morgan and others, and led some early travelers to report that in some societies people did not know their true relatives. Even Robert Lowie, an anthropologist of long experience, was apparently caught off balance when he heard a sixty-five-year-old Crow Indian man call a twenty-one-year-old relative "father" and a child of four call a two-year-old cousin "daughter."

Among the Hopi Indians of the American Southwest, a father raised the food for his family but did not really belong within it. He was a friend to his children, but he was the authority figure for his *sister's* youngsters. He was one of a kin group traced through his mother—the Bear or Sun group, perhaps. His wife and children were members of a different group. He had been born into a group that traced its descent through women back to one of the people who came to this world from the underworld at the time of Creation. He worked with others of this kin group to maintain the Hopi universe by participating in group rituals and other activities.

The farm lands that the Hopi father tilled were controlled by his kin group in his village. Some of the Hopi kin groups were descendants of ancestors who had been siblings, and so their members felt a closer kinship tie to each other than to the members of groups whose ancestors had not been as closely related. One could rely for help on members of these "sister" groups more than on Hopi from other lines.

In contrast, the people of the Rio Grande pueblo of San Ildefonso were born into one of two major groups—they were either Summer people or Winter people. Winter people tended to marry only Winter people, and Summer people, only Summer people; so, of course, children belonged to the same group as both their parents.

Some of the most intriguing complications of kin affiliations are found among many Australian aborigine groups. Scholars describe the same kinship divisions among these people, but their explanations are rarely the same. A child was born as a member of one of two major groups in some societies, becoming either an A or a B, according to the group to which its father belonged. In some other aboriginal groups, the child would also be a member of group C or D, depending on its mother's affiliation. No person could marry anyone who was a member of either of his or her own lines: The son of an A father and a D mother could only marry a girl who had B and C parents; AC and BD combinations were ineligible. In other Australian groups further complexity was added by recognizing the groups of grandparents, a procedure that resulted in a total of eight sections, of which a person was born into four. Clearly, the kinds of groups that people form on the basis of kinship can be varied and complex.

Important kinship groupings can be recognized at times of stress: Who helps to resolve conflict? In the event of a murder among the Tlingit, a person's kin group takes over the case. Among the Swazi, ordinary disputes are settled by the head of the household group, or if the conflict involves people beyond one household, among the heads of the groups concerned. But if murder is involved, the matter will be taken to the king, the head of the highest-ranking kin group.

Sometimes the ownership and use of land are concerns of kin groups. In the case of the Hopi, for ex-

ample, land was controlled by the matriline. The people of Rapa did not distinguish between "we" and "they" groups on the basis of ancestry through men or women, but unlike the Vasilikans, they were born with potential rights in several named kinship divisions with land-use rights. Exercising one set of these rights brought an individual into residence with a group of people who could all trace a relationship back to a common ancestor who was connected to that land. It did not make any difference whether the tie was through males or females; the important thing was that each member had some tie of descent from the ancestor. Other Polynesians made even more of their genealogical connections to the founders of their groups. The genealogies were perpetuated in legend, and "we" groups were often formed on the basis of people's common ties back to one or another of these ancestors. Social ranking, land-use rights, marriage rules, and often religious activities were governed by these kin ties.

Theory

Systems

People acquire three kinds of kin: *consanguineal* kin by birth, *affinal* kin by marriage, and *fictive* kin by such practices as adoption, godparenthood, or blood-brother rites. Kin may be further classified as *agnatic*, related to one through males; *uterine*, related to one through females; *collateral*, those relatives in one's own generation on both sides of the family out to some culturally defined limit; or *cognatic*, those relatives of all generations on both sides of the family to some culturally defined limit.

If you sketch out a model of your genetic relationships, including all possible relations of each of your relatives, you will see that the total universe of possible kin is almost infinite. But actual kinship systems and the words (kinship terms) people use to refer to their relatives reduce the field to those relationships that are considered significant in each society.

A few major principles of descent and affiliation have widespread use and help to identify and describe kinship systems. A person may be born into a named kin *category,* a universe of kinsfolk with whom one rarely gets together, even though one is socially defined as a member. One may also be affiliated with a kin *group,* those people with whom one does interact on the basis of their being relatives.

Affiliation and descent may be defined by ties that are *unilineal*—that is, the continuity of a group is defined through links of one sex on one side of the family. These ties are *patrilineal* where descent is traced through males, and *matrilineal* where descent is traced through females. *Double descent,* found in some societies, is where an individual belongs to both a patriline and a separate matriline. However, the person usually exercises the rights of membership in each group separately according to the situation. For example, religious affairs may be the domain of the patriline, while economics may be the concern of the matriline. A much-used principle for defining kin is the *bilateral* form, in which an individual is linked equally to relatives of both sexes on both sides of the family.

Greenland Eskimo family sitting near a sealskin tent in the summer. Compared to many groups, the Eskimos have a very low degree of social organization. Thus for them kinship is a much less important mechanism for the structuring of social behavior than it is, say, for the Tlingit.

Anthropologists are particularly interested in corporate social groups—groups of varying size that persist through time—and some of these are *descent* groups maintained by marriage and family formation. These are the groups of relatives, including but going beyond the family, that define one's ancestors, social position, rights, privileges and duties, respect relationships, and inheritance.

A major form of descent group is the *lineage*, unilineal consanguineal kin group tracing descent from a known ancestor. There are two forms of lineage: *patrilineages*, in which the relationship is traced through males, and *matrilineages*, in which descent is traced through females. A larger grouping, the *clan*, in matrilineal or patrilineal form, is an exogamous unilineal kin or descent group tracing descent from an unknown, perhaps legendary, founder. Sometimes certain clans are believed to be related, some more closely than others; such groups of related clans are called *phratries*. Occasionally a society is divided into two parts, both of which are usually, but not always, based on unilineal descent. Each part is termed a *moiety*.

In bilateral systems we find groupings known as *kindreds*, which are not descent groups. Rather, kindreds are networks of meaningful relatives of any *one person*; consequently, they differ for each person and do not endure beyond the life of that person.

The forms of all these groups are reflected in systems of kin terms—the words people use to identify the kin relations that are considered significant in their society. Some of these terms, such as our term *mother*, are *descriptive* and identify a particular role as well as a position in the kinship network. Other terms, such as our *aunt* and *uncle*, are *classificatory* and apply to a class of relatives. Systems vary in the extent to which they use classificatory principles.

One way to view the variation is to note the kinds of information conveyed by a kin term. The terms may tell us the sex and perhaps the generation of the relative mentioned, the sex of the persons through whom the speaker and the person referred to are related, and sometimes even the sex of the person identifying the relative. The terms may also tell us whether the relationship is affinal or consanguineal, lineal or collateral,

and in some societies whether the relative is dead or alive. Kinship terms can indicate the relative age of the subject, and they can signal a reciprocal relationship between the two people—both may be called by the same term. In defining their kin, each society systematically emphasizes some of these aspects over others. However, every kinship system roughly approximates one of about a dozen basic types. In the next section we will introduce a few of these types to show how these systems work.

Anthropologists generally use the following system of notation to diagram kin relationships:

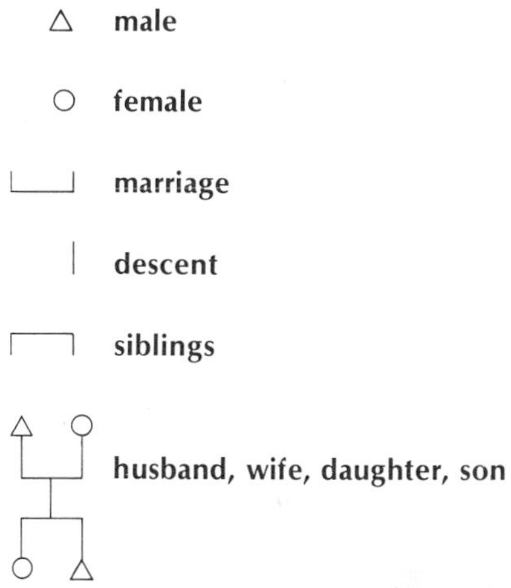

△   male

○   female

⎣___⎦   marriage

| descent

⎡___⎤   siblings

husband, wife, daughter, son

Even in contemporary, mass industrial society kinship retains some of its previous significance. It is hardly trivial that, for example, workers united in common struggle refer to their fellow union members as "sisters" and brothers." What do you think is being conveyed by this usage?

Local kin terms are translated into symbols that identify positions on a genetic chart. These symbols are supposed to be free of the meanings we attach to the English words from which they are derived.

Ego	The speaker	B or Br	Brother
M	Mother	Z or Si	Sister
F	Father	H	Husband
S	Son	W	Wife
D	Daughter		

These symbols are combined to identify the position of other relatives. For example, MB identifies Ego's maternal uncle, MF signifies maternal grandfather, and MFZDS yields mother's father's sister's daughter's son (figure that one out!). These symbols are used to show which genetic relationships people socially define as worth identifying in their kin terminology.

Processes

With these concepts in mind, imagine how your circle of close kin would look in an anthropologist's diagram. Figure 9-1 shows which relatives would probably fall into your kindred if your kinship system is bilateral, with some variations depending how often you saw some of these people. In American English we would speak of our parents, brothers, sisters, aunts, uncles, grandparents, children, nieces, and nephews. You can see from figure 9-1 that other people's kindreds would exclude some of yours but would include others you do not consider kin.

If yours is also a cognatic descent group, you would be most interested in those relatives who could trace their descent through ancestors of either sex to a venerable ancestor—say, George Washington or Queen Victoria.

However, if you belong to a group based on the patrilineal principle, the "we" group would be composed quite differently, as shown in figure 9-2. Not all members of your family or household would belong to your kin group—your mother, her relatives, and all spouses of your people belong somewhere else. If the chips are down, they are apt to join their people against you. While you are your mother's child, you are not one of her descendants, not one of her "people."

Figure 9-1 (below)
Bilateral Kindred for Both Male and Female Egos

Kinship is traced through both female and male links.

Figure 9-2
Patrilineal Kindred for Both Male and Female Egos

Kinship is traced exclusively through male links.

Figure 9-3
Matrilineal Kindred for Both Male and Female egos

Kinship is traced exclusively through female links.

Key:

△ = male
○ = female
└──┘ = marriage
┌──┐ = sibling tie
| = descent

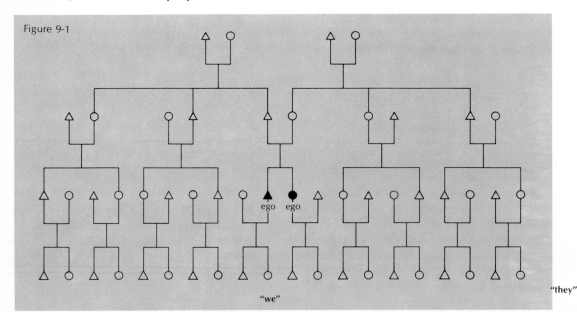

Figure 9-1

"they"   "we"   "they"

If the principle of organization is matrilineal, things switch again, as shown in figure 9-3. Now it is your father, his kin, and the various spouses of your people who are the outsiders, who must choose between you or their people in disputes. Father may be a good friend, but his major loyalties may lie with his brother, his mother, and his sisters and their children. It is your mother's brother who has authority over you and must come to your aid in time of trouble.

Where double descent is the rule, you become enmeshed in both lineal situations, but conflicting loyalties are separated according to the situation. You

Figure 9-2

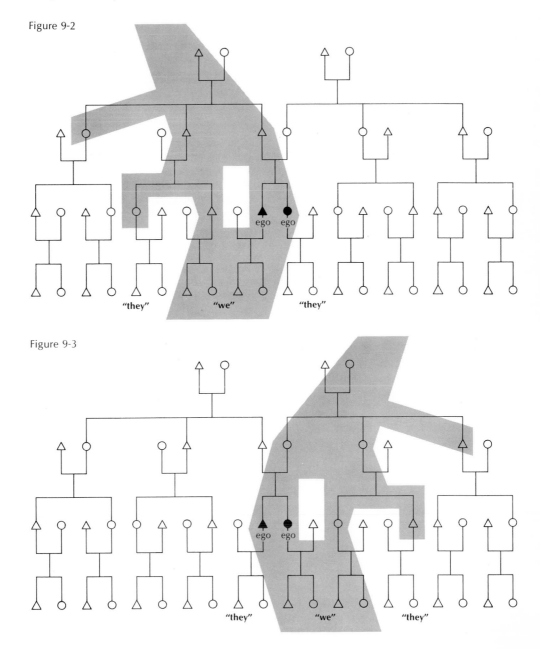

Figure 9-3

Figure 9-4
Patrilineages, Patricians, Phratry

A *lineage* is a kin group whose members can actually trace their descent through either a line of males (patrilineage) or a line of females (matrilineage). Shown here are six skeletal patrilineages (A, B, C, D, E, F); females are omitted for simplicity.

A *clan* is a kin group composed of two or more lineages, all of which *believe* they can trace their descent from a common ancestor but need not actually demonstrate their ability to do so. A clan composed of patrilineages is a patriclan, of matrilineages, a matriclan. Shown here are two patriclans (I, II).

A *phratry* consists of two or more clans that *believe* they can trace their descent from a common ancestor but need not actually demonstrate their ability to do so. The largest kin group shown here (included within the dashed line) is such a phratry.

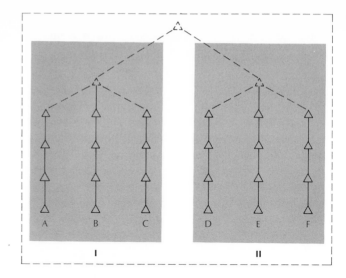

may join your matriline for religious ceremonies and inherit your guardian spirits through this line, but when rights in land are at issue, you might group with members of your patriline. You would often have to find a marriage partner outside both groups.

The groups we have diagramed could represent lineages. They could also be extended back to some legendary common ancestor to represent a clan. The clans could be related to other clans in a phratry relationship, or they could compose moieties. In studying any society, the anthropologist tries to seek out the named, meaningful social units that approximate these definitions (see fig. 9-4). The analysis of kinship terms is too complex to be handled in a few pages, but we can prepare you to read more detailed accounts.

In the simplest bilateral system, called the *Hawaiian* system, the kindred is divided by terms that tell the sex and generation of the relatives in relation to Ego, the person speaking (see fig. 9-5). Within these distinctions the terms are classificatory: Two terms at the grandparent generation could be translated "grandmother" and "grandfather" but would include the siblings of these. At the parental level there are again two words, one for males (lumping F, FB, MB, FZH, MZH, and so on), and one for females (M, MZ, FZ, FBW, MBW, and so forth). In Ego's own generation, siblings and cousins are classed together, with one word for males and another for females, and children and grandchildren are treated in the same fashion.

A slightly more complicated bilateral form, called the *Eskimo* system, is more familiar to you. In this system the aunts and uncles are called by different terms than those used for parents, and cousins are distinguished from siblings (as we have just done with the English words in this sentence).

The *Iroquois* system introduces a new distinction: the difference between *cross* and *parallel cousins*. You are linked to your cousins by members of your parents' generation. One link is one of your parents, the other link is a sibling of your parent. If both links are of the same sex (FB, MZ), you and your cousins are parallel cousins; if the two links are of different sex (FZ, MB), you and your cousins are cross cousins. This is an im-

Figure 9-5
Some Typical Systems of Kinship Terminology

Letters equal kinship terms used by ego; heavy lines mark distinctions made by terminology.

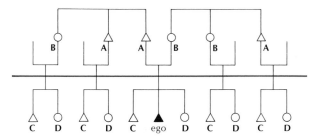

Hawaiian: emphasizes generation membership.

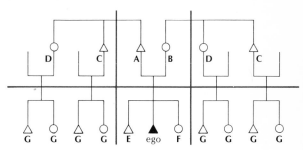

Eskimo: emphasizes both lineal descent and generation membership.

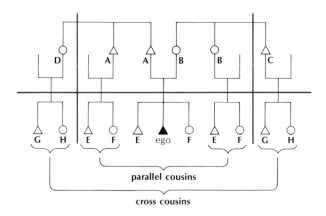

Iroquois: emphasizes lineal descent, generation membership, and the distinction between cross and parallel cousins (and thus also cross and parallel aunts and uncles).

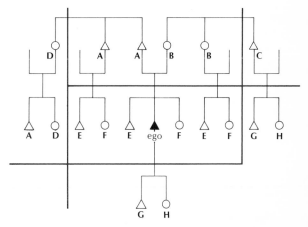

Crow and Omaha: emphasize lineal descent more strongly than generation membership; maintain distinction between cross and parallel cousins. These two systems of terminology are mirror images of each other: **Crow** is matrilineal, **Omaha** patrilineal. Illustrated here is the **Crow** terminology as used by a male ego.

portant distinction because in a unilineal system, your parallel cousins are members of your lineage and hence are usually not eligible marriage partners. In contrast, your cross cousins are not members of your lineage, and as "outsiders" are often eligible and even desired spouses.

Other unilineal systems are more complex and varied, but in most cases, terms distinguished by sex and generation are used for people in one's own line, whereas a few classificatory terms are employed for other significant lines. Thus in the *Crow* type of matrilineal system specific words exist for relatives in one's own line but men of the father's matriline are called by the term used for father, and women, by the term used for father's sister, regardless of generation. People related through men of one's own line and one's mother's line are called by the terms used for daughter and son.

A model patrilineal system, the *Omaha* system, makes similar use of classificatory terms for generational and sex divisions within one's own line, and lumps males of one's mother's line in the same classification as one's mother's brother.

Arguments abound over whether or not we can adequately or properly translate the classificatory kin terms in the way we have just done. In the folk perspective, are men lumped *with* MB, or is MB just one of a class? We will return to this problem later.

Analysis

The Folk Perspective

The Tlingit kin groups were central to the definition of proper relations between the Tlingit people and between the people and their environment. The kin groups tied people to the past and to the supernatural. A Tlingit might have seen his or her kin universe much as follows (based on deLaguna 1972:450 -454, 475-496; Oberg 1973:23-54):

/ ɣ í ɫ k̓ʷ	Grandparent
/ ʔic /	Father
/ sʌni /	FB, FZS, and all older males of father's line not called ɣ í ɫ k̓ʷ or húnx
/ ʔàt /	FZ, FZD, and all older women of father's line not called ɣ í ɫ k̓ʷ or cʌtx
/ t ɫ a /	Mother
/ t ɫ akʷ	"Little mother": MZ, and all older women of mother's line not called ɣ í ɫ k̓ʷ or cʌtx
/ kak /	MB
/ húnx /	Used by males for elder brother and elder parallel cousins
/ cʌtx /	Used by females for elder sister and elder parallel cousins
/ ʔik̓ /	Used by females for brother and male parallel cousins of same relative age
/ t ɫ ák̓ /	Used by males for sister and female parallel cousins of same relative age
/ kík /	Younger siblings of same sex as Ego and parallel cousins of same relative age
/ yɪt /	Son; also used by males for MBS
/ si' /	Daughter; also used by males for MBD
/ ké ɫ k̓ /	Used by males for sister's children
/ ka ɫ k̓ /	Used by females for brother's children and MBCh
/ xox /	Husband
/ cʌt /	Wife

The child lived in a section of a long plank house with its / ic /, / t ɫ a /, and siblings. It learned that it belonged to one of two major kin categories, the Wolves and the Ravens. The child was perhaps a Wolf, and thus considered itself better than "those others"— the Raven people—even though it lived in a house

The kinship terminological systems of Eskimos and Americans are strikingly similar. What feature of social organization would you think these societies might have in common which would help to explain the similarities of kinship system?

where all the men were Ravens. / ʔic / was a Raven, too, a friendly man who cared for his children, punished them if necessary, but could not teach them the history and lore of their line. He could do this for his sisters' children; he had greater responsibility for them than he did for his own children. His sisters' children were Ravens, too, and in his direct line.

The child also learned that it was a member of a particular line of the Wolf division, perhaps the Teqwedi (the Bear House line). This was the line of the child's maternal uncle. If the child was a boy, he would move to this uncle's house at age six or seven and would take his place in a household of Teqwedi men and their Raven wives of differing lines— / T ʎ ʔuknaxʌdi /, / kʷackqwan /, or / T l ukʷaxʌdi /. A girl would remain in her parents' house until she left to join her husband in his house.

The child was told the history of its people, a story that should not be told to people who are not Teqwedi or Wolf. The child never got to know all the other members of the Wolf people, for they never met as a group, but it did know the Wolf and Raven people in the house and village. Raven people helped in important ways at birth, marriage, death, and at potlatches (ceremonial feasts), just as Wolf people served the Ravens; and one was required to marry a person of the other division. The child's sister would marry a Raven man, and their children would be Wolf and Teqwedi. An older brother would watch over these children, but his own children would be Ravens like their mother.

The child called several older men / ʎ í ʎ kʷ /, but one (in English, its mother's maternal uncle) was most important. He was head of the Teqwedi in the village as long as he lived, and on his death he was replaced by his younger brother or his sister's oldest son. The man who was most important to the growing child was its / kak /, the older one of several men called by this name who was responsible for the child's good behavior and for training it in the lore and ritual of the Teqwedi. A girl's / ʔik / was supposed to watch over her, protect her, and treat her with great respect, but her / kak / had greater responsibility. If she should disgrace the line by becoming pregnant before marriage, her / kak / had the power to force a marriage with the man responsible, or he could kill the girl and her child to clear the family name. He took the boys into his home in their childhood to train them in their adult roles. He punished the children more often than did their / ʔic /. An / ʔik̓ / continued to watch over his / t ʎ ák / as long as they lived, and so great was her respect for him that she was never to be alone in the same room with him, nor was it right for them to speak directly to one another after they reached puberty.

Children were also respectful toward their / ʔàt /, who had helped at their birth and who often gave them presents throughout their lives. And in case a child began to get the idea that kin were a pretty solemn bunch, it gradually learned that a certain class of people joked and teased with it, and that it could joke with these people, too. These people were / yʌtxi /, members of one's own sex and generation whose / ʔic / had the same line name. Thus the child learned how to distinguish the people who were kin, how to call them by the proper terms, how to behave toward them, and how they could be expected to act in return.

The Analytical Perspective

The Tlingit kin terminology structure closely fits the matrilineal type called Crow, which expresses the greatest specificity when denoting relatives within one's own line and uses classificatory terms more extensively for others. This tendency can be seen in three ways: the kinds of information thought important enough to be included in the terminology, the relative number of descriptive and classificatory terms used for various kin types, and the particular relatives who are classed together under single labels.

All relatives in the generational levels between grandparent and grandchild are distinguished by sex— that is, females and males are called by different terms. Differences in generation are noted to a greater degree in one's own line than elsewhere, and within generations, relative age is stated in the terms people use for their collaterals. It is interesting to note that an emphasis on relative age overrides other factors in the definitions of / sʌni /, / ʔàt /, / t ʎ ak̓ʷ /, which are not used if the relative indicated is old enough to be classed with grandparents or young enough to be classed with one's collaterals.

The sex of the intervening relative is shown in the terminological separation of FB, FZ, and their line collaterals from MB, MZ, and one's own line collaterals. It is evidently important for a Tlingit to note through which relative a connection is made.

Tlingit indicate the speaker's sex in talking about members of the same generation and of one's own line: Males and females use different terms for similar relationships, and they make the same distinction in talking of children of these relatives.

If we look carefully at the kin types that the classificatory terms lump together, we find that those so grouped share some simple attributes in common. The people called / sʌni /, for instance, are all males of the same relative age and are related to F through females. The most economical and perhaps least ethnocentric translation of this term would be "males of father's line." Similarly, / t ɬ a / and the diminutive / t ɬ akʷ / mean "women of the parental generation in one's own line." The sibling terms that include parallel cousins essentially denote "males or females of one's own generation and line."

The inclusion of MBS and MBD with the terms for S and D, a common feature of Crow systems, has generated a number of explanations. Perhaps it is sufficient to note that these relatives are not of one's line but nonetheless are children of males of the line. Their inclusion in the same terms used for S and D implies that / yɪt / and / sí / would be translated more accurately as "males and female children of the line."

The terminological system clearly signifies that descent is matrilineal and also gives some clues to the form of social organization, but it does not tell all. The Tlingit lived in a rich environment where their fishing and gathering technology supported sizable populations and made sedentary living possible. The people lived in villages beside bays and estuaries, in large plank structures capable of housing several families. Some organization was needed to order village activities.

The data show that the Tlingit had a moiety system. Each division was exogamous, and membership was transmitted through women. The moieties had reciprocal obligations—that is, people of one moiety performed services for members of the other. These moieties were kin categories rather than groups, because neither Ravens nor Wolves interacted as a group. Tlingit in other villages were similarly divided, so that category loyalties went beyond the village to other people one might never have met.

Teqwedi and the other names stood for clans. The clans were in fact matriclans and were exogamous. The clans were important in political matters; they owned and allocated rights to house sites, trails, and fishing locations. Each village had members of several clans in residence, and clan members tended to group their houses together and to act cooperatively on occasion. Each clan had its totem (an object serving as the clan's emblem), history, lore, and ritual. Clan membership located the individual in the Tlingit ideological and social world.

The household, based on a group of men who were related through women, approximated a lineage; in effect, it was a segment of the clan under the direction of a senior male house leader. This unit owned the house slaves, canoes, and ritual objects and worked together for the good of the household members (Oberg 1973:20–30). The village was loosely structured. House groups of different clans tended to compete more than they cooperated, and when they did cooperate it was usually on a moiety basis.

Factors of prestige and relative age further ordered the society. While these are not kinship factors, they operated through the Tlingit kinship organization. Each clan was ranked within a moiety, and each household within a clan; in general, the higher honors, particularly the ranking within the household, went to older people.

Among the Tlingit, then, there was a moiety, a clan, a lineage, and a household system based on matrilineal principles but in the control of matrilineally related males. A child was born into its mother's categories but inherited duties and privileges from the mother's brother.

Conclusions

Schools of Thought

As they did in the case of marriage and family, the experts disagree over the utility of each other's studies and the conclusions they reach. Some say terminology reflects social relations; others disagree. Some believe that analysis of terms based on algebraic or formal logical models creates artificial universes of terms, or gives a system a more complex and integrating logic than it really has, or is guilty of both errors at once.

Perhaps the most debated current issue is what kin terms actually "mean" to the people who use them. One approach, well established in both British and American anthropology, centers kinship terminology in the roles of the nuclear family and sees the use of classificatory terms as extensions of these roles along genealogical lines to a wider universe of kin. For example, if I call one man "father," others whom I might address by the same term would be "like fathers to me." I would expect them to treat me as "son," and I would owe them the things expected of a son by a father. This *extensionist* approach is used by some writers for finding a way through the unilineal kin term systems. Ernest Schusky, for example, employs this approach in such statements as "Sib/clan/members, in one sense, are thought of as brothers and sisters" (1965:27); "Anyone who is a sib brother to my father is a brother to my father" (1965:29); and "Anyone I call 'father' will call me 'son'" (1965:31).

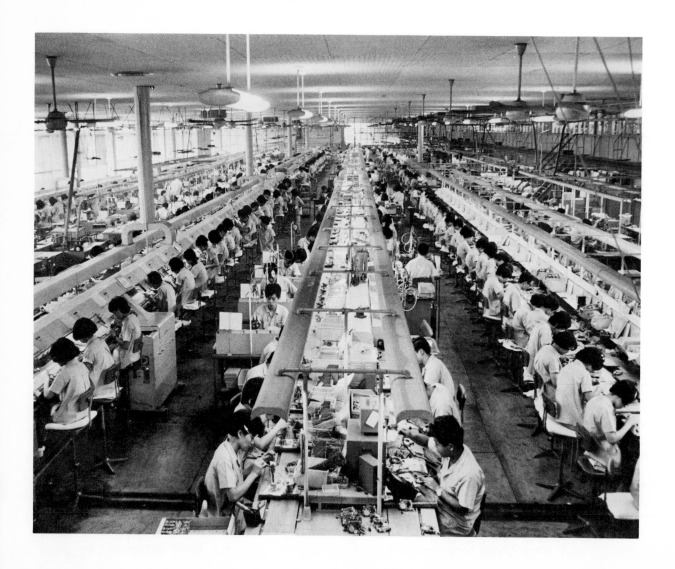

Although the family and kinship relations are still important to us, kinship is too limited a mechanism of social organization to be sufficient for the organization of behavior in mass, industrial society. However, in Japan appropriate social behavior—though not organized through kinship—nevertheless uses kinship relations as a *model* for good behavior. For example, the boss-worker relationship is patterned after the father-son relationship of pre-industrial times.

Floyd G. Lounsbury (1956, 1965) and others have used logical models—componential analysis—to prove that an analysis starting with the terms applicable to the nuclear family can generate the rest of the terminology by the use of extension principles.

Edmund Leach (1958, 1966) and Rodney Needham (1962), among others, disagree with these assumptions. The extensionists, they say, are ethnocentric; they are misled by the convention of using English kinship terms as translations of the words of others. These writers take a *categorist* approach. For instance, in their view, the Rapan—who use one term, *metua tane*, for F, FB, MB, FFBS, MZH, and so on—are not saying "all these are like fathers to me" and extending their affections in circles out from F. They do not sit down and figure out just how each man is related to them through whom in order to determine what to call them. Rather, *metua tane* would be translated most accurately as "men of the parental generation," a category; the one term reminds people of the appropriate behavior toward all men (including one's father) of this category.

Debates about alliance and descent are present in the study of kinship as they are in discussions of marriage. Extensionists tend to be more concerned with the rules of affiliation, with the channels of rights and duties, and with the problems of descent—how economic, political, material, and ideological aspects are transmitted from one generation to the next. They study the role relations, cooperative endeavors, and conflict resolutions that are handled by what Fortes has called "the web of kinship" (1949). The categorist position tends to include those who take an alliance point of view. They look from outside the larger system and treat the groups within as exchangers of women and goods and as groups vying for power. The task, as they see it, is to describe the alliances and the groups involved, and to determine how economic and political ends are met and the alliances perpetuated.

Author's Conclusions

The categorist versus extensionist arguments seem to me to produce more smoke than fire. The real issue is how to get inside the heads of the people who use the terms. But this may not be possible, and so the strengths of the positions might be better judged by how well they help the reader understand another system.

Lounsbury seems to present a good case for the extensionist perspective in his logical models, but it is not clear whether his results are neat because of the internal logic of his analytical model or because it most closely represents how the people concerned really think. From the perspective of the people, the model would surely seem complicated and cumbersome in just those respects in which the categorist approach seems simple and reasonable. A child could more easily learn the words and the categories they define than build a Lounsburian logical model in its mind. But then, models we can easily develop may turn out to be complex when viewed by another people. Also, we may underestimate the logical complexity a child can handle.

The main attraction of the categorist model is that it requires fewer assumptions and is thus a better general model with which to begin the study of a particular system. The investigator can then uncover the assumptions of the people and use them to modify the models; the conclusions would reflect people's requirements rather than the requirements of our logic. It might, or might not, turn out that they had an extensionist view of their kin.

The complex logical analysis of kin terms can become an intellectual game, an end in itself, but it can also produce valuable insights. If nothing else, formal analyses can help the investigator to anticipate some possible gaps in the terminology collected, and he or she can then check to see if words for a particular relation are present or not. The analyses might also be used to generate extension rules that could be checked with the people themselves to see whether they take an extensionist or categorist view.

We have to remember, too, the dual problem of first trying to understand what our subjects' view of kinship is and then trying to tell someone else, in English, what that view is. The two perspectives, extensionist and categorist, may supplement each other in clarifying the reality of another kinship system. Of late the long frowned-on concept of empathy—putting oneself in the other person's place—seems to be gaining favor as a means to this end.

The relationship of terminology to ongoing social organization is still not adequately understood. As mentioned earlier, many factors—change, optional usages, and others—make a one-to-one fit with an analytical model unlikely. Research on how people use the same terms in varying contexts should be illuminating. In one examination of the problem, Harold Scheffler emphasized that people often use the terminology to achieve diverse ends, with the result that a word may have different referents in different situations (1965).

Other studies should show some of the reasons for discrepancies between our ideal models and actual behavior. In particular, more studies are needed on how terminology is modified under conditions of change. The ties of kinship may weaken everywhere under the impact of industrialization and urbanization, and other social features, such as networks of interpersonal relations, may become useful in explaining prevalent social organization (Barnes 1972). But kinship ties will nonetheless persist and remain important, and they should not be overlooked.

Remember "my uncle, the judge."

Summary

Kinship is one of the most important organizers of human behavior. Marriage and the family lie at the heart of the institution.

A considerable though finite variety in the forms of kinship is found around the world, but a few basic patterns recur. Like marriage and the family, kinship is a social form resting on a biological base, but kinship structures may depart significantly from a purely genetic model of kin relationships.

Some of the major kinship patterns are exemplified here by the Greek village of Vasilika, the Blackfoot Indians, the Tlingit of Alaska, the Swazi of Africa, the Rapa islanders of Polynesia, the Hopi Indians, and the Australian Aborigines. These systems show very marked differences from each other in important respects.

People acquire three kinds of kin: *consanguineal kin* by birth, *affinal kin* by marriage, and *fictive kin* by such practices as adoption.

Affiliation and descent may be *unilineal* (patrilineal or matrilineal), *bilateral,* or defined by *double descent.*

A major form of descent group, the *lineage,* may be traced through males (patrilineages) or females (matrilineages). Other, larger forms of kin or descent groups include the *clan,* the *phratry,* and the *moiety.*

Anthropologists use a special system of notation for constructing diagrams of kin relationships. Some of the basic kinship types—Hawaiian, Eskimo, Iroquois, Crow, and Omaha—are analyzed here in anthropological terms.

Two main schools of thought have developed on the issue of kinship terminology. Extensionists are mostly concerned with the rules of descent or affiliation, whereas categorists tend to take an alliance point of view on kinship systems.

Annotated Bibliography

Bohannan, Paul, and Middleton, John, eds. (1968) *Kinship and Social Organization.* Garden City, N.Y.: Natural History Press. Contains a good summary of the development of kinship studies and includes significant papers that contributed to this development. Provides a sampling of papers addressed to a professional audience so that the reader can participate in the raising of issues and the generation of theories to resolve them.

Schusky, Ernest L. (1965) *Manual for Kinship Analysis.* New York: Holt. A primer of concepts and their use in diagraming and describing kin groups and terminological systems.

(1974) *Variations in Kinship.* New York: Holt. A useful companion to the manual that goes over the same ground with examples that show how real societies vary from the descriptive models. In many ways an expansion of parts of this chapter. The bibliography is a useful source of case studies.

A sense of the richness of variation and the complexities of kinship in actual life can be best gained by reading ethnographies. A few good ones with which to start are:

Balikci, Asen (1970) *The Netsilik Eskimo.* Garden City, N.Y.: Natural History Press. Balikci has worked with contemporary Netsilik to reconstruct the traditional way of life. His chapters on "Man and Society" provide an excellent example of description and analysis of marriage, family, and kinship in their context of a subsistence pattern of hunting migrating land and sea mammals.

Beals, Alan R. (1962) *Gopalpur: A South Indian Village.* New York: Holt. A good description of marriage and kin relations, with an inside view of family life and the role of patrilineal kinship in village life.

Hart, C. W. M., and Pilling, Arnold R. (1960) *The Tiwi of North Australia.* New York: Holt. A short case study of Tiwi life and culture; of major interest here because of the rules that require all females to be married. Baby girls are born married; widows are remarried. Through marriage, women play an important role in the political and economic power games of elderly men, but one over which they have little control. Old men have many wives; young men must work and wait, hoping to have a wife at least by middle age.

Hogbin, Ian (1964) *A Guadalcanal Society: The Kaoka Speakers.* New York: Holt. Marriage, family, and kinship are described in a way that contributes to a better understanding of them in their full social and cultural context. Matrilineality, subclan, and clan are seen as meaningful groupings in the social, economic and religious life of people rather than as abstract concepts. The reader feels what it is like to be a member of this society.

Kuper, Hilda (1963) *The Swazi: A South African Kingdom.* New York: Holt. This case study rounds out and brings alive the material presented in these chapters. Marriage, family, and kinship are parts of a complex political organization; kinship is related to other principles of social organization.

10
Subsistence and Trade: *Economic Anthropology*

The World Context

Origins and Development through Time

As we saw in Chapter 2 human biological and cultural evolution are intimately interrelated. The story of cultural evolution is written to a large degree in the means people devised to solve the problems of subsistence posed by their environments. As subsistence techniques developed and hominid groups were able to move into an increasing range of environments, social forms—especially the relationships between males and females—evolved in response to adaptive pressures. Tasks were gradually differentiated and parceled out among cooperating individuals.

The invention of agriculture was one of the most significant events in the story of human social evolution. Our early ancestors subsisted by hunting animals and foraging for vegetable foods. By the time of *Homo erectus*, they had developed both the technology and the forms of social organization necessary to be successful big-game hunters: Hoofed animals and other large mammals, such as the mammoth, make up about 90 percent of the killed animal remains we find. This pattern continued among groups of modern *Homo*

Tea-picking machines on the Ingirsky collective farm in Georgia, U.S.S.R. Securing material needs and wants is a matter not only of technology, but of ownership of resources, the means of production, and of the mechanisms through which goods are exchanged and distributed. The forms a society chooses in these domains become the foundation for the society's whole social organization.

sapiens until about 22,000 years ago. At that time, at least in the Middle East, a shift in subsistence strategy occurred. Kent Flannery describes the change from a narrow spectrum of food resources to a much broader one:

> pressure for the use of invertebrates, fish, water fowl, and previously ignored plant resources would have been felt most strongly in the more marginal areas which would have received overflow from the expanding populations of the prime hunting zones, raising their [population] densities to the limit of the land's carrying capacity. At this point they would tend to turn . . . to those smaller resources which are readily and predictably available in some quantity at certain seasons for the year. These are water fowl, fish, mussels, snails, and plants. (1969:57)

Archaeological data indicate that such a shift did occur, that it was nutritionally sound, and that it was caused by population pressures in marginal areas to which people had migrated from the more crowded favorable regions. The evidence also suggests that the innovation was taken up by populations in the more favorable areas. It is also worth noting that the "new" animal and vegetable foods were of a kind that could easily be collected by women and children, while the men could continue to hunt larger game (Flannery 1969:57–58). This broad-spectrum subsistence strategy persisted until the invention of agriculture.

Agriculture was invented at least three times in three different areas of the world: the Middle East, East Asia, and the New World. In each place we can identify a geographic center where entire complexes of plants and animals were domesticated and from which they diffused outward as a group. We can also identify noncenters, broad regions where different plants and animals were each domesticated separately and from which they diffused individually throughout the entire region. Systematic communications probably existed between each center and its associated noncenter area (Harlan 1971).

The Middle East is the area in which the food tradition that we associate with European society origina-

ted some 10,000 years ago. Its center is gradually being defined to include the arc along the mountain flanks from Iran through southeast Turkey to the southern Jordan highlands (Harlan 1971:468) (see fig. 10-1). The plants domesticated in this area include wheat, barley, rye, peas, lentils, flax, and chick-peas; domesticated animals were sheep, goats, pigs, dogs, and probably cattle somewhat later. A broad belt stretching 4,200 miles across sub-Saharan Africa is the corresponding noncenter where, possibly shortly after 4000 B.C., sorghum, millet, okra, cowpeas, and yams were domesticated (see Harlan 1971: table 1). Agriculture spread outward from this Middle Eastern center across the Anatolian peninsula into Greece, across the Sinai to North Africa, up the valley of the Danube River into Europe, and down into the alluvial valleys of the Tigris and Euphrates rivers (Harlan 1971:469).

Investigators are currently debating the location of the East Asian center. Some evidence points to China, about 4000 B.C., as the center (Harlan 1971). However, Wilhelm Solheim argues that the center is to be found

in ancient Thailand (1972). He concludes that the evidence suggests a domesticated food tradition in Thailand possibly as early as 9000 B.C., based on rice but also including chiles, beans, soybeans, peas, cucumbers, chickens, hump cattle, and water buffalo. The corresponding noncenter is scattered from eastern India across Burma, Indochina, southern China, Indonesia, the Philippines, Borneo, and New Guinea; it may even have extended into the Pacific as far as the Solomon Islands and New Caledonia. The most important crops domesticated in this noncenter were root crops, especially yams and taro; other foods included bananas, sugarcane, citrus fruits, and the coconut (Harlan 1971:472).

In the New World, the center appears to have been Mesoamerica, and South America as a whole the noncenter. The dominant crop of the center was maize (corn). In the Mexican highlands maize was domesticated between 7000 and 4000 B.C. (Meggers 1972:29). The bean seems to have been domesticated throughout both center and noncenter areas in a 3,000-mile

Figure 10-1
The Origins of Agriculture
Shown on this map are the centers and noncenters of agricultural origins: A1, Near East center; A2, African noncenter; B1, Chinese center; B2, Southeast Asian and South Pacific noncenter; C1, Mesoamerican center; C2, South American noncenter.

right
Inca men and women harvesting potatoes, a crop domesticated in the New World.

band from Mexico to Venezuela. Other domesticates include cassava, lima beans, avocados, peanuts, and sweet potatoes. These crops diffused northward to Mesoamerica, from which elements of the complex spread into North America (Harlan 1971:473). Tobacco, one of the most widely used nonfood crops, was also domesticated in South America and has diffused from there to every region of the world.

Why and how people developed agriculture and animal husbandry is still unresolved. The eminent archaeologist and theorist V. Gordon Childe advanced the so-called "oasis hypothesis" for the Middle East: The increasingly arid environment at the end of the Pleistocene forced human and animal populations to concentrate around sources of water, where they developed symbiotic interdependence. Humans harvested wild grains, especially wheat; wild sheep and goats came to depend on the stubble as a source of food; humans started to make systematic use of these wild herds, and also attempted to perpetuate what had previously been a wild harvest (1951, 1952).

Geographer Carl Sauer contended that agriculture was invented only once in Southeast Asia, and had diffused from there to all centers (1952). Although this radical diffusionist position is still controversial, his point of view that agriculture represents an adaptive strategy through which peoples interact with the environment remains a fundamental theme in the theoretical perspective called *cultural ecology*, which is currently popular.

Robert Braidwood, one of America's most prominent archaeologists, rejects the materialist and ecological approaches of Childe and Sauer. He argues that the climatic changes that took place at the end of the Pleistocene had occurred several times previously during late Pleistocene interglacial periods—but without generating an agricultural revolution as an adaptive response. Braidwood envisions the development of agriculture as a natural result of the broader evolutionary processes by which human society was becoming increasingly differentiated:

In my opinion there is no need to complicate the story with extraneous "causes." The food-producing revolution seems to have occurred as the culmination of the ever increasing cultural differentiation and specialization of human communities. Around 8000 B.C. the inhabitants of the hills around the fertile crescent had come to know their habitat so well that they were beginning to domesticate the plants and animals they had been collecting and hunting. At slightly later times human cultures reached the corresponding level in Central America and perhaps in the Andes, in Southeastern Asia and in China. From these "nuclear" zones cultural diffusion spread the new way of life to the rest of the world (1960:134).

The problem with Braidwood's hypothesis is that it never tells *why* knowing the environment well should lead to the development of agriculture: Why, if people were subsisting adequately, would they change their whole life-style? Also, as Thomas Meyers points out, the hypothesis cannot be tested; it is based on assumptions about human nature that must either be accepted or rejected on philosophical—but not empirical—grounds (1971).

Perhaps the most sophisticated theories about the origins of agriculture are those of Kent Flannery. In his discussions of both the Middle East (1965) and Mesoamerica (1968), Flannery agrees with Braidwood that climatic changes alone cannot account for the shift in subsistence activities from foraging to agriculture. However, he does not abandon the search for ecological and adaptational elements that might have contributed to this process. Flannery argues that the shift to agriculture was part of a slow process by which hunting and gathering populations gradually reduced the number of their subsistence resources. These people began to concentrate their foraging into decreasing ranges and adapted to the use of a few selected plants and animals.

In Mesoamerica, people came to depend more and more on wild ancestors of maize (corn) and beans. Gradually this concentration on the harvesting of wild maize and beans led to the deliberate sowing of seeds. The genetic changes in the plants that led to their full domestication was only a matter of time and selection. In the Middle East, people concentrated on the large stands of wild grasses that were ancestral to wheat and barley. The resulting life-style was so successful that they could begin to concentrate into rather permanent settlements by around 7000 B.C. The population began to rise, approaching the carrying capacity of these abundant areas. This forced people to migrate into marginal areas, where they attempted to re-create the more abundant environments they had left behind by sowing the cereal grains they had carried with them. The "invention" of agriculture was underway. Animals may have been domesticated somewhat by chance, but once the process had been started, there was good reason to continue it: Animals are both an immediate source of food and a way of storing food for times of need when crops fail.

Although we are far from knowing the exact causes of the domestication of plants and animals, we do know that this adaptive strategy was very successful. It spread across the ancient world and became the material basis for the development of all civilizations. Agricultural food production has also contributed to: a reduction in the sizes of territories that people need to provide themselves with food; an associated increase in population densities; the conversion of land from a communally owned resource to privately owned property; the development of new social forms based on property ownership and laws of inheritance; and a tremendous amplification of the impact of human beings on the environment (Fagan 1974:189–192; Thomas 1956).

Contemporary Examples

It has long been a common anthropological assumption that the life of nomadic and seminomadic hunters and gatherers is dominated by the never fully satisfied quest for food:

> The nomadic hunters and gatherers barely met minimum subsistence needs and often fell far short of them. Their population of 1 person to 10 or 20 square miles reflects this. Constantly on the move in search of food, they clearly lacked the leisure hours of nonsubsistence activities of any significance, and they could transport little of what they might manufacture in spare moments. To them, adequacy of production meant physical survival, and they rarely had surplus of either products of time (Steward and Faron 1959:60; cited in Sahlins 1972:3).

This point of view is being increasingly attacked. It is based on the folk assumptions of our own culture; that people should produce and own more goods than they need to subsist; that time not spent on subsistence pursuits should be "properly" spent in "activities"; and that agricultural subsistence (which is the evolutionary basis of our own civilization) is the only subsistence form that can provide sufficient goods and leisure to satisfy the "basic human need" for both.

Arnhem Landers and the !Kung San   The facts, it seems, are different. As more and more studies of hunting and gathering societies become available, anthropologists are having to reassess their image of these groups. Reporting on some studies of Australian aborigine groups living in Arnhem Land, Marshall Sahlins finds: "The most obvious, immediate conclusion is that people do not work hard. The average length of time per person per day put into the appropriation and preparation of food was four or five hours. Moreover, they do not work continuously. The subsistence quest was highly intermittent. It would stop for the time being when the people had procured enough for the time being, which left them plenty of time to spare" (1972:17).

Furthermore, it is clear that the aborigines procure *less* food than they could; they choose to stop when their immediate demands have been met. The labor is not particularly exhausting, and the Arnhem Landers themselves do not consider their work to be onerous or unpleasant. Moreover, these people do not simply scavenge anything they can find but consciously look for some diversity in their foods, even though this means some extra work. Even at their leisurely pace, however, the aborigines are able to ensure themselves of a more than adequate amount of food (Sahlins 1972:17–18).

These aboriginal groups have significant amounts of free time. They tend to spend their leisure hours chatting and resting rather than manufacturing more products. We must once again question our folk assumptions: Why *should* they produce things they do not need—especially when carrying possessions would hamper their mobility? These groups see the world quite differently from the way we do. We foster almost unlimited wants—and assume that all people share these "needs." Their wants are few and easily satisfied. Their opportunities are limited by their technology, of course, but this is in terms of *our* standards.

A tragic paradox seems to characterize the evolution of more advanced subsistence methods: Technological progress has made it *less* easy for people to get what they want, rather than what they need. Also, probably more people are starving in the world today, when some societies have the technological ability to produce more food than the entire world population could consume, than 15,000 years ago, when all the world was still at the hunting and gathering stage of subsistence.

Although this research on the Arnhem Landers was undertaken in the late 1940s, recent research on other hunting and gathering groups has yielded similar findings. In chapter 21, Richard Lee describes the lives of the !Kung San (Bushmen) living in the Kalahari Desert of southern Africa; they also have the ability to adequately meet their needs in a less than bountiful environment.

If many contemporary hunting and gathering groups do have subsistence difficulties, the fault probably lies not with their own technology but rather with the expanding industrial civilization that is driving them out of the environments to which they had adapted and displacing them into areas with ever fewer natural resources.

The Ik   A case in point is that of the Ik, a tribe of nomadic hunters and gatherers who roamed through parts of what is now Kenya, Uganda, and the Sudan until just before World War II. Their tragic story has been documented in painful detail by Colin Turnbull (1972). What had been their major hunting and foraging territory is now a national park. The Ik have been permanently settled in some seven Ugandan villages, each containing from four to fifty huts. The government encourages the Ik to cultivate gardens, but these often fail because of poor soil and frequent severe

An Australian Aborigine family in northern Queensland, c. 1920. The man at right is preparing to roast a kangaroo. Their shelter is obviously not a permanent structure, reflecting the group's commitment to mobility as part of their subsistence strategy.

droughts. Thus many old and sick people starve to death, and others survive on government handouts.

Under these conditions the fabric of Ik social life has been irreparably damaged. Parents no longer bring up their children. They expel them from their hut by the age of three, leaving them to roam, uncared for, in scavenging peer groups. The old and infirm are also ejected and left to die, partly because the traditional funerary requirements are beyond people's means, but more importantly, because food and medicine are reserved for those who can most benefit from them.

When the weather is good enough for Ik gardens to produce a reasonable yield, the people glut themselves and do little to preserve or store their surplus. Storing, they feel, would be a waste of time: They would merely steal from each other as soon as times became hard. Moreover, they do not wish to look too prosperous, because the government would then reduce or cut off desperately needed aid. The Ik, according to Turnbull, have lost the most central institution of human society: the family. They have rejected as too costly the binding forces of parent-child love and concern. The constant condition of hunger has destroyed the fiber of their social structure. Deprived of those qualities that we think of as the nobler human characteristics, the Ik continue their wretched existence—an existence in which each person's overriding concern is simply and solely his or her survival.

Theory

Systems

The natural environment is the origin of all the resources people use to secure their material needs and desires. However, societies have only limited access to the range of resources nature has to offer. These limitations are imposed by *where* the people live, *who* they trade with, and the *technology* at their disposal. Moreover, no society uses all available elements in the environment. All groups are selective, choosing to utilize certain resources and to ignore others.

As we shall see, societies approach the problem of subsistence with very different strategies. Some groups forage for food and supplement their vegetable diets with various kinds of game; other groups emphasize fishing; still others concentrate on agricultural food production. The nature of the subsistence strategy a society emphasizes determines which natural resources are of principal importance—that is, which resources cannot be done without. If a society is primarily agricultural, land is such a crucial resource. For a fishing society, materials to build boats and fishing equipment are primary. Thus the subsistence strategy and the environment interact to create a category of resources that are vital to the group's survival—their *strategic resources.*

In order to exploit the natural environment, all societies use skills (including knowledge), implements, and sources of power. Together these elements constitute a group's *technology.* Let us look at each in turn.

The range of subsistence *skills* human beings have developed is vast. Obvious categories are skills for hunting (tracking, trapping, use of weapons, butchering, and so on), foraging (vegetation recognition, ecological knowledge, tool use, and so forth), fishing (use of boats, tackle, ability to predict the behavior of fish, knowledge of winds and tides, and so on), horticulture (preparing land for planting, tending crops, harvesting, and so on), pastoralism (animal breeding, herding, care, and so forth), or agriculture (land drainage, clearing, terracing, irrigation, planting, harvesting, storing, and so on). Each group develops its own range of such skills and passes them on to the next generation.

The skills a society develops are intimately related to the *implements* it uses. Some of the major categories of implements are:

1. Tools: These are implements designed to facilitate the performance of a particular work activity. They can include implements for killing animals, for modifying the environment, and for manufacturing other tools and objects.

2. Clothing: These are materials worn on the person, primarily to protect the body from the natural environment. Clothes are worn to protect against the cold (the sealskin parkas, pants, and boots of Eskimos), the heat (the flowing white robes of Arab desert tribes), or dampness (the knit wool clothing of nordic

Danakil camel- and goat-herding nomads of Ethiopia searching the desert floor for salt. They subsist mainly on goat's milk and the loot they can steal from unwary victims. Salt is the only commodity they can produce for cash; hence it becomes a vital strategic resource, even though it lies for all to find on the desert floor.

European groups). However, groups living in similar climates do not necessarily produce and wear the same types of clothing. For example, the Eskimos cover themselves almost entirely, whereas the Yaghan of Tierra del Fuego in Antarctica wore almost nothing. They merely rubbed their bodies with grease for insulation.

3. Shelter: These are structures built by people to protect themselves against the environment. There is enormous cross-cultural variety in the complexity of the structures that people build. Consider the windbreaks of the Australian Aborigines, the half-open brush huts of the !Kung San of the Kalahari Desert, the multistoried adobe dwellings of the Pueblo Indians of the American Southwest, the snow-built igloos of the Eskimos, the skin tepees of the Great Plains Indians, the felt tents of Siberian reindeer herders, and the split-level suburban houses of the industrial United States. The diversity of human architectural ingenuity expresses itself in countless ways.

4. Transportation devices: These include all the mechanical devices people use to facilitate their own movement and the movement of their goods. These devices include containers of all sorts, nets and sacks that can be slung over the shoulders or looped around the forehead, skis and sleds, rafts and boats of all shapes and sizes, wheeled vehicles such as carts, cars, and trains, and flying vehicles such as gliders, airplanes, and spacecraft. (Interestingly, although Mesoamericans knew of the wheel and incorporated it into children's toys, no New World civilization used the wheel for transportation or any other "practical" purpose.)

The remaining element of a society's technology is the sources of power that it harnesses. All societies employ human muscle power and have devices to amplify it, such as digging sticks or levers. Some human groups have no other sources of power. Others use animal power for transportation and sometimes for modifying of the environment, as in plowing. Other groups have learned to control the forces of nature, such as the power of wind and water (windmills; dams and water mills). Some groups have learned to create sources of power by converting natural resources such as crude oil or uranium into energy. Sources of power are so important to a society's success that some anthropologists use the amount of per capita energy a society can control as an index of its level of cultural evolution.

Among primate groups in general, each mature individual is responsible for gathering its own food and meeting its own subsistence needs. In contrast, all human societies divide subsistence tasks among their members, making each individual in the group dependent on the cooperation of others to secure his or her subsistence needs. Human societies have evolved a number of different modes for this organization of work.

The Organization of Work Age and sex (and kinship) are universal bases for the organization of work, although their relevance varies from culture to culture. Among the less technologically advanced societies, especially those that subsist primarily through hunting and foraging, age and sex are the most important determiners of work. There is little or no technical specialization of labor; all the mature males of a group do what is considered appropriate for men to do, while all the women engage in women's work. The nature of the work considered appropriate to each sex varies from culture to culture and depends on such factors as the natural environment, the subsistence technology, and the local traditions. Nevertheless, some general cross-cultural patterns do exist in the division of labor between men and women (see Chap. 3). The age dimension is significant in that all societies recognize a period of childhood during which individuals are not expected to engage in subsistence activities. In most societies, however, children are enculturated at early ages into the subsistence roles expected of them when they mature. The old, too, are usually exempted from at least the more strenuous subsistence activities.

Kinship, particularly in the nonindustrial world, is one of the major devices by which people organize their social existence (Chap. 9). Not surprisingly, kinship organization is also an important means of organizing work, especially in societies with relatively simple technological systems. Among the hunting and gathering !Kung San described in Chapter 21, each man hunts primarily for his own wife and children but shares whatever meat he has among his consanguineal relatives. Each woman shares her portion of the meat with her own relatives, too, but shares the vegetable foods she has gathered primarily with her husband and children. Among the Swiss peasants described in Chapter 20, food is produced and consumed entirely within a household unit consisting (ideally) of a three-generation, vertically extended family.

Age, sex, and kinship criteria are universally used as a basis for the organization of work. However, a society can divide various tasks among its members in many other ways. Tasks may be ascribed on the basis of *caste* (see Chap. 15), with certain occupational roles being tied to hereditary membership in particular castes or subcastes. Such a system has existed on the Indian subcontinent for thousands of years. Another basis similar to caste for organizing work is *skin color* or *ethnicity*. The division of labor along these lines may take place in the shape of subtle discrimination, a form widely applied against minority groups in the United States today. Or occupational roles may be explicitly and formally assigned on the basis of what are believed to be "racial" criteria. This form of work organization was practiced in many colonial situations and still persists in the contemporary Republic of South Africa, for instance, where all skilled and most semiskilled jobs are reserved by law for members of the ruling white minority.

In stratified societies, work may be organized in such a way that *social class* effectively allocates job roles to individuals. In practice, little social mobility is possible in most class societies, and the work opportunities of most people are largely determined by the socioeconomic status of their parents. In technologically advanced societies that have highly specialized occupational roles, *individual characteristics*—skills, knowledge, training, experience, personality attributes—become very important in the division of labor. However, the opportunity to acquire these individual characteristics depends to a great extent on one's class background.

Not all labor is voluntary, nor is all work in the worker's own best interest. Especially in stratified societies, forms of work organization based on coercion appear. In such situations, people work solely to avoid punishment, not to gain anything for themselves. Coerced work can be divided into several different types.

Forced labor deprives people of their freedom for a specified period during which they are compelled to perform specific tasks. Chain gangs of prisoners are one example. Another form of forced labor was the *corveé* in feudal Europe, a system whereby the lords could compel their vassals to work on their farms for a certain number of days a year. Yet another form of forced agricultural labor is *tenancy*, under which farmers plant their crops in the landowner's fields but owe him a certain (and often very high) proportion of the crops they harvest. Although the tenant is in theory a free person, in practice tenancy often becomes a system of perpetual indebted (and hence forced) labor. A tenant family may become so heavily indebted that the obligations bound to them are passed on from generation to generation. This condition is known as *peonage*. When a system of peonage operates through the mechanism of land residency, the term *serfdom* is used. Serfs owe their landlords work simply because they live on lands to which he holds legal title. The landlord not only owns rights to the land; he owns rights to the labor of his serfs as well. The serfs do not have the right either to leave the land or to refuse their labor.

The most extreme form of coerced work organization is *slavery*, in which others own not only rights to people's labor but also rights to the people themselves. Generally, the positions of both slave and master are inherited. Not all forms of slavery were as brutal and dehumanizing as the form that evolved under plantation systems. In some African, Asian, and classical European societies, slaves had limited but real legal rights, could sometimes own property and hold public office, and might occasionally marry into the society of free people. Nevertheless, slavery is the most coercive form of labor that human beings have managed to devise.

It is clear that the way a society organizes its work is intimately related to such factors as the nature of its technological system, the problems posed by the natural environment, and the form of sociopolitical organization it has adopted. One way of measuring social complexity is to count the number of specialized occupational alternatives a society offers its members: the more alternatives, the more complex is the society. You might try looking through the case studies presented in chapters 20 through 25 to see if you can arrange these societies in a continuum of increasing complexity as indicated by their organization of work.

Processes

Two major processes are crucial to the securing of material needs: *subsistence strategies* and *methods of distribution.* Let us examine these in turn.

Subsistence Strategies   **In Chapter 3, five major** classes of subsistence strategies were identified: hunting and gathering (or foraging), horticulture, pastoralism, agriculture, and industrialism. Because of its enormous complexity, we shall not discuss industrialism as a subsistence strategy and instead will focus on the first four.

Hunting and gathering is an adaptive strategy that relies on minimally amplified human muscular energy

alone. Collecting wild foods with a few tools, such as a digging stick, or fishing and hunting with knives, spears, boomerangs, bows and arrows, traps, nets, and so forth are typical activities. This subsistence strategy usually, but not always, means a semi-nomadic lifestyle, with small bands of fifty to a hundred persons ranging across their territories in quest of food. Groups that live near relatively plentiful and reliable sources of food, such as streams with seasonal salmon runs, tend to be somewhat more sedentary (Cohen 1968:59).

Horticulture, like hunting and gathering, relies primarily on muscular energy to meet subsistence needs. Horticulturalists generally cultivate garden plots, using either a digging stick or a hoe, and plant tubers, seeds, shoots, and roots. Although many horticulturalists also hunt and gather other foods, their basic subsistence strategy represents a fundamental break with the hunting and gathering way of life. As

Cameroun women clear and prepare a field using iron-bladed hoes. They purchase the blades at the market. Such hoe cultivation is called horticulture.

such societies come to rely more and more on cultivated plants and domesticated animals for food, their population densities rise, their settlements become increasingly permanent, their division of labor grows more specialized, and their political organization becomes more complex and centralized (see Chap. 3).

Pastoralism is a subsistence strategy mostly adapted to semi-arid open grassland environments; it involves a primary dependance on herding and animal husbandry to satisfy many of the people's material needs and wants. Pastoralists exploit their herds for milk products, but use their animals for much more: Dung provides fuel for fires, skins of deceased animals are made into leather products, sheared fur is processed into wool or matted into felt (for clothing or tents). Although deceased animals are eaten, pastoralists avoid butchering their animals for meat since this would tend to deplete herds. For vegetable foods pastoralists frequently also practice limited horticulture; those groups that do not (like, for example, the Mutayr Bedouins described in Chapter 22) have long-standing trading relationships with settled agricultural peoples. Pastoralism demands a certain degree of mobility from its practitioners, as the animals are herded cyclically through a sequence of ecological niches (frequently from lowlands to highlands and back—termed *transhumance*) as the seasons change. Of the strategic resources—grazing lands, water, and the herds of animals themselves—the former is often more available to all members of the society, whereas individuals' access to the latter two varies greatly from one society to the next. Thus differences in individual wealth—though not outright class stratification—are quite common in pastoral societies. Class stratification and centralized political organization seem to appear in pastoral societies as an adaptation to deal with the pressures exerted by neighbors at the state level of sociopolitical organization.

In *agriculture*, the hoe and digging stick are replaced by the plow, an innovation that allows agriculturalists to turn the soil deeper and vastly increases crop yields. The use of the plow, however, necessitates the use of draft animals, which must be bred, raised, and distributed. Agriculture may also require some form of centralized irrigation system. And because agriculturalists often produce more than a single household can consume, the resulting surpluses can be stored, carted off to market, or paid in taxes, all of which implies increasingly elaborate communications networks and systems of political regulation. Thus the productive potential of advanced horticulture and agriculture is significant far beyond the narrow issue of subsistence: It brings with it the material base to sustain new social forms, including stratified social classes and centralized state authority. Increasingly specialized and differentiated forms of social organization develop. The division of labor becomes complex: People fill a wide range of specialized craft and service roles, and entire groups of individuals can engage in non-food-producing work.

As we have seen, the development of more "advanced" subsistence strategies does not necessarily result in the saving of time or labor. Marvin Harris has drawn together careful quantitative research on five different groups (1971:203–217). Comparing the amount

of calories of food produced for each calorie expended in food production, he found the results indicated in figure 10-2. The data suggests an increasing "techno-environmental efficiency" as we move from such hunting and gathering groups as the !Kung San to peasant peoples such as the prerevolutionary Chinese irrigation farmers. However, when we compare the !Kung San with the horticultural Genieri, we find that the most striking difference between the two energy systems is the twentyfold increase in total calorie output. Most of this difference is accounted for by the increase in size of the labor force. Note that the factor of technological efficiency is only slightly higher and that the hours of work are essentially unchanged. "The advantage of rudimentary forms of agriculture [that is, horticulture] over most hunting and food-gathering lies in *the ability of agricultural routines to sustain nucleated settlements rather than in any immediate labor-saving improvement* in . . . technoenvironmental efficiency" (Harris 1971:207; emphasis added). In fact, considered in an evolutionary context,

$$E = m \times t \times r \times e$$

Society	Annual Calories Produced	Food Producers	Hours Per food Producer	Calories Expended Per hour	Techno-Environmental Efficiency	Subsistence Technology
!Kung San (S. Africa)	23,000,000	20	805	150	9.6	hunting and gathering
Genieri (W. Africa)	460,000,000	334	820	150	11.2	hoe horticulture
Tsembaga*, (Highland New Guinea)	150,000,000	146	380	150	18	slash-and-burn horticulture
Luts' un (Yunnan China)	3,780,000,000	418	1,129	150	53.5	irrigation agriculture
U.S.A.	260 trillion	5,000,000	1,714	150	210	industrial agriculture

* The data only includes vegetable food production. The formula for pigs is:
$$\underset{18,000,000}{E} = \underset{146}{m} \times \underset{400}{t} \times \underset{150}{r} \times \underset{2.1}{e}$$ Thus meat production is much less efficient.

Kikuyu market north of Nairobi, Kenya. It is a weekly affair, with both local food producers and importers of foreign trade items congregating to bargain, barter, and exchange their goods.

Figure 10-2
Comparison of Technoenvironmental Efficiency of Five Societies
Increasing technoenvironmental efficiency (e) has *not* meant increased leisure, contrary to popular belief. Rather, with the exception of the remarkably undemanding subsistence technology of slash-and-burn horticulture, increased efficiency has also meant increased work (*t*) for more people (*m*), who produced more and more food (*E*). (Condensed from Harris 1971:203–17.)

the data in figure 10-2 strongly indicates that when labor-saving food-production techniques have been developed, they have been used to *increase production* rather than to decrease work effort.

Distribution Methods   Let us now consider distribution methods, another crucial system that operates to help human beings secure their material needs and wants. We shall examine three major distribution systems: reciprocity, redistribution, and market exchange.

Reciprocity is probably the oldest form of distribution and the one that still predominates in technologically simple societies. Reciprocity is the giving and receiving of gifts. Such gifts may consist of material items, favors, or specific forms of labor. When people give each other gifts without expecting anything in return at that time or in the immediate future but assume that they will receive *equivalent* value in return over the duration of the relationship, we speak of *generalized reciprocity*. The straightforward exchange of goods or services that both parties regard as equivalent at the time of the exchange is termed *balanced reciprocity* (Service 1966:15). An example of generalized reciprocity in our own society is the giving of birthday presents among friends. Balanced reciprocity is the kind of trading children engage in—marbles for baseballs, stamp collections for comics.

All societies practice forms of reciprocal exchange, and such exchanges are often fundamental to the survival of groups with simple technologies. In these societies the principal item exchanged is food; and it is only because reciprocal exchanges of food constantly take place (primarily along kinship lines) that every group member is ensured sufficient food to survive.

Redistribution involves the movement of goods toward some kind of center of allocation and then outward again. Redistribution requires some central authority with sufficient power to compel people to surrender to it a portion of their goods in accordance with the rules of the system. The central authority subsequently redistributes a portion of what is collected, but has discretionary power over how to do so and hence has the ability to enforce allegiance through selective "generosity." In state societies redistribution often takes the form of taxation, the proceeds of which are used to support the administrative bureaucracy, to underwrite centrally controlled projects, and to provide public services.

Redistribution systems operate prominently in stratified societies; indeed, redistribution provides a mechanism, once a society has the technological ability to produce a surplus beyond its subsistence needs, whereby an elite can secure or maintain its social ascendancy in economic as well as in sociopolitical terms.

Market exchange is the third major process through which goods are distributed. It is useful to think of markets not only as *places* where goods are exchanged but also as *mechanisms* that operate to set prices on such goods. Market systems develop only in societies that have the technological capacity to produce more than each food-producing unit can consume. When a society's food producers can supply a surplus, other members of the society can specialize in the production of craft items. Artisans and food producers bring their respective wares to market, where they negotiate over the worth of what they have to offer. Unlike reciprocal relationships, the intent of each person

at the market is to maximize his or her gain at the other's expense; impersonal considerations such as the supply of and the demand for items influence prices. Sometimes the goods themselves are exchanged, a transaction that is termed *bartering*. But frequently all payments for goods are made through the vehicle of money. *Money* is a medium of exchange that is fungible (easily replaceable and/or exchangeable for another of like kind), portable, divisible into combinable units, and accepted by all participants in the market system in which it is used.

In the more complex societies, all three processes—reciprocity, redistribution, and market exchange—coexist, each in its own sphere. In some societies market systems are peripheral and are dominated by redistributive and reciprocal exchange processes. In societies with the simplest technology (primarily hunting and gathering societies), reciprocity remains to this day the dominant mode of distributing goods.

Analysis

The Folk Perspective

Let us see how some of the concepts we have presented can be used to understand how people secure their material needs and wants, and how these processes mesh with other aspects of the social and cultural systems. The case we shall focus on was described by Paul Bohannan (1955). The people he studied are a tribal group called the Tiv, who live in northern Nigeria. Their mode of food production is subsistence agriculture, and the dominant form of distribution is a network of markets.

The Tiv divide goods into two categories: "gift" goods and "market" goods. "Gift" goods are exchanged between individuals who have long-standing and affectionate personal relationships. It is considered bad form for people to carefully tally the values of the gifts they exchange; rather, they should trust that things will even out in the long run—a perfect example of generalized reciprocity.

"Market" exchanges involve no personal feelings between individuals; in fact, because each person is determined to trade to his or her best advantage, previous relationships get in the way, and people therefore avoid trading with relatives in markets.

Several Tiv concepts are lumped together in the word *kasoa*, which we are translating as "market." The word refers primarily to any exchange that is not a "gift" exchange. It also refers to the physical place where people meet regularly at scheduled times to exchange goods. Finally, it refers to an aspect of a person's "luck," for some people have good "market luck," and others, bad. The Tiv believe that such factors as one's ritual condition, promises one might have broken, and the curses of witches may operate to impair an individual's "market luck."

The market operates in a classic way as a price-setting mechanism, although traditionally price was not set in terms of a third factor (money) but rather in terms of the inherent values of the goods themselves. Bargaining, then, did not involve dickering around with abstract prices but rather determining the relative "equivalent," or "value," of the items being exchanged. Actually, the Tiv language does not neatly discriminate, as does English, between bartering goods and selling them for money.

The Tiv system of exchange also has the peculiarity that not all items should—or even can be—traded for any other commodity. The Tiv have at least three distinct, exclusive categories of traded commodities:

1. Subsistence items: All locally produced foodstuffs, such as peppers, yams, guinea corn, and so forth, are appropriate items to exchange for one another in market bartering. The category also includes such animals as chickens and goats, household utensils, tools, and some of the raw materials necessary for producing these items. Prices of items in this category are not predetermined: The "deal" each individual is able to close is a reflection on his or her "market luck."

2. Prestige items: Associated with the concept of prestige, this category includes slaves, cattle, a certain kind of prized white cloth, and metal bars.

3. Dependent persons: This category consists of "rights in human beings other than slaves, and particularly rights in women" (Bohannon 1955:62). For practical purposes the category usually refers to rights in wives and their children. The values of these "commodities" were expressed in terms of Tiv kinship and marriage norms.

(It is interesting to note that land—the ownership of which is for many peoples the ultimate expression of wealth—is not and cannot be traded among the Tiv; land rights reside in entire, corporate kinship groups. See Chaps. 8 and 9.)

These three categories are in a hierarchical relationship to one another—"to convert subsistence wealth into prestige wealth and both into women is the aim of the economic endeavor of individual Tiv" (Bohannon 1955:64). Thus exchanges *within* categories—conveyances—are morally neutral, but exchanges *between* categories—conversions—are marked by a strong moral component for the Tiv.

There are many social sanctions for conversion of one's wealth to higher categories: Tiv are very scornful of a man who is merely rich in subsistence goods (or, today, in money); they say that if he has not converted his goods the reasons must be personal inadequacy. Tiv also say that jealous kinsmen of a rich man will bewitch him and his people by means of certain fetishes in order to make him expend his wealth in sacrifices in order to "repair" the fetishes. Once the conversion is made, demands of kinsmen are no longer effective—at least, they must take a new form.

A man who persists in a policy of converting his wealth into higher categories instead of letting it be dispersed by his dependents and kinsmen is said to have a "strong heart" (*taver shima*). He is both feared and respected: because he is strong enough to resist the excessive demands of his kinsmen, but still fulfills his kinship obligations generously, he is feared as a man of special potentially evil, talents (*tsav*) (Bohannan 1955:66).

The Analytical Perspective

By the time Bohannan started his research, money had been introduced into Tivland for some twenty-five years, and all conversions and most conveyances were enacted through the medium of money. The Tiv are far from happy with money, it should be emphasized, for they see it as "the root of much of their trouble." Desiring money but yet not truasting it entirely, the Tiv have attempted to relegate it to a fourth category of exchange—at the bottom of the hierarchy. The logical conclusion would be a system in which money could only be exchanged for money, or for European industrial trade goods. The older and more traditionally oriented Tiv maintain that this is exactly what has happened, but the facts do not fit this folk perspective.

Two separate processes intersect to cause the Tiv a great deal of difficulty. On one hand, an occupational group of male semiprofessional traders, who specialize in dealing in goods that must be transported over long distances, has emerged. Subsistence goods such as smoked fish, camwood, and kolas may be purchased for money and carried as far as 150 miles to market, where they are sold at higher prices, again for money. These traders' purpose is simply to increase their money, an enterprise that the Tiv consider to be legitimate.

On the other hand, women trade in *local* subsistence goods. They, too, use money as the medium of exchange rather than bartering. This enterprise is also seen as legitimate, because the Tiv say that the use of money is beside the point as long as the women are not making conversions from one class of goods to another, but are selling one type of subsistence good to be able to purchase others.

The Tiv difficulties arise out of the fact that the highly mobile semiprofessional male traders now actively trade in the foodstuffs that had formerly been exclusively traded among women. Thus goods that used to circulate locally are now being channeled away from communities every market day.

[The Tiv] . . . say that food is less plentiful today than it was in the past, though more land is being farmed. Tiv elders deplore this situation and know what is happening, but they do not know just where to fix the blame. In attempts to do something about it, they sometimes announce that no women are to sell any food at all. But when their wives disobey them, men do not really feel they were wrong to have done so. Tiv sometimes discriminate against non-Tiv traders in attempts to stop export of food, but their actions are seldom upheld by the courts to which the outsiders scurry, and in any case Tiv themselves are occupied in the export of food (Bohannon 1955:69).

But money has not only affected the ability of the Tiv to feed themselves and to trade well. Of even more concern to them is the effect that money has had on their marriage system. The administration had legally abolished exchange marriage and substituted for it the system whereby a husband's family pays a bride's father a cash brideswealth. The problem is that money has no inherent prestige value: Every father who thus "sells" his daughter feels that he has converted downward in the categories of exchange, thereby depreciating his social position. Nor is the person who thus "buys" a wife necessarily better off. The paradox is:

It is easy to sell subsistence goods for money to buy prestige articles and women, thereby aggrandizing oneself at a rapid rate. The food so sold is exported, decreasing the amount of subsistence goods available for consumption. On the other hand, the number of women is limited. The result is that brideswealth gets higher—the price of women becomes inflated. Under these conditions, as Tiv attempt to become more and more wealthy in people, they are merely selling more and more of their foodstuffs and subsistence goods, leaving less and less for their own consumption (Bohannan 1955:70).

The case of the Tiv is interesting for several reasons. It demonstrates that very diverse items (including people) can be strategic economic resources. It also illustrates how systems of reciprocity and market exchange can exist side by side. Finally, it is an example of how the introduction of money into a market system that originally functioned without money has not only distorted the operation of the system but has also profoundly influenced major aspects of the society's social organization.

Conclusions

Schools of Thought

It is customary to credit Bronislaw Malinowski with being the major pioneer in the development of economic anthropology. In his classic study *Argonauts of the Western Pacific* (1922) and also in a detailed article in the journal *Man* (1920), he described in magnificent detail the system of exchange operating among a small group of Melanesian Islands lying off the eastern end of New Guinea. He focused his attention on the ritual exchange of two items: white cowrie shell armbands called *mwali*, and red shell necklaces called *soulava*. The principle was very simple: *Mwali* could only be exchanged for *soulava*, *soulava* only for *mwali*. The result was that *soulava* and *mwali* moved between islands in two great circles rotating in opposite directions; *soulava* moved clockwise, and *mwali*, counterclockwise (see fig. 10-3).

This system of exchange, called the *kula*, involved large expeditions of men sailing on long voyages between islands in wooden outrigger canoes powered by lanteen-rigged sails. Malinowski described minutely

Figure 10-3
Kula Ring
Routes for the reciprocal exchange of *soulava* and *mwali* in the kula exchange system described by Malinowski. (after Hammond, 1971)

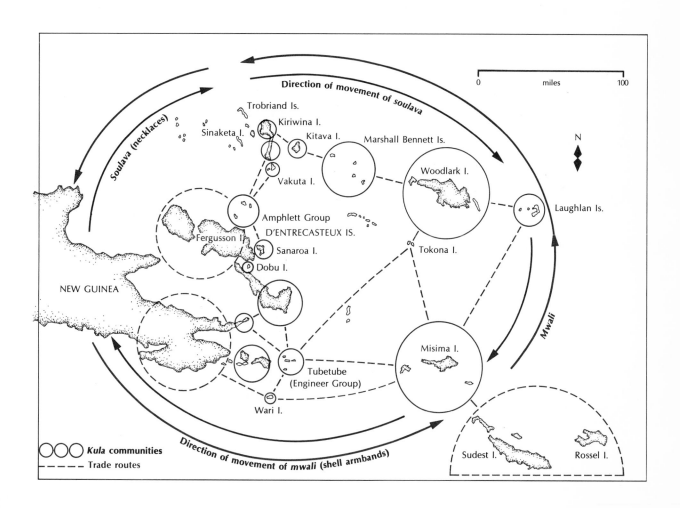

the ritual preparations for such journeys and discussed at length the participants' attitudes and their hopes to rise in the prestige system as a result of their *kula* exchanges. However, as Marvin Harris points out, we "learn only incidentally, never in detail, that the whimsical voyagers circulate not only armbands and necklaces but coconuts, sago, fish, vegetables, baskets, mats, sword clubs, green stone (formerly essential for tools), mussel shells (for knives), and creepers (essential for lashings)" (1968:563). Contemporary economic anthropologists would certainly focus on the latter aspects, seeing the *kula* as a supportive mechanism that facilitates the trading of important subsistence items and provides a network of meaningful personal relationships through which the exchange of strategic materials can be undertaken in a friendly environment.

Two of Malinowski's students, Raymond Firth (1929, 1939) and D. M. Goodfellow (1939), advanced

Trobriand Islanders. Anthropologist Charles Julius is shown examining a bailer for use with this kula ceremonial canoe. Note the carving and cowrie shell decoration on the canoe.

the development of economic anthropology. They argued that people's economic behavior must be studied in terms of the choices they make, and that people everywhere make choices in terms of maximizing their returns. They assumed

> that people make choices among alternatives in a rational fashion, according to determinable principles. . . . Out of this simple initial premise is built, largely by deduction, a highly elaborate set of propositions which, in their initial formulation, purport to show how an *economic system, such as that existing in the United States,* functions. In effect . . . [they] were arguing that *the basic premises of this system of thought were valid everywhere and not merely in Western industrial-commercial societies* (LeClair and Schneider 1968:6; emphasis added).

Their work, along with that of Melville Herskovits (1940, 1952), has led to the development of what is called the *formalist* position in economic anthropology. Formalist writings are counterposed by a group with another perspective, the so-called *substantivists*. The substantivists deny that rational economic models derived from developed market economies can be applied to economic activity in all societies. Instead, they believe that anthropologists should examine the economic behavior of other peoples in their own cultural terms, focusing on the substantive social and technological processes through which humans interact with one another and with the environment to meet their subsistence needs.

The leader of the substantivist attack on formalist theory was not himself an anthropologist. Karl Polanyi was an economic historian, but he produced, with colleagues, a volume entitled *Trade and Market in the Early Empires* (1957), which had a strong impact on anthropologists. Polanyi disagreed with the formalists and denied that economic theory could be applied to anything other than market economies. He contended that the relatively recent invention of the price-making market in Western civilization had irretrievably distorted the patterns of social relations among people by artificially isolating the economic sphere from the rest of social behavior, and had induced people into "maximizing" and "economizing" modes of thought (LeClair and Schneider 1968:10–11).

The formalist counterattack was predictable; it is forcefully argued by Scott Cook (1966). He claims that substantivists misunderstand and oversimplify economic theory and analysis, and ignore concrete data which demonstrate that nonmarket economic systems do indeed involve "economizing" on the parts of their participants.

Many economic anthropologists are currently trying to steer the middle course, using formalist conceptions when they apply, but being careful to investigate the substantive cultural systems and networks of social relationships within which economic activities are played out.

Author's Conclusions

It seems to me that the formalist-substantivist debate obscures some basic aspects of human existence:

1. The environment in which a group lives will pose problems and also offer possibilities for securing a group's material needs.

2. The customs and traditions of groups—their culture—define for them what is possible and desirable in the realm of subsistence activities.

3. The technology and the system of distribution that each group creates are adaptive mechanisms that solve the problems posed by the environment, make use of its possibilities, and provide the material basis upon which each society is organized.

4. Within the cultural structuring of choices, human beings will make rational decisions that can be described in terms of formal logic; if they did not make logical decisions, they would not survive.

5. The issue of whether or not people maximize their economic potentials is a false one. In markets, where individuals are pitted against each other in a competitive system, maximization will express itself in the form of price haggling. In systems of generalized reciprocity, such as characterizes the !Kung San (see Chap. 21), *the system of reciprocity itself maximizes the economic possibilities of each person:* The individual gets the greatest economic security through cooperation and sharing.

Thus whether subsistence activities and modes of distribution are embedded in kinship systems (as in technologically simple societies) or relatively differentiated into their own spheres (as in industrial societies), the primary issue is not sentiment, mental state, values, or beliefs, although these are all important aspects of the human condition. The issue, as more and more research suggests, is how societies adapt to their environments and thus secure their subsistence needs (Gouldner and Peterson 1962; Harris 1974). From this material base all else follows.

Summary

All human groups must secure their material needs and wants. Our early ancestors were hunters and foragers, but they eventually invented agriculture, and the centers where the invention was made have been identified. The explanation for this crucial invention has been debated extensively.

The subsistence strategies of more developed societies do not necessarily make it easier for their members

to fill their wants, however. Research shows that many hunting and gathering peoples enjoy an adequate subsistence and expend relatively little effort in obtaining it. Where they experience hardship, as in the case of the Ik, their plight often results from the impact of industrial society.

All societies use a technology to exploit the environment. A technology consists of knowledge and skills, implements, and sources of power. All societies also employ some organization of work, at least along lines of age and sex and usually on the basis of other criteria as well.

The five main subsistence strategies are: (1) *hunting and gathering;* (2) *horticulture;* (3) *pastoralism;* (4) *agriculture;* and (5) *industrialism.* Each entails the use of distinctive technologies to exploit the natural environment. The fruits of these subsistence strategies are distributed among the population by means of one or more of three major distribution systems: *reciprocity,*

redistribution, and *market exchange.* The Tiv provide an example of the operation of a market exchange system.

Considerable debate arises in economic anthropology between the formalists, who attempt to apply models derived from developed market economies to other economic systems, and the substantivists, who argue that the economic behavior of nonmarket societies should be analyzed in its own terms. The author believes that this debate obscures the main issue: how societies adapt to their environments and thus secure their material wants and needs.

An Equadorian Indian youth learns to sharpen an arrow. The technology which every society creates to exploit the environment, and the system of distribution it utilizes to circulate goods among its members, are adaptive mechanisms which solve the problems posed by the environment, make use of the environment's possibilities, and provide the material base upon which each society is organized and because of which its culture can flourish.

Annotated Bibliography

Dalton, George, ed. (1968)   *Primitive, Archaic, and Modern Economies.* New York: Anchor. A collection of Karl Polanyi's essays, many of them classics, presenting the substantivist point of view in the formalist- substantivist controversy. Part 1 consists of theoretical articles, part 2 of case studies.

Fried, Morton H. (1967)   *The Evolution of Political Society.* New York: Random House. A sophisticated attempt to reconstruct the sequence of sociopolitical evolution. Fried constructs a four-step typology: egalitarian society, rank society, stratified society, and the state. Among other cultural systems, patterns of subsistence and trade are examined in this perspective.

Herskovits, Melville J. (1952)   *Economic Anthropology.* New York: Knopf. A major classic in its field; lays the groundwork for the formalist approach to economic anthropology.

LeClair, Edward E., Jr., and Schneider, Harold K., eds. (1968) *Economic Anthropology.* New York: Holt. Probably the best single collection of papers covering historically important classics, the theoretical formalist-substantivist disputes, and a nice sampling of case studies.

Sahlins, Marshall D. (1968)   *Tribesmen.* Englewood Cliffs, N.J.: Prentice-Hall. A condensed yet readable discussion of tribal social groups, including useful discussions of subsistence and exchange activities.

Service, Elman R. (1966)   *The Hunters.* Englewood Cliffs, N.J.: Prentice-Hall. A useful introduction to hunting and gathering societies, with an extended discussion of subsistence activities and reciprocal exchange systems.

11
Power in Society:
Political Anthropology

The World Context

Origins and Development through Time

In modern society, political power—the power to make the decisions of public policy—is very unequally distributed. Some people—the heads of government bureaucracies and large business enterprises—have a great deal of power. Others—such as those whom the bureaucracies administer and the enterprises employ—have very little. This unequal distribution of power is so familiar that we take it for granted. We even tend to assume that it is an inevitable feature of human society.

The comparative study of societies across the world and through time has shown that the hierarchical distribution of political power is by no means universal. On the contrary, it is fairly recent in human history. Our best estimate is that such hierarchies first appeared between 4000 and 3000 B.C., when a centralized state organization arose in Mesopotamia (Adams 1960). For tens of thousands of years before that time (and until much later in many areas of the world), political systems were much less hierarchical than they are now. Complete equality may not have existed in Paleolithic and early Neolithic society, but if modern ethnographic accounts of small-scale societies are any indication, the average individual had much more influence over policy decisions in the earlier stages of social evolution than in the complex urban civilizations of the last few thousand years.

The simplest and least hierarchical political systems known to the anthropologist are those of hunting and gathering societies. Such societies as the !Kung San of the Kalahari Desert (see Chap. 21) and the Eskimos of the Arctic have no strictly political institutions: There is no legislature, no court system, no police force, and no administration. Indeed, the nomadic hunting and gathering mode of subsistence could not support such specialized institutions. Nor do these societies contain such differences of wealth or privilege as would make strong political institutions necessary for the maintenance of social order. Instead, political decisions are made by informal discussion leading to consensus. In

President Ford and his cabinet. Because we have always lived in a society in which the system of political organization is strictly hierarchical, we take this for granted and project it easily onto other political systems when we encounter them. This makes analyzing diverse forms of political organization very difficult.

Features Of Society	Egalitarian Society	Rank Society	Stratified Society	The State		
				Feudalism	Capitalism	Socialism
Subsistence Activities	hunting and gathering	hunting and gathering; horticulture	horticulture; pastoralism	agriculture; pastoralism	industrialism; agriculture	industrialism; agriculture
Distribution System	reciprocity	reciprocity; redistribution	redistribution; reciprocity	market exchange; redistribution; reciprocity	market exchange; redistribution; reciprocity	redistribution; market exchange; reciprocity
Classes	none	none	chiefly class; peasants	landed aristocracy; peasants (plus emerging merchant class)	capitalists; workers (plus small business-people)	none (but often bureaucratic elite)
Governing Body	whole society: consensus	whole society: but leaders have more influence than others	chiefdom	monarchy	government bureaucracy	people's government bureaucracy

direction of sociopolitical evolution

such discussions the opinions of different people may be given different weights, depending on their reputations for clear thinking or knowledge of the subject under consideration. But no decision is reached unless everyone agrees to it or those who disagree hold their own opinions in abeyance, at least temporarily.

Consensus decision making can prevail among hunters and gatherers for two reasons. First, there are no fundamental social cleavages among groups with radically different interests. Second, relatively few issues exist on which strong differences of opinion are likely. Such decisions as where to hunt or gather and when to move the camp engender no serious difficulties; disagreements are settled either by discussion or by temporarily splitting up the group. Some potentially difficult decisions—for example, how to divide up the meat of a large animal killed—are settled by fixed customary rules and so do not generate political problems.

One area in which strong emotions and differences

Figure 11-1
Sociopolitical Evolution

right
An Eskimo community, photographed in 1915 by Diamond Janness, migrating to a new winter location in the vicinity of Coronation Gulf in north central Canada. Such highly mobile hunting and gathering groups tend to have the most egalitarian forms of political organization.

of interest regularly arise, causing the politics of consensus to break down, is sexual infidelity. If the aggrieved party takes revenge on the sexual trespasser and the kinfolk of the two parties then come to the defense of their own, a blood feud may develop. Such feuds are costly to hunting and gathering communities, and groups have developed cultural means of containing or preventing them. Classically, these mechanisms are duels or contests between the parties to a dispute, with the winner of the contest determined by community consensus. For example, the central and eastern Eskimos have song contests in which the disputants make up insulting songs about one another. The audience picks as winner the person who has invented the best insults (Rasmussen 1929). Among the Walbiri of Australia, disputants may engage in spear-throwing duels; the person who is first hit by a spear is the loser (Meggitt 1962).

Because their political decisions are made and their disputes are settled by consensus, simple hunting and gathering societies have been termed *egalitarian societies* (Fried 1967). The term is useful for comparing these groups to the more complex, hierarchically organized societies that follow them in social evolution, but it obscures certain inequalities that exist even at this level of development. These inequalities are based on age and sex. In no known hunting and gathering society do women or youths have an equal role with adult men in decision making. The subordination of women in these societies is not nearly as severe as it is in most of the more complex societies, but it does exist. Inequality based on age is reflected not only in the lesser weight given to the opinions of the young but also in their lower ritual status. Moreover, in some groups older men have preferential access to marriage partners.

We should note that our evidence on age- and sex-based inequality in modern hunting and gathering groups does not tell us whether this inequality was present in Paleolithic society or whether it developed later. The hunting and gathering groups in the ethnographic record have been in contact with more hierarchical societies for thousands of years, and we cannot determine what might have been borrowed in that time. Anthropological opinion on the question of whether there was ever a period of human history in which inequality did not exist is divided, and we may never have the evidence to settle it.

At the other end of the continuum of political systems is the highly complex and hierarchical state organization of modern society. Whether it is a parliamentary democracy or an authoritarian government, the modern state is an elaborate bureaucracy with many specialized functions of administration and social control. Since its inception in Neolithic Mesopotamia, the state has grown ever more elaborate, and state societies have extended their control over more and more of the earth's people.

The political institution we call the *state* arose to maintain social order in societies where great differences in wealth had developed. These differences resulted from the adoption of agricultural production, which enabled people to produce much more food than they needed for subsistence. This surplus production made possible a new and separate class that no longer did productive work but rather compelled the rest of the population to pay tribute to it. A society that contains such a dominant class has been called by anthropologists a *stratified society.*

According to Morton Fried (1960, 1967), a stratified society is one in which members of the same sex and equivalent age status do not have equal access to the basic resources that sustain life. Those who control the basic resources have enormous power because other members of the society must in some way pay them for access to the resources. This payment may be in the form of rent for land, enforced taxes or tribute, or the sale of one's labor for less than the value it produces.

In order for the emerging ruling class to *compel* the rest of the population to relinquish its surplus production, a coercive mechanism of enforcement had to develop. The state was that mechanism. In the words of Fried, the state is:

> a collection of specialized institutions and agencies, some formal and others informal, that maintain the order of stratification. . . . Usually, its [the state's] point of concentration is on the basic principles of organization: hierarchy, differential degrees of access to basic resources, obedience to officials, and defense of the area. The state must maintain itself externally as well as internally, and it attempts this *by both physical and ideological means* (1967:235; emphasis in original).

The development of state organization revolutionized human social relations. It allowed a much larger population to live under a single political system, because where obedience can be compelled, a small centralized administration can make political decisions for a very large group.

Once in existence, the newly organized states continually expanded in both territory and population. Indeed, the history of the last five thousand years has been a history of the extension of state societies all over the globe. The territorial ambitions of state societies soon brought them into collision with one another, and the resulting wars caused destruction and slaughter on a scale unknown in earlier tribal raids or feuds. In the course of their expansion, state societies incorporated or exterminated other societies on lower levels of social evolution. A less stratified society that came into contact with an expanding state could hope to escape incorporation or extermination only by adopting this mode of organization itself.

The reasons for the expansiveness of early state organizations are easy to see. The social position of those at the top of the hierarchy depended on the payments they exacted through their control of essential resources. The size of these payments depended in large part on the number of people and the amount of territory under their control. Expansion strengthened the power of the elite and made it better able to handle competition or revolts from below.

Between the simple hunting and gathering society and the states of the ancient and modern world lay, of course, a long process of social and political evolution. We can get some idea of this process by looking at the modern ethnographic record, which provides many examples from all parts of the world of societies that are between the two types. These societies are generally based on some form of horticulture or agriculture. Termed *rank societies* by Fried, they exhibit widely differing amounts of political hierarchy. In general, however, the differences among adult men are differences in influence and prestige rather than the absolute distinctions between the powerful and the powerless typically found in state societies.

In the simplest horticultural societies, political power tends to lie in the hands of the male elders of the community. The source of their political power is their kinship ties to women and to younger men. They have domestic authority over the local residential group, and although they cannot act tyrannically without driving people to live elsewhere, their word is generally followed. Outside the domestic sphere, the elders as a group have control over rituals, and in societies where labor is communal, they allocate that labor.

The degree of inequality possible in simple horticultural societies has two major limitations: Every male eventually becomes an elder, and the elders cannot deny others access to the crucial resource in the society —land. When, as a consequence of population increase or other factors, land becomes scarce, the position of the elders grows stronger, and they may begin to take on aspects of a true ruling group. Adults who cannot get the land to which they are theoretically entitled may attach themselves as clients to wealthy elders who can provide land. In exchange for access to this resource, the clients become ritually and politically subordinate to their hosts. Eventually the wealthy elders and their close kin become chiefly families, and the clients become political commoners. When this happens, a simple horticultural society has reached a new stage of political organization, the chiefdom. From there the evolution to the state level of political organization requires only the steady erosion of the rights of the commoners and a corresponding increase in their obligations to the chiefly group.

Contemporary Examples

In this century anthropologists have compiled a rich ethnographic record of the political institutions found at all levels of social evolution. A brief look at some examples illustrates the different ways in which human beings have organized their political life. It must be remembered, however, that these political institutions were not "pure" when discovered by anthropologists. In every case they have been profoundly affected by contact with outside forces, particularly Western colonialism. This contact has destroyed some societies and has incorporated the rest, even the most remote, into a world economic and political system. When we describe the traditional political institutions of a Melanesian island or an African horticultural society, we are reconstructing the past from what remains in people's memories and in the contemporary patterns of their lives.

Sometimes anthropologists have given the impression that the traditional systems still exist, intact and undisrupted. This picture downplays the drastic changes caused by Western penetration. Moreover, it obscures the distinction between what has been observed at first hand and what has been reconstructed, making critical evaluation of ethnographic description difficult. Therefore, for the examples that follow, we have chosen ethnographies that distinguish clearly between reconstructed and current practices.

Lugbara Let us begin by examining the relatively nonhierarchical (although not egalitarian in Fried's sense) political system of the Lugbara, a simple horticultural society in the East African country of Uganda. According to John Middleton, an anthropologist who did extensive fieldwork among the Lugbara from 1949 to 1952, no chiefs or other central authorities existed in their traditional political system (1958, 1960, 1965). (When the colonial powers arrived in Lugbaraland, however, they appointed some of the wealthier men of the area to be "chiefs," or local representatives of the centralized colonial administration. Considerable resentment developed among the Lugbara toward the government-appointed chiefs and the authority they exercised.)

In the traditional system, with which we are concerned, political power was wielded by elders, the male heads of lineages. The Lugbara are a patrilineal people who live in family clusters scattered over their plateau territory. These clusters contain an average of about twenty-five people headed by an elder. The core of the family cluster is a group of patrilineally related men living together with their wives and children. The senior member of the core patrilineage is the elder of the cluster. He exercises domestic authority and is also in charge of religious rituals that are performed to propitiate the ancestral ghosts of the core lineage.

A cluster sometimes contains other people in addition to the core group. For example, it might include a married female member of the patrilineage and her husband, or even a sister's son of a patrilineage member. Such people become attached to a cluster when, for one reason or another, a man decides to leave his father's kin and to live with either his wife's or his mother's people. In addition, if an elder is well-to-do, he may attract clients, unrelated people who live with him and to whom he may give his daughters in marriage to keep them in his household.

Beyond the family clusters are three levels of political groupings, which Middleton calls minor sections, major sections, and subtribes. A minor section is a group of family clusters; a major section is a group of minor sections; and a subtribe is a group of major sections. A minor section is created when family clusters that were a single unit segment because adult men have asserted their independence in order to achieve the status of elder. In the traditional system, the major section was the feuding unit. Feuds could never occur within major sections because people in a single major section were considered to be too closely related to use force against one another. The subtribe is the largest effective unit of the Lugbara political system.

The units of the Lugbara system are held together by their organization around a core of patrilineally related men. Thus the patrilineal cores of the family clusters in a minor section consider themselves to be descended from a common patrilineal ancestor. Similarly, the minor sections in a major section consider themselves to be descended from a single more distant ancestor. The same relation holds between the major sections of a subtribe. Disputes between members of a single subtribe but of different major sections can lead to feuds, but these feuds must ultimately be ended by agreement. However, the traditional system offered no means of settling feuds between members of different subtribes, and they continued indefinitely.

Each of the political groups up to the level of the major section has its elder. The elder of a minor section is the senior elder of its constituent family clusters, and the elder of a major section is the senior elder of its constituent minor sections. These higher level elders have traditionally had no political authority over the other elders of their sections. They act as representatives of their sections on ritual occasions, but they have no secular authority over family clusters other than their own.

Although the political organization of the Lugbara is decentralized and nonhierarchical, all members of the society are not politically equal. Real (though limited) differences in influence among adult male

heads of family clusters exist, and there is considerable inequality within the cluster based on age and sex. Women and younger men are expected to obey and show respect toward elder male kin. This domestic authority of senior males has a ritual as well as a pragmatic basis: The elder of a family cluster has the exclusive power to invoke the ancestral ghosts to punish an erring member of the lineage.

The Trobriand Islands   Let us now consider a chiefdom, a society at a more "advanced" level of political evolution. The society of the Trobriand Islands of Melanesia was described by Bronislaw Malinowski (1922, 1929, 1932, 1935).

The Trobriand Islands are a small archipelago located about a hundred miles north of the easternmost tip of New Guinea. When Malinowski did his fieldwork in the second decade of this century, the traditional way of life of the islanders had already been substantially altered by European rule. Many of the islanders were working for wages, especially as pearl divers, and the authority of the local chiefs had been considerably undermined. Enough remained of the previous social system, however, for Malinowski to give a clear picture of how it had worked.

The Trobrianders depended for their livelihood primarily on the produce of their gardens, where they grew yams as the staple food and a variety of other crops, including taro, coconut palms, and bananas. They depended for protein on fish and domesticated pigs.

The Trobrianders lived in villages, and each village (in large villages, each village section) was dominated by a local branch, or subclan, of one of the four matrilineal clans to which the islanders belonged. Membership in a local subclan entitled an individual to farm the land in proximity to the village or village section.

Some village headmen had authority that extended beyond their home village. Such men were known as *guyau*, "chiefs." Among these chiefs, one, the chief of the village of Omarakana in the district of Kiriwina, was considered to be the paramount chief of the whole Trobriand archipelago. The relative status of each chief and village headman was determined by an elaborate system of subclan ranks. In theory, each subclan had its place in a hierarchical ranking system, with the subclan of the chief of Omarakana at the top. High rank carried with it considerable prerogatives, and those who enjoyed such status were treated with elaborate respect. For example, high-ranking people were always supposed to be physically elevated above people of lower rank; chiefs would sit on platforms to be above their subjects. If a person of high rank was sitting down and a person of lower rank came by, the person of higher rank would stand up and the one of lower rank would bend over so the proper physical relationship could be maintained. The basis of the ranking system, of course, was economic. Chiefs appropriated much of the surplus yam production of the common people's gardens. With this surplus they paid artisans to fashion decorations and implements for them and magicians and sorcerers to cast spells. They also distributed largess to close kinsmen.

Perhaps the most interesting feature of Trobriand social organization was the way the kinship system served as the mechanism through which the chiefs appropriated the surplus. As we have seen, the Trobriand descent system was matrilineal. Residential groups consisted basically of a core of men of the locally dominant subclan, along with their wives and immature children. Young men left their fathers' households at an early age to live in their own subclan village —that is, with their mothers' brothers. Women, on the other hand, went to live with their husbands when they grew up and married and so did not ordinarily live in their own subclan villages. This residence pattern was linked to a system of *urigubu* payments made by the men of the subclan to their married sisters' households. These payments compensated for the fact that married women could not directly cultivate land in their own subclan villages. Between a third and half of the produce of a man's garden went in such payments to the households of his female matrilineal kin.

This system of *urigubu* payments was the source of the surplus accumulated by a chief. Unlike a commoner, a chief had more than one wife. In fact, he would have a wife from the dominant subclan of each village under his authority, and if one of these wives were to die, her village would provide a replacement. Thus the members of all of the dominant subclans of a district would owe *urigubu* payments to the chief, providing a chief with an enormous supply of yams

The exchange of yams for fish is an important business in the everyday life of the Trobriand Islanders. Yams are also used to make *urigubu* payments to the local chief by his wives' kindred. The chief stacks these yams in front of his house to display his accumulated wealth. Through his control over the redistribution of this surplus food, the chief solidifies his centralized political power.

and other goods—especially as the *urigubu* for a chief was not only larger and of higher quality than that for a commoner but also came from a wider group of the wife's kin.

The political system of the Trobriand Islands was clearly an intermediate stage between the egalitarian and state levels of political organization. Like the latter, it was based on the extraction of a surplus from the population by a well-defined ruling group. On the other hand, this surplus was extracted not by tribute, taxes, or other coercive measures but rather by reliance on kinship obligations like those found in egalitarian or simple horticultural societies.

Bunyoro   Finally, let us turn to an example of a state-level political organization, the East African kingdom of Bunyoro. Our account is based on the work of the British anthropologist John Beattie, who did fieldwork among the Bunyoro people between 1952 and 1955 (Beattie 1960).

Bunyoro is now incorporated into a modern state society, the Republic of Uganda. The kingdom lost its independence with the British conquest in the 1890s, and its political system has since undergone enormous changes. Although the Bunyoro state had ceased to be an independent political entity, it had not completely disappeared when Beattie did his research. The king of Bunyoro and his chiefs were still recognized, although they executed the rule of the colonial administration.

The king of Bunyoro, called the *mukama*, is a member of an aristocratic ruling clan called the Bito. The social division between the Bito and Bunyoro commoners is greater than any distinction of rank we have considered thus far. Unlike the Trobriand chief, for example, the *mukama* is not considered to be a kinsman of his people, and he does not receive his tribute on the basis of kinship ties. Instead, the king traditionally had legal control over all land and natural resources in Bunyoro. He granted dominion over tracts of land and over the people who farmed it to his chiefs, who collected tribute from the peasants, keeping some and passing some on to their sovereign. Thus the Bunyoro peasants supported the entire political structure through their compulsory economic contributions.

African states such as Bunyoro have been called *feudal* because they resemble in many ways the political systems of medieval Europe. In both Bunyoro and feudal Europe, the king granted land and the right to exact tribute from the peasantry to vassals (chiefs or lords) in exchange for promises of loyalty and service. In both cases the king was faced with the prospect of rebellions by powerful vassals, and he tried to minimize the danger by requiring them to spend much time in court. In both cases, too, the positions of chief or lord—originally granted to an individual in recognition of some service—tended to become hereditary. Of course, many differences existed between African and European feudalism, but the basis of the political structure—the funneling of tribute through vassals to a central monarchy—was the same in both systems.

In order to rule his extensive kingdom and maintain his supremacy over possible rivals among the great chiefs, the *mukama* had a number of court officials. Among these was the *okwiri*, the *mukama's* official brother. This man was by tradition the eldest son of the late king and hence was usually a half-brother of the new king (of different mothers). The *okwiri*, appointed by the new king after his installation, was said to rule the Bito clan, and his office served to detach the king somewhat from the Bito aristocratic group. The king was supposed to represent the whole kingdom, and the *okwiri*, the special interests of the aristocrats.

Another important Bito official was the king's official sister, the *kalyota*. She was chosen by the king and ruled the women of the Bito clan, settling disputes, judging inheritance cases, and deciding matters of social precedence among them. She was also a chief, and her appointment to office included the grant of tribute-producing estates. Another woman with considerable power and influence, as in many other African monarchies, was the king's mother, who kept her own court and ruled estates. As a check on these titled officials, the king maintained a large group of informal advisers and retainers who frequently had considerable influence over him. They were often rewarded by the king with the grant of a chieftainship.

Through his Bito officials and territorial chiefs, the *mukama* gathered tribute from a large population. This tribute enabled him and his chiefs to maintain sizable establishments and to enforce their political will on the subject population. In spite of this state apparatus, however, the daily life of the Bunyoro commoners was not very different from horticulturalists in nonstate societies. They spent most of their time farming and socializing with their neighbors and kinfolk. Apart from the compulsory payment of tribute, the main way in which the Bunyoro state affected the lives of its subjects was by substituting the authority of the state for that of the local kin group in the regulation of political affairs. The anarchic independence of the family clusters and the settlement of disputes by community elders found among the Lugbara were absent in Bunyoro. Serious disputes went to the chief's court, and the chief had the power to enforce his decisions on the litigants. Feuds, which were common in Lugbaraland when disputes crossed kinship boundaries, were greatly curtailed in Bunyoro. Blood vengeance could not be taken unless the king judged such vengeance to be appropriate.

In summary, the Bunyoro state, like all other states, reserved for itself the right to make important political decisions and enforced this right through its administrative apparatus and the threat of the sanctions it could impose.

Theory

Systems

When anthropologists study political organization, they try to determine how the decisions of public policy, whether large or small, routine or extraordinary, are made and enforced in different societies. In the course of their investigations, they and other social scientists have defined a number of key concepts. The most basic of these is the idea of *political organization* itself. The political organization of a society is a subsystem of its overall social organization. In societies with little hierarchy, political organization and social organization might be considered coextensive. In general, however, the two concepts should be distinguished, since in large-scale societies a big gap often exists between the organization of daily life and the administration of public policy. One useful definition of political organization has been offered by Fried: "political organization comprises those portions of social organization that specifically relate to the indi-

The Prime Minister of Bunyoro (Katikiro), Martin Mukidi, and the Judge of Bunyoro, Laurenti Muganwa, are garbed in their formal robes of state for the festivities in honor of the 30th anniversary of their king's accession to the throne.

Chairman Mao Tse-tung of the People's Republic of China. He emerged as a leader of the Chinese Revolution of 1948, and has held the people's affection and commitment ever since then. In this sense, he has consistently held *leadership* in the People's Republic. However, his *power* has fluctuated as various factions fought for control of the party. At one point his power had diminished so much that he could not even get an article published in the organ of the Chinese Communist Party in Peking. It was partly, at least, in order to regain his political power that Mao helped launch the Cultural Revolution in the mid 1960's which indeed did succeed in retrenching his position at the apex of the Chinese political organization.

viduals or groups that manage the affairs of public policy or seek to control the appointment or action of those individuals or groups" (1967:21).

Political organization is not equivalent to government. The term *government* refers to the administrative apparatus of the political organization in a state-level society. Government does not exist in nonstratified societies, nor does it include those aspects of political organization, such as political parties, that are outside the formally defined state structure.

Some anthropologists distinguish between leadership and power. A person or group is said to hold political *leadership* if his or their opinion tends to be followed. Political leadership exists in all societies, even simple ones without coercive sanctions to enforce obedience. In chiefdoms and states, however, political leadership is backed by *power,* the ability of leaders to compel compliance with their wishes. The ultimate source of this compulsion is the threat of the physical force available to the political leadership if their decisions are resisted. (See Swartz, Turner, and Tuder 1966 for one discussion of some of these concepts.)

Another central notion in political anthropology is that of *legitimacy.* Power is said to be legitimate to the extent that it is accepted by the general population as morally right (Hoebel 1954). The use of force or other sanctions is not the only or even the primary way that obedience to decisions and laws or customs is maintained. In all societies, except those going through a rapid and revolutionary transformation, political institutions are considered by most people to have some moral justification. Obedience to them is seen, at least to some extent, as a duty as well as a practical necessity. When a political system loses its legitimacy, it cannot long continue.

Processes

Anthropologists who study political organizations have generally been impressed by the smoothness with which political institutions function in most nonstate societies. The political system is generally accepted as legitimate, and force is rarely needed or used to achieve political ends or to maintain social order.

A number of explanations for this phenomenon have been offered. Some anthropologists stress that the political systems of nonstate societies function smoothly because their people share a common set of values, which makes disputes less likely. Others point out that in nonstate societies everyone has access to basic resources. Under these conditions, there is no need for a struggle over the control of these resources, nor for the criminal behavior that poverty engenders in stratified societies (Fried 1967). Of course, stateless societies are not without their political disputes. But at least within the local political unit, disagreements can be resolved by social consensus, and no special police apparatus with coercive powers is needed to enforce the social order.

An interesting question arises at this point: Why have anthropologists been so impressed by the successful functioning of noncentralized, nonhierarchical political systems? The reason is that the maintenance of social order is difficult in modern, complex societies,

Figure 11-2
Functional Relationships in State Society
Read any capitalized label. Follow any arrow leaving that label; read the text along that arrow. Then read the capitalized label the arrow leads to. This will result in a sentence explaining one of the relationships delineated by this model. This model generates twelve such statements.

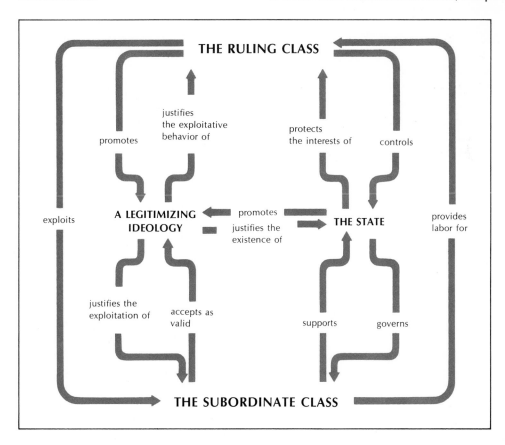

and investigators tend to project this difficulty onto simpler, less hierarchical systems.

Political strife in complex societies derives from the fact that such societies are generally based on class divisions and on the extraction of a surplus from the mass of the producers by the dominant or ruling class. Because state societies typically have this social basis, political harmony in them has depended on convincing people to accept inequality as moral and legitimate, a difficult task requiring the creation of sophisticated ideologies. These legitimizing ideologies have taken many different forms in the course of human history. In some societies the rulers have been invested with divine characteristics to buttress their social superiority. At other times and places, the masses in a society have been regarded as "radically" inferior to their overlords. In still other places, the rulers have based their position on the notion that the privileged group is by nature more able to make good political decisions than poor people. And the coercive power of the state has always been available for use against those who reject the ideologies and disturb the political "peace."

A central theoretical problem for anthropology is that of defining the circumstances under which political power and leadership are or are not legitimate. We know that legitimacy is a necessary attribute of any political system and that force by itself cannot long maintain a political system. We know that legitimacy has different bases in state and nonstate society. However, we know a great deal less about the conditions under which the legitimacy of a political system deteriorates, or how changes in ideology might be related to political change.

Analysis

The Folk Perspective

One of the most interesting recent empirical studies of political legitimacy was conducted by Talal Asad (1970), who examined the structures of political domination among the Kababish Arab nomads of the northern Sudan. This study indicates that the ideological justification of the political system is perceived independently and differently by the rulers and the ruled,

Statue depicting Ramses II, Egyptian Pharaoh. The kings of ancient Egypt were believed to be living embodiments of deities; hence to disobey a king was the same as disobeying a god, an unthinkable act in a devout society. Divine kingship is one of the ideological mechanisms through which political organizations legitimize themselves. Others include racist dogmas and theories about the innate inferiority of the lower social strata in society. One such mechanism is the appeal to order: rejecting the political order is tantamount to inviting forth chaos. This form of psychological blackmail was used, for example, by President Ford when he campaigned for Republicans in the fall of 1974. A vote for the Democrats, he argued publicly, could well jeopardize world peace and the ability of this nation to function.

and that the notion of legitimacy itself assumes different meanings in both cases.

Before the conquest of the Sudan by the Anglo-Egyptian forces at the end of the nineteenth century, the Kababish Arabs were a loose confederation of tribes. Each tribe was ruled by a *shaykh* under a political system about which we have little information. At the time of the conquest, one of these *shaykhs*, Ali at-Tom, was able—with the help of the colonial power—to extend his domination over many of the other tribes and to become recognized as the paramount ruler, or *nazir*, of the Kababish in the eyes of the colonial administration and of the people themselves.

Once in power, Ali at-Tom deprived the old tribal rulers of most of their powers, largely by eliminating their traditional functions as judges. Instead, he established a central administration and judiciary around

his own lineage, the Awlad Fadlallah. The Kababish have been ruled by the senior men of this lineage ever since. The political rule of the Awlad Fadlallah involves not only administration on behalf of the Sudan government but also the collection of a tribute, called the ʔawaid, which is paid by the Kababish to the *nazir* in addition to ordinary government taxes.

Both the mass of ordinary Kababish and the members of the ruling Awlad Fadlallah believe that the rule of the latter is legitimate. The senior members of the ruling lineage say that they are the *ahl al-mulk*—that is, the people with "authority" and "ownership." In using this expression, the rulers are claiming to be the owners of the Kababish territory, not in the sense of legal ownership (that is in the hands of the Sudanese government), but in the sense of having the right as descendants of Ali at-Tom to rule over the territory.

Two Kababish girls tying skins full of water on the pack saddle of their donkey for transport to the semi-desert region in which they live. Shaikh Ali at-Tom cooperated with the invading colonial powers and secured political power for himself and his descendants over all the Kababish people. To this day all *nazirs* (paramount *shaikhs*) are descended from Ali and continue to keep their centralized political power.

The leaders of the Awlad Fadlallah believe that the Kababish have binding obligations to follow their rule because their ancestors agreed to follow Shaykh Ali when the present political organization was established. Thus they speak of the *wajb,* or "duty," of their subjects to follow them.

Ordinary Kababish see the legitimacy of the political system in quite different terms. They refer to the members of the Awlad Fadlallah as *ahl as-sulta,* the people of political "power" or "might." They see their payment of tribute as legitimate because the rulers have the power to take it. Similarly, they say that they obey authority out of "compulsion," *jabr,* rather than duty.

The Kababish do not believe that this compulsion is necessarily immoral, but neither do they believe that it derives from any consent given by their forefathers to the political system. They often describe themselves as liars, thieves, and deceivers. By this they mean that they tend to resist the authority of their rulers through indirect means because they cannot resist it directly. The fact that they use denigrating terms to describe this process of evasion indicates that they do not believe it to be proper to resist authority, although it may often be a practical necessity.

To summarize, the Awlad Fadlallah leaders see themselves as the legitimate rulers of the Kababish because of a historical contract made by the Kababish people to follow their lineage ancestor Ali at-Tom. They believe that this contract gives the common people a duty to obey them. The Kababish commoners, on the other hand, consider themselves compelled to obey because the Awlad Fadlallah leaders have the power to make them obey. They do not believe that consent enters into the relationship at all, and they do not believe that the history of the rise of the political system is relevant to their obedience.

The Analytical Perspective

The political ideology of the Kababish poses a challenge to the analytical tools of the political anthropologist. Asad points out that political anthropology has traditionally based the notion of political legitimacy on the consent of those governed by the political system. His own description and analysis of the Kaba-

bish, however, indicates that consent plays no role in the legitimation of authority in their society. Asad argues convincingly that the mass of the Kababish do not conceive of themselves as having given consent to the political system; nor do they feel that such consent is necessary for the political system to be legitimate.

The political history of the Kababish shows a gradual narrowing of the group of people who participate in the political process, even to the extent of merely giving political consent. Before the rise of Shaykh Ali, political power was held by a large number of tribal chiefs and their close lineage kin. The political role of the common people also seems to have been greater, although information on the extent of their participation is lacking. Due to Ali's efforts, political power has become restricted to the Awlad Fadlallah, and within this lineage to its genealogically senior members. High administrative offices are now given to members of the ruling lineage without any participation by nonlineage Kababish. Even supposedly elected officials such as members of the parliament are not elected by vote. The candidates are selected by the senior Awlad Fadlallah and are declared elected without polling because they run unopposed. The fact that there is no objection to this procedure indicates that the Kababish do not expect to be asked their opinion or to give their consent on political matters.

Asad argues that the question of whether or not consent is involved in political legitimacy depends on the particular political system in question. In some, such as the modern parliamentary democracies, people do not believe that their government is legitimate unless they have given consent to it through an electoral process. In others, however, legitimacy may have different sources. Among the Kababish, the legitimacy of the political system rests on the belief of the ordinary people that the rulers have the power to enforce their political authority and that they generally do not act unreasonably or oppressively. (By "oppression," *zulm,* the Kababish mean acting in a way that deprives the ordinary members of society of their ability to make a living—for example, through exorbitant taxation.) The view of legitimacy held by the ruling lineage, on the other hand, is the same consensual view put

Kababish camel caravans are outfitted from El Obeid, the capital of Kordofan. The Kababish do not think of themselves as being governed through their consent. Nevertheless, they do not think that the political organization which governs them is not legitimate. Unlike Americans, for instance, the Kababish do not perceive a need to tie together political legitimacy with consent by the governed.

forward in the writings of political anthropologists. This is hardly surprising, since an ideology in which people consent to the distribution of power is obviously more likely to be effective than one in which people feel compelled to submit to it.

Asad points out that a major reason for the political legitimacy of the rule of the Awlad Fadlallah lineage is that the ordinary Kababish have no alternative to rally

around. They are a pastoral, nomadic people, and their economic organization is based on individual households. Larger groups that might have acted together have not existed since the destruction of the political integrity of the tribes and their chiefs. In contrast to the ordinary Kababish, the Awlad Fadlallah do not live in scattered households; they live in a camp called the *dikka*. This *dikka* also moves over the countryside according to the seasons, but it is much larger than an individual household. In Asad's census, the *dikka* numbered about 860 people divided into 60 households. Of these, twenty-eight were Awlad Fadlallah households, and the rest were mostly the dependents or clients of the Awlad Fadlallah. The organization of the lineage into a residential group reinforces its political power because by living together the members of the Awlad Fadlallah are able to run the administration from day to day. It is hardly surprising that the ordinary Kababish household head sees no alternative but submission to the power of the *nazir* and his lineage, or that he sees their power to compel obedience as the main reason why he should obey.

Conclusions

Schools of Thought

Political organization has two major functions: maintaining social order and making the decisions of social policy. Anthropologists have studied these functions from a variety of theoretical perspectives. Most work in political anthropology has used the theoretical framework of *functionalism*, a perspective associated with the British anthropologist A. R. Radcliffe-Brown and the American sociologist Talcott Parsons and their many followers. The functionalist approach to the study of non-Western political systems is well illustrated by the introductory essay by Meyer Fortes and E. E. Evans-Pritchard to the classic work *African Political Systems*, which they edited (1940).

They hold three principles to be true of all African political organization, at both the state and nonstate level. The first principle is that everyone has an interest in the maintenance of the political system, no matter what his or her position in society. This interest derives from the fact that the political system guarantees social order, which is necessary for the continued economic production on which all depend for their livelihood. The second principle is that the political system is based on the consent of those living under it. The third principle is that all the various interests in African society have either direct or indirect representation in the conduct of political affairs.

In African political systems, according to this view, these various influences interact in a system of checks and balances that prevents any one force from becoming all-powerful. In Fortes and Evans-Pritchard's view, it follows from these three principles that a political system is a mechanism for harmonizing the various interests of society to produce a more or less smoothly functioning whole.

In recent years some scholars have seriously challenged functionalist theory. The challenge is based on a set of assumptions very different from those outlined by Fortes and Evans-Pritchard; it draws instead on the insights of Marxist and other materialistic approaches to political systems. This view, represented by the work of Morton Fried and others, sees political systems in all but the earliest levels of social evolution as mechanisms for ensuring the domination of certain interests over others in society. *Materialist* theorists tend to argue, therefore, that a fundamental difference exists between the political institutions of state societies and those of egalitarian and simple horticultural societies. In the latter, something like the system described by functionalists may operate. But in the state societies, the political system subordinates the interests of the many to those of the ruling few rather than harmonizing those interests (Engels 1968). From this perspective, the primary problem for a state organization is neither the maintenance of a system of checks and balances nor the preservation of consent by the ruled, but rather the maintenance of political domination by the ruling class.

One of the clearest examples of the debate between the functionalist and materialist (also called *conflict theorist*) schools of thought is over the definition and use of the concepts *state* and *law*. Functionalist anthropologists tend to argue either that the term *state* should not be used (Easton 1953) or that states exist in all societies (Hoebel 1949). The materialists, on the other hand, argue that the state is an institution that arises only at a certain point in social evolution (with the development of classes) and that it transforms the nature of political power. Similarly, functionalists tend to argue that law is universal to human society since all societies have rules for behavior (Pospisil 1958, 1971). The materialists argue that a distinction must be made between rules that are backed by the coercive power of a government and rules that are enforced by community consensus. Only the former should be considered law (Fried 1967); to use the same term in both cases obscures the qualitative differences between them.

The United States Senate in session. Often referred to as "The Most Exclusive Club in the World," it is interesting to ask: in whose interest does it govern?

Author's Conclusions

Although many people have attempted to reconcile functionalist and materialist approaches to the study of political organization, the two views have remained remarkably distinct and opposed for a long time. In the end, the anthropologist who works in this area must decide which of the two approaches seems more valid if he or she is to have any theoretical position.

I believe that the materialist criticisms of functionalism are valid. In particular, I would stress that in all societies on which we have first-hand information, those who are relatively privileged and those who are relatively unprivileged are in political conflict. At the level of class society, this conflict becomes an all-encompassing political problem requiring an elaborate mechanism of coersion, the state. However, it is present (although in weaker form) even in horticultural and hunting and gathering societies whose division of labor and differential access to political authority are based on age and sex. Moreover, the fact that the Trobriand chief has armed attendants who can kill a commoner who offends him shows that a fully developed class society is not necessary for the sort of conflict we are talking about to exist. In other words, I am arguing that although the state is, as materialists point out, a qualitatively new form of political organization in social evolution, the seeds of it are present wherever there is systematic social inequality. The state is merely the culmination of a long evolutionary history of political conflict and the related attempts by those in authority to control society.

Summary

Political organization has evolved from the simple consensus decision making of hunters and gatherers to the complex institutions of the modern state. The state, now the dominant form of political organization in the world, occurs in all stratified societies.

Various forms of political organization are exemplified by several societies: the Lugbara, a relatively egalitarian society; the Trobrianders, a rank society; and the Bunyoro, a society at the state level of political organization.

A central notion in political anthropology is that of legitimacy. Power is said to be legitimate to the extent that it is accepted by the general population as morally right; the use of force alone is not enough to ensure the legitimacy of the system. A system that loses its legitimacy in the minds of the people cannot long continue. The political structures of the Kababish Arab nomads of the northern Sudan provide several insights into the problem of legitimacy. In particular, it seems that the ideological justification of the system is perceived differently by the rulers and the ruled.

Considerable controversy exists among anthropologists about the precise nature of the state. Functionalist theorists contend that it exists primarily to guarantee social order; conflict theorists believe that it exists mainly to preserve the interests of the ruling class. The author favors the latter view.

Annotated Bibliography

Asad, Talal (1970) *The Kababish Arabs.* London: Hurst. An innovative study of a recently created system of stratification among a nomadic people.

Beattie, John (1960) *Bunyoro: An African Kingdom.* New York: Holt. A traditional, social anthropological description of an African kingdom, with an emphasis on the effects of the British colonial rule.

Fried, Morton H. (1967) *The Evolution of Political Society.* New York: Random House. A theoretical introduction to political evolution from a materialist perspective.

Hoebel, E. Adamson (1954) *The Law of Primitive Man.* Cambridge, Mass.: Harvard Univ. Press. Traditional anthropological treatment of law discussed critically by Fried.

Malinowski, Bronislaw (1932) *Crime and Custom in Savage Society.* New York: Harcourt. Valuable information on social control among the Trobrianders.

Middleton, John (1965) *The Lugbara of Uganda.* New York: Holt. A descriptive monograph on a decentralized African horticultural society.

12
Control of Behavior:
Formal and Informal Sanctions

The World Context

Origins and Development through Time

So far we have studied different aspects of how societies work—how people manage to communicate with each other, marry and arrange themselves into families, establish kinship networks, organize their social existence through kinship groups, coordinate their subsistence activities, and assign positions of power in society. At various points we have indicated that things may not always run smoothly, but we have generally taken it for granted that, regardless of difficulties, societies manage to keep arranging, organizing, and coordinating themselves—and, in fact, this assumption is for the most part true.

In this chapter we consider *how* societies maintain themselves, not on the grand scale of political organization, but rather in the daily life of each person as he or she participates in society. For it is clear that if society is to function, each member must conform to social expectations, must participate in social institutions, must adjust his or her behavior to prevailing patterns. We cannot take this conformity for granted.

We must assume that it is induced by social mechanisms, that people's actions are in some way socially controlled.

The adjustment of individual behavior to patterns is a major feature of social life in the animal world. But human beings are somewhat special in the sheer amount of behavior they must learn and the subtleties they must observe in their relationships with others. As we have seen (Chaps. 3 and 4), some of our social behavior may be traced to generalized primate patterns. But these patterns are highly flexible; they are constantly being adapted to pressures from the natural and social environments. Let us see to what extent we can reconstruct the evolution of social control over individual behavior in the hominid line.

We have very limited knowledge about *Ramapithecus,* the first hominid, who lived between 10 and 14 million years ago in the open woodland areas of the Old World (see Chap. 2). These creatures appear to have been at least somewhat terrestrial, perhaps even walking on their hind legs when foraging for food in open areas. Much smaller than many of the other animals who shared this habitat, and therefore subject to the predatory attentions of larger and heavier carnivores, the ramapithecines must have developed minimal patterns of cooperation for the defense (or at least warning) of the group. It is not unreasonable to imagine that individual behavior was at least as socially learned and patterned as it is among contemporary apes and monkeys (see Chap. 3).

We know rather more about the organized behavior that had developed by the time of *Australopithecus,* some 5 million years ago. Some of these ancestors of ours produced conventionally patterned stone tools. We also have evidence that they were able to organize group behavior enough to drive a primitive elephant into a swamp and beat it to death, butchering it on the site (Butzer 1971:427). Cooperative hunting could not have taken place without systematic sharing of the spoils, which in turn means that individuals must have had to subordinate their personal wants and needs to the collective will of the group.

These implied patterns of social control were considerably elaborated by the groups of *Homo erectus* that emerged some 1 million years ago. Producers of

Adult male baboon grooms his adult female consort in Nairobi Park, Kenya. The more scientists study primate societies, the clearer it becomes that individuals participate in patterned social behavior and that these behavior patterns are learned. In many cases, juveniles have been observed to be threatened by adults when they have violated accepted patterns of behavior (e.g., hurt infants). Thus the issue of the control of behavior seems to be an important one in every social group—human or not—in which role behavior is learned rather than genetically programmed.

precisely patterned tool complexes that persisted over hundreds of thousands of years, developers of the controlled use of fire, and skilled hunters of large game, these ancestors of ours were clearly organizing their social existence to a rather high degree. Some of the later sites of around 400,000 years ago show the division of space into separate work (tool-producing) and living areas, evidence of individual adjustment to group norms. At Terra Amata, near Nice, we find shelters constructed by our ancestors at about that time; these shelters are subdivided in a way that suggests the emergence of family groupings (Watson and Watson 1969: chap. 5), in which case the patterning of individual behavior in terms of group expectations must already have been substantial.

There can be no doubt that by the time *Homo sapiens* evolved between 300,000 and 100,000 years ago, group behavior was highly patterned, with well-defined social roles that both stimulated and constrained individual behavior. Stone tool technology was becoming increasingly sophisticated, religious beliefs and practices emerged, and groups could be flexible in meeting the special needs of individuals—for example, caring for a cripple such as the one-armed individual of 46,000 years ago found by Ralph Solecki in Shanidar Cave, Iraq.

Among modern *Homo sapiens,* these patterns have been vastly elaborated over the last 40,000 years. In chapter 3 we explored the ways in which adaptive pressures helped mold the evolution of social forms, especially the social roles of men and women in societies practicing different subsistence modes. In order to understand how groups induce their members to behave in certain ways, it is necessary to introduce two basic concepts of social science: *status* and *role.*

No human group is seen by its members to be socially homogeneous. The members recognize differences between individuals that go beyond individual physiques or personalities. Specifically, *sets* of persons who occupy *socially defined positions* are recognized: Child, adult, male, and female are basic social positions identified in every society. All societies also recognize additional social positions that an individual may occupy during the course of his or her lifetime—father, mother, shaman, professor, carpenter, student, actor,

This photograph taken in 1905 depicts a group of Ainu, natives of the island of Hokkaido (the northernmost island of Japan), seated according to rules of etiquette during a ceremony. The functionaries are all men; women remain discreetly in the background. The statuses of women and men are different in all societies, and are *ascribed* regardless of differentiating personal characteristics.

and so forth. Each society has a unique constellation of such social positions, called *statuses*. Social scientists often distinguish between two kinds of status: ascribed status and achieved status.

An *ascribed status* is the social position a person comes to occupy simply by being born into and growing up in a given social group. Infant, child, adolescent, teenager, young adult, adult, middle-aged person, elderly person are some of the ascribed statuses we can all expect to pass through in American society. Other ascribed statuses are the various kinship positions we occupy without any action on our part; by being born we become somebody's child, perhaps someone else's cousin, niece, nephew, sibling, aunt, or uncle. Every society has its own inventory of such ascribed statuses and its own set of cultural meanings that it attaches to them.

Achieved statuses are the social positions a person comes to occupy by virtue of intent and some degree of effort. Every society has a range of such positions, some of which are rather easy to achieve (becoming a parent, for example), and others that are quite difficult (mastering a craft, trade, or profession). Societies that make all achieved statuses equally accessible to all adult members are called *egalitarian societies;* those that limit access to certain achieved statuses are *rank societies;* and those in which access to selected achieved statuses is virtually impossible for members

of certain social groupings within the society are said to be *stratified societies* (Fried 1967). These forms of society are further discussed in chapter 15.

Every status, whether it is ascribed or achieved, has a set of behaviors attached to it by the society. To be more precise, persons occupying specific statuses are *expected* by members of the society to behave in specific ways under certain circumstances. The expected (normative) behaviors that every society associates with each of its statuses are the *roles* the society recognizes. Roles, then, are culturally defined and organized norms for behavior that persons occupying specific statuses are induced to enact.

Before we explore the specific mechanisms that societies use to induce their members to perform the behavior appropriate for their roles, let us first observe some social behavior that has been described in the ethnographic literature.

Contemporary Examples

The BaMbuti   The BaMbuti are a pygmy people who live in the Ituri rain forest in the northeast corner of Zaire (formerly the Belgian Congo), Africa. They subsist primarily by hunting and gathering in the moist, cool jungle. One of their preferred hunting techniques is to drive game into nets that they string in a large arc through the jungle. Some individuals are responsible for driving the animals toward the nets, and others kill the trapped prey. For the hunt to be a success, individuals must stay at their assigned places and perform their designated tasks. This is a crucial requirement even though on any given hunt a particular individual or even a family might not kill a single animal. The BaMbuti share all food reciprocally, and in the end everyone eats an equivalent amount.

The BaMbuti are an egalitarian society. They have no chiefs to give commands, no state agencies to enforce conformity to social norms. Although they understand very well the importance of cooperation among individuals, this understanding alone does not always ensure cooperation. As among all groups, people's vanities, desires, moods, resentments, or pettinesses sometimes make it difficult for them to submit to group expectations. Not surprisingly, such incidents

occurred even among the easygoing, peaceful BaMbuti (see Chap. 17). The one we shall discuss is the story of Cephu, who, according to Colin Turnbull, committed one of the gravest offenses possible among the BaMbuti: He abandoned his assigned position and set up his own net in front of the group's net (1962: Chap. 5).

Cephu was always a bit of an outsider. He and some others had set up their huts a little to the side of the main camp. His reclusiveness was accepted by the group as a personal peculiarity. They even tolerated his refusal to contribute food to and attend the evening ceremony commemorating a deceased woman, although his behavior aroused hostile feelings in some group members. Despite his eccentric and socially divisive ways, Cephu was seen as a member of the group, a person who could be counted on to participate in the organized group hunting, a person who would share his spoils and with whom everybody would share theirs.

One day Cephu apparently became disgruntled over the fact that for the past few days his net had remained empty, while other nets in the line seemed to attract game. Pretending to be confused, he positioned his net where it would be sure to trap game, though at the expense of others' nets a distance behind him. He was discovered, and his feigned ignorance was not accepted for a moment. Nor could the group afford to ignore such brazen antisocial behavior.

All the men were called at once to a general meeting to discuss breaking camp and moving, because the existing camp had been defiled by Cephu's behavior. This was a very serious issue, and even Cephu dared not avoid the meeting. Entering the gathering late, he found that all seats were taken and his juniors refused to make room for him. Cephu shook one young man to get him to rise, but was told: "Animals lie on the ground." Furious, Cephu began a long harangue about this lack of respect. Only Bantu villagers, he argued, are like animals. He, Cephu, was a respected hunter and elder of the group and thus should be accorded social courtesies.

A group elder spoke up, supporting Cephu and telling the young man to give Cephu his seat, which he did grudgingly. Then another elder said that if the situ-

BaMbuti pygmies of the Ituri Forest in Zaire, shown here wearing bark cloth clothing. Considered to be among the most egalitarian of human societies, the BaMbuti use an organized, primary process (see text) of social control to deal with a serious offender of their practices.

ation was as Cephu said, why did he live apart from the group and why had he not participated in the commemorative feasting? Cephu, not perceiving the drift of the comment, answered that the feasting was none of his business. Why not? he was asked. He had been glad enough to receive the food of such feasting when his own daughter had died; why did he not wish to contribute to the feast commemorating his "mother"? Cephu replied that Balekimito was not his mother. That was his big mistake, for two reasons. First, he had uttered the dead woman's name, a grossly inappro-

priate act. Second, although he and the dead woman were only distant relatives through marriage, denying that she was his "mother" was equivalent to saying he was not a member of her group—the group that was meeting at that very moment.

One of the group's most respected elders leaped to his feet, shook his fist at Cephu, and raged that he hoped Cephu would fall on his own spear and kill himself because "who but an animal would steal meat from others?" Outraged cries from others supported this tirade. The real issue was finally out, and now that it was put so starkly, Cephu knew he was defeated. He broke into tears and confessed his guilt, protesting his innocence of intent, however. But the group was not yet satisfied; the recklessness of Cephu's behavior had to be driven home.

Another elder rose and made a long speech, saying that Cephu was indeed a great leader of his own group, which apparently did not need the larger group at all: It could go off on its own and hunt elsewhere, with Cephu as its chief. The implied threat of group expulsion was extremely serious, for everyone knew that it would be tantamount to a sentence of death; no group as small as the one clustered around Cephu could adequately provide for itself.

Cephu apologized profusely. He went over to his wife's hut and, over her loud protests, took all their food and gave it to the group. The group then expropriated all the food in the huts of Cephu's circle. Cephu began to wail and cry, claiming he would starve to death, but he was ignored by most of the men and ridiculed by the women of the main group. Later that night, however, one of Cephu's kinsmen quietly brought Cephu and his family some stew. All was forgiven. Cephu had admitted the error of his ways, had paid the price, and could be counted on to conform to group norms once again. That was sufficient. The group was once again whole.

The Kapauku   The Kapauku Papuans are a horticultural group living in the Wissel Lakes region of the central New Guinea mountains. They are a patrilineal, patrilocal society, and they occupy villages containing some 150 persons living in about 15 households.

Inhabitants of one or several neighboring villages constitute a localized lineage that, if large

enough, may be subdivided into sublineages. . . . Members of two, three, or more localized lineages of different sibs [aggregates of lineages tracing their relationship back to an hypothesized common ancestor] unite themselves for defense and offense into relatively permanent political confederacies, which may comprise as many as 600 individuals, living in from four to seven villages. . . . Within the . . . [confederacy], law and order are administered by wealthy headmen. Every lineage and sublineage has its headman, and the most influential of these is elevated to the confederacy leadership (Pospisil 1969:210).

The main character in the incident that concerns us is Awiitigaaj, a courageous, shrewd person who was the headman of Botukebo village and whose exploits are described by Leopold Pospisil (1969). The tale starts with a love affair of a familiar sort—an illicit romance. Awiitigaaj fell in love with a beautiful young woman who also happened to be his third paternal parallel cousin (see Chap. 8), which made her a member of his sib. Kapauku law explicitly defines and prohibits incest: It is forbidden to marry one's sibmate. Yet the brash Awiitigaaj was not to be denied his love, and the couple eloped.

Needless to say, this behavior precipitated a crisis. The young woman's father, Ugataga, ruled that both sinners must pay the price of incest—execution. His decision was upheld by the headman of the confederacy, and the patrilineal relatives of both fugitives dutifully fanned out through the entire region in an attempt to find the couple and bring them to justice.

Awiitigaaj and his beloved hid out in the bush, awaiting the time when Ugataga's anger would blow over. Pospisil lays out the logic of Awiitigaaj's reasoning:

Ugataga was a clever businessman and politician; he would see the personal disadvantage of killing his daughter and forfeiting a handsome bride-price; he would end up with no daughter and no money—a very hard prospect to be contemplated by even a very moral Kapauku. It was much more likely that Ugataga would show great anger in public and make exhausting expeditions into the forest until he tired out the patrilineal relatives and bored the other tribesmen. If he eventually gave up the search and accepted the inevitable, he would preserve the public's high opinion of his morality, the life of his beloved daughter, and the prospect of an unusually large brideprice. . . . The acceptance of the brideprice would make the marriage formally valid and would legally absolve him [Awiitigaaj]. The only problem seemed to be to play the socio-political game properly and avoid detection by his patrilineal kin who were combing the forests. To accomplish this, Awiitigaaj cleverly utilized the . . . [conventions] that require maternal relatives, especially mother's brothers, to protect a fugitive from Kapauku justice; these relatives supplied him with food and with information about the plans and movements of the searching parties of his paternal kin (1969:213).

Awiitigaaj seems to have been very astute, for the scenario he envisioned came to pass. The patrilineal kinsmen made a big show of their search. They spent evenings around the fires of other Kapauku and dramatically lamented their plight: They had to do the "right" thing and pursue the fugitives, but had to kill their own close relatives in the interests of justice. In time, of course, they grew weary and their audience became bored. This apathy signaled the end of the drama, for it represented a collective (though nonexplicit) decision that sufficient energy had been expended to defend the society's moral code. The parties concerned could read the society's decision; the headmen of two uninvolved confederacy lineages began to call for an end to the hunt and a peaceful settlement. Ugataga, of course, resisted for a while longer in the name of moral outrage, but finally gave in to calmer minds and sound economic sense. He asked for a brideprice from Awiitigaaj's paternal relatives, thus publicly legitimizing the incestuous union.

Many a man in Awiitigaaj's position would have been more than pleased to proceed with Kapauku custom and pay the brideprice. But Awiitigaaj was not content merely to have successfully violated Kapauku law and married his parallel cousin. He intended to get her without paying any brideprice at all. Thus he let it be known among his patrilineal relatives that he was in

Awiitigaaj: Kapuku Papuan (New Guinea Highlands) rebel and conformist, making a political speech.

fact a very poor man and could not afford the expected brideprice. If they wished the whole affair to be over, they would have to raise the brideprice among themselves. Awiitigaaj's plan worked; his paternal relatives refused to pay, insisting once again on the imposition of the death penalty. This turn of events so infuriated Ugataga and his sublineage that they attacked Awiitigaaj's sublineage with sticks, inflicting several bloody wounds on the culprit's relatives. The attack absolved Awiitigaaj's relatives from having to pay a brideprice to the aggressors. Under Kapauku law, an individual may either accept a brideprice or avail himself of the opportunity of physically punishing the offending party—but he may not do both.

Once his patrilineal relatives were absolved from having to pay a brideprice, they no longer had any reason to oppose settlement of the issue, and they consequently accepted the marriage. Awiitigaaj thus had the pleasure of his incestuous marriage, the acceptance of his relatives, and the material benefit of not having paid a brideprice.

However, as a sublineage headman and a Kapauku businessman who appreciated the necessity of a good public image, Awiitigaaj knew that he could not afford to be considered negligent of the law. In his official capacity as a headman, he therefore promulgated a new law. It was permissible, he declared, to marry within the same patrilineal sib—even within the same patrilineage or sublineage—provided that the two people were at least *second* cousins (he and his wife were third cousins). Because of his social position, and perhaps because it was simply more convenient to do so, his fellow confederacy members accepted this modification of their incest law. Awiitigaaj, the bold social innovator, was once again within the social fold.

This example might be interpreted as evidence that individual behavior is not in fact determined by group expectations. Awiitigaaj was able, after all, to induce the group to accept his deviant behavior and even to change one of its norms. But Awiitigaaj was successful precisely because he so clearly understood the way his society worked, particularly the role behaviors that were incumbent upon individuals occupying specific statuses (for example, patrilineal and matrilineal rela-

tives). He cleverly manipulated the situation in terms of these statuses and roles, exploiting contradictory interests. And even Awiitigaaj recognized that his social position was in jeopardy unless other Kapauku saw that he was a fundamentally moral, law-abiding person. So he promulgated the new law. In fact, the new law did not represent a great change from the previous law; it was a modification that people could accept.

Awiitigaaj did not make public his real beliefs, which he confided to Pospisil: "Please don't tell the others. They wouldn't like me and I would lose influence. As far as I am concerned, it would be all right if first cousins were to marry. To marry your sister is probably bad, but I am not convinced even of that. I think whoever likes any girl should be able to marry her. I set up the new taboo in order to break down the old restrictions. The people . . . are like that. One has to tell them lies" (1969:215-16).

Theory

Systems

Two separate sets of mechanisms induce individuals to conform to group expectations. One such set consists of each person's beliefs and values; to the extent that these mirror the beliefs and values of the group, they will induce people to behave in ways appropriate to the group culture. Because each person carries such beliefs and values around "inside" his or her mind, social scientists sometimes refer to them as *internalized controls*. But nobody spontaneously creates his or her own set of such control mechanisms. They develop in each person as part of enculturation (see Chap. 14), the process by which each person acquires his or her identity as a group member and learns the content of the group culture. Thus the ultimate source of internalized controls is the group rather than the individual.

The other set of mechanisms that induce individual conformity to group expectations are called *external controls*. All external controls involve *sanctions*—that is, the responses a social group makes as a consequence of an individual's behavior. Social scientists recognize at least four types of sanctions, which are generated by the intersection of two dimensions: *positive/negative* and *formal/informal.*

Positive/Negative Sanctions   **Social sanctions can be used either to reward or to punish an individual's behavior. When the social response is some form of reward, we speak of** *positive sanctions.* **The nature of the rewards depends, of course, on the situation and the significance the culture attaches to it. In our society we reward people with a smile, trophies, cash, automobiles, promotion to positions of prestige, and so on. Positive sanctions, or the anticipation of receiving them, make a person feel good and increase the probability that he or she will continue to act in the manner that elicited this response from society.**

On the other hand, societies also punish people for behavior that does not meet with group approval. In such instances we speak of *negative sanctions.* **Here, too, the nature of the sanction may vary from the relatively mild (a frown) to the extreme penalties of imprisonment or death. It is obviously in the interest of society never to have to impose negative sanctions, since the undesired behavior must have occurred before the sanction is applied. This points to a very important difference between positive and negative sanctions. Although both operate on people's** *expectations,* **imposition of the former means that those sanctions have been successful, whereas imposition of the latter indicates their failure (the undesired behavior has not been prevented).**

Formal/Informal Sanctions   **When sanctions (either positive or negative) are invoked in response to a person's behavior, they may be applied in a visible, patterned ritual under the direct or indirect leadership of social authorities. We call these organized, public rituals** *formal sanctions.* **When sanctions are enacted by group members with minimal organization by social authority, we speak of** *informal sanctions.* **Formal sanctions, then, are generally applied by a subgroup of the larger society and represent a conscious decision on the part of authority; informal sanctions are carried out by all members of the society who individually choose to do so. Figure 12-1 shows the four types of sanctions that derive from the intersection of these two dimensions, positive/negative and formal/informal sanctions.**

	Positive	Negative
Informal	1 informal positive: smiles, pats on back, and so on	2 informal negative: frowns, avoidance, and so on
Formal	3 formal positive: awards, testimonials, and so on	4 formal negative: legal sanctions

Figure 12-1
Types of Social Sanctions

Informal positive sanctions consist of such behaviors as encouraging smiles, pats on the back, and congratulations. Cephu, the antisocial Mbuti whose story was presented earlier, received some informal positive sanctioning when a relative of his brought him some stew after the whole affair was over. His decision to make a clean breast of things and pay the price of his crime was informally but significantly reinforced by that action.

Informal negative sanctions are overt displays of displeasure, which may take the form of frowning, impolite treatment, avoidance of the culprit, or even group ostracism. Cephu suffered various forms of informal negative sanctioning before the implied threat of the sanction of group expulsion finally broke him down. The informal style used by the BaMbuti to deal with deviant behavior should not be underrated; it can be as harsh an experience for its target as the more formal, organized sanctions used in other societies.

Formal positive sanctions are public affairs, ceremonies conveying social approval of a person's behavior. Examples are the awarding of medals, graduation ceremonies, or ticker-tape parades for national heroes. By promulgating a new law on incest, Awiitigaaj ensured that in the future people who married within their own patrilineal sib, lineage, or sublineage could receive a formal positive sanctioning of their behavior—a legitimate and publicly attended wedding ceremony.

Law   *Formal negative sanctions* usually take the form of *law*. There are many theories and disputes about the nature of law (see Nader and Yngvesson 1973). Perhaps the clearest formulation, and one that is well adapted for use in cross-cultural comparison, is that advanced by Pospisil (1958, 1971). He sees law as a mechanism for settling disputes and suggests that law has the following four attributes:

1. Authority: "A decision, to be legally relevant, or in other words, to effect social control, must either be accepted as a solution by the parties to a dispute or, if they resist, be forced on them" (Pospisil 1971:44). The authority may be a designated politically empowered ruler, or it may be the entire group. With Awiitigaaj, the authority issuing the death sentence was the headman of the entire confederacy; his decision was enforced by the patrilineal relatives of the culprits.

2. Intention of universal application: **For the decisions of authorities to qualify as legal decisions (as opposed to, for instance, political decisions), they must be made on the understanding that the authorities intend to make the same decision in all similar cases (Pospisil 1971:79). The decisions regarding both Cephu and (initially) Awiitigaaj met this requirement. Both decisions were phrased in universalist terms:** *No Mbuti should hunt individualistically if this interferes with the group hunt; no member of the Kapauku confederacy should marry another member of his patrilineal sib.* Of course, Awiitigaaj changed this law, but he replaced it with a new law that once again applied to all members of the society.

3. Obligatio: **Legal decisions make obligatory relationships between two parties explicit. The guilty party has a** *duty* **imposed on it. The vindicated party (which might well be the whole society) has a** *right* **conferred on it (Pospisil 1971:81–82). Thus marriage law among the Kapauku stipulates the following obligatio (a term coined by Pospisil to denote both the rights and obligations that devolve upon parties to a legal dispute and decision) between the groom's party and the bride's party: The groom's party has the duty to pay a brideprice or accept corporal punishment; the bride's party has a right to receive a brideprice from or administer a beating to the groom's party.**

4. Sanction: **Failure to comply with the law must have identifiable, negative consequences for the offender. These unpleasant consequences, which are meant to compel compliance with the law and with legal decisions, are called** *legal sanctions.* **Awiitigaaj and his lover were threatened with the legal sanction of execution for their crime of incest. Legal or formal negative sanctions need not be so extreme, however. Public shaming, temporary deprivation of liberty, the imposition of work tasks, and the payment of fines are among the many forms these sanctions take.**

Processes

Exactly *how* **are sanctions applied to individuals? Through what processes do social groups enact their sanctions? Just as we were able to identify two dimensions of sanctions (positive/negative and formal/infor-**

mal), so we can identify two dimensions of processes through which sanctions are applied: organized/diffuse and primary/secondary.

Organized/Diffuse Processes   A society can apply sanctions in a formally organized manner. It can make a visible and conscious decision to do so, it can decide on the specific form of the sanction, and it can even decide who is to enact the required behavior. When such a process takes place, we speak of *organized processes.* For instance, a group decision to expel Cephu and his subgroup would have been an organized process, as was the decision that Awiitigaaj and his illicit lover should be hunted down and executed.

On the other hand, because all members of the society share assumptions about appropriate role be-

The public execution of Lim Seng, a heroin manufacturer and peddler, by the Philippine military. A formal, negative sanction.

havior, each person may react negatively toward someone who violates these expectations, with the result that group patterns of sanctions are applied to the offending individual. In such cases we speak of *diffuse processes* because the process flows from individuals' shared expectations rather than from a deliberate, organized decision. Diffuse processes can also be positive—spontaneous expressions of approval of individual behavior by group members. An audience's standing ovation after a brilliant concert performance is an example.

Primary/Secondary Processes   In applying either positive or negative sanctions, a group may act in its entirety (or close to its entirety). We refer to this collective process as *primary*. For example, Cephu encountered the hostility of the entire BaMbuti encampment. However, the group can also delegate responsibility for the positive or negative sanctioning of behavior to a subgroup—or even to a single person. This is called a *secondary process*. The person or subgroup that applies the sanction is backed up by the group. Awiitigaaj and his wife, for example, were hunted only by their patrilineal relatives, not by the entire confederacy. However, these relatives were acting with the moral and political support of the entire group. A secondary process does not necessarily have less group support than a primary process. Figure 12-2 presents the intersection of these two dimensions. Four possible types of processes result, but only three of these actually exist.

Diffuse primary processes are the more or less spontaneous actions by individuals that express their commitment to the group culture. Gossip, avoidance, expressions of appreciation (such as applause) are all diffuse primary processes for applying sanctions.

Diffuse secondary processes do not exist because secondary processes require group organization and collective decision making. Otherwise no responsibility could be delegated, and the group could not consciously back those delegated to apply the sanctions. Because organization by definition cannot be diffuse, this cell in the matrix represented in figure 12-2 is empty.

Organized primary processes are consciously arranged, collective events. These processes can only be

	Primary	Secondary
Diffuse	1 diffuse primary: actions by individuals	2 none
Organized	3 organized primary: actions by groups as wholes	4 organized secondary: actions by group representatives

Figure 12-2
Processes for the Enactment of Sanctions

right
A Mau Mau general under police trial in Nyeri, Kenya. In their status as police, these individuals are delegated by society to apply secondary sanctions (see text). Although it is commonplace to say that they represent society as a whole, in stratified and state societies (such as ours) such public agents act in the interest of the ruling class(es), rather than in the interest of the broad base of society.

carried out by relatively small, homogeneous groups. The smaller and more isolated the society, the more likely it is to use organized primary processes—such as group expulsion—in the enactment of sanctions. In larger, more heterogeneous societies, these processes are possible only within subgroups—ethnic groups, communities, kinship groups, and so on.

Organized secondary processes typify large, heterogeneous societies. In such societies, especially those that are stratified, delegated subgroups typically assume responsibility for applying sanctions. These groups can become very highly specialized, as in our own society. Police enforce laws and legal decisions; courts adjudicate disputes both between individuals and between an individual and the wider society.

Analysis

The Folk Perspective

Chapter 20 describes a community of Swiss peasants living in the alpine foothills. It was difficult to identify the boundaries of this community because it consists of outlying areas of three distinct townships. The existence of the community and its boundaries were established by noting how community members placed their behavior in the community context, using community norms and expectations to evaluate both their own and other people's behavior.

The community recognizes a variety of social statuses within its membership and appreciates the fact

that these same statuses have different meanings in relation to the outside world. They consequently expect community members to behave differently toward each other than they would toward individual outsiders or toward more impersonal outside presences, such as governmental institutions and agencies of law enforcement.

In order to illustrate how shared expectations organize individual behavior, let us briefly examine the community's assumptions about various forms of illegal conduct—that is, acts expressly forbidden by Swiss federal law or the law of their own canton of Bern.

Several federal and cantonal laws are regularly broken by many local people. A large number of the men poach deer, an offense that is subject to a stiff fine in the cantonal court. They justify their behavior by arguing that the deer eat their crops and that many of the local people care for the deer during harsh winters—for example, by carting loads of hay out into the forests. Why, they ask, should they have to pay for a license to hunt? What right does the state have to interfere? Shouldn't the state reimburse them for their damaged crops before demanding that they purchase hunting licenses?

Many community households violate an even more serious law: They brew liquor from potato mash, producing a clear, colorless, but very strong alcoholic beverage. They clandestinely sell the brew at great profit to city folk with whom they have long-standing relationships, sometimes extending over several generations. But the brewing of liquor is very tightly controlled by federal law, and conviction for the offense brings an automatic fine large enough to bankrupt many a local household. Consequently, potato liquor is brewed at night during the worst winter storms in order to reduce the likelihood of discovery by federal agents. The brewing itself is done in the houses, and it produces such a powerful odor that all the neighbors within a half-mile radius know when a household is engaged in the process. Yet even though the practice is clearly illegal, and even though the government offers rewards for information leading to the arrest and conviction of moonshiners, neighbors never turn each other in to the authorities—even neighbors who are feuding and who often make life miserable for one another in other ways. When the peasants

were asked what they would think of a person who would turn in his or her neighbor for brewing, the general consensus was that such an act would be *gemein*—"nasty and contemptible."

A number of formally illegal acts are not only tolerated but even encouraged; however, many other forms of behavior are not tolerated and receive severe negative sanctions within the community. One such act is stealing. The most frequent accusation is that a neighbor has stolen trees—that is, he has cut down trees which did not belong to him. Heated arguments frequently arise about the locations of boundary lines, and vicious gossip circulates about individuals who are regarded (rightly or wrongly) as consistent wood thieves. Occasionally these arguments lead to fist fights outside the local tavern. More frequently, they result in various degrees of ostracism by large numbers of community members. Rarely, however, are the legal authorities called in; the community has a massive distrust of and dislike for the police, the courts, and the cantonal and federal governments. Whenever possible, the community prefers that deviant behavior be handled internally.

One domain the community will not intrude upon is the household. Although behavior outside the home is subject to constant community observation, comment, and sanction, behavior inside the home is held to be almost inviolate. Even known cases of father-daughter incest, although they disgust many people, are thought to be beyond community control. The external authorities are rarely called in in such cases, a fact that reflects community aversion to outside interference, even in areas the community cannot bring itself to intrude upon.

The Analytical Perspective

How can we use the theoretical framework presented earlier to analyze the folk views of this group of Swiss peasants? Let us examine the illegal practices of poaching and moonshining that are accepted by the community as perfectly reasonable behavior. How can behavior be at the same time formally illegal and highly punishable, yet socially accepted and common practice? The answer lies in the context: Poaching and moonshining are supported as acceptable behavior patterns in the immediate group; the laws of the can- ton and federal governments represent the views of a wider society that is both psychologically and geo- graphically distant. According to Alfred Lee: "In any reasonably 'normal' life in . . . society, group models for thought, affect, and action have an especial urgency and priority in decision making upon those who find themselves in a group's context. The compulsions associated with societal models in their context are frequently more formal, less immediate and pressing, more easily pushed aside socially and repressed men- tally" (1966:14). It is clear that a distant group's sanc- tions will not be as effective as those of the immediate group; people have less incentive to conform. This fact brings out an important point. Every group that is a constituent part of a larger society has its own cul- tural system—its own values, beliefs, sanctions. In a complex society, each person might belong to many groups, and it might become difficult for a person to meet the increasingly conflicting demands for con- formity that each group attempts to impose on its members.

At least one scholar has even argued: "Every func- tioning subgroup of . . . [a] society *has its own legal system* which is necessarily different in some respects from those of the other subgroups" (Pospisil 1958:272; emphasis added). Although Pospisil's position is prob- ably extreme, his view does alert us to the fact that different subgroups *may* have their own legal systems and legal sanctions. It may therefore be permissible to speak of the internal legal system of a corporation, a revolutionary guerrilla group, or even perhaps a street gang as well as that of the entire society. When we study a society, we must investigate the sanctions and sanctioning processes of all its subgroups before we can claim to understand how individuals make their daily decisions—or how in each particular in- stance society is able to control individual behavior.

Conclusions

Schools of Thought

Most anthropologists who address the problem of social control operate within the branch of the profes- sion known as *legal anthropology* or the *anthropology*

of law. Thus their view of social control tends to em- phasize societal structure (specifically the legal frame- work) rather than the drama of individual decision making in concretely described contexts. This "top- down view has, as Laura Nader and Barbara Yngvesson point out, a built-in bias:

> anthropologists have been overly influenced by a model of law as defined by the legal profession, a model that tends, most obviously, to produce works that focus on legal codes, legal procedure, and legal concepts, with minimal attention to contextual data. . . . Investigations of the effects of things legal on social life and of social life on things legal are, of course, significant aspects of anthropological law studies, yet in this partic- ular way of focusing on law and society there is an implicit assumption that legal rules, institu- tions, and ideas are a realm unto themselves, affected by and affecting, but not in fact an as- pect of, ongoing social life. (1973:886)

This bias toward viewing legal systems as fully dif- ferentiated from the rest of society has led to a sharp debate on the universality of law—that is, whether all human societies in fact have legal systems. Among those who support the universality of legal systems are such scholars as E. A. Hoebel and Leopold Pospisil. Hoebel defines law in terms of *legal norms:* "A social norm is legal if its neglect or infraction is regularly met, in threat or in fact, by the application of *physical force* by an individual or group possessing the socially recognized privilege of so acting" (1954:28; emphasis added). On the basis of this definition, Hoebel believes that law exists even among societies as uncentralized and organizationally simple as the Eskimos, and that law is therefore universal. He finds one major differ- ence between the law of complex, stratified societies and what he calls the "private law" of simple societies. In complex societies, court systems intervene between an aggrieved person and the claims she or he may impose on the wrongdoer, whereas in simple societies, this process of imposing claims occurs directly between the two parties—but with the approval and sanction of the wider society (Hoebel 1954:50).

Pospisil, whose definition of law in terms of *legal attributes* has already been presented, argues that scholars who deny the universality of law do so because they insist on locating law at the level of the whole society. If they could shake off the "tremendous influence" of "the well-elaborated and unified law of the Roman Empire" on their thinking and recognize the fact that each level of societal organization has its own legal system (and hence any society will have a "multiplicity of legal systems"), they would be able to see such legal systems operating in all human societies (1971:99–106).

Those who argue against the universal presence of law in all human societies inevitably do so from an evolutionary perspective. Eugen Ehrlich (1862–1922) was one of the founders of the sociological study of law. In his classic work, *Fundamental Principles of the Sociology of Law,* published in German in 1913 and in English in 1936, he argued: "Among primitive races, the law is generally identical with the inner order of

their associations. At this stage of development there are no legal propositions at all. At a somewhat higher stage, they appear in the form of religious commands. And it seems that until man has reached a very high stage of development, he cannot fully conceive the idea that the abstract rules of law can force their will upon life" (quoted in Golding 1966:208).

The argument advanced by Morton Fried is considerably more persuasive than Ehrlich's ethnocentric adventures into the psychology of "primitive minds." He accepts Pospisil's formulation of law in terms of the four attributes that have been discussed. But he argues that even Pospisil's Kapauku Papuan data fail to clearly demonstrate the presence of law in Kapauku society when viewed rigorously in terms of Pospisil's own formulation. Fried believes that law develops as a means of social control as society becomes more com-

plex. The evolution of law is related to the decline of the kinship relations that served these social control functions at an earlier stage of social evolution. Thus law proper is not to be found in what Fried calls egalitarian or rank societies (see Chaps. 10, 11, and 15). Rather, it evolves parallel to social stratification. Discussing egalitarian and rank societies, Fried considers it

> relatively a simple matter to establish the absence of law. . . . The most that can be seen in the available illustrations might well be called "law-like" processes of repairing social breaches. Law-like, because one or more of the criteria of law are present and active, yet at the same time one or more of the criteria of law are absent so that . . . we can analytically distinguish legal institutions from those that fall short, *thereby assisting in discovering what developments go with others in the evolution of general sociocultural systems* (1967:145; emphasis added).

Author's Conclusions

Since Ralph Linton's clarification of the concepts *status* and *role* (1936), these have become standard tools in social science research. All thorough ethnographies include rather exhaustive lists of the statuses and roles to be found in the society being described. But much of this kind of description seems frozen; statuses are often depicted in such a way that they appear static. Although we are offered abundant descriptions of the social mechanisms through which statuses are acquired or achieved, we are rarely invited to observe the difficulties that face an individual who is trying to meet the social expectations attached to his or her statuses.

J. van Velsen sees the rather static images of society that emerge from the pages of ethnographies as a result of the dominance of British structuralist methods: "structural analysis aims at presenting an outline of the social morphology; consequently there is a marked emphasis on consistency so that variations are ignored in its abstractions" (1967:136). As van Velsen points out, this tells us very little about the realities of daily life: "norms, general rules of conduct, are translated into practice; they are ultimately manipulated by indi-

Burial of a Hun. Members of the Boston motorcycle gang called "the Huns" showered the casket in which one of their deceased leaders was being buried with beer and liquor, then threw the "empties" into the grave. Though by the standards of the wider society such behavior is clearly deviant, it is legitimized within the group which counterposes itself to the dominant society in terms of its beliefs, values, and internalized sanctions; all of which control members' behavior.

A group of Bakhtiari tribesmen conducting a trial. The accused is alleged to have employed a professional thief to steal for him. Many anthropologists who study legal systems collect such cases for their data. The author of this chapter argues that cases extending far beyond the trial itself must be collected if we are to come to a complete understanding of how society channels and controls behavior.

viduals in particular situations to serve particular ends." (1967:136).

In order to understand the mechanisms of the social control of behavior, we must free ourselves from the top-down orientation of so much social science. The decisions of each individual are what ultimately make society work. We must attempt detailed analyses of the contexts of individual decision making, of the pushes and pulls that people experience and that shape their behavior. One technique that has been proposed is the extended-case method. The highly detailed descriptions of sequences and contexts of individual decision making employed in this method might enable us to make what van Velsen would call "situational analyses" (1964). Such an analysis would inform us further about the ways society molds individual behavior. We might also make a closer study of *reference groups*—the categories of people individuals use for comparison when they assess their own and others' behavior (Merton 1968: Chaps. 10 and 11). In any event, anthropologists must not limit descriptions to statements of norms, frozen forever in formal renderings of societal structure and organization.

On the larger scale, it seems to me to be imperative that we keep the image of sociocultural evolution constantly in mind. The one great constant is change—and a science of human behavior must embrace the description and analysis of change, identifying its sources, charting its ebbs and flows. The course of recent sociocultural evolution is perhaps most visibly marked in the domain of sociopolitical evolution as described, for example, by Fried (1967). I agree with his argument that, in this instance, law must be understood as an evolving institution, dynamically interacting with other evolving features of society such as social stratification and the emergence of the state.

From the lofty peaks of social organization to the grass roots of individual behavior, it seems to me that the only models that will ultimately be useful in promoting our understanding of the human condition are those in which *process* (dynamics) is built in as an initial condition of all behavior.

or effort. The expected behavior of a person occupying a given status constitutes the role associated with that status.

Examples from ethnographic literature concerning incidents among the BaMbuti of tropical Africa and the Kapauku of New Guinea illustrate some of the processes by which individuals are induced to conform to social norms.

Individual behavior is subject to control by sanctions, the responses the group makes to the individual's behavior. Sanctions may be positive, as in the case of social approval, or negative, as in the case of punishment. They may also be formal, as in the case of legal action against an offender, or informal, when they are not applied in an organized way by social authorities.

The example of a Swiss peasant community reveals how sanctions may be applied or withheld and how a considerable discrepancy may develop between the actual laws of the society and the informal expectations of the local community. In fact, scholars debate whether "law" is universal in human groups or whether the traditional concept of law cannot be applied to norms and expectations that are not enforced by a formal political authority—but that are nonetheless extremely powerful influences on human behavior.

Summary

For a society to "work," each individual must conform to social expectations and adjust her or his behavior to prevailing cultural patterns. This conformity is induced by social mechanisms—that is, people's behavior is largely socially controlled, even when the individuals concerned are unaware of this fact. We know from the available evidence that some measure of socially learned behavior existed among the earliest hominids and that it is a feature of all primate social groups, but these cultural patterns have been vastly elaborated in *Homo sapiens*.

In all human social groups, differences in role and status are recognized among individuals. Ascribed statuses are those social positions that a person is born or grows into; an achieved status is obtained by intent

Annotated Bibliography

Fried, Morton H. (1967) *The Evolution of Political Society.* New York: Random House. A survey of the evolution of sociopolitical forms, making explicit reference to the emergence of law as society becomes complex. An influential book among anthropologists in the evolutionary school.

Hoebel, E. Adamson (1954) *The Law of Primitive Man.* Cambridge, Mass.: Harvard Univ. Press. Still a standard reference text on the anthropology of law, though considerable progress has been made in this area of study since it was published.

Nader, Laura, ed. (1969) *Law in Culture and Society.* Chicago: Aldine. A useful collection of readings on the ethnography and nature of law.

13
Belief Systems:
The Sacred and the Profane

The World Context

Origins and Development through Time

"As members of society, most of us see only what we expect to see, and what we expect to see is what we are conditioned to see when we have learned the definitions and classifications of our culture" (Turner 1964:339). Everyone makes the chaos of the universe understandable and manageable in cultural terms. These cultural terms are learned categories, called *cognitive categories*, that we use to sort out our perceptions. Culturally molded cognition is the way in which we create order in our world.

Culture provides more than just categories that we use to organize our experience of the world. It also furnishes us with *beliefs* regarding the universe—that is, thoughts based on the uncritical acceptance of the inherent "truth" or "correctness" of our culture's cognitive categories. Beliefs do not occur randomly in a society; they are organized and systematically related, even though some beliefs may appear to contradict or even exclude other beliefs that are held at the same time.

Belief systems deal with everything human beings perceive and with everything they can imagine. Indeed,

Sacrificed dogs are impaled by the rein-
deer-herding Koryak of the Kamchatka
Peninsula (U.S.S.R.). They are hung
with their muzzles pointing up and
their bellies pointing East to insure good
hunting. Dogs are also sacrificed to the
evil spirits (*kalau*) to protect the people
from disaster and to ward off disease.
These practices are an expression of
beliefs which are very foreign to us, and
seem, therefore, to be impractical and
even foolish. In this chapter, however, we
explore the importance of beliefs of all
kinds in everyday life for all peoples. It
is also pointed out that all beliefs are
ultimately grounded in one way or
another in material conditions. For
instance, regarding these sacrificed dogs:
the Koryak usually only sacrifice young,
disabled, or sick animals; i.e., animals
which cannot draw the sleighs that
are the people's primary means of transportation. This eliminates the need to
feed unproductive animals—a very practical, economically useful device.

it is through belief systems that human beings give
meanings to their experiences. Belief systems are concerned with a vast number of topics: what to eat, how
to prepare food, the nature of the universe, the position human beings occupy in the scheme of the cosmos. Belief systems deal with very particular and
detailed items, such as what to do about cuts and
bruises. But they also speak to the great mysteries that
have always puzzled human beings—questions about
the meaning of life, the nature of death, the reason for
death, the purpose of our existence, and so forth.

Instrumental, or rational-technical, belief systems
are concerned primarily with the concrete tasks necessary for human survival, such as subsistence activities,
travel, nourishment, medicine, and so on. Such belief
systems provide people with practical guidelines by
which they can structure their day-to-day behavior—
when to eat, how to get food, whom their daughter
should marry, what to do about a sick relative, which
stocks to invest money in, which courses to take in college, which merchants to patronize.

Other belief systems take us beyond daily concerns.
Humans are perhaps the only species in which each
organism is aware that a time existed when she or he
did not exist, and that a time shall inevitably come
when she or he will cease to exist—at least in the form
the person currently assumes. Thus all cultures provide
people with organized ideas about states of existence
beyond the capacities of their senses to register, about
things it is impossible for them to learn from their
personal experience. These beliefs are called *transcendental.* Thus, along with their unique communication
skills (see Chap. 7), humans are unique in the animal
kingdom in that they alone create and deal with
transcendental beliefs.

These transcendental belief systems provide the
structure through which human beings give meaning
and purpose to their existence. They address the central questions of human existence. They provide the
ways in which people come to see themselves and
their societies as important or debased. They define
which tasks of their lives are worthwhile, which ob-
jectionable. They state which of the ways of life people
pass on to their children are significant, and which
need changing. They affirm the spiritual value of some

humans, deny the personhood of others. They extol the virtues of one society, while condemning other societies. They specify which persons are worth what to whom.

In practice, it is sometimes difficult to decide whether a particular belief system is instrumental or transcendental. These labels are no more than concepts that anthropologists use to classify and understand beliefs. Actual belief systems may have both transcendental and instrumental components. For instance, Hopi Indian beliefs about the nature of the universe (transcendental beliefs) tie them firmly into such day-to-day tasks as when to plant their corn (instrumental beliefs). This is an example of the many ways in which beliefs are systematically ordered and connected to one another. In fact, the understanding of these relationships is a major task of anthropology.

Some of the questions about belief systems that interest anthropologists concern their origins and development through time. Where did they originate? How did they evolve? Although some of these issues were dealt with in chapter 2, we shall also consider them here.

In earlier chapters we saw that human beings do not inherit their organized responses to environmental stimuli; they *learn* almost every item of behavior in which they engage. The same holds true for the cognitive categories and beliefs that human groups use to interact with their environments, to impose order on the universe, and to inject meaning into their lives. At what point in the evolutionary sequence did our human or prehuman ancestors use cognitive categories and systems of belief? What kinds of data would we need to be able to guess that our ancestors organized their experience in terms of belief systems?

It is difficult to tell from the skeletal remains of our ancestors to what extent their lives were governed by systems of belief (unless these fossilized remains offer evidence of behavior showing conscious intent, as in the case of body adornment such as head-flattening). However, we can learn a lot more about beliefs from the *cultural remains* our ancestors left behind. These include such artifacts as tools, weapons, and structures; the waste materials from the production of implements, such as stone chips; garbage, such as sea shells; patterns indicating the nature of their living arrangements—the sizes, shapes, and materials of their homes; and evidence regarding the food they ate and their treatment of the dead. When we examine these diverse data, we can observe an evolutionary pattern originating in simple cognitive systems and leading finally to the complex, heterogeneous transcendental beliefs of the diverse religions in the world today.

The remains left by the first hominid, *Ramapithecus*, are limited mostly to facial bones and teeth. No identifiable cultural remains have been found, although these creatures possibly used some tools similar to those used by modern chimpanzees (Pilbeam 1972:99) and probably achieved a level of cultural development comparable to some contemporary primates, such as baboons.

It is at the next stage of human evolution, the australopithecine stage, that we find concrete evidence of cultural remains. About 2 million years ago in East Africa, advanced forms of the gracile line of australopithecines (*Australopithecus habilis*; see chap. 2) were using simple pebble tools. These tools were made by knocking several flakes off fist-sized flint nodules. They were used mostly for hunting small and medium-sized animals, enabling these ancestors of ours to subsist on a reasonably protein-rich diet. These creatures lived in groups, acquiring knowledge and skills and teaching them to succeeding generations. They were, in short, developing culture.

However, neither the complexity of these tools nor the evidence of some degree of group organization (hunting) suggests mental development beyond that of some basic cognitive categories such as we find among modern apes. Although the gracile australopithecines were clearly imposing their sense of order on the environment—using natural resources for tool making, hunting selected animals, and gathering certain roots, grasses, berries, and seeds—there is no evidence to suggest the development of complex organized belief systems.

These systems appear to have developed at the next stage of human evolution. *Homo erectus* evolved roughly a million years ago, with a thoroughly modern body and limbs and a cranial capacity of some 1,100 cc (within the lowest end of the range of modern

Homo sapiens). **For some 800,000 years,** *Homo erectus* **roamed the earth, eventually moving out of the tropical and subtropical African grasslands to occupy the colder temperate zones from western Europe across southern Eurasia and into eastern Asia as far north as Peking. We can infer something about the cultural development of** *Homo erectus* **from their success in adapting to this wide range of ecological niches, the greatly increased complexity of their tools, their control of fire in colder climates, and settlement patterns in some of their sites that suggest the possible division of groups into smaller units like the family (see chap. 2). These data suggest a level of cultural development that probably included the emergence of primitive forms of language (see chap. 7), a division of labor in tool making and hunting, and the development of complex** *instrumental* **belief systems.**

So far we have uncovered no evidence of *transcendental* **belief systems until the emergence of** *Homo sapiens* **at the Neanderthal stage some 100,000 years ago in the Middle East. In Shanidar Cave and in later sites in Europe and Asia, we find the earliest evidence of systematic and ritual burial of the dead. Corpses were tied in fetal positions, buried on their sides, sprinkled with red ocher (and, at Shanidar, even with flower petals), and provided with food in their graves. Their treatment of the dead suggests that these Neanderthal people no longer considered the person as simply a creature among other creatures; for them, at least, other forms of existence awaited after death. Clearly, beliefs about existence beyond that of daily life are transcendental (Solecki 1971). Thus we may conclude that these Neanderthal people had developed transcendental belief systems.**

Of course, we can know very little about the content of these transcendental beliefs. We do know that the beliefs gradually developed and became more complex, as suggested, for example, by the magnificent Upper Paleolithic art first produced between thirty and forty thousand years ago. How these belief systems evolved into fantastically complex cosmologies and religions is a matter of speculation and cautious deduction.

Robert N. Bellah defines religion as "a set of symbolic forms and acts which relate man to the ultimate

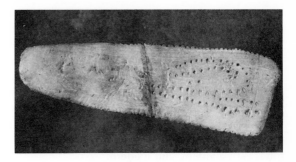

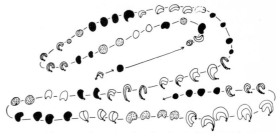

This carved piece of antler bone is approximately 4 inches long and was found at the site of Blancharde, in the Dordogne region of France. It dates from the Aurignacian culture, some 34,000 years old. Many such objects have been found in Upper Paleolithic sites; their markings have largely been ignored and they have been called anything from "spatulas" to "palettes" or "knives."

Recently Professor Alexander Marshack of Harvard has begun reexamining these objects, including the microscopic examination of the details of their manufacture. His accompanying drawing shows some of the details he has noted. The significance of the finds is that these prehistoric people had a notational system; that this system was rather complex; that it was part of an established tradition; and that it expresses complicated cognitive development. It makes sense to further presume that these people would not have taken the trouble to carve these notations unless their belief system told them it was meaningful behavior. Marshack suggests that the 24 changes of point, style of stroke, or pressure used show that the creation of this notation was divided into 24 separated moments, of significance to the maker(s). Computer analysis suggests that this notational system was used to record or predict phases of the moon.

conditions of his existence" (1964:37). He has proposed a scheme of five evolutionary stages, or ideal types, of religion. Each stage exhibits its own forms and combinations of four features: (a) the symbol system, (b) the kind of action it generates, (c) the form of social organization in which the religion is embedded, and (d) the implications for social action that the religious action contains (1964:40). The five ideal types, or levels, of religion are: primitive, archaic, historic, early modern, and modern.

1. Primitive: **The religious system tightly unites the mythical, or symbolic, world and the real world. Religious action entails a mystical participation in this mythical-real world and during rituals the distinction between symbolic and real evaporates entirely. No isolated, specialized institution serves the religion: religious congregation and community are one and the same. At this stage, instrumental and transcendental belief systems are often inseparable. Religion apparently affects social action by reinforcing group solidarity within the society.**

2. Archaic: **Mythical (symbolic) beings have become much more concrete; they have unique identities. Participation takes the form of cult activities in which human beings and supernatural beings are placed in subject-object relationships. Thus worship and sacrifice emerge at this level as means of communicating with supernatural beings. Religious organization and social organization are still fused, although cults differentiate as the society itself breaks up into subgroups and becomes less homogeneous. The social action induced by religion is still the reinforcement of group solidarity.**

3. Historic: **The symbolic system of historic religions is strongly dualistic, emphasizing two hierarchical worlds: that humans and the supernatural world of the gods. Life after death is stressed. These religions are also *universalistic*; instead of stressing the community or tribe, they address themselves to the entire human species. Religious action is centered around the diverse ways of achieving salvation. Historic religions are also characterized by the emergence of specialized, hierarchical religious organizations such as churches. These religions introduced into society new sources of values and authority that could be** counterposed to those of the state. Hence the possibility of conflict between religious and secular hierarchies arose for the first time in the sphere of social action. Secular and religious authorities could also cooperate and strengthen each other's power.

4. Early modern: **This stage arises out of the Protestant Reformation and is defined by the "collapse of the hierarchical structuring of both this and the other world" (Bellah 1964:45). Religious symbolism focuses on the individual's achievement of transcendence in a personal relationship with the supernatural. Religious action becomes identified with the orientation of a person's entire life-style. The hierarchical organization of the Roman Catholic Church is overthrown. One result is that status distinctions derive from an individual's perceived fitness for salvation rather than from a church hierarchy. The social implications of these developments were many and complex. For example, where Calvinist Protestantism flourished, hereditary kingships and aristocracies were undermined, and the Industrial Revolution, with its ascendant merchant class, was born.**

5. Modern: **This stage is the least well defined. Bellah believes that it is characterized by a collapse of the fundamental dualism of earlier stages; religious symbolism itself has become the subject of contemplation and analysis. No simple truths seem to have survived: What had been simple propositions are now awesomely complex problems. An emphasis on coming to personal terms with creeds seems to be a major theme, with religious action focusing on each person's quest for self-actualization rather than salvation. The social implications of these phenomena are difficult to interpret or predict. Some scholars believe that this process represents the disintegration of society as we know it and the degeneration of moral fiber into amorphous hedonism. Others see possibilities for individual creativity and innovation that might lead to new stages of social evolution.**

Contemporary Examples

Belief systems have been with us for at least the last six hundred thousand years. They are what make life meaningful for human beings around the world.

Let us briefly look at a few examples that flourish in our own and other societies.

As we mentioned earlier, human belief systems deal with all aspects of the human condition. For instance, many societies have elaborately organized beliefs about human origins and the nature of the universe. And in some societies—the United States, for example—many competing belief systems on these topics exist, from the biblical version in Genesis to scientific evolutionism.

A Lake City Sect　In the early 1950s in the fictitious Middle American town of Lake City, a group of people formed around a medium by the name of Mrs. Keech. They came to believe that the world would be destroyed on December 21, and that only the "elect" would be saved. They heard that the origin of the earth's population was the planet Car, which had been blown to pieces when the "scientists," under the leadership of Lucifer, ineptly lost control of atomic weapons they had built to fight "the people who followed the Light" in the service of God under the leadership of Jesus Christ. After that cosmic mishap, Lucifer led his legions to Earth while the forces of light retrenched on other planets. Because they had lost their "cosmic knowledge," human beings were intent on following Lucifer and hence were doomed to destruction (Festinger, Rieken, and Schachter 1956).

The Yanomamö　The Yanomamö Indians are a jungle-dwelling tribe of the Amazon basin living in parts of Venezuela and Brazil. In their conception, the cosmos consists of four planes or layers. Human beings live on the second plane from the bottom, supernatural beings live on the plane above them, and a single village of dead spirits occupies the bottom level. The top level is apparently empty. They do not see the universe as having a beginning: The "first beings" have always existed. These first beings contended with numerous catastrophes, including a flood which they escaped by climbing into the mountains. Some first beings built rafts to escape the waters, floated away, and developed "foreign" languages and customs; hence the world became populated with peoples other than the Yanomamö. Meanwhile, a great many of the first beings had died in the flood. One who survived was a cannibalistic creature by the name of Periboriwä, who

descended from the plane above the earth and ate the children. Eventually he was shot by the hero Suhirina, who used a bamboo arrow. The blood from Periboriwä's wound spilled onto the surface of the earth, and the Yanomamö people emerged from this blood. Hence they are very fierce (Chagnon 1968:44–48).

The Kapauku Papuans　As a group, the mountain-dwelling Kapauku Papuans of west New Guinea invest very little energy in thinking about transcendental issues. They leave this activity to a few philosophically inclined individuals. But the Kapauku do have cosmological beliefs. For them the earth is an infinitely deep block of stone and soil surrounded by water and covered by a sky shaped like an inverted bowl. The universe was created by Ugatame, who incorporates masculine and feminine characteristics but at the same time does not exist (for, after all, he/she created all "existence"). Ugatame's act of creation was completely deterministic, so there is no room for the concept of free will. Good and evil are equally Ugatame's creations. Everything is "real," even evil spirits who, though immaterial, manifest themselves as sickness, and whose behavior is governed by the same natural laws that govern human beings and animals (Pospisil 1963:83–88).

The Trukese　Leaving the area of cosmic concerns, let us briefly examine a concrete—though certainly quite marvelous—example of what human beings are capable of achieving with instrumental belief systems. The people of Truk, a small island that is part of the Caroline group in the northern Pacific, have been undertaking ocean voyages in their open sailing canoes since time immemorial. These voyages may span over a hundred miles of open ocean. Their destination is often an island no more than a mile across, a mere speck of land in the vast Pacific.

From the deck of the canoe, the island of their destination is not visible until shortly before the voyagers arrive, because the curve of the earth's surface hides even a forested island below the horizon if it is more than three or four miles away. The responsibility for steering the course that will bring the sailors safely to port rests on the navigator, who has learned his craft by apprenticeship from older master navigators. It should be noted that their traditional techniques make no use of such aids to "modern" navigation as the

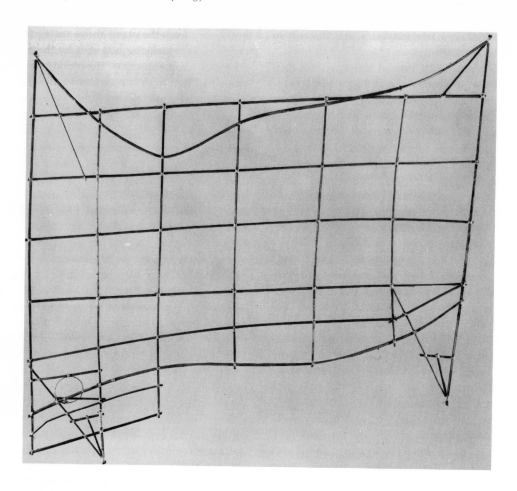

Rattan navigational chart from the Marshall Islands, Micronesian neighbors to the Trukese. Encoded in this elegant device is sufficient oceanographic and astronomical information to enable these people to navigate across hundreds of miles of open ocean.

chronometer, the sextant, star tables or even a compass.

Essentially the navigator relies on dead reckoning. He sets his course by the rising and setting of stars, having memorized for this purpose the knowledge gleaned from generations of observation of the directions in which stars rise and fall through the seasons. . . . Through the night a succession of such stars will rise or fall, and each will be noted and the course checked. Between stars, or when the stars are not visible due to daylight or storm, the course is held constant by noting the direction of the wind and the waves. A good navigator can tell by observing wave patterns when the wind is shifting its direction or speed, and by how much. In a dark and starless night the navigator can even tell these things from the sound of the waves as they lap upon the side of the canoe's hull, and the feel of the boat as it travels through the water. All of these perceptions—visual, auditory, kinesthetic—are combined with vast amounts of data stored in memory (Gladwin 1964:171).

The boat travels along an invisible pathway that exists in the navigator's mind and that can be charted only by his instrumental beliefs—beliefs about the behavior of stars, wind, and water. However, by accepting these beliefs, the navigator can translate his mental images into concrete reality. He can safely guide his canoe across the ocean to distant islands; and he can bring the craft and its crew safely back home again.

Anthropologists   Every group has its own systems of belief as part of its culture. As anthropologists have studied more and more isolated groups living in remote corners of the world, they have been forced to confront the placid assumption of our civilization that our own belief systems are natural and correct.

For that matter, anthropologists, as a specialized subgroup of our society, have their own specific beliefs that they learn as part of their training. One of these is that they should enter fully into the lives of the people they study, using the technique of participant observation (see Chap. 20). It is thought that this task should be accomplished to the point where anthropologists come to see and understand the world in the manner of the people they are studying. However, very few (if any) anthropologists claim to have achieved this perspective, and the goal remains an ideal rather than an accomplished fact. Precisely because cultures are such complex systems of beliefs and behavior, it is doubtful that any anthropologist will ever be able to enter into every aspect of another society's way of life. Thus anthropologists usually settle for partial understanding of fragments of the belief systems of the people they are studying.

One anthropologist who was perhaps more successful than others in achieving full participation in the culture he was studying has come to the attention of the American public. The writings of Carlos Castañeda have shocked some, troubled others, and won the enthusiastic support of many young people. Castañeda wrote about the activities of Don Juan, a self-proclaimed Yaqui Indian sorceror who lives in northern Mexico. Many people have written about witchcraft from the position of outsiders, causing no controversy. However, Castañeda apprenticed himself for a decade to the sorceror and, in effect, *became* a witch himself. In so doing he transformed his identity, and this fact—the threat of identity loss or the promise of identity change—may account for Castañeda's controversial appeal (see Chap. 14).

In a series of four books (1968, 1971, 1972, 1974), Castañeda shares with us the supremely difficult process through which he internalized Don Juan's belief system. In order to "see" what Don Juan could "see," "do" what Don Juan could "do," and "be" what Don Juan insisted that Castañeda could "be," Castañeda was gradually forced to give up the most basic causal assumptions of our industrial society's culture. He had to unlearn all the habits of categorizing, analyzing, and perceiving that had been his natural way of relating to the universe since his earliest childhood. This process meant allowing his entire mental structure to collapse as all its supports—the unquestioned assumptions every culture provides— were subjected to a ten-year assault through the untiring, uncompromising instructions of Don Juan and his friend Don Genaro. Under their tutoring, Castañeda learned to converse with animals, to become a bird himself, to see the world as a nonconcrete web of force fields, to identify supernatural allies and dangerous sorcerors, and to abandon rational-analytical thought as the sole correct perspective on reality. This happened as more and more of the things Don Juan did and showed him defied our culture's definitions of what is possible and real.

Quite understandably, this was an emotional and intellectual experience filed with anguish, confusion, and almost constant doubt. Toward the end of this period, Don Juan insisted that Castañeda would have to make a choice between the two belief systems: He would either have to abandon his quest for understanding of the Yaqui way of knowledge and return to his unseeing, habit-dominated way of life at the university, or allow Don Juan's version of the nature of the universe to take command of his perceptions of himself and the world around him, thereby losing forever his ability to feel himself a part of his own culture. At the end of his third book Castañeda decides to put off his irretrievable conversion to Don Juan's belief system, although we are left with the distinct impression that this conversion will take place. In the fourth book it does.

Although some scholars express doubts about the truth of Castañeda's writings, his story nevertheless serves to make the central point of this chapter: Reality is a cultural construct, a series of conventions through which group members structure the possibilities of their experiences. As each of us becomes enculturated—that is, learns the group culture—through our childhood development, we are learning what reality is and what we should think about it. The reality of every group, then, is unique, and it is taken for granted by those who share it.

This theme is hardly new. Plato represented this point of view in *The Republic* four centuries before Jesus. In his analogy of the cave, he argued that we are like hypothetical cave residents who never leave the cave and who mistake the shadow images on the wall of the cave for the real objects that cast those shadows from a position in the sunlight outside the cave. Reality, for Plato and for present-day anthropologists, must be treated as a culturally relative phenomenon.

Theory

Systems

We have already identified some of the elements of belief systems. We have distinguished between instrumental beliefs and transcendental beliefs, and have indicated that all belief systems are constructed out of the cognitive categories that are provided by culture.

Because instrumental belief systems can often be investigated through references to concrete—real—items in the environment, the major difficulty for anthropologists has been simply to find techniques for identifying exactly what one's informants *mean* when they talk about their instrumental beliefs (Chap. 7).

Naturally this problem also confronts investigators of transcendental belief systems. But before they can

even get that far, they must confront an even more basic problem: defining terms. Unfortunately, anthropologists have not yet been able to agree on the meaning of some of the most basic concepts they use to investigate transcendental belief systems—concepts such as *religion*, the *supernatural*, *magic*, and *witchcraft*. We will attempt to steer a middle course through this definitional tangle, employing terms in accordance with the usage that is most common among scholars.

We shall use the term *supernatural* to refer to all things that are believed to exist but are beyond the reach of the human senses (and such devices as microscopes and telescopes). *Supernatural beliefs*, then, are essentially the same as transcendental beliefs. *Supernatural practices*, it follows, constitute a realm of human behavior that derives its meaning from the relationships that participants or onlookers believe to exist between the behavior and supernatural elements.

One kind of supernatural system is religion. A workable definition of *religion* is: "an institution consisting of culturally patterned interaction with culturally postulated superhuman [supernatural] beings" (Spiro 1966:96). This means that religion consists of both supernatural beliefs and supernatural practices.

Some of the supernatural beliefs that are elements of religion are *animism,* the belief that objects (including people) in the concretely perceivable world have a nonconcrete, spiritual element (for human beings this element is the soul); *animatism,* the "attribution of life to inanimate objects" (Hoebel 1972:689); and *taboo,* the belief in negative supernatural consequences that attach to the performance of certain acts.

A few common supernatural practices that form a part of religious activities are *ritual,* which consists of culturally prescribed, periodically repeated, patterned sequences of behavior; *magic,* the (usually ritualized) behavior that is intended to control or at least significantly influence the basic processes of the universe without recourse to perceptibly instrumental acts; and *shamanism,* in which certain gifted persons establish—usually with the aid of trance or an ecstatic state of excitement—direct communication with the supernatural and thus link group members with the awesome powers of the supernatural universe.

Using this approach, witchcraft and divination are both types of magical activity. *Witchcraft* is the use of

Witchcraft: the use of magic in order to control the behavior of another person or group of persons. Shown here is an Australian Aborigine engaged in "bone pointing," a practice which mobilizes spiritual energy, which is channeled in such a way as to inflict damage on an enemy from a distance.

Divination: the use of magic to predict the future. Takahashi Sanshiro, 80, of the Japanese village of Takatoya (see Chapter 23), demonstrates the use of divining sticks to discover the location of a lost object. He is the last "mountain ascetic" (*yamabushi*); his art combines elements of Shinto, Buddhism, and native folk practices.

magic to *control* the behavior of another person or persons; *divination* is the use of magic to *predict* the behavior of another person or persons, and also possibly the behavior of supernatural entities as well.

Processes

The belief systems a person has learned strongly influence his or her behavior, especially in the area of instrumental belief systems. People eat what they believe they should eat, marry whom they believe they should marry, vote for the party they believe will best represent their interests, take the path they believe will lead most directly or effortlessly to their destination. A belief system can influence behavior effectively only if two basic requirements are met: It must be physically possible for the believer to operate in the world under his or her belief system, and she or he must be unambivalently attached to that belief system. Let us consider these requirements in more detail.

In the first case, belief systems must reflect to at least some degree the material conditions of the people who hold them. For example, the Hopi Indians have an elaborate supernatural belief system in regard to their agricultural calendar. However, their beliefs about such activities as when to plant are rooted in the climatic conditions of the American Southwest and the Hopi's technology. As material conditions change, belief systems must change to accommodate them. One major theoretical issue in social science is the extent to which a society's material conditions (including the environment and the group's technology and economic system) *determine* their belief systems. Marxists argue that a society's material conditions have a primary influence on other elements of the group's culture. Other theorists see the various elements of socioeconomic and cultural systems as being in equilibrium, with no one element having causal priority. All theorists, however, acknowledge that belief systems lead groups to make technological and economic innovations and vice versa.

The second requirement, that an individual must be unambivalently attached to his or her belief system, is often not the case. Indeed, a person may adhere to several conflicting belief systems. This situation is unlikely to involve only instrument systems. Generally, the conflict will be between an instrumental and a transcendental belief system, or possibly between two transcendental systems of belief. This state of conflict is known as *cognitive dissonance.*

Dissonance produces discomfort and, correspondingly, there will arise pressures to reduce or eliminate the dissonance. . . . Such attempts may take any or all of three forms. The person may try to change one or more of the beliefs, opinions or behaviors involved in the dissonance; to acquire new information or beliefs that will increase the existing consonance and thus cause the total dissonance to be reduced; or to forget or reduce the importance of those cognitions that are in a dissonant relationship.

If any of the above attempts are to be successful, they must meet with support from either the physical or the social environment. In the absence of such support, the most determined efforts to reduce dissonance may be unsuccessful (Festinger, Rieken, and Schachter 1956:26).

In order to understand more clearly how belief systems and patterned behavior are interconnected, let us examine the phenomenon of religion more closely. We have said that religion is a system of transcendental beliefs and practices through which people establish relationships with the supernatural. How does this system work? What effects does religion have on human beings?

Numerous types of effects, often called *functions,* have been suggested by students of religion. Among them are:

1. Emotional integration: **Depth psychologists, especially Carl Jung and his followers, have argued that religion provides a symbolic system through which the person can actively participate in his or her emotional development, and which a person can also use for therapeutic purposes when emotional problems erupt (see, for example, Jung 1969; Neumann 1954).**

2. Cultural revitalization: **Some scholars, such as Anthony F. C. Wallace (1966), emphasize the ways in which religion acts to "recharge the batteries" of a flagging culture. These scholars have described what they call "revitalization movements," which sometimes**

occur in cultures that are under attack from competing belief systems (such as when industrial civilization reaches some previously isolated people).

These cultures may retrench themselves by generating powerful religious movements that stress the return to the "good old values" of the "previously uncorrupted" tradition. But people may also come to accept *new* belief systems when the old ones have fallen too far out of phase with historical events; the new belief systems also provide cultural vitality.

3. Provision of meaning: Still other scholars stress the symbolic element of religion, and how it provides a meaningful cultural context for individual behavior. For example, Clifford Geertz sees religion as: "(1) a system of symbols which acts to (2) establish powerful, pervasive, and long-lasting moods and motivations in men by (3) formulating conceptions of a general order of existence and (4) clothing these conceptions with such an order of factuality that (5) the moods and motivations seem uniquely realistic" (1966:4).

4. Social integration: Finally, another major school of theorists takes the path suggested in Émile Durkheim's classic, *The Elementary Forms of the Religious Life* (1915). In this work, Durkheim argues that religion's primary function is to provide human groups with the symbolic forms through which they can ritually enact their group integration—and in doing so become more socially integrated.

Two major vehicles through which religion can have these effects (achieve these functions) are *myth* and *ritual*. Recent writings have dealt with myth and ritual as systems of communication that individuals are taught and that provide the means for reexperiencing the most basic—and usually unconscious—distinctions made by their culture (see, for example, Lévi-Strauss 1964; Leach 1969; Turner 1967). Claude Lévi-Strauss perhaps expresses this view most forcefully, arguing that myths operate on people's thought habits even without their awareness. In a sense, myths are messengers of the culture that teach people the grammar through which they construct their reality. "Myths are anonymous: from the moment they are seen as myths, and whatever their real origins, they exist only as elements embodied in a tradition. When the myth is repeated, the individual listeners are receiving a

Religion as a mechanism of social integration. An old chief washes an initiate before an initiation ceremony among the Xavante, an Amazon Indian tribal group. Such rituals enable social groups to experience their unity and permanence through cycles of renewal.

message that, properly speaking, is coming from no-where; this is why it is credited with a supernatural origin" (1964:18).

Because myths come to all individuals from outside themselves and are perceived as having supernatural origins, people do not attempt to impose their conscious thoughts on myths. Rather, they passively allow the structure of myths to organize their patterns of thought. These patterns will thus be congruent with the fundamental distinctions assumed by the culture. Consequently, members of a cultural group are able to interact with each other through shared meanings.

Victor Turner has a similar perspective on ritual. In his view, ritual is the means through which people are "transformed" socially from one state to another, such as when a single person marries or an initiate becomes a confirmed member of the church. A "space" is left in the social area vacated by the person. The individual and others need some cultural mechanism through which they can integrate this "loss" and adjust to the "addition" of the individual to the social category of which she or he has become a new member.

> I consider the term "ritual" to be more fittingly applied to forms of religious behavior associated with *social transitions,* while the term "cere-mony" has a closer bearing on religious behavior associated with social states, where politico-legal institutions also have greater importance. *Ritual is transformative,* ceremony confirmative (1964:339, emphasis added).

This section of the chapter has necessarily been somewhat abstract. We have explored the fundamentals of belief systems and attempted to see how they operate in cultural processes. Let us now examine some examples of behavior and see if we can understand them by using the theoretical constructs just discussed.

Analysis

The Folk Perspective

When we describe and analyze social and cultural phenomena, perhaps the most difficult thing is keeping separate the different perspectives from which events are perceived. Anthropologists frequently allege that

they can distinguish their point of view (etics) from that of their informants (emics). However, this is a very difficult task, for reasons we have already discussed. Here we consider another source of difficulty: lack of shared perceptions or perspectives among the people we are studying. In such cases it is impossible to describe a single, integrated folk (emic) system.

In order to illuminate this problem and to show the application of theory to the analysis of case materials, let us examine the story of Quesalid, a Kwakiutl Indian from Vancouver Island, British Columbia. Quesalid received his name when he became a sorceror, or shaman, among his people. His account of his activities was recorded by Franz Boas (1930), who was at that time the most famous American anthropologist and who contributed enormously to the development of anthropology by stressing the importance of accurately recording fieldwork materials. This, briefly, is Quesalid's autobiography (following the summary presented in Lévi-Strauss 1963:175–178).

Quesalid had apparently been interested in shamanism for some time, for he deliberately associated with local shamans until he was invited to enter a four-year apprenticeship. Gradually he was instructed in the various elements of the art: sleight-of-hand tricks, pantomime, and empirical knowledge about plants and animals. He also learned sacred songs, how to induce vomiting, some quite detailed instruction in obstetrics and ausculation (the art of diagnosis by listening to various parts of the body, as medical doctors do with a stethoscope), to employ spies to gather information about the nature and origins of patients' symptoms, and how to simulate fainting and trance.

He was also taught one of the most secret of the shamanistic tricks: how to hide a piece of down in his mouth, bite his tongue to cause it to bleed, then produce the "bloody worm" after having "sucked it out of" the patient, effecting a dramatic "cure."

Quesalid was outraged at the deceptive practices he was taught but he kept quiet in order to learn everything. Perhaps he also remained silent because he was troubled. Although the shamans were clearly frauds in that many of their "miracles" were nothing but shabby tricks, the disturbing truth was that they also cured people. As a matter of fact, his initial attempt to cure

Kwakiutl village, c. 1900. It was in the context of such villages that Quesalid rose to fame as a great shaman—and also agonized over his own and other shamans' authenticity.

a sick person using the "bloody worm" technique was a success, and this launched Quesalid on his career as a great sorceror among the Kwakiutl and neighboring Indian tribes.

During a visit among the nearby Koskimo Indians, Quesalid encountered shamans who were even less artful than his own instructors. These practitioners sucked on the patient, then merely spit into their hands and claimed this to be the "sickness"—no "bloody worm," no illusions. Yet these shamans, too, cured some people. How could this be? he wondered.

Observing a curing ritual that failed, Quesalid asked if he might try. He then performed his own ritual, produced the "bloody worm," and succeeded in curing the patient where the resident shamans had been unsuccessful. This feat, of course, enhanced his prestige and propelled him farther along his illustrious career as a shaman.

For Quesalid, however, this episode was very disturbing. Although he was contemptuous of his own system of shamanism as being essentially fraudulent, he had discovered another system that was apparently even more fraudulent: It offered less illusion and apparently achieved less success. But if their system was less valid than his own, did that not mean that his system had at least some validity?

As Quesalid continued his career, his rapidly growing reputation caused anxiety among his colleagues. One old shaman decided to bring matters to a head by challenging all the curers in the entire area to a showdown. This shaman's technique entailed incorporating the patient's sickness into a wooden bird; through a sleight-of-hand illusion, he was able to make the bird appear to float below his outstretched fingers.

At this contest, Quesalid again was able to cure where others, including the old man, had failed. The old shaman became distraught and begged Quesalid in private to tell him whether his "bloody worm" was "real" or merely an illusion. Quesalid kept silent, and the old man subsequently went insane.

As Quesalid pursued his career, a gradual change of mind came over him. Although he continued to be contemptuous of frauds, he did come to acknowledge that there might well be "real" shamans—especially one individual he knew of who never charged anybody for his services.

And what about him? At the end of the narrative we cannot tell, but it is evident that he carries on his craft conscientiously, takes pride in his achievements, and warmly defends the technique of the bloody down against all rival schools. He seems to have completely lost sight of the fallaciousness of the technique which he had so disparaged at the beginning (Lévi-Strauss 1963:178).

What, one might ask, can anthropology add to our understanding of this story?

The Analytical Perspective

The material just presented is obviously complex, the more so because the major protagonist is operating under competing belief systems. How can we as anthropologists analyze these data, making them somehow more understandable in our own terms?

Shaman-Patient Relationship   The shaman has undergone a physically and psychologically difficult apprenticeship and has consequently invested much emotion in his career. He has a great interest in the patient's recovery, as this validates his self-image. The patient is sick, is feeling awful, and wants to get better. Thus she or he has placed trust and faith in the shaman and consequently also has a vested interest in the success of the curing ritual. In the ritual the patient hopes to be *transformed* from a state of disease (separation from the society of healthy people) to a state of health (membership, once again, in the well group).

Shaman-Public Relationship   The shaman has an important social position that he can maintain only if the wider community continues to ascribe this status to him. The public needs the reassurance that illness can be cured and thus wants to define the shaman as a successful practitioner.

Patient-Public Relationship   The patient, as long as she or he is ill, is an "outsider" who experiences "isolation." The patient wishes to be reintegrated into the group of well people. The community experiences a loss when a member becomes sick, and it consequently is best served by a ritual through which the patient can be reincorporated into the group.

This analysis explains the shamans' public competitiveness, their concern with winning public support rather than merely maintaining a statistically high success rate in curing. The curing procedure is a *ritual* in which the shaman uses *magic* to effect a *transformation* in the state of an individual (the patient).

The Shaman's Experience   What of the shaman himself? The shaman, too, passed through a transformation as he left the society of "ordinary" people and became a "different" kind of person with unique social characteristics.

One study suggests that this is a case of religion providing for both the psychological integration of the

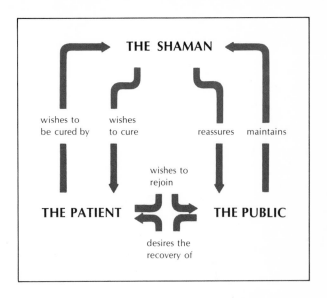

Shaman-Patient-Public Triad

Because the shaman's performance is public and is as important to the community as it is to the patient, much more than the effectiveness of a particular cure is at stake: The shaman plays a crucial role in the maintenance of group cohesion. Thus shamans with only chance-level cure rates are maintained in their social positions.

individual and the social integration of society (Silverman 1967). The author describes five stages that research has shown individuals pass through as they become schizophrenic. He then demonstrates that shamans pass through comparable stages as they embark on their careers.

Stage 1   The precondition: fear; feelings of impotence and failure; guilt

A lot of medical research has shown that people who become schizophrenic have passed through periods that were unbearable—periods in which they perceived themselves as incapable of coping with the world and experienced acute anxiety, frustration, and despair. "Comparable psychological conditions have been recorded among prospective shamans" (Silverman 1967:25).

Stage 2   Preoccupation; isolation; estrangement

The careers of both shamans and schizophrenics come into focus as their attention gradually shifts away from the external world and narrows down to a preoccupation with themselves. This isolates them from others, reinforcing their feelings of estrangement.

Stage 3   Narrowing of attention; self-initiated sensory deprivation

Gradually this focusing inward leads to the perceptual blocking of incoming stimuli—the person perceives

A shaman of the !Kung San (see Chapter 21) in a trance, serving his people through his ability to establish immediate connections with the supernatural world.

fewer and fewer messages from the surroundings. Research has established that sensory deprivation leads to a state of hallucination (see, for example, Heron 1957). The individual thus loses even more contact with the world, and his or her mental processes become distorted.

Stage 4   The fusing of higher and lower referential processes

As this process continues, the person's thought processes become dominated by cosmic, mythological figures representing the most primitive of emotions. Conventional logic and day-to-day concerns are of less and less importance and become represented as parts of this mythological universe.

Stage 5   Cognitive reorganization

The schizophrenic has meanwhile been the object of many negative responses from his or her primary groups. The person is labeled as "sick" and is placed into a variety of "therapeutic" settings, many of which reduce even further the individual's self-esteem and emotional commitment to the surrounding world. In contrast, once it is recognized that the shaman is embarking on his or her career, she or he receives much positive reinforcement and emotional support. Assigned a position of social prominence, shamans are able to reorganize their cognitive systems, their beliefs about who they are and what their relationships to the surrounding world are. Thus shamans can reconstitute themselves and their lives, whereas schizophrenics are deprived of freedom, cut off from significant others, and spiritually undermined so that the chance of their becoming emotionally reintegrated is relatively remote.

Thus shamanistic religion can provide the mechanisms through which potentially severely troubled persons can reintegrate themselves cognitively and emotionally. Also, the society remains integrated in the sense that it is not confronted with a pathological member, but merely a "chosen one" who is opting for a particular career.

Let us return to the special case of Quesalid. We indicated that although he was scornful of shamans and their fraudulent techniques at the start of his career, he eventually came to believe in his own curing powers and even accepted the possible validity of some other shamans. Clearly this is a case of cognitive reorganization. But we can even explain *why* he reorganized his belief system by referring to the theory of *cognitive dissonance* presented earlier. When a person suffers because of cognitive dissonance, she or he can reduce the tension by obtaining new information that negates one of the conflicting belief systems. In this case the information was that he could cure people more successfully than others. Or the person may seek social approval for one of the beliefs, canceling out conflicting beliefs. By winning public competitions in curing, Quesalid attracted public support for the belief that he was indeed a great shaman. His belief that all shamans were frauds was gradually displaced onto shamans other than himself as he and his society came to acknowledge his unique worth. Or perhaps he simply became comfortable with himself as a fraud.

Conclusions

Schools of Thought

No unified theory of or approach to the study of belief systems in anthropology exists. However, many scholars follow the pioneering work of Émile Durkheim, who made the fundamental distinction between *sacred* and *profane* beliefs. He writes: "In all the history of human thought there exists no other example of two categories of things so profoundly differentiated or so radically opposed to one another" (Durkheim 1915:53).

In this chapter we have essentially accepted this categorical distinction. However, we have employed a more neutral vocabulary. The term *sacred* connotes a necesssarily religious content, whereas the term *transcendental* is broader. *Profane*, too, suggests something narrower than the term *instrumental*, which we have substituted. *Profane* also carries a somewhat negative flavor that is lacking in the label we have used. Critics point out that in practice it becomes difficult to distinguish between the two categories. Many societies do not have clearly demarcated churches or sects; religious behavior permeates their lives in the most mundane details of existence. How can one tell what is sacred, what is profane?

Mircea Eliade, the distinguished Rumanian historian of religion, attempts to resolve this theoretical issue by referring to human experience.

For religious man, space is not homogeneous; he experiences interruptions, breaks in it; some parts of space are qualitatively different from others. . . . There is, then, a sacred space, and hence a strong, significant space; there are other spaces that are not sacred and so are without structure or consistency, amorphous. Nor is this all. For religious man, this spacial non-homogeneity finds expression in the experience of an opposition between space that is sacred—the only *real* and *real-ly* existing space—and all other space, the formless expanse surrounding it (Eliade 1959:20; emphasis in original).

Thus Eliade is willing to accept the possibility that, especially in the secularized modern world, some individuals live exclusively in the domain of the profane. For them the world is simply defined by their instrumental belief systems, all stimuli are experienced on this one plane. However, religious people experience the world as sharply divided; their experience of sacred places and things gives them a powerful channel through which they can tap the sacred in order to give meaning to the profane.

There are many other areas of dispute as well. These disputes revolve mainly around the issue of definition: What *is* religion? What *are* magic, ritual, myth, and so forth? Associated with these disputes is the parallel set of disagreements over the ways in which these diverse phenomena affect the nature of human existence—the so-called functions of religion, myth, and ritual. One interesting debate over the nature of rituals and magic took place between two of the most famous anthropologists, Bronislaw Malinowski (the "father of functionalism") and A. R. Radcliffe-Brown (the "father of structural functionalism").

Malinowski argued that although magical rituals refer to things beyond the abilities of human beings to observe, they are basically oriented toward achieving concrete, desirable ends in this world. They do not replace work, but grow out of human beings' realization that some forces that affect their daily lives (such as the weather) are beyond their control. This realiza-

In a funerary rite in Northern India, a man of the Thakur caste offers a ball of cooked (and thereby purified) rice to the spirit of his recently deceased father. He uses only his right (pure) hand; the ball of rice is placed on an altar made of mud which is also pure, having been in contact with water (a primary instrument of purification) in a nearby pond. Thus does the Hindu concept of purity permeate the believer's life; for the Hindu, Eliade's notion of "spacial non-homogeneity" is an experienced reality.

tion produces anxiety, and in their attempts to reduce their anxiety, human beings devise rituals that enable them to control, or to believe they control, these forces. "Magic, therefore, far from being primitive science, is the outgrowth of clear recognition that science has its limits and that a human mind and human skills are at times impotent" (Malinowski 1931:67).

Radcliffe-Brown, on the other hand, argued that such rituals do not function to *allay* anxiety, rather, they *create* anxiety because (in the minds of believers) so much depends on their outcomes. He rejects Malinowski's attempt to account for the existence of rituals on a psychological level; he insists instead that the explanation is to be found on the sociological level.

> My own view is that the negative and positive rites of savages exist and persist because they are part of the mechanism by which an orderly society maintains itself in existence, serving as they do to establish certain fundamental social values. The beliefs by which the rites themselves are justified and given some sort of consistency [for example, beliefs regarding their magical purpose] are the *rationalizations* of symbolic actions and of the sentiments associated with them (Radcliffe-Brown 1939:82; emphasis added).

As in many disputes, the participants were guilty of talking past each other rather than attempting to meet on common ground. George C. Homans has performed the valuable service of distilling the essence of this debate and showing how these positions are compatible within the same framework (1941). He argues that magic rituals do indeed both allay and create anxiety, and that they function on both the psychological and sociological levels—they are symbolic means through which both individuals and groups integrate themselves and thus are better able to continue their existence.

Author's Conclusions

Social scientists are still investigating and debating many other unresolved issues regarding belief systems. Earlier in this chapter, the debate between Marxist theorists and other thinkers was introduced. This revolves around the relationship between belief systems and other sociocultural systems.

In the nineteenth century Karl Marx conceptualized the sociocultural system as operating on two planes: the *material basis*, consisting of the physical environment and the forms of production and distribution through which the society maintains itself; and the *culture*, which is an ideational superstructure rooted in and dynamically dependent upon the material basis. In *A Contribution to the Critique of Political Economy*, Marx spells out his position eloquently:

> In the social production which men carry on they enter into definite relations that are indispensable and independent of their will; these relations of production correspond to a definite stage of development of their material powers of production. The sum total of these relations of production constitutes the economic structure of society—the real foundation, on which rise legal and political superstructures and to which correspond definite forms of social consciousness. The mode of production in material life determines the general character of the social, political and spiritual processes of life. It is not the consciousness of men that determines their existence, but, on the contrary, their social existence determines their consciousness (Marx 1904:138).

Other theorists, including functionalists such as Talcott Parsons (1966), argue that all elements of the sociocultural system are in dynamic equilibrium, no particular subsystem (such as the cultural system, social system, or subsistence system) is determinative. However, a recent study by Alvin Gouldner and Richard Peterson tends to support the Marxist position. Using data from seventy-one primitive or preindustrial societies and sophisticated statistical techniques, they attempted to determine which factor or factors, if any, have a determinative influence on what they call the moral order (or culture) of society. They analyzed eleven factors, including kinship and sexual dominance, and were persuaded that "technology is the single most influential factor, in that it predicts more of the variance in all of the other factors than does any other single factor" (1962:59).

This finding is very important. It underlines the fact that belief systems are not just "floating around" in people's heads, but, like other elements of culture, they are rooted in the basic, material conditions of a group's existence.

I do not mean to suggest that the *particular contents* of any belief system are determined by the economic and technological circumstances of the group. These particular elements are unique to every culture and are passed on from generation to generation with modifications and substitutions. However, although culture

Adam and Eve expelled from the Garden of Eden. *Genesis* is clearly a myth produced by a society with an agricultural material base. ". . .accursed shall be the ground on your account. With labor you shall win your food from it all the days of your life. . . . You shall gain your bread by the sweat of your brow. . . ." With these words God addresses Adam, upon discovering the couple's transgression. Among other things, *Genesis* legitimized the point of view that nature is expressly there for humans to exploit. Addressing Noah, God says: "Every creature that lives and moves shall be food for you; I give you them all, as once I gave you all green plants." This utilitarian stance, placing humans apart from nature, is very different from many world views which place humans within the realm of nature and stress the notion of harmony among all things.

The view of the author of this chapter is that it was the relations of production which stimulated the emergence of this myth, rather than vice versa. The myth explains the origins of the people's way of life and reinforces their perspective on it.

has its own internal dynamics and it certainly influences the economic aspects of social groups, the material conditions of a society do seem to set boundaries on the possibilities of its belief systems—up to and including beliefs about the "inherent" nature of the sexes, as we saw in Chapter 3.

Summary

Beliefs are defined as thoughts that are based on the uncritical acceptance of the inherent truth or correctness of the cognitive categories of one's culture.

Two types of beliefs are described: *Instrumental beliefs* **concern primarily the concrete tasks necessary for survival;** *transcendental beliefs* **involve states and elements of existence inherently beyond the perceptual capacities of human senses—things that cannot be learned about directly from human experience. Both forms of belief systems provide the frameworks through which human beings give meaning and purpose to their existence.**

We can partially reconstruct the evolution of belief systems from archaeological evidence. Some case examples illustrate contemporary belief systems. One such example is concerned with elements of the belief system of anthropology itself.

Some basic concepts used by anthropologists to study belief systems are *ritual, myth, religion, witchcraft,* **and** *magic.* **The problem of conflicting belief systems can be analyzed from the perspective of (cognitive) dissonance theory. These concepts are utilized in the case of a Kwakiutl shaman who displayed an unusual amount of self-critical analysis of shaman role behavior. This example illustrates the problem of keeping emics and etics separated in practice as well as in theory, and further shows how religious systems can function to promote both psychological integration in individuals and social integration in groups.**

The relationships between belief systems and material culture is a controversial one; Marxists contend that material culture determines the content of belief systems, but other social scientists deny that such a causal relationship exists.

Annotated Bibliography

Bellah, Robert N. (1965) "Religious Evolution." In *Reader in Comparative Religion: An Anthropological Approach,* ed. William A. Lessa and Evon Z. Vogt. New York: Harper. Perhaps the best-formulated, most concise, most plausible theory of the evolution of religion.

Castañeda, Carlos (1968) *The Teachings of Don Juan: A Yaqui Way of Knowledge.* New York: Ballantine.

(1971) *A Separate Reality: Further Conversations with Don Juan.* New York: Simon and Schuster.

(1972) *Journey to Ixtlan: The Lessons of Don Juan.* New York: Simon and Schuster.

(1974) *Tales of Power.* New York: Simon and Schuster.

This series is best read in sequence. The books are beautifully and powerfully written, sweeping the reader along even though many of his or her fundamental beliefs are challenged on almost every page. These books tell the story of the decade-long apprenticeship undertaken by an anthropologist under the guidance of a Yaqui shaman. During this period the anthropologist is challenged to give up his (and our) conception of reality and to embrace the separate reality of Don Juan. Because Don Juan is so powerful, the anthropologist is finally able to make that leap.

Lessa, William, and Vogt, Evon Z., eds. (1965) *Reader in Comparative Religion: An Anthropological Approach.* New York: Harper. Perhaps the best single collection of readings on the subject. Includes excerpts from the original writings of many nineteenth century evolutionary theorists and other classic writings on the topic, as well as some of the best and most illuminating contemporary articles. An extremely useful reference book.

14
Culture, Identity, and the Individual:
Psychological Anthropology

The World Context

Origins and Development through Time

A distinctively human level of existence, in contrast to the levels of prehuman or nonhuman species, is based largely on individual feelings of personal and social identity. All of us have a profound sense of who and what we are, and this sense of psychosocial identity influences our behavior and our relationships with others throughout our lives.

Before the invention of speech, humans were bound to immediate experience and were thus severely limited in their capacity to share private experiences with others (Hallowell 1962:250). We call prehuman capacities for communication *intrinsic*—that is, they were bounded by the individual's restricted ability to communicate symbolically; their ideas remained inside them. Most prehuman experience was private and thus unsharable. Like dogs and chimpanzees, prehumans dreamed, but they could not discuss their dreams. Their capacity for thinking was limited to primary process, the style of cognition found in early infancy, in the fantasy world of wordless dreams, and in the thought of some schizophrenics.

Erik H. Erikson, the most eminent scholar whose life work is devoted to the study of identity. He started out as an artist, joined the original circle of students around Sigmund Freud, and became one of the few internationally famous psychoanalysts without having an M.D. degree; much of his thinking has been influenced by his study of ethnographic materials.

With the evolution of speech behavior came the capacity for *extrinsic* communication—that is, communication using arbitrary, external symbols that could be used and understood by many. Speech allowed an entire group to share a common, meaningful world. It freed individuals from the limitations of trial-and-error and imitative learning, and it accelerated cultural and environmental adaptations by making private experiences readily accessible to others. More importantly, speech allowed individuals to become objects to themselves and subjects to others. Humans could now think of and discuss the past, take account of what was remote from present experience, and contemplate the future.

The evolution of language is directly related to the emergence of individual psychosocial identity. An individual's identity is a complex of images about the self—images that are simultaneously private and public, and on which the individual and others focus both thought and strong emotion (Wallace 1968:47; Robbins 1973). This emergence of personal identity as the dominant integrative center of personality had profound implications for the nature of human social life and also produced complications.

With the development of individual identity came the capacity for self-consciousness, self-reference, self-evaluation, self-stimulation, and self-control. The group life of prehumans—based on instinct and modified by social learning—was transformed into the moral orders that distinguish human societies. These moral orders were built around the shared symbols, norms, and ideals that influence individual behavior.

Human social adaptation is characterized by distinctive kinds of experiences and behaviors. A person can be held responsible for both what he or she does or does not do. People can be held responsible by themselves in the absence of others. They can be judged for their covert, private actions (such as dreams, wishes, or intentions) as well as for overt behaviors. They can be known and judged when absent or long dead. Human societies are thus arrangements of persons who are conscious of their own private experience and public behavior as well as the overt behavior and private experience of others. Unlike the prehuman level of adaptation, the human level requires a capacity for self-control, self-correction, and self-adjustment in a shared social environment. People must learn who they are and how to fill their own needs as well as who they are in relation to other people and how they must adapt to allow others the same freedom to fill their needs.

The study of individual identity has had a mixed history in anthropology. Sometimes it has been relegated to what was seen as the lesser science of psychology; more often, it has been submerged in culture-personality studies that hardly dealt with individuals, focusing rather on group patterns. But in the past decade, a new concern with individual identity has emerged, and it is casting light on a wide variety of anthropological problems, from primate studies to cultural change. This renaissance of the individual involves questions and issues that were first raised many years ago and that have lain dormant too long.

A book called *American Indian Life*, first published in 1922 (Parsons 1973), consists of twenty-seven stories about individual American Indians from as many different tribes in Mexico, the United States, and Canada. Read in the 1970s, these stories—which may properly be called fictionalized biographies—are peculiarly flat, superficial, unilluminating, and unsatisfying. They lack psychological penetration; no attempt has been made to offer insights into the motivations, the aspirations, the frustrations, or the self-concepts of the individuals portrayed. Moreover, the stories do not adequately distinguish between individual psychological data and collective cultural data.

These stories are not about individual Indians at all. They are imaginative reconstructions of personal life experiences written from ethnographic data. Their authors were twenty-four (which is to say most) of the first, pioneering generation of professionally trained American anthropologists. Their intention was not to add psychology to anthropology but rather to offer the public a choice between Fenimore Cooper's romantic fables and the pompous dullness of the ethnographies then in print. Writing about individuals was little more than a means of popularizing anthropology.

Until the early 1920s, anthropology had been largely nonpsychological. But within the next fifteen years, the authors of *American Indian Life* were concerned with an entirely new field of study: *culture and personality*. Authors who were not directly involved in developing this new approach encouraged their students to specialize in it; others entered into controversy with psychiatrists and academic psychologists over the issues. Indeed, one of the authors, the brilliant Edward Sapir, underwent something of a professional identity transformation. He abandoned his earlier focus on the collectivist, cultural level of analysis and soon displayed the same genius in comparative psychological studies as he had exhibited in linguistics and ethnography earlier in his career.

Soon Bronislaw Malinowski was questioning some of Sigmund Freud's ideas about the universality of the Oedipus complex;* Margaret Mead was engaged in the first of her fruitful South Seas studies of socialization and sex roles; and Ruth Benedict was thinking about whole cultural systems in psychological terms. The field of culture and personality had emerged as a fresh approach to a number of old concerns, most of which hinged on the characteristics, the determinants, and the range of variability of human nature.

From the start, culture and personality was an interdisciplinary field of study, involving anthropology, psychiatry, academic psychology, sociology, and later history and political science. The earliest findings of culture and personality were so stimulating and the public controversies so rich in new insights that the poet W. H. Auden was impelled to write:

> Malinowski, Rivers,
> Benedict and others
> Show how common culture
>   Shapes the separate lives:
> Matrilineal races
> Kill their mothers' brothers
> In their dreams and turn their
>   Sisters into wives.

(1945:106)

* *Freud claimed that 3 to 5-year old children universally pass through a developmental stage in which, among other things, they work out conflicted sexual feelings toward their opposite-sexed parent. Malinowski claimed that this was an artifact of European society—that it was lacking among the matrilineal avunculocal Tropriand Islanders, where a boy's mother's brother fills the social role equivalent to that of a European father.*

This Finnish Laplander, wearing an old Finnish military jacket and holding a young reindeer by the antlers, is one of the Laplanders now hard at work rounding up the reindeer from snowy mountain pastures for the annual redivision among their owners. The natural environment, their subsistence activities, the patterns of their social relations with others—all go into the making of personal identities for the Laplanders.

Auden's summary of the debate between Malinowski and the psychoanalysts over the universality of the Oedipus complex* reflects the importance of the issues developing in the field of culture and personality. New knowledge about human nature had implications that transcended the boundaries of the several social sciences and captured the public's attention. How malleable, how variable was human nature? How did a common culture shape our separate lives?

Early psychoanalysts and some academic psychologists concerned with personality were heavily influenced by the anthropological theorizing of their day, notably nineteenth century cultural evolutionary thinking. Consequently, their thinking about personality incorporated such ideas drawn from early anthropology as the innate destructiveness of humanity, primitive irrationality, the collective unconscious,* prelogical thinking, and evolutionary stages of psychocultural development. For their part, many anthropologists became consumers of psychological theories and methods as they set out to study the nature and functioning of personality in many different societies (Wallace 1968:41). This vigorous interchange of ideas and research findings continues to this day. But for many years, anthropologists did not notably contribute to new theories of personality.

Until the 1960s, only a few anthropologists had used the biographical approach to the study of individual lives that was first tentatively and naïvely employed in *American Indian Life*. Some anthropologists collected, helped edit, and published autobiographies, while others systematically obtained facts for and published biographies of individuals from different cultures. It should be noted that the difference between an autobiography and a biography rests on the same distinction, emic versus etic, that anthropologists use in studies of cultures. An autobiography is an individual's life story told by herself or himself and interpreted in personally meaningful terms. A biography should be a person's life story told by someone else and systematically interpreted and explained with general ideas.

Few of the autobiographies and biographies published by anthropologists have included sophisticated psychological interpretation. In preparing these life stories, anthropologists have most often used cultural materials and interpretations, setting the ethnographic scene in which the individual lived or explaining exotic customs and beliefs. The exceptions to this generalization—life histories enhanced by both cultural and psychological interpretations—have either been the work of individuals who were extensively trained in both anthropology and psychiatry or psychology (for example, Leighton 1949; Devereux 1961), or they have been the product of a collaborative effort between an

* A term developed by Jung to designate his conception of the biologically inherited mental experiences of our evolutionary ancestors, which structure the possibilities of human thought.

above
Don Talayesva, also known as Sun Chief, is a Hopi Indian whose autobiography was recorded and edited by Leo W. Simmons. This account of the emergence of Sun Chief's identity as a Hopi in Oraibi, Arizona, is structured, however, not in the folk categories of the Hopi, but rather in terms of the categories and processes posited by psychoanalysis. The book *Sun Chief*, then, tells us as much about the ways in which psychoanalysis views identity formation as it does about the experience of becoming a man in Hopi society.

right
A quiet moment among the BaMbuti pygmies of the Ituri rain forest, Zaire. The men share with the women the care of small children. Here, the group is listening to a story being told aloud. The identity formation in an intimate, close, face-to-face environment has been the normal process for human beings for most of our evolutionary history. Scholars are beginning to investigate the impact of mass society on identity formation—a phenomenon which is apparently causing our own society a great deal of trouble.

anthropologist and a psychologist (for instance, Gladwin and Sarason 1953; Clifton and Levine 1962).

However, the preparation of individual life stories has been only a minor theme in culture and personality studies. Most research and theorizing has expressed the basic anthropological concern with groups and collectivities. Thus the major question has concerned the relationship between culture and the typical personality of the society studied. *Typical personality*—those personality characteristics most commonly shared in a society—has been given various terms: *modal personality, basic personality, cultural character, social character, national character,* and so on. The descriptions of typical personality seem to concern an individual, but they do not. Rather, they are abstractions, synthetic descriptions of a supposedly typical (but nonexistent) person. And although other anthropologists have in effect added a psychological

perspective to their studies of cultures by researching and writing about themes, guiding beliefs (ethos), values, world views, and the like, their psychological materials are submerged in the cultural, and little effort is made to keep the individual human being in view.

What all the typical personality approaches have in common is a disregard for the individual, who is studied and discussed only as a sample of the members of a society, as a way station toward statements that are true of the Tuscarora Indians, the Great Russians, the Hutterites, or the Japanese. The conceptual problems with this approach sometimes generate great confusion. For example, we find discussions of the impact of "culture" upon "personality" that on close examination are actually statements about the effects of people-in-general (that is, the values, roles, or themes of a tribal culture) upon people-in-general (that is, the basic personality of the members of a tribe). One ex-

ample of such confusion is an effort to explain that a high incidence of hostile, suspicious, antisocial individuals is caused by a "paranoid" culture. As Alexander Leighton has indicated, this is rather like saying that a drop of seawater is salty because of the salt in the sea from whence it came (1959:189–190).

It is important to recognize the cause of this confusion and how to avoid it. The problem derives from the different focus of psychologists and anthropologists. When the psychologist is studying an individual, he or she is comfortable thinking about that person and his or her relationships with other specific individuals. In contrast, the anthropologist generally studies the characteristics of a group without much concern for the wishes, aspirations, or motives of the individuals involved. But when the psychologist and the anthropologist come together in a joint enterprise, they are apt to forget that they may be studying the same kinds of things in different ways. The solution is to conduct the research and analyze the data carefully and systematically in both psychological and cultural terms.

Another problem is that of reducing cultural facts to psychological ones, a prospect that some anthropologists find threatening. But it is misleading to state the issue in this fashion. All ethnographic descriptions and theories invariably contain many psychological elements and assumptions, either implicitly or explicitly. The real issue is one of economy and relevance: At what point is it most profitable to shift from the study of individuals to the study of groups (Devereux 1961)?

A further difficulty involves the confusion of anthropological or sociological models of behavior with psychological ones. If anthropologists attribute to individuals the models of motivation and cognition that the anthropologists have themselves created to explain a group process or a cultural system, they get into difficulty. This is precisely why the "natives" get upset as they become literate and read what ethnographers have written about them. No real individual is motivated or thinks in exactly the ways that are described in generalized ethnographic reports. Although the behavior of two or more people may seem similar or the same to an observer, it may not be the same when viewed from the subjective perspectives of the individuals concerned (Devereux 1961:235).

Contemporary Examples

Let us look at the identities of some specific individuals in their cultural context. Each of the following examples is from a biographical or ethnographic work published within the last two decades.

A Winnebago Indian Mountain Wolf Woman, a Winnebago Indian in the United States, learns that a woman's body makes her unclean.

When Mountain Wolf Woman visited her grandfather's house, her mother told her what happened to little girls when they became women. "When that happens to you," she said, "you should not look at anyone, not even glance. If you look at a man you will contaminate his blood. Even a glance will cause you to be an evil person. When women are in that condition, they are unclean." Soon afterwards her menses started, and frightened, she ran far into the woods. There she sat under a fallen tree, her blanket pulled over her head, for she had been forbidden to glance at anyone. She cried and cried until, later, her sister and sister-in-law found her and made a shelter for her. She stayed in the small wigwam in the woods four days, never eating, lonely and frightened. After she slept the third time, she dreamed of a large clearing filled with horses of many colors. Ever after, her relatives and friends knew that horses were very special to her (Lurie 1961:23).

An Ojibwa Indian Hole-in-the-Day, an Ojibwa Indian in the United States, learns something about despotism and its consequences.

At the Treaty of Fond du Lac in 1847, Hole-in-the-Day spoke forcefully to the treaty commissioners. Like his father, he was a man proud and domineering, quick and impatient of temper, more feared than respected by his fellow Chippewa in the Mississippi bands of which he was chief. He was also grasping and avaricious. He told the treaty commissioners it was useless for them to call all the chiefs from the many Chippewa villages to negotiate a treaty selling the Chippewa lands. They did not own the land, he said. He—Hole-in-the-Day—was the sole owner, by right of inheritance from his father, who had acquired the land by conquest from the Sioux. He added, "The Indians here have nothing to say, they can but do my bidding." Through the years Hole-in-the-Day continued to prosper, amassing considerable wealth, always at the expense of other Chippewa. Finally, the Chippewa revolted against his despotic rule, first plundering his wealth and burning his house and farm, then assassinating him. In the end, the Indians did have something to say (Smith 1973:20–21).

A Native American of the Southwest   This is the tale of Mabel, a Native American woman of the southwestern United States.

For many years Mabel had earned her good reputation and a respectable income as the town whore. Reputed to be content and expert in her work, she was a pleasant, vivacious lady who kept regular hours and donated annually to the United Fund. Then the federal government terminated supervision over Mabel's tribe and her per capita share of the tribal assets suddenly made her a wealthy woman. On the day after a share was deposited in her name at the local bank, she arrived at the teller's window with a shopping bag under her arm. "I want to withdraw my money," she demanded of the teller.

"Oh, hello, Mabel," he answered. "How much would you like? Fifty . . . a hundred dollars, maybe?" "All of it," she said. "All of it?" "Yes, all of it . . . forty-seven thousand six hundred and eighty-seven dollars and thirty-three cents. That's what it says here on the deposit slip from the Department of the Interior. Put it right here in my shopping bag." "But, Mabel," the teller retorted, "you don't want all that money. You can't *have* all that money, not at once!" "What do you mean I can't have my money? It's my money isn't it? It's deposited in my name isn't it? What's the matter with this little bitty bank of yours? Don't you have any money in it?"

The teller, intimidated, called for the head cashier's advice. The cashier consulted with the President, the President with the bank's attorney. Yes, the attorney opined, it was Mabel's money, and short of closing their doors, they had to pay it out to her . . . all of it. "You have got money in the bank, don't you?" he asked. The chief cashier handled the transaction personally. "Just give me the green stuff, Eddie," said Mabel, pointing to the teller, "Give Billy there the change, he always was sweet to me."

Mabel strolled demurely out of the bank, her arms wrapped around the bulging brown bag. Once on the sidewalk, she whistled up the cab parked across the street. As she slid into the back seat, she said to the driver, "Joe, I want you to take me to Mexico City, but there's a few places I want to stop along the way." "Stop bulling me," said the driver, "it's a hot day and business is bad. Where do you want to go? The Thunderbird Lounge?" "Mexico City is where we're heading," said Mabel. "Joe . . . take a look in my shopping bag." "Mexico City it is!" said Joe. "You don't mind if I stop first, tank up, pick up a spare tire, and call the wife to let her know I'll be missing in action for a while?"

Mabel and Joe stopped first at Las Vegas and then Reno, where Mabel studied the mysteries of the roulette and faro tables. In the late mornings, over a hearty breakfast, she and Joe played a few hands of blackjack or cribbage. Mabel wasn't good at cards. She was worse at faro. They never made Mexico City. The last stop was Tijuana. By this time, Mabel's shopping bag had disappeared, but her purse was still fat. The Tijuana racetrack and the Fronton palace slimmed that—the horses Mabel was fair at, but jai alai betting was an enigma to her. In the end, Joe sold his cab, bought Mabel a ticket back home, and advanced her eating money until she could resume her profession. He then disappeared.

Back home, people stopped Mabel on the street to inquire unctuously, "Mabel, where have you been? What have you been doing with yourself?" Mabel always replied, "Traveling . . . and having a ball . . . a real ball." Privately, all the townsfolk deplored the bad example Mabel had set. Even more privately, in the depths of their nine-to-five souls, they envied her desperately. None of them had ever had . . . none could ever even hope to have a real ball. How could she? A sympathetic social worker observed how obviously Mabel lacked foresight and skill for rational planning. Poor unfortunate!

Privately, Mabel had her own thoughts, too. "What use did I ever have for all that free money?" she said. "What good would it ever do me? It'd only make my men friends uncomfortable. How'd I ever know that they might not just be interested in that money and not really interested in me? And I've still got my War Bonds. That's *my* money. I earned it. Besides, I enjoy my work. But I do miss Joe—I know his wife does, too.

I am sorry he couldn't handle the strain" (*Western Americana Notes* 1959).

A New Guinea Tribesman   Let us turn to Paliau, a New Guinea tribesman of the Admiralty Islands, and note how a great man's reputation goes before him.

Paliau was the leader of the New Way, a cultural revitalization and modernization movement in the Admiralty Islands. His presence on the scene at the right historic moment transformed a movement that might have ebbed to discordant discontent into a vital wave of development. A man of gifted mind, he became a prophet to many outside his own society. He sought no utopia for his part of the earth. It was his duty, he believed, to model and teach the ways of bettering his people's lives. His means were to carefully modify and shape changing institutions into useful instruments that would aid the people of the Admiralties in crossing a great cultural gap. He sought to unify hostile societies, to promote economic development, to encourage community growth. He successfully countered both the local elders and the Australian officials. A man made dramatic by his brilliance and his modesty, he was a great and spellbinding orator, if a quiet one. But few knew Paliau. All knew of him. Many had seen him only at a distance, most not at all. Nonetheless, his teachings spread widely, borne on the strength of his reputation to those who were strangers to him. Throughout the islands, people knew that Paliau had been responsible for their successes. Thus his New Way became their way. His reputation, the powerful, positive image of his person, preceded him (Mead 1956:188–211).

A Mapuche Indian   Finally, let us look at the education of Esmeralda, a member of the Mapuche Indian tribe of Chile.

Although Esmeralda's mother was a *machi* (shaman, native curer), she was an unsuccessful one. She did not train her daughter herself. She was so lacking in powerful spirits that when boils covered all of Esmeralda's body, she could not help. Esmeralda cured herself with her own power. She got some of her mother's knowledge, but she had in her own right more power than her mother. One day she had a vision of a white lamb which came and followed her endlessly. Then she saw a sacred white *kultrun* (drum) in the bushes. It was

then she knew she was herself to be a *machi*. When she again became sick with boils, she went to live with a famous old *machi* in Marquigua. Her cure, and her education were very expensive, but her family paid for them. The old *machi* would not teach Esmeralda all. But again, as with her mother, Esmeralda's special power made her greater than her teacher. She now knew she had a very powerful *pillan* (familiar spirit); and so, as others recognized this, she prospered. But her work was dangerous. Often, when her *pillan* possessed her, she lay near death. And evil spirits came to harm her as well. The souls of men she had killed had come to fight her (Faron 1968:78–79).

This limited sample suggests how culture can influence individual identity, how identity and culture can interact, and incidentally, how fascinating the anthropological study of personality can be.

Theory

Systems

When anthropologists view cultures and communities as wholes, they often lose sight of the individual humans whose actions are the materials for their ethnographic models. Yet each individual is a complex whole, a system of processes in his or her own right. Indeed, social and cultural systems and processes depend in large part on identity processes. For example, individuals learn to use organizational roles to serve their own needs. When these roles are no longer satisfying, and especially when they generate intense frustrations, individuals manufacture new roles, create new values, define new goals, and refashion their views of the good life. The fundamental organizational principle of identity is striving, which always occurs in some social setting, on some cultural scene, old or new.

The development of a mature identity is contingent upon personal growth in a community in which individuals find significant values. The processes of identity formation depend on a set of roles that an individual can confront, learn, master, and assume. But the mere existence of *any* traditional roles and values is not

A Peronist crowd in Argentina chanting the slogan "Peron or death." Mass behavior: a group identity is more than the sum of the identities of the individuals who compose it.

sufficient for the ultimate growth of an individual's personal identity. Only when the maturing individual finds an integrated set of roles and values that encourage personal development and promote satisfying adaptation can she or he realize the fullest personal potential. Living in a community that has a meaningful place in history is a necessary condition for full personal growth. Individual identity formation and sociocultural integration thus become complementary processes. The individual's sense of effective being and personal worth is the subjective dimension of a community that is itself well integrated (Erikson 1968).

Community integration and the growth of mutually meaningful identities are created out of and depend on the idiosyncrasies of numerous individuals. But there seem to be limits to the social tolerance of personal uniqueness. For, as Clyde Kluckhohn and H. A. Murray wrote, "Every man is in certain respects, (a) like all other men, (b) like some other men, and (c) like no other man" (1954:53). Some features of personal identity are shared throughout the species. They are determined by the universal aspects of human biology, by the terrestrial environment we inhabit, and by the fact that all humans are born and mature in *some* cultural setting. Other features of identity are products of adaptation to and learning within particular human groupings.

Yet the universals of human biological nature and the communal nature of cultural experience do not produce sameness between the members of any group—not even in the smallest, simplest society. Organized social life and cultural change are possible not only because the participating individuals are quite like one another but also because they differ from one another. Social life depends on and must deal with variations in the personalities of individuals. The individual members of a community share motives and needs, perceptions and ideas that are never fully equivalent to one another. Every person has an inner core of unconscious motives and feelings that shared cultural teachings hardly touch.

But each individual also organizes his or her behavior largely on the basis of socially provided and shared motives. Cultural values may sanction the expression of subjective, personal, idiosyncratic motives,

or they may not. Nonetheless, individuals are creative enough to find outlets in the common culture for their diverse personal desires. As George Devereux once observed, mass movements are like great boilers generating energy. They can consume a variety of different kinds of fuels. When enough persons are unable to find outlets for their personal hopes, when the full development of many identities is thwarted, when the loyalties and energies of the young are not sufficiently engaged, communities may fall into grave disrepair. Or they may correct themselves.

Human identity thus has both a private-individual side and a public-collective face. The organization and the functioning of a group rely on the meshed identities of individuals who are committed to it, and the development of personal identities in turn depends on involvement in groups.

Processes

These points can be better understood if we look at how the several dimensions of an individual identity fit together. The individual's *private identity* (sometimes called *ego-identity*) consists of the subjective sense of personal continuity through time and some awareness of his or her own characteristics. A sense of private identity requires a complex cognitive-perceptual capacity and a memory to provide continuity of self-experience. Private identity is the oldest dimension of individual identity. Clearly, contemporary apes have private identities. But their private identities are limited by their incapacity to communicate to others their subjective experiences, as humans have been able to do since the evolution of speech.

Social identity is the position of an individual in a community. A person's roles, status, name, rank, and identification number are some markers of social identity. These features of identity enter into the individual's perceptions and memories of who and what he or she is. Social identity thus has both private-subjective and public-collective aspects. An individual who is a stranger to others may have to document his or her social identity by displaying appropriate badges, symbols, or behaviors. These constitute public notices of who, what, and where a person is socially (Goffman

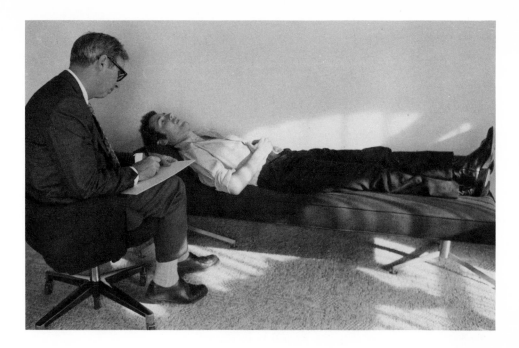

A patient in psychoanalysis attempting to remember events of the past. However, even the most earnestly attempted recollections are structured by the individual's self-conception—his or her identity perceived and enacted within a socio-cultural matrix.

1963:57–60). Social identity consists partly of other people's expectations of a person, but these images enter into the private experience of the subject as a result of communication with others. A person may have a difficult time maintaining a consistent, coherent image of herself or himself without such communications from others; and such images will change as the judgments others make of her or him change.

Psychosocial identity has a more elusive meaning. According to Erik Erikson, it is simultaneously "subjective and objective, individual and social" (1968:61). The subjective experience of psychosocial identity involves more emotion than that of social identity. It is an intense sense of finally becoming oneself, of "getting it all together." However, this experience may be only half conscious or even unconscious, and it may be temporary. In some societies many individuals never have such an experience, but all—at least up to a certain point in their lives—grow in anticipation of its possibility. Individual psychosocial identity is a developmental, maturational process. In Erikson's words, it is

> not feasible before and is indispensable after the end of adolescence, when the grown-up body

Vinobha Bhava, the most "orthodox" disciple of Gandhi living today, advocates Gandhian principles to a crowd of villagers in Bihar state. The goal of all meditational practices and disciplines is "enlightenment." Those who have experienced it have a great deal of difficulty communicating the experience to others. However, often suggestive images such as "oceanic oneness" are used. This may mean that such persons have developed their identities in such a way as to maximally include their deepest unconscious images as well as the images of the world around them. The psychologist Carl G. Jung called this "individuation"; the author of this chapter attempts to discuss this process using the concept of psycho-social identity.

grows together, when matured sexuality seeks partners, and when the fully developed mind begins to envisage a historical perspective and seeks new loyalties—all developments which must fuse with each other in a new sense of sameness and continuity. (1968:61)

Many people never attain this quality of identity experience, for not all cultural settings offer the opportunity for such a degree of personal and social integration.

Other aspects of identity processes supplement the three types of identity we have mentioned. *Self-concept* is the individual's conscious views of self, appearance, strength, beauty, capabilities. A person's self-concept is generally compared to the views others have of the person and his or her qualities. A *model identity* (or ego-ideal) is one's private view of the ideal person one might become; it is the standard against which one can measure oneself. Model identities have public versions as well as private ones. The explicit, culturally expressed view of the ideal man or woman is one example.

Conversely, there are *stigmatized identities*—private and public images of the kind of person who is to be deplored or despised. Elements of such stigmatized identities are often found in the unconscious worlds of an individual; these are sometimes called *negative identity* fragments. They can lie hidden like small emotional cancers, ready to prompt the individual into irrational hatreds when they think they see in other people features that they are too fearful to admit lie hidden in themselves.

Identity confusion is a state of acute emotional and intellectual impairment. Such breakdowns in normal identity integration are associated with prolonged, unusually painful life experiences, such as repeated victimization, war, imprisonment, or migration from familiar to alien cultural scenes (Erikson 1968:62). What anthropologists call *culture shock* is a mild, transitory form of identity confusion.

Several dimensions of identity create problems when the anthropological distinction between folk and analytical models is applied to understanding a specific individual. Before we introduce and try to explain a man called Weasel, this tangle should be partly unraveled. We have likened emic (folk) to autobiographical and etic (analytical) to biographical versions of an individual's life story. But the issue is somewhat more complicated. Every individual has an autobiography that generally consists of highly selected elements pieced together to form some kind of unity. But most such personal autobiographies are semifictional, invented to suit personal (model identity) needs. Moreover, the individual rarely reveals all of his or her autobiography to anyone. Usually pieces of it are handed out to suit the situation. Personal autobiographies are composed and interpreted as personalized versions of culturally available explanations. Hence they are "folk" or emic statements.

"Similarly, other people know parts of a person's biography, and these, too, are built of culturally available materials. The point is: although the anthropologist should know and appreciate what others in the community think and believe about a person, he or she does not have to believe what they say. The anthropologist accepts these images and judgments for what they are, part of a set of folk ideas used to judge a person's worth or explain his or her behavior. If, for example, people were to explain aspects of Weasel's behavior or features of his identity by saying that he was infested with evil spirits, or that his mother had violated an incest taboo in conceiving him, we should make note of these opinions. These, too, are folk, or emic, statements, but they are of a collective rather than an individual nature. But we are obliged also to seek general—etic—ways of interpreting Weasel's identity. The distinction is important: It is between folk interpretations of identity and behavior and generalized scientific interpretations and evaluations. As we read about Weasel, we shall have to keep this distinction in mind.

Analysis

The Folk Perspective

I had seen Weasel and knew of his reputation in the reservation community where he lived well before I met him. Weasel and I first talked in jail, the morning after he was arrested for seriously assaulting a frail old man with a blunt instrument, the blunt instrument being the old man's crutch. Local people, Native American and Anglo, pointed Weasel out as the star example of the stereotype of a worthless, indolent, drunken, hostile Indian. He always spoke of himself as worthless (and helpless), although his manner spoke otherwise. He carried an aura of violence about him, which to many people was disturbing, if not frightening.

Soon after we started talking, Weasel told me about a recurrent dream he had. In his dream he was faced with an impossible task: "I'm supposed to cross over this wire—a steel wire stretched up high over the ocean. I want to walk it, but I can't. I got this big load to roll along the wire. I just can't do it. I get up on it [the wire], but I can't make it." Weasel did not know what the burden was or what awaited him on the other side. He was certain the course was impossible for him; he was going to fall off his life and drown (Clifton 1960:219).

Weasel was born and raised, more or less, on a reservation ranch. For more than twenty years—as child, adolescent, and young adult—he existed there in the midst of a group of older brothers, half-brothers, and stepbrothers. All of them were older, stronger, and more effectively aggressive than he. He said that his brothers "tended to die young." Six of them had done so as a result of alcoholic violence and car accidents. Weasel's education ended at age fifteen, in the ninth grade, when he was arrested and imprisoned on a burglary charge. Since then he had spent six years in prison and several more years on probation. Jail was nothing new to him.

Prison had made Weasel quite suave about personality tests and psychological interviewing: He had been through all that many times before. One might suspect that his habitual troubles with the law had some (unconscious) function for him. But Weasel thought otherwise. One day we talked about getting into trouble. Something he had read in jail had made him think about it: "This guy Freud wrote it—he said when it seems like a guy is always locked up maybe he is afraid to be on the outside. He said they won't admit it to themselves—that they want to be locked up, because down deep inside they feel insecure. I don't feel that way. I don't like it on the inside."

Outside, Weasel had made repeated attempts to get up and stay on that wire, but he always fell off. He once moved away and started a professional boxing career. But he was battered into insensibility and lost all his fights. His face showed the mark of that failure. Once he got married, for thirteen weeks. He remained sober all of that time, the longest spell since he was fifteen. But his wife deserted him. He was only trying to impress her, he said, but "I was joking myself—trying to make myself think I wasn't . . . that I was a halfway decent person—I have my doubts about that." After his wife left, Weasel was back on the bottle, and soon the boxing commission suspended him for bad conduct. Weasel took an odd pleasure from this: He had to have been a "professional boxer" in order to get suspended for "conduct unbecoming."

Weasel and a gang of his brothers and cohorts regularly made a circuit of nearby towns. Their visits had the appearance of hostile raids. In the bars and alleys of these towns they always got in trouble, Weasel particularly. He was always "asking" for trouble, never avoided its consequences, and generally lost his battles. He never gave much evidence that he could back up threat with force, not with anyone his size and not even with those who were smaller and weaker—not face to face. Once or twice Weasel applied for vocational training, indicating that he wanted to better himself. The first time it was for barber training, the next as a butcher's apprentice. He slyly hinted both times that he wanted to exploit his native talents with sharp instruments. Always he tried to give the impression of submerged, volcanic violence.

Oh, he was violent, no doubt—a danger to small boys, incapacitated drunks, and old men, but never to women: Women simply were not Weasel's thing, and he had little to do with them. But such attacks as he carried out bought him a reputation as something of a dangerous criminal. Not everyone believed this; the local sheriffs easily saw through him. Yet he rather gloried in his "rep." After all, a man has to get recognition somehow. And he did satisfy the needs of some people: He made himself an object of contempt and a target for the aggressions of others. His end was inevitable: Everyone saw it, and so did he. Indeed, he himself predicted the manner and conditions of his passing.

The Analytical Perspective

In addition to numerous interviews and conversations, Weasel consented to the Rorschach test and the Thematic Apperception Test (TAT), both of which allow the subject to project his or her unconscious hopes, fears, or fantasies. The Rorschach test consists of a series of inkblots, many of them with elaborate shapes. The subject is asked what the blots represent, and the responses often reveal his or her underlying concerns and anxieties. The Thematic Apperception Test consists of a series of drawings of people, usually in situations of interpersonal interaction. The subject is asked to make up stories about the various pictures, and the themes of these stories give the analyst clues to the subject's basic concerns. These tests together with the biographical materials and the assessments of others in the community are the basis for this formal view of Weasel's identity. The evaluation was the joint product of an anthropologist and a clinical psychologist (Clifton 1960; Clifton and Levine 1962).

The sale of alcohol is frequently prohibited on Indian territories, so most of the drinking is done in nearby towns. The conflicting pulls of their traditional culture and the wider society poses agonizing problems for these Native Americans. If they stay in their own community, they can count on social validation of their identities, but must accept severe limitations on their economic possibilities. If they attempt to enter into Anglo society, the dream of possible success crashes up against prejudice and discrimination, and their identities are under constant, hostile assault. Alcohol can relieve the hurt and anger temporarily.

A murderous kind of aggressiveness was the major overall impression one got from Weasel's Rorschach record. But it was plain that Weasel was uncomfortable with his hostility. He was blatantly preoccupied with bloody, personalized violence. He lacked control of his impulses, and intellectual considerations entered little into his behavior and relationships. He was moved by crude, strong feelings and urges. His style of relating to others was marked by guarded suspiciousness. He saw life as violent and full of struggle, but his feelings about people were strikingly shallow and ill defined. Close friendships or satisfying interpersonal relationships of any kind were weak. However, he was concerned with overt signs of status, with how he might appear to others. He was a man seeking attention by whatever means were available to him, and his resources were few.

There could be no question as to whether Weasel was aggressor or victim. He was both. He trusted no one; no one trusted him. He was an isolated, rejected person. But under his belligerent facade was some gentleness, sensitivity, and passivity. He probably had moments of deep, if crude, aesthetic feeling. More than likely, he was a bluff. Together, these observations suggest a diagnosis of paranoia, with a repressed and projected homosexuality. This might account for the *targets* of his aggression. In any respect, Weasel manifested profound sexual disturbance—he continually projected an image of bodily mutilation. Moreover, he was a chronically tense, anxious, frightened man with violent moods that he was likely to act out, and these moods made him most uncomfortable.

All of Weasel's TAT stories had a hollow, empty ring to them. The figures he described were like puppets, moved by forces they did not understand and over which they had no control. Personal desires, wishes, intentions, or goals were rarely stated. The overriding moods in his stories were depression, hopelessness, apathy, and inertia. Rarely did any story have a definite outcome.

In his TAT stories, Weasel showed that he did not understand how people make successes of their lives, except perhaps by "magic" or "having confidence." None of Weasel's heroes—the central figures in his stories—showed consideration for other people, and others showed none for the heroes. Throughout, Weasel projected his doubts about his own manhood, his confusion about the means for effective striving. Sometimes this tendency was extreme: He could not tell if this figure were a "man or a boy," that one "a man or a . . ." This is profound ambivalence. And throughout, Weasel told us he could not tolerate being unmasked, revealed for what he was or was not. The core of his private identity was self-punishment, self-destruction. Relations with others were unstable, erratic, unsatisfying. Weasel never got it all together, not even part way, not with himself or with others.

Card 16 in the Thematic Apperception Test series is blank. It is generally the most threatening card to subjects, who are thrown back entirely on their own resources. Many people reject this card or make some bland, diffident comment about it, such as "Looks like a snow storm." But for Card 16, Weasel told his most coherent story, one with a definite outcome:

I see a man standing in front of a judge. He's feeling bad, too. And they're trying him for fraud. He knows he's going to get a sentence, but he doesn't know how much. The judge is a stern old man. And he deals with people's life like it didn't have no meaning at all. He puts out time like, well I dunno, like he figures he's an old man and he's going to make an old man out of someone else. He gives the man 20 years . . . and it doesn't make him feel too happy. They take him back and put him in a cell. He thinks he can't do no 20 years. The next morning they come in there, they find him hanging up there by his neck (Clifton 1960:210).

A year after I last saw Weasel he was arrested on another charge of assault with a deadly weapon and sentenced to three years in the state penitentiary. Released on probation after two years, he was arrested again within a few months on the same charge. This time the stern old man gave him ten years. Shortly after his term began, one "morning they come in there, they find him hanging up there by his neck." This might be his epitaph: *Weasel: Born 1931—Died 1963. He lived—not willingly, and not well.*

The yard at Clinton Prison in New York, where inmates can go for a few hours each week for recreation. They are permitted to cook out after buying food from the commissary. Although we know that prisons are "bad," the statistics and theories we use to describe the situation get between us and the real life dramas being enacted within prison walls. By not being able to acknowledge prisoners as *people*—individuals with real identities—we can avoid taking our share of responsibility for the forces which have shaped and continue to shape their lives.

Conclusions

Schools of Thought

A. F. C. Wallace suggests that the recent upsurge of interest in identity processes grew out of anthropological studies of themes, world views, ethos, national character, and values (1968:47–49). This cannot be disputed, but there is another side to the matter. Research using such concepts as cultural themes or ethos originated in an earlier effort (during the 1930s) to inject a more dynamic perspective into the then static nature of ethnographic studies. The tactic employed was to psychologize anthropology.

Anthropologists were concerned with the limitations of the piecemeal, mechanistic descriptions of cultures that were characteristic of early anthropology. This concern led to an effort to show more clearly how cultures function. One outcome was psychological studies of individuals and groups. However, the fundamental anthropological emphasis on whole societies and whole cultures caused a deemphasis of the individual. Anthropology did get psychologized, but once again the discipline lost sight of the individual. The current growing concern with individual and collective identity probably represents an effort to improve our understanding of certain problems that are as yet imperfectly grasped, particularly at the individual level.

However, stating that anthropologists have become interested in individual identity again does not explain how or why this interest erupted in the 1960s. Writing about the development of identity studies in psychiatry, Erik Erikson makes a point that applies to anthropology as well:

> Intricate life processes often reveal themselves first in epidemiological states of dysfunction. Thus in our time the significance of the identity process first became apparent to psychopathologists who recognized psychosocial factors in several disturbances of the individual sense of identity (alienation, identity confusion, depersonalization) and to diagnosticians of social upheavals (role, conflict, anomie). (1968:62)

In psychiatry the focus of theoretical interest had shifted from the statics to the dynamics of personality,

Takahashi Shizue tends the pine tree
in front of her house while her grandson sleeps in the traditional baby's sling
on her back. During the day, Japanese
infants are nearly always carried by their
mother, a grandparent, or a sibling,
rather than being left in a crib. The
problem confronting those scholars who
study the relationships between culture
and identity is to find some way to use
theories in a non-alienating manner, to
allow the individual people they are
studying to emerge from the statistics
with their identities intact and
communicable.

from psychological defenses to adaptive mechanisms,
from infantile determinants of behavior to adult adaptations. This theoretical shift coincided with the great
upheavals of the post–World War II era in Europe and
the Americas.

A comparable theoretical shift occurred in anthropology as well, away from static descriptions of social
and cultural elements to a concern with the dynamics
of whole sociocultural systems, and especially of
change and adaptation. Events in the postwar colonial
world forced anthropologists to give increased attention to studies of change—that is, cultural adaptiveness.
This trend is represented by a growing emphasis on
innovative processes, acculturation, migration and
conflict, intergroup relations, factionalism, cultural
revitalization movements, and the like. Once anthropological attention focused on the dynamics of cultural systems, it was difficult not to pay attention to
identity processes. For example, it is nearly impossible
to understand the basic processes involved in inventing
new cultural ways, much less to understand the origins
and course of revitalization movements, without coming to grips with individual identity processes.

This change in emphasis leaves the current field of
identity studies wide open and growing rapidly. Anthropology, psychiatry, and clinical psychology remain
locked in the creative embrace that began when
Sigmund Freud first provoked Bronislaw Malinowski.
Richard H. Robbins even suggests that the concept of
identity offers an entirely new way to approach a wide
variety of old problems—a way that promises a new
synthesis of the findings of many fields of study, and
a possible new paradigm for anthropology and its
related disciplines (1973).

Author's Conclusions

Some anthropological models of human behavior
actively block efforts to understand the doings and
sayings of real people—for example, kinship studies.
Others, such as the new ethnography, offer elegantly
formalized models that seem to promise certainty but
may in fact protect us from genuine, personal contact
with the meaning of individual humans. An overem-
phasis on rigorous methods, mathematical modeling,

computer simulation, and the like may gain favor with the hard sciences, but they are also efforts to intellectualize everything at the expense of other dimensions of the human condition. A narrow and exclusive use of intellectualization as a mode of coping with people is, in fact, a well-recognized ego defense mechanism! Intellectualization defends people from unwanted recognition of aspects of themselves and others that they might find disturbing. What is there about people that anthropologists are unwilling to face?

Close personal study of individual human situations and lives might take us more directly to where the significant human action is. The several ways available for thinking about identity processes can help us understand what we see and hear. On the other hand, structural-functional approaches, cultural themes, and computer models force us to think in abstracted categories. They put too much distance between ourselves and other people. Individuals become stereotyped, become only representatives of a class, are spoken of as "culture bearers" (as if this was all men and women were good for, to bear as a burden the "culture" anthropologists are bent on studying). Every person deserves a better hearing than this.

Summary

Anthropology's preoccupation with populations, groups, and collectivities has submerged the individual, who receives little attention. This chapter discusses the individual, particularly several dimensions of individual identity. The broad field of culture and personality studies should have contributed much to an understanding of the relationships between individuals and their cultures, but it did not. Except for a relatively few biographies and autobiographies, the idea of personality was turned into a device for characterizing the psychological functioning of groups. Hence such concepts as basic or modal personality came to dominate the field. The consequence of this approach was to characterize what was typical, not what was individual.

But in the past decade, anthropologists have become concerned with individual identity. This development has coincided with an equal concern in the fields of psychiatry and clinical psychology. The results of this interdisciplinary convergence have led to a better understanding of cultural change, individual adaptations, and matters seemingly as far removed as human behavioral evolution and primate studies.

The chapter outlines some of the key dimensions of identity—public and private, psychological and social, conscious and unconscious, model and stigmatized. In this discussion, the distinction between emic and etic creates a special problem. An individual has a personal "explanation" of himself or herself cast in private, idiosyncratic terms that are only partially shared and imperfectly validated in public terms. At the same time, the outsider—anthropologist or psychiatrist—also imposes his or her categories and terms in an "objective," analytical effort to comprehend the individuality and identity of one person.

Annotated Bibliography

Barnouw, Victor (1973) *Culture and Personality*. Rev. ed. Homewood, Ill.: Dorsey. The best introduction to the field available; especially valuable for a full discussion of cases and methods.

Erikson, Erik (1968) *Identity, Youth, and Crisis*. New York: Norton. Erikson's masterwork; the most profound treatment of identity issues and problems available. Most other current treatments of identity derive from but do not improve on this book.

Fitzgerald, Thomas K., ed. (1974) *Social and Cultural Identity*. Athens: Univ. of Georgia Press. A good variety of essays on group identity processes that illustrate conventional anthropological approaches to the topic. However, the book's treatment of aspects of individual identity is weak.

Goffman, Erving (1963) *Stigma: Notes on the Management of Spoiled Identity*. Englewood Cliffs, N.J.: Prentice-Hall. If the clarity of his conceptualizations matched the sharpness of his insights, this interesting book would be even more valuable. Nonetheless, Goffman's fine perception of individual identity processes make important reading.

Part IV

Issues in the Contemporary World

15
Social
Stratification

The World Context

Origins and Development Through Time

Social inequality has always been a feature of the human condition. In all societies, past and present, some people have enjoyed a higher status than others. The determinants of an individual's status vary from one society to another, but two criteria are universal: age and sex. In every society, the status of the mature differs from that of the young; and there is no society in which the statuses of males and females are identical in all respects. Additional criteria for according differential status depend on the personal attributes that are valued in a society. Beauty, strength, courage, wisdom, or particular manual, intellectual, and artistic skills are not equally distributed among a population, and wherever some such characteristic is highly (or negatively) valued, its possessors tend to be accorded a higher (or lower) status, at least in some respects, than those who do not possess it.

In some societies, however, social inequality takes a much more elaborate and structured form: the institutionalized inequality of entire categories of people. Such a society is organized into a hierarchy of two or more strata, the members of which have quite different

Hunting and gathering societies, like that of the Tasaday (Philippines) shown here, are frequently referred to as "egalitarian." What this means is that there is no social stratification, there is equal access by all members to strategic resources, and equal access to valued social positions. However, this does not mean that there are no differences perceived to exist between people. All societies have a degree of social inequality: even egalitarian societies make social distinctions with regard to age and sex, and also recognize superior talents and abilities.

rights of access to the strategic resources and fruits of the society's economic activities. A society of this type is said to be *stratified*—that is, it is "one in which members of the same sex and equivalent age status do not have equal access to the basic resources that sustain life" (Fried 1967:186). Inequality between individual human beings is universal, but social stratification is not.

Anthropologists distinguish two basic types of stratification, caste and class. A *caste* system is highly rigid: The social strata within it are hereditary and endogamous (individuals may marry only within their caste). An individual is born into a specific caste and can never change his or her status because membership is automatic and lifelong. The entire system is sanctioned by the mores, the laws, and usually the religion of the society. In a *class* system, the boundaries between the strata are more blurred. An individual's posi-

tion is usually determined by the economic status of the family head, but a person can potentially rise or fall from one class to another through his or her own efforts or failings.

Social stratification is a relatively recent phenomenon in human history. We can guess from archaeological evidence that little or no stratification existed in Neolithic society. All the dwelling units in Neolithic settlements were of roughly the same size, whereas in the archaeological remains of early urban civilizations, we usually find that some houses are markedly larger than others and that these houses are situated together in one part of the city. Neolithic graves, too, are generally very similar to one another; they contain few if any grave goods—personal possessions buried with the corpse, presumably for use in the afterlife. The graves of early civilizations, in contrast, display considerable variety in size and in the amount and quality of the personal goods they contain. In fact, in ancient Mesopotamia and Egypt, the personal servants of a dead member of the royal family were sometimes killed and buried close by so that they could continue their service on his or her journey into the next world.

How did social stratification develop? Anthropological research has clearly demonstrated that the emergence of caste and class systems is directly related to the degree of complexity of a society. Morton Fried, for example, distinguishes three basic societal types that form an evolutionary sequence from simple to more complex and less egalitarian social forms: *egalitarian* societies, *rank* societies, and *stratified* societies (1967).

An *egalitarian* society, according to Fried, "is one in which there are as many positions of prestige in any given age-sex grade as there are persons capable of filling them. Putting that another way, an egalitarian society is characterized by the adjustment of the number of valued statuses to the number of persons with the ability to fill them" (1967:33). Egalitarian systems are found primarily among hunting and gathering peoples and very occasionally in simple horticultural and pastoral societies. The egalitarian society was dominant before the development of agriculture, and the few remaining hunting and gathering peoples in the world,

such as the !Kung San, give us some idea of what such societies were like (see Chap. 21).

These simple societies have no elaborate differentiation in the roles and functions of individuals. Accumulation of private wealth is not possible; everyone has equal access to the strategic resources of food and shelter. Each individual may have a slightly different status in the community from everyone else, but such differences do not exist among entire categories of people except on the basis of age and sex. Status cannot be gained by amassing wealth; indeed, a highly valued form of behavior in these societies is the sharing of goods, especially food. There is no prestige or power to be gained from keeping goods to oneself.

Rank societies have a more complex social structure and generally practice agriculture or pastoralism. Fried defines a rank society as "one in which positions of valued status are somehow limited so that not all those of sufficient talent to occupy such statuses actually achieve them" (1967:110). In a rank society, then, individuals have equality of access to land and other economic resources but unequal access to positions of high status. Privilege and power are to some extent restricted to certain groups. The position of chief, for example, can be aspired to only by some members of the community, for it is at least partly based on heredity. The major process of economic integration in a rank society is redistribution; goods flow steadily to and from a center of authority, which is the pinnacle of the rank hierarchy.

Historically, rank societies have generally existed among horticultural and early agricultural peoples. A substantial number of rank societies still exist in the modern world, such as the Mutayr of Saudi Arabia (see Chap. 22) and many African tribal societies. The rank system tends to be replaced by full-scale stratification with advanced agriculture or industrialism, which generate large economic surpluses (but see the discussion of the Trobriand Islanders in Chapter 11).

The *stratified* society, which over the last few thousand years has become the dominant social form in the world, is characterized by structured inequality of access not only to power and prestige but also to the basic, strategic resources that sustain life. These societies are almost universally agricultural or industrial, and their stratification systems are founded on a surplus production to which the dominant stratum has a prior claim. In such societies, statuses and roles become increasingly specialized, and rewards are more and more unequally distributed. A centralized authority structure, the state, emerges to administer the complex social order and to maintain the system of stratification.

Stratified societies are of many different types. In many societies, particularly in Africa and in the classical civilizations of Greece and Rome, the stratification system included slavery. In other societies a feudal form of stratification arose, based on a rigid division between the nobility and the peasantry, whose respective rights and obligations were defined by their very different access to control over land. Feudal systems predominated in medieval Europe for centuries, but similar systems also existed in other parts of the world. Aztec society in Mexico, for example, displayed many similarities to European feudalism, as did west African kingdoms.

Excavation of the Royal Cemetery at Ur (see Chapter 18) in Mesopotamia, under the direction of Sir Leonard Wooley from 1922–1929. Towards the end of his excavation Woolley found a rather extreme expression of social stratification: in front of the entrance to the tomb of one king there were 74 corpses of women, lying neatly in rows next to each other. Careful analysis of the positioning of the bodies, and the fact that each had a small cup nearby, led Woolley to the conclusion that after the king had been buried, the women had entered the chamber and drunk poison—some 4,500 years ago.

Coatlicue: Mother Earth figure revered
by the Aztecs. A giant statue was found
in the center of the main plaza in Mexico
City. This rather forbidding figure, with its
double serpent head, necklace of severed
human hands and hearts (with a human
skull as a pendant), stood in the great
courtyard of the temple at the Aztec
capital Tenochtitlán. As its skirt of
corncobs suggests, it reminded the
peasants that the fertility of the earth
required their participation in the
religious system—which legitimized the
harsh Aztec system of social stratification.

Rigid preindustrial stratification systems have tended to crumble under the impact of industrialism. An industrial system requires a skilled and mobile labor force; its efficiency is impaired if arbitrary barriers restrict the potential work contribution of large segments of the population. The spread of industrial society around the world has created new forms of stratification, transforming the rural peasantry of country after country into an urban proletariat who offer their labor to an entrepreneurial class in return for wages (see Chap. 16). In the more developed industrial societies, there are clear class distinctions between the affluent owners of strategic resources and the means of production and the less affluent groups who sell their labor. However, in the socialist countries the state is explicitly committed to the equal distribution of wealth and the elimination of social stratification.

Contemporary Examples

As we have seen, a few egalitarian societies and rank societies still exist. The overwhelming majority of contemporary societies, however, are stratified and have a state form of government. Caste or castelike systems are now relatively few in number, as they are incompatible with modernization. Class societies are found almost everywhere and are rapidly replacing the rank societies that still exist in areas of the Third World. Most contemporary developing societies already have marked class divisions. The elite class is typically composed of such disparate elements as traditional chiefs, new entrepeneurs, and political leaders. The middle class in these societies is usually very small, for the vast majority of the inhabitants—in Africa and Asia, primarily peasants—fall into the lower class.

In developed societies, on the other hand, class distinctions appear to be becoming less evident in some respects than they were even half a century ago. Universal suffrage has greatly increased the power of the ordinary person. The lower class in these societies has shrunk and the middle class has expanded rapidly, for a large part of the population has shared, even if unequally, in the immense wealth that modern industrial economies produce. Gerhard Lenski estimates that in stratified agrarian societies, the top 2 percent of the population generally receives about half the total income of the society; in modern industrial societies, the top 2 percent receives, on the average, about 10 percent of the income (1966).

Let us look more closely at the social systems of three contemporary societies: India, which still has a caste system; the United States, a capitalist industrial society; and the Soviet Union, a socialist state that claims to have abolished classes.

India   The caste system has been a fundamental feature of Indian life for over 2,500 years (Hutton 1963). Although the system was officially abolished by the Indian government in 1949, it is still an important element in the social life of the country, especially in rural areas.

In theory, India has four main castes, or *varnas:* the *brahmins,* or priests; the *kshatriyas,* or nobles and warriors; the *vaishyas,* or merchants and craftsmen; and the *shudras,* or common laborers. Beyond these four *varnas* are the outcastes, or "untouchables"—so

In the anonymous, crowded conditions of modern, urban India, the caste system is slowly breaking down because it is simply impossible to observe all the ritual and social requirements which are part of it. In the countryside, however, the caste system still rigidly structures peoples' lives.

344 Issues in the Contemporary World

called because merely to touch an outcaste, or even to be brushed by his or her shadow, is a form of ritual pollution for members of the higher *varnas*. The avoidance of such "pollution" is one of many practices of social distance that ensure the continued segregation of the castes and thus buttress the system. Strict endogamy is also maintained within each caste, and intercaste sexual relations are a matter of defilement, especially for the upper-caste partner.

In practice, the four castes in India are divided into literally thousands of subcastes, or *jati*. These *jati* are sometimes confined to local areas, but membership in some of them is spread across India. A *jati* is often linked to a particular occupation, and all members of that *jati* are expected to follow a specific line of work. An individual cannot change his or her status, since status is determined by caste and one's caste is that of one's parents. However, the relative status of an entire *jati* may change slowly over time.

The Indian caste system is closely intertwined with the Hindu religion, which is explicitly concerned with the maintenance of the stratified social order. Each of the four *varnas* has appropriate rules of behavior that each member must follow. According to the Hindu doctrine of *karma*, an individual is reincarnated again and again through a series of lifetimes, and one's status in the next lifetime depends on one's behavior in this one. Failure to live up to the requirements of the stratification system may result in reincarnation as a member of a lower *varna*, or perhaps as an outcaste, or even as an animal. Thus the Hindu religion is both an expression of the caste system and a mechanism for its maintenance.

The Indian caste system is breaking down rapidly in urban areas, where the difficulty of recognizing another person's caste in an anonymous, crowded environment makes it virtually impossible for people to observe the complicated rules of ritual distance or to avoid ritual pollution. In the villages and the countryside, however, this highly rigid system still dominates the lives of millions of people.

United States   Equality is a core value in American culture. Unlike most other Western industrialized societies, the United States has no feudal history; indeed, the official American ideology of human equality had its origins in European liberal Enlightenment writings—John Locke's and his followers'—aimed at the overthrow of privileged elites. Yet American society has considerable structured inequality. More than 200,000 people are millionaires, and more than 3,000 families have an annual income of over a million dollars. And yet more than 38 million Americans live below the official poverty line, or incomes acknowledged by the federal government to be inadequate to meet the basic requirements of food, clothing, and shelter. Another 28 million live in a condition of economic deprivation. Some 1 percent of the American population owns almost a third of the country's wealth, while the bottom 20 percent owns only slightly over 2 percent (Lerner 1973:9–10). Two percent of private stockholders own two-thirds of all stock held by individuals. The upper fifth of the families in the United States receive over 40 percent of the nation's annual income, whereas the lowest fifth receives 5.5 percent—a proportion that has remained almost constant for at least the last thirty years (McKee and Robertson 1975).

Power in American society is also very unequally distributed. Social scientists tend to take one of two basic views of the distribution of power in the United States. Some theorists, such as C. Wright Mills, contend that the power structure is pyramidic and dominated by an informal "power elite" of corporate and bureaucratic interests that makes the most important decisions and does so largely in terms of its own interests (1956). Other theorists, such as David Riesman, argue that the power structure is pluralistic; a variety of powerful interest groups struggle for advantage and balance one another out (1969). We do not yet have sufficient empirical data to prove or disprove either of these views, but it is significant that the ordinary citizen does not feature in either of the models. Most people in the United States have no direct involvement and usually very little indirect involvement in the major economic or political decisions that affect their lives. Indeed, they are usually unaware that these decisions are being made.

Social scientists agree that the United States is a stratified society, but the exact contours of the stratification system are difficult to determine. Some analysts contend that two classes exist; others say three classes;

and still others find as many as eleven. Some even argue that the United States does not have distinct classes, but rather a continuum of unequal statuses. However, most social scientists take the conventional view that American society falls into three main classes: a very small upper class, a very large middle class, and a fairly small lower class. For some analytical purposes, each of these classes may be subdivided into upper and lower substrata.

A major problem in analysis is that the analytical categories of the investigator and the (folk) perceptions of the individuals concerned do not necessarily coincide. When asked, most Americans declare themselves to be middle class. Analysis of the class structure is made more complicated by the fact that ethnic, regional, and religious affiliations crosscut economic differences and inhibit individuals' identification with any one class.

Moreover, the American stratification system contains some castelike features. The various "racial"

Although American egalitarian ideology and ideals make it difficult to acknowledge, social class is probably the most powerful single determiner of the course of life a person will lead in the United States.

minorities are largely endogamous and are accorded lower collective status than the dominant white majority. To the extent that status is linked to the particular "races" recognized in American folk taxonomy, it is generally hereditary and lifelong. In addition, American racism has a long history of the observation of social distance (formalized in segregation statutes) and also of ritual pollution (as evidenced by segregated washrooms and by taboos on "interracial" sex, particularly if the female partner is a member of the higher status group). To complicate matters further, each of the American "castes" may contain an internal, class-based stratification system.

Soviet Union   The government of the Soviet Union has abolished private ownership of the means of production and distribution and maintains it is working toward the construction of a totally egalitarian communist society. Although the USSR sometimes is described as communist in the West, no society in the world *describes itself* as communist: The Soviet Union claims only to have reached the intermediate stage of socialism, in which classes have been formally abolished but strong centralized government is still needed to guide the transition to the future communist society (see fig. 15-1).

There is no doubt that the Soviet Union does not have a dominant entrepreneurial class such as those found in all capitalist societies. But whether the Soviet Union has successfully abolished classes is a matter of intense debate. In the USSR, as in all other Eastern European socialist societies, the incomes of the officials at the top of the bureaucratic hierarchy are several times those of ordinary people (Djilas 1957). The bureaucrats enjoy many privileges denied to the masses, such as better housing and the use of free automobiles. Political power, too, is very unequally distributed. The Soviet Union is ruled by a small elite consisting of the upper echelons of the Communist party and government departments—officials who have only a fictive responsibility to the general population. The ruling elite is significantly more powerful than any comparable elite in the West for two reasons. First, it

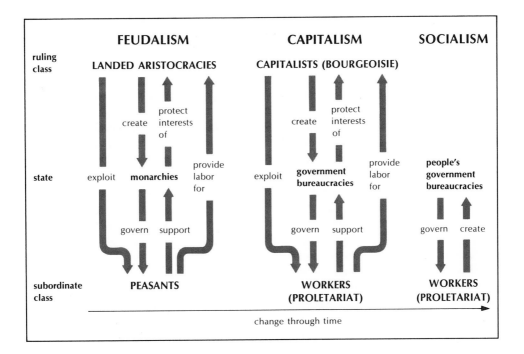

FEUDALISM

CAPITALISM

SOCIALISM

ruling
class

LANDED ARISTOCRACIES

CAPITALISTS (BOURGEOISIE)

create
protect
interests
of

create
protect
interests
of

state

exploit

monarchies

provide
labor
for

exploit

**government
bureaucracies**

provide
labor
for

**people's
government
bureaucracies**

govern
support

govern
support

govern
create

subordinate
class

PEASANTS

**WORKERS
(PROLETARIAT)**

**WORKERS
(PROLETARIAT)**

change through time

Figure 15-1
**Social Stratification and the State:
Marxist Analysis**
This model illustrates how the state
maintains the status quo in a stratified
society. However, in the end the state
cannot keep class conflicts suppressed;
it is this conflict that is the source of
social change over time—until with
socialism the exploitative ruling class
is eliminated.

left
Leonid Brezhnev and Gerald Ford meet in
Vladivostok. Although as perhaps the
most powerful person in the Soviet Union
Brezhnev enjoys great social prestige,
his own personal economic position is
not so very high above that of the
average Soviet citizen. Nor will he be
able to pass either his position or his
wealth to his heirs. Do you think
the Soviet Union has a system of social
classes? Why?

has both political and economic power concentrated
into its hands, whereas in capitalist societies power is
more diffuse. Second, the Soviet elite is not subject
to periodic free elections, and its policies are not effectively subject to public criticism.

Whether the Soviet elite actually constitutes a class
is a matter of definition. If a class is defined by its control over strategic resources, then the Soviet elite is
clearly a class, and a very powerful one. However, if
we specify that the ruling group must use its control of
resources primarily for its own benefit, as in capitalist
societies, then the Soviet elite cannot be considered
a class. There is certainly no indication that the bureaucrats think of themselves as a class, or that the ordinary
people consider their society stratified in any way.
The Soviet system differs from all other class systems
in that it has no "leisure class" that lives off accumulated wealth. Perhaps most importantly, people cannot
inherit large sums of money or even high status from
their parents. It remains to be seen whether the Soviet
Union—or any other society with a different interpretation of communism, such as the People's Republic of
China—will achieve an unambiguously classless society.

Theory

Systems

Social scientists have developed several useful concepts to describe and analyze stratification systems.

A stratified society invariably develops a *state* form of government. Fried defines the state as "a collection of specialized institutions and agencies, some formal and others informal, that maintains an order of stratification" (1967:235). The state, then, is the source of political authority in a stratified society, and it functions not only to maintain the social system as a whole but also to maintain the stratification system itself (hence defending the interests of the ruling class).

A stratification system may be either closed or open. In a *closed* system the boundaries between the strata are sharply drawn, and an individual cannot change his or her societal status. Under such conditions, a person's status is said to be *ascribed* (see chap. 12), for it is attributed on the basis of criteria over which the individual has no control, such as the social origins of one's parents. In an *open* system an individual may legitimately hope to change his or her status through personal efforts. A person's status under such a system is said to be *achieved,* for the individual has some access to statuses other than that into which he or she was born. Movement from one stratum to another is termed *social mobility.* Closed societies allow little or no mobility, but open societies offer at least some possibility of mobility.

Caste systems, then, are clearly closed, and the societal statuses within them are ascriptive. In these systems, the social strata are frozen by endogamy and the practice of hereditary transmission of status. Most anthropologists apply the term *caste* to any rigid, closed, ascriptive system. However, some prefer to restrict its use to the Indian social order and use the term *estate system* for castelike hierarchies such as that of feudal Europe. Under the estate system, the nobles granted military protection and tenure of land to the peasants in return for the right to call on them for military service, for labor, and for rent payments, frequently a part of their produce. Analagous systems have

been recorded in other parts of the world, particularly in Mesoamerica and many parts of Asia.

Class systems are to a greater or lesser extent open, and at least in principle, the statuses within them can be achieved. The analysis of a class system, as we have seen from the example of the United States, presents many more problems than the analysis of a caste system. To determine an individual's caste is easy: It is simply a matter of definition. But to determine someone's class is much more difficult. What criteria can the social scientist use to distinguish one class from another and to determine an individual's class position?

To Karl Marx, a class consisted of all those people who share a common relationship to the means of production (1967, orig. 1867–1894). Those who control the means of production—slave owners, feudal lords, or capitalist entrepreneurs, as the case may be—constitute the dominant class; those who work for them—slaves, peasants, industrial laborers—compose the subordinate, exploited class. The economically dominant class, Marx argued, invariably has the greatest social prestige and political influence as well as disproportionate wealth. The Marxist definition of class has been profoundly influential, and anthropologists often find it convenient to regard as a class any group of people who have a similar degree of control over and access to basic resources.

Marx's definition is less useful in marginal cases, particularly those found in industrial societies, which have changed considerably since Marx's time. What, for example, is the social class of a hippie, who does own or control the means of production but who does not work either? Of what class is a penniless aristocrat, who may enjoy prestige because of birth rather than his or her relationship to the means of production? How does one classify skilled manual laborers who have higher incomes than some professionals? What is the class of the Soviet bureaucrat, or the wealthy black American who suffers the effects of "racial" prejudice and discrimination throughout his or her life?

One influential analysis that confronts these problems is that of Max Weber (1946), whose multidimensional approach has found favor among many American

Vice President Nelson Rockefeller. As a private citizen, Rockefeller commanded enormous wealth and tremendous power to make decisions which affected all our lives. Then he entered into a position of great public prestige as well. Many question the advisability of concentrating so much wealth, power, and prestige into the hands of one person. What do you think about this?

social scientists. Weber breaks the unitary concept of class into three distinct but related elements: political status, or *power*; economic status, or *wealth*; and social status, or *prestige*. Clearly, a person may be politically influential but have little wealth (such as Ralph Nader), or may be wealthy but have little society-wide prestige (such as the head of a Mafia family), or may have prestige but no wealth (the penniless aristo-crat). But although wealth, power, and prestige may to some extent be independent of one another, in prac-tice, the three are usually closely associated. Weber's distinction is useful in some ambiguous cases, but for most purposes, Marxist analysis of class by economic position alone is adequate.

Processes

How does structured social inequality work? At first sight, it would seem improbable that any strati-fication system could endure for long, since in every case a small minority enjoys disproportionate access to strategic resources and thus deprives the majority of an equal share in what the society produces. Yet stratification systems do persist, and some of the most rigid and inegalitarian—such as the European feudal estate system or the Indian caste system—last for many centuries. What processes sustain caste and class systems?

Any successful political system requires some kind of *legitimacy*: If the people do not perceive the social order as legitimate—that is, valid and justified—the system will soon collapse (see Chap. 11). In a state society the ruling group can try to apply force to ensure the maintenance of the social order, but most stratification systems persist without the necessity of using force or even the threat of force. In practice, the state and the stratification system it upholds are accepted as legitimate for the simple reason that they are taken for granted; they are perceived as natural by all concerned—both the dominant stratum and usually the subordinate stratum (or strata) as well.

As was shown in Chapter 11, the legitimation of a political system is provided by the dominant *ideology* of the society—the belief system that explains and justifies the existing order. The role of ideologies in the legitimation of stratification systems was first systematically explored by Karl Marx, and his viewpoint has since been very widely accepted, even by social scientists who reject other Marxist theories. Marx's argument was simple: The dominant belief system in any society is always the belief system of its ruling class, and the belief system of the ruling class is always one that legitimates that class's economic interests. Other belief systems may exist in the society, but an ideology can never become dominant or widely accepted unless the class that holds it, and whose own economic interests it legitimates, becomes the dominant class. In a society dominated by capitalists, therefore, the dominant ideology will be one of capitalism, not socialism. In a society dominated by socialists, the dominant ideology will be socialism, not capitalism. In a society dominated by a slave-owning class, the dominant belief system will legitimate the institution of slavery, not promote social equality for all people.

It is easy to see why the dominant stratum should believe in the dominant ideology, but what of the members of the subordinate stratum? In general, they also tend to accept the legitimacy of the system, a phenomeon that Marx termed *false consciousness*—a subjective consciousness that does not accord with one's objective situation. Thus the industrial worker accepts the legitimacy of capitalism, the low-caste Indian accepts the legitimacy of the caste system, the feudal serf accepts the legitimacy of the estate system. Only when the members of the subordinate stratum gain *class consciousness*—an awareness of their common exploitation—do they begin to question the legitimacy of the system and to develop a new ideology, one that serves their own economic interests. *Class conflict* is likely to follow (see Chap. 17).

An ideology is a complex belief system that typically includes religious, political, and economic elements. The feudal system, for example, drew its ultimate legitimation from the political and religious doctrine of the divine right of kings—the notion that the monarch derives his authority directly from God. Peasants seem to have accepted this doctrine as unquestioningly as the kings and the lords. The king delegated some of this authority to the lords, and it followed that the peasants were under a divine imperative to obey them. When the feudal system was finally overthrown, the agent of its demise was an emerging class of urban capitalists who offered a new ideology, that of political liberalism, economic laissez faire, and the "Protestant ethic" of hard work and deferred gratification—all of them legitimating a new social order that was fitted to the new mode of production that emphasized the individual entrepreneur.

The ideology of colonialism, too, provided a justification for the acts of the colonists. They saw themselves not as exploiters of raw materials and sweated labor but as bearers of the "white man's burden"—the noble but demanding task of civilizing "inferior races." Often the subject peoples, too, seem to have accepted the colonial view that they were genuinely inferior; their belief in the legitimacy of the system made it easier for small European minorities to dominate vast populations until the emergence of a nationalist ideology in the developing nations after World War II. The Indian caste system is another example; it was legitimated primarily by religion (Hinduism) and has been unquestioningly accepted by all the castes, and even the outcastes, for thousands of years.

Less dramatic than the Indian case, but of no less interest to the social scientist, is the lower-class American's deep belief in the virtues of the capitalist system. The existence of inequality in American society is legitimated by an ideology (though not the fact) of equal opportunity. Everyone has a chance to get rich by working hard, and inequality is justified as a means of rewarding individual achievement. Those who do not get rich (that is, most people) therefore have only themselves to blame—not the rich, and not the system as a whole. In practice, very few Americans of manual working-class origins make it to the corporate elite. Marvin Harris estimates the chances of doing so at less than one in a million (1971:431).

The boundaries of classes or castes are preserved by norms and practices that maintain *social distance* between the groups. The Indian institution of ritual pollution is an extreme example of such a practice, but an upper stratum can distinguish itself from the lower strata by many other devices. Dress may indicate rank; the imperial purple of ancient Rome, the gold ornaments of Inca rulers, the sword of the medieval lords, the silk clothing of the ancient Chinese nobility—all were forbidden to commoners. The rules of endogamy found in many stratified societies also maintain social, economic, and political differences and preserve over many generations the dominant group's differential access to resources. Ritualized forms of obeisance—bowing, kneeling, and using respectful terms of address—continually remind the lower strata of their subordinate status.

In modern industrial societies, the upper classes are more discreet and do not demand, nor could they enforce, such acknowledgment of their superior status. But they do maintain social distance and assert their superior status in more subtle ways. In Britain, for example, a person's exact social status is evident as soon as he or she speaks, for accent is the most important single indicator of class status in that country. In the United States, the wealthy display their status and maintain social distance between themselves and their social inferiors by their "conspicuous consumption" of expensive goods and services (Veblen 1954;

Orig. 1899). They also spend a great deal of money on walled and guarded estates, "exclusive" apartments, and employees who ensure their employers' privacy. It is hardly an accident that social scientists know a great deal about the poor and the powerless—but very little about the extremely rich and powerful.

Analysis

The Folk Perspective

It is clear that folk perceptions of a stratification system may differ markedly from the perceptions of the investigator, who (at least when studying societies other than his or her own) is unlikely to view the system as inevitable or its legitimating ideology as self-evidently valid. Moreover, the investigator's analysis may have to contend with a number of *different folk perspectives* on the stratification system: Individuals will offer quite different viewpoints, depending on their own position in the social hierarchy and the degree to which they perceive the system as legitimate. A study of aspects of South African society provides an example of one such conflict of folk perspectives (Robertson 1973).

South Africa is a modern industrialized society. Its population consists of some 17 million people defined as "blacks," some 4 million "whites," and about 3 million members of other minorities, primarily people of Asian ancestry and persons of "mixed race." As is well known, the society is dominated by the white minority, which exerts total political and economic control over all other groups through the most rigid system of segregation recorded in human history. The system of white domination and "racial" segregation is termed *apartheid* ("separateness").

Blacks have no vote in national elections and are not represented at all in the central parliament. Their only political rights are in their impoverished reserves, covering 13 percent of the land area of the country. Blacks may leave these areas only to work for whites, but they may not bring their spouses or children with them unless they too can obtain work permits. All skilled and most semiskilled jobs are reserved by law for whites, and it is a criminal offense for black workers to go on strike. The income of blacks averages less than a seventh of that of the whites, who in turn enjoy a standard of living similar to that of white North Americans.

The "races" are rigidly segregated in every conceivable sphere of human activity: schools, transport, residential areas, eating places, beaches, and other public facilities. Marriage across the "color line" is illegal, and even sexual relations between blacks and whites carry a punishment of up to seven years imprisonment and a whipping of up to a dozen strokes. Civil liberties are very few for whites and virtually nonexistent for blacks; the police may detain any person indefinitely in solitary confinement without trial.

The politically dominant group among the whites are the Afrikaners, descendants of early Dutch settlers who now number about two-thirds of the white population; the remainder are of British origin. The Afrikaners are strongly nationalistic and are mostly members of a fundamentalist Calvinist sect, the Dutch Reformed Church, which preaches that "racial" segregation in South Africa is in accordance with the will of God. The belief system of the Afrikaners includes the following basic ideas: The Afrikaner people are chosen by God to work his will on the African continent; Western civilization is an attribute indissolubly linked to (white) skin color; the culture of the blacks is inferior and derives from the "racial inferiority" of the blacks themselves; "race purity" is a moral imperative, to be maintained at any cost through segregation; and evil forces abroad in the world are determined to subvert Christian white South Africa. Let us look at some statements by Afrikaner leaders to gain insight into their folk perspectives on the South African social order.

The last prime minister, H. F. Verwoerd, explained his policies to Parliament: "We want to make South Africa white. . . . Keeping it white can mean only one thing, namely, white domination, not 'leadership,' not 'guidance,' but 'control,' 'supremacy'" (quoted in Robertson 1973:44–45).

Another prime minister, D. F. Malan, spoke about the special role of the Afrikaner in God's plan for the universe: "The history of the Afrikaner reveals a determination and a definiteness of purpose which make

South Africans working in a diamond mine. These men work in 120 degree temperature, miles below the earth's surface. They live in company barracks and are kept very far away from the "white"-dominated urban centers. Can you explain why "black" Africans continue to participate in this exploitative system even though their wages are kept very low?

one feel that Afrikanderdom is not the work of man but a creation of God. We have a divine right to be Afrikaners. Our history is the highest work of art of the Architect of the ages" (quoted in Robertson 1973:43).

The cabinet minister responsible for the "development and administration" of the blacks explains that apartheid accords with the divine plan: "Every nation has its own nature and its own avenue of development. . . . We have been put here in a constellation of units, each peculiar to itself, and we have to protect the natural harmony and order" (quoted in Robertson 1973:42).

The Afrikaner elite is well aware that international opinion is highly critical of the apartheid system, but this criticism is taken as evidence that something is wrong with the rest of the world, not South Africa. The main organ of the ruling Afrikaner Nationalist party comments in an editorial:

In Britain and America, the spiritual capitulation of the White man is the order of the day, to such an extent that the British are apparently prepared to become a bastard race within a few generations. . . . The liberalistic sickness will not continue. . . . The liberalistic striving after equality will be rejected. When liberalism disappears and a normal situation rules again, common South Africa will be praised because it did not want to go with the stream. (Quoted in Robertson 1973:41)

The socialization process for white children inculcates in them a belief in this ideology and so makes the apartheid system seem legitimate and become taken for granted. School textbooks systematically explain and justify the existing stratification system. One high school book declares:

Many of our country's racial attitudes between whites and non-whites are entrenched in law. Our forefathers believed that like must seek like. Also, the non-whites do not like the bastardizing of their people. During the years gone by the whites therefore remained white and the non-whites, non-white. It has become the traditional principle that although white and non-white share a common fatherland, there is no blood-mixing, and there is no eating, drinking, or visiting together. This principle is also entrenched in various laws. The living together of white and non-white is not only a great shame, but it is also forbidden by law (quoted in Robertson 1973:121).

Another text urges the maintenance of white supremacy:

It is actually not only the white South African's skin which is different from that of the non-white. The white stands at a much higher level of civilization and is more developed. The whites must so live, so learn and so work that we do not sink to the level of civilization of the non-whites. Only then will the control of the country be able to remain in the hands of the whites.

The religious legitimation of *apartheid* as a manifestation of God's will is explained in yet another school text:

The Creator has a purpose in the placing of a people in a determined place. We as a people are not fortuitously here in Africa. It is the will of our Father who is in Heaven. . . . Taking all the circumstances into account, the coming into existence and the continued existence of the white Christian civilization in spite of the mass of the non-whites, can be seen as nothing less than a providence of the Almighty. . . . We believe that Providence planted us more than three centuries ago on the southern corner of

Africa because He had a definite purpose with us (quoted in Robertson 1973:146).

What of the black majority's perceptions of the system? Since the blacks have few opportunities to express their opinions on the subject, and since social science research on such a topic is not easily conducted in South Africa, little empirical evidence of the views of the subordinate group is available. The denial of political rights to the blacks and the general apparatus of oppression make it clear, however, that the system is not considered legitimate by the majority of the country's inhabitants. Nelson Mandela, the man generally acknowledged to be the leader of the black resistance movement, is currently serving a life prison sentence for attempting to overthrow the regime. His remarks at his trial provide a sharply contrasting folk view of the South African stratification system:

South Africa is the richest country in Africa, and could be one of the richest countries in the world. But, it is a land of extremes and remarkable contrasts. The Whites enjoy what may well be the highest standard of living in the world, while Africans live in poverty and misery. Forty percent of Africans live in hopelessly overcrowded and in some cases, drought-stricken reserves. . . . Thirty percent are laborers, labor tenants, and squatters on White farms, and work and live under conditions similar to those of serfs in the Middle Ages. The other thirty percent live in towns. . . . Yet most Africans, even in this group, are impoverished. . . . The complaint of the Africans . . . is not only that they are poor and the Whites are rich, but that the laws that are made by the Whites are designed to preserve this situation. . . .

The lack of human dignity experienced by Africans is the direct result of the policy of White supremacy. White supremacy implies Black inferiority. . . . Whites tend to regard Africans as a separate breed. They do not look upon them as peoples with families of their own; they do not realize that they have emotions—that they fall in love like White people do, that they want to be with their wives and children like White people want to be with theirs, that they want to earn enough money to support their families properly, to feed and clothe them and send them to school. . . . Africans want a just share in the whole of South Africa (Mandela 1970:19–22).

The Analytic Perspective

From the analytical perspective, it is clear that South African society contains a castelike stratification system. Status is ascribed on the basis of skin color and is lifelong and unchangeable; no social mobility whatever exists between the strata. The economy is based on a "racial" division of labor, and the whites derive immense economic benefits from the maintenance of the existing social hierarchy. They keep blacks' wages suppressed, monopolize wealth, power, and prestige in the society, and have evolved an elaborate ideology to legitimate their privileged position and to make it seem a morally justified one, both to themselves and to others.

The various segregation practices represent institutionalized strategies for the maintenance of social distance, which enhances the awareness of differential status among both strata. The insistence on endogamy, even to the extent of policing private sexual acts, is fundamental to the preservation of the social order. Unlike many other stratification systems, apartheid is based on observable phenotypic differences between the dominant and subordinate castes. Any interbreeding would blur the boundaries between the groups and thus undermine the entire system. Furthermore, endogamy ensures the transmission of status from one generation to the next. The concern over sexual contact also represents a fear of ritual pollution, which may be seen as a projection of the fear of blurring of phenotypic differences—a real threat to this particular system of social stratification.

Naturally, not all cross-strata contact is avoided, only that which suggests "racial" equality. It is considered defiling for a white to eat with a nonwhite, but it is perfectly permissible, and indeed expected, that the nonwhite should cook the meal, serve it, and wash the dishes afterward.

The belief system of the dominant caste includes an ideology of "race" which specifies that one group is "racially superior" to another. As Manning Nash has observed, several preconditions are necessary for the emergence of an ideology of "race": a conflict of interest between "racial" groups; the subordination or systematic disprivilege of one group; the unwillingness of the subordinate group to submit; and the structuring of the division of labor along "racial" lines (1962). Clearly, these conditions are met in South Africa.

Like the dominant ideologies of many stratified societies, apartheid is legitimated by religious belief, in this case a particular interpretation of fundamentalist Christianity. When Calvinist Dutch settlers arrived in South Africa three centuries ago, they faced many challenges that they surmounted with great courage—material deprivation, arduous treks into the unknown interior of the continent, conflict with the indigenous Africans, and a bloody war with British imperialist forces. Believing already (as Calvinists) in the predestination of individuals, the Afrikaners came to believe also in the predestination of entire peoples, and they developed the conviction that their mission was to rule South Africa. The historical experience of the Afrikaners has led to the creation of a highly nationalist, strongly authoritarian, and extraordinarily ethnocentric group, clinging with desperate tenacity to the precarious control of a country in which it is a tiny minority and attempting to preserve its hard-won privilege through a rigid system of stratification based on skin color.

Recent analyses of South Africa take the view that the members of the subordinate stratum do not regard the stratification system as legitimate, although they may have done so to some extent in the colonial past (van den Berghe 1970; Adam 1971). Increasingly, therefore, the system rests on the threat or use of force. As we said earlier, once people's perception of the legitimacy of the state evaporates, only massive force on the part of the state and the ruling stratum can preserve the existing social order. Mandela's view, cited earlier, represents a radically different perception of apartheid from that of the ruling caste, and if his views are indicative of a general consciousness of oppression among blacks, a likely prediction for the future must be conflict between the dominant and subordinate strata. In any event, analysis by an outsider finds Mandela's perceptions, not those of the Afrikaner ruling caste, to be in accord with social reality.

Conclusions

Schools of Thought

Two general theoretical perspectives on the phenomenon of social stratification exist. One approach, espoused primarily by functionalist theorists under the influence of Talcott Parsons (1951), views stratification as an inevitable and even necessary feature of social existence. The other approach, adopted by conflict theorists under the direct or indirect influence of Karl Marx, regards stratification as modifiable, avoidable, and the source of unnecessary injustice and deprivation.

The functionalist perspective on society and culture regards most elements in the social structure as contributing to the survival of the society as a whole. Those elements that generate conflict or instability are considered dysfunctional and detrimental to the system. Stratification exists in most societies, and it must therefore fulfill some valuable function in the maintenance of those societies. The classic statement of this position is that of Kingsley Davis and Wilbert Moore, who contend that some form of stratification is necessary in any society, although they take pains to point out that they are merely trying to explain this situation, not to justify it (1945).

The functionalists argue that some social roles require scarce talents or prolonged training. Not everyone can be a surgeon or a professor of anthropology. All societies must have some method of distributing these positions among members of the population, and those roles that impose greater stress, responsibility, or sacrifice than others must be better rewarded—through wealth, power, prestige, or some combination of the three. In a society that values the services of warriors more highly than the services of priests, the warriors will be better rewarded; a society that values film stars more than garbage collectors will give film stars greater rewards. In this way, people are motivated to train for and to accept the more demanding and socially valued roles. The entire society benefits, because roles that

South African cooking dinner for "white" guests. It is not unusual for such typical middle class South African families to have two or three "black" servants. When interviewed, such families maintain that their servants care for them deeply, feel like part of the family, are glad to be working there. What do you think of this?

demand skills and talents have been matched with the people who offer those skills and talents. Stratification is the inevitable result.

Conflict theorists generally reject the functionalist model of society as a harmonious, well-integrated system in which conflict is abnormal. Instead, they regard conflict over social goals and group interests as intrinsic to any society and as the dynamic for social change. Marx argued that history is essentially the history of class conflict—between the rich and the poor, between those who exploit and those who are exploited (see fig. 15-1). Social stratification, in his view, is created and maintained by one group of people in order to serve their own economic interests. Marx believed that class conflict is the key to historical progress. Every ruling class is eventually overthrown by the subordinate class, which then becomes a new ruling class. The process repeats itself until the final confrontation of capitalists and workers. The victorious workers establish a temporary "dictatorship of the proletariat" to create a new classless society in which the means of production and distribution are communally owned and in which people contribute according to their ability and receive according to their need. Few Western social scientists accept the Marxist

view that historical forces will lead inevitably to a classless society, but modern conflict theorists have been profoundly influenced by Marx's emphasis on conflict between economic interests as the underlying feature of statified societies. And the implication of this conflict perspective is clear: Stratification is merely the product of a particular form of economic organization, not a functional social necessity—although it is certainly convenient for those who benefit from it.

Author's Conclusions

I do not believe that a dogmatic adherence to either a conflict or a functionalist perspective is helpful in the analysis of stratification, or indeed, of any other issue in the social sciences. In general, I do not find functionalist explanations of social and cultural phenomena persuasive; explanations in terms of conflict theories seem more fruitful. But functionalist explanations are by no means useless in every case, and they can even be combined with conflict analyses in some instances. For example, we might analyze the functions of ideology in maintaining a stratified social system, while acknowledging that the system is itself an arena of conflict between the various strata.

It seems to me that functionalism may provide a partial explanation for some forms of social *inequality*, but that it cannot account for social *stratification*. Some differentials in the statuses of individuals, such as those between different age groups in society, can certainly be explained on the grounds that these status distinctions serve some social function. But the more complex phenomenon of social stratification cannot be explained in these terms.

A casual glance at any stratification system will reveal weaknesses in the functionalist argument. The vast earnings of top movie stars, for example, cannot be explained on the grounds that it is functional to pay them more than teachers, police, or the president of the United States. These stars would perform just as well if they were paid much less; they earn a great deal merely because—through their talents, luck, or valued physical appearance—they are in a position to share in the profits of the American film industry. Many people who perform no discernible functions to society are highly rewarded, such as the "jet-setting" inheritors of family fortunes.

The functionalist argument is least convincing in cases where social status is based on hereditary factors, as in caste systems and to a somewhat lesser extent in class systems. Even in the most open class systems, the rate of social mobility is very low. *Stratification does not operate to ensure that the fittest people train for and fill the most appropriate roles; it functions to ensure that most people stay where they are.* People may hold a status for reasons that cannot be explained on a functionalist premise and may then pass this status on to their heirs. Inequality diffuses and increases over time until its ultimate form bears no relationship to its origins, functional or otherwise. In fact, the inheritance of status may be highly dysfunctional for society because it ensures that people do not have equal access to various social roles and so prevents the allocation of positions by merit. Indeed, all stratification systems are fundamentally unjust for this very reason. Consequently, stratification does not necessarily contribute to the maintenance of social order, as functionalists claim. It can, and very often does, bring about a conflict that destroys the entire political and economic system.

However, I cannot accept the Marxist view that historical processes are leading inevitably to a classless society. The idea that some "dialectic" force will bring about this blissful state seems to me to be a piece of mysticism that has no place in the social sciences. This does not mean, of course, that a substantially classless society is impossible to achieve. But it is difficult to see how a complex modern society could function without some concentration of political authority, even if there were equal access to economic resources. I do regard as entirely valid Marx's basic insight into social stratification: that conflict over control of and access to economic resources is the source of all caste and class systems, and that in every case the interests of the dominant stratum are served by the apparatus of the state.

What we must realize is that the issue of social stratification is not only anthropological but also moral. A stratified society is not necessary or inevitable; it is not part of the natural order. Castes and classes are social constructs created in society after society by countless men and women. And since stratification is socially constructed, it must in principle be socially modifiable as well, provided that people are aware of their own capacity to transform the social order.

Summary

Inequality between individuals is found in every human society, but structured inequality between entire categories of people is not universal. This structured inequality, or social stratification, varies considerably in form from one society to another. Most stratification systems can be roughly categorized as either class systems or caste systems.

Social stratification is virtually unknown among hunting and gathering societies, which are generally egalitarian. Distinctions of rank commonly appear in horticultural, pastoral, and early agricultural societies.

Structured inequality based on unequal access to vital resources is found predominantly in mature agricultural and industrial societies. These latter systems are always associated with the state form of government, which upholds the system.

The Indian caste system, the United States class system, and the supposedly classless system of the Soviet Union provide examples of different forms of structured inequality.

Stratification systems may be open, with the opportunity for individual mobility, or closed, without such opportunity. Class systems are therefore open, whereas caste systems (and estate systems, such as that of feudal Europe) are closed.

A stratification system is upheld by the state. The lower strata generally accept the ideology of the upper strata, which makes the system seem inevitable and legitimate. Norms of social distance reinforce the system. South Africa is a striking contemporary example of a castelike stratification system based on race. Its ruling white minority holds an ideology that justifies its rule as being in accordance with God's will. Increasing numbers of the subordinate black majority perceive white rule as illegitimate and unjust. The etic perceptions of the anthropologist accord with the emic perceptions of the subordinate majority rather than with those of the dominant minority.

Some theorists take a functionalist view of social stratification: They believe it is inevitable because it performs important functions in the maintenance of any society. Other theorists take a conflict perspective and believe that social stratification is the outcome of conflict between groups for scarce resources. The author finds the latter view more persuasive.

Annotated Bibliography

Bottomore, T. B. (1966) *Classes in Modern Society.* New York: Pantheon. A short, readable analysis of social classes from the sociological viewpoint. Includes comparative material from both "capitalist" and "socialist" societies and examines the important issue of whether the political elite in "classless" societies is in reality a new form of social class.

Davis, Kingsley, and Moore, Wilbert E. (1969) "Some Principles of Stratification." In *Structured Social Inequality*, ed. Celia Heller. New York: Macmillan. The classic statement of the "functionalist" perspective on classes and castes. The functionalist theory advanced by Davis and Moore has sparked a good deal of controversy, but it remains a seminal contribution to the field.

Fried, Morton H. (1967) *The Evolution of Political Society.* New York: Random House. An influential evolutionary perspective on social stratification. Systematically relates different forms of social and political organization to the level of technological and economic development of the societies concerned.

Hutton, John H. (1963) *Caste in India: Its Nature, Function and Origins.* 4th ed. London: Oxford Univ. Press. The classic analysis of the Indian caste system. Includes much descriptive material, as well as a historical account of the development of castes and an investigation of their current functions and the processes that sustain them.

Lenski, Gerhard (1966) *Power and Privilege.* New York: McGraw-Hill. Lenski provides a critical review of stratification theories from the earliest times and presents his own account of the phenomenon. Like Morton Fried, he systematically relates forms of stratification to modes of subsistence and levels of economic development. He argues further that structured inequality will inevitably tend to diminish in modern industrial societies.

16
Modernization in the Third World

The World Context

Origins and Development through Time

Modern industrial society is rapidly spreading across our planet. Its material success has immensely attracted peoples all over the world; everywhere traditional societies are being transformed by the process of modernization. Until the last few hundred years, human societies tended to institutionalize tradition; today they tend increasingly to institutionalize change and to accept rapid social, economic, and scientific innovation as the norm.

The modernization process is generally considered to have first occurred in western Europe around A.D. 1500. Other societies, notably the classical civilizations of Greece, Arabia, and China, had earlier reached a high level of mathematical, scientific, and technological achievement. But for reasons about which we can only speculate, they did not advance toward industrial modernization. Only in the West was scientific knowledge harnessed to a production-oriented economy, thus launching the process of industrialization that was to transform the world.

The modernization process has involved several distinct but related elements. One of the most important has been the change in the *social* structure of modern and modernizing societies. Unlike so-called traditional societies, modern societies tend to be urban, to have literate classes, and to have an economic system in which industrialism is a major component. They have low birth and death rates and, at least for the higher social strata, a relatively high standard of living. Their expanding economies support mass media and extensive communications networks. People no longer behave primarily as members of a relatively small social group, such as fixed kinship or other traditionally structured social relationships. Nor do they unquestioningly accept the ancestral beliefs, customs, and social statuses handed down to them by their parents. The modern world emphasizes individualism. Social life is based not on hallowed values but rather on freely contracted associations and utilitarian considerations. The impersonal and universal standard of

Sao Paulo, Brazil; such photographs are often used to illustrate "progress" and "modernization" in the Third World. However, we seldom stop to ask ourselves such basic questions as: "Are progress and modernization really the same thing"? "What are our criteria for measuring progress"? "Why do we accept the idea that modernization is inevitable"?

the control of money becomes a yardstick of prestige and worth, replacing such measures as positions in kinship networks and the enactment of traditionally valued behavior.

Another important element in the modernization process is *psychological*. Many writers contend that traditional peoples enjoy close personal attachments and meaningful labor whereas urbanized individuals, isolated from their kindred and converted into mere units of labor in an impersonal productive or bureaucratic machine, are said to lead lonely, atomized lives. Lacking religious or other traditional values and commitments to channel behavior, the modern secularized individual is constantly confronted with moral dilemmas for which the only acceptable guide is his or her own reason. *Alienation* is a persistent theme of those who write about the psychological costs of modern living. To be alienated is to feel oneself isolated in the social world that humans themselves have created.

A third element is the *political* implications of modernization. In most traditional societies, people do not contemplate radical change. As Edmund Leach has observed, their notions of time tend to be repetitive rather than linear, reversible rather than directional and evolutionary (1972). But when people begin to see that they can shape and control their natural and social environments, their attitudes change from acceptance to activism. Political authority can no longer be based on divine right or tradition; it requires a more rational basis. Political modernization involves the differentiation of new, specialized structures out of older and more diffuse ones, and the development of a strong nation-state that demands the loyalty and obedience of its citizens (Huntington 1966:383 ff.).

The final important element in modernization is the *economic* factor. The modern economy is secularized—that is, it functions in accordance with utilitarian rather than religious, sentimental, or traditional requirements. Surplus resources are reinvested in order to further development and are not simply consumed for immediate gratification (see Chap. 10). Scientific knowledge becomes a dynamic, central component of the modernized economy, in which increasingly sophisticated technology is applied to the processes of production and distribution. The owner-ship of strategic resources becomes critical, and as that happens, their ownership by kinship groups gives way to ownership by impersonally organized corporate groups—private enterprise, the state, or a partnership of the two. The modern capitalist economy must continually expand and, to do so, it continually seeks new markets, new sources of energy, and new materials.

The modernization process in Europe was generated by internal factors operating over several centuries. The modernizing forces that have confronted the Third World (Africa, the Middle East, Asia, and Latin America) since the colonial period have been largely external in origin and have resulted from contact with an alien culture introduced by industrialists, plantation managers, conquering armies, missionaries, teachers, administrators, and other colonists. Transformations of whole societies have taken place, not in hundreds of years but abruptly, within a few decades.

The European powers severely dislocated the traditional societies they colonized. Missionaries drew people away from their traditional religious views and attacked cultural patterns of which they did not approve, such as polygamy. Colonial administrations destroyed existing political structures wherever these were seen as a threat to colonial interests. An economic infrastructure was established to exploit the raw materials of the colonies, and local people were drawn into this new sphere of activity as laborers—often simply in order to pay the head taxes imposed by the colonial administration (Dalton 1971:3). A money economy first coexisted with, then superseded, the traditional (frequently subsistence) economies. Severe cultural discontinuity has resulted from the rapid transition from traditionalism to modernization, and the now-independent Third World countries are still beset with problems generated by this headlong process.

Modernization was essentially a Western phenomenon until relatively recently, when it spread outward from Europe to the rest of the world. However, it can no longer be regarded as a process of "Westernization" or the mere transplanting of Western institutions to developing countries. Modernization now takes many forms; the methods, the goals, and the processes involved are markedly different from country to country.

Contemporary Examples

The current transition to modernization is primarily a phenomenon of the Third World, which comprises over a hundred nations in Asia, Latin America, Africa, and the Middle East. These new nations must face many problems that were not confronted by Western Europeans. They often have to adopt and modify foreign models for which there are no indigenous analogies, such as schools, hospitals, and bureaucracies (Black 1966:104). Improved health care has resulted in an unprecedented population growth, which is severely taxing limited resources. Illiteracy rates are still very high in most Third World countries, and the expanding urban areas are being flooded by rural migrants who lack the basic skills required in a modern economy. The developing nations are attempting to modernize by crash education and industrialization programs, but in many cases they lack the means for industrial expansion, and their new school systems create a literate and semiliterate class that has great expectations but few means of satisfying them (Hunter 1969:12–13). Let us look at some anthropological case studies of modernization.

Turkey   D. Lerner and his associates studied the Turkish village of Balgat in 1950 and returned to it four years later (1958). They found that many changes had taken place in the intervening period. The meaning of the complex processes of modernization to ordinary people is well illustrated by Lerner's study of two men in Balgat, a grocer and the village chief.

The grocer, who in 1950 was the only nonfarmer in the town, tried to be Western in his dress and manner and had for years led a life different from that of the other villagers. He yearned for the things of the city—for more modern clothes, a better store, more information about the wider world. When he was asked if there was anywhere else he might like to live, he replied: "America, because I have heard that it is a nice country, and with possibilities to be rich even for the simplest persons" (1958:25). Although the Balgat peasants publicly avowed their allegiance to the traditional ways, some were quietly seeking the grocer's advice on what to do if they went to the city.

In contrast, the Balgat chief venerated the traditional Turkish virtues of obedience, courage, and loy-

Mr. and Mrs. Gerald Conn, missionaries in Ecuador, at their mission at Des Rios with a Quechua woman. Missionaries were among the earliest agents of modernization in the Third World. They were frequently in the vanguard of invading colonialist forces, quickly setting up schools and building churches. The combination of military might and the missionaries' assault on native world views, belief systems, and values often was very effective in demoralizing and facilitating the domination and exploitation of Third World Peoples by imperialist nations.

alty. He did not want any radical social changes, and he hoped that his children would live by the same standards that he did. He attempted to restrain and control change in Balgat. In 1950 he was the only person in the village who had a radio, and he permitted others to listen to it only if they would also stay to hear his official interpretation of the news. When asked if there was anywhere else he would like to live, he replied: "Nowhere. I was born here, grew old here and hope God will permit me to die here" (1958:25).

When Lerner revisited Balgat in 1954, the first change he observed was that the village was now connected to Ankara by road and had its own bus station. The village also had electricity, piped water, and new buildings, and it had come under the jurisdiction of the district police of Ankara, the Turkish capital. In 1950 all the villagers but the grocer had been farmers, but in 1954 most of the male population were wage earners in factories and on construction sites in Ankara. They were spending their new income on food (since they no longer produced their own), machinery, and appliances, especially radios. The chief's sons, who he had hoped would become traditional military men, had become shopkeepers in Balgat instead. One was even a grocer.

The grocer himself had died in the period between Lerner's visits, but he was remembered by some villagers as a "person who saw what lay in the path ahead," even as a "prophet" (1958:41).

Indonesia   Clifford Geertz describes two different forms of modernization in two towns in Indonesia: Modjukuto, a town of about 24,000 people in east central Java, and Tabanan, a smaller town of some 12,000 inhabitants in southwest Bali (1962).

Modjukuto is a highly commercialized market town and is also an administrative center for the surrounding region. During the colonial era, a large trading class developed around the region's plantation economy. Modernization in Modjukuto takes the form of a change from the traditional bazaar economy to one centered on commercial firms. A bazaar economy is characterized by a high turnover of easily portable goods, an irregular clientele, and constantly fluctuating prices that are determined by individual bargaining. Every transaction involves many middlemen, each of

whom takes his own risks and profits. The bazaar has a somewhat ambiguous position in the Javanese social structure, so the status of a bazaar trader is not highly esteemed.

In contrast, an economy centered on commercial firms specializes in shops catering to modern tastes and is oriented toward a steady clientele of people who occupy modern roles, such as teachers and government workers. Firms have fixed prices—an impersonal, stable basis of exchange. By establishing regular relationships with factories, the firms avoid the uncertainties created by the multitude of middlemen involved in the bazaar economy. The entrepreneurs who are trying to set up these firms are generally reformist Muslims whose beliefs resemble the Protestant ethic in that they emphasize the acquisition of material possessions through rational and dedicated work—an orientation that is in direct contrast to the fatalistic ethic of the traditional bazaar.

The Balinese town of Tabanan was traditionally centered around the palace, not the market. Although many egalitarian reforms have swept the country in the course of the century, the nobility are still influential in the region. Balinese belong to many *seka,* or social groups that are organized for some specific goal—temple congregations, residential units, irrigation societies, kinship groups, and the like. Traditionally the nobles were closely linked with the villages; they led some of the important group ceremonies and even called out *seka* for war. The nobles now call on the traditional loyalties of the villagers for their own economic ventures.

The town's largest commercial corporation illustrates this relationship between nobles and villagers. It was founded by local Balinese nobles who assessed village household heads in their area for "contributions" and in return awarded them a share in the business, which was to handle all imports coming into the town. Other businesses, such as a weaving factory, a bus service, and a bookstore were started in similar ways. The villager shareholders do not expect a voice in governing the businesses, and many sell out to larger shareholders. As Geertz points out, corporations built on villager support would not be feasible in parts of Indonesia that are heavily influenced by Western ideas.

There, many traditional institutions have been changed significantly and the emphasis is on individualism and self-determination, not on collectivity and allegiance to nobles. Tabanan's commercial leaders, unlike those of Modjukuto, do not have values resembling the Protestant ethic; rather, they adhere to ancient Hindu values that stress the mutual obligations between people in different social strata.

Innovative leadership in both towns has come from a homogenized group—Islamized traders in one case and traditional nobles in the other—who view themselves as moral leaders of the community. The groups from which the innovators emerge are experiencing cultural stress: displacement of the nobility in Tabanan and the declining esteem of bazaar traders in Modjukuto. In both these transitional but preindustrial societies, the function of the entrepreneur is to adapt customary means to new ends.

Nigeria   In the early 1960s the Nigerian nation and especially its predominantly Ibo eastern region seemed excellent examples of the positive effects of mass literacy, technical education, commercial and industrial development, and other factors associated with modernization. By 1966, however, two national coups had occurred, the Ibo state of Biafra had seceded from Nigeria, and a civil war had started which lasted until the defeat of Biafra in 1970. What was the significance of Ibo modernization and its relationship to the war of secession?

In the early colonial era, it seemed to many outsiders that the Ibo were one of the least likely of Nigeria's ethnic groups to become firmly dedicated to modernization. Unlike the Hausa of the northern and the Yoruba of the western regions of Nigeria, who possessed large walled cities and a tradition of centralized state systems, the Ibo lacked political unity beyond the village-group level until about 1900. The village group, usually a few thousand strong but occasionally including as many as 20,000 people, shared a central meeting place, one or more marketplaces, and various ritual and political institutions, but in most cases there was little centralization of power (Forde and Jones 1950:16). The people were generally poor; the highest population densities were in areas of low fertility.

A major method of achieving social status and prestige among the Ibo was to offer gifts—yams, cowries, and ceremonial feasts—in order to obtain a title that enhanced the bearer's social influence. Ibo society was open in the sense that any freeborn man with initiative and skill could obtain high social status through his own efforts. Unlike many other ethnic groups in what later became Nigeria, the Ibo valued personal economic initiative and individual self-assertiveness more highly than obedience to authority or dependent relationships of the patron-client type.

In retrospect, it seems obvious that the Ibo were in some ways eminently preadapted to accept and exploit the institutions introduced by the British colonists: mission schools, local governments, and an economy formally based on free wage labor and trade. As soon as the British had extended their rule over the whole of Nigeria, the Ibo began to migrate out of their heavily populated areas to other regions in search of new economic opportunities. During the first half of this century, the Ibo population in the Nigerian capital city of Lagos rose from a few hundred to 26,000. Similar migrations to many other Nigerian cities took place, and the Ibo obtained jobs as laborers, traders, craftsmen, and clerks. In the years before independence, many of these people began to occupy positions formerly held by British colonials (Coleman 1971:70–71).

The Ibo were quick to grasp the intrinsic relationship of Western education to the diverse economic and political opportunities that were becoming available. They welcomed the Christian missions and schools, raised funds for school expansion, and sought opportunities in higher education. Although they entered the Nigerian educational system later than some other Nigerian groups, the Ibo were soon disproportionately represented in Nigerian secondary schools. By the early 1950s, the number of Ibo (from the east) at the major university in the western region almost equaled that of the indigenous and prosperous Yoruba, who had begun the modernization process considerably earlier than the Ibo (Coleman 1971:70), and who had a very profitable cash crop economy centered around the production of cocoa. In contrast, the vast, primarily Islamic northern region did not encourage either Christian missions or Western-style schools, which were

viewed as sources of undesirable change. The northerners were consequently soon underrepresented in
the colonial administration and in other positions
requiring literacy.

The Ibo were very prominent in the emergent Nigerian nationalism, and together with the Yoruba, they
produced the first effective leaders of the movement.
The Ibo came mostly from stateless societies, and the
question of why they developed such a strong interest
in an independent national state perplexed some of
their colonial overseers. An obvious socioeconomic
reason is that most of the Ibo homeland was in a relatively poor physical environment. Thus it made financial sense for emigrated Ibo to develop a strong interest
in freedom of movement and room for social and economic advancement inside the country as a whole
where they could share in the benefits of better natural
resources (Coleman 1971:76; Ottenberg 1958:130-131).
Further, J. Coleman has observed that the Ibo's
achievement orientation, assertiveness, independence,
antiauthoritarian views, and tradition of relatively
democratic political organizations equipped them well
for their role in political modernization (1971:73-74;
see also Ottenberg 1958:136-140).

After independence, political unrest increased
steadily in the 1960s and was aggravated by a disputed
1963 census count that greatly increased the population
of the northern region relative to the south. A blatantly
rigged election in the western region in 1965 was followed by anarchy in the area. The first coup d'etat of
1966 was led by Ibo officers and directed against the
central Nigerian government. The new leaders claimed
that the government had been weak and corrupt and
that the coup was in part a movement against regionalism and exploitation of the masses by the privileged
few. The new military government promised to suppress tribalism and corruption, but when it began to
unify the civil service in all regions, it was ousted in
a countercoup directed mainly by northern (Hausa)
army officers (Sklar 1971:49-50).

The easterners, and especially the Ibo, reevaluated
their position in the country in light of the countercoup and its aftermath, which included a pogrom
launched against all Ibo living in the northern region.
The Ibo seceded, thinking their region, now called

Mass starvation was the gruesome result
of the Biafran war. In the West the
Biafran war was "explained" as the result
of traditional tribalism once more inter-
fering with "progressive" modernization.
However, as the author of this chapter
indicates, the causes of the Ibo secession
lay as much with the inherent nature of
the modernizing process as with the
"reactionary" and divisive nature of
ongoing African tribalist sentiment.

Biafra, could form a viable nation.* The United States maintained a position of formal neutrality. The Soviet Union saw support of the northern leaders as part of its backing of the Arab world. Other African nations, fearing that the example of Biafra might encourage secessionist movements among their own ethnically diverse populations, refused to recognize the new nation and strongly supported the federal government. Biafra was slowly defeated.

Throughout the recent history of Nigeria, some forces have pulled toward unity, whereas others have pulled toward ethnicity and regionalism. The process of modernization has emphasized the differences between the Ibo and other Nigerians. The Ibo enjoyed a differential access to education and exploited this advantage. Northerners and other Nigerians resented the technically skilled Ibo, whom they stereotyped as clannish, selfish, and aggressive (Melson and Wolpe 1971:14). The Ibo, the ethnic group so prominent in the drive for a modernized Nigeria, seceded from the nation and were defeated in a civil war that left them impoverished and politically impotent.

Theory

Systems

Theories of modernization, though derived primarily from the experiences of Western Europe, are generally applicable to all modernizing societies. Perhaps the key concept in modernization theory is *differentiation*, the transformation that occurs when a single institution performing many functions is superseded

* One reason the Ibos thought Biafra would be viable was because it laid claim to great oil deposits. The Ibos assumed Britain and the oil corporations would back them to gain access to the oil; but they overlooked several factors: Britain's commitment to "one Nigeria," the nation it had created from a patchwork of hundreds of different ethnic groups; the support of the Nigerian federal government by the big oil companies, who feared that the educated Ibos would nationalize the oil; the oil companies, in addition, did not want to offend the Arab states, who backed the Hausa-dominated federal government because the Hausa are Islamic.

by two or more specialized institutions that divide up the tasks. For example, in traditional societies the family is the basic social unit with a wide range of tasks, including enculturation, production, and consumption. In modern societies, however, many of the family's traditional functions have been taken over by specialized social institutions, such as the schools, and the family itself has become more specialized.

Differentiation can be seen in virtually every element of the modernizing social system. In the economic sphere, a traditional society displays relatively little division of labor, but modern societies produce a proliferation of highly differentiated and specialized occupational statuses and roles. The belief systems of traditional societies are often to a great extent religious in nature, but in modern societies a considerable differentiation in the belief system usually exists, with clear distinctions between religious and secular beliefs (see Chap. 13). The values that guide the conduct of individuals no longer rest primarily on religion for their legitimacy, but may be explicitly derived from instrumental, utilitarian considerations. The political system, too, undergoes marked differentiation: military, legislative, judicial, and administrative functions are often separated, and the administrative arm of government always includes a large number of highly specialized bureaucracies (Smelser 1971:357–364).

A related concept is that of system *integration*. Modernization is not simply the creation of increasingly differentiated institutions and role systems, for these systems must be related to one another if the modernized society is to function. Modernization thus entails a continuing integration of diverse and often novel elements into a rapidly evolving and increasingly complex social system. Many integrative mechanisms may be at work in a modernizing society, such as the national, secularized state and the accompanying ideologies that bring hitherto disparate individuals and groups together in a more encompassing social order.

Three elements are of particular importance in the modernization of a social system: *industrial* and *technological innovation*, the development of *mass education*, and the provision of *mass communications*. Industrialism greatly increases productivity and so provides the economic basis for the development of differentiated, specialized institutions. Directly or indirectly, technological innovation creates a variety of new statuses and roles, new opportunities, and demands for new skills. Modernizing nations must therefore develop an educational system that will teach people the skills, values, and attitudes that will enable them to participate in and contribute to the transformation of their societies (Apter 1965:60, 70–72). Entrepreneur, technician, teacher, administrator, politician—all are new social positions for a traditional society. People occupying these positions are needed, and their skills, motives, and standards of judgment may have to differ markedly from those of their parents. Mass communications play an important part in encouraging people to aspire to modernization and modern roles. Through newspapers, movies, radio, and television, people gain a vision of the possibilities that lie beyond their immediate confines; their orientation changes from immediate to more universal (Lerner 1958:56). Mass communications enable nation-states to reach, influence, and unite their members.

Processes

Modernization is everywhere associated with certain essentially similar processes:

1. **Subsistence farming gives way to cultivation of agricultural products for the market. New jobs are created in trade, manufacturing, and administration.**

2. **The use of simple tools and traditional techniques gives way to the use of applied scientific knowledge and advanced technology.**

3. **Human and animal power becomes an insignificant factor in production as new sources of energy are exploited and individual wage earners operate machines within the industrial system.**

4. **Specialized educational institutions bring literacy to the mass of people and impart skills that are unknown to the parent generation.**

5. **Urban areas develop very rapidly as rural migrants flow into the cities in search of economic opportunities. Urban dwellers are separated from their extended kin, freed from traditional restraints, and placed in new social roles.**

Figure 16-1
Processes of Differentiation

Sociocultural Items	Predifferentiated	Differentiating
subsistence activities	subsistence farming	cash crop agricultural production for markets
technology: tools techniques power sources	hand tools traditional human and animal	mechanical tools scientific machine
education	centered in home	formal institutions
living environment	rural	urban
statuses and roles	few and multi-purposed (ascribed)	many and narrowly defined (achieved)
psychological state	integrated internally and with culture and society	alienated from self and new sociocultural patterns
family	unit of both production and consumption; also primary unit of socialization and other broad functions	unit of consumption only; functions very specialized and narrow
social organization	based on kinship	based increasingly on formal institutions

change to →

6. **The functions of the family change.** It now specializes in limited areas such as the primary socialization of children. Also, wives tend to have more equality with their husbands than they had in the traditional setting (Dalton 1971; Smelser 1971).

Another process that is associated with differentiation and that seems particularly common in urban contexts is *alienation*. The concept of alienation was developed by Karl Marx to refer to the individual's loss of sense of belonging to or controlling the social world. Clearly, any widespread feeling among people that they are strangers in their own society will weaken the force of social norms over individual behavior. Alienation may be encouraged by feelings of relative deprivation—of having less of the good things in life than others. Deviant and criminal behavior, which are everywhere more common in urban than in rural contexts, may result (Aberle 1962:219; Frankenberg 1966:277).

During modernization, some organizations, such as urban mutual aid societies, political parties, labor unions, state and national religions, work to tie individuals into wider systems of common interests (Smelser 1971). Yet modernization may also disrupt the social structure. One effect is the population explosion that has accompanied modernization in every country of the Third World. The extension of modern medical knowledge and facilities to the peoples of these countries has resulted in a dramatic drop in the death rate, especially among infants, but the birth rate has remained high. The continuing poverty of many Third World nations stems partly from their economic inability to keep pace with their unprecedented population growth.

Another major cause of Third World poverty is the systematic destruction of indigenous subsistence economies. The imperialist colonizers converted these economies to specialized cash crop economies. Thus peoples who previously could meet their subsistence needs were forced to participate in an economic system that (a) is beyond their control, (b) keeps the raw materials they produce at artificially low prices, (c) makes them dependent on the purchase of imported manufactured goods for their subsistence, (d) keeps these manufactured goods at artificially high prices, and

The human cost of modernization. This woman is the last surviving member of the Yaghan tribe who lived in *Tierra del Fuego,* the southernmost tip of South America. This group of Native Americans was decimated by contact with Europeans and the new states they created. Measles killed a good many of them; but also they were pushed out of their lands by the expanding societies of Argentina and Chile, who occupied the territory for the purposes of sheep farming, gold mining, and (more recently) oil drilling.

(e) keeps low the wages with which they must purchase these imported goods.

Tension also results when Western-style education has been provided without sufficient availability of modern occupational positions. People who have had some formal schooling are generally not satisfied to return to the life of an agricultural laborer, but they are often unable to find work at the level to which they aspire. The frustration of the youth, who are more eager to modernize than any other segment of the population, is often an important element in Third World national political life (Apter 1965:80).

Analysis

The Folk Perspective

Economists, sociologists, and historians have usually studied the modernization process at the societal or even the international level. Anthropologists, however, have been especially interested in the cultural impact of modernization, and in the adaptations that human groups make to their changing environment. These cultural processes can often be conveniently studied at the small-scale level of case studies of specific groups.

A common response to the disruption of traditional cultural patterns by modernization is the formation of voluntary associations, whose members provide mutual assistance. Two rather different West African urban voluntary associations are useful examples. The first is a "company" of young men and women in Freetown, Sierra Leone; the second is a young people's church group in eastern Nigeria.

Sierra Leone   The voluntary associations of Sierra Leone are described by Michael Banton (1957). In the early nineteenth century, freed slaves from various parts of Africa were settled in the port of Freetown. Years of social interaction with British colonists gave the descendants of these freed slaves a self-concept that was heavily influenced by the social and religious standards of Victorian England. They evolved a distinctive version of English called *Krio*, which had an African syntax but incorporated many European as well as African words, and came to call themselves *Creoles.*

In their attempt to adapt the urban styles of England to the conditions of Freetown, the Creoles established voluntary associations. They took as their models the working-class clubs or societies of industrial England, whose activities included the pooling of savings and mutual aid among members. The Creoles participated in the missionary penetration of West Africa, and their voluntary associations were widely adopted by West Africans, who modified the organizations to fit their own diverse needs. Early in the twentieth century, Africans from the hinterlands of Sierra Leone migrated into Freetown in search of jobs as wage laborers and evolved social groups called *compins* ("companies"). These Africans added innovations of their own, further developing the Creole model.

Banton made a special study of one of the earliest clubs formed among one of the ethnic groups in Freetown, the Temne. The Temne youths who founded the club called it *Ambas Geda, ambas* being the Temne word for "we have" and *geda* the Creole word for "together." Thus the title of the group proclaims: "We (Temne) have people and are bringing them together in a Creole way" (1957:166).

The Ambas Geda association had an elaborate roster of officers, including the following titles: the Sultan, who served as the chief executive official; the Mammy Queen, his counterpart for the women's branch; the *Pa Kumrabai*, a patron who represented the elders and gave fatherly advice; the Second Sultan, who supervised funeral collections; the Second Mammy Queen, who supervised women's dancing; the Judge, who heard major disputes between members of the group; the Doctor, who examined prospective members for disease, attended them with patent medicines when they were sick, and washed the corpse of a dead member before his or her funeral; the Manager, who took charge of seating and lighting arrangements at company meetings; the Cashier, or keeper of the funds; the Secretary, who looked after accounts and correspondence; the Leader, who directed the dancers; the Conductor, or supervisor of the band; and the Sister, who was in charge of a number of "nurses" who dressed in white with red crosses on their caps and provided soft drinks at the club meetings (Banton 1957:169–172).

Nigeria   **The Nigerian church group was the subject of my own study in the early 1960s. In eastern Nigeria, the particular form that a church youth group takes depends on the needs of the community it serves. The group under study, here referred to as the Youth Fellowship, was founded by a bank clerk from a rural Ibo village. He migrated to the city of Onitsha, where he attended a religious training course and was inspired to establish a society for young people of the church. The fellowship began in 1957 with 57 members and was 460 strong by 1962. Most of its members were traders at the Onitsha marketplace, but carpenters, mechanics, printers, bookshop clerks, blacksmiths, shoemakers, electricians, mattress makers, news agents, and shopkeepers were also represented. Very few of the members had been born in Onitsha; most had immigrated from Ibo rural villages, leaving their families and friends behind.**

Onitsha Waterside showing a small shop complex. On the left, a provision store; center, a shoemaker's workshop; right, a battery-charging shop.

The officers of the society were termed *ministers*, titles the founder believed would build interest in the group because they paralleled those used in the national government. The chief officer was the Premier, who formulated policies and represented the group to the public. The Minister of Labor was responsible for building arbors for the Thanksgiving Harvest Festival. The Minister of Evangelism led Bible discussion groups. The Minister of Information informed members when their fellows were ill and also had "intelligence" tasks, such as investigating the religious affiliations of local political leaders. The Minister of Education organized a literary society among the members, and the Minister of Finance took charge of all fellowship funds.

The formal programs of the organization included hospital visits, home visits to sick members, Bible study, choir practice, and games. A stated aim of the group

A view up New Market Road in Onitsha Waterside. On the left a photographer advertises his work.

was to contribute to large projects, such as school construction, in a rural district from which many fellowship members came. On their own initiative, members might start an addition to a church or school building, with one person giving a bag of cement, another free labor or money. The fellowship also took responsibility for the burial costs of a deceased member, including the expense of transporting his or her body to his or her home village—the proper place for burial. Some of the youth fellowship members would accompany the body home.

The activities of the fellowship fostered unity and mutual loyalties among the members. Attendance at weekly church services was strongly encouraged. The services stressed moral instruction, self-discipline, brotherhood, and love. Members were urged to come to the Premier and other ministers when they were in trouble to discuss possible solutions to their problems. The ministers were regarded as "fathers" to ordinary members.

The Minister of Finance would attend weekly youth fellowship meetings. The organization did not officially make loans to members, but when informed of a member's financial plight, the Minister of Finance might ask the group to "put something extra into the contribution box for the needy fellow." In this way a person would be helped but would not feel indebted to any individual. The Minister of Finance also encouraged members to loan money directly to their fellows beyond the church context.

The help the fellowship could provide was widely known. One youth made this appeal to the Premier in 1961: "I have gone to the people for help in getting school fees but could not get. If you can give me a shilling it is a help. Anyone will tell you I am in adversity. From where will the help of my God come? I want to be educated and do something good for my country Nigeria before I die, but who is to help me? Oh, please help me."

A strong feeling of unity existed among members. One informant said:

> Members are my most intimate friends, and this is the general rule. We in the Youth Fellowship call each other brother and have a special handclasp and greeting. We have a common sign, a badge, and we help each other. If there is a job available, I will know my fellow member would do it well for me. If I need a shoemaker and my fellow is one, I will know for certain that he will do the work best and will charge me the least possible amount.

The traders in the Onitsha market who belonged to the youth fellowship also helped each other in the market. As one of them remarked, "If I am a trader and I see my fellow member in a dispute, I must see that that dispute does not become serious. If the police enter in, I must help my fellow member with money to keep him out of trouble."

The Analytical Perspective

Both voluntary associations were formed under the impact of immigration into an urban and modernizing social context. Differentiation and integration are relevant processes here. The individuals involved were entering into role networks that were wider and more diverse than those of the traditional village group. They encountered many economic, occupational, political, and social problems that they were ill prepared to solve.

The desire to achieve prestige, the need to accumulate money, and the demand for Western educational attainment all forced the individual to pursue nontraditional goals. The migrants needed to learn appropriate role behavior in a context where the declared emphasis is on personal achievement rather than the ascriptive status evident in a traditional rural village. Since most immigrants came from families of no great wealth or prominence, they were often without extensive contacts in the city to help them adjust to the unfamiliar environment. They tended to feel alienated in the absence of their former friends and relatives. The immigrants feared that in case of indebtedness, sickness, or death, they might be without friends to help them, visit them, or take their bodies back to their village of birth for proper burial. They wanted to be able to view themselves as important, worthy persons in their new social context, and they attempted to affiliate themselves with organizations that were widely respected.

The voluntary associations provided new organizational and value frameworks into which an urbanizing person could become integrated and so find solutions to his or her most pressing problems within a secure social network. Thus the youth fellowship encouraged members to help one another and to widen their urban contacts by bringing new members into the group. Fellow members provided reliable business contacts and a steady clientele for traders and businessmen. Contacts made through the youth fellowship could help an individual in problems with the police; the ministers could also suggest ways of handling legal

In many ways the Youth Fellowship and the Sierra Leone "company" provided modern substitutes for the social status and social welfare functions traditionally performed by rural kinship networks or village communities. Male and female members could meet suitable mates at fellowship or company activities. Individuals could achieve prestige and status by performing their organizational roles as well. Marriage and farewell ceremonies honored the individual at important points in his or her life. The sick were visited and the dead returned to their villages. The voluntary associations offered a basis for common identity among people coming from different villages; the various group activities and the ritual paraphernalia solemnized the new relationship of "brotherhood."

Both the Nigerian Youth Fellowship and the Sierra Leone *Ambas Geda* were innovative in that they combined new and traditional cultural elements. This tendency can be clearly seen in the names chosen by the Sierra Leone society: The name *Ambas Geda* is composed of both Temne and Creole words, and English, Creole, and Temne names appear in the titles of the officers. The modern title of *Pa Kurumbai* is that of a traditional Temne secret society office; the title *Mammy Queen* was originally applied by the Creoles to Queen Victoria. Some of the other offices, however, had strictly modern titles, such as cashier and secretary. Although the original models for both organizations are European, the African voluntary associations are not mere replicas of their Western counterparts. Their structure, activities, orientations, and functions have been adapted to the unique demands of the modernizing African environment.

The youth fellowship and the company were especially important in the field of role socialization. As Banton has shown, such organizations were "pressure groups for modernization" that proclaimed they were not interested in tribal superstitions (1957:175). In both organizations, the members emphasized self-restraint, industriousness, and the virtues of modernization. They disparaged people who followed traditional values, regarding them as lazy and primarily interested in self-gratification. Both organizations took people who were unfamiliar with the skills of modernization and instilled in them appropriate values, such as the importance of loyalty to their new associates as well as, or even in preference to, their home village group.

Members were given a chance to exercise responsibility in the voluntary association and to gain experience in a variety of unaccustomed roles. The organizations honored individual members when their behavior fit a modernized rather than a traditional ideal, and they encouraged self-discipline and conformity to group standards. The titles of the officials in the Nigerian fellowship were taken from the national political system; familiarity with these offices and their functions helped people become more knowledgeable about participation in the political life of their nation. Similarly, the titles of officials in the Sierra Leone company gave members familiarity with such new roles as doctor, secretary, and judge while building on more familiar concepts such as Mammy Queen and Sultan.

Conclusions

Schools of Thought

Modernization involves not only economic planning and investment of surpluses in new development but also important political and social questions for societies that want to change from their traditional styles of life. Two basic kinds of politico-economic systems can engender and sustain modernization: *capitalism,* which is the private ownership of the means of production and distribution, and *socialism,* the public control of production and distribution. Of course, many varieties of each system exist, and some developing countries have adopted elements of both. But most developing societies are oriented toward one or the other of these

Smoke billows from the oil city of Hamadi in Kuwait. Looks can be deceiving. Although modernization in the Third World often exhibits an impressive technological face, its benefits (in the form of vast new sources of wealth) do not necessarily spread equally throughout the modernizing societies; rather, the benefits of income and high living standards tend to be concentrated in the hands of the ruling classes.

systems, and considerable debate arises over which will best serve their interests.

The capitalist model has many advocates who believe that it can continue to contribute to modernization and economic growth in the Third World. Cyril E. Black, for example, points out that colonialism and imperialism have played a vital part in the development of the Third World in the past (1966). He concedes that high profits and massive resources have been taken

from underdeveloped countries, but he argues that this exploitation did not impoverish the colonies because "they were too poor to produce much wealth per capita or to absorb large quantities of consumer goods" (1966:125). Many of the colonies were not nation-states before their contact with the West, and their cultures were not at a level of technological development that would have enabled them to take advantage of their own resources.

According to Black, the worst "pillaging of wealth" has been done by the new post-independence leaders, who have profited greatly while attempting to move their countrymen from agrarian to industrial ways of life (1966:125). Rather than depriving the colonies of their proper due, Black argues, the imperialist powers gave them the benefits of modernization—new institutions and a technology that gave them the means to develop themselves (1966:125-127).

Black does not see any one form of political system as inevitable in modernizing societies. An authoritarian concentration of power, for example, has generally occurred where the culture had already emphasized extreme political centralization, as in Russia and China prior to their revolutions. According to Black, the weakness of one socialist view of modernization, that of the Soviet Union, is that it projects the Russian experience of central planning and collective agriculture onto countries with vastly different traditions. Underdeveloped nations, Black argues, cannot simply transfer institutions and values developed in one context, whether it be capitalist or socialist, without generating conflicts in their traditional ways of life.

Writing from a socialist point of view, Paul Baran argues that monopolistic concerns have taken the economic surplus produced by underdeveloped or colonial nations and have either sent it abroad, applied it to their own interests in the underdeveloped country, or used it to provide resident foreigners and the native elite with extravagant standards of living (1957). Expatriate enterprises have not used these resources to build or develop native enterprises or markets. When money has been spent on social services for workers, its purpose has been to increase the efficiency of the workers so they could produce more for their exploiters (1957:205). According to Baran, the wealth of the capitalist countries has been based on economic

expansion during times of imperialism, on war, and on systematic waste. The kind of modernization that will help the Third World cannot be achieved in systems where the "means of production remain under the control of private interests which administer them with a view to their owner's maximum profits" (1957:xxix). In a capitalist system, Baran argues, the individual consumer is the prey of profit-hungry exploiters, whereas in a socialist system, people can be taught to want a world "determined by and oriented toward solidarity, cooperation and freedom" (1957:xvii).

Baran further argues that modernization can best be accomplished by expropriating the resources held by capitalists and thus reducing excessive consumption of nonessential items (1957:262-263). The use of the economic and social resources can then be planned within the framework of the socialist economy itself. He contends that massive industrialization and agricultural change must be accomplished together, although industrialization should be given priority in terms of investment. The growth of industry will give agriculture technical resources, and, in turn, agriculture will provide food for industrial workers and raw materials for industry. Socialist governments, Baran argues, must not permit agriculture to develop at the expense of industry, because this would continue the old pattern of providing raw materials for imperialist countries at the expense of domestic economic progress.

Another source of contention is whether or not the effects of modernization are predominantly positive or negative. Some writers believe that people living in small, isolated, nonliterate communities following traditional life-styles experience a richer and warmer existence than those who leave their traditional roots and try to take up modern styles of life in the city. Robert Redfield saw peasants as characterized by "an intense attachment to native soil; a reverent disposition toward habitat and ancestral ways; a restraint on individual self-seeking in favor of family and community; a certain suspiciousness, mixed with appreciation, of town life; a sober and earthy ethic" (quoted in Lopreato 1967:435).

Modern societies generate impersonal and anomic relationships, which often put a heavy strain on individuals. Robert F. Murphy strongly expresses this prob-

Mahatma Gandhi (right), the architect of India's independence from Great Britain, talks to his eventual successor Rashtrapati Jawaharlal Nehru in 1946. Gandhi's name has become synonymous with nonviolent opposition and political leverage, and his struggle in India has served as a model for political struggles around the world.

Mao Tse-tung welcoming Soviet President Voroshilov to Peking in 1957. Mao is Chairman of the Central Committee of the Communist Party, People's Republic of China. The Chinese have not been content to modernize simply in the area of technology. Their revolution of 1948 overturned the previous social order and gave them the opportunity to experiment with new social forms. Their search for economic, social, and political structures which allow for (and encourage) the maximum participation of all citizens in the work and benefits of society, while maintaining efficient and productive organization, is a social experiment far larger in scope than any previously attempted in the history of the world.

lem: "Progress is brought about by the impoverishment of human relationships, for the ability to adapt to the unanticipated must be predicated upon a corresponding lack of attachment to one's established ken and kin" (1967:16).

Many writers take the view that industrial economy and bureaucratic society depend to a considerable extent on objectifying humans as things. An extreme statement of this perspective has been offered by J. H. Bodley, who regards our contemporary "consumption culture" as a transient feature of human history: "If humanity survives, primitive culture will be restored as the most viable human adaptation" (1975:174). Bodley urges that tribal people be allowed to choose whether or not they want to modernize, and that national governments and international organizations support tribal rights to land and resources. Only the people themselves should decide what outside contacts, if any, they want. Bodley cites such negative effects of modernization as malnutrition, urban poverty, various forms of discrimination, and imbalanced ecosystems.

The question of whether industrial society will survive, and if so, in what form, has become more pertinent as people begin to recognize that economic growth has limits—limits set by finite resources, pollution, and expanding populations. For several hundred years, technological progress has permitted humans to raise their general standard of living while multiplying the world's population and taking irreplaceable resources from the earth. In 1650 the population of the earth was 0.5 billion. By 1970 it was 3.6 billion. The world's population is now growing at the rate of 2.1 percent annually and is expected to double again within thirty-three years (Meadows et al. 1972:41). It has been estimated that at the present rate of exploitation of nonrenewable natural resources, raw materials will be so scarce and their cost will be so high that the limits to growth will be reached within 100 years. The question is: Should we attempt to live within our natural limits by controlling population growth and economic development, or should we continue growing as before and hope that new technology will push back the limit and allow even more growth? (Meadows et al. 1972:75, 158–159).

Despite the alleged drawbacks of modernization, almost everywhere the peoples of the Third World seem to have radically new conceptions of what their lives *should* be like. These ideas are often derived from the mass media, accounts of migrants to the city, or the campaign promises of politicians that they will no longer accept "misery, starvation, and disease" as their "ineluctable fate" (Baran 1957:xxx). They believe that economic progress is possible, and they want it in their lifetimes. Joseph Lopreato cites an Italian peasant's view of his traditional life-style: "We peasants are poor earthworms. We live with the animals, eat with them, talk to them, smell like them. Therefore, we are a great deal like them. How would you like to be a peasant?" (1967:434). Baran derides the "anthropological and quasi-philosophical writing" which argues that people of the Third World may "prefer their present state to economic development and to national and social liberation" (1957:17). Such writers, he claims, support what is "backward, moribund and medieval" (1957:253), while accusing proponents of modernization of being ethnocentric.

Author's Conclusions

It seems that rapid modernization in the Third World has most often been achieved through one-party political systems with a high degree of centralized state planning. The cost to individuals, who are deeply tied to their traditional beliefs and ancestral land, has been high. The balance between costs and gains is not easily measured.

I believe that limits should be set on the massive propagandizing of the "new" that makes people want to do the "modern" thing even if it results in diets rich in sugar and fats, machines that are created to make life easier but that destroy the natural environment, or excessive rises in energy consumption. International corporations should not be the ones to set future tastes with their unrestricted advertising campaigns.

I do not wish to make grand predictions about the future of modernization. My own experiences among the Ibo of Nigeria before the Nigerian civil war perhaps gave me a falsely optimistic view of social change. While living in a crowded, noisy Nigerian city, I naïvely asked some local residents if they liked living in the city. The gist of their answers was that the city offered lights, piped water, social services, and entertainment. Unexpected things were happening there. Although some people said they wanted to retire to their traditional villages, they tried to bring modern changes to those villages as well.

I would agree with Bodley that ideally people should have a choice as to what outsiders come to their traditional villages and what changes, if any, are made. But for most of the Third World, the inhabitants have already sampled modernization and have incorporated it into their cultural goals. And would any government be willing to permit traditionalist minority groups to maintain their way of life on large areas of land, a scarce and valuable resource?

I am strongly impressed by the arguments for the natural limits to growth. A research team that has made computerized projections of these limits advocates a state of global equilibrium, in which population and economic growth would be maintained at a finite, stable level (Meadows et al. 1972:177). This should not necessarily mean that the rich nations of today stay rich while the poor stay poor, but rather that "high plateaus of development" can only be justified as "staging areas from which to organize more equal distribution of wealth in the world" (Meadows et al.

1972:197). Technology could continue to work toward recycling resources, decreasing pollution, harnessing solar energy, making more efficient and durable products, and advancing medical science.

This is indeed an optimistic picture. Whether and how such a global equilibrium could be achieved before we have polluted and plundered the earth beyond remedy is a great question. It is difficult to see how any government that is heavily influenced by private corporate interests, or any government, democratic or totalitarian, that is determined to be strong and rich (at the expense of others who will, perforce, be weak and poor), can have the foresight to make radical adjustments in the name of future generations.

Summary

Modern industrial society is becoming the dominant social form in the world. It originated in the West, but a host of social, economic, political, psychological, and cultural changes are now taking place in the Third World as societies move from a traditional to a modern way of life.

Turkey, Indonesia, and Nigeria provide examples of Third World modernization and reveal both the unique problems faced by particular peoples and the common difficulties they must face. Not all societies, however, choose to adopt a Western model of modernization, and in some areas there is considerable resistance to the modernizing process in general.

The major concepts used in the analysis of modernization are *differentiation* and *integration*. Important elements in the modernizing process are the *development of industry, technology, mass communications, mass education, urbanization,* and *changes in kinship structure*. Case studies from Africa exemplify folk perspectives on modernization and modes of adaptation to the modernization process. These can then be subjected to anthropological analysis.

Capitalism and socialism offer two contrasting approaches to modernization. Each claims particular virtues for itself and disadvantages for the other, but most developing nations have opted for some form of socialist society.

Modernization has extremely far-reaching effects, both positive and negative. One pressing problem is that industrialism now poses a growing threat to the natural environment.

Annotated Bibliography

Black, C. E. (1966) *The Dynamics of Modernization.* New York: Harper. A clearly written book that attempts to clarify the major processes of modernization and relate them to their origins in Europe in the Middle Ages. Black outlines seven main patterns of growth and discusses the modernization experiences of numerous countries in relation to these patterns. He also appraises the abilities of Third World countries to adapt to rapid social change.

Geertz, Clifford (1963) *Peddlers and Princes: Social Development and Economic Change in Two Indonesian Towns.* Comparative Studies of New Nations Series. Chicago: Univ. of Chicago Press. A detailed study of Modjukuto and Tabanan, focusing on social and economic change with a strong historical emphasis. The book examines the complexities of the transition from the traditional ways of life to those of industrialization.

Little, Kenneth (1973) *African Women in Towns: An Aspect of Africa's Social Revolution.* Cambridge: Cambridge Univ. Press. This book concentrates on urbanizing women—their various roles as wives, migrants, and workers, and their contemporary problems.

Meadows, D. H.; Meadows, D. L.; Randers, J.; and Behrens, W. W., III (1972) *The Limits to Growth.* New York: New American Library. A book to be read in conjunction with other, more sanguine approaches to modernization; it outlines impending global disaster unless population growth is checked and an equilibrium attained.

17
Peace and Conflict

The World Context

Origins and Development through Time

The problem of aggression is very much on people's minds. Despite international peace-keeping efforts, devastating wars continue to be fought; despite more heavily armed police forces, the incidence of violent crime in our cities continues to rise. Many influential social scientists seem to offer little hope for the solution of these problems. In his modern "classic," *On Aggression*, Konrad Lorenz paints a gloomy picture:

> Unreasoning and unreasonable human nature causes two nations to compete, though no economic necessity compels them to do so; it induces two political parties or religions with amazingly similar programs of salvation to fight each other bitterly, and it impels an Alexander or a Napoleon to sacrifice millions of lives in his attempt to unite the world under his scepter. . . .

> All these amazing paradoxes, however, find an unconstrained explanation, falling into pieces of a jigsaw puzzle, if one assumes that human behavior, and particularly human social behavior, far from being determined by reason and cul-

Karate, the Japanese art of self-defense, is gaining popularity around the world. For some scholars, this is an example of the enactment of basic human aggressive "drives"; for sports enthusiasts, it is a lightning-fast, exciting test of the athletes' superiority; for the devoted karate practitioner, such contests are a context for testing the progress they have made in integrating mind and body: for them, karate is "moving Zen," one of many ways to gentleness. Once again it is clear that what one "sees" is a matter of one's perspective.

tural tradition alone, is still subject to all the laws prevailing in all phylogenetically adapted *instinctive behavior* (1966:228-229; emphasis added).

In his review of human evolution, Lorenz portrays violent beginnings. He sees the emergence of australopithecine hunting weapons as the moment when we fell from grace. Inevitably we turned these weapons on each other while losing the genetically programed rituals that keep other social animals from killing one another. He laments that *Homo erectus*, "the Prometheus who learned to preserve fire, used it to roast his brothers" (Lorenz 1966:231). Upper Paleolithic big-game hunters and collectors of food are portrayed as "warriors" who discharged their aggressive "drive" on a large number of "hostile neighbors."

What hope does Lorenz perceive for us, the descendants of these innately aggressive hominids? If we study ourselves honestly and realize our inherent

aggressiveness, if we use such social devices as intensely competitive sports to displace destructive urges, and if we use humor as a major propaganda vehicle to promote humanistic ideals—over the next century or two the human species might evolve *biologically* to the point where aggressive drives are muted and cooperative forms of social organization are possible (Lorenz 1966:266 ff.).

In Chapters 2, 3, 4, and 5 we presented both facts and arguments that refute Lorenz's position. The major thrust of anthropology is to insist that human behavior is explicable in its own terms and cannot be reduced to innate "drives." Indeed, the human species lost most of its biological programing as it evolved over several million years into a creature that adapts to the problems of existence through learning—that is, through culture.

However, the problem of unpeaceful conditions is real, and as social scientists, we are obliged to address it. We must investigate the contexts of unpeaceful conditions and take careful notice of peaceful conditions as well, so that we can contribute to attempts to create a world where peaceful rather than unpeaceful conditions predominate.

Peaceful conditions are those under which "the individuals or groups concerned gain more advantage than disadvantage. Ideally, it means something even more positive: the harmonious and constructive collaboration typified by a happy marriage, or an effectively run common market" (Curle 1971:1). Unpeaceful conditions are those "in which human beings are impeded from achieving full development either because of their own internal relations or because of the types of relation that exist between themselves (as individuals or group members) and other persons or groups" (Curle 1971:1). In Chapters 13 and 14 we dealt with individuals' internal conflicts; here we focus on relations between individuals and between groups.

What do we know of the origins and development of unpeaceful behavior during the course of human evolution? We have seen (Chap. 4) that aggression plays a significant role in the organization of social life among our nonhuman primate relatives, and it was probably an element in the course of human evolution. Lorenz is correct in pointing out that *Homo*

erectus apparently engaged in cannibalism; in Choukoutien cave we find, among the cooked remnants of horse, elephant, and deer, the remains of some roasted *Homo erectus* skulls with their bases bashed out, presumably to enable the cave occupants to remove and eat the brains (Williams 1973:162–163). But we have no way of interpreting this behavior. Was the cannibalistic feast the result of a raid against a hostile group? Or was it merely the eating of the cave dwellers' own relatives after their natural death—a funeral practice, found among some preliterate populations, that is supposed to ensure the perpetuation of the departed persons in the continuing life of the group?

As we explained in Chapter 2, the evolution of human beings relied heavily on the development of complicated forms of *cooperation*—that is, of peaceful conditions. Thus the story of our evolutionary history tells us little more than what we already know about contemporary social life: Both peaceful and unpeaceful conditions existed and continue to exist. However, as human beings evolved, so did human society; and as social forms and institutions became increasingly complex and differentiated, so too did the forms of human aggression.

This tendency is particularly well illustrated in the evolution of warfare. War has been defined as "armed combat between political communities" (Otterbein 1970:3). A political community is a group of people who occupy a common territory and who have at least one official whose function it is to announce group decisions. Not all human societies practice warfare. A recent study of 652 preliterate societies found that approximately two-thirds do not engage in war (Broch and Galtung 1966). When we examine the distribution of warfare among groups that have been described in the ethnographic literature, a well-defined pattern in the evolution of warfare emerges. Morton Fried has identified four levels or stages in the evolution of society: egalitarian society, rank society, stratified society, and the state (see Chap. 15). Let us examine the nature of warfare as it is conducted at each of these levels of sociopolitical organization and assume (along with Fried) that this sequence represents an evolutionary development, not just the different levels of sociopolitical organization found in the world today.

Figure 17-1
Stages of Sociopolitical Evolution

Sociopolitical Stages		Defining Social Features	Subsistence System	Property Forms	Exchange System	Political Organization
egalitarian society		all members have equivalent access to positions of prestige	unspecialized (beyond age and sex) hunting and gathering; no surpluses	private property limited to nonstrategic forms	generalized reciprocal exchange of food	amorphous
rank society	unstratified rank society	differential access to positions of prestige	development of craft specialists with the production of food surpluses, generally through domestication of plants and animals	private property includes strategic forms	reciprocity plus addition of redistribution	varied but with tendencies toward centralization
	stratified rank society	same as above	same as above	ownership of strategic forms including means of subsistence and production concentrated in hands of one subgroup	same as above with development of incipient market economies	same as above
stratified society		class differentiation based on the exclusion of one (or more) class(es) from access to ownership of the means of production	production of food surpluses through agriculture; elaboration of diverse occupational specialties	all subsistence and productive resources owned or controlled by one subgroup	same as above with elaboration of market economy	transitional—must move toward forming centralized state to protect society from rupture due to inevitable conflicts between the classes
the state		presence of state form of political organization	same as above plus centralized irrigation, road construction, etc.	same as above	same as above	state: centralized institution which maintains social order by protecting interests of ruling class

Egalitarian Society   **In egalitarian societies, which provide valued social positions for every member, subsistence activities are limited to food collecting— that is, hunting and gathering. Living in loosely defined territories at population densities approximating perhaps three people per square mile, these societies make all of nature's strategic resources available to all members; only nonstrategic resources (such as personal adornments) are regarded as private property. This situation obviously makes irrelevant one of the major origins of conflict in more complex society: "The significant sources of food available to simple societies are not foreclosed to any member of the group and . . . usually are available to outsiders as well" (Fried 1967:71).**

Given these features of social life, and given that no power hierarchy exists, the following characteristics of the very limited amount of warfare waged at this . level of sociopolitical development are hardly surprising: (1) No time is devoted to preparing for war; (2) no fortifications are built; (3) no food or supplies are stockpiled; (4) nobody engages in specialized training in the arts of war; (5) there is no specialized military technology—ordinary hunting weapons are used in warfare; (6) combat intensity is low; (7) prolonged actions such as sieges or campaigns do not occur; (8) the most typical action is a raid, involving a brief clash between the two sides; and (9) there is a complete absence of a command hierarchy and consequently minimal combat organization (Fried 1967: 101–105).

Rank Society   **In such societies "positions of valued status are somehow limited so that not all those of sufficient talent to occupy such statuses actually achieve them" (Fried 1967:109). Although in rank societies the labor is divided mostly in terms of age and sex, as in egalitarian societies, work itself is confined to smaller, well-defined geographical territories and generally involves the planting and harvesting of domesticated plants.**

All the sources of interpersonal conflict found in egalitarian society persist in rank society, as indeed they persist in all subsequently evolved types of society. Certain kinds of irritation not present in egalitarian society make their ap-

Crow warriors in Montana. With the introduction of the horse and the development of the immensely successful buffalo hunting subsistence strategy, the Plains Indians evolved into rank societies—and like so many other rank societies, were preoccupied with warfare, especially around the raiding of neighboring groups for horses and the display of great personal valor in fighting. Killing, however, was not of great significance: cleverness, the successful stealing of horses, and a stoical ability to bear pain were valued far more.

pearance in rank societies, although their expression may be relatively subdued. For example, while access to basic resources within the corporate unit is not significantly altered, there tends to be much more consumer's property in rank society. Patterns of reciprocal exchange do operate to keep these things in circulation, but there is a qualitative break with egalitarian societies as accumulation of nonstrategic values is often the basis or means of validation of rank distinctions (Fried 1967:141-142).

An outstanding feature of rank societies is their combativeness. Many seem to be in a relatively constant state of warfare, with group anxiety about war providing a psychological mechanism through which social cohesion is maintained—a crucial factor in the competition for survival. In rank societies, then, warfare is quite intense, and there are distinct military leadership roles. It appears that societies at this sociopolitical level interact with other such societies primarily in terms of military confrontation. However, the actual wars are generally quite brief: Periods between clashes are much longer than the clashes themselves. Thus Fried argues that rank societies are more

accurately described as "oriented around war" rather than as continually *at war* (1967:179).

Stratified Society   At this level of evolution societies are organized in such a way that "members of the same sex and equivalent age status do not have equal access to the basic resources that sustain life" (Fried 1967:186). In other words, basic resources that are still available to all individuals in rank societies have been converted from shared, communal property to privately owned property in stratified societies. At this stage, warfare is even more frequent than among rank societies, and stratified societies have the resources in food surpluses to support military specialists and to wage highly sophisticated combat. "What is more, the cultural development of warfare is more likely to receive special attention in a stratified society as owners can make economically rational decisions to divert resources and labor into military activities" (Fried 1967:215).

The State   Once social stratification emerges, conflict develops between the ruling classes, who control access to basic resources such as land, and those classes who must pay for the right of access to these resources. At this point the state—"a collection of specialized institutions and agencies, some formal and others informal, that maintains an order of stratification" (Fried 1967:235)—arises as a mechanism by which the ruling classes maintain their position of advantage. The state protects itself against both internal and external attacks. It has the social, economic, and organizational resources to engage in extended and highly advanced forms of warfare and has the political flexibility to engulf and administer conquered peoples and territories. The state, not surprisingly, is the most warlike of all sociopolitical forms.

Contemporary Examples

We shall now examine two societies that exemplify different levels of sociopolitical development. The BaMbuti are an egalitarian foraging society; the Jalé are a rank society. The BaMbuti stress cooperation and an overriding concern for the welfare of the group; they adopt a stance of passive resistance toward outside groups. The Jalé are in a constant state of tension induced by the perpetual cannibalistic feuds that structure their social existence. Finally, we contrast these groups with a modern state society, the United States.

The BaMbuti   In 1961 Colin Turnbull published a remarkable account of a group of people living at almost the exact geographical center of Africa, in the heart of the Ituri Forest of the Congo (now Zaire). Here, in the quiet jungle, far from the plantations of the horticultural Bantu villagers, live seminomadic bands of pygmies whom the villagers call the BaMbuti.

The pygmy bands—to whom we were introduced when we considered the case of Cephu in Chapter 12— roam through the jungle, hunting animals both small and large (including elephants) and carefully collecting the many different vegetable foods that grow abundantly in the forest. Although they do trade with the settled villagers for such things as steel knives, they essentially subsist solely through their skill at exploiting the animal and vegetable resources in their environment.

To be sure, it is not an easy life. Bands must move camp frequently, carrying all they possess with them and each time building their huts anew. One con-

sequence of this life-style is: "Old and infirm people, amongst the pygmies, are regarded not exactly with suspicion or mistrust, but with apprehension. In a vigorous community of this kind where mobility is essential, cripples and infirm people can be a great handicap and even endanger the safety of the group. Hence there are numerous legends of old people being left to die if they cannot keep up with the group as it moves from camp to camp" (Turnbull 1961:27). Needless to say, this attitude puts pressure on old people to continue to work hard as long as possible and also makes it less likely that individuals will indulge their infirmities.

One aspect of BaMbuti life that struck Turnbull was the pygmies' free-flowing expression of their feelings. "The pygmy is not in the least self-conscious about showing his emotions; he likes to laugh until tears come to his eyes and he is too weak to stand. He then sits down or lies on the ground and laughs still louder" (Turnbull 1961:50).

The BaMbuti deal with disputes very differently than we do. Quarrels—as we saw in the case of Cephu— are usually settled "with little reference to the alleged rights and wrongs of the case, *but chiefly with the intention of restoring peace to the community*" (Turnbull 1961:118; emphasis added). For example, late one night Kenge stole quietly into Manyalibo's hut in order to consummate a heavy romance with one of the latter's daughters. Unfortunately for Kenge, he was discovered and sent running by the enraged father, who pursued him, hurled sticks and stones after him, and denounced him as an "incestuous good-for-nothing." The charge of incest was untrue, but the second charge, that Kenge had been brazen enough to attempt to crawl over him on his way to his daughter, was indeed something the community considered to be insulting, since etiquette generally required that lovers entertain each other through prior arrangement and away from the camp.

Interestingly enough, Kenge felt little need to defend his uncouth behavior. Laughing almost beyond control, he shouted back that Manyalibo was "making too much noise!" Finally Moke, one of the respected elder males, decided to end the dispute. Whistling for silence, he announced that the noise was giving him a headache. Addressing Manyalibo, he quietly in-

A BaMbuti encampment in the Ituri rain forest, Zaire. The BaMbuti are an egalitarian society; they place a great value on group cohesion and the maintenance of peaceful conditions as do the !Kung San described in Chapter 21.

sisted: "You are making too much noise—you are killing the forest, you are killing the hunt. It is for us older men to sleep at night and not to worry about the youngsters. They know what to do and what not to do."

Whether Kenge had done something wrong or not was relatively immaterial. Manyalibo had done the greater wrong by waking the whole camp and by making so much noise that all the animals would be frightened away, spoiling the next day's hunting. The pygmies have a saying that a noisy camp is a hungry camp (Turnbull 1961:119).

A grumpy Manyalibo finally returned to his hut.

The Jalé   The Jalé live in compact villages in the valleys of the Snow Mountains of west New Guinea. They are cannibals. A major theme of their life, as described by Klaus-Friedrich Koch (1970), is warfare and revenge.

Disputes generally arise over women, over pigs (very important for ceremonial meals), and over garden plots (in which families grow their staples). Any such dispute "may generate enough political enmity to cause a war in which many people will lose their lives and homes" (Koch 1970:47). When two villages are at war, the fighting is sporadic, with agreed upon "cease-fires" to enable the members of the fighting villages to tend their gardens. Even with pauses in the combat, however, after several weeks of fighting, both villages face the threat of famine because their cultivated gardens have been insufficiently cared for. This common danger often induces the combatants to agree to and even maintain a somewhat fragile truce. But although the fighting ends, at least for the time being, tensions remain high because both sides fear the possibility of a preemptive strike by their enemies.

If an invasion appears to be imminent, the women and children leave the village while the men stay behind to defend their territory. The attacking forces will press the battle until the defenders are driven into the men's communal hut, which the attackers are prevented from entering or burning by a taboo. The vic-

torious attackers then often plunder and burn the other village houses, and the defeated side usually abandon their homes and move to another territory. However, hostilities remain a possibility until a formal peace is arranged between the two groups at a ritual pig feast, after which both sides exchange a large number of pigs.

Although these wars are conducted with impassioned brutality, the Jalé generally will not violate specific "rules" for the conduct of warfare. Thus, for example, they believe that "people whose face is known must not be eaten" (Koch 1970:47).

Consequently, cannibalism is normally not tolerated in wars between neighboring villages, and the few incidents that did occur during the lifetime of the oldest . . . men are remembered as acts of tragic perversion. In wars between villages separated by a major topographic boundary

The Jalé are a rank society and exhibit the constant preoccupation with warfare and revenge so frequently associated with this level of sociopolitical evolution.

such as a mountain ridge, however, cannibalistic revenge is an integral part of the conflict (Koch 1970:47).

Wars between neighboring villages usually end within a few years, but interregional wars can easily last more than a generation. In this period both sides send raiding parties into enemy territory. The task of these parties is not to engage in overt confrontation with comparable enemy forces; rather, it is to surprise lone hunters or unarmed groups of women at work in isolated garden areas. These victims are quickly shot with bamboo arrows and, if possible, carried home by the raiders. If an alarm is raised and the raiding party is driven off, they attempt to carry at least one of their victims' limbs home with them. Either the entire corpse or the retrieved limb is then presented to a kin group of one of the raiders who has lost a member in the war. The kin group rewards the party with gifts of pigs, and the heroes are treated to a victory feast in which the victims are steam-cooked in an oven dug in the ground near the village.

> Before the butchering begins, the head is specially treated by ritual experts: eyelids and lips are clamped with the wing bones of a bat to prevent the victim's ghost from seeing through these apertures. Thus blinded, it will be unable to guide a revenge expedition against its enemies. After the head has been severed, it is wrapped in leaves. To insure more revenge killings in the future, some men shoot reed arrows into the head while it is dragged on the ground by a piece of vine. Then the head is unwrapped and swung through the fire to burn off the hair. This is accompanied by loud incantations meant to lure the victim's kinsmen into sharing his fate (Koch 1970:49).

After the body has been butchered and cooked according to custom, the raiders distribute the meat—mostly to the relatives of the person whose death has been avenged by this killing. However, all present get to partake in the feast, and shares of food may even be sent to eligible relatives in other villages.

After the festivities, the host group performs rituals designed to rid the area of the victim's ghost and to protect the village from retaliatory raids. This is the only aspect of Jalé cannibalism that may be considered even remotely religious. Jalé attach no transcendental meaning (see Chap. 13) to eating the flesh of enemies; they eat human flesh because it happens to be delicious—"as good as pork if not better" (Koch 1970:49)— and also because the enemy group had previously eaten members of their own village.

United States What of our own society? How should it be characterized? There can be little doubt that a great deal of unpeaceful behavior is commonplace, that violence in human relations permeates every level of our society.

We support an immense military with sophisticated hardware capable of massive human destruction. We are willing to make overt military struggle a systematic element of our international politics, as in the Bay of Pigs invasion of Cuba and in the Indochina war. We sponsor disruption and even civil conflict in nations whose political system we do not care for, as evidenced by the Central Intelligence Agency involvement in successful and unsuccessful assassinations and coups around the world. A staple of our mass media is the depiction of violent relations between people, from agonizingly realistic movie representations of gory murders and rape to the Saturday morning television cartoons, in which every frustrating situation is "dealt" with by resort to violence: Characters shoot each other, smash each other, blow each other up, disintegrate each other with ray guns, flatten each other with steamrollers, punch, trip, strangle, deep-freeze, and attempt to drown each other. In the streets, the incidence of violent crimes continues to rise, even though our police forces are armed with clubs, Mace, pistols, and shotguns. This high level of violence is also expressed in family life; significantly, many police officers consider their most dangerous task to be the quieting down of domestic quarrels.

On the other hand, we can also observe peaceful behavior in our society: homes in which family members take great pleasure in each other's company, friendships that remain meaningful for a lifetime, cooperative ventures in which people participate with feelings of sociability and goodwill, festivities where warm feelings lift entire crowds into exhilarated moods, moments when individuals are quietly alone

and at peace with themselves, lovers' interludes, Thanksgiving Day dinners, family celebrations, and "blissed out" ashrams of different religious and ethical persuasions.

Both peaceful and unpeaceful conditions exist in our society, as indeed they exist in most, if not all, societies in the world. But it is apparent when we compare societies, as we have done with the BaMbuti and the Jalé, that unpeaceful relations between groups and individuals are not *equally* distributed across all social groupings. In the following section the theoretical tools that anthropologists use to analyze peace and conflict are examined, and some reasons for this unequal distribution of conflict are suggested.

Theory

Systems

As we have indicated, peaceful conditions exist when *all parties concerned gain more advantage than disadvantage;* unpeaceful conditions exist when *individuals or groups are impeded or prevented from achieving their potential development.* But several other central concepts need to be examined. These concepts and the perspective adopted here have been developed by Adam Curle (1971). The following, then, are elements in systems of peaceful and unpeaceful conditions.

Conflict Ultimately, this situation reduces to fundamental incompatibility: "conflict develops when one individual, community, nation, or even supranational block, desires something that can only be obtained at the expense of what another individual or group also desires. This is a conflict of interest, which can all too easily lead to a conflict in the sense of war or strife" (Curle 1971:3–4).

Awareness of Conflict When we think about conditions of conflict, we often envision situations in which all parties concerned share a perception of the issues involved—that is, they agree on the *fact* of the existence of unpeaceful relations, though they may (and indeed often do) disagree on the *causes.* Such situations may be termed conditions of *high awareness of conflict.*

On the other hand, individuals and groups may also be in states of conflict but be only minimally aware that this is the case. We shall call such situations conditions of *low awareness of conflict*. However, it is improbable that all parties involved in a conflict will have a low awareness of the situation. This fact suggests that a dimension of inequality exists in social situations; we refer to this dimension in terms of *balance* and *imbalance*.

Balanced Relationships   **When relationships are balanced, all parties concerned share in an equal division of *power*. They need not have the same *kind* of power, but regardless of the nature of the power each party wields, they *are able to control each other's behavior* to an *equivalent* degree. Thus a stronger person may invoke the threat of physical violence against a weaker person. But the weaker person may take advantage of the fact that both their goals can be attained only through cooperation, and he or she may threaten to withdraw from the relationship if the physically stronger in fact uses violence. The two individuals' sources of power are different but equivalent.**

Unbalanced Relationships   **When persons or groups have the ability to control the behavior of others, this is an unbalanced relationship. The means of control may vary from psychological pressures to threats of violence or economic deprivation. Some pressures are extremely subtle: The ability to keep the other party in a state of uncertainty may often be enough to control the other's actions (Schelling 1966).**

By using these concepts, it is possible to work out a scheme that formulates the systematic relationships between various forms of peaceful and unpeaceful conditions. In figure 17-2, four fundamental types of peaceful relationships are represented. The distinction between *positive* and *negative* peace is important here. *Positive peace* involves the interaction of all parties to their mutual benefit. *Negative peace* entails the avoidance of interaction between parties. This avoidance may be due to external factors, such as geographical obstacles, or may be the result of a deliberate decision to be circumspect made by all involved parties.

Cell 1 of figure 17-2 represents balanced, positive, peaceful conditions. Groups joining together in co-

Figure 17-2
Peaceful Relations
(Adapted from Curle 1971)

	Balanced	Unbalanced
Positive	1 peaceful and constructive associations	2 ongoing relationships of a harmonious nature between unequal partners —for example, parent-child
Negative	3 mutual avoidance by equals	4 avoidance by subordinate of the more powerful

President Ford discussed limitations of nuclear weapons with Soviet General Secretary Leonid Brezhnev at Vladivostok in 1974. U.S.–Russian detente is an example of balanced negative peace.

operative efforts, successful marriages, harmonious federations of states—all are examples of this type of relationship. Cell 2 represents unbalanced, positive, peaceful relationships. There are differences in power between the interacting persons or groups, but the result is harmonious and mutually beneficial. Examples of this type of relationship are healthy parent-child relationships, the successful interactions of state and federal governments, and the vertical relationships in bureaucratic structures (as long as they remain peaceful).

Cells 3 and 4 represent negative peaceful conditions, and it must be pointed out that negative peaceful conditions are probably inherently unstable and may easily deteriorate into unpeaceful conditions. Cell 3 represents balanced, negative, peaceful conditions. Here parties with equal power avoid conflict and at least preserve the appearance of peace; they may even undertake cooperative endeavors. It is perhaps fair to use these terms to describe the current détentes between the three great political powers in the world today: the United States, the Soviet Union, and the People's Republic of China. Cell 4 represents unbalanced, negative, peaceful conditions. In such situations the weaker parties attempt to preserve their integrity by avoiding interactions with the dominant forces—in effect, avoiding conflict in order to survive. Extreme examples are such groups as the Kalahari Desert !Kung San (see Chap. 21); also the Amazon Basin Kreen Akrore Indians, who constantly retreat deeper into the Brazilian jungles rather than allow contact with the expanding industrial society that would eventually exterminate them or incorporate them into its lowest socioeconomic levels, with little hope for anything but a miserably deprived existence. The BaMbuti are another example of this phenomenon. Each incursion into their jungle by another road or new plantation represents for them the death of the forest—and ultimately their own death. "The forest is our home, . . ." they say; "when we leave the forest, or when the forest dies, we shall die. We are the people of the forest" (Turnbull 1961:272).

A similar matrix may be constructed to illustrate forms of unpeaceful relationships. Figure 17-3 also has four cells. Cell 1 represents balanced, unpeaceful relations characterized by a high degree of awareness. The conflict between the Axis powers and the Allies of World War II exemplifies this type of relationship, as do the Jalé groups described previously. In cell 2 we find unbalanced, unpeaceful relations characterized by a high degree of awareness. Conflicts in this category include the initial stages of rebellions and revolutions (which have the *potential* of becoming balanced or even unbalanced in the opposite direction), civil rights movements, and other situations in which the "underdog" is attempting, through direct confrontation, to achieve a balance of power with a view to eventual victory.

Curle identifies cell 4—unbalanced, unpeaceful relations characterized by a low awareness of conflict—as a category that describes cases such as the condition of the Faqir Mishkin of Chitral (a small state nestled high in the Pamir, Karakoram, and Hindu Kush mountains). This peasant class is "one of the most depressed and oppressed groups in the world, but are so dominated, miserable, and ignorant that they are unaware of the abjectness of their position: they accept and endure it as a fact of nature like the bitter winters and

	Balanced	Unbalanced
High Awareness of Conflict	1 approximately evenly matched overt conflict —for example, the Axis powers and Allies of World War II	2 rebellions and revolutions
Low Awareness of Conflict	3 inherently unstable condition; will probably convert to cell 1 or cell 3 of fig. 17-2 or cell 1 of this figure	4 politically unaware groups exploited; inherently equivalent to cell 4 of fig. 17-2

Figure 17-3
Unpeaceful Relations
(Adapted from Curle 1971)

the annual time of hunger" (Curle 1971:12). However, Curle also describes the hatred in the peasants' eyes as they bow before their ruler when he passes. Thus it appears that the Faqir Mishkin are to some extent aware of the conflict of interest between themselves and their feudal ruling class, but they perceive themselves as politically powerless to engage in overt conflict. In a sense the Faqir Mishkin behave in a manner similar to the Kreen Akrore and the BaMbuti, described by cell 4 of figure 17-2, except that they withdraw through sham submissive behavior rather than through flight into the jungle since they have nowhere to go. Thus it appears that the fourth cells of both figures 17-2 and 17-3 are equivalent and constitute a single category that links peaceful relations and unpeaceful relations into a continuum.

The question remains whether the conditions described in cell 3 in figure 17-3—balanced, unpeaceful relations with a low awareness of conflict—exist in the real world. Probably one could make a case that they represent certain very temporary conditions that are inherently unstable—conditions that will, depending on circumstances, either improve in the direction of cell 1 in figure 17-2, become clarified into the conditions of cell 3 in figure 17-2, or erupt into the open conflict of cell 1 in figure 17-3.

Processes

In order to discuss some of the processes involved in the systematic relationships between various peaceful and unpeaceful conditions presented in figures 17-2 and 17-3, let us refer to types that lie at opposing ends of the continuum: cell 1 of figure 17-2—balanced, positive, peaceful relations; and cell 1 of figure 17-3—balanced, unpeaceful relations characterized by a high awareness of conflict.

Perhaps the most obvious form in which the latter manifests itself is warfare, a topic to which anthropologists are devoting increasing attention. Keith Otterbein has produced one of the first statistically systematic cross-cultural studies of warfare, and he arrives at the following conclusions (1970:104–8; the order is altered):

1. "As a political community evolves in terms of increasing centralization, the more evolved [becomes] the manner of waging war."

2. "The more evolved the manner of waging war, the more likely that the political communities . . . will be militarily successful." Thus "it is the military ability of . . . political communities, not simply the level of their political centralization, that determines military success." For example, due to superior military abilities, the politically less developed Indo-European "barbarians" of the third millenium B.C. were consistently able to conquer (at least temporarily) the more sophisticated civilizations of Mesopotamia and the Mediterranean area.

3. The "development of an efficient military organization appears to be a necessary condition for a political community to remain viable in intersocietal conflicts; whereas the development of a centralized political community which is not supported by an efficient military organization will not prevent . . . [it] from being engulfed by militarily more efficient neighbors." Otterbein cites Quincy Wright's observation: "Out of the warlike peoples arose civilization, while the peaceful collectors and hunters were driven to the ends of the earth, where they are gradually being exterminated or absorbed, with only the dubious satisfaction of observing the nations which had wielded war so effectively to destroy them and to become great, now victimized by their own instrument" (Wright 1942:100; cited in Otterbein 1970:108).

4. Contrary to the slogan of the Strategic Air Command—"Peace is our profession"—military development does not guarantee peace. Otterbein found that societies that are highly developed militarily are frequently involved in warfare with their neighbors and consistently suffer high casualties. Thus "no evidence was found to support the theory that a well-developed military system will deter the attacks of enemies."

Anthropologists have been concerned to distinguish between warfare and other forms of violence. One of the more systematic approaches to this problem is the set of distinctions offered by Leopold Pospisil (1971).

Feuding involves prolonged violence (which may be of an intermittent nature) between two groups that are in some form of intimate relationship to each

The Strategic Air Command's motto "Peace is Our Profession" does not square with what we know about warfare: what prevents war is not military preparedness, but rather such things as both sides' perception of mutual interests.

other—often a kinship relationship. The level of violence may range from beatings resulting in minimal injury to armed conflict with resulting deaths. However, an important element of feuding is that the fighting is conducted within the culturally established conventions that both groups recognize (Pospisil 1971:3-4). Otterbein narrows the definition of feuding somewhat to include only those instances of *armed* combat *within* a political community in which, if a person is killed, the kin take revenge by killing either the killer or any member of the killer's kin group (1973:923-24).

Warfare always involves conflict between two or more politically unrelated groups or units. However, it is only one of two types of conflicts that can take place between members of separate political groups. *External self-redress* involves violent actions taken by members of one political group against particular members of another political group; this form of conflict might also be termed *retaliation*. *War*, on the other hand, involves an action or series of actions taken by members of one political entity *in the name of their political group* against members of another politically unrelated entity (Pospisil 1971:6-7).

What are the processes or mechanisms through which it is possible to convert unpeaceful into balanced, positive, peaceful situations (cell 1 of fig. 17-2)? Curle suggests the following (1971:173 ff.):

Research: Any would-be peacemaker must discover all the pertinent facts. This entails not only the list of grievances that both sides harbor but also the economic, social, political, and even ecological elements that have contributed to the conflict.

Conciliation: The peacemaker attempts to alter both sides' perceptions or definitions of the situation. It is hoped that this will lead to changes in attitudes and in the end to changes in behavior.

Bargaining: Eventually disputants must negotiate with one another. If the conflict is unbalanced, the settlement will generally have to be lopsided in favor of the stronger of the two sides.

Development: Sometimes unpeaceful relations can be restructured so that a new situation is created in which both parties have the opportunity to develop their various interests and goals while meeting basic needs. In practice, unless development can be achieved, it is unlikely that any settlement process short of a clear-cut victory for one side will lead to an enduring peace.

Education: **If either or both parties involved do not have access to all the pertinent facts, these should be made available to them—even at the risk of moving a dormant conflict in a situation of low awareness into the arena of highly aware, open hostilities. This process will often lead to the following one.**

Confrontation: **This very wide category includes all the means by which weaker groups in unbalanced relationships attempt to change the distribution of power so that they have at least equivalent power and thus cause the situation to become balanced. The means employed include passive resistance, propaganda, political maneuvering, and armed rebellion.**

Revolution may either produce peace or create new conditions of conflict. If the weaker group in an unbalanced conflict succeeds merely in turning the tables on what had been the dominant group, then unpeaceful conditions continue to prevail. The newly suppressed group will resist the loss of its power and seek to regain it. However, if the weaker group succeeds in depriving what had been the dominant group of access to power, then conflict cannot continue since one side can no longer fight. It is therefore hardly surprising that all successful revolutionaries seek to protect their position by eliminating their enemies' access to power—or by eliminating their enemies.

Let us now examine some case material concerning an extremely unpeaceful situation to illustrate the ways in which anthropologists apply theory to data.

Analysis

The Folk Perspective

The Yanomamö Indians live in the Amazonian jungle region in the vicinity of the Orinoco River in northern South America. Their territory includes the southern part of Venezuela and the northern part of Brazil. They have been reported on principally by Napoleon Chagnon (1968) and Judith Shapiro (1971). In addition, a young woman who was kidnaped by them as a girl, was married to a Yanomamö, and finally was able to escape has written a remarkable document (Biocca 1970).

All accounts of the Yanomamö are in agreement: They are one of the most aggressive, unpeaceful groups of people anywhere in the world. Fighting and intimidating others is a constant feature of their existence. The men demand immediate obedience from their women and frequently beat them to ensure it. The men also constantly "test" each other's "fierceness" and often fight among themselves over issues ranging from real or imagined insults to charges of committing adultery with each other's wives. Moreover, villages frequently wage war against each other, when the men's continual challenges and provocations lead to the ultimate aggressive behavior, the killing of human beings.

Both husbands and wives accept the bullying of the women as a natural form of behavior.

Women must respond quickly to the demands of their husbands. In fact, they must respond without waiting for a command. It is interesting to watch the behavior of women when their husbands return from a hunting trip or a visit. The men march slowly across the village and retire silently to their hammocks. The woman, no matter what she is doing, hurries home and quietly but rapidly prepares a meal for the husband. Should the wife be slow in doing this, the husband is within his rights to beat her. Most reprimands meted out by irate husbands take the form of blows with the hand or with a piece of firewood, but a good many husbands are even more brutal. Some of them chop their wives

The United Nations. Although the U.N. is well-intended, its peace-keeping record is terrible. Why is this? In trying to keep the peace the U.N. makes use of five out of the six mechanisms for converting unpeaceful into peaceful conditions: research, conciliation, bargaining, development, and education. However, more and more oppressed peoples are resorting to the sixth: confrontation—because the first five tend to perpetuate the status quo to a greater or lesser degree. And although confrontation can eventuate in the creation of peaceful conditions, the process is inherently unpeaceful.

with the sharp edge of a machete or axe, or shoot them with a barbed arrow in some nonvital area such as the buttocks or leg. Many men are given over to punishing their wives by holding the hot end of a glowing stick against them, resulting in serious burns. The punishment is usually, however, adjusted to the seriousness of the wife's shortcomings, more drastic measures being reserved for infidelity or suspicion of infidelity. *Many men, however, show their ferocity by meting out serious punishment to their wives for even minor offenses.* It is not uncommon for a man to injure his errant wife seriously; and some men have even killed wives.

Women expect this kind of treatment and many of them measure their husband's concern in terms of frequency of minor beatings they sustain. I overheard two young women discussing each other's scalp scars. One of them commented that the other's husband must really care for her since he has beaten her on the head so frequently (Chagnon 1968:82–83; emphasis added).

When the men fight with each other, they follow a clearly defined hierarchy of levels of violence. At the lowest level, they hurl insults back and forth. If the issue cannot be resolved, the fighting escalates through the following stages.

Chest Pounding   Only two combatants engage in this form of duel at any given time, although they usually represent the honor of larger groups such as families, lineages, or entire villages. One man presents himself to the other, standing upright with legs spread apart, his hands behind his back. The other man sets himself up, carefully measures the distance, rears back, and punches the former as hard as he can in the chest. The recipient of the blow is urged on by his followers to accept another and another. When he can stand it no more, he is entitled to hit his attacker back as many times as he was hit. Thus the more blows he can stand initially, the better his change of "winning"—which he does if his adversary surrenders before receiving the full number of return blows.

Needless to say, chest pounding is excruciatingly painful, especially as the duelers concentrate on

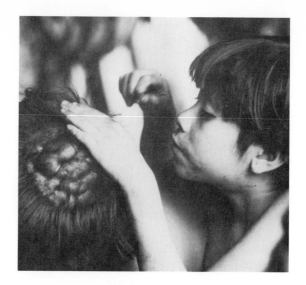

Yanomamö girl delousing her brother's head, which is shaved to display the network of scars he has acquired dueling in many club fights.

Two Yanomamö men chanting to each other right after having engaged in a chest-pounding duel.

Yanomamö side-slapping duel. Here the recipient is in a kneeling position. Note how he holds his arm high to give his adversary a clear target.

hitting each other on exactly the same spot, so that their blows raise great welts on each other's chests. The duel takes an even more painful form if the combatants hit each other while clenching rocks in their fists. After such a duel both fighters will often cough up blood for days.

Side Slapping   The rules are the same as for chest pounding, and in fact, Chagnon suggests that the Yanomamö include it in the same category. Here, however, the duelers hit each other on their sides (rather than on their chests), using their open hands to slap. This duel form may also be escalated, with the combatants hitting each other with machetes or axes—but they strike with the flat side of the weapon since the object is not to draw blood but rather to hurt one's opponent so much that he will withdraw from the contest.

Club Fights   This is the most violent level of non-lethal dueling, and it usually arises from disputes over sexual affairs with women. The rules are essentially the same, but now the combatants present their bare heads to each other and alternately hit each other over the head with eight- to ten-foot-long wooden clubs. This exchange results in split scalps for both, and men pride themselves on the scars that crisscross their heads, attesting to their demonstrated ferocity. In fact, some men keep the tops of their heads shaved and rub red pigment on their scars to make them especially visible. (This behavior resembles that exhibited by some upper-class male German university students before World War II; they used live blades in fencing competitions with the express intent of sustaining prestigious facial scars.)

Spear Fights   Occasionally men agree to fight with spears. They agree in advance not to use their more deadly bows and arrows, but fatalities can and do occur. Any such fatality will usually precipitate the highest level of violence: feuding between groups related to the original combatants.

The highest level of violence in Yanomamö society is about to be enacted: a group of raiders exchange arrows among each other as a mark of solidarity just before setting out to raid a nearby village.

Raids   This form of combat takes place only be-tween villages. Both sides send armed groups of men to raid the other village. An important goal is to abduct women and sometimes children, who are incorporated into the victorious village's social order. A raid usually terminates when a combatant is injured or killed, but occasionally a major massacre of the male population of a village takes place, and the village is destroyed. Those males who survive and those women and children who manage to escape must try to attach themselves to the villages of their relatives (Chagnon 1968:113–137).

The Yanomamö accept this ongoing violence as in-herent in the order of things. They attribute most duels, feuds, and other outbreaks of violence to dis-putes over women. Women are in short supply—the ratio of men to women is 1.2 to 1, even though ap-proximately a quarter of the men die in combat—partly because the infanticide of females is a frequent oc-currence. Further, headmen and others who have cultivated a reputation for ferocity have as many as four or five wives at any given time; about a quarter of the men have two or more wives. Thus sexual access to women is difficult for many young men to achieve through marriage—and they would rather risk the violent confrontations that follow if their secret liaisons with married women are discovered than accept the sexual favors their married elders offer them in return for future services to be rendered.

The Analytical Perspective

The state of affairs that exists among the Yanomamö is hardly pleasant, and if anthropology is to have any credibility as a social science, it must be able to ex-plain why this unpeaceful condition exists, what ends it serves. Anthropologists insist that all patterned be-haviors—even conditions of endemic conflict such as we have described—represent attempts to solve real problems. The solutions chosen by a group of people to solve a particular set of problems may not be the best, but they are often the only solutions available. Once this fact is appreciated, anthropologists can perhaps be of help in the creation of alternative solu-tions (see Chap. 25).

Chagnon describes three levels of alliance between Yanomamö villages: reciprocal trading, mutual feasting, and the reciprocal exchange of women through marriage.

These are cumulative levels in the sense that the third phase implies the first two: allies that ex-change women also feast and trade with each other. Likewise, allies that merely feast together also trade, but do not exchange women. At the lower end of this scale of solidarity lie those villages with which one fights to kill, while at the upper end are those villages from whom one's group has recently separated. Frequently the scale is circular rather than linear: A village's mortal enemy is the group from which it has recently split (Chagnon 1968:101).

Neighboring villages clearly have a stake in main-taining peaceful relations; the ravages of continuous feuding over short distances would be very difficult to bear. Such wife-exchanging villages often deliberately stage chest-pounding duels at feasts. This, Chagnon believes, allows the two villages to display their friend-ship by communal feasting and at the same time to ritually demonstrate their respective ferocity and their unwillingness to be trifled with. This explains some of the systematic conflict of Yanomamö society, but hardly all.

We may push considerably further by examining not only the political context of Yanomamö conflict but the ecological context as well. In using this approach, we shall attempt to answer two questions: What prac-tical ends are achieved by the kind of deadly feuding that is practiced by the Yanomamö? and What is the adaptive significance of the violent male domination of Yanomamö women? In both instances we follow the arguments developed by Marvin Harris in his pro-vocative book, *Cows, Pigs, Wars, and Witches: The Riddles of Culture* (1974).

Harris proposes that the endemic combat of the Yanomamö may be seen as a cutoff mechanism—a device that helps populations maintain their state of equilibrium in relationship to their natural environ-ment, their ecological niche. However, this achieve-ment is not accomplished through the deaths of the male warriors. Even the holocausts of modern mechanical warfare do not deplete populations by killing off soldiers. Despite the massive, intense ground and air war in Vietnam, for instance, the population of that country increased steadily throughout the 1960s. Rather, the ecological equilibrium is maintained for the Yanomamö through conflict because (1) local groups are forced to abandon their gardens before they have exploited the environment to its ultimate capacity, and (2) *female* infant mortality is increased. We will discuss both reasons more fully.

The Yanomamö practice a slash-and-burn style of gardening, in which they cut down trees and other vegetation, burn them, and plant crops in the ashes. However, this practice depletes the soil. The cyclical invasion and destruction of villages and the resulting evacuation of villagers is one social mechanism that helps move populations around, forcing people to allow garden lands to lie fallow. This, of course, enables the soil to replenish itself, maintaining the region's carrying capacity.

In a state of perpetual combat, societies must produce fighters or face extinction. This requirement puts a premium on the raising of male children since men are the warriors. This is true even in a society like that of the Yanomamö, in which women do most of the work related to food production.

Warfare inverts the relative value of the contribution made by males and females to a group's prospects for survival. By placing a premium upon maximizing the number of combat-ready adult males, warfare obliges primitive societies to limit their nurturance of females [because, among other things, there are severe limits on how much protein a nursing mother can provide her children, and this environment is extremely protein deficient]. It is this, and not combat per se, that makes warfare an effective means of controlling population growth (Harris 1974:77–78).

In fact, the Yanomamö attitude toward females as social inferiors to men amplifies this tendency. Chagnon reports that women are greatly pressured to bring boys rather than girls into the world (1968:81); consequently, female infanticide through direct methods such as strangulation or through indirect methods such as abandonment or abusive treatment are frequent

occurrences, especially if the girl is a first-born child. (Normal boy babies are killed relatively infrequently.) A shortage of women therefore exists, and this rather than the male combat deaths regulates the regional population growth: A few men can keep many women pregnant, but limiting the number of females inherently restricts population growth.

This brings us to our second question: Why are Yanomamö males so violent, and why do they direct their violence toward the women? Harris argues that this is simply the extension of the pattern of male dominance that pervades every aspect of Yanomamö life. The question then becomes: Why do Yanomamö women raise fierce, dominant males? After all, as the primary agents of child rearing and enculturation, the women have ample opportunity to raise benign, nonviolent males. The answer is conflict. The women could no doubt dominate the males of their own group, whom they had reared, but once a cycle of conflict with neighboring groups develops, and once males (for whatever reason) assume the burden of carrying on that conflict, the raising of large numbers of fierce males becomes a priority activity for the women of all groups involved.

The fiercer the males, the greater the amount of warfare, the more such males are needed. Also, the fiercer the males, the more sexually aggressive they become, the more exploited are the females, and the higher the incidence of polygyny—control over several wives by one man. Polygyny in turn intensifies the shortage of women, raises the level of frustration among junior males, and increases the motivation for going to war [which includes, among other things, the abduction of women]. The amplification builds to an excruciating climax; females are held in contempt and killed in infancy, making it necessary for men to go to war to capture wives in order to rear additional numbers of aggressive men (Harris 1974:87).

But what is the source of the warfare? Both Chagnon and the Yanomamö themselves argue that it is competition over a scarce resource: women. But the scarcity of women is clearly an artifact of the culture of warfare. Thus another factor must underlie this cycle. Harris suggests that this independent factor is the competition for another scarce resource: protein. Female infanticide does more than make women scarce. It spaces out protein-needing infants and creates a higher ratio of men to women—and it is the men who are the hunters and who consequently provide meat, the major source of protein in the Yanomamö diet (Divale 1970). Warfare creates the conditions (given the tropical environment and the limitations of Yanomamö technology) under which female infanticide will flourish.

Conclusions

Schools of Thought

We feel little compulsion to explain the "normal." When things are going smoothly, peacefully, and harmoniously, we seldom question them. Thus it is not surprising that most of the anthropological literature dealing with peace and conflict focuses on the broad category of violent behavior loosely referred to as "warfare."

Otterbein has reviewed the anthropological literature dealing with warfare and classified it according to the theoretical approaches used (1973). He finds that essentially eight themes run through the literature, each theme consisting of postulated *causes of war* linked to postulated *effects of war*. These linked pairs are listed in figure 17-4 along with the variable that characterizes each pair or theme. "For each pair, the variable that is responsible for warfare (first column) is essentially the same variable that is affected by warfare (second column). For example, the 'innate aggression' approach finds in biological man the cause of war, while the 'effects on species' approach examines the effects of war upon man viewed biologically" (Otterbein 1973:927).

Let us examine each of the approaches identified by Otterbein.

1. Human biology: Books by Konrad Lorenz (1966) and Robert Ardrey (1966) have suggested that human warfare is an inevitable behavior system rooted in our genetic makeup. The general response of anthropologists has been to refute these works on the basis of both theory (they are circular in reasoning and sim-

Figure 17-4
Approaches to the Study of Warfare
(Derived from Otterbein 1973:927.)

	Causes of War	Effects of War	Common Variable
1	innate aggression	on species	human biology
2	frustration-aggression	ethnocentrism	hatred of enemy
3	diffusion	acculturation	spread of invention
4	physical environment	ecological adaptation	natural environment
5	goals of war	patterns and themes	human values
6	social structure	on social organization	social groupings
7	military preparedness	survival value	efficient military organization
8	cultural evolution	origin of the state	sociopolitical complexity

plistically reductionistic) and particular ethnographic data that these works cite but which are apparently incorrect (for example, Lorenz's discussion of the Ute Indians). A useful collection of these critical essays is Ashley Montagu's *Man and Aggression* (1973).

Studies of the effects of warfare on human populations have become more frequent since the 1960s. For instance, William Divale demonstrates that in many primitive societies, female infanticide creates an initial male-to-female ratio of 3 to 2, but this is reduced to an even ratio among adults due to male deaths in war (1970). Frank Livingstone suggests that warfare may provide an environment in which the adaptive qualities of size, strength, and hairiness (for ferocious looks) may be selected for in males (1968). Alexander Alland argues that warfare increases disease among human populations by destroying forested areas, which drives diseased wild animals into contact with domesticated animals human beings use for food, contaminating the food source (1968).

2. Hatred of enemy: **Typified by John Dollard and his colleagues (1939), scholars using this approach argue that, given a military structure, the more frustrated a people become in their daily lives, the more likely they are to go to war. Hatred of the enemy—an extreme form of ethnocentrism—is the consequence of warfare.**

3. Spread of invention: **Some students of warfare are concerned with its invention and the spread of its practice. Perhaps the most extreme diffusionist was W. J. Perry, who argued that warfare was invented in Egypt and spread from there to all other human groups (1917). Acculturation studies focus on how particular societies pick up specific traits of warfare from their neighbors.**

4. Natural environment: **Although few scholars argue that the natural environment is an actual *cause* of war, ecologically minded anthropologists such as Marvin Harris (1974), whose arguments we just explored, do emphasize the ecologically adaptive functions of warfare.**

5. Human values: **An approach that has found favor among anthropologists views warfare as a mode of behavior in which groups of men attempt to actual-**

India tests her own atomic bomb: the spread of military invention.

ize their goals at the expense of other groups. Andrew Vayda argues that only if one understands the thoughts and feelings of Iban headhunters can one satisfactorily explain why they go to war (1969). Such goals of war can spill over into other areas of the daily lives of groups, eventually becoming dominant themes and patterns in their existence. The theoretical groundwork for this approach derives from Ruth Benedict's classic *Patterns of Culture* (1934), which presents a theory of cultural configurations unique to each group.

6. Social groupings: **Structural factors within societies can act as causes of warfare. For instance, in a cross-cultural study, J. van Velzen, H. U. E. Thoden, and W. van Wetering demonstrate that fraternal interest groups (men's "societies") are a recurring source of conflict within local groups (1960). Conversely, the effects of warfare on social groupings can be profound: "it may produce cohesion, stratification, or disorganization" (Otterbein 1973:940).**

7. Efficient military organization: **The fact of being in a state of military readiness can itself be considered a cause of war. This process can operate in two ways: (1) Once a group is prepared to go to war, it is tempted to do so; (2) a neighbor's state of preparation may precipitate a group into a preemptive strike (Otterbein 1973:942). Two sets of cross-cultural studies refute the notion that military preparedness lowers the probability that a group will become involved in conflict (Naroll 1966, 1969; Otterbein 1970). But Otterbein demonstrates that military preparedness does increase a group's survival potential (1970).**

8. Sociopolitical complexity: **A lot has been written relating the causes and nature of warfare to levels of social complexity and political centralization. Fried's efforts (1967), which were mentioned earlier, typify such concerns. Some scholars look at the problem the other way around and investigate how the practice of warfare contributed to the development of the state. The classic statement of this position is by Gumplowicz: "States have never arisen except through the subjugation of one stock by another, or by several in alliance" (1899:119; quoted in Otterbein 1973:947).**

Author's Conclusions

The study of peaceful and unpeaceful conditions is obviously of great social importance. Indeed, the future of the human species may well depend on our gaining an understanding of the circumstances that create conflict and on our developing social, economic, and political forms that lead to peaceful conditions and channel unpeaceful conditions toward productive resolution.

In order to achieve this end, no perspective is expendable, no approach can be neglected. However, we must do more than merely add to the specialized studies described above. A coherent body of theory must be developed that does not isolate the study of warfare from other human behavior; rather, it must conceptualize human behavior on a continuum from the thoroughly peaceful and cooperative to the state of massive violence characterized by war. The work of Adam Curle points in this direction (1971, 1973).

The other requisite for approaching these issues is to resist the all-too-easy pessimistic shrug of the shoulder. Neither peaceful nor unpeaceful conditions should be mystified: There are causes for both. The spirit of Marvin Harris's (1974) down-to-earth search for the material bases of human behavior must inform all productive work on the topic of how human beings can create the conditions under which they can build societies that are inherently healthy and satisfying for all members. To speak of peace under any other condition is a hollow sham.

Summary

This chapter explores the concepts of peaceful and unpeaceful conditions. Two societies are briefly described. The BaMbuti pygmies of the Ituri rain forest have a social system that stresses the ultimate of peaceful conditions: cooperation and an overriding concern for the welfare of the group. The Jalé of New Guinea, in contrast, live in a constant state of tension induced by the perpetual cannibalistic feuds that structure their social existence.

Basic concepts for dealing with these issues are *conflict, awareness of conflict,* and *balanced* and *unbalanced relationships.* These elements are combined into a typology of peaceful and unpeaceful relationships. Three kinds of unpeaceful relationships are defined: *feuding, self-redress,* and *war.* But a series of mechanisms for converting unpeaceful conditions into peaceful conditions exists. These mechanisms include *research, conciliation, bargaining, development, education,* and *confrontation.*

The case of the violent and aggressive life-style of the Amazonian Yanomamö Indians is presented in some detail, including the brutal ways in which men treat women and the endemic state of feuding between villages. The materials are analyzed in an attempt to identify the adaptive significance of these behaviors.

Finally, eight approaches to the study of warfare are explained. The author calls for a synthetic, holistic approach to the study of peace and conflict.

Annotated Bibliography

Ardrey, Robert (1970) *The Social Contract.* New York: Dell. The most recent attempt by the playwright, journalist, and pop ethologist to promote his ethological restatement of Hobbe's *Leviathan.* Beautifully written, dangerously seductive. Montagu (1973) is recommended as an antidote.

Harris, Marvin (1974) *Cows, Pigs, Wars, and Witches: The Riddles of Culture.* New York: Random House. Written with wit, charm, and a deft logic. Harris insists that even perplexing and apparently contradictory behavior is susceptible to explanation. His chapters "Primitive War" and "The Savage Male" are especially pertinent. His approach is a refreshingly nondeterministic ecological materialism.

Lorenz, Konrad (1966) *On Aggression.* New York: Harcourt. The ethological position taken to extremes. All human behavior—especially aggressive and "territorial" behavior—is portrayed as instinctual. Alarming jumps from stickleback fish to human beings are made with the greatest of ease. See Montagu (1973) for perspective.

Montagu, Ashley, ed. (1973) *Man and Aggression.* 2d ed. London: Oxford Univ. Press. An updated collection of responses by anthropologists and biologists to the writings of Lorenz, Ardrey, and Desmond Morris (*The Naked Ape*). All the articles are critical: of the theory of instincts, of the ethnographic data used (especially Lorenz's data on the Ute Indians), and of these authors' profound lack of understanding of the significance of culture.

18
Urban Life

The World Context

Origins and Development through Time

We tend to take urban living very much for granted. Seven out of ten Americans live in urban areas, and their number will probably increase to nine out of ten within the next decade. Yet cities were unknown a mere six or seven thousand years ago, and large-scale global urbanization is almost exclusively a phenomenon of the present century. Our ancestors and their hominid predecessors evolved over an immense period in the context of small groups, but today more than a quarter of the world's population lives in urban areas of 20,000 or more inhabitants. The teeming anonymity of the modern city is a relatively novel experience for our species, but, as we shall see, urbanization is one of the most significant events in the history of human social evolution.

A city is a concentration of a large number of people who engage in specialized activities and exchange their specialities for food produced beyond the urban boundaries. A city can exist only in a society that practices organized agriculture, because a reliable food surplus is necessary if a substantial part of the popula-

An artist's conception of the wall and hanging gardens of Babylon. Babylon still stirs our imagination: the site of the Tower of Babel, which was built and rebuilt numerous times by vain rulers who sought to rival the heavens, Babylon was a small town founded by a desert sheik which grew to be the capital of the empire dominating the entire Middle East in the 18th century BC. Now desert sands drift where once lush, irrigated fields supported a proud people.

tion is to be freed from direct dependence on the land. It is no accident that the earliest fully developed cities occurred after the domestication of plants and animals in such areas as the rich subtropical valleys of the Tigris, the Euphrates, the Indus, and the Yellow rivers.

The earliest cities developed from the technological base of Neolithic agriculture (see Chap. 10). As human beings learned to raise crops and domesticate animals, they were able to produce food in larger quantities on smaller areas of land. This development led to an increase in population density on reduced territories, with a corresponding increase in political and social complexity.

Some time between 6000 and 5000 B.C., the Neolithic revolution crystallized in the hills to the north and west of the valley of the Tigris and Euphrates rivers, near the present boundary between Iraq and Iran. The villages of early agriculturalists gradually spread down into the huge, flooding river valleys as their inhabitants adapted to this novel ecological setting. Date palms were cultivated, and new forms of wheat and barley were developed as staple foods. Marshes provided fish and reeds for building materials. Robert Adams believes that the care of herds of cattle and donkeys became the concern of temple priests, who organized the cultivation of fodder for the animals and took them to pastureland along the riverbanks during the hot, dry summer (1966). Cuneiform records indicate that sheep, goats, and pigs were also raised and that temple artisans wove wool into cloth.

Towns grew up around the temples, and the priests seem to have been the first socially differentiated high-status group. As labor and service specialization increased, trade and redistribution systems developed. More and more people left agriculture to take up non-food-producing occupations in the growing cities. The inhabitants of these cities constructed walled fortifications, initially to defend themselves against wandering nomads bent on plunder but later for protection against attacks from other city-states. Councils of elders chose military commanders, who gradually developed into full-time political leaders.

Palaces were built in Mesopotamian cities about 1,200 years after the temple cities first appeared. Like the temples, the early palaces were large institutions; they had many retainers, including harems, and their grounds contained fields and orchards. An early text from the city of Ur, dated 2900 to 2500 B.C., mentions musicians and craftsmen in at least periodic service to the palace, as well as masons, potters, reed weavers, carpenters, smiths, millers, and brewers.

As Adams emphasizes, the development of these early cities in Mesopotamia was not a uniform process (1972). Even within the center of the region, in classical Sumer, the cities of Uruk and Ur, for instance, had remarkably different histories. Uruk was initially a ceremonial center that by about 3500 B.C. was surrounded by small agricultural villages and settlements. Around 3000 B.C. its population expanded rapidly,

incorporating an estimated forty to fifty thousand inhabitants on the thousand acres that were contained within its defensive wall. This increase in urban population occurred at the same time as a general abandonment of the surrounding villages and settlements. The rural population apparently moved into the city in response both to military threats from the outside and to the consolidation of political authority within the society. In contrast, the biblical city of Ur was never surrounded by intensely developed settlements; nor, apparently, was it ever the recipient of a massive transfer of rural populations (Adams 1972:739). However, Ur did become one of the principal cities of the Sumerian civilization.

In the Nile River valley of Egypt, stratification and kingship developed before cities. In the late fourth century B.C., when the cities of Mesopotamia were already flourishing, Egypt was still populated for the most part by agricultural food producers who lived in scattered villages that were organized into royal estates. But when Upper Egypt conquered Lower Egypt around 3200 B.C., a capital for the newly united empire was established near the border of the two Egypts at Memphis. However, the new capital did not really become a city until the early dynastic period (3100–2686 B.C.); and although these Egyptians were capable of magnificent undertakings, such as the construction of the pyramids, they built no other urban settlements. Cities emerged for the first time in the development of Egyptian civilization during the New Kingdom, which flourished and revitalized Egyptian culture from 1567 to 1085 B.C.

In the New World, the Olmecs built massive temple centers in eastern Mexico around 1000 B.C., but these complexes had no permanent populations. By the time of Christ, however, the city of Teotihuacán was established high in the Valley of Mexico, near the site of present-day Mexico City. The pattern of urbanization was similar to that in Mesopotamia. Agricultural villages developed into temple-centered towns; population expanded, and economic specialization increased; religious and political authority were differentiated; and a kingship and state form of government based on conquest finally cemented the structure of urban life.

Ecologically, Mexico is more varied than Mesopotamia. Although the lakes in the Valley of Mexico provided a good environment for some crops, other staples had to be obtained by trade with other regions. Land was held communally in kinship groups. Warfare was the main way of obtaining new land and resources, and the king, who controlled the army and distributed land to the nobles, was able to keep tight control over the major sources of wealth.

The Toltecs and the Aztecs built many other cities in the next 1,500 years. We have little information about the earliest cities, such as Teotihuacán, and in fact, there is some controversy over whether they were really cities or simply vast ceremonial centers. In contrast, we have a relative wealth of information about the late cities of the Aztec empire because the invading Spaniards recorded many of their initial impressions. However, most of the evidence of the culture was systematically destroyed when the Spanish tried to consolidate their rule and convert the Aztecs to Christianity.

The city of Tenochtitlán, the Aztec capital, stood in a lake on an artificially filled island, square in shape and with sides nearly two miles long. The island was connected to the mainland by three causeways, which had bridges at intervals to let the waters of the lake flow in and out. The city was divided by many canals, and the various parts of the island were connected by drawbridges. Canoes were used to transport people

Urban civilization in the New World. This scale model of Tenochtitlán is on exhibition at the National Museum of Anthropology in Mexico City.

and goods within the city and to the mainland. The most important places in the city were the main temple, containing a religious and educational complex of seventy-eight buildings, and a huge square housing a market that sixty thousand people attended every day. There were also botanical and zoological gardens. The population of Tenochtitlán numbered over a quarter of a million (Diaz del Castillo 1956).

The Aztecs were divided into two main social strata, nobles and commoners. Warriors, artisans, and merchants were all commoners but had higher status than farmers. Children of the nobility were educated in reading, writing, theology, and astrology, whereas the sons of commoners were educated in the fundamentals of religious belief, agriculture, and warfare. Land, the main source of wealth, was tightly controlled by the king.

The archaeological record of other early urban settlements is more limited. We know that cities developed at Harappa and Mohenjo-Daro in western India between 3000 and 2500 B.C., but by 2000 B.C. the empire and cities of the Indus Valley had been destroyed. We also have evidence that city-states developed along the Yellow River in China between 2000 and 1500 B.C. However, little is known about the design of these cities because the buildings were made of wood rather than brick or stone.

There has been considerable speculation about exactly why the earliest cities flourished so spectacularly once the urbanization process was under way. It seems likely that religion played an important part in the process. Priests were probably the first group to develop specialized roles. The earliest city settlements were organized around central temple complexes, which seem to have been the focus of economic and political life as well as religious activity. These temples became centers for economic redistribution, and large dependent populations of artisans and craftsmen developed around them. Eventually political leaders were differentiated from religious functionaries, and the state form of political organization emerged. The early political elites or aristocracies were supported by taxes and tributes, and they built vast projects—pyramids, roads, monuments, canals—by the use of conscripted or corvée labor. These elites sponsored the development of writing, record keeping, the sciences, and specialized arts and crafts. The emergence of stratification gave a tremendous impetus to the urbanization process.

In a controversial study of traditional societies, Karl Wittfogel suggests that in most early states outside Europe, stratification systems developed because an elite group controlled and regulated irrigation (1957). Once a single group could control water, a strategic resource, stratification was ensured, and the elites could consolidate their position through militaristic expansion and the development of a vast redistributive bureaucracy. Wittfogel suggests that because these oriental empires were based primarily on agricultural output and whatever trade the elites themselves fostered, control could be kept concentrated in the hands of the ruling group. The elites were able to perpetuate their power by encouraging a conservative, traditional way of life. Any changes in these hydraulic, agrarian societies were precipitated by pressures from outside the system rather than forces within the society. However, many anthropologists are critical of any theory that attempts to explain early urban development or stratification in terms of any one factor. The processes involved are more likely to have been very complex, and it is probably most useful to consider economic, political, technological, and religious influences as parts of an interacting system.

The earliest cities were relatively small by modern standards: The important city of Babylon covered only 3.2 square miles, and Ur occupied only 220 acres. Later the Romans developed a sophisticated administrative system and even engaged in some methodical town planning, but at its greatest size in the third century A.D., the city of Rome covered only about 4 square miles and had a population of about 800,000. Medieval and Renaissance cities rarely approached even these proportions; the city of a million or more inhabitants did not emerge until the Industrial Revolution. Industrialism vastly increased productive capacities and so made possible a significantly greater ratio of urban dwellers to the agricultural workers who fed them.

By 1800 only one city, London, had more than a million inhabitants, and only 2.4 percent of the global population lived in cities of more than 20,000 people.

Since then, urbanization has increased at an accelerating rate and shows no signs of slowing down. By 1900 some 9.2 percent of the world's people lived in cities. In 1950 the proportion was 20.9 percent and by 1970 it had risen to 27.8 percent. The populations of the United States and Japan are now over 70 percent urban; the urban population of Europe is 64 percent; of Latin America, 36 percent; of eastern Asia, 30 percent; of Africa, 22 percent; and of southern Asia and the Middle East, 21 percent. Now over 140 cities have more than a million inhabitants. By current projections, more than 500 cities will have a population exceeding 1 million by the end of this century, and several cities will have over 25 million inhabitants. By the year 2000, some four-fifths of the world's population will live in cities (Davis:1966). Clearly, any science that hopes to comprehend contemporary human societies must come to grips with the problems of urban life.

Rapid urbanization, which is invariably coupled with industrialization, characterizes both developed and developing nations. In the developed nations, the urban environment is often in a state of physical and social decay. City centers, particularly in the United States, are no longer the focus of the urban community; they are being abandoned by those who can afford to flee to the rapidly expanding, more congenial suburbs. But in the developing world, urban problems are frequently even more acute. Cities often have a high proportion of terribly poor shantytown dwellers, and urban services are commonly inadequate to meet even the basic demands of the inhabitants. Population growth rates are much higher in developing than in developed countries, and the natural population increase in the cities is complemented by a steady stream of impoverished rural migrants, most of them poorly educated and ill equipped to meet the challenges of urban living. The densely populated cities of the Third World typically lack the amenities that we associate with urbanism in the already industrialized West.

Urban anthropology is a relatively new branch of the discipline. Several factors have caused the growing anthropological interest in cities. The traditional subjects of anthropology—the so-called primitive societies—are rapidly disappearing under the impact of industrialism and urbanization; it is now virtually impossible to find any people, however remote, who have not been affected in some way by these processes. The consequences of urbanization for traditional societies are necessarily an important concern of modern anthropology. Another reason for the growing interest in cities is the sense that anthropology should be relevant to our own society, which is primarily urban. Although they have had some problems in adapting their field methods—which were originally developed to describe small-scale communities—to the modern urban context, anthropologists are now applying their distinctive paradigm to contemporary mass societies.

Contemporary Examples

Anthropologists studying modern urban complexes usually focus on one or more segments of the population and stress urban cultural differences. Virtually the entire range of anthropological concerns can be studied in cities, but the subject of urban anthropology proper is those aspects of human behavior that are unique to city living or are somehow different in large-scale urban contexts than in small-scale rural ones. Anthropologists have been particularly interested in patterns of modernization as traditional agrarian towns become industrialized, spurring migration from the countryside and creating neighborhoods of "urban villagers." The cross-cultural study of the poor in urbanizing and industrializing societies has also become an important anthropological concern. Let us look at some examples of anthropological studies describing these phenomena.

Lima, Peru   One of the most common results of rapid migration into the cities of the Third World is the appearance of squatter settlements on city fringes. These neighborhoods usually develop haphazardly, but William Mangin gives an interesting account of the deliberate creation of such a squatter settlement, or *barriada,* in Lima, Peru (1973). Mangin traced the fortunes of two squatters, Blas and Carmen.

Blas, the son of a plantation laborer, came to Lima with a friend and found a job as a waiter. He moved in with Carmen, who had originally come to Lima as the unpaid domestic servant of a dentist who owned property near her rural village. They rented a two-room adobe house in a crowded area. Living conditions were wretched: Only one filthy bath with a frequently clogged water tap served ten houses, and crime was rampant. A fellow waiter told Blas about a planned squatter invasion of some state-owned land—the site of an annual folk music festival. The invasion was planned for the middle of the night on the eve of a national holiday. The group concerned was composed mainly of people from one of the highland Indian clubs, which provide migrants with opportunities to meet new friends and learn about the ways of the city, and a number of soldiers stationed at a nearby base. Blas and Carmen decided to join the group.

Just before the invasion, the group wrote a letter to the wife of the Peruvian dictator, stressing their patriotism and explaining that their terrible poverty had driven them to this desperate action. The members had planned the streets and assigned lots beforehand. Thirty-one families arrived quietly during the night in taxis and borrowed trucks and quickly set up huts of straw mats, each with a Peruvian flag in front. The police came the next morning and told them to leave, but everyone stayed and no violence occurred. In the next few days the original families were joined by twenty or thirty others who had heard about the invasion.

Blas and Carmen soon built a concrete house facing the street and constructed a brick wall around their spacious lot. Carmen established a small shop in the front room, and Blas continued his job as a waiter. The residents elected a committee to govern the settlement, particularly to control the movement of families in and out of the barriada. Most of the adults in the barriada were born in highland Indian communities and speak Quechua, but their children reflect their parents' urban commitment and speak only Spanish. Parents have high aspirations for their children and insist that they go to school in order to get good jobs. If their aspirations are frustrated due to a lack of job opportunities in the city, Mangin predicts that these now-patriotic citizens may become more revolutionary.

Bombay and Bangalore, India   William Rowe describes a difference in migration patterns between two Indian cities (1973). In Bombay the migrants are generally closely tied to their villages, whereas in Bangalore they tend to cut their rural ties and become urbanized.

Rowe studied the rural village of Senapur, which sends many sons and husbands to Bombay to work, primarily as factory or tramway laborers. Several men from the village, usually relatives, migrate together, choosing the area of the city that has a high percentage of people from their caste and local area. Relatives help them find jobs and housing, and the migrants' wages are sent back home to their families, who often need the additional income to survive. Although the Bombay migrants spend most of their lives in the city and come back to the village for only a month or so each year, they retain their identity as members of the village and of their rural extended families. Their wives and children often remain in Senapur, and all their associations in Bombay are with kinsmen in similar situations.

In contrast, the majority of migrants to Bangalore are rather poor, landless members of the untouchable caste who do not have obligations to their native villages. They migrate from villages in the rural south in which the untouchables are isolated rather than incorporated into the local social network. These migrants move with their wives and children to mud hut slums around industrial cities such as Bangalore. Kinship ties are important in the process of migrating to the city, but once they are in the city few migrant families ever return, and few send any money back to their villages.

In both cases the city is used as an extension of village needs. The two urban migration patterns differ according to the social organization and caste relationships of the rural villages concerned.

Washington, D.C.   Ulf Hannerz, a Swedish anthropologist, studied aspects of the culture of the black ghetto in Washington, D.C. (1969). He describes several general kinds of ghetto life-styles. Some people are "mainstreamers," following what is essentially a white, middle-class life-style within the ghetto. They are concerned with being respectable, having nice homes, and raising well-educated children. The men are the authority figures in the family, and they spend most of their leisure time with their wives and children. These families enjoy the highest income and the greatest job stability in the community.

On a street in the city of Bangalore, a woman in the traditional *sari* passes a woman in a miniskirt. Each has adapted to urban living in a different way.

The pottery seller makes his living in the urban environment of Bombay by utilizing a traditional craft and marketing technique.

A second life-style is that of the "swingers." These are young people who spend most of their free time in the company of their peers, partying, drinking, and flirting. Wives may divorce their husbands if they leave home too frequently in their attempts to maintain a swinger life-style after marriage. Swingers change jobs and are unemployed more frequently than mainstreamers.

Another life-style is that of the "street families," whose members spend a great deal of time on the ghetto street corners in order to escape their squalid, crowded apartments. These households are often headed by a single or divorced woman. Street-family women tend to bear children from their mid-teens until middle age, so three generations may live in a single household. The members of street families are often oriented more toward their peers than toward the loose household unit, and husbands and wives often have separate spheres of friends.

A final life-style is that of the "street-corner men." They are often peripheral members of street families, but they conduct most of their lives outside the context of the family. Poorly educated, these men are often unemployed or hold very low-paying jobs. They spend much of their time on the streets, talking to friends, drinking, and gambling. Although they talk about their friendships as being strong and loyal, most of their relationships with other people are superficial and temporary.

Most of the ghetto life-styles are not considered respectable by middle-class white society, but Hannerz argues that they are socially structured responses to poverty and lack of job opportunities rather than a matter of a culture without values or standards.

Medan, Indonesia   Edward Bruner reports on the significance of ethnic identification in the city of Medan on the Indonesian island of Sumatra (1970, 1973a, b). Medan has many competing minorities rather than a single, dominant ethnic group. Bruner studied one ethnic group, the Batak, and found that their social world changes drastically when they migrate from the village to the city. In the village everyone is Batak and can be placed in some kinship relation to everyone else; even non-Batak strangers can be accounted for by adopting them into a clan. Batak migrants to the city

establish permanent residence there, but since they can no longer classify all their associates on the basis of kin ties, they have to reorganize their view of the social world. By experience and by the creation of stereotypes, they learn what to expect from members of other ethnic groups.

On the whole, Batak try to avoid contact with ethnic strangers, whom they perceive as dangerous: One never knows what might make them angry and drive them to use poison or magic in revenge for some imagined insult. Bruner suggests that the most amicable relations exist between ethnic groups that do not compete directly for jobs and other resources, while the most intense hostility is between competing groups. Since Indonesia has no dominant or national ideal for cultural behavior, each ethnic group maintains its own language and customs, and communication with members of other groups remains limited.

Los Angeles, California   Another example of ethnic interaction is provided in an unpublished sociolinguistic study by Shirley Fiske (19--). The Navajo are the largest tribe among the approximately 60,000 Native Americans in Los Angeles, and they are also the most segregated, both from "Anglos" and from other Native Americans. The Navajo women whom Fiske studied categorize ethnic strangers along two dimensions: dark-skinned/light-skinned and belonging/strangers. Navajo are classed as dark-skinned and belonging, whereas Anglos are light-skinned and strangers, with the extra stigma of being termed *anaa'i*, "enemy." Other Native Americans are categorized as being more like Navajo or more like Anglos, depending on their degree of acculturation to white society. Mexicans are identified as being close to Indians; blacks and Asian-Americans arouse more ambivalence.

Most of the social interactions of the Navajo women are with people they consider most like themselves; they say that they do not know how to act with people they consider different. When they do have contacts with Anglos, Navajos use terms of address that reflect the separation and status differences they perceive. They are likely to address an Anglo as "Mr. Jones," but tend to address a Navajo of the same status by his or her first name. (This may be because most Navajos come into contact with Anglos through Indian boarding schools, where harsh Anglo teachers emphasize the superiority of Anglo customs and language.)

Fiske describes two very different Indian neighborhoods in Los Angeles. The central city, where most new immigrants arrive by bus, is made up of old and often dilapidated apartment buildings. The only place for children to play is in the heavily congested streets, so mothers try to keep their children at home. Social contacts among these Navajo are almost exclusively restricted to other Navajo, primarily neighbors and kinfolk. Although most households contain a single nuclear family, the boundaries are flexible enough to accommodate relatives and the children of relatives. Kin often live very near one another.

The southeast district, by contrast, is much more suburban. The Navajo here are somewhat wealthier and live in duplexes and low stucco apartments. The children often have yards to play in. Navajo in this area are more likely to interact with other Native American groups but social contact with Anglos is still restricted.

Most Navajo in Los Angeles plan to return to the reservation, and many return every summer for extended visits. Like the immigrants to Lima, Bombay,

Living in the inner city of Los Angeles means moving more often, accepting more dilapidated housing, keeping possessions to a minimum; a less comfortable environment than in suburban Los Angeles, where Native Americans are more settled and usually more affluent.

Suburban living in Bell Gardens is the choice of many Indians as an alternative to the inner city environment.

and Medan, they have come to the city to seek economic opportunities that are not available in the countryside. (Fiske has found that the average family of 6.2 persons has an average income of $5,420, yet even this meager income is more than could be earned in Arizona on the Navajo reservation.) Yet the Navajo persist in trying to maintain their separation from other ethnic groups and to preserve their own language and way of life.

Theory

Systems

A major problem in urban systems analysis is the definition of the boundaries of the city and the relationship of the city unit both to its environment and to its own subunits. Anthropologists have not reached any consensus on how to define the basic units of urban study. Some anthropologists argue that the city must be defined in relationship to the rural, national, and international social systems of which it is a part. There is also controversy over whether urban boundaries should be considered in geographic, demographic, or social terms. And anthropologists have studied ethnic groups, neighborhoods, social classes, and occupational groups as important subunits of urban populations.

Aidan Southall suggests that cities should be defined socially (1973). He argues that the traditional definitions of density, which are based on area and population size, give an incomplete picture. Southall proposes that the number of culturally differentiated roles and the number of relationships each person has with other individuals on the basis of these roles be used as an index of *social density* to supplement the more commonly used index of *population density* (number of persons per square mile).

The whole idea that localized density is an important defining characteristic of a city is questioned by Conrad Arensberg (1968). Not all cities, he points out, are densely populated centers of political and economic power that are physically and socially distinct from the countryside. Quite separate port towns, pal-

ace towns, and commercial towns existed in sixteenth century Japan, and the literary elite was scattered throughout the countryside. Similarly, Latin American temple centers served as the focal point for dispersed populations that gathered only periodically for markets and ceremonies. In some contemporary cities, such as Bombay, migrant populations make the urban area an extension of a rural social structure (rather than vice versa). And suburbanization in the United States disperses economic and political centers while creating powerless ghettos in the central cities. In all these cases, town and countryside interpenetrate, and social, economic and political power is dispersed rather than focused in a dense city center. Arensberg suggests that we conceptualize cities as large, permanent concentrations of people that link together other communities within the society. His approach ignores the concepts of density and complexity.

Another view, propounded by Anthony Leeds (1968), is that institutional structures—rather than cities as wholes—should be the primary unit of study, both within cities and when examining ties between the city and the countryside. To understand how Lima's *barriada* functions as an institution (an organized set of social roles) in a patterned relationship to the other units of the city, one must study not only a single *barriada* but many different *barriadas* in Lima. *Barriadas* must then be compared to alternative communities of the very poor in Lima and to squatter settlements in other cultures. Only then can the anthropologist arrive at abstract statements about regularities and variations in squatter settlements (if there are any) and show how these units function within cities.

J. A. Barnes points out that we form our concept of an institution by observing patterns of interpersonal relationships (1968). In order to describe urban institutions or the boundaries of the city itself, we might trace the actual networks of interpersonal relationships within the city. Barnes includes both formally defined social roles and casual, fleeting contacts in his notion of relationship. He distinguishes dense networks, where everyone has relationships with everyone else, from sparse networks, where few overlaps exist. He also distinguishes multiplex relationships, where two people have several links, from simplex relationships, where there is only one tie. Network analysis can be used for identifying social units such as ethnic groups within the city because interaction within a unit ought to be intensive, whereas relationships outside the unit should be fewer and more transitory.

Processes

Anthropologists have been particularly interested in the processes of social and cultural interaction in urban contexts and the ways in which these processes differ from those found in small-scale, traditional communities.

In the small community, people live in primary groups and engage in primary, face-to-face contacts (Redfield 1960). Their interpersonal relationships are generally based on emotional ties. In modern urban society, however, people tend to interact with others largely in terms of narrowly functioning segmented roles—as bank tellers, teachers, garbage disposers, commuters (Wirth 1938). Their interrelationships are based largely on utility, and the roles each individual plays are frequently designed to serve his or her personal ends, usually economic ones. The urban dweller often knows many more people than the person living in a rural village, yet he or she has superficial relationships with most of them.

Unlike the small-scale community, the city tends to have a heterogeneous culture; its population is often ethnically, religiously, and socially diverse. The highly specialized urban division of labor leads to the development of corresponding specialized areas within the city, such as shopping or entertainment precincts. Confronted with this juxtaposition of different peoples, values, and modes of life, city dwellers tend to become comparatively tolerant of nonconformity and tend to develop a relativistic perspective on the social world. They are considerably less likely than their rural counterparts to take their own norms and values as unquestioned absolutes (Wirth 1938).

The behavioral heterogeneity that results from the intermingling of diverse cultural elements leads urban residents to depend less on tradition as a guide to thought and conduct; they tend to exercise comparatively greater personal freedom of decision in such questions as their area of residence, choice of spouse, religious affiliation, and selection of occupation. The processes of informal social control that are so powerful in rural communities lose much of their force in the cities and are replaced by formal institutions and processes: laws, courts, judicial procedures, administrative regulations. This reduced influence of traditional social controls is reflected in the sharply increased rates of socially disapproved behavior of every kind: suicides, drug addiction, sexual variance, mental disorders, prostitution, property crimes, and interpersonal violence. The kinship system, too, is profoundly affected. It no longer functions as a self-contained economic unit, and the kinship network is less and less the organizer of social behavior.

In examining how social systems operate, the urban anthropologist often encounters the basic problem of how his or her participation affects the processes under observation. This is not simply a methodological problem of personal rapport with informants—it must be analyzed as the systematic interaction of people with very different political and economic allegiances and goals. Anthropologists themselves participate in a sociopolitical system, usually through a university that itself has a systemic relationship with the sociopolitical system they wish to study. The implications of this situation are exemplified by the sources that anthropologists use to find out about the social system under study and the sources from which they get money to support their research projects.

Most urban studies made by anthropologists have been of politically powerless groups, largely because the anthropologist has easier access to these groups than to any others. Numerous studies describe ghettos and squatter settlements, drug addicts and prostitutes, tramps and immigrants, but virtually no studies delineate the subcultures and life-styles of urban political and economic elites. This omission is significant, because many anthropologists have seen the concentration of wealth and political power as the spur to city development. Some anthropologists have recently called for more studies of elites and government bureaucracies (for example, Hymes 1974), even though such studies are difficult to accomplish. It is important to remember that "objective" analysis of social processes is impossible, since the observer always has a relationship at some level of analysis to the system he or she is observing.

Urban anthropology also brings the problem of ethical responsibility into sharp focus. Urban populations are usually literate and can read anthropologists' accounts of their communities. They quickly become aware of the political implications of studies of poverty and other controversial issues and may be unwilling to cooperate with an observer who will not let the community leaders have veto power over what is put into print. The poor, for example, often do not wish to be "described" from someone else's point of view; instead, they want anthropologists to document information that will be useful to them. In an urban context, knowledge is a political resource, and the anthropologist has to be aware of the interrelationships of his or her own needs (notably the need to publish in order to get or keep a job) and the needs of the people under study.

Some approaches to urban systems have focused not on social roles and structural units but on action processes and decision making. Luther Gerlach and Virginia Hine have studied social transformation movements such as the Black Power and ecology movements, both of them primarily urban phenomena (1970). Gerlach and Hine focus on the processes by which these movements recruit members and maintain commitment to an ideology that redefines the members' view of the world and serves as a program for social change.

Analysis

The Folk Perspective

Any urban social behavior can be viewed through the concepts of the observer (such as "social roles" or "decision-making strategies"), or it can be viewed through the concepts of the participants (such as the Navajo categorization of Anglos as light-skinned stranger-enemies). My own study of hostility between

J. P. Morgan and sons at a Harvard Commencement. The very rich are the least studied people. Why, do you think, does social research focus so heavily on the *powerless* rather than on those who actually rule society?

right
Police tend to over-react in controlling Chicano political protests. The police perceive a threat to social order while Chicanos believe they are merely exercising their right to free expression.

Chicanos and the police in San Jose, California (Geilhufe 1972), illustrates the way in which folk and analytical perspectives can be used to analyze social interaction.

Mexican-Americans, who make up about 20 percent of the population of San Jose, are concentrated in the poorer areas of the city. There is widespread hostility between Mexican-Americans, particularly the youth, and the municipal police. Chicanos are a segment of the Mexican-American population who use their ethnic identity for political ends. The study was concerned only with those Chicanos who were politically active and trying to influence the San Jose Police Department.

Chicanos saw the police as racists who discriminated against Mexican-Americans. They' believed that the police harassed Mexican-Americans by intensive and unnecessary surveillance and brutalized Mexican-Americans by beating them or using other means of force. Chicanos accused the police department of racist policies because less than 5 percent of its officers were Mexican-American and because it did not respond to community complaints about harassment and brutality.

The police denied practicing discrimination and declared that they wanted to hire Mexican-American officers, but Mexican-Americans did not perform as well as Anglos on the qualifying tests. The police officers pointed to their Community Services Unit as an innovative attempt to encourage community dialogue and participation, and to their Internal Affairs Unit, which investigates complaints against individual officers, as an indication of their sensitivity to community complaints. The officers who were interviewed dismissed the Chicanos as self-serving radicals who were seeking publicity and who did not represent the community.

In response to Chicano pressure, the municipal government attempted to mediate between the community and the police. The city's Human Relations Commission, composed of a small investigative staff and seventeen volunteer commissioners, examined

complaints against the police and other city agencies. Yet the views of the members of the Human Relations Commission reflected the tremendous differences in the perceptions of Chicanos and Anglos, even when the members supposedly had access to the same information. A Chicano commissioner told me:

During the Labor Day parade, a guy named ——— was beaten [by police] and after that some militants broke some windows at the Police Department. Human Relations was instructed to let Internal Affairs handle it because the officer was supposed to be wrong, but now [three months later] we can't get a report on it because the case is still pending (Geilhufe 1972:131).

Government institutions are often caught in the middle of conflicts between Chicanos and other constituents, or between Chicanos and members of other government agencies such as the police. Not wanting to antagonize either side, government representatives often do nothing.

An Anglo commissioner told me:

> There was a riot or near riot on Labor Day. A Chicano dame started yelling that her son had been beaten. The police are so paranoid that they won't make the investigation public—after all, the officer said the boy's leg was already broken when he got there and the ambulance was already on the scene, but Internal Affairs still refuses to release the report (Geilhufe 1972:132).

When the perceptions of both "sides" conflict like this and there is no way for a third party to judge between them or to add still another perspective, analysis is very difficult. The attempts by the city government to mediate between the two groups were usually interpreted by each as partisan, and there seemed no way to reconcile the polarized viewpoints.

The Analytical Perspective

My strategy for analyzing the situation was to ignore the issue of who was right and who was wrong and to focus instead on why the two groups held such divergent views of the problem. I found that the situation could be viewed in terms of ideology and the functions of ideology in regulating social interaction. Both the Chicanos and the police were employing strategies to maximize the social distance between themselves and the "enemy" group. Each group defined its goals in terms of political control over police activity. The police wanted independence and autonomy; the Chicanos wanted effective control of police behavior and policymaking. The two goals were mutually exclusive, so any cooperation or compromise with the opposing group would contradict the ideological goals. By stereotyping each other as extremists, the Chicanos and police could dismiss each other as less than human and therefore outside the realm of reason and communication. Both groups were then free to focus their political strategies on the city council and city manager, who held the ultimate authority over the police department, its officers, and its budget.

The council and city manager were reluctant to impose policies on the police department, and they tried to give the appearance of responsiveness to the community while avoiding any direct confrontation with the police chief. Both Chicanos and the police could communicate more effectively with the council than with each other; the council responded both to informal political pressure and to public demonstrations. Both groups were frustrated because the council and manager were not strong, decisive mediators; they tended instead to move slowly and hesitantly, trying to satisfy all the parties involved. But by directing the political contest to the arena of the council and manager, the Chicanos and the police avoided intensifying the existing hostilities.

Thus the concepts of stereotypes, ideologies, political strategies, and the distribution of political power help us to analyze this situation. Chicano and police stereotypes of each other directed their political strategies toward a third group (the council), which had to respond to both of them; all three groups seemed to wish to restrain the political conflict to a socially manageable level. As long as this continued to be the case, we could expect a lot of "sound and fury" but little violence or direct confrontational politics.

Conclusions

Schools of Thought

Oscar Lewis first introduced his notion of the *culture of poverty* in *Five Families* (1959), a study of the poor in Mexico City. He refined and expanded it in *La Vida* (1966), a study of a Puerto Rican urban family. Lewis suggests that the urban poor in industrial nations share "a subculture, with its own structure and rationale, as a way of life which is passed down from generation to generation along family lines" (1970:68). He argues that the poor are socialized into this subculture and its limited expectations, which restrict their options and prevent their escape from poverty. The culture of poverty emerges, Lewis contends, after long periods of deprivation in stratified, capitalist societies, and it perpetuates the plight of those who are born into it.

Lewis describes the culture of poverty with a list of seventy interrelated social, economic, and psychological traits. The most important of these are negatives: that the poor *do not* participate in the wider social,

Urban poor in Rio de Janeiro, Brazil. Often social research reflects the values of the dominant society and produces theories such as Oscar Lewis's "culture of poverty" which winds up "blaming" the victims themselves for the structure of the society which victimizes them.

economic, and political institutions of the society; that they have *little or no* social organization beyond the nuclear family; that they profess middle-class values but *do not* live by them; that at the family level there is *little* personal support and much disorganization; and that individuals are characterized by "a strong feeling of *marginality,* of *helplessness,* of *dependence,* and of *inferiority*" (1970:72).

Lewis's formulation has been extremely influential, and it was widely used in the public policy analyses that resulted in the federal "war on poverty" during the mid-1960s. However, his concept has been much criticized on both methodological and theoretical grounds.

For example, Charles Valentine suggests alternative interpretations of Lewis's data by arguing that the lack of participation of the poor in the major social institutions is not due to a culturally perpetuated life-style but rather to the structure of the society as a whole, *which is beyond the control of the poor* (1968). Valentine argues that the poor actually have a differential participation in social institutions. For example, they have a higher rate of participation in the police-courts-

jail complex than the rest of the population, but they participate less in desirable or steady employment. As we have seen, evidence shows the existence of social organizations among the poor beyond the family, such as migrant voluntary associations, *barriada* self-government, and grass-roots social change movements.

Some critics have taken the view that any distinctive subculture of the poor is the *consequence* and not the cause of their continuing poverty. The poor, it is argued, have abandoned middle-class behavioral standards because middle-class culture is utterly irrelevant to their immediate situation. Elliott Liebow (1967) and Ulf Hannerz (1969) have studied ghetto residents of Washington, D.C., and contend that the discrepancies between the middle-class values often professed by the poor and their actual behavior is the consequence of a lack of money. Hannerz points out that when ghetto dwellers have a stable source of income, they tend to become "mainstreamers" concerned about middle-class respectability. He attributes the varieties of family organization and disorganization in the ghetto to external conditions, such as limited job opportunities. Carol Stack argues that the black family is organized differently from that of the white middle class because it must be flexible enough to provide support for its members through all the fluctuations imposed by a life of poverty (1970).

Anthony Leeds criticizes Lewis for making generalizations about culture on the basis of family studies and autobiographies only (1971). A culture would have to include linkages of families

> through such networks as true and fictional kin ties, friendships and neighborhood links; through associations and agencies; and by virtue of real or attributed membership based on race, ethnicity, or other criteria. . . . Such a system is neither conceptualized nor analyzed [by Lewis] with respect to the postulated culture of poverty so it is impossible to determine . . . why [in Lewis' work] one is not dealing with, say, family neuroses (1971:232).

Leeds also calls for more rigorous cross-cultural comparison of communities of the poor, beyond Lewis's studies of a few families in Mexico and Puerto Rico.

Author's Conclusions

I believe that anthropologists bring to any research a bundle of cultural attributes that strongly influence the way they select behavior for observation and the way they explain the behavior they have observed. Anthropologists need to pay as much attention to their own values and assumptions as to those of the people they are studying. Social research itself is rapidly becoming another urban phenomenon, and the structural interrelationships between anthropologists and the community are an integral part of any study.

Einstein's conceptualization of the physical universe as relative, depending on the position and speed of the observer, holds equally true for the urban social universe. A multiplicity of perspectives exist within the city, and there is no guarantee that the analytical perspective of anthropologists has more validity than the folk perspectives of the people they study. The perspectives simply serve different purposes in different social contexts. Unfortunately for the poor, the analytical notion of the culture of poverty was more useful for the policy makers who planned the war on poverty than the folk perspective of ghetto populations—that they should receive money or employment directly instead of being taught a "new" culture.

The critiques of Lewis's work reflect the problems of defining adequate units for study and constructing generalizations about their structure and functioning. Urban anthropologists have not adequately defined the subunits of cities, and they do not agree upon the best techniques for generalizing about vast urban populations. Valentine's critique also raises the problem of the analysis of whole systems and whether or not a subculture can be understood if it is isolated from the larger social structure of which it is a part.

In order to understand urbanization processes, I think Arensberg's conceptualization of the city as an institution that links together other communities is most useful. The development of early cities was spurred by linkages created by political and economic elite groups rather than by the poor. Cities are better seen as specialized systems of relationships rather than as physical concentrations of people, and urban phenomena should be studied in terms of a wider framework than has been used thus far.

Anthropologists will have to use interdisciplinary techniques if they are to understand cities from a systemic perspective. Institutional linkages imply politics, economics, ideology, values, psychology, and so on, and an evolutionary view implies ecological adaptation. Participant observation is not an adequate tool for such comprehensive analyses, although it is valuable in providing case study validation. Supplementary sources of information must be used if we are to look at entire social structures.

If urban anthropologists are to be effective, they must become more involved in policy-making studies and in carrying out policy based on anthropological research. For instance, anthropologists have produced scathing critiques of the culture of poverty, but those critiques were not adequately presented to government agencies. Systemic interdisciplinary research requires more involvement if it is to be useful.

Summary

Urban society first arose some five or six thousand years ago, for reasons that are still debated. Urbanization is one or the most significant developments in the history of human social evolution; by the end of this century, about four-fifths of the world's population will live in cities.

A major concern of urban anthropology is the impact of urban life on migrants from traditional rural communities. Examples from Peru, India, Indonesia, and the United States reveal some of these problems.

Many problems of urban life are profitably analyzed by paying attention to the vested interest and ideologies of groups, such as the police and Chicanos of San Jose who find themselves in conflict.

Urban anthropology is a relatively new field of anthropology, and anthropologists are still adapting their methods—originally developed for the study of small communities—to the requirements of urban research.

The urban environment differs from the rural environment in several important respects: it is more anonymous, more tolerant, more heterogeneous, and more diversified and specialized. The incidence of all forms of social pathology is higher in cities than in rural areas.

A major focus of anthropological research in urban areas is poverty. An important concept in this area of research is that of the "culture of poverty." Some anthropologists contend that the urban poor all over the world share a distinctive culture whose value system tends to trap them and their children in poverty. This view has been strongly criticized by other anthropologists, who deny the existence of such a "culture" or assert that it is an adaptive response to, rather than an inherent feature of, poverty.

Annotated Bibliography

Breese, Gerald, ed. (1969) *The City in Newly Developed Countries: Readings on Urbanism and Urbanization.* Englewood Cliffs, N.J.: Prentice-Hall. A useful demographic survey that relies heavily on urban geography. Also contains some data on migration and social change and a section on the changing economic roles of cities.

Leon-Portilla, Miguel, ed. (1962) *The Broken Spears: The Aztec Account of the Conquest of Mexico.* Boston: Beacon. Perhaps the only emic account of an early urban civilization. The narrative focuses on the Spanish invasion but includes much information about social life.

Mangin, William, ed. (1970) *Peasants in Cities: Readings in the Anthropology of Urbanization.* Boston: Houghton Mifflin. A valuable collection of readings, with an emphasis on Latin America and migration.

19
Social Research and Ethics

The World Context

Origins and Development through Time

Modern anthropology was born in the second half of the nineteenth century, a product of an expanding Western society bent on bringing the entire globe into its political and economic orbit. The discipline grew out of attempts by Euro-American scholars to understand the diverse cultures that the conquest of the world was bringing to their attention. No longer were the options of human existence limited to the customs of Europeans, past and present. New vistas of human potential were opened up to the scholarly imagination.

From the outset, however, the attitudes of anthropologists toward the peoples they were studying were adversely affected by the fact of Western conquest. The first anthropologists were armchair scholars who relied on the reports of soldiers, missionaries, and adventurous travelers for their information. Both these reports and the anthropologists' interpretations of them were laden with prejudiced judgments about the supposed "racial" and cultural inferiority of the newly subjugated populations. Later anthropologists tried to avoid the errors of armchair scholarship by going into the field and gathering firsthand information. These fieldworkers produced much more detailed and less biased accounts, but they were nonetheless representatives of conquering colonial empires among the conquered. By and large, they accepted the rightness of Western domination.

Only since World War II, as the peoples of the non-Western world have successfully challenged the colonial system, have anthropologists begun to examine with a critical eye the historical and political context of their research. The now almost complete disintegration of the European colonial empires and the continuing resistance of non-Western peoples to Western economic and political domination are forcing anthropologists to give up long-held assumptions about their relations to the peoples they study and to redefine their role in light of new social realities.

As a first step in redefining their discipline, some anthropologists have begun to analyze the field's his-

British colonial Basil Duke, who designed all of the buildings in Yei, speaks with his Sudanese successors to the rural council. The French and the British took very different approaches to colonial rule: the former utilized "direct rule" under which all political offices were filled by French people; the British used "indirect rule" under which they appointed members of native populations to enact their policies. Although on the surface the British system appears to be less oppressive, this is inaccurate: the local forms of social and political organization, usually based on kinship networks, became distorted and caused a great deal of confusion and bitterness on both sides. Thus the British were often very disillusioned at the "dishonesty" of their native appointees who insisted on favoring their relatives; and the native groups resented the attaching of formal political power to what had previously been merely positions of social prestige, and felt betrayed when their politically powerful relatives, under great pressure from the British, tried to resist granting them favors.

tory and leading ideas (see, for example, Hymes 1969; Asad 1973). This self-examination has centered on two issues: (1) the extent to which anthropological research has contributed to Western imperialism by providing information and analyses to policy makers engaged in the suppression of popular revolt, and (2) the extent to which procolonialist and proimperialist commitments have distorted the development of anthropological theory.

In the last decade numerous studies have documented the close relationship between anthropology and government policy making. Many of these studies have focused on the role of British social anthropology in colonial Africa, where the relationship was particularly explicit. Not only did the colonial administration use the results of anthropological research in designing policies aimed at maintaining British rule (Feuchtwang 1973), but also, many anthropologists helped in the tasks of administration. In a series of frequently quoted articles, Bronislaw Malinowski, a leader of British anthropology, contended that anthropologists could and should offer practical help to colonial administration (Malinowski 1930, 1945). Malinowski argued against some of the more flagrant injustices committed by the Western powers (James 1973), but he accepted the colonial system itself without question. Marvin Harris, the best-known contemporary historian of anthropological theory, has observed: "The basic premise of Malinowski's position involved him in the assumption that the Europeans had a right to be governing the Africans" (1968:557). Nor was Malinowski's position rare among British anthropologists. Support for colonial rule was a universal tenet of functionalist anthropology under the British empire (Feuchtwang 1973; Stauder 1974).

American anthropology has played a social role similar to its British counterpart, especially since World War II, when the United States has been the dominant Western power. Although the United States does not have an extensive colonial empire, it has exercised political and economic domination over other countries, especially the Third World states of Africa, Asia, and Latin America. U.S. hegemony, like earlier British colonialism, has used social scientific research to aid in policy planning to protect its supposed international interests. Over the past several years, a series of exposés has revealed that the U.S. government has re-

cruited social scientists, including anthropologists, to do research for the planners of counterinsurgency operations in Latin America, Southeast Asia, and elsewhere. These projects have included empirical studies of "sensitive" areas of the world where anti-U.S. movements had developed as well as theoretical research aimed at predicting future trouble spots (see Jorgensen and Wolf 1970; Horowitz 1967).

When we turn to the influence of proimperial ideology on the development of anthropological theory, some striking parallels between social practice and social theory emerge. The common presumption of anthropological thinkers of the nineteenth century was that non-Western peoples were inferior to Europeans in their ability to organize civilization and carry out intellectual activity (Harris 1968). It was supposed that the European "race" and its society had reached a higher stage of evolution than the non-Western "races" and cultures. In the words of the eminent Belgian anthropologist Jacques Maquet:

> The reader of the ethnological literature of that time [before World War I] was under the impression that savages were very different from the Europeans, that they had queer if not repugnant customs, that they lived in a pre-logical world of curious superstitions, that their strange behavior—deemed a submission to instinctive impulses—was explainable only by a theory of racial inferiority, and that their ways of life were therefore inferior to "civilized" ones. All ethnographic books were far from blunt in expressing these ideas, but of the writings of that time, most were more or less explicit in their assertion of these views (1964:50).

This racist view of non-Western peoples was not simply the product of prejudiced scholars' imaginations. It was an academic version of the ideology of expanding colonialism. The conquest of the world needed moral justification, and the image of non-Western peoples, especially Africans, as barbarous and uncivilized freed Europeans from any obligation to treat them as equal human beings. To quote Maquet once more:

> The partition of Africa into "spheres of influence," military expeditions into the dark continent of "cannibals," and establishment of

colonial rule were made morally acceptable—even virtuous activities—since the colonized peoples were so different, so inferior, that the rules of behavior for intercourse with civilized peoples were obviously not applicable. Indeed, the "savages" were considered fortunate to be put under the rule of a Western country, to be obliged to work, and to be forbidden to engage in their immoral practices. The colonial expansion required that a certain image of the non-literate peoples be accepted by Western public opinion. On a more refined level, ethnology supported that picture (1964:50).

Early anthropologists' acceptance of the ideology of colonial conquest prevented the development of sound theories of social evolution and functioning. The ideology blinded anthropologists not only to the brutality of colonial subjugation but also to the complex history and social organization of conquered peoples, whom Western ideology had defined as "savages" without history or culture. By 1910, however, the period of colonial expansion had ended, and a period of consolidation was well under way. In this new era the crude racist ideology of conquest was no longer appropriate (Stauder 1974). Populations that had been conquered had to be administered, and to be administered, they had to be understood. The colonialists had to come to grips with the details of the social organization of their new subjects in order to integrate them into the colonial economic and political systems. In these new circumstances a new, more objective anthropology developed, particularly in Britain. Termed "functionalist anthropology" by its founders, Bronislaw Malinowski and A. R. Radcliffe-Brown, it sought to understand how non-Western societies worked, how their various institutions fitted together to produce a stable social order.

The growth of the new functionalist anthropology was greatly stimulated by the prevalence in the British colonies of a policy of "indirect rule" (Stauder 1974:38-40). Under this policy, adopted to provide efficient and cheap administration of the far-flung British Empire, native political leaders and institutions were to be used as far as possible to carry out colonial policy. The studies produced by functionalist anthropologists provided much of the necessary background information on how these native institutions worked.

Functionalist anthropology was an improvement over earlier approaches, if only because it had more respect for the facts of social life. Nevertheless, it had serious theoretical weaknesses related to its colonialist origins. Most importantly, it was uninterested in the dynamics of social development and change and focused instead on how societies maintained their structures over time. This theoretical orientation reflected an intense practical concern on the part of anthropologists and administrators, who saw that the effects of colonial rule were destroying traditional society and opening subject peoples to the appeals of anticolonial political movements (Radcliffe-Brown 1930). By discovering the conditions for stability of native institutions, many anthropologists hoped to arrest the political process that ultimately led to independence for the British colonies and the end of the British Empire (Stauder 1974:36). Once again the theoretical orientation of anthropology turns out to have been more influenced by the requirements of the colonial system than by those of scientific understanding.

At the time the functionalist school of anthropology was developing in Britain, another school, the "historical particularist" school, arose in the United States. Led by Franz Boas, sometimes called the "father of American anthropology," the historical particularists were especially vehement in their rejection of the nineteenth-century evolutionist universal socio cultural "stages." They argued that every culture should be studied as a unique whole and that the discovery of general processes of social development was difficult or impossible. The dominant ethic of Boasian anthropology was *cultural relativism* (see Chap. 1). According to this doctrine, an anthropologist is not permitted to make value judgments on social institutions or cultural systems or to compare cultures on a moral plane.

For half a century cultural relativism and historical particularism dominated American anthropology. By adopting this approach, anthropologists hoped to avoid the denigrating judgments on non-Western peoples that had permeated the discipline in its origins. However, in recent years a number of investigators have argued that the historical particularist approach, like British functionalism, has distorted anthropological understanding (Harris 1968). The most striking of these distortions was a tendency to ignore the oppressive relationship between the societies studied (in America, primarily Native American ones), and the anthropologists' own society. Cultural relativism may have protected non-Western cultures from invidious comparisons with the West, but it also protected Western society from a clear exposure of its aggressive and exploitative acts against the non-Western world. Historical particularism may have promoted respect for the cultural integrity of peoples in the abstract, but it also blinded anthropologists to the need for studying the forced integration of non-Western peoples into the modern industrial world, often with brutal and destructive consequences.

The recent critical evaluation of anthropology has revealed extremely serious flaws in its research practices and theoretical orientation. However, to be fair, these flaws do not give the whole picture. Many anthropologists have been deeply concerned with the welfare of the world's peoples and have made serious efforts to influence government policy in a progressive direction. For example, Franz Boas was an active opponent of

Advertisement placed by the Navy in the August, 1968, issue of the *American Anthropologist.* This ad touched off a great controversy: should the official organ of the internationally respected American Anthropological Association tacitly give support to anthropologists' engaging in counterinsurgency fieldwork by publishing this kind of ad? Current editorial policy is to refuse such ads.

scientific racism in the United States (Gossett 1964). Most anthropologists did not intentionally construct their theories with the objective of legitimating the colonial system; rather, they were the victims of the assumptions (folk perspective) of their own cultures. And we must not forget that some of the harshest critics of anthropology have been anthropologists themselves.

Furthermore, insofar as it has accurately portrayed the life ways of non-Western peoples, anthropology has always posed an implicit challenge to the pretensions to superiority of Western civilization (Diamond 1964). Indeed, the ethical and political crisis in modern anthropology derives precisely from the existence of two opposed tendencies in the discipline: accepting the dominant values of Western capitalist society, and siding with the peoples studied. As the demands of the oppressed peoples for social change have grown stronger, anthropology has also inevitably come under pressure to change.

Contemporary Examples

Examples of ethical and political dilemmas and controversies in modern anthropology are numerous. Of particular concern in recent years, due to the Vietnam War, has been the recruitment of anthropologists to do research designed to serve U.S. government counterinsurgency programs around the world. One of the best-documented cases of a link between anthropological research and counterinsurgency comes from work done in Thailand in the 1960s.

During the 1960s the U.S. government spent considerable money for social science research on minority ethnic groups in the northern border region of Thailand. This research was funded by a number of government agencies, including the Defense and State departments, and its aim was to provide information useful for the containment and suppression of a Communist-led rebellion in the border area.

Delmos Jones, one anthropologist who worked in Thailand, reports that the information gathered by anthropologists and others was assembled by the Advanced Research Project Agencies of the Department of Defense in a storage and retrieval system for counterinsurgency intelligence data called the Thai Information Center (Jones 1971). Jones believes that most of the anthropologists who worked in Thailand were unaware that their research was being used to further counterinsurgency and once he had discovered this, he decided not to publish his data. His reason was that he was by no means sure that the people he was studying would not be better off under a communist government than they were under the royal Thai government. On the basis of his experience, Jones argued that contemporary anthropological fieldwork is politically dangerous because *the publication of field data is almost always more beneficial to the policy planning of powerful national governments than to the local communities about whom the information is obtained.* Thus neutrality in fieldwork is impossible: Where national governments and their local communities are in conflict, to publish field data is to side with the former against the latter.

Jones forcefully stated the dilemma faced by the fieldworker who wants to do justice both to the people she or he studies and to the scientific goals of the profession. But a larger issue was involved in the anthropological work in Thailand. In 1970 student radicals at the University of California at Berkeley obtained and photocopied documents from the files of an anthropologist that implicated anthropologists in counterinsurgency activities in Thailand. Copies of these documents were sent to the ethics committee of the American Anthropological Association and were simultaneously made public. In the opinion of Joseph Jorgenson and Eric Wolf, two prominent members of the ethics committee at that time (1970), these documents demonstrated that at least some anthropologists working in Thailand were aware that their research would further counterinsurgency and were willing to help with this goal. Jorgensen and Wolf condemned the willingness of anthropologists to participate in counterinsurgency projects and charged that the entire discipline was damaged when its members provided professional support for U.S. military objectives in another country halfway around the globe.

After considerable internal debate, the executive board of the American Anthropological Association established a committee chaired by Margaret Mead to investigate the Thailand controversy, and the report of the committee was debated at the 1971 annual meeting of the association. The report found that the criticisms against anthropologists were exaggerated: "The controversy within the American Anthropological Association is linked to wider political struggles in our society, but its vehemence is disproportionate to the acts of any anthropologist in Thailand" (Davenport, Olmsted, and Mead 1971:4). This conclusion was extremely controversial. Many members of the association believed that it covered up the issues of counterinsurgency research by anthropologists, and after prolonged debate the report was voted down. But the vote did not settle the controversy, which will doubtless continue as long as there are disagreements over U.S. policy toward the Third World. Those who oppose cooperation with government counterinsurgency efforts will argue that anthropologists must take the commitment to the people they study more seriously than the advancement of their own careers or the collection of scientifically useful data. Those who believe that the government's needs for research and information should be met by anthropologists will argue that if anthropologists do not cooperate, the data that is collected will be of poorer quality, and the policy decisions of the government will be made on a less informed basis.

Once again we see how the personal values and attitudes of anthropologists can influence their work and theoretical orientation. Those who believe that the policies of the U.S. government in the Third World are basically progressive, or can be made so by the addition of information and logical argument, may see nothing wrong in participating in U.S. government intelligence projects. On the other hand, those who view U.S. government intervention in the Third World as basically wrong and damaging may oppose research that could enable U.S. government policies to be carried out more efficiently on the basis of better information.

The Thailand case is not the only one in which anthropologists have been recruited for ethically debatable purposes by government agencies. Much of the concern over that case came from the perception by many anthropologists that their profession was being damaged by repeated scandals involving governmental policies for research sponsorship. Perhaps the best-known such scandal erupted in 1965 over Project Camelot, an army-funded research project aimed at learning how to prevent social revolution (Sjoberg 1967; Horowitz 1967). In the words of a letter sent to social scientists being recruited for the project, its goal was "to make it possible to predict and influence politically significant aspects of social change in the developing nations of the world. . . . The U.S. Army has an important mission in the positive and constructive aspects of nation-building in less developed countries as well as a responsibility to assist friendly governments dealing with active insurgency problems" (quoted in Horowitz 1967:47–49).

Project Camelot collapsed before it got started. An American anthropologist visiting Chile made informal efforts to establish working relationships with Chilean social scientists. However, some of these men had previously been made aware of the nature of the project by a Norwegian sociologist then in Chile, and the approaches of the American anthropologist caused a public explosion. The American ambassador to Chile, embarrassed by this outcry, called for the cancellation of the project. In June of 1965 then Secretary of Defense Robert McNamara announced the project's demise (Sjoberg 1967:142–143).

The American Anthropological Association and other professional social science associations were quick to condemn Camelot. The project, it was charged, would make it more difficult for American social scientists to do research in foreign countries because they would all be subject to the suspicion that they were actually spies for the American military. Largely in response to Camelot, the American Anthropological Association adopted a code of ethics entitled "AAA: Principles of Professional Responsibility." This code prohibits secret research and requires anthropologists to do everything in their power to protect the welfare of those they study. The code reflects a consensus among anthropologists that government misuse of research is a serious problem.

It should not be thought, however, that research by American anthropologists has always been concerned with preserving the status quo. This is not the case. Indeed, the field of applied anthropology has been

Irving Louis Horowitz, well known sociologist, wrote the critical expose entitled *The Rise and Fall of Project Camelot.*

largely concerned with the promotion of change in local communities (see Chap. 25). One well-known applied anthropological project that attempted to initiate and direct change was the Cornell Peru Project, jointly established in 1952 by Cornell University and the Peruvian Institute for Indigenous Affairs (Holmberg 1970a, 1970b).

Vicos was an unproductive Peruvian hacienda of forty thousand acres with a population of 1,800 Indians. Cornell rented the Vicos hacienda from the owners, the Beneficencia Publica de Huaraz. The Indians were originally serfs on the estate, and under the traditional hacienda system, the owner or renter of the estate had the right to farm the most fertile land and to demand a certain amount of labor from the population. In exchange for this labor, the population was allowed to use the marginal land on the estate for subsistence farming.

The aim of the project was to transform Vicos into a modern, economically productive community and to give the Vicosinos the opportunity to make crucial decisions affecting their lives. The Cornell anthropologists first shared their power with members of the community and eventually transferred to them the legal prerogatives of renters. The project was successful. Cornell's profits from running Vicos were reinvested in the community to improve agricultural productivity and to construct health and educational facilities. New agricultural techniques were introduced to the Indians, who adopted them for use in their own fields. The standard of living of the people of Vicos rose. Of course, the results of the Cornell Peru Project were limited. The internal differences of wealth and power in Vicos were not diminished by the project, nor was the economic subordination of the Vicosinos to nearby *patrons,* for whom they worked as part-time wage laborers. The Vicosinos were freed from the archaic and semifeudal bonds that tied them to the hacienda system but not from more modern, capitalist forms of social inequality (Stein 1974).

When Cornell's lease on Vicos ran out in the late 1950s, a local power group in the area tried to prevent the people of Vicos from buying the estate for themselves. They saw the existence of an independent (Indian) community as a threat to their own social system, based as it was on serfdom and peonage. However, national political pressures for ending the hacienda system were already growing, and the Vicosinos were eventually able to purchase the estate in 1962. Indeed, by 1964 the Peruvian government had instituted land reform aimed at the hacienda system, and after the military coup d'etat of 1968, widespread expropriations of haciendas were undertaken.

The Cornell Peru Project has been seen as a positive example of anthropological intervention in the social life of a community. The project showed that a peasant population, once freed from the tremendous economic burden of serfdom, will respond to the opportunities of modern life and economic independence. But in order for the Vicosinos to become economically better off, it was necessary for Cornell to intervene and spend money without the hope of profit in return. This could be done by a university at the level of one estate, but it could not be done for a whole country. On such a large scale, determined government action to abolish the traditional social system would be required; the applied anthropologist cannot produce that kind of social change. Indeed, since the changes introduced by applied anthropologists must be sponsored by the governments that enlist their services, those changes cannot be more progressive than the governments themselves are.

Theory

Systems

Any discussion of social research and ethics must address the issue of values: What system of values shall be used to assess the ethics of a research project? Two opposed sets of values claim the allegiance of social scientists. One approach holds that social science must be (or at least must strive to be) *value free*—objective and detached, uninvolved with the objects of research. The other—we might call it the *"value-centered"* approach—maintains that because the "objects" of social research are people, researchers cannot be "neutral"; all social acts (including social research) have political and ethical consequences, and social scientists have an obligation to plan their research explicitly with a view toward achieving clearly stated social consequences. These opposed points of view have generally been integrated into the broader ethical and political perspectives of the scholars who have expounded them. The "value-centered" approach is compatible with a wide spectrum of political positions from conservative to radical, depending on what social ends scholarship is directed to serve. On the other hand, the "value-free" approach is usually associated with liberal social ideology. It reflects the constant attempts by academic liberals to protect their discipline from interference by outside social forces.

The clash of "value-free" and "value-centered" ideologies has been a part of modern social science from its beginnings. One of the most famous instances of this clash occurred in Germany in the first years of the twentieth century (Dahrendorf 1968). At that time the dominant position among German social scientists was that research should serve the needs of the German empire. The leaders of the profession were men who had been designing social policies for the government since the Bismarck period (1871–1890). However, the famous German sociologist Max Weber opposed this position and argued for "value-free" sociology. In 1909 Weber and his colleagues formed the German Sociology Society to further this goal. They proclaimed: "It is the purpose [of the society] to advance sociological knowledge by undertaking purely scientific investigations and surveys, and by publishing and supporting purely scientific studies. . . . *It rejects all concern with practical (ethical, religious, political, esthetic) goals of any kind*" (quoted in Dahrendorf 1968:2; emphasis added).

Interestingly, Weber was accused by the social science establishment of being a political radical who was seeking to deprive the German government of social scientists' expertise. In fact, Weber was a political moderate and a fervent German nationalist. His concern for "value-free" social science was motivated by the classic liberal aim of protecting the discipline from political "contamination," not by radicalism. Indeed, radicals, at least since the time of Marx, have argued for a "value-centered" rather than a "value-free" approach to research. Certainly today's "radicals" in the realm of social science promote precisely the opposite value system from that of Weber. They ask that social science come to grips with its social character and assess its practice in the light of current sociopolitical realities,

especially of the role it has played in selectively promoting certain social interests.

All of the controversial ethical and political issues within anthropology have been generated by the social context in which anthropological research and theorizing are carried out. Because the work of anthropologists is more useful to some people than to others, various groups have always had different estimates of the value of anthropology. These groups are often in conflict and may see anthropological research either as potentially useful to their own political interests or as part of the enemy's arsenal of material and ideological weapons. Anthropologists have generally tried to steer a middle course between such conflicting social interests, arguing that in the long run an increase in knowledge will benefit everyone. As conflicts between interests in Western countries and peoples in the Third World have grown sharper, however, this position has become more and more difficult to maintain.

The considerations that led Jones to suppress his Thailand research data are instructive here: How is it useful to a hill tribe in Southeast Asia to have its social structure recorded in books that are available to Western policy makers? Most of the information in the book, after all, is information that the tribe already knows. Even if the tribe had access to the report that the anthropologist writes (which is usually not the case), it certainly would benefit less from that monograph than the Pentagon planners who know nothing about Southeast Asia except what is collected for them by researchers in the field. If a political conflict arises between the hill tribe and the U.S. or Thai government, it is hard to see how anthropological research benefits *all* the parties concerned. In the long run, of course, humanity might benefit from the increase in knowledge gained from field research, but in the short run that increase in knowledge contributes to a policy that may well be detrimental to the group being studied.

Processes

Our discussion so far has been based on the assumption that anthropological research is scientific, that its research results are more or less true statements about social life. Given this assumption, the political or ethical question becomes one of process: Who has access to these results? To what end are these truths used? However, the basic premise itself is surely an oversimplification. Much social scientific research is seriously flawed by the ideological assumptions—folk perspective—of the society in which the researcher lives. The history of anthropological thought reveals pervasive flaws of this nature. This fact poses a rather different ethical problem, involving another process—that process whereby researchers' biases are transmitted through teaching, publication, and media coverage to a wide audience. Some anthropologists, for example, Margaret Mead, reach millions of people through their professional activities. We shall briefly examine some contexts in which these processes are played out.

The misconceptions and mistakes of anthropologists are not unethical in themselves. Science cannot exist unless the scientist is free to speculate and to make mistakes. However, the mistakes of social scientists are in some ways potentially more dangerous than those of many natural scientists. The theoretical and observational mistakes made by social scientists are nearly always biased by an acceptance of the ideology of the dominant group in a society. Sometimes consciously and more often unconsciously, social scientists become agents of the elite in conflicts of interest between the powerful and the powerless.

Those who feel themselves oppressed by a social system sometimes attack social scientists as the agents of that system. The researchers often answer these attacks by citing their academic freedom to pursue the truth as they see it. Here again we are faced with a difficult problem. The dilemma cannot readily be resolved by appealing to an abstract moral principle such as the freedom of research. If academic freedom turns out to help certain social groups and hurt others, then it will not be accepted by everyone as an absolute right. Many anthropologists have recently tried to reevaluate anthropological theory and research to find out what its real scientific value and content is. These scholars believe that only by exposing those aspects of the field that are unduly influenced by ideological preconceptions can the interests of both science and human welfare be safeguarded. Of course, since no one has a guarantee that his or her ideas are true, the critical analysis of anthropology is not easy to carry out.

Margaret Mead, world famous contemporary American anthropologist. As a social scientist with a great deal of exposure in the mass media (having written numerous books, countless articles, and appearing frequently on TV talk shows), Professor Mead's pronouncements on social issues have a potential for great impact, hence she has the ethical responsibility to weigh very carefully the possible political or social consequences of her words.

right
This shot of S. F. Nadel was taken in Heiban in 1938 shortly after his arrival there to study the Nuba.

Currently such critical rethinking is being undertaken with regard to many specific issues, some of which have been discussed previously. Others include:

1. To what extent should the people being studied play a role in the planning of research?

2. To what extent should the people being studied have a say about the uses to which the research is put?

3. Is the act of research itself—with its inevitable introduction of new elements—justifiable in remote societies where people are living what we must presume are satisfying lives in relative isolation from the industrial world?

4. How far should we go to get data? For instance, should museums traffic with grave plunderers to obtain rare artifacts?

Gradually even the most established anthropologists are beginning to struggle with these and similar questions. No longer can many anthropologists unthinkingly follow in the footsteps of S. F. Nadel, whose approach to anthropology we shall now consider.

Analysis

The Folk Perspective

British social anthropology of the colonial era clearly reflects the relationship between anthropology and the wider society. Let us look at the case of one famous British anthropologist, S. F. Nadel, to discover how he carried out his work. We base our analysis on a study by James Faris (1973), an American anthropologist who received his training in Britain and did extensive fieldwork among the Nuba peoples of the Sudan, one of the societies also studied by Nadel.

Nadel understood and approved of the British government's desire to use anthropological research in the service of colonial administration. In fact, all of his fieldwork was done at the explicit request of colonial government agencies. In his first book, Nadel says: "It has been said that modern anthropology is destined to be of great assistance to colonial governments in pro-

viding the knowledge of the social structure of native groups upon which a sound and harmonious Native Administration, as envisaged in Indirect Rule, should be built. Let me say that I for one firmly believe in the possibility of such cooperation between anthropologist and administrator" (Nadel 1942:vi, as quoted in Faris 1973). He did not believe in social research for its own sake. Indeed, his view that anthropology cannot be value free but must in some way relate to the wider society seems quite modern except for the fact that his loyalty was to a colonial order.

Nadel was sent to do fieldwork among the Nuba of the Sudan in 1938 because the government was having great difficulty in controlling them. The Nuba were a horticultural population of 300,000 people with no political hierarchy of their own. The government had created local native chiefs, but the Nuba remained rebellious. The research priorities of Nadel's fieldwork were determined by administrative need: Nuba groups that had caused problems were investigated before others.

When Nadel published his book on the Nuba in 1947, he saw it as "primarily planned to be of practical value to administrators and others" (Nadel 1947:7). In particular, he believed his work would facilitate the implementation of the British colonial policy of indirect rule, under which the government relied as much as possible on local customs for its administration. By doing this, the British government hoped to maintain its colonial presence more cheaply and also to minimize political opposition to colonial rule. The British administration was particularly concerned to retard the spread of Islam in the Sudan. The Nuba are the farthest north of any of the pagan societies in the Sudan, and the British wanted to turn them into a buffer between the Islamic north and the pagan south because they feared the political unity of an all-Islamic Sudanese society. Interestingly, Nadel was almost as opposed to fundamentalist Christian missionaries as he was to Islam. He believed that their lack of understanding of modern social realities made these missionaries more of a hindrance than a help in educating the Nuba to proper behavior in the colonial system.

Nadel's description of the Nuba groups gives the impression that he thought them an unpleasant people.

"From our description a Tullishi (Nuba) society emerged fraught with tension and conflict" (Nadel 1947:356). The Mesakin (Nuba) are labeled as "dour," "reserved and suspicious," and are said to have a "pessimistic, neurotic mentality." Nadel's hostile judgments of the Nuba may be related to his fieldwork techniques. He avoided using educated local people as informants or researchers because he felt that they had a distorted view of their customs. He preferred "raw savages" and used what he himself called "bullying" in talking to his informants. In an article on interviewing techniques he said flatly:

As a rule the most successful approach lies in stimulating the informant emotionally and thus overcoming his indolence or his reluctance to discuss certain points. . . . I have found it most profitable to stimulate the emotionality of a few chief informants to the extent of arousing almost violent disputes and controversies . . . a "bullying" technique of this type amounts to deliberate introduction of leading questions, a practice against which fieldworkers are frequently warned. But the leading question has its legitimate place in the anthropological, as in other interviews, provided that it is handled carefully and, above all, with full knowledge of its dangerous nature (Nadel 1939:322, as quoted in Faris 1973).

In his theoretical framework, Nadel was a committed functionalist. His focus was on systems of control and regulation in the societies that he studied, and he believed that social control was the primary concern of all societies. He was interested in the conditions under which a society could be said to be well adjusted or maladjusted because, like other functionalists, he believed that "healthy" societies were "well integrated"—that is, free of internal conflict. Nadel's definitions of maladjustment clearly reflect his social circumstances and ideology. Thus a raid on a government outpost, resistance to recruitment for forced labor, refusal to obey a government "chief," or opposition to the payment of taxes were easily interpreted as examples of maladjustment.

Nadel's explicit theoretical aim was to understand how the Nuba had maintained social order in the past and what changes would be needed to produce a new, integrated social system under colonial conditions. He was particularly interested in determining which customs could be codified into law and which should be discouraged or destroyed. He tended to see law as simply an extension of traditional custom rather than a new mechanism of social control—necessary to prevent rebellion in colonial society but nonexistent in the traditional Nuba social system. Nadel thought

Three Nuba girls standing above their village in southern Sudan.

that if some of the morals of classless Nuba society were dropped and a few new principles were added (law and centralized authority through government-appointed chiefs), then Nuba social structure would support the colonial political system. Toward this end he urged:

> The education of the Nuba, as of all primitive groups, should be guided thus: let moral education take the form of a teaching of tribal history, modified, and weighted in accordance with modern values. The principal tenets of social morality as we visualize them, and as they are embodied in tribal structure and the tribal past, are often the same, only their terms of reference, the social range to which they refer, need reinterpretation (Nadel 1947:512, as quoted in Faris 1973).

The Analytical Perspective

In addition to describing Nadel's approach to anthropology, Faris subjects it to a critical analysis. He points out that while many anthropologists may have done their work without understanding its political significance, Nadel was not one of these. He was a convinced colonialist. However, although Nadel knew very well what he was doing, he could not grasp the real meaning of the social process he was enmeshed in. For example, he confused the attitude of the Nuba toward him and the British government with their basic personality. When he argued that various Nuba groups were dour, suspicious, and pessimistic, he did so without realizing that these so-called character traits might be no more than expressions of hostility toward himself and what he stood for.

Faris argues that a careful reading of Nadel's Nuba study reveals that the groups Nadel labeled as most unpleasant were also those that had had the worst experiences with the British administration. In one case Nadel unfavorably compared the psychological characteristics of one group, the Mesakin Nuba, to another, the Korongo. Investigation reveals that the Mesakin had suffered punitive police action, whereas the Korongo had been spared armed encounters with the colonialists. Faris points out that Nadel "was serving an administration that physically attacked local societies,

Kordafan dancing girls of the Kau Nyaro Nuba, dancing with rawhide whips and accompanied by drums.

driving them from their homes, forcing migrations, imprisoning (and very frequently hanging) their men and women, and he was an apologist and defender of that system" (Faris 1973:160). In addition, Faris argues, Nadel's self-admitted "bullying" interviewing techniques and the fact that he had access to the police and could summon informants at will would have made the Nuba "unpleasant" to Nadel even if their relations with the British administration had otherwise been better.

Faris argues that Nadel's attitude toward colonialism was the determining factor in his theoretical outlook as well as in his practical activity. Nadel could not explain social change or come to grips with the social processes unleashed by colonialism. By describing the relationship between the colonial power and the subjugated population as needing adjustment, Nadel was

claiming that a properly formulated colonial policy could eliminate conflict between colonizers and colonized. He did not and could not understand that colonialism inevitably generated opposition and that eventually the system would have to change.

Conclusions

Schools of Thought

The dilemma of anthropology is that its moral justification depends on its ultimate value to humanity as a contribution to human welfare through knowledge, but in the social circumstances of today, even the best anthropological research can have the opposite result. In attempting to solve this dilemma, anthropologists have taken three major positions, which we might

label the "ethics" position, the "political policy" position, and the "activist" position.

The first, or "ethics," position is reflected in the guidelines of professional responsibility for anthropologists that were adopted by the American Anthropological Association. According to this position, the crucial question is whether anthropologists behave in an improper way or directly contribute to harming the peoples they are studying. To avoid this possibility, anthropologists are urged to behave ethically. Thus they are to avoid secret research that is in principle available only to the sponsor and not to the peoples being studied. They are to avoid lying to the people they work with about what they are doing. They are to avoid misrepresenting the results of their research to their sponsor or to the public. By adopting such a code of ethics, many anthropologists hope to reassure foreign governments and others about the dangers of anthropological research. They also hope to separate themselves from possible undesirable consequences of research—by being able to claim that the anthropologist behaved decently even if someone else misused the work. People who hold the "ethics" position generally argue that no scientist has control over the results of his or her research and that therefore no science can put requirements on its practitioners that go beyond their own personal moral behavior.

The second position, the "political policy" position (see Piddington 1970), argues that anthropologists must be professionally involved with the practical results of their research. It therefore proposes that anthropologists become active policy consultants to the sponsors of anthropological research, in particular to the government. By arguing in government and other circles for a moral and progressive policy, the anthropologist discharges his or her ethical obligations and also has some hope of having a real, positive effect on the welfare of the people he or she studies. According to this position, a code of ethics is fine, but alone it is insufficient to deal with the social context of anthropological research.

The third, or "activist," approach is based on a radical critique of Western society and its relationship to the non-Western world. Western countries are seen as imperialist in their relations with the non-Western world; they seek to dominate the economies and the political organizations of non-Western countries in order to exploit their labor and natural resources. Government and private agencies that fund anthropological research are held to be subservient to the political and economic interests of the forces that rule Western society. No matter how many anthropologists do research and make policy recommendations, this basis of policy formation will not change. Some who hold this view argue that anthropologists should do no field research at all, but should devote themselves to a political struggle against imperialism. Others (see Gough 1968) argue that anthropologists should do fieldwork that will be useful to the forces that oppose imperialism.

Author's Conclusions

In this chapter we have presented a wide spectrum of opinions on the ethical and political dilemmas of modern anthropology. This was unavoidable because no consensus exists within the field as to what constitutes ethical research, and no agreement has been reached on what the relationship between social science and society is or ought to be. Neither are there well-defined schools of thought that clearly reflect the different shades of opinion held by various anthropologists. However, I believe that anthropologists can be grouped according to their attitudes toward modern capitalist society, attitudes which then largely determine the positions they take on certain questions of ethics and the kinds of research they are willing to engage in or support. These attitudes cluster around two opposite poles: basic trust in the dominant institutions of Western society, and opposition to and suspicion of those institutions.

I find myself much closer to the latter pole than to the former. The war in Southeast Asia and the treatment of minority groups in this country, to name but two issues, seem to me to make trust in our political institutions a rather bad bet. This is especially true since the social system under which we live, advanced industrial capitalism, appears to generate insoluble social problems by its very nature.

Because of the way our sociopolitical system works, I do not think that the ethical dilemmas of modern social science can be solved in the context of present social arrangements. The best, most moral, most scrupulous, and most theoretically advanced research can always be misused if its results are controlled by the wrong people. Furthermore, good research can always by stymied if those who hold the purse strings are so inclined (see Gough 1968 for an example). Since the rulers of our society are so clearly willing to abuse research, no anthropologist can practice the profession without fear of undesirable consequences. Many natural scientists have known this about their work for some time—at least since the development of the atom bomb—but social scientists are taking longer to come to the same conclusion.

In my view, the only solution to the ethical problem of science is for us to change the structure of the wider society in which the scientist and everyone else does his or her work. The moral obligations of scientists are fundamentally no different than those of citizens who participate in social life as factory workers, schoolteachers, white-collar workers, and others. Almost anyone's work is potentially either useful or harmful, depending on who controls it and how its results are used. We all have an obligation to strive for the kind of society in which our work is beneficial instead of destructive to our own welfare and to that of humanity. Only by taking this obligation seriously can we claim to behave ethically.

Summary

The issue of social research and ethics concerns the ethical dilemmas and controversies of modern anthropologists and places them in historical context.

Anthropological theory and research, it is now realized, was for a long time distorted by the relationship between British functionalist anthropology and the British colonial administration in subject territories. This relationship between dominant political interests and social science research has persisted, as the examples of Project Camelot and the Thailand controversy in the American Anthropological Association reveal.

Anthropology need not be the servant of the dominant ideology of the anthropologist's society, however, as the Peru project of Cornell University shows. In this case, anthropological principles and methods were applied to the intended benefit of the community concerned. However, even here the results reflected political realities more than anthropological intentions.

An analysis of the work in the Sudan of S. F. Nadel, a famous British anthropologist, provides insight into the relationship between colonialism and anthropological research and highlights both the ethical problems involved in this kind of research and its practical and theoretical shortcomings that resulted from a committment to colonial ideology.

Annotated Bibliography

Asad, Talal, ed. (1973) *Anthropology and the Colonial Encounter.* London: Ithaca. A collection of critical articles on the social role of British social anthropology, including several useful case studies.

Clifton, James A. ed. (1970) *Applied Anthropology: Readings in the Uses of the Science of Man.* Boston: Houghton Mifflin. A spectrum of opinions on the proper role of applied anthropology.

Gossett, Thomas (1964) *Race: The History of an Idea in America.* New York: Schocken. A survey of racist ideas and opposition to these ideas in the U.S. intellectual tradition.

Horowitz, Irving Louis (1973) *The Rise and Fall of Project Camelot.* 2d ed. Cambridge, Mass.: MIT Press. A detailed account of the most famous recent scandal in U.S. social science.

Hymes, Dell, ed. (1969) *Reinventing Anthropology.* New York: Random House. A collection of articles on innovative, sometimes radical approaches to redefining anthropology in the contemporary world.

Malinowski, Bronislaw (1930) "The Rationalization of Anthropology and Administration." *Africa* 3:405–29. A pro-colonialist statement of the value of collaboration between anthropology and colonial administration by one of the founders of functionalism in Britain.

Stauder, Jack (1974) "The Relevance of Anthropology to Colonialism and Imperialism." *Race* 16:29–51. A pointed critique of the role of anthropology in supporting colonialism and imperialism.

Part V

Case Studies

20
Fieldwork I:
Participant Observation in a Swiss Peasant Community

Introduction

To reach the area of Switzerland known as the Emmental, one travels eastward from the Swiss capital of Bern on winding Route 10 toward Luzern. Within half an hour one passes through quiet farming towns and heads into the heart of an area that is justly famous for its rugged green hills, steeply walled valleys, dense pine forests, and a peasant population farming slopes that appear to be impossibly steep.

All along the way one passes peasant homesteads strung out along the hillsides. For the most part, the homesteads are isolated from each other, but occasionally they cluster together into hamlets and—in the larger valleys—into towns centered around picturesque churches. The dwellings are of weathered pine. Grayish brown, broad, and low roofed, they cling to the valley walls, dotting the quiltlike pattern created by the small, exquisitely manicured fields the peasants till in even the steepest and most remote places.

The Emmental peasants are famous in Switzerland for their gruff ways, stubborn independence of spirit, and aggressive informality (they address even total strangers with the informal pronoun *du* instead of the "correctly formal" pronoun *Sie*, which all other

left

Loading wheat. Farming on the steeply walled valleys of the Emmental region is very difficult. Some slopes, such as the one shown here, are so steep that horses and tractors cannot be used to haul loads such as this. The local peasants have devised a complex system of cables, movable blocks, and electric-powered winches to transport loads of grain, hay, etc., up and down the hillsides.

Figure 20-1
The Emmental Area of Switzerland

German-speaking Swiss use to address people they do not know). Here, in the alpine foothills, they pursue a way of life that is quickly fading from the European scene. They plant grains, potatoes, and grass for hay; most of their cash income is earned by selling the milk they produce, generally to cheese-producing plants that are locally owned and operated. This cheese, called *Emmentaler* cheese in Switzerland, is what the rest of the world knows as Swiss cheese.

The Environment

The Emmental is the area of the canton of Bern, in central Switzerland, that lies in the foothills of the Alps and whose waters drain into the Emme River. The very rugged character of the terrain derives from its geological history. The wider valleys were cut by glacier tongues during the Würm glaciation, which finally receded some 10,000 years ago. The myriad of smaller,

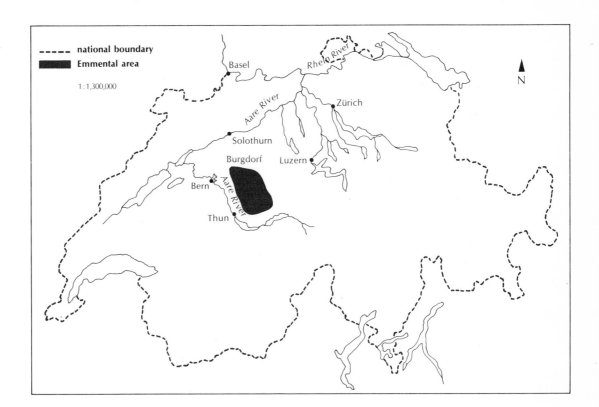

steeply walled side valleys were cut by erosion and still harbor thousands of brooks and streams that flow into the Emme and its tributaries. Most of these valleys are covered with pine forests on their northern slopes, but the southern slopes are clear and are used for farming and pasturing (Berger-Kirchner 1964:30).

It is interesting to note in this context that the endings of place names often have topographical significance. Places with names ending in -*au* (Langnau) are usually located on the floors of the broader valleys; those with names ending in -*wil* (Bowil) are generally on terraces above broad valley floors; and names ending in -*egg* (Heiteregg) or in -*weid* (Brüschweid) most often refer to places found toward the crowns of hills.

The climate of the Emmental is raw, with an average December-January temperature of 31° Fahrenheit and a midsummer average of 63° Fahrenheit. The entire Emmental lies within the area that receives more than 39 inches of rain per year. Snow falls in all but four months of the year (June, July, August, and September), and in the winter drifting snows can cut households off from the outside world for days at a time.

The community I studied lies at an altitude of about 3,100 feet along the crown of a ridge running east to west which I call Mülenberg (all place names and names of persons have been changed to keep the identity of the community anonymous). Strung along a portion of this ridge, interspersed among the pine forests guarding the steep slopes are twenty-eight households. Most of them are quite isolated, but about a third of them are grouped into hamlets such as Sattelweid, which consists of five homesteads nestled into a saddle of the ridge.

Some ten minutes' walk from Sattelweid is another hamlet, called Kriegsweid, which consists of a three-room schoolhouse, a general store and bakery run by a local peasant, a blacksmith, a wheelwright's shop, and a peasant household run jointly by two brothers, one of whom is the local pig butcher. A new addition to Kriegsweid is a ski lift completed in the winter of 1968/69, which represents a considerable entrepreneurial risk taken by eleven local men.

Another ten minutes' walk along the packed gravel road brings one to the Bären Inn, which overlooks the steeply sloping hillside leading down to the town of Ilistal in the valley below. The inn is quite well known throughout Switzerland, and many Swiss vacation there because of its excellent "country" cuisine and its magnificent view of the stark cliffs of the fore-Alps and the dazzling, snow-covered high Alps behind them. The inn is also an extremely important local institution, serving as a main focus for the integration of the local community.

The land in this area is far from ideal for farming. Only about half the nonforested land is considered arable, and only one-fifth is rated optimal. Much of the land is in shade because of the rugged topography of the area and the presence of the forests; a lot of the land is very steep; some of the soil is quite shallow; some places are prone to landslides; and some areas are far too wet to be suitable for agriculture without being drained.

The Swiss federal government has developed a complex method of determining three levels of difficulty for "mountain farming." Among the factors considered are altitude, exposure to wind, steepness of terrain, temperature, summer precipitation averages, soil composition, vegetation period, type or types of agriculture possible in the area, sizes of local farming homesteads, percentage of cows as opposed to other farm animals owned by households, percentage of cows sent to mountain pasture, costs of milk delivery to collection points, and general access to traffic connections. On this scale the local community falls within level 2—that is, it is in a moderately difficult "mountain farming" zone.

The Group

In the summer of 1966 I traveled to Switzerland to look for a community in which I could engage in the research that interested me: What social and cultural elements operate to create a community, and what factors determine community boundaries? Through friends of my family I was able to make contacts in the community reported on here, and I spent much of the summer getting to know a few of the peasant households, making arrangements for a place to live when I came back for my full year's research, and studying the language intensively.

The blacksmith's house in Kriegsweid. Like most local artisans and craftsmen, the blacksmith is a full time agriculturalist as well as a blacksmith. His shop is on the ground floor, his residence upstairs. He and his wife and children live with his parents in this house. His father, who used to be the blacksmith, has retired and now helps his son.

In June of 1968 I returned with my wife, Carolyn, and we moved into the two attic rooms of a widowed peasant woman's farmhouse. Since all her children had grown and left home, she was lonely and hence more than delighted to have us, both for our company and as a dependable source of income (we paid $35 per month rent).

After allowing ourselves a few days to settle in, to adjust to our somewhat cramped quarters (we had to stoop under the ceiling beams as we crossed our rooms), and to adjust to the fact that we were now completely cut off from the lives we had led in New Haven, Connecticut, we slowly came to grips with the issue of how we were going to lead our "new" lives. Carolyn clearly did not have the inclination or the knowledge of the language to involve herself in my research. She began to orient herself away from the community, traveling to Bern (a fifty-minute drive in good weather) several times a week for dance lessons, movies, and other recreation. However, she also decided to spend several mornings a week visiting the local first grade to make friends with the young woman who was the teacher and to improve her speaking ability in both "High German" and the local German dialect. With Carolyn's routine falling into place, I had to confront my own work. What exactly did I want to do? What could I do? How should I go about doing it?

The local peasant folk were used to having "city people" around. Some of the peasants rented rooms or even small houses to vacationing Swiss; and the Bären Inn—the local pub—was a popular place for city folk to visit on Sunday afternoons for drinks, ice cream for the kids, and a pleasant stroll through the woods and fields after lunch. I knew from my previous stay here that the local people did not particularly like these city folk, whom they regarded as "soft," inconsiderate, and condescending in their attitudes toward peasants. It occurred to me that I might win their confidence if I could demonstrate that I, too, worked hard and valued hard work for its own sake, as they did.

Thus I set forth into the fields throughout the months of June and July. I made a point of leaving my camera, tape recorder, and note pad at home and simply made myself available as a very unskilled laborer to families that I knew had labor shortages. At first the people offered to pay me full wages for a full day's work. However, it was obvious to all concerned that I had neither manual skills nor stamina and could barely do the work of a ten-year-old. I emphasized this fact, saying that the opportunity for learning their work skills—so that I could write an accurate book about their way of life—was more than enough pay for me. In this manner, then, I spent two months working in the fields, being taught such elementary techniques as how to rake hay with a long-handled rake, how to turn hay with a pitchfork, and how to gather and load the hay. At first a curiosity, I was gradually accepted as a somewhat valued helper, and slowly the men included me in their gossip and explained local social, political, and economic issues to me while we worked and when we took breaks.

Subsistence Activities

Early on it seemed to me that all local households practiced the same form of "mixed farming"—that is, they grew cereal grains and potatoes for their own consumption and produced milk for sale as their major source of cash income. Daily routines seemed to be pretty much the same from household to household.

The peasants rise at 4 or 4:30 A.M., and the men clean the cow stalls and milk the cows while the women cook breakfast on wood-burning stoves. The men (or teenage sons) then deliver the milk to the local cheese-making cooperative and return to join the rest of the family for a breakfast of bread and butter with home-made jam and coffee lightened with hot milk. By 9 A.M. the fields are dry enough to be worked; at 10:30 or so there is a morning break for some coffee and bread, after which work is resumed until lunchtime at around 1 P.M. By 2 o'clock the peasants are back in the fields. They take an afternoon break for some bread, sausage, and tea or beer at around 3:30 or 4 P.M. and finish their work (while the male head of the household milks again) by supper at around 6 o'clock. After supper the men cut a load of fresh grass to be fed to the cows before the entire family retires at around 9 P.M.

This is essentially the routine followed by most local households, although there are variations depending on the season: In winter the pace is much slower. The major meal of the day is lunch, at which it is customary to eat soup, meat, at least one vegetable (usually from the garden planted and tended by the women), a salad, bread, cheese, and finally black coffee that is often fortified with some liquor. Each person eats the entire meal from one broad soup plate. Supper is smaller and consists of leftovers from lunch, bread, maybe some eggs or home-fried potatoes or both, and again, coffee with schnapps.

However, I learned that although all the peasant families' routines are similar, three different forms of mixed farming are practiced, not one form as I had at first assumed. The form practiced by most households is the oldest, and it also requires the most intensive application of labor. These households sell their milk to the local dairy and cheese-making cooperative. But because the bacteria which grow in grass that is stored in silos cause cheese to bloat, the peasants following this form of agriculture must feed their cows only hay and fresh grass. In consequence, they must cut hay twice each summer, and they therefore must spread and turn the hay—a heavy, time-consuming job—twice each summer as well.

Instead of selling their milk to the cheese-making

cooperative, some local households sell to the giant Alpine Milk Corporation, which pasteurizes the milk and produces a wide variety of dairy products. The bacteria produced by grass stored in silos is not a problem for milk that is pasteurized. Thus these households have to go through the process of making hay only once each summer; the second cut of hay grass is simply gathered and dumped into the silo to be fed to the cows when it is needed in the winter.

Both these approaches to agriculture and milk production have the virtue of guaranteeing the households a relatively fixed income because the Swiss national government subsidizes the price of milk and maintains the price at a steady level. However, these approaches have the liability that no spectacular financial gains can be made either. The third approach, practiced by a few local peasant households, is more speculative. Instead of selling their milk, these people feed it to calves that they purchase when a few months old and sell to butchers about a year later as veal. They have to contend with price fluctuations both when they purchase the calves and when they sell them for cash. They can earn or lose more money than do households that prac-

Spreading manure. A local woman uses a pitchfork to spread out the manure which has been distributed in piles on the field. Her husband and son, shown in the background, are plowing under this natural fertilizer. The plow is drawn up the hillside using the cable and winch arrangement which was described earlier.

Splitting wood. A husband and wife split pre-cut wood into sections which he will then carefully hand-split into roofing shingles. He holds an axe in place, she hits it with a mallet. This couple is very unfortunate because they never had any children and can barely work their farm any more.

tice one of the first two approaches described, but they usually come out more or less the same.

For all three approaches the yearly agricultural cycle is similar. Hay and grass are cut in the summer, cereal grains are harvested in the fall, and shortly thereafter comes the digging up of the potatoes. The potato harvest is back-breaking work for most households because they do not have motorized equipment and consequently must do all the work—ripping out the stalks, hoeing up the potatoes, and sorting the potatoes—by hand. As winter approaches, the harvested grains are threshed; the cereal is used to make flour for bread and feed for cattle, and the stalks become straw for the cow stalls. At this time, new fields are also prepared and sown with winter grains, primarily spelt (a variety of wheat) and rye.

During the winter the men cut trees to sell to paper mills and lumber companies to mill for lumber and use for house repairs, or cut into sections for firewood. Some local men still practice the traditional craft of making wooden roof shingles by hand, which they sell for additional cash. The winter also provides a special feast. This is the time of year when pigs are butchered, and parties are held among neighbors to eat and celebrate. In the spring the peasants sow the summer grains, and the following year's hay mixture is sown between the rows of the winter grains, which by this time are several inches tall. Fields are also plowed and prepared for the setting in of the potatoes, which must be planted well before haying begins in the summer. At this time, the women plant their vegetable gardens, which provide most of their family's lettuce, cabbage, chard, tomatoes, carrots, and string beans.

This, then, is the agricultural cycle that governs the lives of the people I was attempting to get to know. It is the basic principle by which they structure their lives, organize their time, and coordinate their thinking and planning. The cycle is their pulse, their life rhythm.

Social Organization

The approach I chose for my research among these people, called *participant observation*, has been developed primarily by anthropologists, who have

Splitting wooden shingles. Using a specially shaped knife and a small mallet, this local peasant is adding to his meager cash income during the winter months by hand-producing shingles. For a whole winter's work, he will gross some $150. From this sum, however, the cost of the shingle wood must be subtracted. The reason he does this is due to what economists call a *low opportunity cost*: his opportunities to earn money by spending his time otherwise are for all practical purposes nil.

traditionally focused their attention on relatively small, somewhat isolated communities. In contrast to research based on surveys, participant observation entails the building of quite personal relationships between the researcher and the people being studied. In contrast to laboratory research, the researcher has no control (or at best, minimal control) over social and cultural variables. Participant observers try to immerse themselves in the life of the community or group being studied; they constantly walk a tightrope between intense subjective involvement with their subjects as individuals who are becoming increasingly meaningful to them, and a coolly dispassionate, scientific, analytical view of the social life of the group that is the object of study.

Through this process of immersion, the researcher hopes to penetrate deeply into the maze of local social relationships and come to understand the world view and social life of the group. This process takes time; most such studies continue at least a year, and many last much longer. If the researcher's interest is primarily focused on the nature of the local society and culture—if she or he is attempting to describe and analyze aspects of the local sociocultural systems—we call this *ethnography*. If the aim is to directly affect the community—to introduce planned social and cultural change—we call this *applied anthropology* or *action anthropology* (see Chap. 25).

Developing the relationships that enable one to engage in participant observation involves many levels of difficulty. One of the most relevant variables is the researcher's personality and public identity: his or her habits, values, standards, pet peeves, likes, dislikes, prejudices, orientation toward research, marital status, and so forth. Another is the nature of the community he or she is trying to investigate: whether the local culture is relatively open or closed to strangers, whether people feel they have time to "waste" answering the questions of an outsider, whether the community can materially support the presence of a nonproducing temporary resident, and so on. Most field researchers come to see their period of participant observation as one of the crucial episodes in their lives—a time when they had to confront fundamental questions of who they were, why they were engaged in what they were doing, and what they wanted to become.

I found that getting to know the Swiss peasants I had decided to study was both easy and difficult. By working with them in the fields, I won a grudging respect; by drinking with the men in the local tavern almost every evening, I gradually came to be included in the group of "regulars" who sat around the *Stammtisch* (the table reserved for regular patrons at each tavern in Switzerland). I thus became privy to gossip and overheard many stories that provided me with a great deal of information about community affairs and particular items of interest about individuals. After each such evening I would spend hours at the typewriter recording what I could remember.

However, the basic unit of the local community is the household, and I found that although I got to know many of the men quite well, gaining relaxed access to their homes was another story. Having Carolyn with me helped, since we were occasionally invited as a couple to winter pig-butchering feasts and a few other festivities in some of the local homes. But men do not spend much time with women outside their own household, and even after a year's residence in the community, I was on a "drop in anytime" basis with only four or five of the twenty-eight households I came to know.

As I mentioned at the beginning of this chapter, the community I chose to study is strung out along a ridge in the alpine foothills of the Emmental area of Switzerland. It is more or less in the center of a triangle formed by connecting (in one's imagination) the three closest towns in the valleys below. The boundary lines of the three townships actually come together in the heart of this community, in a hamlet called Sattelweid, which is composed of five peasant households. The community itself, then, consists of outlying portions of three politically distinct townships; the township boundary lines are clearly not the community boundary lines. I had some sense of this fact but had not been able to pin it down because although each homestead and each local hamlet had a name, the social unit that I came to see was a functioning community *has no name at all*—at least it has no single, easily identifiable term that clearly refers specifically to it (Hunter 1975).

My research problem was to describe the form of the local community. By August of 1968, I had made some progress in identifying important local institutions, such as the three-room schoolhouse at Kriegsweid (the other hamlet that was part of the community); the Bären Inn, where many of the local men spent a lot of their evenings drinking and playing cards; some fundamentalist Christian sects, which met in certain peasant homes; the general store and bakery at Kriegsweid, run by a very popular local figure; the local ski and women's clubs; and the local cooperatively owned cheese-making plant and association. But I still did not have a real "handle" on the nature of and boundaries that delineated what I was convinced was in fact a community. The fact that it did not have a name and consequently was difficult to refer to in conversation made the task of investigating its nature still more formidable.

Then, late one summer evening as I sat at the *Stammtisch* drinking and playing cards with some of the local men, the Bären innkeeper, Kratzer Gerhardt, started a monologue which he repeated numerous times during the following two weeks. It seems that on a cold but sunny day during the previous winter, he had been driving up from the town of Oberwil in the valley below. Spotting two vehicles moving down the steep, narrow road toward him, he chose an area where the road widens to pull over and let the vehicles pass. The first of the two was a Land Rover driven by Holzer Fritz, a local peasant living at Sattelweid, whose vehicle was pulling a trailer in which a cow was being transported. The second car was a Volkswagen "beetle" driven by a woman he vaguely knew who lived in the town of Oberwil.

Holzer Fritz had waved and passed him, but the woman had stopped beside him and asked the name of the fellow who was preceding her down the mountain. Gerhardt had told her that the man's name was Holzer Fritz. Much to his chagrin, the woman then informed him that Fritz had backed into her with his trailer, crushing in the hood of her car and leaving the scene after soundly cursing her out and refusing to give her his name. The furious woman informed Gerhardt that she intended to take Fritz to court and that he, Gerhardt, would be called in to testify to the identity of the culprit.

The schoolhouse at Kriegsweid. The large building houses three classrooms; each classroom has three grades in it, all taught by the same teacher. One of the three locally employed teachers lives in the schoolhouse itself. He has a private garden which his wife plants and tends, a very important resource, since he is paid less than three thousand dollars per year. The school is one of the most important local institutions, a centralizing influence which helps constellate the community, otherwise geographically quite dispersed. At the left is one of the local farmhouses.

Now, in August, Gerhardt had received a subpoena. And to put it mildly, Gerhardt was upset. Night after night he sat at the *Stammtisch,* explaining over and over how he had been called in to testify against Fritz and insisting that it was not his fault, that he could not have read the woman's mind, that had he known there would be trouble he would not have identified Fritz that morning, that he had just been trying to be polite to the woman.

Then, growing angry at the person whose "stupidity" had put him in this position, he began to attack Holzer Fritz, criticizing his driving ability and the fact that, as the infamous local tightwad, he did not have automobile insurance like everybody else did. If he had insurance, then it would have been a simple matter because the company would have paid, and Fritz would not have attempted to dodge responsibility. Now the police were involved, there would be a trial, he (Gerhardt) would have to testify against Fritz, and Fritz would have to pay a fine as well as pay the original damages.

Why was Kratzer Gerhardt so upset? Why did he protest his innocence over and over? He answered that question himself when he proclaimed that he did not want anybody to be mad at him, that he did not want people to think he had turned Fritz in on purpose. Clearly, he was addressing a group of people who were very meaningful to him, a group whose norms he apparently felt he might have violated, a group whose negative response he wished to head off.

Thinking about this story, I realized that his loyalty clearly was to the group of people living up here on the top of the ridge rather than to the township to which he belonged. For the woman in question lived in the town of Oberwil, within the township of which the Bären Inn was situated, whereas Holzer Fritz lived in the township of Buchen. Yet Gerhardt obviously felt that his first loyalty belonged to Fritz rather than to the woman. At this point I remembered a phrase I had heard many times: *Wir da oben* ("we up here"). I had taken it to be merely a topographical reference, but now it occurred to me that this phrase might also be the cover label that referred to the local community.

Gerhardt's anxiety stemmed from his fear of local people's reactions to his involvement in the court case. He was clearly concerned about the response of what for him was a *reference group*—that is, a group that sets and maintains values and standards for individuals and provides a context in which individuals assess their positions and behavior relative to others. It made sense to me, then, to avoid the arguments of a lot of community study theory (see, for example, Arensberg and Kimball 1965; Freilich 1963; Hiller 1941; Kaufman 1959; Redfield 1960; Simpson 1965; Sutton and Koloja 1960a, 1960b) and conceive of the *community* as a *reference group with households as the constituent units.* A

left

Pig butchering. All peasant households raise pigs for meat. These are butchered outside in the wintertime. A few of the local men have mastered the craft of pig butchering, and one of them is always called in to oversee the operation. Cows and calves, on the other hand, are taken to professional butchers down in the towns below.

A local pig butcher (left) and his son scrape the bristles off a pig they have just killed. Pig butchering is a way to supplement their agricultural income during the relatively unproductive winter months. When a pig is butchered, the household whose pig it is throws a party that evening, serving many of the delicacies from the butchering: freshly made blood and liver sausage, cutlets, and boiled snout, ears, and feet. Neighbors are often invited, as is the butcher.

community could therefore exist without a formal name; a community could consist of outlying parts of three politically distinct townships because it affected the patterns of local social interaction and was of great cognitive and emotional significance to its residents. To refer to this community, members used one sense of (or one level of contrastive meaning of) the phrase "we up here." Knowing this, I could finally begin to set about systematically investigating not only the major institutions within the community but also the nature of the community itself, including its boundaries and cultural system.

Culture

When one first arrives in the community one hopes to study, one faces many more or less mechanical but necessary tasks that involve active work even though one does not yet have many contacts with local people. I had engaged in quite a bit of this somewhat mechanical work: drawing rough maps of the community; locating households and institutions such as the school, store, and blacksmith shop; taking a census; and so forth. I had visited the cheese production plant and—in return for promising the cheesemaker a copy of the complete set—had taken a series of photographs detailing the stages of cheese production. I also paid visits to the town clerks of the three townships, gathering some demographic data. All these tasks were necessary, but they did not require intimacy between me and the local people.

Gradually, of course, I was able to get closer to the community residents by working with them in the fields and drinking with them in the local tavern. But this was a difficult, time-consuming process during which I often despaired of ultimate success. In fact, on some days I could hardly force myself to get out of bed, and when I did get up, Carolyn and I would flee to the city to escape from the community in which we were both under constant public observation and the subject of continual gossip (a widely believed rumor had me down as a Russian spy infiltrating via America on a phony passport).

One particular problem I had not anticipated was the psychological strain. My identity as a man was threatened because the props that supported my self-definition at home were lacking in this new situation (see Chap. 14). What I was doing had a great deal of social support among my colleagues in America, but in the local value system, in which hard, physical labor was extremely valued, my research was tolerated but certainly was not respected. And it did not help matters when it became obvious that I could not do a "man's share" of work in the fields.

The local men appeared to be developing an attitude toward me that seemed condescending, and I decided that my entire research project would be in danger of disintegrating if I could not win the men's respect. On the one hand, they would not be candid with me when I asked questions, and on the other hand, I felt my emotional strength and determination gradually evaporating so that my work was becoming more and more listless and dissipated. In this state of crisis, I spent quite a bit of time reflecting, and I was able to think through the situation and decide on a course of action.

It was clear to me that I needed to do something that would win me some esteem in terms of the local culture, so that the subtle assaults on my masculinity would stop and I could get on with my research—accepted as a competent, adult male. And in thinking about how to do this, I gradually realized that in my five months of residence I had learned a great deal about the community, that I knew a lot both about individuals and about the values and world view shared by members of the community.

My research had involved identifying the existence of a local community—a community that had no "name" but rather was referred to by one level of meaning of the often-used phrase "we up here." However, although I had established a definite pattern of in-group feeling (the Holzer Fritz case being my first solid evidence), I still hadn't decided whether the group identity was in any sense positive or was merely an aggregation of negative identity feelings—feelings of being discriminated against as "small farmers" or peasants by the national government's agricultural subsidization programs; feelings of having a much more difficult way of life than the valley farmers, who had level land and larger holdings; feelings that they,

Examination day. Every spring, the local school celebrates the graduation of one class of students and the promotion of the other classes. Parents visit the school and watch (carefully rehearsed) classes. Afterwards, at the local tavern, the graduating class is served alcoholic beverages for the first time—in public, at least. That evening there is a dance, with waltzes and other traditional music provided by a local accordian duo. Virtually the entire community attends.

as isolated, rural farmers were being discriminated against by their own townspeople in the valleys below. One sentiment often expressed at the Bären Inn, for example, was that good, paved roads are built primarily in the towns for the use of townspeople, whereas it would take "forever" until the roads leading up to the local area would be paved.*

These negative feelings were certainly very important elements of the local people's in-group feelings. But such cases as the Holzer Fritz affair indicated that some positive elements of group belongingness must be present as well. Thus I started to look for indications of such feelings, and once I had adopted this course, numerous instances presented themselves.

In one case a local peasant who made some extra cash by acting as a guide to deer hunters from the city was the target of a great deal of local hostility.

The community felt that local deer were to be hunted by local people (with or without licenses), not by "outsiders." Another instance was the fact that many local households engaged in the strictly illegal and very heavily fined practice of brewing liquor from potato mash. However, despite the fact that many bitter feuds constantly raged between households, nobody would have dreamed of turning in his or her antagonist to the cantonal (state) or federal police. In fact, sentiment against involving police in community matters was an extemely strong element of the local value system. These and other cases argued for the existence of a locally operating moral code—a community code that had much more meaning for local residents than did the formal legal systems of the town, canton, or federal governments.

An important question arose at this stage of my research: Was this moral system attached to a cognitively bounded area? In other words, was there in fact a local community with boundaries that could be identified? Did the reference group I had found occupy

---

* This folk perception is quite accurate. However, as of the summer of 1971, the township of Ilistral in fact paved the road leading from the town proper all the way up to the Bären Inn.

a "place"? Or was it merely a suggestive element, a vague notion in the minds of the local people?

I investigated this question by asking residents of what I believed to be the community to tell me "exactly" the area to which the phrase "we up here" referred. I had not expected this process to bear much fruit; I expected responses to be varied and idiosyncratic, if there were any responses at all. To my surprise (and delight), I found that this question made sense to people, and better yet, their responses were highly patterned. *Within* hamlets, individuals' responses were *identical*. Since I investigated three hamlets, I received three somewhat different sets of data. But when I superimposed these answers onto a map (see fig. 20-2), a "core area" that all three groups of people had included as being contained within

"up here" was revealed. Peripheral zones that showed decreased agreement were also delineated.

What is surprising, I think, is not the fact that transitional zones exist but rather the great amount of agreement over the core area. The transitional zones all lie along roads (see fig. 20-2) to the towns below, which means that communication or access is not broken at any obvious places. These transitional areas may be thought of as zones in which the "polar pulls" of the hilltop community and the towns in the valleys below are more or less balanced, so that individuals in these zones vacillate in their social interaction with and commitment to the local community versus the towns.

Along the agreed-upon borders of the core area, three dimensions that structure the cognitive boundary line emerged: limitation of visibility, limitation of ac-

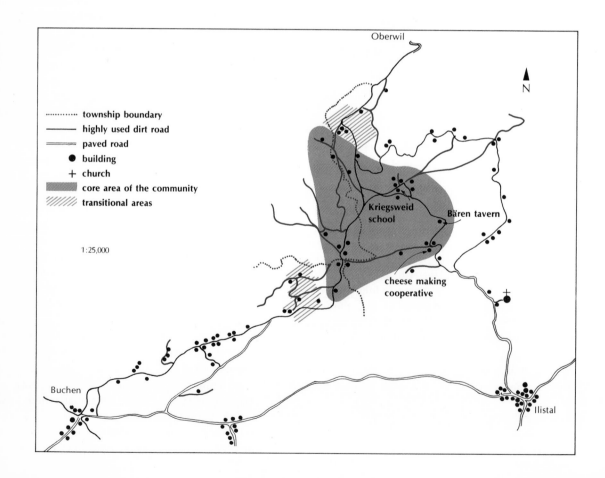

township boundary
highly used dirt road
paved road
● building
+ church
core area of the community
transitional areas

1:25,000

Oberwil

N

Kriegsweid school

Bären tavern

cheese making cooperative

Buchen

Ilistal

Figure 20-2
The Local Community

cess, and local animosity toward a particular household.

The eastern and western edges of the community core area are bounded by dense pine forests through which no major road pass. Thus in both access and visibility outward they represent "natural" cutoff lines, which are clearly represented in the local cognitive system. The part of the northern boundary that is sharply drawn is a very steep slope running down from the core area into a valley hidden from view. The transitional zone lies along the road leading down to the town of Oberwil.

The transitional zones on the southeast and southwest ends of the community also lie along major roads, linking the core area with the towns of Ilistral and Buchen, respectively. The southern boundary is partly delineated by a steep slope similar to the one in the north, but also by local animosity toward a family which lives halfway down the mountain. This particular household has had more than its share of troubles with the local moral code—and the cantonal and federal authorities as well. Consequently, this household is so despised that nobody included it as being inside the community boundary line.

Much has been theorized on the subject of deviant behavior. Many theorists believe that *deviants are necessary to communities* because, in effect, they are moral boundary markers by which the community "stakes out" its identity (see, for example, Becker 1963; Erikson 1966). This seems to be the case here; the community cognitive system draws a concrete, geographically expressed boundary line excluding this household.

Thus my research was bearing fruit. I had been able to identify a community, to delineate its boundaries in the local cognitive system, to identify components of its moral system, and as time went on, to demonstrate that people's interactions were patterned by this community—that is, community members tended to interact much more (and in predictable ways) with each other than with neighboring households that were outside the boundary line.

I also was finally able to establish my identity as a man to be reckoned with in terms of the local cultural system. At a pig-butchering feast, amid a great deal of drinking and bawdily boisterous behavior, one of the most obese local men made an ill-designed pass at Carolyn in my presence. Seizing the moment, I leveled him in the earthy imagery that characterized local humor. "Listen," I said, gazing pointedly at his bulging stomach, "it wouldn't matter even if you were alone with Carolyn: Your cock could never reach her anyhow." The prolonged hilarity and the nature of the jokes that followed left no doubt: What had started out as a putdown of me (via Carolyn) had been turned around at the other's expense, and I had won respect from the group for asserting myself and taking him on in terms of *their* value system.

Problems and Prospects

In A.D. 1600 the total population of Switzerland was 1,000,000. By 1850 this had risen to 2,393,000; by 1900, to 3,316,000; and by 1960, to 5,495,000 (of which 495,638 were foreign workers, mostly from Italy, Spain, and Greece) (Tschäni 1967:10). However, although the total population of the country has spiraled upward, since the turn of the century the cities have grown at the expense of the countryside. In Switzerland, as in most—if not all—industrializing nations, both absolute and percentage figures leave no doubt: The rural, agricultural way of life is being abandoned.

In 1900, 32 percent of the population of Switzerland depended on agriculture for its way of life. Thirty years later this had shrunk to only 21 percent; by 1950, to 17 percent; and by 1960, to 15 percent (Dovring 1965:84, extracted from table 11). In the canton of Bern itself, the picture is similar. In the fifty years between 1905 and 1955, the absolute number of male agricultural workers declined from 76,353 to 59,149, a drop of 22 percent. During the same period, the number of females engaged in agriculture declined even more starkly, from 61,889 to 28,696, a drop of 53 percent. These figures (*Statistiches Handbuch* 1964:76) dramatically show the major problem confronting the local community and other similar peasant communities in Switzerland: It is harder and harder to convince peasant boys that they should keep on farming in the traditional way, and peasant girls want even less to marry peasant boys who stay on farming homesteads.

Grim prospects. Because of deteriorating economic conditions, more and more homesteads are being abandoned as the young generation refuses the hardships of the peasant way of life and seeks relatively better living standards in the towns and cities.

Many of the eligible young men in the vicinity of the community I studied are unable to find wives. Much to the consternation of the older generation, the relatively easier way of life offered by the city overshadows the satisfactions of living away from the noisy crowd, on one's own property, farming one's own land. And if their sons cannot find brides, how can one expect them to stay? The peasant way of life is organized around the household, and the household is organized around the family. A single person cannot run a homestead unless he joins together with a brother, for instance. But, say the local people, what satisfaction is there in that?

Community members are unanimous in their gloomy predictions for the future. They see many small homesteads being consolidated into large commercial concerns, with pasturing replacing the labor-intensive, agricultural way of life. In the future the land will not be worked by tightly knit households committed to the traditional peasant life-style; instead, the countryside will become an extension of the industrial organization of the cities.

In my daily interactions with the community members, I became aware of the extent to which this gloomy picture preoccupies them. It makes them actively hostile toward outsiders, especially foreign workers who have immigrated into Switzerland, but also toward Swiss city folk. They feel betrayed by the national government, which maintains a public posture of attempting to preserve the small peasant households as a "national heritage," but is in fact helping along the destruction of their way of life through subsidization programs that favor the large, more mechanized farms in the broad valleys and flatlands. The peasants point to the increasing number of abandoned farmhouses dotting the countryside, falling apart, used by nobody. They discuss the difficulties facing local men who are trying to carry on even though they cannot find wives,

and they are bitter over the "frivolity" of this new generation of girls. "Nobody wants to work anymore," they lament.

The theme of hard work being good work is a major component of the local culture. Hard work keeps people honest, trustworthy. They see in the threat to their way of life an even larger threat—the decline of the moral fiber of the entire country. They point to government scandals with an expression of "What do you expect?" They see the emergence of vast, multinational corporations as the concrete embodiment of the disappearance of concern with the productivity of the individual, the application of standards to individual achievement and accomplishments. "Soon," they say, "Switzerland will be no better than any other country."

On the other hand, they are enamored of America. Every time I visited a family or drank away evenings at the local tavern, I was asked to describe life in the United States. My attempts to give a balanced picture that included poverty and slums were dismissed. What they enjoyed most of all were my descriptions of cattle ranches and midwestern farms. The immense size of these operations fascinated them, and even though they despised these very trends in Switzerland, they could indulge in daydreams about how it must be to own and work such mechanized operations in a setting far removed from their immediate environment.

The cold statistical facts appear to bear out the community's view of the future, although it may take more than fifty years for their way of life to pass from the scene. Not only is the rural population dwindling, but the percentage of local people engaged in agriculture is also declining. Even those individuals who do not leave the area are changing their means of livelihood. They are becoming municipal employees, taking jobs with the light industries that are moving into the valleys, and even commuting to the larger towns for jobs in the commercial sector.

As a foreigner who spent some fourteen months in this community, getting to know the people and becoming close friends with some, the vanishing of this way of life has personal meaning for me. I feel bad about it, for I can appreciate the positive aspects of their life-style. However, farming on these mountain slopes obviously does not "pay" (in the economic sense), and if it were to be preserved, it would take a massive financial commitment from the national government. This is unlikely.

However, I did make available to a local representative to the national government a copy of my dissertation (Hunter 1970), in which I argue strongly that this expenditure would be worthwhile. I think it is very sad—if not dangerous—that the ever industrializing world is loosening its relationship to its roots, to its heritage. What of Switzerland? Will the tenacity, the strength, the honesty that have characterized Swiss national character and culture for so long survive the destruction of her peasantry? The old people of the community sadly shake their heads . . .

Summary

The people discussed in this chapter are a relatively isolated community of Swiss peasants living in the alpine foothills of central Switzerland. The environment and the community itself are described, with emphasis on the subsistence activities, social organization, and culture of the group.

A major element is the description of the process of fieldwork itself. *Participant observation* is contrasted with other forms of social scientific research. The author tells the story of his fieldwork experience in the first person so that students can envision themselves in the peasant community—confronting the problems of initial acceptance, the difficulties of obtaining useful information, and the identity crisis the researcher undergoes in a social situation that lacks the supports of his usual life. Fieldwork engages and challenges both the researcher and the people being studied.

In the final section the author foresees the eventual disintegration of the community; he senses the personal meaning this has for him as well as for the native population. Thus fieldwork is often more than merely a research exercise; for many anthropologists it becomes a crucial episode in the person's life, a period of emotional and intellectual growth of great importance in the process of identity formation.

Annotated Bibliography

Arensberg, Conrad, and Kimball, Solon T. (1965)   *Culture and Community.* New York: Harcourt. A readable collection of essays on the nature of human communities. Of special interest is their sense that the community is the locus where person and culture intersect.

Becker, Howard (1963)   *Outsiders.* New York: Free Press. A classic in modern sociological literature. It discusses the ways in which people become labeled as "deviant" and the consequences this has for both the person so labeled and the wider society.

Hillery, Goerge A., Jr. (1955)   "Definitions of Community: Areas of Agreement." *Rural Sociology* 20:111–23. A must for any student interested in community study theory, this article examines a great number of definitions of the term *community* and systematically displays areas of difference and agreement.

Redfield, Robert (1960)   *The Little Community* and *Peasant Society and Culture* (in one volume). Chicago: Phoenix. Another classic. In the first essay Redfield looks at the community from different points of view and discovers that with each point of view the community becomes something else. This has profound implications not only for the study of communities but for all social research as well. In the second essay Redfield attempts to specify the nature of peasant societies.

Wax, Rosalie H. (1971)   *Doing Fieldwork: Warnings and Advice.* Chicago: Univ. of Chicago Press. A sensitive anthropologist writing about her responses to participant observation. She discusses her research in Japanese-American relocation centers during World War II and also two periods of research among American Indian groups. Wax clearly faces the crucial issue posed by this research technique: What do the subjects gain from this interaction?

21
The !Kung San:
A Hunting and Gathering Community

Introduction

Until ten to fifteen thousand years ago, hunting and gathering was the universal mode of human existence. Today this way of life persists in only a few marginal, isolated parts of the globe: deserts, tropical rain forests, and arctic tundra.

One of the best known and largest of the remaining hunting and gathering peoples are the San (once known as the "Bushmen"). Some 45,000 San live in and around the fringes of the Kalahari Desert of southern Africa. As recently as the early 1960s, when I began my fieldwork, about 20 percent of the San still subsisted on wild plant foods and game. Today the proportion of the San who subsist on hunting and gathering has shrunk to less than 5 percent, largely as a result of the rapid expansion of ranching and mining in the countries of Namibia and Botswana, where most of the San are currently found.

* The author gratefully acknowledges the financial support of the National Science Foundation, the National Institute of Mental Health, the Canada Council, and the Wenner-Gren Foundation for Anthropological Research.

The San are culturally and physically distinct from the neighboring Bantu peoples. They are quite small: Adult males average about five feet two inches in height, and adult females are about an even five feet. Their skin color is a coppery yellow at birth, darkening to a deeper brown in later years. The faces of the San appear to age and wrinkle very rapidly, probably because of a lack of subcutaneous fat, so to Westerners, they often seem to be much older than they are. The eyelids frequently have mongoloid folds. The females often display a condition known as steatopygia—that is, noticeably protuberant buttocks as a result of an inherited tendency to accumulate fat on that site rather than around the abdomen.

The various languages of the San belong to the Khoisan family, along with those of the distantly related Hottentots, who were virtually exterminated in the seventeenth century by Dutch settlers and smallpox. These languages possess an unusual phonetic feature called clicks—sharp popping sounds made by drawing the tongue sharply away from the roof of the mouth. The !Kung, the San people I have studied, have four different clicks: the dental (/), alveolar (=), alveopalatal (!), and the lateral (//) (see Chap. 7). Some Khoisan languages have as many as six separate clicks.

This chapter deals with the !Kung, a San people living in the northern Kalahari Desert. My own field-

left

The search for water. A !Kung hunter probes the hollow hole of a *Mongongo* tree for collected rainwater.

Figure 21-1

Major Study Sites of the San

The shaded area represents !Kung distribution.

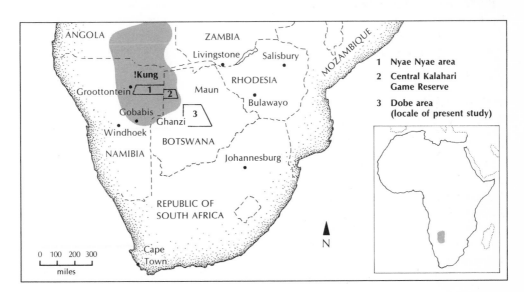

1   Nyae Nyae area

2   Central Kalahari
    Game Reserve

3   Dobe area
    (locale of present study)

work was with the !Kung of the Dobe area, a geo-graphically remote region in the northwest corner of Botswana. It is separated from the rest of the country by a belt of waterless territory about sixty-five miles wide. Some 460 San reside in the area, and they share their nine waterholes with several hundred members of the Herero, a tribe of Bantu pastoralists. Members of the Tswana, another Bantu tribe, are also scattered throughout the area. My fieldwork began in 1963, and since then I have spent over three years living and working with the !Kung in their own language.

The Environment

The Dobe area is part of a sandy plain lying 3,200 feet above sea level on the northern fringe of the Kalahari Desert. The region is about 20 degrees south of the equator, so that winter falls in July and August, and Christmas occurs in midsummer. The summers are hot and rainy, whereas the winters are dry and moder-ately cool. The annual rainfall in the northern Kalahari is highly variable, ranging between seven and forty-six inches. The area has no permanent rivers, but during exceptionally heavy rains, the low-lying regions may be flooded. After the floodwaters subside through evaporation and seepage into the deep sand, large scattered pools may remain for as long as six months after the rains have stopped. The year-to-year variabil-ity in the amount of surface water poses a continuing problem for the !Kung.

The Dobe area supports a particularly rich vegeta-tion characterized by broad-leaved trees and shrubs on the sand dunes, and acacias or other thorny species in the dry river courses. Some of the twenty species of excellent shade trees grow to fifty feet in height. Unlike most of the Kalahari Desert, which has sparsely wooded open plains, the Dobe area contains mature woodlands with abundant deep shade. The habitat thus provides the !Kung with an unlimited supply of firewood, cover from the hot sun, and a wide variety of hardwoods for making weapons, tools, and domestic articles.

Because of the broken nature of the vegetation, the area does not support the large herds of migratory plains game that are found on the open stretches of the southern Kalahari. Of the forty species of resident larger mammals, the most prominent are kudu, wilde-beest, and gemsbok. Giraffe, eland, roan antelope, and hartebeest are also present. Warthogs, ant bears, por-cupines, steenbok, duiker, and spring hares are also found and are of particular importance to the San as game.

The major African predators—lions, leopards, chee-tahs, wild dogs, and two species of hyena—are all repre-sented in the area. The smaller carnivores include caracal, wildcats, genets, jackals, and several species of mongoose. Birds, reptiles, amphibians, spiders, and insects are varied and abundant.

Almost 500 species of local plants and animals are known and named by the !Kung. Of these, the !Kung find some use for about 150 species of plants and 100 species of animals.

The Group

Subsistence Activities

The "hunting and gathering way of life" has some-times assumed a misleading connotation in the ethno-graphic literature. Especially in reference to the San, the term has come to imply a random and precarious existence of searching for food and eking out a living on odds and ends. In fact, however, the hunting and gathering Dobe !Kung have a reliable subsistence that is founded on a systematic exploitation of abundant food resources. Very little of their food getting is left to chance. They have an exhaustive knowledge of the local environment, of the habits of game, and of the growth phases of food plants. They rapidly disseminate information about food through a dense communica-tions network based on intercamp visiting. They know where the food is at each season of the year, and they know how to get it. They do not allow themselves to run short of food resources; even during the period of scarcity at the end of the dry season, the gatherers never come home empty handed.

For their subsistence the Dobe !Kung rely primarily on more than a hundred species of edible plants in the Dobe area. These include thirty species of roots and bulbs, thirty species of berries and fruits, and an assortment of melons, nuts, leafy greens, and edible gums. The most important of the food plants is the mongongo nut, a superabundant staple whose fruit and kernel are both edible. The kernel contains 600 calories per 100 grams and has a protein content of 27 percent, a nutritional value comparable to the richest cultivated foods, such as groundnuts and soybeans. The !Kung consume thousands of pounds of these nuts each year, yet thousands more rot on the ground for want of eating. Not all the San foods are attractive, however. Some of the larger roots and melons have a decidedly bitter taste and a high proportion of roughage, and the San eat them only when more desirable foods are in short supply.

However, vegetable foods are so plentiful for most of the year that the !Kung can afford to exercise selectivity in their diet. They tend to eat only the most attractive foods available during a given season and bypass those that are less desirable in taste or ease of

Women gather the berries of the buffalo-thorn tree. Over 100 species of wild plant foods are eaten by the !Kung.

collection. Twenty-three species of plants account for about 90 percent of their annual vegetable diet by weight, and one species, the mongongo nut, accounts for at least half the total.

Game resources are less abundant and less predictable than plants. Meat provides from 20 to 50 percent of the diet by weight, depending on the season and the number of men hunting in the camp. The big antelopes—kudu, wildebeest, and gemsbok—are regularly hunted with poisoned arrows, but a hunter feels he has done well if he kills as many as six of these in a year. In addition, the hunters stalk warthogs with hunting dogs. The owner of a well-trained pack of four or five dogs can count on a yearly catch of twelve to fifteen of these animals, which weigh 110 to 155 pounds. Duiker and steenbok, small antelope weighing 20 to 35 pounds, are next in importance; the hunters take them with dogs, trap them in rope snares, or shoot them with poisoned arrows. Spring hares, ant bears, and porcupines are sought in the underground burrows they sleep in during the day. Game birds are caught in snares and are considered a delicacy. The big leopard tortoise, which weighs up to nine pounds, is a great favorite. In general, the San of the Dobe area despise snakes, lizards, and insects.

The organization of work is simple. Members leave camp each day and work through the surrounding range, either individually or in small groups. They return in the evening and pool the collected resources. The sexes are almost always segregated in food-getting activities. The women go out in groups of three to five, usually with the intention of collecting a particular species. Each woman takes a *kaross,* a leather wrap-around, one-piece garment-cum-carrying device, and when these have been filled, the group returns home by the middle or late afternoon. The women never stay out overnight.

Hunting is reserved for men and is a more individualistic activity; the hunters go out alone or in pairs. Luck plays a large role in the hunt, and not every day's work is rewarded with success. In fact, in one study the men averaged only one kill for every four days of hunting. The key to large-game hunting is an arrow poison that the San make from the larva of a particular beetle. The poison works effectively but slowly, killing a large

A ten year old girl and her grandmother relax in the camp during an afternoon. Contrary to popular assumptions, these hunters and gatherers must devote only three days per week to the finding of food.

Two hunters have found an ostrich nest. The eggs will be carefully emptied; after the contents are cooked and eaten the shells themselves will be made into containers for carrying and storing water.

antelope in twelve to eighteen hours. Although a hunter may kill six or fewer large antelopes a year, a 650-pound kudu can feed a camp of thirty persons for three days, and visitors converge from far and wide to join in the good fortune.

Despite the fact that hunting and gathering is the main means of subsistence, very little time is actually spent on the quest for food. During one month, I kept a record of the work activities of the twenty-eight members of the Dobe camp and their visitors. The results showed that both men and women devoted between two and three days per week to getting food. The rest of the time was spent resting, house cleaning, visiting other camps, and entertaining visitors. The low level of work effort is doubly impressive considering that this was a year of serious drought. The crops and herds of their pastoral neighbors suffered serious losses, but the hunting and gathering subsistence of the !Kung seemed hardly to have been affected (Lee 1968a, 1969).

Social Organization

The definition of !Kung living arrangements presents a challenging problem to the observer. The !Kung commonly live in camps containing from ten to thirty individuals, but the composition of these camps changes from month to month and from day to day. Intercamp visiting is the main reason for this fluctuation, but each year about 15 percent of the population shifts permanently from one camp to another. Another 35 percent divide their time equally between two or three different camps, both in and out of the Dobe area.

The constant circulation of population makes it appear at first that residential life has no stable basis and that the !Kung are a mobile people who can live anywhere and with anyone, but in no one place for long. Yet closer observation reveals that the !Kung living arrangements are stable and are based on underlying principles of association.

At the center of each camp is a "core" of siblings and their offspring of both sexes, who share a claim to the ownership of their waterhole. These owners are simply the people who have lived at the waterhole longer than any others, and they are generally recognized as the "hosts" whom one approaches when visiting a camp. Each camp is gradually built up by the addition to the group of the spouses of the core siblings. These spouses, in turn, may bring with them their siblings and their siblings' spouses, so that the basic genealogical structure of the camp assumes the form of a chain of spouses and siblings radiating from the core, as shown in figure 21-2.

The core siblings of camps are of both sexes. An analysis of twelve camps showed that a brother and sister formed the core in four cases, two sisters and one brother in two cases, and two brothers and one sister in one case. In addition, four camps had cores composed of two sisters, and one had a core composed of two brothers. These varied combinations are to be expected in a strongly bilateral society such as the !Kung, a society without a strict rule of descent through either the male or the female line.

The relatively short-lived ownership of the waterholes is related to the bilateral nature of the group structure. In all but two of the twelve camps, the present owners of the waterholes were born elsewhere. Typically, the core sibling group moved into the waterhole area twenty-five to fifty years ago, when one of them married a young woman or man of the previous core group. The previous owners then died or moved away, leaving the newcomers in possession of the waterhole.

The causes of this high turnover may be found in demographic factors, particularly in the variations of family size and sex ratios that may occur among the very small populations. Because of the small family size and the likelihood of disparities in sex ratios, a family would have great difficulty in maintaining its numbers at an ecologically viable level if it had to depend solely on natural replacement. For example, if the rule of residence were strictly patrilocal—with women marrying out and the men bringing their spouses in—a waterhole group that had only daughters would soon be put out of business; and a waterhole group with a preponderance of male offspring would

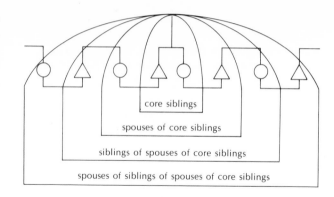

core siblings

spouses of core siblings

siblings of spouses of core siblings

spouses of siblings of spouses of core siblings

Figure 21-2
The Building of a !Kung Camp
The development of a camp by the addition of spouses and spouses' siblings to the core siblings.

have more hunters on hand than the limited game could support.

A far more adaptive way of maintaining group size and distributing population evenly over the resources is to allow many different avenues of group affiliation. The flexible group structure found in the Dobe area is the result. The !Kung do not resort to elaborate fictions to make their living arrangements conform to an ideal model. They simply leave group and geographic boundaries open and allow the most effective subsistence unit to emerge anew in each generation.

Coupled with the flexible group structure is an ingenious kinship system that is organized through a network of shared personal names. The !Kung have a limited repertoire of personal names: Only thirty-five men's names and thirty-four women's names were in use in the Dobe area. All names are sex-specific, and there are no surnames. Personal names are transmitted from grandparent to grandchild according to strict rules of precedence. There are no "new" names, and the current repertoire appears to have been handed down over many generations. A first-born male is named after his father's father, and a first-born female after her father's mother. The second-born child of each sex is named for her or his maternal grandparent. If further children are born, they are named after siblings of their parents or more distant relatives. Parents may never name children after themselves.

This naming system enables the !Kung to extend primary kinship ties far beyond the boundaries of personal genealogical kindreds. In fact, the thousands of speakers of the !Kung language are connected by name relations into a network of fictive kinship that extends from Angola in the north to central Botswana, 500 miles to the south. The principle is that bearers of the same name have a special affectionate relation with one another, regardless of the biological connection. In fact, the relationship obtains even if no biological connection is traceable.

The !Kung believe that all persons holding a particular name are descended from the original bearer of that name. In the Dobe area, 22 of 223 men are named ≠oma, and whenever ≠omas meet, they enjoy the familiarity of a joking relationship (see chaps. 8 and 9). The bonds are particularly strong among men who know that they share a common ancestral namesake.

For instance, 9 of the 12 men named /i!ay in the Dobe area are descended from a single prolific /i!ay. Of him it can truly be said that his name is legion. With 70 percent of the population using only 20 of the personal names in use, it is almost always possible for a person to establish a name kinship connection with another even if he or she comes from a far distant camp. In fact, several possible name routes from one person to another usually exist. This ambiguity is useful to the !Kung, for it enables them to keep the kinship system flexible in the face of frequent changes in group structure.

The far-reaching ties made possible by the name relation <u>are</u> of particular importance in the arrangement of marriages. The !Kung are unusual among hunters and gatherers in that they extend the incest taboo collaterally and forbid marriages between actual cousins. Moreover, a man may not marry a girl with the same name as his mother, his sister, or in the case of second marriages, the same name as his daughter or his first mother-in-law. Similarly, a girl may not marry a man whose name is the same as that of her father, her brother, her son, or her father-in-law. These prohibitions send the young men and women far afield when seeking a spouse.

Men marry between the ages of twenty and thirty, usually after they have served a period as cattle herders for their Bantu neighbors, the Herero. Girls marry around the time of menarche, which among the San tends to occur between the ages of fourteen and sixteen. Parents try to arrange a match while their children are still young, and one of the more pleasant topics discussed during intercamp visiting is betrothal. Most of these arrangements go by the board, however, because the adolescents of both sexes often have ideas of their own. In current practice, young people frequently go through a period in which they may have several temporary liaisons before they settle down with a lifelong partner.

The qualities a girl's parents look for in a son-in-law are hunting ability and a pleasant, nonaggressive personality. To prove himself, the young husband may serve a period of "bride service" in the camp of his wife's parents. However, because of the fluidity of group structure, the young couple may spend as much as half of their time living elsewhere.

Divorce is common in the early years of adult life. Arranged marriages often fail, and divorce is initiated as frequently by the women as by the men. A wife may pack up and go if her husband is adulterous, if he beats her, or if he insists upon taking a second wife. Divorce is a simple matter, since there is no community property and no bride's wealth (see Chap. 8) to dispute about. Children always remain in the "custody" of their mother. In general, divorce does not leave the same bitterness among the !Kung that it often does in our society. Ex-spouses usually maintain cordial relations and may even continue to live in the same camp after one or both have remarried.

The Dobe !Kung are a society that manages its own affairs without a state structure and without even an authority figure such as a chief or a headman. Leadership, like ownership of land, is collective and is shared by both men and women.

Personal qualities may make some waterhole owners informal leaders. Such a leader may persuade and set a good example, but he or she possesses no authority to enforce decisions. In fact, the !Kung are fiercely egalitarian and become resentful if any member of their society tells them what to do. This absence of authority may seem like anarchy, but it works. In the event of serious conflict within a !Kung group, the members often prefer to split up and go their separate ways rather than let a dispute become violent. But the !Kung are by no means pacifists: They argue frequently and loudly. I recorded over fifty instances of fistfights between !Kung during my three years of fieldwork and even homicide is not unknown. But the strong crosscutting kinship ties and the wide-open spaces at the doorstep are two factors that keep arguments from escalating into feuds and warfare. I felt safer living with the anarchic !Kung, 185 miles from the nearest police station, than I have felt at night on the streets of large American cities.

Culture

To understand the ideology or conceptual organization of !Kung culture, we must start with the basic facts of their isolated hunting and gathering way of life, for their material conditions have shaped their

Hunting and gathering requires mobility. Children are carried hundreds of miles by their parents (and older siblings) each year. This four year old is accompanying her mother, who is foraging for food.

values and character. Let us begin with the communal nature of !Kung camp life.

When food is brought into a camp at the end of the day, it is distributed so that everyone receives an equitable share. There is a constant flow of people and foodstuffs from camp fire to camp fire as the !Kung eat, catch up on the day's events, and relax with good company. Of course, not every ounce of food is divided equally among every individual; that would be far too cumbersome. Vegetable foods are usually eaten at the gatherer's hearth or passed to adjacent hearths, but meat is far more formally shared. Men do much of the cooking and carefully distribute the portions of cooked meat according to kinship and the food taboos of the individuals present.

The !Kung camp is a unit of sharing, and when sharing breaks down, it ceases to be a camp. Parties in disagreement will split up and seek another camp where the relations are more congenial. Stinginess and hard-

A !Kung delicacy! Giant truffles (long treasured by European *gourmets*) are collected by !Kung children as an afternoon's diversion.

heartedness are regarded by the !Kung as cardinal sins, but "generosity" is not rewarded with praise or congratulations: it is merely considered elementary good manners. The !Kung have no word for "thank you," and when they encounter Europeans who expect it, they borrow the Afrikaans word *dankie* to please their visitors.

The importance of sharing is related to the face-to-face nature of !Kung social life. A !Kung camp has no walls, everyone's daily life is lived in full view of thirty or more neighbors. The !Kung build small grass huts, in which they may store their possessions and which they may use when it rains, but they do not live in them. All cooking and socializing and most sleeping and sex take place in front of the hut at the camp fire. There are no secrets in the life of the !Kung; everyone knows everyone else's business. When I asked a !Kung married woman with two children how she and her husband made love under those circumstances, she replied, "Very carefully!"

"But doesn't that mean that everyone can see you doing it?" I countered.

"That is true," she said, "but you are not supposed to look!"

The !Kung rarely sleep alone. Father, mother, and young children sleep by the fire under the same blanket. As a boy or girl grows older, he or she may share the blanket of an older sibling or cousin of the same sex. Widows team up with unmarried young women, and even teenage boys and young men sleep three or four to a blanket in the larger camps. In fact, only some widowed older men sleep alone regularly. Inevitably, the intimacy of eating and sleeping behavior strongly affects the style of interpersonal relations.

How are the !Kung able to live up to the demands of their communal existence? This is a complex question, and I can only suggest a few tentative answers about the style of their interpersonal relations. Observers have been struck by the directness of communication between !Kung. Rather than treading lightly and avoiding sensitive areas, !Kung come right to the point and confront one another with the issues. These confrontations are sometimes shocking to North Americans, who are schooled to politeness to the point of deviousness. If a woman's sex life is not going well,

she announces to the group, "My husband can't get it up!" The argument takes off from there. The discussion moves through accusation and counteraccusation until all parties—husband, wife, and others—have stated their positions. Everything is "up front" and out in the open, and the airing of grievances opens the way for understanding and progress.

The !Kung strongly discourage two behaviors: sullen withdrawal and boastful arrogance. Neighbors and kin quickly bring the sullen one out of his shell, usually by provoking his anger and then his laughter. And the !Kung have effective techniques for bursting the bubble of conceit and enforcing humility. When a large animal is killed, the !Kung always belittle the value of the kill, saying, "Oh, what a wretched piece of skin and bones" or "You call this an animal? It is hardly worth carrying back to camp!" To this the hunter must reply, "You are right: let's leave this mess for the hyenas and hunt for something else." Then the men settle down to butchering the meat and carrying it back to camp to be eaten. If a man is allowed to boast unchallenged, say the !Kung, his arrogance may lead to his killing someone. To counteract this tendency, in the words of one !Kung, "We insult his meat, to cool his heart and make him gentle."

!Kung attitudes toward headmanship highlight the strong egalitarian ethos of their life. The existence of a hereditary headman for the !Kung had been reported (L. Marshall 1969). But when I asked the !Kung about it, they invariably denied that they ever had a headman. If such a person now exists, they argue, it is only a product of their contact with their Bantu neighbors, the hierarchically organized Tswana. One !Kung summed it up best. When I asked him if the !Kung have headmen, he surprised me by answering, "Of course we have headmen!" But then he added: "In fact, we are all headmen—each one of us is headman over himself."

The !Kung envision a universe in which an intimate relationship exists among their two gods, the ghosts of ancestors, and the community of living people. The high god, ≠*guan!a*, is a rather remote force, the creator of the world and the ultimate source of misfortune and death. //*gangwa*, the lesser god, is a trickster who is the chief protagonist in a rich series of myths about the distant past, when animals and humans were not yet differentiated and lived together in a single society. //gangwa's escapades are still hilariously retold today by gifted !Kung storytellers but //gangwa himself plays little role in human affairs. Of far greater importance are the //gangwasi, the ghosts of the recently dead. These shadows may hover in the vicinity of !Kung camps for years after a person has died. The !Kung believe that the //gangwasi are the principal bringers of sickness and death to the community. Indeed, until recent times, the !Kung always abandoned a campsite in which a death had occurred.

The role of the healer, or shaman, is to pull sickness out of sick people and drive malevolent ghosts out of the vicinity. The famous !Kung healing dance is a dramatic setting in which the forces of good represented by the medicine people struggle with the forces

The women's healing dance. Two healers work on a patient; all three are in a trance.

of evil, the //*gangwasi* (L. Marshall 1969; Lee 1967, 1968b; J. Marshall 1969; Katz 1974). The dances begin after sundown and may last until dawn. The women sit in the center of the camp around a sacred fire, and the men dance in a tight circle around the perimeter. There are several medicine dances, each with its distinctive melody and intricate rhythmic pattern.

In the early part of the evening the atmosphere is relaxed, but the atmosphere intensifies as the evening progresses, and gradually one or more of the shamans begins to enter a trance state. The dancer's body becomes rigid, the shock waves of his footfalls ripple through his body, he sweats profusely, his chest heaves. When he is fully in the trance state, he moves around the group from person to person, laying on hands, pulling sickness from the bodies and casting it into the darkness with characteristic blood-curdling shrieks. Everyone present at a dance receives this treatment as a form of supernatural protection, but sick people are given special attention, with the healer returning again and again to lay on hands. Two or more healers may work on the same sick person for over an hour. In a case of severe illness, an all-out effort may be made, with healers converging from far and wide to work on a patient. I have seen five healers, male and female, working simultaneously on a single patient and carrying on an extensive dialogue with each other and with the ghosts.

The content of these dialogues reveals an intricate and sophisticated folk belief system of misfortune and death and the ways of counteracting it. According to the !Kung, the society of the dead reduplicates exactly the society of the living. The dead live in camps in family groups and subsist by hunting and gathering. In death the !Kung lose their contact with the living world but are reunited with all the loved ones who have predeceased them. Nevertheless, a ghost may feel intense longing for those he or she has left behind. Because of these longings, the ghost may send sickness or injury to a living loved one, so that the person will die and move into the world of the dead.

The living resist the efforts of the ghosts. In the trance state, the shamans have the ability to see the ghosts and to argue, negotiate, and even grapple with them until they go away and leave the living in peace.

"Begone!" they shout at the ghosts. "Go where you belong! Beat it! Scram!"

The !Kung conceive of the process of dying as a struggle between two groups of loving relatives for the possession of an individual. When a patient recovers from a severe illness, it is regarded as a triumph of the living over the dead. Even when he dies the !Kung console themselves by saying that his dead loved ones wanted him so much that the living were powerless to stop them.

Since nine-tenths of all diseases are self-limiting, the healers enjoy a very high success rate. This high recovery rate reinforces the belief that the !Kung traditional method of curing is indeed powerful. The !Kung *are* effective in their struggles to preserve the health and well-being of their communities. The evil forces (ghosts) are not all-powerful and can be defeated. Thus the !Kung extend the egalitarianism of their society even to their relations with supernatural beings.

Problems and Prospects

In January 1974, twenty-two !Kung children aged five to ten, dressed in khaki shorts and crisp new dresses, sat down timidly in a classroom in the recently opened !Kangwa Primary School. These youngsters were the first of the Dobe area !Kung to receive any formal education. This event typifies the accelerating changes that have overtaken the !Kung in the past twenty-five years. Today hunting and gathering, though still the dominant mode of subsistence, is no longer the sole support of the !Kung. Sharecropping of the cattle of the neighboring Tswana, wage work, and independent farming and herding now provide up to half of the income of the !Kung camps.

Sharecropping is practical under the *mafisa* system, in which cattle are farmed out to poor people who manage and increase the herd. The system has been practised by the Tswana for centuries and has more recently been introduced to the !Kung and other San peoples. Under the *mafisa* system, a !Kung family agrees to maintain a small herd of from five to twenty cattle at their waterhole. The !Kung water and graze the animals and protect them from predators, and in return, they drink the milk the cows provide. If an animal dies they eat the meat, but the owner must be informed. All the calves born are the property of the owner, with the exception of a single calf that is the traditional annual payment to the !Kung family. Because the worker manages a resource owned by others and consumes only a share of the products of his labor, *mafisa* can be regarded as a system of sharecropping. *Mafisa* relations are semifeudal in nature; the arrangement may last for many years, and the obligation may be handed down from father to son.

The Herero, the Bantu pastoralists who share the waterholes of the Dobe area, practice a system of cattle herding that is somewhat different from the *mafisa* system of the Tswana. In the Herero system, a !Kung boy works out a contract of one or two years. He receives clothing and rations during this period, and he is given a calf upon completion of the term of work. Most of the !Kung men have been employed

Scraping the hair off a *kudu* hide to make a *kaross*.

under the *mafisa* or the Herero system at some time. Even older !Kung men who are now full-time hunters and gatherers describe a period of their lives when they herded cattle.

Many of the Dobe !Kung are now engaged in wage labor. In 1967 a store was opened in the !Kangwa Valley, and today about a dozen !Kung men work there for wages. The store offers a small range of goods and basic commodities such as sugar and cornmeal at inflated prices, but its main purpose is to buy cattle from the highly successful Herero and Tswana pastoralists. Every six weeks or so the purchased cattle are driven out to the marketplace 180 miles to the east. In 1973, despite the high rate of inflation, the !Kung working in the store were earning under $7 per week.

Migrant labor is another source of cash. Since the early 1960s a steady stream of young men has trekked out to the depot of the Witwatersrand Native Labour Association to be airlifted to the gold mines of the neighboring Republic of South Africa, from which they return nine months later with the equivalent of ten to twenty-five dollars in their pockets; most of the remaining wages has been spent on beer, prostitutes, and gambling in the mine towns. Despite a 500 percent increase in the price of gold since 1963, the wages paid to the !Kung and to thousands of other nonwhite migrant mine workers has risen by less than 50 percent. This widespread exploitation of African labor contributes to the continued prosperity of white South Africa.

Cash has had a dramatic impact on !Kung life. For example, a number of women brew beer called *khadi* from store-bought sugar, wild berries, and bee earth. They charge five cents a cup for this potion, and they always sell out the bucket within a few hours. The entire concept of payment for goods or services is foreign to the !Kung ethic of sharing, but the *khadi* entrepreneurs, modeled after their Tswana and Herero sisters, nevertheless do a thriving business. The principle of cash payment has not yet extended to other spheres, however; after selling her beer, a !Kung woman may then share her gathered foods in the traditional way with her former customers!

Independent farming is an increasingly important subsistence activity. The !Kung are no strangers to agriculture. Over the years they have learned the techniques from their Bantu neighbors, and a number of families have harvested crops. In years of good rainfall some !Kung experiment with agriculture, but when the crops fail as a result of the frequent droughts, they fall back on hunting and gathering. Simple dry-farming techniques yield a maize and millet harvest only two or three years in five, but mongongo nuts never fail completely.

Without irrigation, agriculture may never form a stable basis for life in the Dobe area. But stock raising in these vast, sparsely grazed grasslands could provide a reliable living for the !Kung. After fifty years of contact with the Bantu, however, very few !Kung have become established as herders. Many men who have worked for the Tswana or Herero have received calves in payment, but over 90 percent of these have been lost through natural causes, sold, consumed, or paid as a fine for some breach of law. Moreover, a minimum herd of from five to ten animals is required before a family can support itself by pastoralism. Such a starting herd would require years of *mafisa* service, as well as much good luck to ensure the animals' survival. Fewer than 10 percent of the Dobe area !Kung families have successfully made the transition to pastoralism.

One of the most severe problems facing the San stems from recent changes in the Botswana land tenure system. In 1968 the Botswana legislature passed the Tribal Land Act, a measure intended to take land out of communal tribal tenure and allot it to private individuals and groups. The stated purpose of the act is to put agriculture and stock raising on a more rational and scientific basis to prevent overgrazing and to ensure the continued production of livestock for the export market. Similar changes in land tenure have taken place in all developed nonsocialist countries, and such a move is regarded by some economic theorists as a prerequisite to economic development. But the change could have disastrous consequences for the San and other peoples, in effect making them squatters on the land they have traditionally occupied. Unless they establish land rights, politically impotent people like the San can be evicted at will by the "owner" of the land. Such evictions have already taken place in parts of Botswana when land has fallen into freehold tenure (Biesele and Lee 1974).

What is to prevent the San themselves from obtaining a tract of their own land? The answer is that the San have not yet mastered the literacy and legal skills required to present and carry through an application to the relevant government board. They cannot compete in this respect against their Bantu fellow citizens, who have had access to schooling for many years.

For centuries the !Kung San of the Dobe area were a proud and independent people. Today they are beset by problems: exploitation through low wages in the mines; discrimination through lack of education and subordinate status in a society dominated by the Tswana majority; and now the threatened loss of their land base. Native Americans, Australian Aborigines, African peasants, and many other indigenous peoples face similar problems in the modern world.

It is a tribute to the fierce independence and tenacity of the Dobe area San that they continue to pre-

Probing underground burrows. A hunter crawls into the burrow of an antbear in an attempt to spear the creature, which sleeps deep underground by day. Meanwhile, his partner is poised to quickly pull him out if the animal should attack.

A musical bow. The !Kung have adapted the form of their major hunting weapon to make several versions of musical instruments. The bow shown here uses a strip of palm frond as the string; the person's mouth acts as the resonating chamber.

serve their culture, hundreds and even thousands of years after most of the world's people have become incorporated into larger and more technological societies. The San and other hunting and gathering peoples therefore have something to teach us, not as living fossils or historical curiosities but as a people living in harmony with themselves and their environment.

Epilogue

It becomes increasingly difficult for scholars to remain completely detached from the plight and struggles of the people they study. In recent years a group of anthropologists and others who have studied the !Kung San have agreed that our responsibility to them goes beyond simply publishing the results of our studies in the appropriate journals. In 1973 the Kalahari Peoples Fund of Cambridge, Massachusetts, was formed to give shape and direction to this extended responsibility. The KPF has two purposes: to work with the San in their struggle for self-determination, and to make our knowledge and financial resources available to the San to develop their communities.

In January, 1974, the Kalahari Peoples Fund provided the scholarships for the twenty-two !Kung schoolchildren mentioned earlier in this chapter. Part of the proceeds of this and other publications on the San are being contributed to the KPF to finance educational and development work with the San. If you are interested in learning more about the work of the KPF, write:

Kalahari Peoples Fund
c/o Cultural Survival, Inc.
10 Divinity Avenue
Cambridge, Massachusetts 02138

Summary

The !Kung San of the Republic of Botswana are one of the last remaining hunting and gathering societies. They live by gathering wild plant foods and hunting game animals with bows and poisoned arrows. Food is not scarce, nor is their life precarious. Over 100 plant and 50 animal species are eaten. An intimate knowledge of their environment and the strong emphasis on sharing are two factors that make the !Kung way of life secure.

!Kung live in flexible, multifamily camps of ten to thirty people. Camps frequently change in size and composition through the comings and goings of people in intercamp visiting. At the core of each camp are several older people who are the acknowledged "owners" of the waterhole and its resources.

Political independence, egalitarianism, and sharing are three basic features that mold !Kung life and character. The !Kung are by no means nonviolent, but the frequent arguments and fights usually dissipate rapidly. A rough form of bawdy good humor helps to clear the atmosphere and to maintain communication.

In recent years great changes have overtaken the !Kung. Wage work, migrant labor, and the cash economy have become increasingly important. Many young men work for a period herding cattle for their Bantu neighbors, and a few families have made a successful transition to independent stock raising. Whether the !Kung will survive in an increasingly uncertain future depends on their educational opportunities and the preservation of their land base.

In 1973 a Cambridge-based group of anthropologists who have studied the !Kung began to provide the !Kung with material support to aid their efforts to determine their own future.

(1969) "!Kung Bushmen Subsistence: An Input-Output Analysis." In *Environment and Cultural Behavior: Ecological Studies in Cultural Anthropology,* ed. Andrew P. Vayda, pp. 47–79. New York: Natural History Press. Energy and exchange relations of a hunting and gathering society.

(1972) "The !Kung Bushmen of Botswana." In *Hunters and Gatherers Today,* ed. M. Brechieri, pp. 327–68. New York: Holt. A detailed ethnographic account of the Dobe area !Kung.

Lee, Richard B., and De Vore, Irven, eds. (1968) *Man the Hunter.* Chicago: Aldine. Fifty contributors discuss the world's hunter-gatherers: their current status, organization, economy, and future. Includes results from recent field research.

(1976) *Kalahari Hunter-Gatherers.* Cambridge, Mass.: Harvard Univ. Press. Field studies of the San by fifteen authors, including specialists in ethnology, ecology, archaeology, demography, ethology, child behavior, folklore, and social change.

Marshall, L. (1957) "The Kin Terminology System of the !Kung Bushmen." *Africa* 27:1–25. An excellent introduction to the complexities of !Kung kinship and the name relation.

(1959) "Marriage among !Kung Bushmen." *Africa* 29:335–65.

Thomas, Elizabeth M. (1959) *The Harmless People.* New York: Knopf. A charming account of the Marshall family's residence among the Bushmen.

Turnbull, Colin M. (1965) *Wayward Servants: The Two Worlds of the African Pygmies.* New York: Natural History Press. Contemporary African hunters with a rich food base and flexible social organization.

Annotated Bibliography

Jorgensen, J. and Lee, Richard B. (1974) *The New Native Resistance: Indigenous Peoples' Struggles and the Responsibilities of Scholars.* New York: MSS Modular Publications. Native political activists from three continents talk of their struggles while anthropologists listen.

Lee, Richard B. (1967) "Trance Cure of the !Kung Bushmen." *Natural History,* November 1967, pp. 30–37. Bushman ritual curing, trance performances, and theory of disease causation.

22

Mutayr: *A Tribe of Saudi Arabian Pastoral Nomads*

Introduction

What, or who, is a Bedouin? Westerners in the Middle East habitually and rather casually call almost any country person wearing Arab garb a Bedouin. But the Bedouins themselves have a much stricter definition. First, a Bedouin must be a nomad who breeds and owns camels. Any nonnomad is ruled out, and so are the thousands of tent-dwelling nomads in Syria and Iraq who breed primarily sheep, goats, and donkeys. In addition, Bedouins must be able to trace their descent from certain Arab tribes recognized as being purebred or noble (*asīl*). Thus, in the strictest sense, a Bedouin is an Arab camel-breeding nomad belonging to certain specified tribes, one of which is the tribe of Mutayr (moo-TEHR).

No official population census of Arab Bedouin tribes has been published to date. In the Arabian peninsula, they probably number about 800,000 people. Various sources (von Oppenheim 1952; Dickson 1949) seem to agree with my own observations that the tribe of Mutayr is approximately 25,000 strong. But the population of Bedouin tribes is difficult to ascertain. From time to time, a winter traveler in a tribal area will encounter small Bedouin camps consisting perhaps of

This tribesman poses with some of the articles commonly found in a Bedouin tent such as the one behind him. Sitting on a tent-divider which also serves as a rug, he holds several handleless coffee cups and a coffee-roasting "spoon." Before him are, left to right: a stone pestle and silver-studded brass mortar, used for grinding cardamom seeds (the mortar also used as an incense burner); wooden bowl with pouring spout, used to hold ground ingredients for coffee; stirrer, used with the large spoon in roasting coffee; tongs for handling hot embers; brass mortar-and-pestle for grinding roasted coffee beans; coffee pots, the blackened ones for boiling water, the smaller brass one for serving coffee; a small chest of carved wood for storing valuables; and a bellows for making or reviving a fire.

only six or seven tents and will conclude that the tribe has fewer people than it actually does. However, in the summer a traveler may suddenly reach the edge of a scarp and see in the depression below hundreds of black tents row upon row, clustered around a group of low, conical mounds that mark the locations of water wells. Moreover, if our summer traveler happens to reach this point shortly before sunset, he or she will notice in addition thousands of camels, sheep, and goats, converging from all directions, bleating, braying, and kicking up dense dust clouds as they make for their watering places. These, in al-Lihābah, are but some of the tents and the livestock of Mutayr. At this time of the year the traveler will conclude that the tribe of Mutayr is much larger than it actually is.

Hardly anything is known with certainty about the origin of the tribe of Mutayr. Frequently among nomadic tribes, many years of peace and favorable envi-

ronmental conditions produce a large increase in population. As a result, the tribe may become segmented. What had previously been tribal sections may become independent tribes claiming their own territory, although normally the new tribes will retain a sense of common origin and will keep the old allegiances. Conversely, unfavorable conditions—such as famine, pestilence, drought, or war—over a number of years may shrink the size of a tribe from several thousand members to perhaps only a few hundred. These remnants may survive for many years as small tribes. At times, however, some of them may become allies and may eventually fuse into a single, larger tribe. It is generally believed (von Oppenheim 1952:72) that this is how the tribe of Mutayr came into being: as the result of a fusion of various tribal remnants and splinter groups of earlier Qahtāni and 'Adnāni tribes. Qahtān and 'Adnān are the two legendary ancestors of all noble Bedouin tribes, and because of this descent, the tribe of Mutayr is considered noble. Their earlier home seems to have been in the west-central Najd, a considerable distance to the west and south from their present habitat. They are reported to have been in the old location in the fourteenth century and to have moved to their present range at the end of the eighteenth century (von Oppenheim 1952:72).

The Environment

Every Bedouin tribe in Arabia, like many nomadic peoples elsewhere, "owns" a *dīrah*, or tribal grazing land, over which it roams throughout the year in search of grass and water for its livestock. However, this ownership is not to be thought of as direct, personal, and documented possession of real estate in Western terms; nor are the boundaries of a *dīrah* to be taken as well defined, surveyed, and monumented, let alone immutable. Rather, the extent of a tribal *dīrah* is the area that includes all permanent water wells and adjacent grazing lands traditionally belonging to the various sections of the tribe. The boundaries of a *dīrah* are not permanently fixed. Tribal wars, for instance, may result in changes in the ownership of wells, or certain wells may dry out and be abandoned. But such changes in the area of a *dīrah* generally occur over a long period of time.

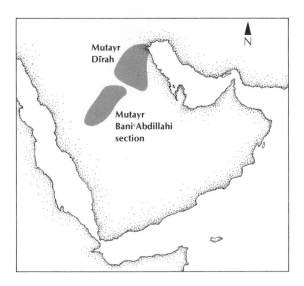

Figure 22-1
The Saudi Arabian Peninsula Showing the Location of the Mutayr Dīrah

Figure 22-2
Major Geographical Locations in the Mutayr Dīrah

The *dīrah* of Mutayr is in northeastern Saudi Arabia, stretching from approximately the points of convergence of the boundaries of Iraq, Kuwait, the Kuwaiti Neutral Zone, the Iraqi Neutral Zone, and Saudi Arabia to the two main centers of the Qasīm: the settlements of Buraydah and 'Unayzah (see fig. 22-2). This grazing area of approximately 21,000 square miles is bisected by the sands of the Dahna, a gently curving, relatively narrow band of sandy desert that joins the two largest sand areas of the Arabian peninsula, the Great Nafūd to the northwest and the Empty Quarter to the southeast. A generally rocky desert lies west of the sands, a large gravel plain extends to the north, and to the east lies a highly dissected sedimentary area where the limestones and sandstones have been subjected to considerable erosion. In this area are a large number of mesas, buttes, and cliffs separated by low-lying sections covered by a relatively thin sand mantle.

In late summer this part of the country looks quite desolate, even forbidding, but the *dīrah* of Mutayr is in fact a choice one, and in years of normal rainfall, it produces a plentiful amount of the kinds of desert grasses and shrubs that camels prefer. There is an adequate supply of firewood and, in a normal year, of water. Except for the oases, the desert area of Mutayr offers only two vegetable products for human consumption: a rare variety of wild onion and a white truffle that grows plentifully in years of abundant rainfall and is considered a delicacy. Hares, lizards, and the lesser bustard are the most common edible varieties of fauna. Gazelles, once plentiful in the area, have been hunted almost to extinction. The Bedouins consider

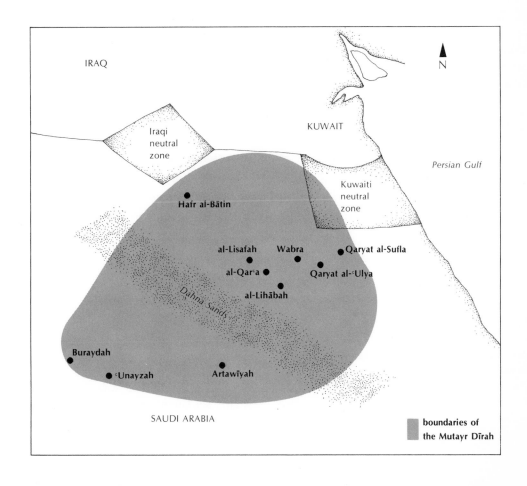

locusts a valuable supplement to their diet and eat the insects either raw or roasted in those years when locust swarms appear in Arabia.

Because the *dīrah* of Mutayr is an interior desert, it is subject to extremes of temperature. In winter the minimum can hover around the freezing point; in summer temperatures of 110° Fahrenheit are common, and readings of 120° Fahrenheit are quite frequent. Of course, these are shade temperatures; surface temperatures in the sun can reach 180° Fahrenheit.

Of greater significance to the Bedouins than thermometer readings is the amount and distribution of rainfall. The *dīrah* of Mutayr, like most of the Middle East, has rainy winters but no rainfall during the rest of the year. The winter rains are scant and erratic and generally fall between early November and late February. The total annual precipitation in the area of Mutayr, according to the weather data gathered over the last twenty-five years, averages two and three-fourths inches—hardly enough to call a season "rainy." This average annual figure is extremely misleading, as differences from year to year tend to be quite marked. In the winter of 1970/71, total rainfall for the area was only six-tenths of an inch, whereas that of 1973/74 reached a total of six inches. In addition, most of the rainfall in this area occurs in the form of sudden, heavy cloudbursts, which fill the riverbeds immediately and

cause considerable erosion. The water disappears just as suddenly through evaporation and through seepage into the sands of the interior drainage basins. Some of the water may collect in small pools, but most of it is of no benefit to the nomads.

The Group

Subsistence Activities

The ecological features of temperature and rainfall are two main determinants of the subsistence cycle of Mutayr, as well as of other Bedouin tribes. The third main determinant is the food and water needs of the Bedouins and their livestock.

When the rainy season has brought a normal amount of rain—that is, about three inches—some water accumulates in a great many small pools all over the desert, and vegetation flourishes. This is the time for Mutayr and other tribes to "disappear"—they split up into small groups and spread out over the full extent of the *dīrah*. These winter camps consist of only six or seven tents. Often these tents are occupied by the members of one extended family, but this is not necessarily so. Some members of a very large extended family may camp elsewhere, and conversely, if an extended family is very small, portions of another, related

left

This is an unusual picture. Two traveling Bedouins (first and second from the right; note the dark water skins) have met two other Bedouins and stopped to exchange news. A Bedouin herding sheep and goats is at left. Normally camels and sheep do not graze together, and would not be found together at about noon, when this picture was taken.

A group of Bedouins ready to ride out in the morning. Three of these men (first two at right, and first at left) are going to a neighboring settlement to trade. The others are about to take the camels out to pasture. Note the elaborate woven strips and tassles hanging from some of the saddle blankets.

extended family may be attached. For this reason, one should refer to the smallest wandering Bedouin unit as a "camping group" rather than a family.

The pools of standing water become depleted fairly soon, or the animals that tramp about the water's edge render the liquid unappetizing. The grasses in the vicinity of the camp are soon exhausted, and the camp itself becomes unhealthy because of the accumulated human and animal refuse. When this happens, about every ten days to two weeks, the Bedouins move to another location. These moves, as well as later ones involving larger numbers of people, are always carried out according to an established pattern. When the adult male members of a camping group have agreed—informally and frequently over their cups of evening coffee—that the grass around the camp and the nearby waterholes has been depleted, two or three camel-mounted scouts are sent out to explore for another suitable site. Upon their return (which in early winter may be only two or three days later) and subsequent report, the most prestigious man of the camping group decides to move camp.

At daybreak the women strike down the tents (packing the tents and setting them up are also women's tasks). The caravan sets out in a strict order. First are

the scouts, who guide the group to the new location; following them are a few adult males with the women, children, camping gear, and some camels, sheep, and goats; third come the main herd of sheep and goats with their herdsmen; and finally come the rest of the camels—a total of ten or twelve adult males, about twenty women and children, perhaps one hundred camels, and twice as many sheep and goats. The distance between each of these groups may be only a few hours' march during the winter, but later in the year it may be as much as half a day. The standardization of such Bedouin moves is further illustrated by the practice of *baraza,* a trem used to describe the usual "false start" of a caravan starting on a long journey. The caravan usually leaves town in late afternoon and makes camp only a little while later, going through all the necessary motions. Should a shortcoming (such as a lack of salt, sugar, or coffee) be discovered, it can be made good relatively easily. It would be much more difficult to do so at a long distance from the source of supply (Dickson 1949:97-101).

The routine of daily life in the winter camps varies little. Bedouins rise at about dawn, and after their morning prayers, they take the young lambs to their mothers. Breakfast is a skimpy meal of bread, perhaps with some clarified butter, a few dates, and coffee. Then the day's work starts. The sheep and goats go out to pasture, generally in the charge of teenage boys. Later the older herdsmen guide the camels out. The women and girls stay in camp, where they busy themselves with household chores, fetching water, and collecting firewood. Bedouins do not usually eat at midday, although the herdsmen may take a piece of their breakfast bread with them and may help themselves to some camel's milk.

In the afternoon those women and girls who are not preparing the evening meal may spin wool, or weave black or black-and-white striped tent cloth or colorful tent dividers (Dickson 1949:67-68, 1956: illustration opposite p. 484). At sunset the animals return and are immediately watered. The camels are hobbled to prevent them from straying and are generally bedded down in a semicircle, within which the sheep stay during the night. Dinner is the main meal in a Bedouin camp, but it is also a frugal affair consisting mainly of

boiled rice and a sauce made of clarified butter with perhaps some canned tomato paste. Meat is eaten only on special occasions, such as when a guest is visiting, unless one of the herdsmen has shot some game, in which case his bag is added to the pot. The rice dish is often followed by dates, perhaps dipped in buttermilk, and the whole meal is washed down with fresh camel's milk. Coffee may be brewed after the milk, but unless a guest is present it may be dispensed with because Bedouins retire early. The meal is served to the men first, and then the tray is taken by the head of the household to the women's section of the tent for the women and the younger children.

In winter the camps are totally devoid of men during most of the day (except for those who are very old, crippled, blind, or otherwise incapacitated). This fact soon becomes apparent to even the most casual observer, although the many reasons for it are less obvious. Winter travel in a tribal range is relatively easy. Thus this is the time when Bedouins who are not occupied with the grazing livestock may go scouting for the next best grazing area or may travel to the permanent settlement in the *dīrah* or to other marketplaces to trade. However, the legendary hospitality of a Bedouin tent remains the same even though the men are gone.

Westerners who have been conditioned by tabloid writings about the seclusion and veiling of women in the Middle East and the raging jealousy of the men should forget these stereotypes. The hospitality of the tent is paramount. News travels fast in the desert, and any Bedouin—and his tribe—would soon find out that the women in his tent had not been hospitable to a stranger. Because of his tent's failure, he would be exposed as stingy, the worst insult that can be hurled at a Bedouin. On the other hand, if a stranger who had been welcomed to a Bedouin tent had overstepped the boundaries of propriety with the women in the tent, the news would travel just as fast, and he would probably not reach the boundary of the *dīrah* alive.

Thus far we have been looking at Bedouin camps in the winter. As the year progresses, these camps acquire a different configuration. When the smaller pools of rainwater and the surrounding grazing become depleted, the small camping groups move to the vicinity of larger and still well-filled pools where good grass is

A section of the Mutayr summer camp at al-Lihābah. The wells are close, but the grazing has long been exhausted. The picture shows the concentration of tents, as well as their different sizes. Compare, for instance, from front to back, the first two tents on the right. The first, a onepole tent, is probably only used as a storage shed; the one behind it, a three-pole tent, is the main family dwelling. There are several white canvas tents in this picture; they are army tents. This does not mean that the camp includes a military detail. Generally it would mean either that one of the Bedouins has purchased such a tent from army surplus (or perhaps from another Bedouin), or that a prominent tribesman, having visited the royal court, was given a white tent from the king's stores as a departure present.

still available. Bedouin camps in these areas become progressively larger until even here the water and grass are exhausted. Finally, late in the spring, the tribal subsections move to their permanent water wells where they try to survive the heat of the summer.

Thus the two mainstays of nomadic life in this part of the Arabian peninsula, pasture and water, determine Bedouin displacements during the year. In winter, when the grass is green and laden with moisture, grazing areas are the determinant of Bedouin moves; in summer, when the grass and brush are dry, the availability of plentiful water determines the nomads' camping sites. This pattern is understandable. In winter watering needs are minimal, but in summer, particularly if a normal amount of precipitation has fallen during the preceding winter, the camels can survive off the fat stored in their humps but need a minimal amount of water. Even in midsummer, however, camels

need to be watered only every third day. Sheep and goats must be watered daily, but healthy camels (and today pickup trucks) can take water to them. The camels themselves may be rather thin and emaciated at the end of the summer, but they have survived, and simple survival is a victory over the desert environment.

From a Bedouin's point of view, and particularly from the view of Mutayr and a few other tribes not far from centers of government power, summer is a bad time indeed. The obvious hardships—lack of good grazing and a barely sufficient water supply—have already been mentioned. But there are other difficulties. The summer heat is oppressive to both animals and human beings. Camels, cantankerous beasts at their best, become difficult to manage. Among men, tempers grow short, and a minor dispute over whose camels are to be watered first may grow from name-calling to fisticuffs to bloodshed, with the ensuing need for revenge and eventually perhaps intratribal or intertribal warfare.

In days past summer brought another danger: Enemy tribes always knew where Mutayr were watering their livestock (something they would not know in the winter) and therefore knew where to strike. This danger is not feared today, but on the other hand, the government's tax collectors also know where the tribes are camped for the summer. Having traded one bad situation for another, the tribesmen of Mutayr could not tell me which one they preferred.

Considering all the obstacles a desert environment puts in the way of human survival, how have the Arab Bedouins been able to survive at all? An important factor is the Bedouins' own adaptation to the desert—their Spartan hardihood, their scant material culture, their extreme mobility, their knowledge of the environment, and a value system that places great emphasis on cooperation. A second but equally important factor is the presence of the camel, with whom the Bedouin has a symbiotic relationship: Neither could exist without the other. The Bedouin supplies an ability to navigate and track and a knowledge of the location of water wells; the camel supplies the needed transportation.

The camel, or more specifically, the dromedary or one-hump camel (*Camelus dromedarius*), is a marvelous example of biological adaptation to a desert environment. Instead of hooves, the camel has soft-

cushioned pads that spread out when the camel walks, making it easier for the animal to move over sand without sinking. A camel can retain large amounts of fat in its hump, a reserve storage that enables the animal to survive the poor grazing of the summer. Furthermore, a camel has a prodigiously large stomach and can drink up to fifty gallons in a single watering. Another adaptive feature is the camel's ability to recycle and re-metabolize its own urea to levels of concentration that would poison other animals. Consequently, the camel does not need to dispose of the urea by urinating so frequently and can conserve the precious water (Schmidt-Nielsen 1959:140). Moreover, camels are able to drink filthy, saline water that Bedouins would not consider potable, and in return, they give perfectly drinkable milk. In effect, the animal is a self-propelled water purification plant. And camels have many uses: They provide transportation and occasionally meat, their hair can be spun and woven, their skin is used to make containers, the long hairs at the tip of their tails are used to make ropes, their manure is used as fuel, and their urine is a very effective delousing agent used by the Bedouins (in particular the women) to wash their hair. Camel breeding and the sale of some camel-derived products are also a source of cash, which is hard to come by for these desert nomads.

Of course, not all camels are alike. A Westerner may think that the only difference between camels is whether they have one hump or two (Arabian camels have only one). But in the eyes of a Bedouin there are as many or more differences among camels as there are among horses in the eyes of a Western horse lover. In the desert there are pack camels and riding camels, purebreds and mixed breeds, milk camels and racing camels, and so on, and Bedouins have developed a large vocabulary to designate these and other differences. Camels are also branded to mark their ownership by a particular tribe or tribal section (Dickson 1949:420–425).

A special purebred strain of camels is specifically associated with Mutayr. This particular herd of dark-coated, almost black camels numbers some two hundred head at present and is collectively called the *shurūf*, meaning "the noble ones" or "the honored ones." They are the pride of Mutayr. They are in the care of and are actually the property of the lineage of al-Duwīsh, from whom the paramount shaykhs (chiefs) of Mutayr are chosen. However, their association with al-Duwīsh, and therefore with the entire tribe, goes back for such a long time that the *shurūf* have become a symbol of Mutayr—rather like a regimental flag or the standard of a Roman legion. Their importance, both as a fine herd and a symbol of Mutayr, cannot be denied. When the tribe rebelled against King Ibn Saud between 1929 and 1930 and was finally defeated, the king imposed two main punishments on the rebels: the imprisonment of Faysal al-Duwīsh, the paramount shaykh of the tribe, and the surrender of the *shurūf*. Not until 1958, many years after Faysal's death in captivity (which Mutayr took a long time forgetting), were the *shurūf* returned to the tribe, and the resentment of Mutayr against the central government subsided.

A group of camels at the Mutayr water wells of al'Lisāfah in the summer. Occasionally, as here, when the grass supply has been exhausted for miles around, some of the animals will not be taken to pasture at all, but be allowed to rest near the wells. Thus, while conserving energy and water, the camels may still survive by drawing sustenance from the fat stored in the hump.

Social Organization

The tribe of Mutayr is divided into two sections, ʿIlwa and Burayh, each of which has three subsections. In turn, the subsections are composed of a number of maximal lineages, each containing a number of extended families. The basic block of Bedouin society, as is true almost everywhere in the Middle East, is the patrilineal, patrilocal, patriarchal, and endogamous extended family. This means that the family includes the head of the household and his wife, their married sons with their wives and children, their unmarried sons and daughters, and possibly a few other relatives. Descent is reckoned through the males; the undisputed authority is the head of the household; and when a son marries, he brings his wife to live with his father's household or in the case of a Bedouin, with his father's camping group. Middle Eastern endogamy rules that one's preferred marriage partner is one's paternal parallel cousin—that is, one's father's brother's son (or daughter). Of course, it does happen, particularly among Bedouins, whose families tend to be smaller than rural or urban families, that no such cousins are available or that they are of the wrong sex. In this case a mate will be chosen from among the most closely related families of the same maximal lineage or even of the tribal subsection.

Bedouin society is basically egalitarian within each tribe. But differences exist between "noble" tribes and nonnoble ones, or between Bedouins and the small groups of ignoble Sulubbah, the gypsylike bands of people of unknown origin who travel among the Bedouins and serve as hunters, trackers, tinkerers, and pot menders. There is no professional specialization among Bedouins; each man must engage in the same kind of work as the others. The only division of labor is that dictated by sex or age. It has often been stated that Bedouin society was "democratic," that a Bedouin shaykh was only the first among equals. This is not quite true. The egalitarian basis of Bedouin society is unquestionable, but equally unquestionable is the fact that a leader's power and prerogatives will, upon his death, be inherited by a member of his patrilineage, though not necessarily by his first-born son. This pattern, followed over many generations, has resulted in the establishment of a number of "shaykhly" families, a sort of aristocracy of the desert who are recognized by all tribesmen to be somewhat superior, even though they may lack any aristocratic trappings, are spoken to without any signs of subservience, and are indistinguishable by their dress, their manners, or their work from any other Bedouin.*

In the Arabian desert no special term is applied to members of such a lineage, although in Morocco they are referred to as "sons of the big tent." Among Mutayr, the lineage that has for many years held the leadership of the tribe is al-Duwīsh, the most famous of whom was Faysal al-Duwīsh, who headed the tribe during the first third of the present century. His successor was his second-born son, Bandar ibn Faysal al-Duwīsh, who is still the paramount shaykh of the Mutayr.

Like other Bedouin tribes, Mutayr have what is called a *segmentary* tribal structure. In such a society, particularly one that is widely dispersed for the greater part of the year, the political leadership must find a way to assert itself down to the most remote tent. Among Bedouins, this is informally but effectively achieved by means of a system of shaykhs. Extended families have a head of household, maximal lineages

Al-Lihābah wells, near the end of a summer day. The sheep and goats, having drunk first, have been led away. Now the camels are clustering around the water. At the left and the extreme right, parts of the Shuruf black herd of the Mutayr wait to be watered.

---

* Thus according to the terminology presented in chapters 11, 15, and 17, Mutayr would be classified as a rank society.

have a lineage shaykh, and so do the subsections and the sections of the tribe, right up to the paramount tribal shaykh—a hierarchical type of authority structure that rests on levels of increasingly inclusive tribal segments, and seems to be of considerable antiquity in the Arabian desert (Exodus 18:17–23). But this authority is hardly ever, if at all, exercised in a dictatorial manner. At all levels of the Bedouin social structure, the shaykh, even when he receives directions from a superior shaykh, will consult with an informal "council," generally composed of the older and more prestigious males in his group, before taking any action.

What of the position of the women? Much has been made of their subordination to men, their seclusion, their veiling, and their overall "second-class" status in the Arab world. It is true that women occupy a social position that is inferior to that of the men, but their fate is not quite as harsh as it might seem, particularly in the desert. Among rural and urban populations women are kept under strict controls because they are exposed to a multitude of occasions when interaction with men (salesmen, postal clerks, repairmen) is required. They are thus subject to an increased number of opportunities to transgress the prevalent, admittedly double-standard moral code and thus forever to besmirch the Arabs' sacred 'irdh, or family honor.

Such opportunities are lacking in the desert, and the offer of rest, food, and lodging to travelers is a para-

mount duty. Therefore women are not as strictly controlled as in rural or urban areas. Veiling is practiced in the desert, although less so than in towns and villages. When all her chores are done, a Bedouin woman may join the group of men and participate in the discussion, although she sits down at the farthest corner of the tent. Such a situation would not occur among settled people. Even so, proprieties must be observed. I have been in Bedouin tents when the wife of the head of the household joined the male group, and I have talked with her—but only indirectly. She spoke to her husband, who spoke to me, and my answer was similarly relayed. All the while we all spoke in Arabic.

Women not only influence decisions but often make them. When Bedouin men return to camp after raiding, guiding caravans, or trading in the permanent settlements, they may find that a pending problem has already been solved by the women who have stayed in camp.

When the head of the household is absent, his wife is the undisputed overlord of the tent, responsible not only for the day-to-day management of family affairs but also for maintaining the prestige of her husband. I once visited the summer camp of al-Duwīsh to call on Shaykh Bandar, the paramount shaykh, and was told that he was absent. So I made my way to the tent of his nephew, the acting shaykh. I stayed in his tent for three days, the minimum stay prescribed for someone not in a hurry. I had brought a set of binoculars with me as a present for Shaykh Bandar, and not wanting to leave them with the nephew, I stopped at Bandar's tent on my way out of camp to give them to his wife. She received me, veiled but alone. I explained the purpose of my visit and handed her the binoculars. But when I wanted to take my leave, I was not allowed to. She knew, of course, that I had been in camp and that I had "stayed with the Arabs" three days, but now that I had called on Bandar's tent, as an old friend of his, I must stay with her for the prescribed three days. A Bedouin tent in August is not the most comfortable place in the world, but my protestations that I had commitments elsewhere and my promises to be back soon were of no avail. She knew I had a radio-equipped truck with me and could report my delay. Furthermore, as she put it, "The son of my uncle will be very angry

with me and also with you, if you do not stay here." I never saw the woman again on this visit, but I complied with the rules of hospitality.

Culture

The poverty of Bedouin material culture has already been mentioned. This lack does not mean that Bedouins are inherently inept or unimaginative but is rather a reflection of the paucity of raw materials the desert offers and of the requirement of portability that a nomadic life imposes. The principal item in a Bedouin's material culture inventory is the tent (called "house of hair"). It is made of lengths of cloth woven of camel and goat hair, generally with a very dark brown roof and striped dark-and-white sides. Tents are of various sizes (Dickson 1949: Chap. 4), depending on the wealth of the owner, and each tent is classified according to the number of its vertical poles—a two-pole tent, a three-pole tent, and so on; the angled poles at either end do not count. Depending on the tent size, one or more colorful, striped tent dividers partition the whole space into two or more "rooms," one of which is the women's side and includes the cooking hearth. Another "room" is the *majlis* (literally, "sitting room"), where the men usually get together and where guests are received. The *majlis* also serves as the bedroom for the entire household.

Inside the tent are all of a Bedouin's possessions: some containers of skin, wood, or metal; camel saddles and trappings; utensils for making and serving coffee and tea; a firearm or two; some sacks of provisions; pieces of matting; a few rugs, perhaps some thin bedding; the parts of a horizontal, frameless loom; a child's cradle; and a couple of metal footlockers to hold spare clothing items and valuables such as frankincense or aromatic sandalwood. These possessions are the total of a Bedouin's material goods, and their portability fits the requirements of nomadic life.

This requirement of portability is also largely responsible for other aspects of Bedouin life. An obvious one is the lack of three-dimensional art forms, a lack which becomes immediately understandable if one recalls that such art forms are generally too heavy or too breakable or both to be carried around. Even their

In the summer camp—al-Lihābah in this case—young children are not as busy as they are in the winter; larger herds of sheep and goats can be taken to graze by fewer herdsmen. But at the end of the day when the livestock come back, all the youngsters congregate near the well-heads, where they socialize and are often put to work drawing water, pouring it into the drinking troughs, or just trying to control the thirsty and unruly camels.

musical instruments—a drum and a one-string fiddle—are simple and lightweight. The Bedouins express themselves artistically through the most portable of all art forms, language. Thus one finds among Bedouins a rich development of poetry, singing, storytelling, recitation of genealogies, and the like.

Most of a Bedouin's tent furnishings and clothing are not of desert manufacture. The Bedouins, if left alone, could not stay alive, no matter how skillfully they know how to exploit the desert. Most of the things a Bedouin needs—clothes, tent poles, containers, and most importantly, staple foods—cannot be obtained in the desert. The presence and survival of the Bedouins can be understood and explained only with reference to trading, in which the Bedouins sell their livestock, skins, or woven tent cloth and obtain the rice and dates that are the mainstay of their diet as well as other food items and household utensils. Conversely, an "oasis culture" in the Arabian desert could not have survived. Through intensive cultivation, oasis dwellers can produce a surplus of food, notably dates, as well as a variety of artifacts. However, all these products would be of little value if they could not be moved out of the oasis to other settlements. The Bedouins provided the camels and the knowledge of the desert necessary to transport the products of an oasis. Today the situation is somewhat different. The Bedouins still need to buy foodstuffs and utensils in an oasis or other settlement, but the introduction of motor transport capable of crossing sandy deserts, the development of a network of surfaced, all-weather roads, and the availability of imported food have freed the oases from dependence on the Bedouins.

The Bedouins' inability to survive by themselves means that they cannot be considered exclusively as pastoral nomads. The link between the terms *pastoral* and *nomadic* in anthropological literature occurs so frequently that one loses sight of the fact that these two terms refer to widely different aspects of life. *Nomadism* describes a certain pattern of habitation; *pastoralism* refers to a specific way of exploiting a natural resource. It is true that the two are often found together, from the Arabian deserts to Lapland, but they can exist separately. Many groups of hunters and gatherers, such as the San of the Kalahari (see Chap. 21) or the Australian Aborigines are nomadic but not pastoral; Western Hemisphere ranchers are pastoral but not nomadic (Salzman 1971). Even Mutayr, who are undoubtedly pastoral nomads, make many moves that are not concerned with the needs of their livestock. The regular trips to the marketplace, the caravan trade, and the raiding and tribal warfare of the past are examples of such displacements.

What of the Bedouin value system? What is the moral code by which they live? First, the Bedouins have a strong sense of pride and honor. A Bedouin takes pride in being an Arab, a Bedouin, and of noble descent; and he takes pride in having kept or increased his personal honor (*sharaf*) and maintained his family honor ('*irdh*), which implies the good name and spotless behavior of the women in his family. With this feeling goes a deep sense of family loyalty, as expressed in the saying: "I and my brothers against my cousins; but I, my brothers, and my cousins against the world."

Second, the Bedouins are deeply religious, a characteristic found elsewhere in the Middle East regardless of the particular denomination involved. Mutayr and other Bedouins are Muslims, and their religion requires that they fulfill the obligations imposed by the Five Pillars of Islām: (1) Profess that there is only one God (Allah), and that Muhammad is his prophet; (2) pray five times a day: morning, noon, afternoon, sunset, and evening; (3) give alms to the needy; (4) observe the rules of fasting in Ramadhān (the ninth month of the Arab lunar year), which require that believers abstain from all kinds of food and drink as well as from sexual intercourse between sunrise and sunset; and (5) perform the pilgrimage to Mecca once in one's lifetime if one is financially and physically able to do so.

Bedouins are seriously religious, but the desert environment produces conditions that make it difficult for them to comply strictly with the ritual requirements of the Five Pillars. Islām was not born of the desert but of the town, and it is a religion for the town rather than for the desert. The Bedouins not only deeply believe but often profess their faith (the First Pillar), and the name of Allah is continuously on their lips. But the other Pillars are a different story. For instance, prayer should be preceded by ritual ablutions, and although one can substitute sand for water when no

water is available, ablutions with sand are second-best. A Bedouin may go for months without being able to use water for his ablutions. Moreover, although prayer is a direct communication between a faithful Muslim and his God, requiring no intermediary, it is more meritorious to pray in a mosque with other people than to do it outside and alone. There are no mosques in the desert, and a Bedouin must pray alone many times.

When it comes to the obligation to give alms to the poor, the Bedouin is in another quandary, for there are no needy people in the desert and no traveling people who are not taken care of within the bounds of family and tribal loyalties and the laws of hospitality. The Bedouins always take care of their own and their visitors.

Keeping the fast during Ramadhān also puts Bedouins in a difficult position. It is relatively easy for townspeople to keep the fast; they do not need to move around much and can stay in their cool houses. But not so the Bedouin: The needs of his herd require that he go out into the sun, and if the month of Ramadhān (being a lunar month) falls in the middle of the summer, the commandment to abstain from water cannot very easily be kept. The rules say that a traveler does not have to keep the fast on traveling days but can make up for it at a later date. Bedouins are perennial travelers and can never quite catch up with the missed fasting dates. This again makes them deviate from strict orthodoxy.

Something similar applies in the case of the Fifth Pillar, the pilgrimage to Mecca. The center of the *dīrah* of Mutayr is approximately 750 miles from Mecca. A Mutayr tribesman in good health could certainly cover the distance there and back with little difficulty by camel, but the whole trip would take him some two and a half months. Bedouins live very close to a bare subsistence level, and it is rarely possible for a Bedouin to take such a long vacation from his chores. To save time, he could go by camel to Hafr al-Bātin or to Artāwīyah (see fig. 22-2) and then take a "pilgrimage bus," but normally he would not have the necessary cash. The result is that few Mutayr tribesmen have been on the pilgrimage. On the whole, therefore, even given their deeply felt religious beliefs, the total en-

One of the well-heads at al-Lihābah, with one pulley. Even though the animals are out to pasture during the day, the wells remain in operation. Water must be drawn for family consumption, and to fill the troughs for the first group of animals to arrive. Here a camel, with rider, pulls up a water skin. A traveling Bedouin has arrived (at right) and his pack camel (front center) is also waiting for water. At other times the rope hauling up the water may be pulled by men or women, rather than by camels.

vironment of the Bedouins is such that they cannot be very good *practicing* Muslims.

The Bedouins' value system also dictates that they observe a series of rules that derive from the fact that they live in the desert. First, they must observe the rules of hospitality. Given the vast area of the Arabian desert, the chances are that any traveler who approaches a Bedouin tent has been riding for quite a distance and still has a long way to go. The traveler will welcome an offer to rest; this offer is invariably made and almost as invariably accepted. After all, the people of the tent will be traveling at some other time and will expect the same treatment. An added element of self-interest in offering the hospitality is that while the guest enjoys his rest he is expected to furnish information, not only about the news from the town (if he came from one) but also about his observations during the trip. How is the grazing at *X?* Has it rained at *Y?* Are there any Arabs at *Z?* The answers may be very valuable to the host in deciding the next camp move.

Next, a Bedouin must observe the obligation to protect his tent neighbor and his traveling companion. The tent neighbor is strictly defined as one who pitches his tent within the distance one can throw a camel-stick. Normally a man's tent neighbors are his relatives

and as such are bound together by family ties. The rules
of "tent neighborhood" apply mostly in cases when a
Bedouin pitches his tent near one belonging to a man
from another lineage, another section, or another
tribe. The latter then becomes, as it were, the new
arrival's host. Such a "tent host" has a number of duties.
For example, he must protect the new arrival against
all comers, and if the new arrival's camels or personal
belongings are stolen, the host must either find them
or make good for them (Dickson 1949:126–132).

The rules governing behavior toward a traveling
companion (*rafīq*) are just as strict as the rules of hospitality and possibly stricter, because the honor of
the whole tribe is at stake, not just that of an individual. In recent years the protection of a traveling
companion has not been as onerous a task as it once
was. Before the establishment of powerful central governments, the Bedouin tribes were largely independent,
and a traveler or a caravan might have to cross the grazing areas of Mutayr and perhaps several other tribes.
The traveler or travelers would first obtain a *rafīq* from
Mutayr as guide and protector, usually for a small fee.
The Mutayr tribesman would guide the traveler safely
across the *dīrah* of the Mutayr to the edge of the area,
where the *rafīq* would turn the traveler over to a *rafīq*
from the next tribe, and so on to the end of the journey. The role of the *rafīq* as a protector has practically
disappeared with the pacification of the desert and
the establishment of a road network, but his role as a
guide is still maintained, particularly for off-the-road
travel.

Finally, a Bedouin must observe the laws of personal
protection and sanctuary. This ancient and honored
practice, followed much more stringently in the desert
than in settled areas, requires that an Arab being pursued or in imminent danger may enter another Arab's
tent, and by uttering one of several standard phrases
(all roughly meaning "I enter into your safekeeping"),
he can place himself under the latter's protection. The
protector must then defend the suppliant, even if it
means sacrificing his own life, or see that he gets to
a place of safety. Even if the fugitive happens to enter
the tent of the brother of a man he has murdered and
asks for sanctuary, he will be safe for three days. Then
the protector must take him safely to his next destina-

Another well-head at the Mutayr summer
camp of al-Lihābah, this one equipped
with three pulleys. The well-head is
slightly higher than surrounding terrain.
A roughly conical mound is formed by
the dirt dug up from the shaft (here, as
elsewhere, lined at the top with rocks),
and its dark color is the result of the
accumulation of camel dung over the
years.

tion, after which the protector is free to resume his blood feud. This practice was observed much more frequently in the past, when tribal wars, raiding, and family feuds were common. The custom became very unpopular with the authorities when strong central governments started consolidating their position, because many fugitives claimed sanctuary and placed themselves out of reach of the pursuing police. Today the practice has all but disappeared.

It is easy to see not only that the Bedouins' activities are governed by their environment but also that their most important values revolve around an ideal of close cooperation. A human being alone against the desert is doomed to perish.

Problems and Prospects

Crucial changes have affected Bedouin society during the first half of the present century. Two forces have been especially relevant: the emergence of central government authority and the development of a modern economy.

The consolidation of central authority in Arabia started a process of change that from the Bedouin point of view has two important effects. One is that the significance of the *dīrah* as a tribal territory has declined. Today, because all tribes owe allegiance to the sovereign, the entire country has become a sort of "super-*dīrah*," and all tribes can (and do) move back

and forth without having to worry about tribal allies or enemies and without having to secure permission to move across neighboring tribal *dīrahs*. The second important effect is the change in the exercise of leadership. Before the consolidation of the central government, a Bedouin's supreme ruler was the paramount shaykh of the tribe, and command was exercised thoughout the segmentary society of the tribe by means of a chain of shaykhs at various segment levels. But today even Shaykh Bandar of the Mutayr, the paramount shaykh of a tribe, is no longer this kind of tribal leader. Rather, he is a courtier who spends a great deal of his time in attendance on the king, from whom he receives an annual dole—partly in return for the tribe's allegiance and partly to make up for the lack of revenue that warfare and raiding used to bring. In turn, the paramount shaykh distributes the dole downward to the various tribal units. The segmentary power structure has now been converted into a patronage chain.

The Bedouins have also had to adjust (and still are adjusting) to economic changes. One of the most significant is the deteriorating importance of the camel. Another is the attraction offered by new or growing settlements in the wake of industrialization. Before the development of the oil industry, camels were a primary export of the Arabian peninsula, particularly among the Mutayr and the other northern tribes. Camel traders made annual tours of the tribes, purchased camels, and sold them in Cairo or Damascus, sometimes as meat but mostly as pack animals for the caravans. The automobile put a quick end to this trade. Mutayr no longer breed camels as a business enterprise; in fact, Saudi Arabia has been a net importer of camels since about 1950. The Arabian range land is now badly overgrazed, and the relative economic deprivation of the Bedouins grows increasingly noticeable.

It has been thought that the best future for the Bedouins, who have a long military history, would be in the army. This is difficult to believe. Bedouins have not fought a war for over a generation, and warfare is becoming alien to them; moreover, the typical Bedouin is lacking in the group discipline, self-assertion, and technical expertise, qualities essential in a modern soldier.

Practically all governments in the Middle East consider that the solution to the "Bedouin problem"—that is, the alleviation of their present economic condition—lies in transforming them into settled farmers. No doubt the Bedouins, or at least most of them, will eventually settle. They have long been exposed to the attractiveness of settled life: the cash-paying jobs in the oil industry, more varied foodstuffs, a secure source of water and hay, and—perhaps foremost—the availability of schooling for their children and of health services for all. However, the chances are that this change from nomadism to sedentary life will occur only slowly; the forcible settlement of Bedouins, as advocated in many Middle Eastern countries, is not likely to succeed.

Summary

The Bedouins are Arab camel-breeding nomads belonging to certain specified tribes, one of which is the tribe of Mutayr.

Mutayr roam the desert in winter in search of forage for their herds and congregate in tribal sections in the summer at the site of the main wells belonging to the tribe. The daily life of the people and the pattern of their movements are described in detail.

Mutayr social organization is built on the patrilineal extended family; numbers of these form maximal lineages, which in turn form tribal subsections, then sections, and finally the entire tribe. The people are relatively egalitarian, but there is a structure of political authority based on the system of shaykhs. Women occupy a social position that is markedly inferior to that of men.

The material culture of Mutayr is limited because they must carry their possessions with them, but poetry and storytelling are richly developed. Their value system is marked by a strong sense of pride and honor; they are also deeply religious, although the desert environment makes it difficult for them to observe Muslim rituals.

Like many nomadic peoples, the way of life of Mutayr has been severely affected by industrialism and modernization. The prospects for the survival of their culture are slight.

Annotated Bibliography

Dickson, H. R. P. (1949)   *The Arab of the Desert.* London: George Allen and Unwin. A masterpiece in its description of life among the Bedouins of northeastern Arabia; it should rank with Philby, Oppenheim, and Lorimer as one of the primary sources for the area. Unfortunately the book is poorly organized and on occasion repetitious; it was not subjected to thorough editing and is thus exasperating to read.

(1956)   *Kuwait and Her Neighbours.* London: George Allen and Unwin. Another monumental work, but it suffers from the same shortcomings of Dickson's earlier work. Includes many references to Mutayr, not all of them accurate. But Dickson's personal involvement with desert Arabs easily overrides the faults of his writing and gives a vivid picture of the life of Bedouins in the Arabian Desert.

Rentz, George S. (1951)   "Notes on Dickson's 'The Arab of the Desert.'" *Muslim World,* January 1951. This review by perhaps the world's foremost authority on the history of the Wahhabi movement, who is also familiar with eastern Arabia, is more than the usual appraisal of a book. It contributes to the detailed knowledge of the tribes in eastern Arabia, including Mutayr.

Von Oppenheim, Max Freiherr, with E. Bräunlich and W. Caskel (1939-53)   *Die Beduinen.* Leipzig and Wiesbaden: Otto Harrasowitz. This is the major work (in German, no translation available) on Middle Eastern Bedouins. It is mostly an account of tribal histories and does not dwell on cultural differences or similarities, but up to this time nobody has assembled as much data on Bedouins.

23
Takatoya: *A Japanese Peasant Community*

Introduction

Takatoya is a small farming village of fifty-two households, presently some 220 people, which lies stretched along the slope of one of the lower mountains of the Mikuni range in northern Gunma Prefecture. Gunma, in turn, forms the northwestern border of the great Kanto Plain near the center of the main Japanese island of Honshu. Takatoya itself is nestled in the mountains forming the northern rim of the Kanto, about an hour by road from the plain and four hours from Tokyo.

The Kanto area, the widest significant regional and cultural context for the people of Takatoya, is now in some ways the heartland of the nation. It is the chief source of rice for Tokyo and its satellite towns, and its mountainous fringe is a major silk-producing area. In modern times its manufacturing towns, mainly the coastal cities of Tokyo, Yokohama, and Kawasaki, have come to produce about 25 percent of Japan's industrial output. When the national capital was moved from Kyoto to Tokyo in 1868, the dialect of the surrounding Kanto was made the national standard language, which enables Kanto natives to feel a slight linguistic superiority.

Takahashi Nami, 72, pulls up rice seedlings from her household's seedbed, for transplanting. Transplanting is laborious but greatly increases the crop by ensuring that all plants have equal space.

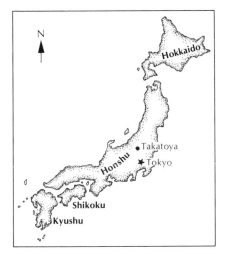

Figure 23-1
The location of Takatoya on Honshu, Japan's Major Island

Although Takatoya is part of the Kanto, it is marginal to the area in several ways. Hemmed in by mountains, the village is cut off from the main flow of Kanto commerce and industry and is limited in agricultural land. As a result, many young people are now leaving the village to work in the cities. The village population is declining, and some traditional village activities and organizations, such as the young men's association, have been abandoned for lack of participants. On the other hand, Takatoya's isolation from the more modern life of the cities of the plain has helped preserve the traditional village intimacy, cooperation, and household continuity valued by many of the villagers.

The Environment

Geologically, the Kanto as a whole is an uplifted plain that has been tilted, eroded, and broken. Most of it is now rather flat, owing to layers of deposits from the rivers, but the northern circumference in which Takatoya lies is dominated by low but rugged mountains. The village lies 2,170 feet above sea level along a narrow, tilted plateau on the eastern slope of a low mountain ridge. The plateau is bounded in the east by a steep, wooded embankment dropping 100 feet down

to the Katashina River. To the west it is bounded by the steep upper flank of the mountain; to the north and south both ends of the plateau are pinched off by convergence of the river and the mountain. To the east of the river, a narrow valley of a few hundred yards' width provides the only extensive land that is flat enough for irrigated rice farming.

The climate is temperate. The yearly weather pattern is monsoonal. In winter heavy, cold air sweeps outward from the eastern Asian mainland, bringing freezing temperatures (a mean of 36° Fahrenheit in February, for instance) and moderate snowfall to the village. In summer the wind direction is reversed, bringing heavy rainfall with occasional typhoons. The total yearly precipitation is moderately heavy, about 39 inches, and provides ample water for irrigation. Summers are warm and humid but not hot (the average temperature in August is 73° Fahrenheit). The village is protected by the mountains from the highest winds of both winter storms and late summer typhoons. Since this area is also relatively stable geologically (the great Kanto earthquake, which virtually destroyed Tokyo in 1923, did little damage here), Takatoya has little to fear from either earthquakes or typhoons, the two most common natural perils in Japan.

The principal natural vegetation, a mixed forest including oak, maple, spruce, fir, and larch trees, covers about 80 percent of the land owned by villagers. Until recent times much of the hardwood was used locally as cooking fuel, either directly or as charcoal, but this function is now largely filled by bottled gas. Reforestation is done mainly in coniferous trees suitable for lumber and pulp.

Game animals in the vicinity include deer, bear, grouse, and pheasant, which are hunted by members of one or two households in the village. Small trout and a few other kinds of fish in the Katashina River provide sport for boys with spears. However, none of these animals is taken in sufficient quantity to be a significant part of the diet.

The most important aspect of the environment from the villagers' viewpoint is the scope it gives for agriculture. As noted above, arable land is limited by the mountains. The average area of cultivated land here is 3.1 acres per household. Although this is more than the average in Japan, only about 5 percent of the land is irrigated rice paddy, the most productive kind of land. This proportion of paddy land to unirrigated land is one-tenth that of the nation as a whole. The growing season, with about 200 frost-free days, is long enough to permit using some of the land for more than one crop a year, but it is not long enough for the double-cropping of rice practiced in southern Japan. As a result, only enough rice can be grown for local consumption. However, both climate and soil (the latter supplemented with chemical fertilizers) are well suited to a number of other cash crops, including soybeans, pole beans, strawberries, tomatoes, tobacco, and most importantly, silk. The silkworms are fed on the leaves of mulberry trees, which are well adapted to the sloping land. Subsistence crops, in addition to rice and soybeans, include wheat, barley, buckwheat, sweet potatoes, corn, Chinese cabbage, giant radishes, cucumbers, and a variety of other vegetables.

The Group

Subsistence Activities

Work in the village follows a yearly round of events set by the seasons. The broadest pattern is the alternation of the agriculturally busy summer with the slack winter. Within this pattern are shorter cycles, such as the raising of silkworms three times (in the spring, summer, and early fall) and the daily round of work and rest.

The agricultural season begins in late April, when seedbeds are prepared for planting rice, and ends in November, when the rice is harvested and threshed. Meanwhile, silkworms have been raised and their cocoons sold, and the major series of other cash and subsistence crops have been planted and harvested. This is the period of long hours and intense work. The four cold and snowy months that follow are a time of relaxation for most households.

Rice production outlines the schedule and typifies the intensive labor of the busy season. In late April or early May the seedbeds are prepared in small plots near each farmer's house. The ground is plowed with a small diesel-powered hand tractor, flooded, and

Two old friends talk while picking bits of chaff from rice in the hopper of the motor-driven rice polisher.

harrowed until a smooth mud is produced throughout. The seed rice is broadcast by hand on the mud and covered by a thin layer of soil, then by a thin layer of straw, and finally by a translucent sheet of plastic. This temporary shallow greenhouse for sprouting the seedlings admits light, retains heat, and keeps out birds.

In about a month, the seedlings are eight to ten inches tall, and it is time to transplant them to the main rice paddies. This is laborious, time-consuming work, but it ensures that the plants will be evenly spaced and that the area of the paddy will thus be used as productively as possible. The seedlings are pulled up from the seedbed, bundled, and removed to the main fields, which have also been fertilized, flooded, and churned to liquid mud. The rice seedlings are set out in groups of three at carefully marked intervals of about eight inches. In order to transplant evenly and quickly, several households cooperate to provide a single line of workers stretching across each field. Each person plants in front of herself or himself and a few steps to each side, at intervals marked on a string stretched across the width of the field. When the row is completed, the string is moved on and a new row begun. The fields of the whole village are transplanted in about a week. As each household finishes its work, it holds a feast of celebration for the people who helped.

From then until harvest time, the rice must be protected against birds and such insect pests as the rice borer; it must also occasionally be weeded. Birds are dealt with by scarecrows, ribbons stretched across the fields, and noisemakers that periodically explode a charge of acetylene gas. A number of pesticides are used against insects.

Early in November the rice harvest brings another flurry of work as the rice plants are cut, bundled, and hung on racks to dry. Most of the cutting is done by hand with the traditional small sickle, although a few households are experimenting with small hand or motor-driven machines which cut and bundle in one step. After drying, the rice is threshed, winnowed, and hulled by a motor-driven machine and placed in bags in the household storehouse.

Meanwhile, almost everyone in the village has been busy at the cultivation of the other cash and subsistence crops. The most important of these is silk, which provides about 70 percent of the cash income of the farming households. It is produced by three generations of silkworms each year in the spring, summer, and fall. Each generation of silkworms starts with eggs hatched by the agricultural cooperative (to which almost all farmers belong) in a humidity- and temperature-controlled hatchery in the neighboring village. After a week of careful nurturing with chopped mulberry leaves, the small white caterpillars are sold by the gram to individual households and are transferred to their second-story lofts. For the next two and a half weeks, the growing caterpillars eat their weight in mulberry leaves each day. All members of the household are kept busy cutting mulberry leaves and bringing them back to the loft for three feedings a day.

Mrs. Takahashi sets out tobacco seedlings in a miniature greenhouse, using a pair of chopsticks. Her household resells the plants when they are larger to other farmers.

Takahashi Yoshino picks mulberry leaves to feed her silkworms.

When the silkworms are ready to begin spinning, they stop eating. They are placed on frames containing a number of lattices forming cubicles. Each crawls into a cubicle and begins to spin its cocoon. In about three days the cocoons, each spun of a single continuous thread about a thousand yards long, are finished. They are pushed from the frames with a wooden key, cleaned of their excess silk floss, bagged, and taken to the warehouse of the agricultural cooperative. Here they are given a preliminary inspection and weighed for later payment to each household. The cooperative then sells them as a lot to one of the raw silk factories in southern Gunma, where they are boiled, unwound, spun into heavier thread, and resold through the Yokohama Raw Silk Exchange.

Every able-bodied member in the household takes part in agricultural work. During the nine years of compulsory education, work done by schoolchildren is limited to the summer vacation month and to the hours following school. The heaviest work, such as plowing, is done by men, and most domestic work, such as cooking, sewing, and washing, is done by women. However, most farm labor is divided equally between men and women. Only infants and the aged are exempt.

The work day varies in length with the season. The hours worked are difficult to estimate, but they probably range from about twelve hours per day in the summer to six hours in the winter. In any case, work is roughly from sunup to sundown. Agriculture in Takatoya, as in the rest of Japan, is labor-intensive (100 times as many person-hours are spent in Japan as in the U.S. to grow a bushel of wheat, for instance), and working hours are long during most of the year. During the four winter months, however, most households are underemployed. Members of many of them take on work farmed out from small factories, such as making buttons, assembling watchbands, and making quilts.

Social Organization

The principal units of social organization in Takatoya are residential: the household, the neighborhood association, and the village as a whole. These three are crosscut by a number of common-interest groups, such as the voluntary fire-fighting force, the women's association, and the agricultural cooperative. Ties of kinship between households also structure social organization to some degree.

The basic unit of organization is the household. Traditionally the Japanese household has been "corporate"—that is, its property, debts, and other rights and obligations are held in common by all members. The head of the household (normally the eldest son of the prior head) manages but does not "own" its property in that he cannot do with it as he wishes but must take the other members into account. Under the postwar constitution, written by Americans, the individual adult has replaced the household as a basic legal unit, and inheritance legally is equal to all children. But in practice household members still share many social rights and obligations, and the eldest son inherits the house and its land intact. The other children are compensated by receiving more education, cash, or other benefits.

The corporate nature of the household may be seen in its relations with other households and with the village as a whole. For instance, gifts are exchanged between households rather than between individual members of the households. The use of loan words from English, such as *puresento* ("present"), to refer to them indicates that "individual" gifts, to the extent that they are possible, are a new phenomenon. At village festivals or work projects, each household is expected to send a representative, who may be any physically and mentally capable person. The same principle is evident in the language. A speaker will use the term translated as "my household" to refer either to himself or herself or to her or his household collectively, and the term translated as "your household" to refer to the listener or his whole household; with the possessive, the terms will be used to refer to possessions either of individuals or of all members.

Membership in the household normally is either by birth or (for brides) by marriage. But actual kinship is neither strictly necessary nor sufficient for membership. For instance, adult males may become members of another household as "adoptive grooms" by marrying a daughter and taking the household name. They may even become household members as employees in the household enterprise.

The neighborhood association is the unit of organization next larger than the household. This is a group of households sharing an area and a number of mutual rights and obligations. The fifty-two households of Takatoya are divided into six such associations. The member households of each association perform a number of services for each other. The most frequent of these is the passing of the "circular notice," a clipboard containing notices of village events, from house to house in a fixed order. Most of these messages originate at the district town hall and are given to the headman of each village. He in turn gives them to the household of the head of each association, a post that rotates each year in the same direction as the circular notice. The head of the association passes the notice on to the household next in sequence to his own, and so on around the association until it returns to the association head.

Other reciprocal services include preparations for weddings, funerals, and memorial services, which are undertaken jointly by all households on behalf of the one concerned. There is also a degree of cooperation in such activities as house building, reroofing, and rice transplanting, and gifts of food are frequently exchanged. Relations within the neighborhood generally are intimate and familial. A popular saying is that "neighbors are more intimate than siblings who live apart."

The village as a whole is the largest unit that involves many regular face-to-face relationships. All of its adult members know each other as individuals and know even the children either as individuals or as members of a particular household. The village is the level at which the fire-fighting force, the women's association, and most of the other common-interest groups operate. It is also the level at which community Shinto festivals are held. Its inhabitants are conscious of their identity as members and readily say that Takatoya is a good place to live, adding or implying that it is a better place to live than the neighboring villages.

Politically, Takatoya, like its neighbors, was once a legal self-governing unit as well as a geographic and social one. Now it has been superseded as the lowest formal political level by a larger "administrative village," an aggregate of twenty-two villages like Takatoya.

The aggregate has a council and a mayor. Although the village is not a formal unit of government, it regularly votes as a bloc to elect a villager to the administrative village council. In each of the small villages a "headman" is also elected each year, but he serves as an administrator on behalf of the council, not as a decision maker. He is spoken of by villagers as a "messenger."

Within the village as a whole, as within neighborhoods, differences in household status are universally recognized, although they are not formally acknowledged. The principal components of status are seniority (and with it, breadth of kin relations), wealth, education, and to some extent personality. Households with strong combinations of these are leaders and are frequently elected to local office. One household in particular is known (and evidently respected) for its wealth and traditional political leadership. Its landholdings are four times the village mean, and the head of its house is regularly elected to the council and is expected to become mayor when he is somewhat

Figure 23-2
Households and Neighborhood Associations of Takatoya

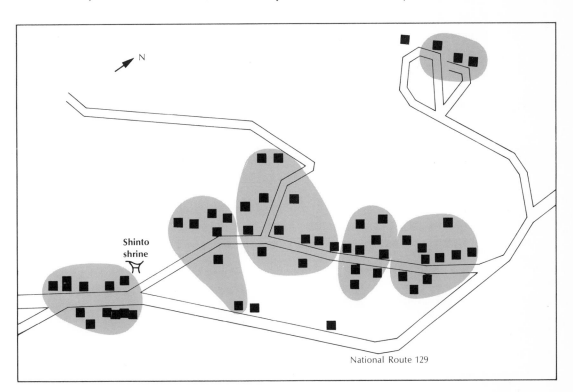

older. At the other end of the social scale is a household consisting of a single, indigent old woman with no kin and no means of support but government welfare.

Crosscutting the residential units of household, neighborhood association, and village, and using them as levels of organization are the common-interest groups. Among these are the Shinto shrine, the firefighting association, the women's association, the agricultural cooperative, the communal property association, the children's association, and the people's association.

The Shinto shrine, taken to include its parishioners, is in several ways typical of the common-interest groups. Its purpose is to secure the general welfare of the whole village by holding three yearly festivals for the deity that has the guardianship of the village. All villagers are by definition members of the shrine, but

The members of the Takatoya "old people's association" pose in front of a historic marker they have just erected in front of an ancient pine tree on their annual outing. The pine tree, a symbol of longevity in Japan, is said to have been planted 600 years ago, at the founding of the village.

An 80-year-old Shinto priest prays to a god before the altar in a shrine in Takatoya, at the shrine's annual festival. Some people say the festival is for good crops; others say it is to ward off colds. The boys looking on are members of the "children's association," which is responsible for gathering food and offerings for the festival.

the responsibility for preparing for the festivals and overseeing and maintaining the shrine building and grounds falls upon the "shrine parishioners' delegation." This delegation is composed of six people, one for each neighborhood association, with one member designated as head each year. For the maintenance of the shrine grounds, the delegation decides on a date and then requests all households to provide one member each for a morning of work.

More important, however, are the preparations for festivals. About a week before each of the festivals, the delegation members go from house to house within their neighborhoods collecting donations for the offerings to the deity and for the food and drink to be consumed after the offering. Each household is expected to give in proportion to its standing in the village. The delegates carry with them a small booklet in which someone from each household records the amount they wish to contribute. That amount is then given to the delegate. The booklet, passing from house to house within the neighborhood, notifies everyone within the association what everyone else has contributed and hence encourages generosity. Each household is expected to contribute not only money but also one member to attend the festival. It is a measure of the effectiveness of the household and neighborhood as elements of village organization that even in the present era of declining village solidarity and weakened faith in the deities, almost 100 percent of the households contribute money and about 90 percent send a member to the festival.

Like the shrine, the fire-fighting association usually functions at the village level and is internally organized by neighborhood association. It expects every household that can to participate by providing an able-bodied male as an active member. Membership entails practice drilling several times a year, and in the event of a fire in Takatoya or in a neighboring village, running or driving to the shed housing the little bright red, gasoline-powered fire pump, loading the pump into a pickup truck, and racing to the fire to combat it.

In addition to its obvious role in public safety, the fire-fighting association, like the shrine, also serves as a locus of communal sentiment in the village. The regular fire drills require the cooperation of all members, and the occasional actual fires further strengthen the bonds by requiring and rewarding intense, coordinated effort in a context of crisis. After a fire, the men retire to a small communal hall next to the equipment shed for an hour or more of relaxation with sake, snacks, and convivial banter.

Members of the firefighting association dismantle a burning house located near Takatoya. Characters on their jackets identify them as members of the Tone Administrative Village Division, to which Takatoya belongs.

As with the shrine, most households that are able contribute a member to the fire-fighting association, but one or two conspicuously do not. One of these households is the local meeting place for the members of a new Buddhist sect which has been the focus of some antagonism in the village. The fact that this household does not contribute either of its two able-bodied men is an indication of its marginal position in the village. Otherwise, the head of each household serves as a fireman until his oldest son is able to take his place.

The women's association, like the fire-fighting association, is organized principally at the village level, with smaller units consisting of the members of each neighborhood. It too serves as a channel of village news and sentiments, and each household is encouraged to participate, although a few households abstain. The group's activities are diverse. If the men of the village are fighting a prolonged forest fire, for instance, the women's association prepares food and carries it to the site. Twice a year the members go from house to house to sterilize the toilets (which are simply wooden casks sunk in the ground) with chemicals. Once a year the group takes a day's outing to some point of interest. There is a women's folk dance at the annual administrative village field day, for which the association of each village practices for several weeks in advance and at which all members wear identical costumes. In recent years the association has also hired a nutritionist to hold a one-day cooking class in the area. To plan these activities, numerous meetings are held throughout the year. These often end with some sake and hilarity, indulgences not otherwise enjoyed in daily life.

For boys of middle-school age (about nine to thirteen) and for older people who have retired from active economic life, there are two more associations that also are organized by village and neighborhood and are diverse in function. These are the children's association, which is charged with organizing two minor Shinto festivals a year and maintaining a fire watch for a week before New Year's, and the old people's association, which makes an annual excursion. Both of these also carry out a variety of other, minor activities throughout the year, but they both seem to be as important for socializing as for carrying out specific tasks. They incorporate the members of the village who are too young or too old for the major activities of economic life into a social network larger than the household.

Other crosscutting organizations, again organized by village and neighborhood, are the agricultural cooperative, the communal property association, and the Parent-Teacher Association (PTA). The agricultural co-op provides its members with seed, fertilizer, pesticides, and other materials at cost, offers expertise, and markets most of the cash crops. The communal property association, which includes about two-thirds of the village households, owns a tract of forest land that is maintained, managed, and replanted by members at a number of meetings and work parties each year. Finally, the PTA, a postwar import from the United States, carries on much the same activities as in its country of origin, though with somewhat less authority.

Culture

The dominant cultural themes and values in Takatoya may be partly understood in the context of the household, neighborhood, and village as social units and in terms of the subsistence system that supports them. As in the rest of Japan, these themes and values are also shaped by and expressed in the two major religious systems, Shinto and Buddhism, and to a somewhat lesser extent by Confucianism. Prominent among these values are (in no particular order) hard work, respect for parents and ancestors, kindness and consideration for others, and in general, submission of self to the welfare of the group. These are quiet virtues, not flamboyant ones. Ideal behavior calls no attention to itself; moderation is almost always best.

The agricultural economy is the primary context for the value placed on diligent work. The small area of arable land available for each household means that long hours of intensive labor must be spent to coax the greatest productivity from the soil. Energy and perseverance are admired and respected, and "working with might and main" is an expression of praise. In fact, hard work is considered so prevalent that overwork is cited as a leading cause of such maladies as high blood pressure. Stamina and persistence, rather than daring or ingenuity, are the useful virtues in this setting.

Another aspect of the work ethic is found in the importance accorded to education. Where cultivation of the soil leaves off, cultivation of personal resources begins. The people of Takatoya, despite their rural setting, share with other Japanese the eastern Asian, Confucian emphasis on self-improvement through literacy and knowledge. One result is that virtually every adult, with the exception of two or three old women, is literate. Another result is that the desire for a good education is a major impetus for ambitious young people to leave the village after high school, or even after middle school, to go to high school and perhaps a university in Tokyo or some lesser city.

A second major kind of value, that of respect, gratitude, and obedience toward parents and ancestors generally, is related to the place of the household as the basic, continuing social unit. Everyone is entitled to land and to a place in village society as a member of a village household, and in turn, everyone is validated as a household member in part by his or her relationship to the ancestors. This relation need not be one of

descent, but it does require recognition of all who have lived and died in the household before oneself as one's seniors and benefactors. To them is owed, first, the founding of the household and its transmission from generation to generation. At the same time, it is the unbroken presence in the village of these generations of ancestors which gives a household its seniority, its place in the village scheme on the basis of its antiquity. Hence devotions to the ancestors are, among other things, affirmations of one's rights as a villager.

The basic model for descendant-ancestor relationships is the relationship of the child to its parents. It is pointed out that the child owes not only its social place but its very existence to its parents. This debt is by nature too great to be repaid, but the least every person can do is to be conscious of it, to express his or her gratitude, to support his or her parents in their old age, and to plan for the continuation of the household through future generations. "Filial piety," in the Confucian phrase, is expected to be the cornerstone of domestic relationships. The misdeeds or virtue of anyone

Takahashi Nami and a neighbor lay straw over seed rice in the seedbed. This will be covered with a sheet of translucent plastic, forming a flat "greenhouse" to hold heat and moisture, and keep out birds, until the rice has sprouted.

in the household are seen as filial impiety or piety, respectively, because of the grief or joy they cause the parents or ancestors.

Filial piety is also a major theme in village Buddhism (most Japanese practice both Buddhism and Shinto, for the household and community, respectively), which provides the rites and paraphernalia for funerals, memorial services, and daily offerings before the household altar. All of these are occasions for the expression of gratitude and respect for deceased parents and for ancestors generally. For the villagers, in fact, "Buddhism" is virtually synonymous with "praying to the ancestors." Some people think of the ancestors as spirits who maintain an active interest in the affairs of their descendants, whereas others feel they continue to exist only through the effects they had while alive. In either case it is appropriate for the living to show their gratitude, respect, and devotion in minor daily rituals and in the yearly round of Buddhist festivals. After the breakfast rice or noodles are cooked each morning, a small bowl of it and a cup of tea or water are placed on the altar in front of the wooden memorial tablets, and a short prayer is offered. At the spring and autumn equinoxes, special visits are made to the graveyard with offerings of little rice dumplings, and at the All Souls' Festival in autumn, the ancestral souls are welcomed home for three days with food, flowers, and lanterns at a specially constructed altar on which all the memorial tablets are displayed.

In addition to providing for the proper expression of ancestor-descendant relations, Buddhism reinforces the ethical principles of kindness and consideration for others, which are frequently cited in the village as qualities of "good" behavior. Although villagers have little contact with priests or preaching except at funerals and memorial services, the ancestors themselves, the objects of Buddhist devotions, are commonly said to desire and support altruism and community harmony.

The last cultural theme to be described here, the submission of individual concerns to the welfare of the community, is well illustrated at the village level by the Shinto shrine. To begin with, the deity enshrined is said to be concerned with the well-being of the village as a whole, unlike the ancestors, who primarily are interested in their own households. Although individuals occasionally visit the shrine to introduce a new infant to the deity, the important events are the three festivals of spring, summer, and fall, when household representatives from the whole village gather. Everyone enters through a symbolic gateway that purifies their hearts of anger and other defilements. After ritual cleansing by the priest, prayer and offerings are made, and then all sit together in the shrine building to drink sake and sing traditional songs. Local affairs are discussed, and everyone agrees that this particular village is a fine place to live. Disagreements between households are supposed to be forgotten. As one man remarked at a festival, "The people of Takatoya are all good people."

In many villages (the population of Takatoya is no longer big enough for it) a heavy portable shrine is carried all around the village by the young men as the major event of the festival. The beams on which the portable shrine is carried are weighted down with sandbags or other weights, which makes the whole device much too heavy to be budged by one individual or even by several. Only a team, representing the whole village and acting in concert, can manage to carry it. The carrying of the shrine thus appears to be a graphic lesson on the weakness of the individual and the power and energy of the group.

Problems and Prospects

The major problems facing Takatoya, as the villagers see them, are the village's economic and educational limitations and the depopulation that is resulting as the young people leave for employment in the cities. With depopulation, community self-sufficiency declines, and most depressing of all, some household lines become extinct.

The main barriers to economic expansion are the mountains. All but the steepest slopes are now under cultivation, and some of the slopes have even been terraced to grow rice. Further expansion would not pay its own cost. Market prices for the crops are now stable rather than rising, and the price for the main cash crop, silk, may soon decline because silk from China has begun to enter the domestic market.

The mountains are also a barrier to industry and commerce. The nearest railroad runs through Numata City, fifteen miles away over a mountain pass, so it would be difficult to get industrial raw materials cheaply or to market finished products. The two light industries in the area, a small shoe factory and a watch-band factory, are made possible only by the cheap, unskilled labor of local farm wives. Both of these enterprises have been started in the last few years and are modestly successful, but despite the best hopes and plans of village leaders, they are unlikely to be followed by industry of a larger scale. Thus although the national economy of Japan has been expanding rapidly since its recovery from World War II, the economy of the village has not shared this growth. This disparity has led the young people of the village, like those of rural areas all over the country, to leave for city jobs.

In addition to its intrinsic economic limitations, people in Takatoya feel that the village is hampered by marginally adequate education. Most children go through high school within the administrative village, but many parents fear that local standards of education are not adequate to meet the demands of modern careers. Even more than in the United States, in Japan education is viewed as the main route to success. The leading positions in government and industry are largely reserved for graduates of a small group of universities with Tokyo University at the apex. Entrance to these universities is very competitive and is difficult unless the applicant has graduated from a leading high school. But entrance into good high schools is itself competitive, and it depends in part on coming from a good middle school, and so on down to primary school. Even outside the narrow circle of leading universities, this sequence of prerequisites is well established, and parents throughout Japan are anxious to get their children started early in good schools. For children from Takatoya, this often means going to high school in Numata City or even farther away to escape what their parents see as the permanent limitations of a country education. So the road from the village to the city may begin at the end of ninth grade.

Furthermore, many young people now find the intimacy of village life oppressive. Relations between households control relations between individuals, and gossip is a powerful control on freedom of behavior. "You can call it 'intimate,'" as one young man said,

A teacher reads an English lesson to his uniformed students in a public high school near Takatoya. English is the required second language for middle school and high school students.

"or you can call it 'meddling.'" Those who have had a taste of the anonymity and freedom of Tokyo often find it hard to settle in the village again.

As a result of all of these factors, the population has been shrinking steadily for several decades. In the five years between 1965 and 1970, for instance, it decreased by over 12 percent. Everyone predicts further decline. Depopulation affects village life adversely in a number of ways. The fire-fighting association and other community labor forces suffer from a lack of able-bodied young men, and the older men must stay in them longer to compensate for this. Community events such as village folk dances and the Shinto festivals have scantier attendance than before, and the traditional dance of the All Souls' Festival has been abandoned. Similarly, a play that used to be performed at the shrine festival has been abandoned because there are not enough performers to present it, and the costumes and carved wooden masks used in it are moldering in a storage chest. The young men's association, formerly charged with a variety of village tasks, has been dissolved. Overall, the people of the village sense that the general level of talent and innovation has declined as the brightest young people have moved away.

The gloomiest aspect of this depopulation, however, is the gradual extinction of household lines. The household, as the basic social unit, is, of course, a channel of continuity and tradition and a measure of the success of all of its members. Seeing that it continues is each generation's primary obligation to the last generation. It is every member's link to the past and the future, and so it offers a kind of immortality. As long as the household continues, no generation will be forgotten; its graves and memorial tablets will be tended and guarded by its descendants. Hence the preservation of household continuity is a central concern to virtually every villager.

Nonetheless, households continue to die out as the children leave and no one replaces them. In 1950 Takatoya had sixty households. In 1955 there were fifty-seven; in 1970, fifty-six; and 1972, only fifty-two. Of these fifty-two, moreover, five had only one member and no prospect of reproduction. It is not surprising, then, that the villagers are worried about depopulation and its consequences.

A young Takatoya groom poses for a wedding photo with his bride and her family. Men now often wear Western-style dress for formal occasions, while women usually wear the traditional kimono.

In the foreseeable future the population of Takatoya will probably continue to shrink, but at a lower rate than at present. Now the village is simply experiencing part of the worldwide emigration from country to city. However, the gap between its standard of living (or level of consumption) and that of the cities is likely to narrow as Japan's industrial expansion is leveled off by the high cost of oil. To the extent that the na-

tional industrial economy becomes depressed, the economic advantage of the urban areas seems likely to disappear, and the population flow may stop or even reverse. Meanwhile, as communications continue to improve and national culture becomes more homogeneous, Takatoya will become more and more like other segments of the national society. Already most households have television sets (many of them color) and receive on them the same amusement, instruction, and enticements as do households in the rest of Japan.

Economic conditions in the village will probably experience slight improvement as other light industries follow the watchband and shoe factories into the area, offering part-time work to underemployed farm families. In recent years increased tourist traffic headed for a national park and a famous shrine complex several hours north of Takatoya has offered a market for village-grown apples and corn as it skirts the village on a new, hard-surfaced highway. Both of these new sources of income will continue the trend of integration of the village with the regional and national economies. As individual villagers increasingly find part of their income outside the village itself, communal economic and ceremonial activities, such as those of the women's association and the Shinto shrine, will probably decline proportionately. Already several farming households receive more of their cash income from members who commute to jobs outside the village than from their crops.

Despite some economic and social uncertainties and the gradual replacement of village traditions by the modern national culture, life in Takatoya remains tranquil and, by and large, satisfying to the villagers. The seasons still set the reliable round of yearly events, the festivals affirm communal feeling, and most households still confidently project their continuity into the definite future.

Summary

Takatoya is a small mountain farming village in Japan, about four hours by road from Tokyo.

The inhabitants' primary means of subsistence are rice production and the raising of silkworms. The life of the community revolves to a large extent around these two crop cycles, and every able-bodied member of the households takes part in agricultural work.

The principal units of social organization are residential: the household, the neighborhood association, and the village as a whole. These are crosscut by a number of common-interest groups, such as the fire-fighting force, the women's association, and the agricultural cooperative. Member households in the associations perform various services for each other, thus maintaining reciprocal loyalties and bonds.

The culture of the group is profoundly influenced by the two major religious systems: Shinto and Buddhism. The people value respect for parents and ancestors, consideration for others, and submission of personal interests to those of the group. Hard work is especially valued.

The main problems facing the community are its economic and educational limitations and the depopulation that results from the migration of young people to urban centers. Some family lines have become extinct. Still, people feel that life is better than it used to be, and that the village itself will always exist.

Annotated Bibliography

Befu, Harumi (1971) *Japan: An Anthropological Introduction.* San Francisco: Chandler. A well-rounded, readable introduction to most of the range of anthropological information and opinion about Japan.

Benedict, Ruth (1946) *The Chrysanthemum and the Sword.* Boston: Houghton Mifflin. The classic attempt to account for Japanese behavior in terms of a distinctive set of cultural values, based on wartime interviews with immigrant Japanese in the United States. Dated but still important.

Embree, John (1939) *Suye Mura.* Chicago: Univ. of Chicago Press. The classic prewar study of a Japanese farm village, done in 1935.

Nakane, Chie (1972) *Japanese Society.* Berkeley and Los Angeles: Univ. of California Press. A readable, useful analysis of the structure of Japanese society in terms of the principle of "verticality."

24
Onitsha, Nigeria:
An African Urban Community

Introduction

In its lower reaches, the Niger River of West Africa runs southward into Nigeria on its course toward the sea. After flowing along a stretch of forested plains, it cuts through a narrow belt of red sandy uplands and descends into a vast floodplain that gradually fans out to form the great oil-bearing Niger Delta. This point, a geographical crossroads between river floodplain and uplands, has long been a meeting place for diverse peoples of the lower Niger region. Here on the east bank of the river lies the teeming city of Onitsha, which at the time of my fieldwork in the early 1960s, had an estimated population of over 160,000.

This town is also a major social and cultural center for the people whom early European explorers and missionaries labeled *Ibo,* recognizing that they speak diverse dialects of a single language that the people themselves call *Igbo.** During colonial times, the ethnic name *Ibo* gained general currency throughout Nigeria and beyond, and in the political movements which led to Nigerian independence in 1960, it became

* *The term is* Igbo, *which also refers to the language spoken by all of these peoples and is presumably the original word that the Europeans transcribed as "Ibo."*

Onitsha Waterside: covered canoes from northern Nigeria dock by the concrete causeway leading to Onitsha Main Market. In the background, the cranes and warehouses of United Africa Company.

a focus of great pride for the people themselves, since Ibo leaders were in the forefront of the nationalist movement. But today, in the aftermath of a bloody civil war in which all of Ibo country was overrun, this name seems to have lost favor with many of the people to whom it has been applied.

This chapter will explore the structure and process of *community*, here minimally defined as the shared recognition of and commitment to social oneness, or social identity—in this case, among those people who also share the facilities and problems of a single, nucleated civic center. One aspect of that process is, of course, the accepting of certain symbols designating the entity *we*.

The Environment

The "hinterlands" to the east from Onitsha are rolling hills of sedimentary sandstone. The soils are quickly robbed of organic material by the combined effects of leaching from heavy rains and bacterial decomposition fostered by the heat of the tropical sun. Their good drainage makes them suitable to the cultivation of the major staple food, the yam, however, and they are also relatively easy to till with traditional tools. In this region the annual rainfall, though broken by a marked dry season, is nowhere less than 70 inches, and the natural vegetation would be high forest everywhere except for the action of humans. But people are everywhere on these eastern uplands, in densities ranging from 600 to over 1,300 per square mile. By clearing and burning the forests to prepare their farms, the inhabitants have removed most of the large trees and have transformed the vegetation into a mosaic of relatively open "bush" woodlands and savannah grasslands. The soils are strained by overuse, and catastrophic erosions are underway on the eastern margins of the uplands. In a situation almost unparalleled elsewhere in Africa, the densest populations are concentrated precisely on the least fertile and most seriously eroding lands (Floyd 1969:53–54).

The lowlands to the north and south of Onitsha form a striking contrast to the upland patterns of good drainage, low soil fertility, heavy population density, and forest deterioration. They are for the most part regularly flooded, and although their alluvial soils are relatively fertile, they tend to be waterlogged and difficult to farm. Swampy conditions and the disease-bearing tsetse fly discourage settlement. The human population in this zone has remained relatively low, in most places less than 200 per square mile.

The highlands west of the Niger have soils similar to those of the eastern uplands, but their fertility has been much less disturbed because the population density is lower. The area encompasses extensive forests and mixed forest and bush vegetation.

Thus the environment of Onitsha—the area that can be said to compose the primary "urban field" whose people regularly serve and are served by the town—includes three distinctive geographical zones, two of which contrast very sharply. The latter two areas display a remarkable imbalance in the population-to-land ratio: at one extreme, a zone of overworked, deteriorating soils combined with an extremely high population; at the other, a zone of well-forested and fertile but relatively underpopulated land. The western highlands are intermediate between these two extremes.

When Europeans first visited Onitsha in the mid-nineteenth century, it was a group of villages containing perhaps 10,000 mainly agrarian people who occupied the riverbank and adjacent uplands. The people of Onitsha base their rights to this site on the legend that their ancestors invaded it long ago, after leaving their earlier homeland among other people who live on the highlands west of the river. These people are referred to as the "Highlanders." Onitsha people also claim a close cultural and historical relationship with the various settlements on the lowland floodplain, whose people they call "Riverine." Several Onitsha villages claim historical connection with the people whom they believe they originally met on the site but defeated and drove eastward; they refer to these and other groups living on the eastern uplands as "Hinterlanders."* Thus from its beginnings, Onitsha has apparently had relations with the various peoples living in each of its three major urban field zones. Although Onitsha people claim closer ties with the Highlanders and the Riverine people than with the Hinterlanders, they do not identify themselves with any of these groups but simply call themselves "Onitsha people."

The Group

Subsistence Activities

In precolonial times most villages of Onitsha town were loosely clustered around a common center or meeting place. Each village had its own wedge-shaped section of "farmland" spreading out from its "residence land" toward the peripheries of the town's territory. Thus the village social units (organized basically as patrilineal descent groups) were clustered for defense, and the farmland of each village was conveniently situated nearby. As a village population increased, its people could expand their residence land out into the adjacent farmland without coming into conflict with members of other villages. This type of Ibo village-group system fostered an orderly adaptation of people to the environment as long as the population was relatively low.

In Onitsha and its hinterlands, both intensive and extensive farming were practiced. Intensive farming is continuous cultivation of small plots of land with concentrated efforts to maintain productivity by the use of fertilizer, composting, and other methods of upgrading the soil—a pattern of high labor input per acre and individualized effort on small plots. Extensive

Figure 24-1
Onitsha Town and Waterside District.

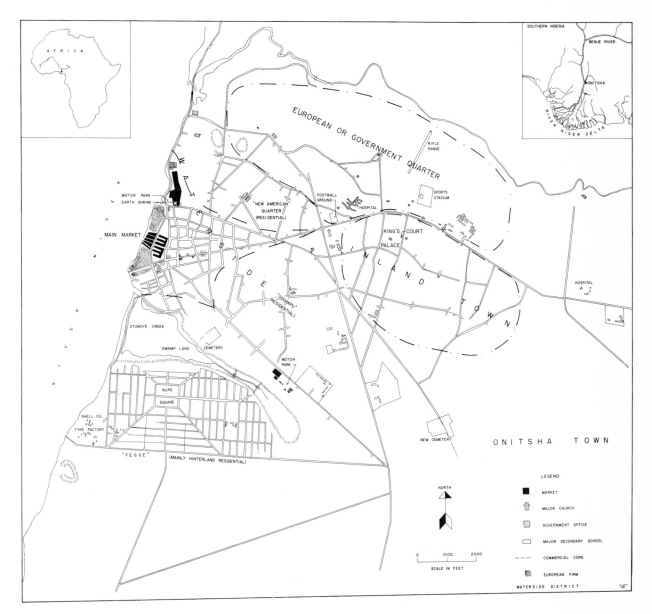

farming entails clearing a rather substantial area of
forest, burning the debris, planting and harvesting on
the plot from one to several years until its productivity
wanes, and then leaving it to fallow until regeneration
of natural plant growth restores its fertility—a pattern
of low labor input per acre and cooperative endeavor
on rather large plots.

In Onitsha town, where the ratio of population to
land was apparently moderate in precolonial times,
intensive farming was limited to areas of village residence land, where individual householders tended
small plots near their compounds. Staple yams, however, were grown on the farmland by cooperating
descent-group men using extensive methods. In the
adjacent hinterlands, similar patterns were followed
wherever the land supply was adequate both to feed
the farming population and to allow sufficient fallow
time, since under such conditions cooperative extensive farming is more productive per unit of labor expended (Netting 1965).

In the hinterlands farther east from Onitsha, however, the rural population density greatly increases,
and in much of the uplands village residence land has
expanded out into farmland until no farmland is left.
Under these ecological conditions, most landholdings
have been subdivided into small individual residential
plots, and all land is intensively farmed. But despite the
continuous, painstaking effort of the individual land-
holders, the land is not productive enough to feed all
of the people who live on it. Even well-tended soil
becomes overworked, and some or all of the people
face hunger. Moreover, the landholdings must be
further subdivided among the children when the
householder dies, or else some of the children must
go without land.

The imbalance between population and food resources is to some extent reversed among the Riverine
people, who traditionally not only produced yams in
the floodplain but also collected fish from the river,
and had more than enough food to support their low
population. Mediating these two very different economic situations were the people of Onitsha, who
were in a position to trade with both groups.

By the time Europeans entered the lower Niger, the
Onitsha waterside market had become an important

Onitsha Main Market: from the top of
the causeway, looking through the
produce market (various grains dry on
the sidewalk and bulk bags of grain are
visible on the side) toward the great
all-weather buildings beyond.

center of international exchange. Products of the oil palm—an economically valuable tree suited to impoverished soils—had become increasingly prominent in the hinterland economy and flowed from the uplands into the Onitsha market. A steady supply of excess people as slaves also came from the same area. The Riverine people exchanged for these and other upland products their fish, yams, salt, and—increasingly during the nineteenth century—European manufactured goods from the coast.

When Europeans settled at Onitsha in 1857, they found the town at war with various groups of Hinterlanders, Riverine traders, and towns across the river. Under these circumstances, the Onitsha people welcomed a European-protected enclave near their waterside market. The site was economically useful to the Europeans because it proved to be the northernmost point at which ocean-going vessels could safely dock year-round and because it was the gateway to an enormous potential market for European goods—the teeming eastern hinterlands. As the European demand for palm oil increased, the Hinterlanders industriously increased their supply, and the long-term growth of Onitsha as a commercial center was assured. In 1905 the British government made Onitsha the site of one of its administrative headquarters. A distinct "European quarter" was established for colonial officials and missionaries to the north of the Onitsha village group, and

the latter came to be known as the "inland town." More non-African trading companies located their warehouses along the riverbank near the main market, and around this complex grew up a native settlement referred to as the "waterside," at first composed mainly of Onitsha people converted to Christianity who had interests in the European trading establishment.

In the early days, trade between the waterside European firms and the Hinterlander palm oil suppliers was mediated by traditional women traders, mainly Onitsha people living in the waterside who intercepted Hinterlander traders on the uplands east of the inland town, exchanging the oil for European manufactured goods obtained from the firms. Some outstanding women traders became very wealthy and supported the Western education of their Onitsha brothers and sons in order to take advantage of the new economic opportunities being opened in the expanding European colonial system.

Western education was at first a monopoly of the various Christian missions in Onitsha. The Onitsha people committed their children to Christianity in large numbers, and they in turn used their educational skills to obtain jobs as catechist-teachers for the missions or as clerks in the European firms and government service. By the 1930s educated Onitsha people were scattered all over Nigeria and had become a permanent and influential part of the social strata of the cities. During the 1940s and 1950s they became some of the most prominent leaders in the Nigerian nationalist movement, and by the 1960s Onitsha men were spread through the highest levels of the Nigerian civil service and the universities. Onitsha people were the first "Ibos" to achieve social mobility through Western education.

Few Onitsha sons forgot their homeland town, however, for in most Nigerian cities they were treated by the local indigenes as "foreigners," and in many places they could not buy land or exercise other civil rights. They felt that it was their duty to help their own people get jobs, and they sent much of their salaried wealth to Onitsha to support family members left behind in the inland town.

Until the end of World War II, nearly all import and export trade in Onitsha was controlled by Euro-

A view down an aisle in the produce section of the Main Market, looking toward the Niger. Women traders fill the interstices, while men from the Hinterlands operate most of the wholesale trade from stalls.

pean or other non-African firms and distributed through their agents, the Onitsha and Riverine market women. A few Onitsha men and other Africans opened shops outside the market, and some pioneered their own business enterprises, such as bicycle repair, truck ownership, printing, building construction, architecture, and private schooling. However, early in the century the colonial government supported the rights of Hinterlander traders to enter the Onitsha waterside, and Hinterlanders began to settle there among the Onitsha people. After the war, road services expanded in the hinterlands, and traders traveled directly to their sources of produce supply, bypassing the old river

trade and the Onitsha women. The success of African privately owned enterprise stimulated investment in local industry and trades, and the economy expanded rapidly, while the population of the town came to be numerically dominated by Hinterlanders.

In the early 1960s, when my wife and I lived in Onitsha, the waterside was teeming with diversified commercial activity. The Onitsha main market contained more than 3,000 separate stalls on some fifteen acres of land, with zones specialized by products. It accommodated the activities of more than 25,000 traders and was reputed to contain a nearly infinite variety of goods. Behind the main market, intermingled

with the scattered warehouses of various European import-export firms, was a plethora of African shops. It is difficult to describe the number and variety of these businesses, but a brief, intensive survey of the shops along seven streets in the commercial core of the town revealed the following units:

Manufacturing, Repair, Processing

26 Blacksmith
 5 Tinsmith
29 Goldsmith
32 Shoemaking, repair
35 Carpentry
 6 Contractor
25 Bicycle repair, rental

 7 Motorcycle repair
10 Automotive repair
 7 Vulcanizing
 8 Welding, battery charging, and so forth
57 Small machine repair (watch, radio, and so on)
71 Tailor
12 Seamstress

 3 Umbrella repair
12 Mattress making
 7 Laundry

 7 Bakery
 4 Flour mill

Product Sales (Mostly Imported)

35 Construction materials
11 Petroleum products
11 Shoes
11 Bicycles (and parts)
 6 Motorcycles (and parts)
 6 Automotive parts
11 Small machine, radio, watch parts
 3 Tires
 4 Sewing machines (and parts)
56 Provision stores
16 Beer, soft drinks
57 Food and drink bars

 4 Hotels
16 Household furnishings (beds, linoleum, and so on)
 4 Dried fish (cod)
11 Hardware
17 Glass cutting, picture frames
 7 Imported leather goods
 5 General goods
11 Fancy wearing apparel
38 Imported cloth
 9 Second-hand clothing
 6 Electrical materials

Social and Cultural Services

12 Photography
16 Art studio
 8 Commercial-technical school
14 Native doctor
 1 Hospital
17 Printing press
 9 Numbers pool

Surprising as the sheer number of shops may be, this list gives no sense of the range in the scale of the businesses involved. Carpentry shops varied from a one-man, hand-tool operation under a thatched lean-to to a multished, mass-production operation using power machinery and employing some thirty apprentices. Blacksmith shops ranged from small, individual operations making mostly traditional iron gongs to large workshops producing substantial and elaborately ornate iron gates. Tailoring and seamstressing varied in scale from one person with a sewing machine under the awning of a shop to an enterprise run by a woman who owned a dozen machines and employed a score of apprentices in a specially constructed building. Most businesses had a similar range in scale, the exceptions being goldsmithing and native doctoring, which were limited to one, two, or three people.

Regardless of the number of workers or the amount of capital involved, nearly all African businesses in Onitsha had a fundamental characteristic in common: They were essentially one-person enterprises in the sense that the owner-manager did not delegate important decision making to those he employed but instead kept complete control. This unwillingness to delegate responsibility, together with the apprentice system of employment, made these businesses markedly different from the Western type for two reasons. First, the inability to delegate authority sets rather low limits on the size and complexity of an organization; one person can directly control only so much activity. The African businessman in Onitsha tended to withdraw capital from his business when it reached a certain level and to invest it in another line of trade (trucks, taxis, real estate) in order to retain full control over his wealth. Second, as a master of several apprentices, the businessman did not ordinarily pay his workers wages. Indeed, apprentices sometimes paid their master, who promised to teach them his methods and to set them up in their own business when their training was completed. Each entrepreneur was thus in effect training, multiplying, and capitalizing his own future competitors. For these reasons, African businesses in Onitsha generally remained relatively small in scale, simple in organization, and intensely individualistic. Many essentially one-person operations competed for a share of an increasingly subdivided pie (Katzin 1964).

Thus Onitsha town had three major economic classes of people, apart from the non-African population. One group made their living as traders in the main market or in shops, in a social context of intensive competition. These traders consisted overwhelmingly of Hinterlanders. In a sense the Hinterlanders were reproducing in their commercial activity an adaptive system analogous to that of their farming kinspeople back in the uplands: intensive, industrious, individualized enterprise, by increasing numbers of workers plying the same line. Second, there were salaried workers employed by the government, the European firms, and the missions. These workers had traditionally been mainly indigenes of Onitsha, but the Hinterlanders were increasingly gaining clerical jobs and had become numerically predominant in the local schools. Third, there were the rentiers of market stalls, of houses, and of land. Onitsha indigenes had also predominated in these economic activities, which sustained their traditional social organization, but Hinterlanders were gaining more ownership of market stalls, owned most of the commercial houses in the

Onitsha Main Market: a view down the street which divides the market. The signboard advertises products of local manufacture.

waterside, and were more or less permanently in control of leased waterside land. The Onitsha indigenes were anxious about these tendencies.

Social Organization

Let us travel briefly to Onitsha town on a Sunday in 1961. We find that the city, in the sense of a community (or as many Africans might put it, as a place of "one-heartedness"), has *two* "hearts": the Onitsha king's palace in the center of the inland town and the Onitsha main market at the waterside.

Let us first examine the palace of the Onitsha king. In traditional local beliefs, high forest is identified with the most fertile earth, and the Onitsha king dwells within high, sacred forest. In the center of that forest is a great open space of cleared, barren earth—the palace meeting grounds, which are entered by a path leading beneath a protective medicinal archway. At the far end of the palace grounds stands the palace complex, a house of many chambers. In front of the main building is a substantially elevated, rectangular, open structure called the "king's breeze house." In times of harvest the king sits here, stripped to his loincloth, painted with white clay, in "dreaming" communion with the forces of the universe and the ancestors of the Onitsha people. This is also where he sits on his throne, robed in splendor and flanked by his chiefs, to receive the salutes of his people after his annual ceremonial emergence from seclusion.

On this day in 1961 the breeze house is empty, though the king's iron war gong hangs suspended from a front rafter, and his twin wooden slit-gongs, which are used to signal the coming of daylight, are set up nearby. The women of the royal family dance before the breeze house in a circle, one of them holding a miniature golden version of the royal sacrificial sword. Nearby, folding chairs are being unloaded from an Onitsha Urban County Council dumptruck. People dressed in fine cloth are walking toward the palace.

We pass the breeze house and enter the palace proper, stepping through an arched entryway into the large open courtyard of the king's public chamber. Here he meets all the people of Onitsha town, but in this context the term *town* means not the wider civic system but rather the people of ancient Onitsha, the indigenes, including their sons and daughters now living elsewhere. Here all "real" Onitsha people may have their say in community affairs at gatherings presided over by the king and his many chiefs or councillors. No outsider, whether European or Hinterlander, has any formal right to be heard. On this day the king's high throne is empty, but his chiefs and men of the town sit along the low edges of the courtyard. They are watching the division of the meat of three cows just sacrificed to announce the death of the king.

The most senior titled chief, or prime minister (a retired bank clerk), supervises the carving and distribution of the meat. Seated beside him in order of rank are the second senior chief (a retired customs official), the third (a retired accountant and a very wealthy man), the fourth (a retired court clerk), the fifth (a retired junior civil servant), and the sixth and last of the senior chiefs (a retired import-export clerk). These are the great men of the inland town, richly robed patricians in their fifties and sixties. Seated beyond them are junior chiefs, and on the floor left of the throne sit some still lesser chiefs, classed as "wives" of the king. All the chiefs, at once holy men and "warriors," are political leaders of their respective villages and subvillages.

At the doorway to the king's private chambers are several representatives of the royal lineage. Also present, in their corner to the right of the king's throne, are some of the most senior patrilineage priests of Onitsha, the representatives of the descent groups that control much of Onitsha's extensive urban and rural lands. Across from the senior chiefs, on the edge of the left flank, sit the ranks of the titled Qzq, holy men of the clans. The end opposite the throne is available for the titled women of the town, but none are seated there today, although a group of them (the traditional wealthy trading women of Onitsha, wearing white robes and great ivory bracelets and anklets) pass through the chamber on their way to salute the corpse of the king.

The next entryway leads into a smaller courtyard where the senior chiefs normally convene with the king, but today it is filled with crowds of mourners waiting to view him lying in state in the next inner chamber: the secluded courtyard reserved for the king and his immediate royal family. His corpse lies on a white, lace-covered brass bed, fully robed and gloved in white, nostrils filled and eyes marked with white clay. A red cap is on his head, and two ornate British-style crowns are placed beside it. Under the watchful eye of the senior daughters of the royal lineage, a line of subjects dressed in richly varied togas and gowns waits to salute the king for the last time with an offering of money.

In the early afternoon a large crowd gathers in the public grounds. The right flank of the field is reserved for the indigenous elite, and the left flank, for non-indigenous dignitaries, who are coming from all over Nigeria to pay their respects. Several Onitsha age-sets—groups of indigenous men and women born within the same three-year span—enter the grounds en masse, colorfully uniformed, to dance in salute. Important officials of the Eastern Region government appear, as do the chairman and town clerk of the Onitsha Urban County Council, of which the king was presi-

In the king's court, Onitsha chiefs sit bareheaded in the sunlight dividing the sacrificial meat of his funeral. Standing and dressed in white the Prime Minister directs the butchers.

dent. Many prominent lawyers and politicians (both Onitsha indigenes and Hinterlanders) are present, some wearing formal European clothes and others wearing African dress. There are turbaned officials from the waterside Muslim community; British expatriate officials; Americans associated with the Pepsi-Cola Company, currently establishing a bottling plant on the edge of town; and an American anthropologist who photographs the scene from a crowded platform built for members of the press.

The climactic moments of the ceremony begin when the senior chiefs, wearing their elaborately feathered headdresses and escorted by the chiefs and men of the villages they represent, enter the palace grounds and perform their war dances in front of the breeze house to the rhythm of the royal war drums. Finally, the king's own sons (a group of educated young men, most of whom reside in urban centers elsewhere) emerge from the palace, wearing their father's royal caps and crowns. When the senior son dances in the crowd and touches the war drums with his father's ceremonial sword to extinguish their sound, the public ceremony comes to an end.

But in this funeral celebration the crowd is so vast (a local newspaper not unreasonably estimated 30,000) that the chiefs and their villagers find it very difficult to make their way through to the palace. At times they are quite engulfed by the spectators—people of all ages, Hinterlanders and indigenes, Africans and foreigners. At times the separation of performers and spectators dissolves into a chaos of milling people. This momentary dissolution of the social groupings might be taken as symbolic of the major social problem of Onitsha as the "real Onitsha" people see it: There are too many foreigners, and few of them seem to know their proper place, which should be one of restraint and respect.

Here we see most of the traditional social structures operating in the town: the patrilineage priests, who control the descent groups' various wedges of land,

The Owelle, sixth senior chief, dances
with his ceremonial sword before the
king's Breeze House.

left
The king's funeral: Members of an
Onitsha age-set (in uniform) escort one
of their members, a daughter of the king.
She holds the black horsetail of
mourning.

now valuable urban real estate; the titled *Qzq* men,
who perform the public acts of priesthood; the three
ranks of chiefs, all selected by the king and regularly
consulted by him; the women's organizations of descent group daughters, wives, and titleholders; the
age-sets, composed of both men and women. Absent
from this ceremony are the "collective incarnate dead,"
the masqueraders representing ancestors. Representatives of this secret organization, to which all adult male
indigenes of the town belong, may never enter the
palace grounds unless the people decide they can no
longer abide the king, when they may send the "long
juju" (or "tall ghost," a giant hooded cobra) to enter
this secluded heartland of the town and depose him.
At this time in 1961, virtually the entire traditional
social structure remains in operation, its main role
players being mostly relatively well educated and also
elderly (see Henderson 1972 for a description of the
precolonial Onitsha social system). In addition, however, the traditional structures have incorporated a
variety of new roles, subgroups, and standards: secre-
tariats and executive committees, constitutions and
rules of parliamentary order.

On the following day, a Monday, the Onitsha main market at the waterside is buzzing with the activity of trade. But this behavior is contrary to the will of Onitsha people, whose representatives on the Onitsha Urban County Council had successfully pressed for a council decree that the main market be closed on the day following the funeral. Announcements to that effect were printed in the two local newspapers, and a bell ringer was sent round the market in the morning to herald its closing. However, after his departure, representatives of the Onitsha Market Amalgamated Traders Association, whose leaders and members are overwhelmingly Hinterlanders, had sent their own bell ringers to announce that the market would stay open, and most stall holders and shop owners did just that. Thus the urban "heart" of the Hinterlanders refuses to honor Onitsha traditional rites.

The everyday lives of the immigrant Hinterlanders in Onitsha are different from those of most indigenes, and their vital statistics are markedly different, too. In a sample of over 100 traders who hold stalls in the main market, all are Hinterlanders and all are men; 75 percent of them are between the ages of twenty and thirty-five; and a slight majority of them are unmarried. The general age range of Hinterlanders is even lower, and the proportion of unmarried men is still higher: Voter registration lists show that some waterside Hinterlander wards have male-to-female ratios of over 4 to 1. Many Hinterlanders have come to Onitsha to obtain money to pay the brideswealth required at home in exchange for a wife and to pay for their own or their kinspeople's educations. In Onitsha they meet intensive competition in all trades, and many of them barely earn a living.

Since they cannot look to their rural homes for support under such circumstances, Hinterlanders must seek social support in the town. They initially do so by participating in voluntary associations, primarily their home "improvement unions"—mutual aid organizations composed of people born in the same hinterland village who have established an Onitsha "branch" of the union. Onitsha has innumerable such unions, ranging in form and scale from tentative groups begun by a handful of newly arrived immigrants to complex, formal organizations divided into multiple subgroups and specializing in different functions.

A view in Onitsha's main lorry park. In the foreground, a "truck" just emptied of bulk produce is being returned to the Main Market; at rear, two lorries, or "Mammy-wagons," the bodies of which are manufactured in local carpentry shops.

These unions train the immigrants to play various kinds of modern organizational roles and to handle money and other assets responsibly in their new urban context. By collecting dues, the unions create a common pool that is used to make loans or to give financial support to members. They also provide information and serve as pressure groups in helping members find work or improve their trade. As they become more successful, these organizations may expand their efforts toward improving and transforming economic, political, and educational conditions in the home village.

During the 1950s the indigene-dominated Onitsha town council tried to limit the infusion of elected Hinterlanders into local urban government. The various Hinterlander improvement unions met and formed a unified political pressure group. They organized Hinterlander support and rode to victory in contested local elections, since the indigenes were far outnumbered in their own town. Once this victory had been won and the Onitsha urban council had been reformed in a compromise that provided for several traditional members with an elected majority of Hinterlanders, this organization was dissolved.

This brief contrast between Hinterlanders, or "non-Onitsha Ibos," and Onitsha indigenes, or "Onitsha Ibos," has so far ignored certain social strata and structures that do not fit the contrast. For example, a num-

ber of fairly well-educated young people living in the inland town are not much interested in traditional activity. These Onitsha people might be expected to share social interests with the enterprising Hinterlanders, but they do not respect the capitalist enterprise or hometown "improvement" practices of the latter and instead seek to organize political groups aimed at advancing the cause of socialism on the national level.

In addition, two important types of organizations in Onitsha crosscut the indigene-Hinterlander division: the church and the political party. Nearly all Ibo people in Onitsha are or have been associated with either the Anglican or Roman Catholic church, as most of them have received some education in mission schools. Both indigenes and immigrants are more or less evenly divided between the two churches, which have long been locked in competition for converts. The competition between the faiths has perhaps to some extent united two different sets of Hinterlanders and indigenes in a common cause. However, the social involvement of the indigenes in their churches is generally different from that of the Hinterlanders. Whereas the Hinterlanders attend their churches quite seriously, often regarding them as sources of support, Onitsha indigenes view church activity as more peripheral. Many inland town men affirm that they have parted with the church, identifying it with colonialism and proposing well-reasoned arguments that indigenous religion is analogous to Christianity or in important ways superior to it.

The majority political party of the Eastern Region of Nigeria at this time has grassroots organizations in every ward of Onitsha town, and both Hinterlanders and indigenes are members and officials of these groups. In order to contest successfully on the national level, this party has worked hard to unify diverse Ibo groups, and within it, the indigenes and the Hinterlanders work together in cautious but mostly cordial cooperation. Among social elite, local lawyers, doctors, politicians, and senior government officials form a night-clubbing set which substantially crosscuts the division, and they mingle in residence areas—many of them living in the former European or government quarter. But fundamentally a deep social gulf remains,

across which the Onitsha indigenes look with a mixture of anxiety and resentment, while the immigrants consider traditional Onitsha concerns as largely irrelevant to their everyday lives.

Culture

Previous sections of this chapter have made numerous references to contrasts between Onitsha indigenes and Hinterlanders that are in an important sense *cultural:* differences in historical and communal relations with other peoples, in self-identification, in economic organization and social class membership, in orientation both to modern insititutions (Christianity, capitalism) and to traditional ones (kingship, indigenous religion). All of these cultural differences are partly reflections of the different situations in which members of the two groups find themselves, but in part the cultural differences themselves define orientations, structure situations, and thus channel behavior. How do the cultural patterns influence social interaction between indigenes and immigrants?

The indigenes have always had a high regard for the kingship and believe that the Hinterlanders, who lack the institution of chieftaincy, are commoners in relation to the Onitsha elite. Even today, kingship and chieftaincy remain pivots of the community for Onitsha indigenes, and their hostility to the Hinterlanders is based on the latter's lack not only of Onitsha-style kings in their own village groups but lack of respect for the value of kingship itself. The Hinterlander population, a substantial majority in the town as a whole, has little sense of the relevance of traditional kingship. These people come from a rural background whose economics are individualistic and whose politics are basically competitive and democratic. Intently involved in educational success and economic survival in the teeming waterside scene, most Hinterlanders have significantly different basic orientations to social life from those of the indigenes (Morrill 1963; Henderson 1966).

One indicator of this difference is the astonishing proliferation of popular literature pouring off Onitsha presses in the waterside printing shops. These pamphlets, written mostly by local Hinterlanders specifically for their elementary-school-educated associates, appeal to the distinctive cultural preoccupations of this group. They are brief, clearly written, and cheaply produced. As Emmanuel Obiechina points out, this popular literature is

a product of a highly mobile consciousness, a consciousness most actively creative where the importance of individuals is recognized and promoted within the social structure. Only to those who accept this belief in the value of the individual could such otherwise anonymous little people as office messengers, petty traders, band-leaders, students, peasant farmers, unskilled labourers, artisans, white collar workers assume sufficient importance to become the subject for literature (1973:8).

The dime novels and guides for social behavior that make up the bulk of this literature cover a great variety of experiences, but two features stand out. First, the pamphlets focus on the problems of the new values and new demands that the Hinterlanders confront in

Escorted and protected by the masked Incarnate Dead, members of an Onitsha patrilineage escort the corpse of an indigenous youth from the Waterside back to his home in the Inland Town.

the city, particularly the prospect of social mobility. Many pamphlets preach a Hinterlander moral code that is similar to the Protestant ethic: self-denial, self-discipline, frugal saving and investment, and avoiding the dangers of self-indulgence, whether in drinking places or in the arms of the opposite sex. Many of the pamphlets are guides to specific means of job advancement; they stress hard work, bold assertiveness, and scrupulous honesty. The pamphlets generally strongly affirm Christian ideals. Although they focus on material wealth, prestige items of Western manufacture, and money and credit standing, they are also pervaded by a Christian idealism: The moral and responsible person, no matter how lowly his or her position, will be rewarded in the end, and the corrupted will ultimately suffer. The individual is everywhere responsible for his or her fate.

A second major feature of the pamphlets is their rejection of tradition wherever it is confronted by the demands of modern life. A prime villain in the novels is the pidgin-speaking, village-dwelling chief, who is pictured as anti-Christian, greedy, and often drunk, and who demands an outrageous brideswealth for his daughter or uses his money to claim as his wife an educated young girl whom an urban Hinterlander wishes to marry. Where the situational demands of life in a modern city meet traditional constraints, tradition must give way.

These two features reflect an overall Hinterlander ideal of Nigerian life, an ideal that may be characterized as secular, individual mobility in the framework of a democratic nation-state. National politics are not much stressed in these pamphlets, but Hinterlanders leave no doubt (in 1961) that their commitment to "one Nigeria" is a fundamental assumption and that their vision of the state is a democratic one: "one man, one vote." They scarcely question the ultimate value of the full range of Westernizing modernization; to them, the Onitsha indigenes seem to have "accepted the wrong side of civilization," for they have failed to be "detribalized."

It would be a mistake to infer from this that the Onitsha indigenes lacked the values of individualism, industriousness, or the Christian version of morality; on the contrary, they have long been exposed to such

values and have evolved a system of standards that reflect these elements (see Henderson 1972 for a discussion of traditional Onitsha values). What they have done is to organize the priorities of their value structures differently. They have also had the experience of relating the values to social reality for a long time—their grandparents were in some cases literate converts to Christianity. They no longer treat the values as absolutes. For example, there is a skeptical cynicism about what Christian standards "really mean" in contemporary Nigeria.

The indigenes on the whole have had longer experience with indigenous systems in other parts of Nigeria, among which they find parallels to their own kingdom. The persistence of traditional political systems in a modern state therefore does not surprise them. Moreover, they do not believe, as their parents or grandparents perhaps did, that Christian morality will lead to a golden age. They are partly disillusioned, having found corruption as widespread among Europeans as among Africans and having learned that Christian or democratic standards cannot always suffice as guides for social conduct in the cities of Nigeria. It is not that they value a "one Nigeria" less—but that they are not so confident that it is moving toward an individualistic, democratic state. For these and other reasons, Onitsha indigenes find the pamphlet literature of the Hinterlanders naïve, unrealistic, and uninteresting.

The fundamental problem, from the viewpoint of the indigenes, is the complex of social forces leading toward the dissolution of the inland town social system: a gradual infiltration of Hinterlanders, the long-term effects of leasing more and more blocks of descent group land to Hinterlanders for commercial purposes, the erosion of Onitsha ownership of stalls in the main market, and the diminution of their political voice in their own urban council. Under these circumstances, many educated young Onitsha people see a general socialist or even communist revolution as the only hope for long-term security in Nigeria.

On the other hand, their elders, though similarly aware of the local pressures toward dissolution and the pervasiveness of ethnic identities in Nigeria, are committed to strengthening the security of their home grounds. They emphasize a self-conscious "nativism" as their highest value. By bringing in educated and prominent elders to fill positions of title and of chieftaincy, they aim at bolstering and effectively reorganizing the only basis of social life on which they believe they can ultimately rely: their own tradition, people, and resources. To both groups, the individualistic capitalism and ultrademocratic politics of Hinterlanders seem unrealistic or threatening. They are threatening because such activities tend to erode the indigenes' social basis of security, and unrealistic because they presume an institutional framework for individualistic competition that is not, in the world of Nigerian cities with which they are familiar, a framework on which people can necessarily rely. Given these major contrasts in social orientation, it is understandable why

On the edge of the Inland Town, two masked Incarnate Dead of the indigenes accost a Hinterlander, intending to extort money from him before allowing him to pass on his way.

interaction between indigenes and Hinterlanders so often leads to insults and hostility. From the Hinterlander viewpoint, many local indigenes are lazy and backward, resting on the laurels of those among them who have attained national prominence. From the indigenes' perspective, many Hinterlanders are naïve, grasping, and disrespectful of the one ultimate basis for security in the dynamic context of Nigerian social life: tradition-based structures rooted in the commitment of people to the land they live upon.

Problems and Prospects

Turning from Onitsha as we found it in 1961 to the present, we survey an intervening time punctuated by cataclysmic disaster for the people living in the city and region just described. By the time my wife and I departed from Onitsha in the summer of 1962, signs of breakdown in the Nigerian federal system had already appeared. Tendencies toward disintegration accumulated over the following years until a military coup—led mostly by Ibo army officers, including Onitsha indigenes—put an end to civilian government in 1966. The government leaders were imprisoned and an Ibo Hinterlander, Major General Johnson Aguiyi-Ironsi, was made military commander of the federation. Six months later a countercoup was aimed largely at the Ibo. Ironsi and many other Ibo officers were killed, and a northern officer, Yakubu Gowon,* became the Nigerian supreme commander. A massive pogrom was subsequently launched against Ibo civilians living in urban centers of the Northern Region, and thousands were slaughtered and perhaps over a million driven as penniless refugees back to their homeland in the Eastern and Midwestern regions (see Chap. 16). Ibos also fled from the other regions, in fear for their lives, and returned home to the east.

After a period of recriminations between leaders of the east and the federal government, the Eastern Region seceded from Nigeria and established the new nation of Biafra, led by the Hinterlander Odumegwu

* Gowon himself was ousted from government in a bloodless coup while attending the annual summit of the Organization of African Unity in Uganda in August 1975.

Ojukwu. Federal troops invaded Biafra and overran Onitsha. They scattered its population, destroyed the main market, and razed the town, and—after years of bitter fighting and starvation—defeated the secessionists and reintegrated them into Nigeria. The former Eastern Region was divided into three states; Onitsha town is now included in the Eastern Central State, which is composed almost exclusively of the core Hinterlander area.

During the war most outsiders (including most Ibos living overseas) believed that the Ibo surrounded by federal troops inside Biafra were as totally committed to Biafra as were those living outside, many of whom organized movements for Biafran relief. However, it gradually became apparent that Onitsha indigenes were not trusted as true Biafrans, and that a number of prominent Onitsha men had never committed themselves to the cause. After the end of the war, it became clear that a substantial number of Onitsha indigenes living inside the country has always opposed the idea of secession, a fact that came as a considerable surprise to the many Onitsha people who had strongly supported it from overseas.

As Onitsha and its main market were rebuilt under military occupation in the aftermath of war, the indigenes mobilized to reconstruct their home community and reassert their control over the market, demanding ownership of the bulk of its stalls. After conflict with the state administration over this issue, they petitioned the national government in 1973 to separate Onitsha town from the East Central State and to include it, along with the Riverine people and the Highlands people living across the river, into a new state that could take root in the historical and cultural relations Onitsha people share with these other groups.

On the other hand, many traders from the hinterlands at first refused to return to the Onitsha waterside after the war and tried instead to relocate commercial activity in their hometowns. A trading center called New Onitsha was established in the densely populated uplands to draw the commercial center of gravity to that site, an effort that suggests deep alienation from Onitsha on the part of the Hinterlanders. With military barracks everywhere, with the old home improvement unions banned and other integrative structures weak or absent, it seemed to the Hinterlanders that the best base of operations would be at home.

It even appears that among some of the people the term *Ibo* itself has fallen into disrepute. An effort is being made by some Igbo-speaking scholars to eliminate its use (they brand it as a colonialism) and to substitute the term *Igbo* as the general category name. It remains to be seen whether the latter word (translated for convenience here as "hinterland" or "Hinterlanders" in its ethnic reference) will prove acceptable to all Igbo-speaking peoples. From the perspective of Onitsha indigenes, both in 1961 and today, the answer appears to be no. Indeed, whereas in 1961 few Onitsha people quibbled about being refered to as *Ibo*, some now question whether *any* ethnic cover term can apply to the various groups. In Onitsha town the problem of *community* is no longer designated by the opposition between "Onitsha Ibos" and "non-Onitsha Ibos"; there seems to be some doubt as to what common terms, if any, remain among the groups involved. If attitudes such as these are now much more widespread, it may be that the people anthropologists have long called *Ibo* and who have become famous for their remarkable feats of modernization, are declaring that the ethnic identity *Ibo* no longer exists.

Summary

Onitsha, a town on the Niger River in Nigeria, has long been a social and cultural center for the people termed "Ibo" by European explorers. In the past the people practiced agriculture, with farming patterns becoming more intensive as the population increased. By the time Europeans first entered the town, it had become an important market.

The Ibo have played an important role in the recent political history of Nigeria, both as leaders of the movement for national independence and in the Nigerian civil war. Their prominence derives largely from their early perception of the importance of education as a route to social mobility.

The inhabitants of the town include both the original residents and the Hinterlanders, who dominate the town market and are increasingly influential in other civic areas as well. The political organization of the town is based on both traditional and modern structures: the institution of kingship and the newer urban government. Hinterlanders are especially active in "improvement unions," which introduce new migrants to the ways of the town. Considerable tension exists between the more tradition-oriented indigenes and the Hinterlanders, who favor modernization and abandonment of tribal ways.

The Ibo suffered severely in the Nigerian civil war, and the town of Onitsha was devastated. The town has subsequently been rebuilt, but its future remains uncertain.

Annotated Bibliography

Achebe, Chinua (1960) *No Longer at Ease.* London: Heinemann. A sophisticated novel by an Ibo intellectual, set mainly in the Nigerian city of Lagos, that traces one man's tragic efforts to reconcile modern desires and ideals with commitments to his home people.

Banton, Michael (1957) *West African City.* London: Oxford Univ. Press. A classic study of Freetown, Sierra Leone, tracing the historical development of the city, migration patterns, ethnic group relations, and the forming of voluntary associations.

Cohen, Abner (1969) *Custom and Politics in Urban Africa.* Berkeley and Los Angeles: Univ. of California Press. An insightful case study of ethnic politics among Hausa settlers in the Yoruba city of Ibadan, Nigeria.

Melson, Robert, and Wolpe, Howard (1971) *Nigeria: Modernization and the Politics of Communalism.* East Lansing: Michigan State Univ. Press. A collection of essays considering the relations among ethnicity, class formation, and political power distribution in Nigeria, together with a theoretical statement on the problem of modernization and ethnicity.

Southall, Aidan (1961) *Social Change in Modern Africa.* London: Oxford Univ. Press. Provides a useful comparative framework for the study of African cities and specific case reports on urban social relations in various parts of the continent.

25
Fieldwork II: *Applied Anthropology Among Wisconsin's Native Americans*

Introduction

This chapter describes an applied program in which I am still very much involved. The University Year for Action Program,* or for short, the Action program, is one variety of applied anthropology. It consists of a set of antipoverty projects, more than half of them in Wisconsin's "Indian" reservation communities.

The people among whom we work are termed *Indians,* but the word *Indian* is a "racial" label that conveys a highly stereotyped, simplified image. The term covers a great range of cultural, linguistic, and social territory, as well as diverse historical experiences. The original "Indians" of the state were very different from one another, and so are their descendants—biologically as well as culturally. A fair number of "Indians" in the state are, phenotypically, more "Caucasoid" or "Negroid" than Native American.

At present there are twelve separate rural "Indian" groupings in Wisconsin, each with its own identity, interests, and political organization. These communities represent three major ancient language stocks

* University of Wisconsin–Green Bay.

ACTION program identity. The young ACTION workers marked their presence on the reservation with this sign. Laurie Larson (left) worked in Economic Development, Linda Simonson in Youth Development, and Jeff Russell (right) as a Public Relations aide. Rusty Wolfe (at center) was their friend and informal advisor in the Chippewa community.

that include seven tribal organizations: the Siouan language family (Winnebago tribe), the Iroquoian language family (Oneida tribe), and the Algonquian language family (Chippewa, Potawatomi, Stockbridge-Munsee, and Menomini tribes). Only two of the major tribes represented, the Winnebago and the Menomini, are native to Wisconsin. The rest are more or less recent immigrants: Oneida from New York State, Stockbridge from Massachusetts, Munsee from Delaware, Potawatomi from Michigan, and Chippewa from Ontario (Lurie 1969:3–4).

The historical experiences and cultural backgrounds of these tribes have been very different, creating cultural and social diversity among Wisconsin's "Indian" populations. The Winnebago and the Menomini were decimated by epidemics and intertribal wars immediately before the first Europeans arrived. The Potawatomi came to the state as refugees from Iroquois invasions of their Michigan homeland. The Chippewa arrived in search of beaver pelts for European markets. The Stockbridge-Munsee and the Oneida were relocated in Wisconsin by the federal government. In addition, extensive interaction has occurred among the different tribes and between the tribes and the

French, Spanish, English, and contemporary Americans. The result is an extremely complex and heterogeneous culture.

The Action program was conceived by a new federal agency, ACTION, and was publicly announced in a presidential speech in July 1971. The official policy was that universities were to be the contracting organizations and students were to be the agents of change. In this way, the know-how and resources of the universities were to be mobilized and put to work in poor communities. Later, once the program was underway, a covert reason for this policy became known. ACTION's director had privately promised legislators that the new program would be much cheaper than other poverty programs because students would work for less and the universities would be induced to meet part of the costs from their supposedly vast storehouses of hidden wealth. In brief, the Action program was started in haste with almost no planning or research, and when it began it was badly underfunded. These are characteristics of virtually every new social program in the United States, although in this instance the problem was perhaps worse than usual.

The Action program has two sides. One, called the *service component*, consists of the delivery of needed (and requested) services to Native American communities. The other side, called the *learning component*, consists of an effort to improve the quality of higher education delivered to a selected group of students. Within the service component, the students, backed up by faculty members and other university resources, are the agents of change, and the Native American communities are the beneficiaries of their work. Within the learning component, the students are the beneficiaries. This is one of the unusual features of the Action program.

Under the supervision of one or more Native American communities, undergraduate and graduate students spend a full twelve months working off-campus in the Action program. During their year of service, these young men and women—whom the "Indians" call Action workers—earn a full year's college credits. The kind of learning they are engaged in is called *experiential*, a word much used but rarely defined. Experiential learning is learning that is accomplished off-campus, outside the context of ordinary classroom lectures and discussions. When we started the Action program, I did not know what experiential learning was. Since then I have discovered that, in part, the student participants are learning on what you now understand as the level of the *folk perspective*.

When the Action program began, it was a particularly ill-defined, ambiguous human enterprise. Nearly everyone involved wanted to reduce this ambiguity by imposing some arbitrary order on the project, but hardly any two people agreed on what this order should be. I urged that we should all cooperate to meet the minimal goals of the program, anticipating that we would make mistakes but also recognizing that we would gain experience and develop workable concepts by solving problems as they arose.

This position involved conceptualizing the project, using a clearly thought out definition of culture and a congruent perspective on the ways organizations work. I saw the Action program as needing a culture of its own—not one lifted quickly from some other, different program, such as VISTA. I was convinced that what we needed was time and experience for all concerned to develop a policy, tacitly and gradually, to further their common interests.

This in itself was a piece of applied anthropology. It meant putting some anthropological ideas to work at the start. This particular view of the way groups work is called an "organization-in-diversity" perspective. It means that all participating individuals need not be duplicates of one another but must accept and work creatively with differences in skill, motivation, viewpoint, and philosophy. The only requirement is a joint commitment to some basic goals. All the participants had to accept that the top priority was to deliver the maximum amount and quality of services to Native American communities and that each participant had to report regularly on what was being accomplished.

A number of subgroups were involved in this program: faculty, who were responsible for academic supervision and evaluation; university administrators, who conducted all programs; students, who studied and worked in the community; Native American representatives, who were responsible for work supervision, program planning, and evaluation; program administrators, who managed the details, ranging from payrolls to insurance; and federal ACTION officials, who dealt with Congress and administered the legislation that created the program. Each of these groups worked for the success of the program, yet their interests and attitudes were often different. They were, in effect, the "subcultures" of the Action program, and they had to fit together if the whole were to function effectively. Creating an appropriate organization out of these diverse interests required that we generate our own culture, one that fitted what we were doing.

When anthropologists assume applied roles, they generally do so on behalf of some powerful government agency, such as a colonial office, the Department of Defense, or the Bureau of Indian Affairs. In recent years this kind of relationship has become highly suspect and subject to criticism. The objection to these relationships is that they are unilateral and asymmetrical. The anthropologist contracts with the outside agency instead of with the community that is the sub-

An ACTION staff meeting. Much of the success of the ACTION program was due to William Wildcat (left), chairman of the Lac Du Flambeau Tribal Council and the Great Lakes Inter-Tribal Council, seen here with ACTION workers Laurie Larson and Bob "The Bear" Wagner. Wagner currently is employed as a development planner by the Great Lakes Inter-Tribal Council.

ject of his or her work. The government agency, not
the community, commands and manages the anthropologist's labor. Our Action program differs profoundly
from other applied programs in these respects. We
have multilateral relationships with numerous groups:
students, other faculty members, university administrators, state agencies, the federal government, the
tribal governments, and others. These relationships,
moreover, are relatively well balanced and symmetrical.
Power, or the capacity to control the allocation of
resources, is fairly equally distributed. In fact, the
largest share of the power to manage resources rests
in the hands of the community groups and the Action
workers themselves. But no one has absolute authority;
without the effective cooperation of all, the program
could not function.

The Environment

Approximately 23,000 Native Americans live in
Wisconsin. Of these, about 10,000 maintain homes in
rural communities; the balance live in urban areas,
mainly Milwaukee. Because the Action projects are
entirely among the rural groups, I will describe only
these environments. It should be noted, however, that
the Native American population is not static; there is
a constant interchange between rural and urban communities. Indeed, a great many "Indians" are commuters, living in one area and working somewhere else,
often many miles distant.

The rural populations consist of groups living on
nine federally recognized reservations plus three
scattered concentrations of Winnebago (see fig. 25–1)
and a scattered group of Potawatomi who live on
homestead, or private, lands. There is also one unique
case, the Menomini. In the 1950s this tribe's federal
relationships were terminated, and their reservation
was converted into a county. Until recently they were
not legally "Indians" at all. But as a result of their
lobbying efforts (with the aid of some Action workers),
their legal status has been restored, and they are now
converting the county back into a federal "Indian"
reservation.

With the exception of the Winnebago, who live in
the farmlands of the southwestern quarter of Wiscon-

Figure 25-1
**Wisconsin Native American Populations,
1974**

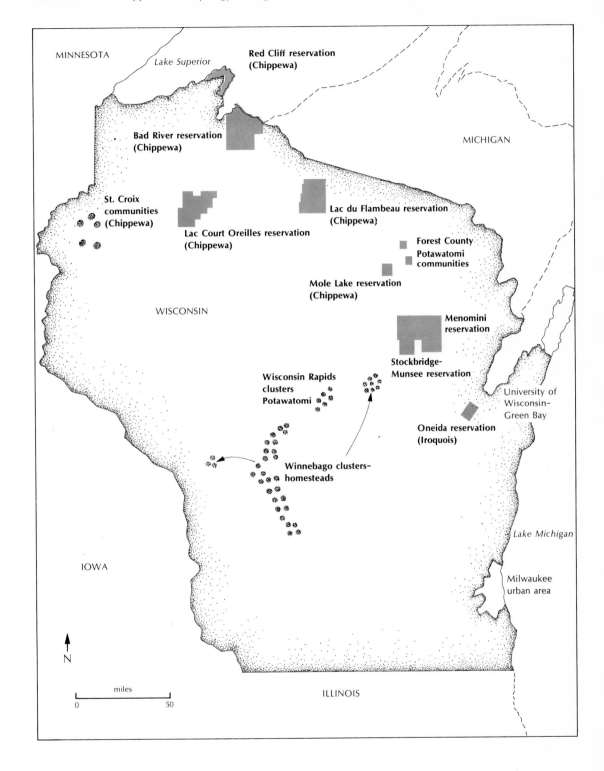

sin, the Native Americans occupy the northern half of the state. All the reservations are in economically depressed areas characterized by high unemployment rates, sudden and frequent failure and migration of industries and businesses, and a constant exodus of economically active adults. Most people in these areas are relatively poor, the "Indians" somewhat more so than others.

The major physical resource in the reservations is timber; five tribes own substantial marketable forests. Three reservations have modest wild rice stands, but these provide only slight income for a few people. One reservation has a small but underutilized area suitable for agriculture, and another has a small cranberry marsh. Two reservations on the Lake Superior shoreline have some opportunities for fishing for both income and subsistence. A few men trap fur-bearing animals, and a few more act as hunting and fishing guides. But for practical purposes, none of the Native American populations earns its living by extracting resources from the physical environment. They gave up hunting beaver a century ago and have since taken up hunting money.

Most Americans are unfamiliar with reservations and think of them as blocks of land surrounded by fences that keep the "Indians" in and others out. This is far from the truth. All of these reservations are heavily checkerboarded, with some of the land owned tribally or by individuals and the balance owned by non-"Indians." Even in their home reservations, Wisconsin's Native Americans live in constant contact with other Americans. A persistent stereotype is that of the "noble savage"—the myth that "Indians" live closely attuned to the rhythms of nature, subsisting off fish, game, and the wild plant foods they obtain by foraging. The truth is that they live closely attuned to the workings of the public and private bureaucracies that provide employment and other opportunities for income or subsistence. The environment from which they extract their livelihoods is social rather than physical. This adaptation involves wage work (full- or part-time, permanent or temporary), as well as the receipt of welfare and Social Security funds, payments from tribal income, and the like. Because a large percentage of this population falls below the poverty

line, and because they obtain substantial aids by virtue of their Native American status, they are also able to supplement their cash incomes with food stamps, tribal housing programs, federal and state programs for health and education, and various other categorical aids.

The Group

Subsistence Activities

The major mode of economic adaptation of Wisconsin's Native Americans is to the social, not the biophysical, environment. This is due partly to the small size of the reservation land and its resource base and partly to an extremely rapid population increase in recent years. But other factors are involved. A lack of appropriate skills, attitudes, values, and opportunities has meant that Native American entrepreneurship has been virtually nonexistent. The opportunities for Native American entrepreneurs have been restricted by outside competition from people with the managerial skills and capital necessary to operate businesses. Whatever the income of the Native American people, nearly all of it drains outward from their community.

But businesses in the northern counties are few anyway, and they are small, marginal, low-paying operations. In consequence, job opportunities in the private sector are very few and undesirable. For these reasons, Wisconsin "Indians" have had to adapt in different directions to survive. One such tack involves the creation and funding of Native American–oriented development and service programs whose resources come exclusively from state, federal, or private agencies. Fund raising is a vital skill for any Native American leader, and grantsmanship is a prime economic activity. (In fact, a major responsibility for Action workers has been to assist with fund raising: In four years they have brought in over $2,800,000 for various Native American projects.)

Statistics on Native American economic activities are generally highly suspect and unreliable, particularly reports of earned income and employment status. Like other Native Americans in the United States and Canada (and like poor people generally), Wisconsin

Conviviality after hours. ACTION workers actually kept no regular hours, but were always on duty. Here Jeff "Custer" Russell and Linda Simonson (right, on top) frolic with the next generation of Chippewa leaders. "Custer" currently is co-director of a Community Action program.

"Indians" are reluctant to report their earned income or employment status for fear of jeopardizing their welfare payments and other categorical aids (Bennett 1969:163). This attitude of concealment or distortion is so pervasive that in the Action program we have had to proceed very cautiously in reporting successes. The specific concern is that if word gets out that Native Americans are not as bad off as some militant leaders make them out to be, the chances of getting new grants and programs would be reduced. "Poor-mouthing"—projecting an image of helpless impoverishment—is an adaptive economic posture in its own right.

Nonetheless, a large proportion of Wisconsin's Native Americans are relatively poor compared to other groups in the state. In the early 1970s unemployment rates in the northern reservations were reported at around 40 percent of the work force. The jobs that are available in the private sector are generally at the minimum wage rate. The best-paying positions are usually held by those Native Americans who are acculturated to the values and standards of white, middle-class America. But this does not mean that the people are without economic resources. They are extremely skilled at extracting small sums of money from employed kinfolk, friends, and acquaintances. And the destitute can always turn to their community government for aid, as this is a primary function of the "Indian" community councils.

As John Bennett has pointed out, wherever people live in circumstances like this, they become very adept at creating and manipulating personal networks (Bennett 1969:166–167). These networks consist of better-off and sometimes influential people who control or have access to economic resources. Indeed, an important role is that of go-between, a person who has numerous contacts with those who control jobs and other resources. The reservation communities may lack substantial physical and economic resources, but they are not without economic devices. They are skillful and ingenious in manipulating their environment. These skills go a long way to make up for the relatively poor resource base and the lack of entrepreneurial skills, capital, and formal education.

Social Organization

Superimposed on the twelve local Native American communities are several statewide organizations. The largest, most complex, and most effective of these is the Great Lakes Inter-Tribal Council (GLITC). Founded in 1961 to provide a united front to deal with outside organizations, GLITC flourished during the years of the federal war on poverty and has since evolved into a highly effective political and administrative organization. GLITC consists of the elected chairmen of the community (or tribal) councils, plus a nonvoting member from Menomini County. The council functions as a kind of legislative branch, discussing, approving, and overseeing the various programs and other activities that make up GLITC's work. Decisions of the council are made by majority rule, and since each community has only one vote (regardless of population size), some interesting divisions, conflicts, and coalitions arise. The basic line of conflict is between the six northern

Chippewa and the Potawatomi communities on the one hand, and several southern communities, such as the Oneida and Stockbridge, on the other. Although they are poorer and smaller in population, these seven northern communities vote together fairly consistently, thus overwhelming much larger populations such as the Oneida.

On the administrative level GLITC is a complex bureaucracy that includes a large number of lesser administrative units, each of which has responsibility for a specific "Indian" service program. The GLITC bureaucracy has become so large that it is now the largest single employer of Native Americans in the state. Because each unit functions throughout the state, administrators constantly travel from place to place. Indeed, some observers receive the impression that many of the administrators spend more time traveling from meeting to meeting than they do at work. So much time spent on the highway may be seen as dysfunctional—but not from the (folk) perspective of the traveler, who is sometimes referred to locally as a "mileage Indian." Although this phrase may sometimes be used with derogatory intent, many Native Americans take pride in the number of miles they log annually, and many others supplement their income in this fashion. The all-time record holder is a senior official who in one year chalked up 97,000 miles in a compact car he leased from an unsuspecting dealer for $67 per month. He was an expert mechanic who did his own maintenance, and he received ten cents per mile (sometimes more when he could arrange to attend two or three meetings in the same city for different organizations). Clearly, a fair amount of disposable income can be generated by such practices. This kind of exploitation of the social environment serves more than economic ends: it also becomes a matter of personal pride and status.

On the local level, two basic and interlocking kinds of structures, very different from each other, shape the social patterns. One is the *local community*—for example, Lac du Flambeau—or alternatively, a dispersed network—for example, the Winnebago. The other kind of structure is the federally chartered membership corporation, a formal political-administrative organization. We will discuss this corporation first.

Each corporation has an elected council of three to seven members. Generally, each council member is elected as the representative of one of the extended kin groups, which function as voting and patronage blocs. A few people who have become unusually expert in obtaining and delivering outside resources for their communities are no longer closely linked to a kin group, and they run as candidates-at-large and are regularly elected term after term. But most of the representatives never manage to extricate themselves from the patronage ties to kinfolk, which are the primary facts of political and social life.

The extended kin groups are often involved in long and bitter rivalries. These tensions may express fundamental cultural differences, such as "traditional" against "modern"; or they may express religious differences between Catholic and Protestant; or they may simply involve personal feuds in which kinship groups have become involved. But the rivalries concern real issues: Who shall belong? Who shall benefit from community resources? Who shall control? The specifics in disputes may include the distribution of payments, allocation of jobs and travel expenses, or rights to timber-cutting contracts.

The corporation is a *fixed-membership* corporation: Membership is for life, and no provisions exist for removing a person who is on the rolls. The membership of the corporation is never coextensive with the membership of the local community. In all cases the majority of the members of the corporation do not live in the base community, whereas the base community includes numerous people who are not members of the corporation (such as non-"Indian" spouses and children). Moreover, the community and the corporation differ in their structures and functions. The local community consists of people who live together and who have strong kinship, friendship, and neighborhood ties. One can become a member of the local community by marrying in, moving in, or being adopted. But one can become a member of the corporation only by birth.

The issue of membership in the corporation, which carries with it the right to share in corporate assets, is probably the most controversial question facing Wisconsin Native Americans. One problem is that membership in the community is based on residence and sentiment. The sentiments and sense of belonging are strong, and thus many nonmembers become convinced that they should have rights in the corporation to which most people in their communities belong. Yet the corporation is a legally bounded group that has strict criteria for membership, and these criteria do not include residence or sentiments. Corporation members are those persons who are descended from previous members, but only to the limit of "one-fourth degree of blood." To become a member of the Lac du Flambeau Chippewa corporation, for example, one must be one-fourth Lac du Flambeau Chippewa, not one-fourth Chippewa, much less one-fourth Native American. Membership in the corporation, and the privilege of sharing in its resources and activities, is a hereditary right. However, children of members of one-fourth "blood" who have married nonmembers legally are not entitled to enrollment, and hence are not considered "Indians." Obviously this is a breeding ground for confusion and tension.

The several Wisconsin "Indian" corporations are responding to the problem in different ways. Some try to patch up difficulties by bending the rules, others have decided to adhere strictly to the letter of their law, and others have changed the rules drastically. The Native American population has a high rate of marriage into other cultural groups, resulting in an infusion of new members who are culturally different from the local community. These "Indian" populations thus face the threat of a growing pressure from a culturally diverse population upon their limited resource base. In drawing up their new constitution, one group has chosen to hold tightly to the one-fourth blood rule so as to restrict membership, control population size, and restrict the flow of outsiders into the membership corporation. Another community is following quite a different policy. Their strategy is to maximize their population size, on the assumption that they will be able to extract sufficient resources from the social environment to support it. Their leaders have, in fact, been extremely adept at obtaining federal, state, and private grants, and they firmly believe that the outside resource base is almost infinitely expansible.

The most important locus of social life in the local

community is the household group, which consists of nuclear or extended families. Indeed, extended kin ties, which are now traced bilaterally rather than patrilineally or matrilineally, are vital for domestic, economic, and political life. Beyond these kin groups are a wide variety of secondary associations: friendship groups, clubs, fraternal orders, militant groups, and so on. Several of the reservations have local chapters of the American Indian Movement, and many people are members of other pantribal organizations on the state or national level. A few Chippewa still hold to the old Midewiwin (spirit doings) cult; several hundred Chippewa, Potawatomi, and Menomini continue to practice the rituals of the Dream Dance cult; and about as many are members of the Native American (Peyote) Church. But the great majority of the "Indians" are Catholic or Protestant.

I have not used the words *tribe*, *band*, or *nation* to describe Wisconsin Native American social orga-

Linda Simonson (second from left) and her Chippewa youth group on an outing. Linda is currently employed as a youth worker in Wisconsin.

nization. Yet these terms are often used by the Native Americans themselves in talking about their social units. I have not used them because I have been describing the organization in general, analytical terms. When words such as *tribe* are used locally, they are used on a folk level—that is, they are folk constructs. The source of confusion is that *tribe* also has a technical, analytical meaning in anthropology. In the strict sense of the terms, no tribes, bands, or Native American nations exist in the state of Wisconsin today.

Culture

The conventional anthropological view of Wisconsin Native Americans is that after centuries of acculturation they have all become quite like one another. My experience suggests that this is not true. The few descriptions of "Wisconsin Indian culture" in the literature seem stereotyped and tend to exaggerate similarities while overlooking important cultural differences. Some of these differences represent the continuity of very old traditions that have been adapted to the realities of the present. Other differences represent something like subcultural strata, ranging from very traditional (tribal) to highly Americanized (acculturated) beliefs and values. These differences are apparent even in the smallest community.

In their studies of the Menomini, George and Louise Spindler identified five levels or types of adaptation or acculturation. Broadly speaking, these categories apply to other communities as well. They are: (1) the *native-oriented* subgroups, consisting mainly of older people who may still speak the language and adhere to a traditional religion; (2) the *transitionals,* people who live and think in alternating ways, sometimes "Indian," sometimes American; (3) the *peyotists,* adherents of the Native American Church; (4) the *lower-status acculturated,* Native Americans who live an essentially lower-class or working-class way of life; and (5) the *elite acculturated,* the upper crust of the reservation community, whose values and life-styles are essentially those of the European-American middle-class (Spindler and Spindler 1971).

I would add two additional categories of people who have increasingly weak ties to reservation communities: the *public servants,* adults who have made their careers out of state-level service to Native American communities; and the *urban alienates,* primarily younger militants and dropouts. These seven categories are analytical ones, imposed by outside observers. But Native Americans themselves recognize similar differences and construct their own categories. One of these, as we have seen, is the *mileage Indian.* This term involves a play on words: it refers to a person who gets a lot of "mileage" out of being a professional "Indian" or celebrity, and it also refers to a person who increases his income with a fat expense account—an "Indian" bureaucrat.

The Native American communities display ancient cultural and linguistic differences, but they have become even more heterogeneous in consequence of acculturation experiences. The Spindlers' five categories represent incipient social classes that are differentiated by wealth, prestige, and power. The Native American communities in the state are not culturally homogeneous, nor are they very egalitarian in practice. The fact that all of these groups are categorized as "Indian" should not obscure these differences.

The social institution that most conditions and encourages cultural diversity within each local community is the fixed-membership corporation. As we have seen, membership status is ascribed: People have to do nothing to become members of these corporations except be born of the right parents. Once certified as an "Indian," the individual does not have to do anything further to retain that status, and nothing she or he does or does not do can cause others to alter it. The membership corporations have no formal provisions or mechanisms for disciplining members or for requiring their conformity to cultural norms. On the other hand, communities, kinship groups, and other Native American organizations often discipline and even expel members, but this does not alter the individual's primary status as an "Indian." This social structural fact alone encourages cultural variety. Extensive contacts with other cultures have guaranteed this variation.

Because they represent continuity with older, different tribal cultures, the traditional people in the various communities tend to be unlike one another in some cultural ways. Thus when one older person tells you how Indian women are and should be influential in tribal affairs, whereas another tells you how dangerous it is to have women meddle in politics, you can be certain that the former is an Oneida (who retain much of their older matrilineal ways) and the latter a Potawatomi (who retain much of their older patrilineal ways). Highly acculturated members of either tribe might pay lip service to the elders, but in practice, they would not be bound by the traditional norms.

In contrast, peyotists display considerable cultural uniformity regardless of tribal affiliation. The reason is that the Native American Church tends to recruit the same kinds of persons, and the converts become participants in a distinctive, pantribal belief system. Similarly, the public servant types tend to resemble one another, mainly because they have become socialized into a distinctive occupational subculture.

These cultural differences are so many and varied that we make little effort to describe them to new Action workers during their orientation program of fourteen days. But they are offered a substantial account of social organization, and thereafter, we try to teach them basic skills of cultural analysis so that they will be able to learn as they work in their assigned community. Here is one example of how this learning process operates.

One of the first Action projects involved the economic development of a small Chippewa reservation. The goal of the project was to triple the income the community derived from the sale of their wild rice harvest. The means included the mechanization of harvesting and processing procedures, the use of a hybrid seed variety, and the development of a Native American–managed marketing cooperative. I was struck by the quality of the Action worker's design of the project: solid economic analysis, sound geography, excellent application of planning principles. But I was also disturbed by what was missing, a basic cultural analysis. What were the past and present practices these Indians used in harvesting and selling wild rice? What value did the practices have to them? What did wild rice mean in their view? How would they react to the new project proposal? I felt that we must get answers to these questions before proceeding.

Essentially the Action worker was proposing that the Chippewa accept an economic-technological innovation. Through their field research in many parts of the world, anthropologists have gained a good understanding of the conditions under which some innovations are accepted and others rejected. We were thus able to apply some anthropological insights to an analysis. We set about asking several questions. Had other Chippewa groups tried to mechanize wild rice production? (This is a basic case comparison.) Yes, they had, and the projects were not very successful. Indeed, the one in Wisconsin had failed totally after two years.

We next asked: What did wild rice mean to these particular Chippewa here and now? The answer to this question was instructive. The annual wild rice harvesting was an important communal affair, with many people going out to gather the fruits of the earth and enjoying every hour of it. There was much socializing and also some ritual. The rice was hand-processed over open hardwood fires, after being properly "danced." And all who participated profited from the sale of the rice. The young boy could earn enough to buy himself a new bicycle, the family, enough to get a new television. Moreover, all the Native Americans concerned were very proud that they continued to produce wild rice in traditional ways, and they took special pride in the distinctive quality of their wild rice as compared with the commercial variety from Minnesota.

We concluded that if we advocated the commercialized, mechanized process, it would be rejected, or it would eventually fail. But how did the Chippewa feel about this proposal? Regardless of our conclusions, it was their rice, and they had the right to deal with the proposal as they saw fit. Their response surprised me, and I learned something about the adaptive strategies of Wisconsin Native Americans that I did not know before.

The Chippewa quickly saw in this proposal an incentive that had quite escaped me and that overrode the disadvantages I had seen (and with which they agreed). This incentive was a substantial federal grant to develop the new process and co-op, and the several salaried jobs for Chippewa that this grant would fund. The Chippewa separated the short-run gain of temporary jobs from the long-run wild rice project proper. They were convinced that they could have these new jobs and then continue to harvest and sell the rice as they always had—a perception that made the proposal desirable and acceptable to them.

What I learned from this experience was that the Wisconsin Native American communities generally analyze new programs with a view to detecting short-run advantages that may or may not have anything to do with the stated program goals. From their folk perspective, they see an advantage if the program will, in the short run, deliver income into the hands of local people, and they are willing to discuss almost any kind of project if there is some possibility of this. They might have some interest in long-term goals as well, but probably only when those are accompanied by immediate benefits.

Problems and Prospects

The most striking aspect of the Wisconsin Native American communities is their near total dependence upon the outside social environment for their economic survival. Without a constant, substantial infusion of resources from outside, these communities would soon cease to exist in their present form. But they continue to exist, and they are expanding in population and improving in quality of life—ample tribute to the adaptive skills and the effectiveness of the basic strategies of these people.

This, then, is the social and cultural context of the Action programs. The general role of students is that of servant to the powerless (although by now it should be evident that "Indians" are not as powerless as many public statements make them out to be). The Action workers contribute their skills, energies, and pragmatic idealism to the service of other people. Their role is complex, difficult, and demanding. Their most challenging problem is to learn what is expected of them in highly fluid, changing, ambiguous situations. Our Action workers learn a great deal. They mature very rapidly. They polish their identities and learn how to commit themselves and their energies to productive work. They gain a solid year's experience in a highly

Much of the ACTION workers' responsibilities involved routine chores such as churning out the paperwork required to keep their programs funded, visible, and functioning. Here, Linda Simonson is busy at the typewriter while Winnebago humorist and caricaturist "Chief" Lowe acts in his role as Youth Services Program Administrator.

responsible, adult work role. They assimilate facts and new ideas, and they develop skills, particularly in human relations. They become very knowledgeable and full of insight about the world view, culture, and social organization of the communities they serve.

However, the Action workers' views become almost exclusively inside ones—that is, they very easily adopt the folk perspective of the people with whom they are working. Theirs is the kind of learning that an anthropologist in an alien community undergoes if he or she consistently fails to record observations and to think about them analytically. The Action workers obtain a rich and varied understanding, on an intuitive level, of the basic values, categories, manners, and styles of the community in which they work. They learn how to behave appropriately. They learn about specifics of the culture from the perspective of the community. But they rarely develop systematic, analytical knowledge; indeed, they are reluctant to attempt to formulate analytical views; they do not draw general conclusions from their specific knowledge. Their faculty supervisors often find this discouraging.

As anthropologists well know, if such learning is carried too far, the learner develops a problem of over-identification and identity transformation. Indeed, several Action workers have taken permanent roles in the local community. And nearly all the students experience some "reentry shock" when they leave the Native American community to return to the campus or to take a job elsewhere.

The Action program faces continuing operating problems, all of them financial. The federal officials who conceived the program wrote into the legislation provisions for the funding to be reduced annually and terminated completely after three to five years. They anticipated that the universities would somehow manage to find enough money to support the program thereafter. Unfortunately, the fiscal realities of university life make this impossible. The economic facts are simple. Universities are funded to deliver conventional educational programs, the ideal being one professor lecturing to several hundred students in a large classroom. Sixteen Action workers enrolled as full-time students and assigned to Native American communities generate only $17,600 in enrollment funding

for the university. Yet their living allowances and travel costs are $61,000 per year, and this figure does not include staff salaries or other operating costs. Both the nation and the universities have now fallen into an economic recession that bodes ill for the future of the Action program and other social programs. Universities are funded to teach students in classrooms, not to engage in social change programs, and the future of the Action program is in jeopardy.

The Native American supervisors are aware that the program is likely to be terminated. As one community leader commented, "We knew it was too good to last. Every time a really good program comes along, Washington cuts it off after a few years." But the leaders are experienced and can adapt to changing conditions. They know how to take full benefits out of the present without worrying unduly about the future.

As to the problems and prospects of the Native American communities themselves, I will offer only one assessment. There are limits on how much cultural variation and how little adherence to recognized norms a community can tolerate and yet survive with any meaningful identity. Some of the communities have approached the outer limits of cultural variation and are torn with divisive conflict that saps their energy and blocks work toward common goals. Too few effective means exist for reaching and enforcing community decisions.

The number of Native Americans enrolled in institutions of higher learning has increased sharply, however, and many of them are now graduating. Within a few years a large group of educated Native American adults will be available for work in their home communities—unless affirmative action programs lure them away from the reservations to high-paying jobs with large corporations. There is already some disturbing evidence of this kind of brain drain. But I believe that many more technically trained, well-educated Native Americans will soon be available, and this will reduce the need for programs like Action.

More needs to be said about applied anthropology. As C. Wright Mills observed, getting involved in applied work means becoming caught up in the political arena (Mills 1973:10–18). Applied anthropology is political because the work necessarily involves decisions that provide advantages for some groups while creating disadvantages for others. Applied anthropologists help some groups to realize their aspirations, but this means denying other groups this same aid. The Action program is no exception. The demand for Action workers has always been greater than the supply. Some communities have students assigned them, others not, and this means political decisions on the allocation of scarce resources must be made.

The basic roles available to applied anthropologists are similar to those Mills outlined for other social scientists (1970:10-12). The anthropologist may try to become the "philosopher-king," may elect to serve as "advisor to the king," or may choose to stand aside and remain independent (see Chap. 19).

Very few anthropologists have sought or achieved enthronement—a situation in which the scholar holds a position of high official authority, such as commissioner of Indian affairs. Many more anthropologists become "advisers to the king"—that is, they take positions in bureaucracies where they can use their special skills, knowledge, and know-how. The dangers of such positions are that anthropologists may easily lose their moral autonomy and may find that the value they place on truth and rationality in human affairs is not widely shared. But most applied anthropology has been conducted through adviser roles.

The great majority of anthropologists have elected the third role discussed by Mills: They prefer to remain independent, secure in their academic positions, wrapped in the protective armor of tenure, guarded by the moat of academic freedom. The conventional role for the great majority of anthropologists is that of the intellectual critic who offers running commentaries on what goes on in the political arena he or she never enters. As a campus-bound critic, the anthropologist seems to remain aloof and uncommitted. The problem with this role is that it may make anthropology irrelevant because the policy recommendations issued from academe are usually unnoticed or ignored. Recent discussions of the ethics of this position make it seem that the role of uninvolved anthropologist is an amoral illusion (see Chap. 19). By not actively employing his or her knowledge and skills responsibly, the anthropologist has in fact taken sides.

Summary

The Action program, aimed at assisting Native Americans in Wisconsin, is one of many varieties of applied anthropology. The agents for change are students, who not only serve the local community but also learn from that experience. Their learning, however, is primarily on the folk level; they learn relatively little on the analytical level. They nonetheless do contribute to improving community conditions.

Poverty pervades the reservations, and the rate of unemployment is extremely high. However, the Native Americans have developed a highly specialized adaptive strategy: the exploitation of the social rather than the natural environment (through wages, welfare, and so on).

The social organization of the people is based on a number of statewide organizations, twelve local communities, and a series of federally chartered local membership corporations. Membership in these is for life, and membership carries with it the right to share in corporate assets. The question of the criteria to be applied in determining elegibility for membership is one of the most controversial problems facing these Native Americans.

The culture of the people has been severly undermined by contact with "Anglo" culture. One finds varying degrees of acculturation among the Native Americans. Many of the older people, in particular, are very traditional in outlook, and traditional religion still has adherents.

Annotated Bibliography

Clifton, James A. (1970) *Applied Anthropology: Readings in the Uses of the Science of Man.* Boston: Houghton Mifflin. A collection of readings, mainly classic essays on various aspects of applied anthropology, as well as on several kinds of applied projects. Stresses the cultural definition of the field.

Foster, George M. (1969) *Applied Anthropology.* Boston: Little, Brown. A standard textbook that emphasizes the social role definition of applied anthropology.

Bibliography

Aberle, David (1962) "A Note on Relative Deprivation Theory as Applied to Millenarian and Other Cult Movements." In *Milienial Dreams in Action,* ed. S. L. Thrupp, Comparative Studies in Society and History Supplement, vol. 2, pp. 209–14.

Adam, Heribert (1971) *Modernizing Racial Domination: The Dynamics of South African Politics.* Berkeley and Los Angeles: Univ. of California Press.

Adams, Robert M. (1960) "The Origin of Cities." *Scientific American,* September, pp. 153–72.

(1966) *The Evolution of Urban Society.* Chicago: Aldine.

(1972) "Patterns of Urbanization in Early Southern Mesopotamia." In *Man, Settlement, and Urbanism,* ed. Peter J. Ucko, Ruth Tringham, and G. W. Dimbley, pp. 735–49. Cambridge, Mass.: Schenkman.

Alland, Alexander, Jr. (1968) "War and Disease: An Anthropological Perspective." In *War: The Anthropology of Armed Conflict and Aggression,* ed. Morton Fried, Marvin Harris, and Robert Murphy, pp. 65–75. Garden City, N.Y.: Natural History Press.

Alland, Alexander, Jr., and McCay, B. (1973) "The Concept of Adaptation in Biological and Cultural Evolution." In *Handbook of Social and Cultural Anthropology,* ed. John J. Honigmann. Chicago: Rand McNally.

Allen, J. A. (1877) "The Influence of Physical Conditions on the Genesis of Species." *Radical Review* 1:108–40.

Altmann, Stuart A. (1962) "A Field Study of the Sociobiology of Rhesus Monkeys, *Macaca mulatta.*" *New York Academy of Sciences Annals* 102:338–435.

Altmann, Stuart A., and Altmann, Jeanne (1970) *Baboon Ecology.* Biblioteca Primatolgia, no. 12. Chicago: Univ. of Chicago Press.

American Anthropological Association (1971) Principles of Professional Responsibility.

Apter, David E. (1965) *The Politics of Modernization.* Chicago: Univ. of Chicago Press.

Ardrey, Robert (1961) *African Genesis.* New York: Atheneum.

(1966) *The Territorial Imperative.* New York: Atheneum.

(1970) *The Social Contract.* New York: Dell.

Arensberg, Conrad (1968) "The Urban in Cross Cultural Perspective." In *Urban Anthropology,* ed. Elizabeth Eddy, Southern Anthropological Society Proceedings, no. 2, pp. 3–15. Athens: Univ. of Georgia Press.

Arensberg, Conrad, and Kimball, Solon T. (1965) *Culture and Community.* New York: Harcourt.

Asad, Talal (1970) *The Kababish Arabs.* London: C. Hurst.

Asad, Talal, ed. (1973) *Anthropology and the Colonial Encounter.* London: Ithaca.

Auden, W. H. (1945) *The Collected Poetry of W. H. Auden.* New York: Random House.

Bachofen, J. J. (1861) *Das Mutterrecht.* Basel: Benno Schwabe.

Banton, Michael (1957) *West African City.* London: Oxford Univ. Press.

Baran, Paul (1957) *The Political Economy of Growth.* New York: Prometheus, Monthly Review.

Barnes, J. A. (1968) "Networks and Political Process." In *Local Level Politics,* ed. Marc Swartz, pp. 107–30. Chicago: Aldine.

(1972) *Three Styles in the Study of Kinship.* Berkeley and Los Angeles: Univ. of California Press.

Barry, H. A., Bacon, M. K., and Child, I. L. (1957) "A Cross-Cultural Survey of Some Sex Differences in Socialization." *Journal of Abnormal and Social Psychology* 55:327–32.

Barth, Fredrik (1956) "Ecologic Relationships of Ethnic Groups in Swat, North Pakistan." *American Anthropologist* 58: 1079–89.

Bateson, Gregory, Jackson, Donald J., Haley, Jay, and Weakland, John (1956) "Toward a Theory of Schizophrenia." *Behavioral Science* 1:251–54.

Beattie, John (1960) *Bunyoro: An African Kingdom.* New York: Holt.

Becker, Howard (1963) *Outsiders.* New York: Free Press.

Bellah, Robert N. (1965) "Religious Evolution." In *Reader in Comparative Religion: An Anthropological Approach,* ed. William A. Lessa and Evon Z. Vogt. New York: Harper.

Benedict, Ruth (1934) *Patterns of Culture.* Boston: Houghton Mifflin.

Bennett, John W. (1969) *Northern Plainsmen: Adaptive Strategy and Agrarian Life.* Chicago: Aldine.

Berger-Kirchner, Etienne (1964) *Zuerwerbs–, Teilerwerbs– und Nebenerwerbsbauern.* Bern: Buchdruckerei Fritz Marti.

Bergmann, C. (1847) "Uber die Verhältniesse der Wärmeokonomie der Thiere zu ihrer Grösse." *Gottingen Studien* 1:595–708.

Biesele, M., and Lee, Richard B. (1974) "Hunters, Clients, and Squatters: The Kalahari San Today." Paper presented at the *Symposium on the Future of Traditional "Primitive" Societies,* December 1974, at Cambridge University. Mimeographed.

Bingham, H. C. (1932) "Gorillas in a Native Habitat." *Carnegie Institution of Washington Year Book* 426:1–66.

Biocca, Ettore (1970) *Yanomama: The Narrative of a White Girl Kidnapped by Amazonian Indians.* New York: Dutton.

Birdsell, Joseph B. (1972) *Human Evolution: An Introduction to the New Physical Anthropology.* Chicago: Rand McNally.

Birdwhistell, Ray L. (1970) *Kinesics and Context.* Philadelphia: Univ. of Pennsylvania Press.

Black, Cyril E. (1966) *The Dynamics of Modernization.* New York: Harper.

Bloomfield, Leonard (1965, orig. 1933) *Language.* New York: Holt.

Blum, H. (1961) "Does Melanin Pigment of Human Skin Have Adaptive Value?" *Quarterly Review of Biology* 36:50–63.

Boas, Franz (1966) *Kwakiutl Ethnography.* Chicago: Univ. of Chicago Press.

(1969, reproduction of 1930 edition) *The Religion of the Kwakiutl Indians.* 2 vols. Columbia University Contributions to Anthropology Series, vol. 10, part 2, pp. 1–41. New York: AMS Press.

Bodley, J. H. (1975) *Victims of Progress.* Menlo Park, Calif.: Cummings.

Bohannon, Paul (1955) "Some Principles of Exchange and Investment among the Tiv." *American Anthropologist* 57:60–70.

Boserup, Ester (1965) *The Conditions of Agricultural Growth.* Chicago: Aldine.

Boughey, A. S. (1971) *Fundamental Ecology.* London: Intertext.

Braidwood, Robert J. (1960) "The Agricultural Revolution." *Scientific American,* September, pp. 130–48.

Broch, Tom, and Galtung, Johan (1966) "Belligerence among Primitives." *Journal of Peace Research,* no. 1, pp. 33–45.

Bruner, Edward M. (1970) "Medan: The Role of Kinship in an Indonesian City." In *Peasants in Cities,* ed. William Mangin, pp. 122–34. Boston: Houghton Mifflin.

(1973a) "Kin and Non-Kin." In *Urban Anthropology: Cross-Cultural Studies of Urbanization,* ed. Aidan Southall. New York: Oxford Univ. Press.

(1973b) "The Expression of Ethnicity in Indonesia." In *Urban Ethnicity,* ed. Abner Cohen. ASA Monograph. London: Tavistock.

Bruner, Jerome (1960) *The Process of Education.* Cambridge, Mass.: Harvard Univ. Press.

Buettner-Janusch, John (1973) *Physical Anthropology: A Perspective.* New York: Wiley.

Burnett, A. L., and Eisner, T. (1964) *Animal Adaptation.* New York: Holt.

Burt, W. H. (1943) "Territoriality and Home Range Concepts as Applied to Mammals." *Journal of Mammalogy* 24:346–52.

Buskirk, E. R., and Bass, D. E. (1960) "Climate and Exercise." In *Science and Medicine of Exercise and Sports,* ed. W. R. Johnson. New York: Harper.

Butzer, Karl W. (1971) *Environment and Archaeology.* Chicago: Aldine-Atherton.

Campbell, Bernard G. (1974) *Human Evolution: An Introduction to Man's Adaptations.* 2d ed. Chicago: Aldine.

Carneiro, Robert L. (1967) "On the Relationship between Size of Population and Complexity of Social Organization." *Southwestern Journal of Anthropology* 23:234–43.

Carpenter, C. R. (1934) "A Field Study of the Behavior and Social Relations of Howling Monkeys." *Comparative Psychology Monographs* 20(48):1–168.

(1965) "The Howlers of Barro Colorado Island." In *Primate Behavior: Field Studies of Monkeys and Apes,* ed. Irven De Vore, pp. 250–91. New York: Holt.

Castañeda, Carlos (1968) *The Teachings of Don Juan: A Yaqui Way of Knowledge.* New York: Ballantine.

(1971) *A Separate Reality: Further Conversations with Don Juan.* New York: Simon and Schuster.

(1972) *Journey to Ixtlan: The Lessons of Don Juan.* New York: Simon and Schuster.

(1974) *Tales of Power.* New York: Simon and Schuster.

Chafe, Wallace (1970) *Meaning and the Structure of Language.* Chicago: Univ. of Chicago Press.

Chagnon, Napoleon (1968) *Yanomamö: The Fierce People.* New York: Holt.

Chang, Kwang-chih (1970) "The Beginnings of Agriculture in the Far East." *Antiquity* 44:175–85.

Chard, Chester S. (1969) *Man in Prehistory.* New York: McGraw-Hill.

Childe, V. Gordon (1951) *Man Makes Himself.* New York: Mentor.

(1952) *New Light on the Most Ancient East.* 4th ed. London: Routledge and Kegan Paul.

Chomsky, Noam (1957) *Syntactic Structures.* The Hague: Mouton.

(1959) "A Review of B. F. Skinner's *Verbal Behavior.*" *Language* 35: Also reprinted in *The Structure of Language: Readings in the Philosophy of Language,* ed. Jerry A. Fodor and Jerrold J. Katz. Englewood Cliffs, N.J.: Prentice-Hall, 1964, pp. 547–578.

(1965) *Aspects of the Theory of Syntax.* Cambridge, Mass.: MIT Press.

(1968) *Language and Mind.* New York: Harcourt.

(1971) "The Case against B. F. Skinner." *New York Review of Books,* December 30, pp. 18–24.

Clark, Graham (1957)   *Archaeology and Society.* New York: Barnes & Noble, University Paperbacks.

(1969)   *World Prehistory: A New Outline.* Cambridge: Cambridge Univ. Press.

Clark, J. G. Desmond (1952)   *Prehistoric Europe: The Economic Basis.* Stanford, Calif.: Stanford Univ. Press.

(1960)   "Human Ecology during the Pleistocene and Later Times in Africa South of the Sahara." *Current Anthropology* 1:307–24.

Clark, Kenneth (1969)   *Civilization.* New York: Harper.

Clifton, James A. (1960)   "Explorations in Klamath Personality." Ph.D. dissertation, University of Oregon, Eugene.

Clifton, James A., and Levine, David (1962)   "Klamath Personalities: Ten Rorschach Case Studies." Department of Anthropology, University of Oregon, Eugene.

Coe, Michael, and Flannery, Kent V. (1966)   "Micro Environments and Mesoamerican Prehistory." In *New Roads to Yesterday,* ed. J. Caldwell. New York: Basic Books.

Cohen, Yehudi (1974)   "Culture as Adaptation." In *Man in Adaptation: The Cultural Present,* 2d ed., ed. Yehudi Cohen. Chicago: Aldine.

Coleman, J. (1971)   "The Ibo and Yoruba Strands in Nigerian Nationalism." In *Nigeria: Modernization and the Politics of Communalism,* ed. Robert Melson and Howard Wolpe. East Lansing: Michigan State Univ. Press.

Conklin, Harold C. (1957)   "Hanunóo Agriculture: A Report on an Integral System of Shifting Cultivation in the Philippines." FAO Forestry Development Paper, no. 12.

(1969)   "An Ethnoecological Approach to Shifting Agriculture." In *Environment and Cultural Behavior: Ecological Studies in Cultural Anthropology,* ed. Andrew P. Vayda. Garden City, N.Y.: Natural History Press.

Cook, Scott (1966)   "The Obsolete 'Anti-Market' Mentality." *American Anthropologist* 68:323–45.

Crook, John H. (1973)   "The Nature and Function of Territorial Aggression." In *Man and Aggression,* ed. Ashley Montagu. London: Oxford Univ. Press.

Crook, John H., and Gartlan, J. Steven (1966)   "On the Evolution of Primate Societies." *Nature* 210:1200–1203.

Curle, Adam (1971)   *Making Peace.* London: Tavistock.

(1973)   *Education for Liberation.* London: Tavistock.

Dahrendorf, Ralf (1968)   *Essays in the Theory of Society.* Stanford, Calif.: Stanford Univ. Press.

Dalton, George (1971)   *Modernizing Village Economies.* An Addison-Wesley Module. Canada: Addison-Wesley.

D'Andrade, Roy (1966)   "Sex Differences and Cultural Institutions." In *The Development of Sex Differences,* ed. Eleanor Maccoby, pp. 174–204. Stanford, Calif.: Stanford Univ. Press.

Daniel Glyn (1963)   *The Idea of Prehistory.* New York: World.

Darwin, Charles (1962, orig. 1859)   *On the Origin of Species by Means of Natural Selection, or the Preservation of Favored Races in the Struggle for Life.* New York: Macmillan.

(1969, reproduction of 1871 edition)   *The Descent of Man and Selection in Relation to Sex.* 2 vols. New York: International Publications Service.

Davenport, W., Olmsted, D., and Mead, Margaret (1971)   "Report of the Ad Hoc Committee to Evaluate the Controversy Concerning Anthropological Activities in Relation to Thailand." American Anthropological Association.

Davis, Kingsley (1966)   "The Urbanization of the Human Population." *Scientific American,* September, pp. 40–53.

Davis, Kingsley, and Moore, Wilbert E. (1945)   "Some Principles of Stratification." *American Sociological Review* 10:242–49.

De Laguna, Frederica (1972)   *Under Mount Elias: The History and Culture of Yakutat Tlingit.* Washington, D.C.: Smithsonian Institution.

Delgado, J. M. R. (1966)   "Aggressive Behavior Evoked by Radio Stimulation in Monkey Colonies." *American Zoologists* 6:669–81.

Denes, Peter B., and Pinson, Elliot N. (1973)   *The Speech Chain: The Physics and Biology of Spoken Language.* Garden City, N.Y.: Doubleday.

Devereux, George (1937)   "Homosexuality among the Mohave Indians." *Human Biology* 9:498–597.

(1961)   "Two Types of Modal Personality Models." In *Studying Personality Cross-Culturally,* ed. Bert Kaplan. New York: Harper.

Diamond, Stanley (1964)   "A Revolutionary Discipline." *Current Anthropology* 5:432–37.

Diaz del Castillo, Bernal (1956)   *The Discovery and Conquest of Mexico.* New York: Farrar Strauss and Company.

Dickson, H. R. P. (1949)   *The Arab of the Desert.* London: George Allen and Unwin.

(1956)   *Kuwait and Her Neighbors.* London: George Allen and Unwin.

Divale, William T. (1970)   "An Explanation for Tribal Warfare: Population Control and the Significance of Primitive Sex-Ratios." *New Scholar,* fall, pp. 173–92.

Djilas, Milovan (1957)   *The New Class: An Analysis of the Communist System.* New York: Praeger.

Dobzhansky, Theodosius (1942)   "Biological Adaptation." *Scientific Monthly* 55:391–402.

Dollard, John et al. (1939)   *Frustration and Aggression.* New Haven, Conn.: Yale Univ. Press.

Dovring, Folke (1965)   *Land and Labor in Europe in the Twentieth Century.* 3d and rev. ed. The Hague: Martinus Nijhoff.

Dunn, L. C. (1970)   *Heredity and Evolution in Human Populations.* New York: Atheneum.

Durkheim, Émile (1915)   *The Elementary Forms of Religious Life.* London: George Allen and Unwin.

Easton, David (1953)   *The Political System.* New York: Knopf.

Edgerton, Robert B. (1964)   "Pokot Intersexuality: An East African Example of the Resolution of Sexual Incongruity." *American Anthropologist* 66:1288–99.

Eggan, Fred (1966)   *American Indian: Perspectives for the Study of Social Change.* Lewis Henry Morgan Lectures Series. Chicago: Aldine.

(1968)   "One Hundred Years of Ethnology and Social Anthropology." In *One Hundred Years of Anthropology,* ed. John O. Brew. Cambridge, Mass.: Harvard Univ. Press.

Eliade, Mircea (1959)   *The Sacred and the Profane.* New York: Harvest.

Engels, Friedrich (1942, orig. 1884)   *The Origin of the Family, Private Property, and the State.* Ed. Eleanor Burke Leacock. New York: International Publishers.

Erikson, Erik H. (1968)   "Psychosocial Identity." In *International Encyclopedia of the Social Sciences,* vol. 7, pp. 61–65. Glencoe, Ill.: Macmillan and Free Press.

Erikson, Kai T. (1966)   *Wayward Puritans.* New York: Wiley.

Evans-Pritchard, E. E. (1951)   *Kinship and Marriage among the Nuer.* New York: Oxford Univ. Press.

Fagan, Brian M. (1974)   *Men of the Earth: An Introduction to World Prehistory.* Boston: Little, Brown.

Faris, James (1973)   "Pax Britannica and the Sudan: S. F. Nadel." In *Anthropology and the Colonial Encounter,* ed. Talal Asad. London: Ithaca.

Faron, Louis C. (1968)   *The Mapuche Indians of Chile.* New York: Holt.

Festinger, Leon, Rieken, Henry W., and Schachter, Stanley (1956)   *When Prophesy Fails.* New York: Harper Torchbooks.

Feuchtwang, Stephen (1973)   "The Discipline and Its Sponsors." In *Anthropology and the Colonial Encounter,* ed. Talal Asad. London: Ithaca.

Firth, Raymond (1929)   *Primitive Economics of the New Zealand Maori.* New York: Dutton.

(1939)   *Primitive Polynesian Economy.* London: Routledge.

Fiske, Shirley (1975)   *Navajo Cognition in the Urban Milieu: An Invesitgation of Social Categories and Use of Address Terms.* Unpublished Ph.D. dissertation, Stanford University.

Flacourt, Etienne de (1661)   *Histoire de la Grande Isle de Madagascar.* Paris: Pierre l'Amy.

Flannery, Kent V. (1965)   "The Ecology of Early Food Production in Mesopotamia." *Science* 147 (March 12):1247–56.

(1968)   "Archaeological Systems Theory and Early Mesopotamia." In *Anthropological Archaeology in the Americas,* ed. Betty J. Meggers. Washington, D.C.: Anthropological Society of Washington.

(1969)   "Origins and Ecological Effects of Early Domestication in Iran and the Near East." In *Prehistoric Agriculture,* ed. Stuart Struever, pp. 50–79. Garden City, N.Y.: Natural History Press.

Floyd, Barry (1969) *Eastern Nigeria: A Geographical Review.* New York: Praeger.

Forde, Daryll, and Jones, G. I. (1950) "The Ibo and Ibibio-Speaking Peoples of Southeastern Nigeria." In *Ethnographic Survey of Africa: Western Africa,* part 3. London: International African Institute.

Fortes, Meyer (1949) *The Web of Kinship Among the Tallensi.* London: Oxford University Press.

Fortes, Meyer, and Evans-Pritchard, E. E., eds. (1940) *African Political Systems.* London: Oxford Univ. Press.

Frankenberg, R. (1966) *Communities in Britain.* Baltimore, Md.: Penguin.

Freilich, Morris (1963) "Towards an Operational Definition of Community." *Rural Sociology* 23:117–27.

Fried, Morton H. (1960) "On the Evolution of Social Stratification and the State." In *Culture in History,* ed. Stanley Diamond. New York: Columbia Univ. Press.

(1967) *The Evolution of Political Society: An Essay in Political Anthropology.* New York: Random House.

Friedl, Ernestine (1962) *Vasilika: A Village in Modern Greece.* New York: Holt.

Gardner, Beatrice, and Gardner, R. Allen (1971) "Two Way Communication with an Infant Chimpanzee." In *Behavior of Nonhuman Primates,* ed. Allan M. Schrier and Fred Stollnitz, vol. 4. New York: Academic Press.

Gardner, R. Allen, and Gardner, Beatrice (1969) "Teaching Sign Language to a Chimpanzee." *Science* 165 (August 15):664–72.

Garraty, John A., and Gay, Peter, eds. (1972) *The Columbia History of the World.* New York: Harper.

Gartlan, J. Steven (1968) "Structure and Function in Primate Society." *Folia Primatologica* 8:89–120.

Geertz, Clifford (1963) "Social Change and Economic Modernization in Two Indonesian Towns: A Case in Point." In *On the Theory of Social Change,* ed. Everett E. Hagan. Homewood, Ill.: Dorsey.

(1966a) "The Impact of the Concept of Culture on the Concept of Man." In *New Views of the Nature of Man,* ed. John R. Platt. Chicago: Univ. of Chicago Press. Reprinted in *The Interpretation of Cultures,* ed. Geertz. New York: Basic Books, 1973.

(1966b) "Religion as a Cultural System." In *Anthropological Approaches to the Study of Religion,* ed. Michael Banton. Association of Social Anthropologists of the Commonwealth, vol. 3. New York: Praeger.

Geilhufe, Nancy (1972) *Ethnic Relations in San Jose: A Study of Police-Chicano Interaction.* Ph.D. dissertation, Stanford University.

Gerlach, Luther P., and Hine, Virginia H. (1970) *People, Power, Change: Movements of Social Transformation.* New York: Bobbs Merrill.

Gladwin, Thomas (1964) "Culture and Logical Process." In *Explorations in Cultural Anthropology,* ed. Ward Goodenough. New York: McGraw-Hill.

Gladwin, Thomas, and Sarason, Seymour B. (1953) *Truk: Man in Paradise.* Viking Fund Publications in Anthropology, no. 20. New York: Johnson Reprint.

Goffman, Erving (1961) *Asylums: Essays on the Social Situation of Mental Patients and Other Inmates.* New York: Anchor Books, Doubleday.

(1963) *Stigma: Notes on the Management of Spoiled Identity.* Englewood Cliffs, N.J.: Prentice-Hall.

(1971) *Relations in Public.* New York: Harper Colophon.

Golding, M. P., ed. (1966) *The Nature of Law.* New York: Random House.

Goodenough, Ward H. (1956) "Componential Analysis and the Study of Meaning." *Language* 32:195–216.

Goodfellow, D. M. (1939) *Principles of Economic Sociology.* London: Routledge.

Gordon, Chad and Johnson, Gayle, eds. (1976) *Readings in Human Sexuality; Contemporary Perspectives.* New York: Harper.

Gossett, Thomas (1964) *Race: The History of an Idea in America.* New York: Schocken.

Gough, Kathleen (1961) "Nayar: Central Kerela." In *Matrilineal Kinship,* ed. David M. Schneider and Kathleen Gough. Berkeley and Los Angeles: Univ. of California Press.

(1968) "World Revolution and the Science of Man." In *The Dissenting Academy,* ed. Theodore Roszak. New York: Random House.

Gouldner, Alvin W., and Peterson, Richard A. (1962) *Notes on Technology and the Moral Order.* Indianapolis: Bobbs-Merrill.

Gumplowicz, Ludwig (1899) *The Outlines of Sociology.* Philadelphia: American Academy of Political and Social Sciences.

Hall, Edward T. (1959) *The Silent Language.* Garden City, N.Y.: Doubleday (Fawcett).

(1966) *The Hidden Dimension.* Garden City, N.Y.: Doubleday.

Hallowell, A. Irving (1962) "Personality Structure and the Evolution of Man." In *Culture and the Evolution of Man,* ed. Ashley Montagu. New York: Oxford Univ. Press.

Hammel, T. H. (1964) "Terrestrial Animals in Cold: Recent Studies of Primitive Man." In *Handbook of Physiology: Adaptation to the Environment,* ed. D. B. Dirrell et al. Washington, D.C.: American Physiological Society.

Hannerz, Ulf (1969) *Soulside: Inquiries into Ghetto Culture and Community.* New York: Columbia Univ. Press.

Hanson, F. Allan (1970) *Papuan Lifeways.* Boston: Little, Brown.

Harlan, Jack R. (1971) "Agricultural Origins: Centers and Noncenters." *Science* 174 (October 29):468–74.

Harlow, H. F., Schitz, K. A., and Harlow, M. K. (1969) "Effects of Social Isolation on Learning Performance of Rhesus Monkeys." In *Proceedings of the Second International Congress of Primatology,* ed. C. R. Carpenter, vol. 1, *Behavior.* Basel: Karger.

Harris, Marvin (1968) *The Rise of Anthropological Theory.* New York: Crowell.

(1971) *Culture, Man, and Nature.* New York: Crowell.

(1974) *Cows, Pigs, Wars, and Witches: The Riddles of Culture.* New York: Random House.

Harrison, G. A., and Boyce, A. J., eds. (1972) *The Structure of Human Populations.* New York: Oxford Univ. Press.

Harrison, G. A., Weiner, J. S., Tanner, J. M., and Barnicot, N. A. (1964) *Human Biology.* Oxford: Clarendon.

Hart, C. W. M., and Pilling, Arnold R. (1960) *The Tiwi of North Australia.* New York: Holt.

Heisenberg, Werner (1971) *Physics and Beyond: Encounters and Conversations.* New York: Harper Torchbooks.

Hempel, Carl G. (1952) *Fundamentals of Concept Formation in Empirical Science.* International Encyclopedia of a Unified Science, vol. 2, no. 7. Chicago: Univ. of Chicago Press.

Henderson, Richard N. (1966) "Generalized Cultures and Evolutionary Adaptability: A Comparison of Urban Efik and Ibo in Nigeria." *Ethnology* 5:365–91.

(1972) *The King in Every Man: Evolutionary Trends in Onitsha Ibo Society and Culture.* New Haven, Conn.: Yale Univ. Press.

Henderson, Richard N., and Henderson, Helen Kreider (1966) "An Outline of Traditional Onitsha Ibo Socialization." Occasional Publication no, 5. Nigeria: Institute of Education, University of Ibadan.

Heron, Woodburn (1957) "The Pathology of Boredom." *Scientific American,* January, pp. 52–56.

Herskovits, Melville J. (1940) *The Economic Life of Primitive Peoples.* New York: Knopf.

(1952) *Economic Anthropology.* New York: Knopf.

Hildes, J. A. (1966) "The Circumpolar People: Health and Physiological Adaptations." In *The Biology of Human Adaptability,* ed. P. T. Baker and J. S. Weiner. Oxford: Clarendon.

Hill, W. W. (1935) "The Status of the Hermaphrodite and Transvestite in Navajo Culture." *American Anthropologist* 37:273–79.

Hiller, E. T. (1941) "The Community as a Social Group." *American Sociological Review* 6:189–202.

Hinde, R. A., and Spencer-Booth, Y. (1967) "Behavior of Socially Living Rhesus Monkeys in Their First 2½ Years." *Animal Behavior* 15:169–98.

Hockett, Charles F. (1958) *A Course in Modern Linguistics.* New York: Macmillan.

(1960) "The Origin of Speech." *Scientific American,* September, pp. 88–96.

Hoebel, E. Adamson (1949) *Man in the Primitive World.* New York: McGraw-Hill.

(1954) *The Law of Primitive Man.* Cambridge, Mass.: Harvard Univ. Press.

(1972) *Anthropology: The Study of Man.* 4th ed. New York: McGraw-Hill.

Höffding, Harald (1955) *A History of Modern Philosophy,* Vol. 2. New York: Dover.

Holmberg, Allen (1970a) "The Research and Development Approach to the Study of Change." In *Applied Anthropology: Readings in the Uses of the Science of Man,* ed. James A. Clifton. Boston: Houghton Mifflin.

(1970b) "The Changing Values and Institutions of Vicos in the Context of National Development." In *Applied Anthropology: Readings in the Uses of the Science of Man,* ed. James A. Clifton. Boston: Houghton Mifflin.

Homans, George C. (1941) "Anxiety and Ritual: The Theories of Malinowski and Radcliffe-Brown." *American Anthropologist* 43:164–72.

Hooton, Earnest A. (1931) *Up from the Ape.* London: George Allen and Unwin.

Horowitz, Irving Louis (1973) *The Rise and Fall of Project Camelot.* Cambridge, Mass.: MIT Press.

Howell, F. Clark (1966) "Observations on the Earlier Phases of the European Lower Paleolithic." *Special Publication of the American Anthropologist,* part 2, vol. 68, no. 2.

Hunter, David E. (1970) *Social-Cultural Interrelations in a Community of Swiss Peasants.* Ph.D. dissertation, Yale University.

Hunter, David E., and Whitten, Phillip (1975) "Anthropology as a Point of View." In *Anthropology: Contemporary Perspectives,* ed. Hunter and Whitten. Boston: Little, Brown.

Hunter, David E. and Whitten, Phillip, eds. (1976) Encyclopedia of Anthropology. New York: Harper.

Hunter, David E. (1975) "To Find a Community." In *Anthropology: Contemporary Perspectives,* ed. Hunter and Whitten, Boston: Little, Brown.

Hunter, Guy (1969) *Modernizing Peasant Societies.* New York: Oxford Univ. Press.

Huntington, Samuel P. (1966) "Political Modernization: America vs. Europe." *World Politics* 18:378–414.

Hutton, J. H. (1963) *Caste in India: Its Nature, Function, and Origins.* London: Oxford Univ. Press.

Hymes, Dell, ed. (1969, 1974) *Reinventing Anthropology.* New York: Random House (1969), Vintage (1974).

James, Wendy (1973) "The Anthropologist as Reluctant Imperialist." In *Anthropology and the Colonial Encounter,* ed. Talal Asad. London: Ithaca.

Jewell, P. A. (1966) "The Concept of Home Range in Mammals." *Symposium of the Zoological Society of London* 18:85–110.

Jones, Delmos (1971) "Social Responsibility and the Belief in Basic Research: An Example from Thailand." *Current Anthropology* 12:347–50.

Jorgensen, Joseph, and Wolf, Eric (1970) "Anthropology on the Warpath in Thailand." *New York Review of Books,* pp. 26–35.

Jung, Carl G. (1969) *Psychology and Religion: West and East.* 2d ed. Vol. II of *The Collected Works of Carl G. Jung,* Bollinger Series XX (Trans. R. F. C. Hull). Princeton, N.J.: Princeton University Press.

Katchadourian, Herant A., and Lunde, Donald T. (1972) *Fundamentals of Human Sexuality.* New York: Holt.

Katz, Richard (1974) "Education for Transcendence." In *Preludes to Growth: An Experiential Approach,* pp. 362–85. Glencoe, Ill.: Free Press.

Katzin, Margaret (1964) "The Role of the Small Entrepreneur." In *Economic Transition in Africa,* ed. Melville J. Herskovits and Mitchell Harwitz. Evanston, Ill.: Northwestern Univ. Press.

Kaufman, Harold F. (1959) "Toward an Interactional Conception of Community." *Social Forces* 38:8–17.

Kellogg, Winthrop N. (1968) "Communication and Language in the Home-Raised Chimpanzee." *Science* 162 (October 25):423–27.

Kellogg, Winthrop N., and Kellogg, Luella A. (1933) *The Ape and the Child.* New York: McGraw-Hill.

Kluckhohn, Clyde, and Murray, H. A. (1954) *Personality in Nature, Society, and Culture.* 2d ed. New York: Knopf.

Koch, Klaus-Friedrich (1970) "Cannibalistic Revenge in Jalé Warfare." *Natural History,* February.

Köhler, Wolfgang (1927) *The Mentality of Apes.* 2d ed. London: Routledge and Kegan Paul.

Krantz, Grover S. (1968) "Brain Size and Hunting Ability in Earliest Man." *Current Anthropology* 9, no. 5.

Krause, Aurel (1956)   *The Tlingit Indians.* Seattle: Univ. of Washington Press.

Kroeber, Alfred L. (1909)   "Classificatory Systems of Relationship." *Journal of the Royal Anthropological Institute,* vol. 39, pp. 77–84.

(1939)   *Cultural and Natural Areas of Native North America.* Berkeley and Los Angeles: Univ. of California Press.

Kuhn, Thomas G. (1962)   *The Structure of Scientific Revolutions.* International Encyclopedia of Unified Science, vol. 2, no. 2. Chicago: Univ. of Chicago Press.

Kuper, Hilda (1963)   *The Swazi: A South African Kingdom.* New York: Holt.

LaBarre, Weston (1947)   "The Cultural Basis of Emotions and Gestures." *Journal of Personality* 16 (September), pp. 49–68.

Leach, Edmund R. (1958)   "Concerning Trobriand Clans and the Kinship Category 'Tabu.'" In *The Developmental Cycle of Domestic Groups,* ed. Jack R. Goody, Papers in Social Anthropology, no. 1, pp. 120–45. New York: Cambridge Univ. Press.

(1961)   *Rethinking Anthropology.* London School of Economics Monographs on Social Anthropology, No. 22. London: Athlone Press.

(1969)   *Genesis as Myth and Other Essays.* London: Grossman.

(1972)   "Ritualization in Man in Relation to Conceptual and Social Development." In *Reader in Comparative Religion,* ed. William A. Lessa and Evon Z. Vogt, pp. 333–337. New York: Harper.

Leakey, Louis S. B., and Goodall, Vann Morris (1969)   *Unveiling Man's Origins.* Cambridge, Mass.: Harvard Univ. Press.

LeClair, Edward E., Jr., and Schneider, Harold K., eds. (1968)   *Economic Anthropology.* New York: Holt.

Lee, Alfred McClung (1966)   *Multivalent Man.* New York: Braziller.

Lee, Richard B. (1967)   "Trance Cure of the !Kung Bushmen." *Natural History,* November, pp. 30–37.

(1968a)   "What Hunters Do for a Living, or, How to Make Out on Scarce Resources." In *Man the Hunter,* eds. Richard B. Lee and Irven De Vore, pp. 30–48. Chicago: Aldine.

(1968b)   "The Sociology of !Kung Bushman Trance Performances." In *Trance and Possession States,* ed. R. H. Prince, pp. 35–54. Montreal: R. M. Bucke Memorial Society.

(1969)   "!Kung Bushman Subsistence: An Input-Output Analysis." In *Environment and Cultural Behavior,* ed. Andrew P. Vayda, pp. 47–79. Garden City, N.Y.: Natural History Press.

Leeds, Anthony (1968)   "The Anthropology of Cities: Some Methodological Issues." In *Urban Anthropology,* ed. Elizabeth Eddy, Southern Anthropological Society Proceedings, no. 2, pp. 31–47. Athens: Univ. of Georgia Press.

(1971)   "The Concept of the Culture of Poverty: Conceptual, Logical, and Empirical Problems." In *The Culture of Poverty: A Critique,* ed. Eleanor Leacock, pp. 226–84. New York: Simon and Schuster.

Leighton, Alexander H. (1949)   *Gregorio the Hand Trembler: A Psychobiological Study of a Navaho Indian.* Papers of the Peabody Museum of American Archaeology and Ethnology, vol. 40, no. 1. Cambridge, Mass.: Harvard.

(1959)   *My Name Is Legion.* New York: Basic Books.

Lenski, Gerhard (1966)   *Power and Privilege: A Theory of Stratification.* New York: McGraw-Hill.

Lerner, Daniel (1958)   *The Passing of Traditional Society: Modernizing the Middle East.* London: Free Press of Glencoe, Collier-Macmillan.

Lerner, Michael P. (1973)   *The New Socialist Revolution.* New York: Delta.

Leroi-Gourhan, André (1968)   "The Evolution of Upper Paleolithic Art." *Scientific American,* February, pp. 58–68+.

Lévi-Strauss, Claude (1963)   *Structural Anthropology.* New York: Basic Books.

(1964)   *The Raw and the Cooked.* New York: Harper.

(1969)   *The Elementary Structure of Kinship.* Boston: Beacon.

Lewis, Oscar (1959)   *Five Families: Mexican Case Studies in the Culture of Poverty.* New York: Basic Books.

(1966)   *La Vida: A Puerto Rican Family in the Culture of Poverty, San Juan and New York.* New York: Random House.

(1970)   *Anthropological Essays.* Pp. 67–80. New York: Random House.

Lewontin, Richard C. (1974)   *The Genetic Basis of Evolutionary Change.* New York: Columbia Univ. Press.

Lieberman, Philip (1975) *On the Origins of Language: An Introduction To the Evolution of Human Speech.* New York: Macmillan.

Lieberman, Philip, Crelin, E. S., and Klatt, D. H. (1972) "Phonetic Ability and Related Anatomy of the Newborn and Adult Human, Neanderthal Man, and the Chimpanzee." *American Anthropologist*—74:287–307.

Liebow, Elliott (1967) *Tally's Corner: A Study of Negro Street-Corner Men.* Boston: Little, Brown.

Linton, Ralph (1936) *The Study of Man.* New York: Appleton-Century.

Livingstone, Frank B. (1968) "The Effects of Warfare on the Biology of the Human Species." In *War: The Anthropology of Armed Conflict and Aggression,* ed. Morton Fried, Marvin Harris, and Robert Murphy, pp. 3–15. Garden City, N.Y.: Natural History Press.

Locke, John (1964, orig. 1690) *An Essay Concerning Human Understanding.* Oxford: Clarendon.

Lomax, Alan, and Berkowitz, Norman (1972) "The Evolutionary Taxonomy of Culture," *Science* 177 (July 21):228–39.

Loomis, W. Farnsworth (1967) "Skin-Pigment Regulation of Vitamin-D Biosynthesis in Man." *Science* 157 (August 4):501–6.

Lopreato, Joseph (1967) "How Would You Like to Be a Peasant?" In *Peasant Society: A Reader,* ed. J. M. Potter, M. N. Diaz, and F. M. Foster. Boston: Little, Brown.

Lorenz, Konrad (1966) *On Aggression.* New York: Harcourt.

Lounsbury, Floyd G. (1956) "A Semantic Analysis of the Pawnee Kinship Usage." *Language* 32:158–194.

(1965) "Another View of the Trobriand Kinship Categories." *American Anthropologist* 67:142–85.

Lurie, Nancy Oestreich (1961) *Mountain Wolf Woman: The Autobiography of a Winnebago Indian.* Ann Arbor: Univ. of Michigan Press.

(1969) "Wisconsin Indians: Lives and Lands." *Wisconsin Magazine of History* 53:2–20.

Lyell, Charles (1833) *Principles of Geology.* London: J. Murray.

Machiavelli, Niccolo (1947, orig. 1513) *The Prince.* New York: F. S. Crafts.

McKee, Michael, and Robertson, Ian (1975) *Social Problems.* New York: Random House.

McKinnon, J. (1974) "The Behavior and Ecology of Wild Orangutans (*Pongo pygmaeus*)." *Animal Behavior* 22:3–74.

McLennan, John F. (1865) *Primitive Marriage.* Edinburgh: Adam and Charles Black.

(1867) *Studies in Ancient History* London: Macmillan.

MacNeish, Richard S. (1964) "Origins of New World Cultivation." *Scientific American,* November, pp. 29–37.

Maine, Sir Henry S. (1861) *Ancient Law.* London: J. Murray.

Malefijt, Annemarie de Waal (1974) *Images of Man.* New York: Knopf.

Malinowski, Bronislaw (1920) "Kula: The Circulating Exchanges of Valuables in the Archipelagos of Eastern New Guinea." *Man* 20:97–105.

(1922) *Argonauts of the Western Pacific.* New York: Dutton.

(1929) *The Sexual Life of Savages.* New York: Harcourt.

(1930) "The Rationalization of Anthropology and Administration." *Africa* 3:405–29.

(1931) "Culture." In *Encyclopedia of the Social Sciences.* New York: Macmillan. Reprinted as "The Role of Magic and Religion." In *Reader in Comparative Religion: An Anthropological Approach,* ed. William A. Lessa and Evon Z. Vogt. New York: Harper, 1965.

(1932) *Crime and Custom in Savage Society.* New York: Harcourt.

(1935) *Coral Gardens and Their Magic.* New York: American Book.

(1945) *The Dynamics of Cultural Change: An Inquiry into Race Relations in Africa.* New Haven, Conn.: Yale Univ. Press.

Mandela, Nelson (1970) "I Am Prepared to Die. . ." London: International Defense and Aid Fund for Southern Africa.

Mangin, William (1973) "Sociological, Cultural, and Political Characteristics of Some Urban Migrants in Peru." In *Urban Anthropology: Cross-Cultural Studies of Urbanization,* ed. Aidan Southall, pp. 315–50. New York: Oxford Univ. Press.

Maquet, Jacques (1964)   "Objectivity in Anthropology." Current Anthropology 5:47–55.

Marshack, Alexander (1972)   The Roots of Civilization. New York: McGraw-Hill.

Marshall, J. (1969)   N/um Tchai: The Ceremonial Dance of the !Kung Bushmen. Film. Somerville, Mass.: Documentary Educational Resource.

Marshall, L. (1969)   "The Medicine Dance of the !Kung Bushmen." Africa 39:327–65.

Martin, M. Kay (1974)   The Foraging Adaptation: Uniformity or Diversity? Addison-Wesley Modular Publication, no. 56. Reading, Mass.: Addison-Wesley.

Martin, M. Kay, and Voorhies, Barbara (1975)   The Female of the Species. New York: Columbia Univ. Press.

Marx, Karl (1904)   A Contribution to the Critique of Political Economy. New York: International Library. Excerpted and reprinted as "The Material Forces and the Relations of Production." In Theories of Society, ed. Talcott Parsons, Edward Shils, Kasper D. Naegele, and Jesse R. Pitt, pp. 136–39. New York: Free Press of Glencoe, 1961.

(1967, orig. 1867–94)   Capital. Ed. Friedrich Engels. Trans. Samuel Moore and Edward Aveling. 3 vols. New York: International Publishers.

Marx, Karl, and Engels, Friedrich (1961, orig. 1848)   "The Communist Manifesto." In Essential Works of Marxism, ed. Arthur P. Mendel. New York: Bantam Books.

Mayr, Ernst (1972)   "The Nature of the Darwinian Revolution." Science 176 (June 2):981–89.

Mead, Margaret (1956)   New Lives for Old. New York: Morrow.

(1961)   "Cultural Determinants of Sexual Behavior." In Sex and Internal Secretions, ed. William C. Young, vol. 2. Baltimore, Md.: Williams & Wilkins.

(1963)   Sex and Temperament in Three Primitive Societies. New York: Morrow.

Meadows, D. H., Meadows, Dennis L., Randers, J., and Behrens, W. W., III (1972)   The Limits to Growth. New York: Signet, New American Library.

Meggers, Betty J. (1972)   Prehistoric America. Chicago: Aldine.

Meggitt, Mervin (1962)   Desert People. Sydney: Angus and Robertson.

Melson, Robert, and Wolpe, Howard, eds. (1971)   Nigeria: Modernization and the Politics of Communalism. East Lansing: Michigan State Univ. Press.

Merton, Robert K. (1968)   Social Theory and Social Structure. Enlarged ed. New York: Free Press.

Meyers, Thomas J. (1971)   "The Origins of Agriculture: An Evaluation of Hypotheses." In Prehistoric Agriculture, ed. Stuart Struever. Garden City, N.Y.: Natural History Press.

Michael, R. P., and Keverne, E. B. (1968)   "Pheromones in the Communication of Sexual Status in Primates." Nature 218:746–49.

Middleton, John (1958)   "The Political System of the Lugbara of the Nile-Congo Divide." In Tribes without Rulers, ed. John Middleton and David Tait. London: Routledge

(1960)   Lugbara Religion. London: Oxford Univ. Press.

(1965)   The Lugbara of Uganda. New York: Holt.

Mills, C. Wright (1956)   The Power Elite. New York: Oxford Univ. Press.

Miyadi, D. (1967)   "Differences in Social Behavior among Japanese Macaque Troops." In Neue Ergebnisse der Primatologie, ed. D. Starch, R. Schneider, and H. J. Kuhn. Stuttgart: Fisher.

Mizuhara, H. (1964)   "Social Changes of Japanese Monkey Troops in Takasakiyama." Primates 4:27–52.

Money, John, and Ehrhardt, Anke A. (1972)   Man and Woman, Boy and Girl: Differentiation and Dimorphism of Gender Identity. Baltimore, Md.: Johns Hopkins Univ. Press.

Montagu, Ashley (1970)   Culture and the Evolution of Man. New York: Oxford Univ. Press.

Montagu, Ashley, ed. (1973)   Man and Aggression. 2d ed. London: Oxford Univ. Press.

Morgan, Elaine (1972)   The Descent of Woman. New York: Stein and Day.

Morgan, Lewis Henry (1870)   Systems of Consanguinity and Affinity of the Human Family. Washington, D.C.: Smithsonian Institution.

(1877)   Ancient Society. New York: World.

Morrill, Warren (1963) "Immigrants and Associations: The Ibo in Twentieth Century Calabar." *Comparative Studies in Society and History* 5:424-48.

Morris, Charles (1938) *Foundations of the Theory of Signs.* International Encyclopedia of a Unified Science, vol. 1, no. 2. Chicago: Univ. of Chicago Press.

Morris, Desmond E. (1967) *The Naked Ape.* London: Jonathan Cape.

Muller, J. (1949) "The Darwinian and Modern Conceptions of Natural Selection." *Proceedings of the American Philosophical Society* 93:459-70.

Murdock, George P. (1937) "Comparative Data on the Division of Labor by Sex." *Social Forces* 16:551-53.

(1949) *Social Structure.* New York: Macmillan.

(1967) *Ethnographic Atlas.* Pittsburgh: Univ. of Pittsburgh Press.

Murphy, Robert F. (1967) "Culture Change." In *Biennial Review of Anthropology,* ed. J. Siegel and A. R. Beals. Stanford, Calif.: Stanford Univ. Press.

Nadel, S. F. (1939) "The Interview Technique in Social Anthropology." In *The Study of Society,* ed. F. C. Bartlett et al. London: Kegan Paul.

(1942) *A Black Byzantium.* London: Oxford Univ. Press.

(1947) *The Nuba.* London: Oxford Univ. Press.

Nader, Laura, and Yngvesson, Barbara (1973) "On Studying the Ethnography of Law and Its Consequences." In *Handbook of Social and Cultural Anthropology,* ed. John J. Honigmann, pp. 883-921. Chicago: Rand McNally.

Naroll, Raoul (1966) "Does Military Deterence Deter?" *Trans-Action* 3:4-20.

(1969) "Deterence in History." In *Theory and Research on the Causes of War,* ed. D. G. Pruitt and R. C. Snyder. New York: Praeger.

Nash, Manning (1962) "Race and the Ideology of Race." *Current Anthropology* 3:285-88.

Needham, Rodney (1962) *Structure and Sentiment: A Test Case in Social Anthropology.* Chicago: Univ. of Chicago Press.

Netting, Robert (1965) "Household Organization and Intensive Agriculture: The Kofyar Case." *Africa* 35:422-29.

Neumann, Erich (1954) *The Origins and History of Consciousness.* Princeton, N.J.: Bollingen Foundation.

Newman, R. W., and Munro, E. H. (1955) "The Relation of Climate and Body Size in U.S. Males." *American Journal of Physical Anthropology* 13:1-17.

Nissen, H. W. (1931) "A Field Study of the Chimpanzee: Observations of Chimpanzee Behavior and Environment in West French Guinea." *Comparative Psychology Monographs* 8:1-122.

Oberg, Kalervo (1973) *The Social Economy of the Tlingit Indians.* Seattle: Univ. of Washington Press.

Obiechina, Emmanuel (1973) *An African Popular Literature: A Study of Onitsha Market Pamphlets.* Cambridge: Cambridge Univ. Press.

O'Brien, Denise (1972) "African Female Husbands." Mimeographed. Philadelphia: Department of Anthropology, Temple University.

Ottenberg, Simon (1958) "Ibo Receptivity to Change." In *Continuity and Change in African Cultures,* ed. William R. Bascome and Melville J. Herskovits. Chicago: Phoenix, Univ. of Chicago Press.

Otterbein, Keith (1970) *The Evolution of War.* New Haven, Conn.: Human Relations Area Files.

(1973) "The Anthropology of War." In *Handbook of Social and Cultural Anthropology,* ed. John J. Honigmann, pp. 923-58. Chicago: Rand McNally.

Otterbein, Keith, and Otterbein, Charlotte Swanson (1965) "An Eye for an Eye, a Tooth for a Tooth: A Cross-Cultural Study of Feuding." *American Anthropologist* 67:1470-82.

Oxnard, Charles (1969) "Evolution of the Human Shoulder: Some Possible Pathways." *American Journal of Physical Anthropology* 30.

Parsons, Elsie Clews, ed. (1973) *American Indian Life.* Lincoln: Univ. of Nebraska Press. Reprint of 1922 edition published by B. W. Huebsch.

Parsons, Talcott (1951) *The Social System.* Glencoe, Ill.: Free Press.

(1966) *Societies: Evolutionary and Comparative Perspective.* Englewood Cliffs, N.J.: Prentice-Hall.

Paul, Lois (1974) "The Mastery of Work and the Mystery of Sex in a Guatemala Village." In *Woman, Culture, and Society,* ed. Michell Zimbalist Rosaldo and Louise Lamphere. Stanford, Calif.: Stanford Univ. Press.

Perry, W. J. (1917) "An Ethnological Study of Warfare." *Manchester Memoirs* 61(6):1–16.

Pfeiffer, John E. (1969) *The Emergence of Man.* New York: Harper.

Piddington, Ralph (1970) "Action Anthropology." In *Applied Anthropology: Readings in the Uses of the Science of Man,* ed. James A. Clifton. Boston: Houghton Mifflin.

Pilbeam, David R. (1972a) *The Ascent of Man.* New York: Macmillan.

(1972b) "An Idea We Could Live Without: The Naked Ape." *Discovery* 7(2):63–70.

Pilbeam, David R., and Simons, Elwyn L. (1965) "Some Problems of Hominid Classification." *American Scientist* 53:98–120.

Polanyi, Karl, Arensberg, C. W., and Pearson, H. W., eds. (1957) *Trade and Market in the Early Empires.* New York: Free Press.

Polo, Marco (1875, orig. 1295) *The Book of Ser Marco Polo the Venetian Concerning the Kingdoms and Marvels of the East.* Trans. H. Yule. London: John Murray.

Pospisil, Leopold (1958) *Kapaukan Papuans and Their Law.* New Haven, Conn.: Yale University Publications in Anthropology.

(1963) *The Kapauku Papuans of West New Guinea.* New York: Holt.

(1969) "Structural Change and Primitive Law: Consequences of a Papuan Legal Case." In *Law in Culture and Society,* ed. Laura Nader, pp. 208–29. Chicago: Aldine.

(1971) *Anthropology of Law.* New York: Harper.

Premack, David (1970) "The Education of Sarah." *Psychology Today,* September, pp. 55–58.

(1971) "Language in Chimpanzee?" *Science* 172 (May 21): 808–22.

Radcliffe-Brown, A. R. (1930) "Applied Anthropology." *Report of the 20th Meeting of the Australian and New Zealand Association for the Advancement of Science,* pp. 267–80.

(1935) "On the Concept of Function in Social Science." *American Anthropologist* 37:394–402.

(1939) "Taboo" (the "Frazer Lecture"). Reprinted as "Taboo." In *Reader in Comparative Religion: An Anthropological Approach,* ed. William A. Lessa and Evon Z. Vogt. New York: Harper, 1965.

Rappaport, Roy A. (1968) *Pigs for the Ancestors.* New Haven, Conn.: Yale Univ. Press.

Rasmussen, Knud J. (1929) *The Intellectual Culture of the Iglulik Eskimos: Report of the Fifth Thule Expedition, 1921–24,* vol. III, no. 1. Trans. W. Worster. Copenhagen: Gyldendal.

Redfield, Robert (1960) *The Little Community and Peasant Society and Culture* (in one volume). Chicago: Phoenix, Univ. of Chicago Press.

Reynolds, Vernon (1966) "Open Groups in Hominid Evolution." *Man* 1:441–52.

Riesman, David (1969) *The Lonely Crowd.* New Haven, Conn.: Yale Univ. Press.

Rivers, W. H. R. (1914) *Kinship and Social Organization.* London: Constable.

Robbins, Richard H. (1973) "Identity, Culture, and Behavior." In *Handbook of Social and Cultural Anthropology,* ed. John J. Honigmann. Chicago: Rand McNally.

Roberts, D. F. (1953) "Body Weight, Race, and Climate." *American Journal of Physical Anthropology* 11:533–58.

Robertson, Ian (1973) *Education in South Africa: A Study in the Influence of Ideology on Educational Practice.* Ph.D. dissertation, Harvard University, Cambridge, Mass.

Robertson, Ian and Whitten, Phillip, eds. (1976) *Race and Politics in South Africa.* Chicago: Transaction/Aldine.

Rose, M. D. (1974) "Postural Adaptations in New and Old World Monkeys." In *Primate Locomotion,* ed. F. A. Jenkins, Jr. New York: Academic Press.

Rouse, Irving (1973) Personal communication.

Rousseau, Jean Jacques (1938, orig. 1762) *The Social Contract.* New York: Dutton.

Rowe, William L. (1973) "Caste, Kinship, and Association in Urban India." In *Urban Anthropology: Cross-Cultural Studies of Urbanization,* ed. Aidan Southall, pp. 211–50. New York: Oxford Univ. Press.

Rowell, T. E. (1966) "Forest-Living Baboons in Uganda." *Journal of Zoology* 149:334–64.

(1967) "A Quantitative Comparison of the Behavior of a Wild and a Caged Baboon Group." *Animal Behavior* 15:499–589.

(1968) "The Effect of Temporary Separation from Their Group on the Mother-Infant Relationship of Baboons." *Folia Primatologica* 9:114–22.

Sahlins, Marshall (1972) *Stone Age Economics.* Chicago: Aldine.

Salzman, Philip (1971) "Movement and Resource Extraction Among Pastoral Nomads." *Anthropological Quarterly,* vol. 44, no. 3.

Sauer, Carl O. (1952) *Agricultural Origins and Dispersals.* New York: American Geographical Society.

Scheffler, Harold W. (1965) *Choiseul Island Social Structure.* Berkeley and Los Angeles: Univ. of California Press.

Schelling, Thomas C. (1966) *Arms and Influence.* New Haven, Conn.: Yale Univ. Press.

Schmidt-Nielsen, Knut S. (1959) "The Physiology of the Camel." *Scientific American,* December, pp. 140–42+.

Schusky, Ernest L. (1965) *Manual for Kinship Analysis: A Study in Anthropological Method.* New York: Holt.

Service, Elman R. (1962) *Primitive Social Organization.* New York: Random House.

(1963) *Profiles in Ethnology.* New York: Harper.

(1966) *The Hunters.* Englewood Cliffs, N.J.: Prentice-Hall.

(1971) *Cultural Evolutionism: Theory in Practice.* New York: Holt.

Shapiro, Judith (1971) *Sex Roles and Social Structure among the Yanomamö Indians in North Brazil.* Ph.D. dissertation, Columbia University.

Silverman, Julian (1967) "Shamans and Acute Schizophrenia." *American Anthropologist* 69:21–31.

Simons, Elwyn L. (1963) "Some Fallacies in the Study of Hominid Phylogeny." *Science* 141 (September 6):879–89.

(1972) *Primate Evolution.* New York: Macmillan.

Simpson, George Gaylord (1949) *The Meaning of Evolution.* New Haven, Conn.: Yale Univ. Press.

Simpson, Richard L. (1965) "Sociology of the Community: Current Status and Prospects." *Rural Sociology* 30:127–49.

Sjoberg, Gideon (1967) "Project Camelot: Selected Reactions and Personal Reflections." In *Ethics, Politics, and Social Research,* ed. Gideon Sjoberg. Cambridge, Mass.: Schenkman.

Sklar, Richard L. (1971) "Nigerian Politics in Perspective." In *Nigeria: Modernization and the Politics of Communalism,* ed. Robert Melson and Howard Wolpe. East Lansing: Michigan State Univ. Press.

Smelser, Niel J. (1971) "Mechanism of Change and Adjustment to Change." In *Economic Development and Social Change,* ed. George Dalton. Garden City, N.Y.: Natural History Press.

Smith, James G. E. (1973) *Leadership among the Southwestern Ojibwa.* Publications in Ethnology, no. 7. Ottawa: National Museums of Canada.

Solecki, Ralph S. (1971a) "Neanderthal Is Not an Epithet but a Worthy Ancestor." *Smithsonian,* May, pp. 20–27.

(1971b) *Shanidar: The First Flower People.* New York: Knopf.

Solheim, Wilhelm G. (1972) "An Earlier Agricultural Revolution." *Scientific American,* April, pp. 34–51.

Southall, Aidan (1973) "The Density of Role Relationships as a Universal Index of Urbanization." In *Urban Anthropology: Cross-Cultural Studies of Urbanization,* ed. Aidan Southall, pp. 71–106. New York: Oxford Univ. Press.

Spencer, Robert E., and Johnson, Eldon (1968) *Atlas for Anthropology.* 2d ed. Dubuque, Iowa: William C. Brown.

Spindler, G. D., and Spindler, Louise (1971) *Dreamers without Power: The Menomini Indians.* New York: Holt.

Spiro, Milford E. (1966) "Religion: Problems of Definition and Explanation." In *Anthropological Approaches to the Study of Religion,* ed. Michael Banton, Association of Social Anthropologists of the Commonwealth, vol. 3. New York: Praeger.

Stack, Carol B. (1970) "The Kindred of Viola Jackson: Residence and Family Organization of an Urban Black American Family." In *Afro-American Anthropology,* ed. Norman Whitten and John Szwed, pp. 303–10. New York: Free Press.

Statistisches Handbuch des Kantons Bern 1964, (1965)   Bern: A. Francke.

Stauder, Jack (1974)   "The Relevance of Anthropology to Colonialism and Imperialism." *Race* 16:29–51.

Stein, William (1974)   "The Struggle for Free Labor in Rural Peru: Vicos 1872–1971." Paper presented to the XLI Congreso International de Americanistas.

Stoltz, L. P., and Saayman, G. S. (1970)   "Ecology and Behaviour of Baboons in the Northern Transvaal." *Ann. Trans. Mus.* 26:5.

Struhsaker, T. T. (1967)   "Ecology of Vervet Monkeys (*Cercopithecus aethiops*) in the Masai-Amboseli Game Reserve." *Ecology* (Kenya) 48:891–904.

Sutton, Willis A., Jr., and Kolaja, Jim (1960a)   "The Concept of Community." *Rural Sociology* 25:197–203.

(1960b)   "The Elements of Community Action." *Social Forces* 38:325–31.

Suzuki, A. (1969)   "An Ecological Study of Chimpanzees in a Savannah Woodland." *Primates* 10:103–48.

Swartz, Marc, Turner, Victor, and Tuder, Arthur, eds. (1966)   *Political Anthropology.* Chicago: Aldine.

Tanner, Nancy (1974)   "Matrifocality in Indonesia and Africa and among Black Americans." In *Woman, Culture, and Society,* ed. Michell Zimbalist Rosaldo and Louise Lamphere. Stanford, Calif.: Stanford Univ. Press.

Tavris, Carol (1972)   "Woman and Man." *Psychology Today,* March, pp. 57–85.

Taylor, R. B. (1973)   *Introduction to Cultural Anthropology.* Boston: Allyn and Bacon.

Thomas, William L., Jr., ed. (1956)   *Man's Role in Changing the Face of the Earth.* 2 vols. Chicago: Univ. of Chicago Press.

Tiger, Lionel (1969)   *Men in Groups.* New York: Random House.

(1970)   "The Possible Biological Origins of Sexual Discrimination." *Impact of Science on Society* 20:29–44.

Trager, George L. (1962)   "A Scheme for the Cultural Analysis of Sex." *Southwestern Journal of Anthropology* 18:114–18.

Tschäni, Hans (1967)   *Profil der Schweiz.* Zürich: Rascher Verlag.

Turnbull, Colin M. (1961, 1962)   *The Forest People.* Garden City, N.Y.: Natural History Press (1961); Natural History Library, Doubleday Anchor (1962).

(1972)   *The Mountain People.* New York: Simon and Schuster.

Turner, Victor W. (1964)   "Betwixt and Between: The Liminal Period in *Rites de Passage.*" Reprinted in *Reader in Comparative Religion: An Anthropological Approach,* ed. William A. Lessa and Evon Z. Vogt. New York: Harper, 1965.

(1967)   *The Forest of Symbols.* Ithaca, N.Y.: Cornell Univ. Press.

Tylor, E. B. (1871)   *Primitive Culture: Researches into the Development of Mythology, Philosophy, Religion, Language, Art, and Custom.* London: J. Murray.

Valentine, Charles (1968)   *Culture and Poverty: Critique and Counter-Proposals.* Chicago: Univ. of Chicago Press.

Van den Berghe, Pierre (1970)   *South Africa: A Study in Conflict.* Berkeley and Los Angeles: Univ. of California Press.

Van Lawick-Goodall, Jane (1968)   "The Behavior of Free-Living Chimpanzees in the Gombé Stream Reserve." *Animal Behavior Monographs* 1:165–311.

(1971)   *In the Shadow of Man.* Boston: Houghton Mifflin.

Van Velsen, J. (1964)   *The Politics of Kinship.* Manchester: Manchester Univ. Press.

(1967)   "The Extended Case Method and Situational Analysis." In *The Craft of Social Anthropology,* ed. A. L. Epstein, pp. 129–49. London: Social Science Paperbacks, Tavistock.

Van Velsen, J., Thoden, H. V. E., and van Wetering, W. (1960)   "Residence, Power Groups, and Intrasocietal Aggression." *International Archives of Ethnography* 49:169–200.

Vayda, Andrew P. (1969)   "The Study of the Causes of War, with Special Reference to Head-Hunting Raids in Borneo." *Ethnohistory* 16:211–24.

Veblen, Thorstein (1954, orig. 1899)   *The Theory of the Leisure Class.* New York: New American Library.

Von Oppenheim, Max Freiherr, with E. Bräunlich and W. Caskel (1939–53)   *Die Beduinen.* Leipzig and Wiesbaden: Otto Harrasowitz.

Wallace, Anthony F. C. (1966)   *Religion.* New York: Random House.

(1968)   "Anthropological Contributions to the Theory of Personality." In *The Study of Personality: An Interdisciplinary Appraisal,* ed. Edward Norbeck et al. New York: Holt.

Wallace, Bruce, and Srb, Adrian M. (1964)   *Adaptation.* 2d ed. Englewood Cliffs, N.J.: Prentice-Hall.

Washburn, Sherwood L. (1960)   "Tools and Human Evolution." *Scientific American,* September, pp. 62–75.

Washburn, Sherwood L., and De Vore, Irven (1961)   "The Social Life of Baboons." *Scientific American,* June, pp. 62–71.

Watzlawick, Paul, Beavin, Janet H., and Jackson, Don D. (1967)   *Pragmatics of Human Communication.* New York: Norton.

Weber, Max (1946)   "Class, Status, and Party." In *From Max Weber: Essays in Sociology,* ed. Hans Gerth and C. Wright Mills. New York: Oxford Univ. Press.

Weiner, J. S. (1971)   *The Natural History of Man.* New York: Universe.

Wendorf, Fred, ed. (1968)   *Combined Prehistoric Expedition to Egyptian and Sudanese Nubia.* Dallas, Texas: Southern Methodist Univ. Press.

Westermarck, Edward (1891)   *The History of Human Marriage.* London: Macmillan.

Western Americana Notes (1959)   Klemup, Oregon.

White, Leslie (1943)   "Energy and the Evolution of Culture." *American Anthropologist* 45:335–56.

(1949) *The Science of Culture.* New York: Grove.

(1959) *The Evolution of Culture.* New York: McGraw-Hill.

Williams, B. J. (1973)   *Evolution and Human Origins: An Introduction to Physical Anthropology.* New York: Harper.

Wirth, Louis (1938)   "Urbanism as a Way of Life." *American Journal of Sociology* 44:8–20.

Wissler, Clark (1911)   *The Social Life of the Blackfoot Indians.* Anthropological Papers of the American Museum of Natural History, vol. 7, no. 1. New York: American Museum of Natural History.

Wittfogel, Karl (1957)   *Oriental Despotism: A Comparative Study of Total Power.* New Haven, Conn.: Yale Univ. Press.

Wright, Quincy (1942)   *A Study of War.* Vol. 1. Chicago: Univ. of Chicago Press.

Yerkes, Robert M., and Yerkes, A. (1929)   *The Great Apes.* New Haven, Conn.: Yale Univ. Press.

Yoshiba, K. (1968)   "Local and Intertroop Variability in Ecology and Social Behavior of Common Indian Langurs." In *Primates: Studies in Adaptation and Variability,* ed. Phyllis C. Jay. New York: Holt.

Glossary

Abbevillean (or Chellean) culture, the earlier of two stages in the hand ax (bifacial core tool) tradition, lasting from approximately 600,000 to 400,000 B.P.; found across southerly and medium latitudes of the Old World, radiating out from Africa to southwest Europe and as far east as India; associated with *Homo erectus.*

Absolute dating, physical-chemical dating methods which tie archaeologically retrieved artifacts into clearly specified time ranges calculated in terms of an abstract standard such as the calendar.

Acclimatization, the process by which an organism's sweat glands, metabolism, and associated mechanisms adjust to a new and different climate.

Acculturation, those cultural changes which come about in each culture when two or more cultures come into contact with each other.

Acheulian, the second stage of the hand ax (chelloid) bifacial core tool tradition; associated primarily with *Homo erectus;* found in southern and middle latitudes all across the Old World from India to Africa and west Europe; lasting *in toto* from about 400,000 to 60,000 B.P.

Achieved status, a social position that a person comes to occupy by virtue of deliberate intent and some degree of effort.

Action anthropology (or applied anthropology), the use of anthropological concepts, methods, theories, and findings to achieve some desired social goal.

Activity cycle, the daily and/or yearly "schedule" followed by an individual or group.

Adaptation, generally, the ways in which individuals become fitted, physically or culturally, to particular environments. More specifically, adaptation is a two-way process in which changes in physiological and social mechanisms are made in order to cope successfully with environments; but organisms are also constantly changing their environments, making them more "livable."

Adaptational approach, a theoretical approach to cultural change with the underlying assumption that, in order to survive, human beings must organize themselves into social, economic, and political groups that somehow fit in with the resources and challenges of a particular environment.

Adaptive grade, a level of primate social organization representing a particular complex of behavioral features that are adapted to those aspects of the environment that form major selection pressures.

Adultery, sexual intercourse by a married person with a person other than the legal spouse.

Aegyptopithecus, an Oligocene fossil series, dating from about 30 million years ago, representing the common ancestor of apes and human beings.

Affinal kin, a kin relationship involving one marriage link (for example, a husband is related by affinity to his wife and her consanguineals).

Age grades, specialized hierarchical associations based on age which cut across entire societies.

Agnatic kin, kin related to one through males.

Agonistic interaction, behavior that is aggressive or unfriendly and includes both the initiator and the recipient.

Agriculture, domesticated food production involving minimally the cultivation of plants, but usually also the raising of domesticated animals. More narrowly, plant domestication making use of the plow (versus horticulture).

Alienation, the individual's loss of any sense of belonging to or control over the social world; particularly characteristic of industrial society, where secondary groups predominate.

Allele, each different version of a gene.

Alliance theory, a theoretical approach to the study of descent which emphasizes reciprocal exchanges among descent groups as the basic mechanism of social integration.

Allomorph, one of the different-sounding versions of the same morpheme (unit of meaning).

Allophone, one of the different sounds (phones) which represent a single phoneme.

Alveolar ridge, thickened portions of the upper and lower interior gums in which the teeth are set.

Alyha·, among the Mohave Indians of the American Southwest, those males who adopted most of the behaviors, rights, and duties typical of Mohave women.

Ambilineal descent, the reckoning of descent group membership by an individual through either the mother's or the father's line—at the individual's option. *See also* Cognatic descent.

Androgens, hormones, present in relatively large quantities in the testes, which are responsible for the development of the male secondary sex characteristics.

Angular gyrus, an area of the brain crucial to human linguistic ability that serves as a link between the parts of the brain that receive stimuli from the sense organs of sight, hearing, and touch.

Animatism, the attribution of life to inanimate objects.

Animism, the belief that objects (including people) in the concretely perceivable world have a nonconcrete, spiritual element. For human beings, this element is the soul.

Anomie, the state of normlessness, usually found in societies undergoing crises, that renders social control over individual behavior ineffective.

Anthropoidea, a suborder of the primates, including monkeys, apes, and human beings.

Anthropology, the systematic study of the nature of human beings and their works, past and present.

Anthropometry, a subdivision of physical anthropology concerned with measuring and statistically analyzing the dimensions of the human body.

Apartheid, the system of segregation practiced in the Republic of South Africa, where a minority of 4 million whites exercises total dominance over some 20 million black Africans, Asiatics, and populations of mixed ancestry.

Applied anthropology, the use of anthropological concepts, methods, theories, and findings to achieve some desired social end.

Archaeology, the systematic retrieval and identification of the physical remains left behind by human beings, including both their skeletal and their cultural remains.

Arcuate fasciculus, the large bundle of nerve fibers in the human brain, connecting Broca's area with Wernicke's area. A crucial biological substratum of speech in humans.

Aristocracy, the privileged, usually landowning class of a society (for example, the ruling nobility of prerevolutionary France).

Articulatory features, speech events described in terms of the speech organs employed in their utterance rather than from the nature of the sounds themselves.

Ascribed status, the social position a person comes to occupy on the basis of such uncontrollable characteristics as sex, age, or circumstances of birth.

Assimilation, the disappearance of a minority group through the loss of particular identifying physical or sociocultural characteristics.

Australopithecine, an extinct grade in hominid evolution found principally in early to mid-Pleistocene in central and southern Africa, usually accorded subfamily status (*Australopithecinae,* within *Hominidae*).

Australopithecus africanus, the original type specimen of australopithecines discovered in 1924 at Taung, Cape Province, South Africa, and dating from approximately 3.5 million years ago to approximately 1.6 million years ago. Belongs to the gracile line of the australopithecines.

Australopithecus boisei, one of two species of robust australopithecines, appearing approximately 1.6 million years ago in sub-Saharan Africa.

Australopithecus habilis, a form of gracile *Australopithecus,* somewhat larger and more advanced than *Australopithecus africanus,* evolving between 1.85 and 1.65 million years ago. Identified by L. S. B. Leakey as *Homo habilis,* this is the only australopithecine with which stone tools have been found in unambiguous relationship.

Australopithecus robustus, one of two species of robust australopithecines, found in both East and South Africa, first appearing about 3.5 million years ago.

Avunculocal residence, the practice by which a newlywed couple establishes residence with, or in the locale of, the groom's maternal uncle. A feature of some matrilineal societies that facilitates the men's maintaining their political power.

Balanced reciprocity, the straightforward exchange of goods or services that both parties regard as equivalent at the time of the exchange.

Band, the simplest level of social organization; marked by very little political organization and consisting of small (50–300 persons) groups of families.

Bartering, the exchange of goods whose equivalent value is established by argument, usually in a market setting.

Basic personality, the central core of adaptive psychological characteristics shared by all or most members of a society.

Bazaar economy, an economy characterized by high turnover of easily portable goods, an irregular clientele, and constantly fluctuating prices that are determined by individual bargaining.

Bedouin, an Arab camel-breeding nomad belonging to certain specified tribes.

Berdache, French term for North American Indian transvestites, regarded as sacred, whose cultural roles included curing and organizing social events.

Bifaces, stone artifacts that have been flaked on two opposite sides, most typically the hand axes produced by *Homo erectus.*

Bifurcation, contrast among kin types based on the distinction between the mother's and father's kinfolk.

Bilateral descent, the reckoning of descent through both male and female lines. Typically found in Europe, the United States, and Southeast Asia.

Bilateral kin, a kin relationship in which an individual is linked equally to relatives of both sexes on both sides of the family.

Bilocal residence, the practice by which a newlywed couple has a choice of residence, but must establish residence with, or in the locale of, one or the other set of parents.

Blade tools, the ultimate technical refinement in stone tool making, characteristic of Upper Paleolithic culture. Blades are long, narrow flakes whose shapes are carefully controlled for when they are chipped off cores. They can be fashioned into a virtual infinity of tools.

Bound morpheme, unit of meaning (represented by a sound sequence) that can only occur when linked to another morpheme (for example, suffixes, prefixes).

Bourgeoisie, the class of factory owners and businessmen that emerged in all capitalist states at the start of the industrial revolution. Often called the ruling class in capitalist society, juxtaposed in interests to those of the working class (proletariat).

Brachiation, the characteristic pongid mode of locomotion which involves swinging by alternate arms under a support (such as a branch).

Breeding population, in population genetics, all individuals in a given population who potentially, or actually, mate with one another.

Brideprice, a gift from the groom and his family to the bride and her family prior to their marriage. The custom legitimizes children born to the wife as members of her husband's descent group.

Broca's area, an area of the brain located toward the front of the dominant side of the brain that activates, among other things, the muscles of the lips, jaw, tongue, and larynx. A crucial biological substratum of speech.

Burin, a chisel-like stone tool of the Upper Paleolithic, produced by knocking small chips off the end(s) of a blade.

Call systems, vocal systems of communication usually referring to nonhuman primates.

Capitalism, economic system featuring private ownership of the means of production and distribution.

Cargo cults, revitalization movements (also designated as revivalist, nativistic, or millenarian) that received their name from movements in Melanesia early in the twentieth century. Characterized by the belief that the millenium will be ushered in by the arrival of great ships or planes loaded with European trade goods (cargo).

Carotene, yellowish pigment in the skin.

Caste, a hereditary, endogamous group of people bearing a common name and often having the same traditional occupation.

Caste system, a stratification system in which the social strata within it are hereditary and endogamous. The entire system is sanctioned by the mores, laws, and usually the religion of the society in question.

Catarrhini, one of two infaorders of the primate suborder *Anthropoidea,* consisting of all Old World monkeys, apes, and humans.

Catastrophism, a school of thought, popular in the late eighteenth and early nineteenth centuries, proposing that life forms became extinct through natural catastrophes, of which Noah's flood was the latest.

Cercopithecoidea, one of two superfamilies of the infaorder *Catarrhini,* consisting of the Old World monkeys.

Chellean hand ax, a bifacial core tool from which much (but not all) of the surface has been chipped away, characteristic of the Abbevillean (or Chellean) culture. Produced by *Homo erectus.*

Chicanos, popularly used name for Mexican-Americans.

Chiefdom, estate, place, or dominion of a chief. Currently the term is also used to refer to a society at a level of social integration a stage above that of tribal society, characterized by a redistributive economy and centralized political authority.

Chimpanzee, along with the gorilla and the orangutan, one of the great apes; found exclusively in Africa; one of *Homo sapiens'* closest relatives.

Choppers, unifacial core tools, sometimes called pebble tools, found associated with *Australopithecus habilis* in Olduvai sequence, and also with *Homo erectus* in East Asia.

Chromosomal sex, the sex identity of a person determined by the coded message in the sex chromosome contributed by each parent.

Chromosome, helical strands of complex protein molecules found in the nuclei of all animal cells, along which the genes are located. Normal human somatic cells have 46.

Circumcision, the removal of the foreskin of a male or the clitoral sheath of a female.

Clactonian culture, Lower Paleolithic assemblage characterized by flake tools, occurring approximately 600,000 to 60,000 years ago in the northern areas of western and central Eurasia.

Clan, an exogamous unilineal kin group consisting of two or more lineages tracing descent from an unknown, perhaps legendary, founder.

Class, a stratum in a hierarchically organized social system; unlike a caste, endogamy is not a requirement (though it is often favored), and individuals do have the possibility (though not the probability) of moving to a neighboring stratum.

Class consciousness, an awareness by members of a subordinate social stratum of their common exploitation.

Classical archaeology, a traditional field within archaeology that concerns itself with the reconstruction of the way of life of ancient, literate civilizations such as Greece, Rome, and Egypt.

Classical evolution, an approach to social evolution that attempted to arrange what was known about different societies in terms of time, in the hope that a universal evolutionary sequence of social forms would be discovered.

Classificatory approach, the identification of structural regularities among the world's cultures, and the subsequent construction of a limited number of types that are arranged in a progressive sequence or a taxonomy.

Class system, a stratification system in which the individual's position is usually determined by the economic status of the family head, but the individual may potentially rise or fall from one class to another through his or her own efforts or failings.

Cline, a gradual series of variations across spacial distribution in some characteristics of a population.

Closed group, a group in which an animal is clearly included or excluded as a member; the group maintains itself in a stable manner through time and in space, and animals often spend their whole lives in the same group.

Closed system, a stratification system in which the boundaries between social strata are sharply drawn, and there is no way for an individual to change his or her societal status (for instance, a caste system).

Cognatic descent, a form of descent by which the individual may choose to affiliate with either the mother's or father's kinship group. *See also* Ambilineal descent.

Cognatic kin, those relatives of all generations on both sides of the family to some culturally defined limits.

Cognition, the process of putting one's perceptions into categories (cognitive categories).

Collateral kin, those non-lineal relatives in one's own generation on both sides of the family out to some culturally defined limit.

Colonialism, the process by which a foreign power holds political, economic, and social control over another people.

Communication, the exchange of information between two or more organisms.

Communist society, a society marked by common or public ownership of the means of production and distribution.

Comparative linguistics, a field of linguistics that attempts to describe formally the basic elements of languages and the rules by which they are ordered into intelligible speech.

Componential analysis, a school of anthropological linguistics, and one of the methodologies collectively known as formal semantic analysis, with which students of the "New Ethnography" seek to analyze their data; involves the identification of contrastive features of categories of folk ideological systems.

Composite family, the situation in which multiple marriages are practiced, or where the residence rule requires a couple to reside with parents. *See also* Extended family; Polygamy.

Conformity, action that is in accordance with some established custom, usage, practice, or tradition.

Consanguineal kin, a kin relationship based on biological connections only.

Convergent evolution, an evolutionary process by which two unrelated social or biological forms develop great similarities as a consequence of occupying analogous ecological niches.

Core tool, a rough, unfinished stone tool shaped by knocking off flakes, used to crush the heads of small game, to skin them, and to dissect the carcasses.

Corporate social groups, groups of varying size in which all members are jurally equivalent vis-à-vis outsiders, which persist through time, and which may or may not be descent groups.

Corvée, state-supported or state-organized form of forced labor recruitment; often viewed as a form of taxation.

Couvade, the custom, in many societies, for fathers to participate in the period of recuperation, after their wives give birth by remaining inactive for a long period of time—often much longer than the women.

Creation myth, a myth, unique to each culture, in which ancestors become separated from the rest of the animal kingdom, accounting for the society's biological and social development.

Cross-cousins, cousins related through ascending generation linking kin (often parental siblings) of the opposite sex (for example, mother's brother's children or father's sister's children).

Crow kinship terminology, a system of classifying kinspeople mostly associated with matrilineal descent organization.

Cultural anthropology, the major subdivision of anthropology that studies the cultural diversity of contemporary societies.

Cultural area, a part of the world in which the inhabitants share many of the elements of culture such as related languages, similar economic systems, social systems, and ideological systems; an outmoded concept that is seldom used.

Cultural evolution, the process of invention, diffusion, and elaboration of the behavior that is learned and taught in groups and is transmitted from generation to generation; often used to refer to the development of social complexity.

Cultural preadaptations, cultural characteristics that permit groups to adapt to new environments and other stresses by elaborating these characteristics into new forms.

Cultural relativism, a methodological orientation in anthropology, the basis of which is the idea that every culture is unique and therefore each cultural item must be understood in its own terms.

Culture, the patterned behavior (both mental and physical) that individuals learn and are taught as members of groups, and that is transmitted from generation to generation.

Culture of poverty, a concept developed by Oscar Lewis referring to a way of life found among the lowest socioeconomic strata of capitalistic countries that allows the individuals involved to cope with feelings of hopelessness and despair that result from their realization that they will not be able to achieve success in terms of the larger society's prevailing values and goals.

Darwinism, the theoretical approach to biological evolution first presented by Charles Darwin and Alfred Russel Wallace in 1858. The central concept of the theory is natural selection, referring to the greater probability of survival and reproduction of those individuals of a species having adaptive characteristics for a given environment.

Debt peonage, a form of forced labor whereby debtors are unable to move about freely or sell their labor on the open market until their debts are settled.

Deep structure, the structure underlying the syntactic relationships among the units of a sentence.

Demographic study, population study, primarily concerned with such aspects of population as analyses of fertility, mortality, and migration.

Dendrochronology (or tree-ring dating), an absolute dating method based on covariation of climatic variables (often rainfall) with annual growth of ring thickness in some tree species.

Dental formula, the number of incisors, canines, premolars, and molars found in one upper and one lower quadrant of a jaw. The human formula, which we share with the apes and Old World monkeys, is shown below:

I	C	P	M
2	1	2	3
2	1	2	3

Deoxyribonucleic acid (DNA), the hereditary material of the cell, capable of self-replication and of coding the production of proteins carrying on metabolic functions.

Depersonalization, a feeling of estrangement from oneself and a lack of clear sense of one's personal identity.

Descent, the practice of bestowing a specific social identity on a person as a consequence of his or her being born to a specific mother and/or father.

Descent group, a corporate group whose membership is acquired automatically as a consequence of the genealogical connections between group members and their offspring.

Descent rule, the principle used to trace lineal kin links from generation to generation. A child is filiated to both of its parents, but the descent rule stresses one parent's line and sex as links with others, over the other parent's line and sex.

Descriptive kinship terminology, the classification of kinspeople in ego's (the individual's) own generation, with a separate kin term for each kin type.

Descriptive linguistics, the careful recording, description of, and structural analysis of existing languages.

Diachronics, the comparative study of culture and society as they change through time in a specified geographical area.

Differentiation, the transformation that takes place when a single institution performing many functions or tasks is superseded by two or more specialized institutions, each of which fulfills highly specific functions.

Diffuse sanction, a social response to individual behavior that flows from individuals' shared expectations rather than from an organized decision, and involves spontaneous expression of approval or disapproval.

Diffusion, the process by which members of one culture learn and adapt to their own way of doing things new items of knowledge, new aptitudes, new solutions to problems, the production and use of new tools, or acquire any other new (to them) element of culture from another group.

Diffusionism, the belief held by some European cultural anthropologists of the nineteenth century and early twentieth century that all culture began in one or a few areas of the world and then spread outward.

Diluvialism, a school of thought, popular in the late eighteenth and early nineteenth centuries, claiming that Noah's flood accounted for the existence of extinct fossil forms.

Diploid number, the number of chromosomes normally found in the nucleus of somatic cells. In humans, the number is 46.

Displacement, the process by which sexual, aggressive, or other energies are diverted into other outlets. When these outlets are socially approved, the process is called sublimation.

Divergent evolution, the process by which an ancestral form gives rise to two or more differing descendant forms.

Divination, the use of magic to predict the behavior of another person or persons, or even the course of natural events.

Division of labor, the universally practiced allotment of different work tasks to members of a society. Even the least complex societies allot different tasks to the two sexes and also distinguish different age groups for work purposes.

Domesticants, domesticated plants and/or animals.

Dominance hierarchy, the social ranking order supposed to be present in most or all primate species.

Dominant allele, the version of a gene that masks out other versions' ability to affect the phenotype of an organism when both alleles co-occur heterozygotically.

Double descent, a form of descent by which an individual belongs to both patriline and a separate matriline, but usually exercises the rights of membership in each group separately and situationally.

Dowry, the wealth bestowed on the bride or the new couple by her parents.

Dryopithecus, a fossil ape that lived during the Miocene and Pliocene; the ancestor of the modern great apes.

Duality of patterning, a feature of human language, it consists of sequences of sounds which are themselves meaningless (phonemes) and also of units of meaning (morphemes).

Ecological niche, features of the environment(s) that an organism inhabits, which pose problems for the organism's survival.

Ecology, the science of the interrelationship between living organisms and their natural environments.

Ecosystem, a system containing both the physical environment and the organisms that inhabit it.

Egalitarian society, a society that makes all achieved statuses equally accessible to all its adult members.

Emics, the cognitive categories, logical constructs, and ideology used by a group in understanding its own culture (the "folk perspective").

Enculturation, the lifelong process of learning one's culture and its values, and how to act within the acceptable limits of behavior in culturally defined contexts.

Endogamy, the custom by which members of a group marry exclusively within the group.

Environment, all aspects of the surroundings in which an individual or group finds itself, from the geology, topography, and climate of the area to its vegetational cover and insect, bird, and animal life.

Estate system, in feudal Europe, the system under which nobles granted military protection and tenure of land to the peasants in return for the right to call on them for military service, for labor, and for rent payments.

Estrogens, the hormones, produced in relatively large quantities by the ovaries, which are responsible for the development of female secondary sex characteristics.

Estrous cycle, the reproductive cycle of the female primate, characterized by a period of sexual receptivity (estrus).

Ethnic group, a group of people within a larger social and cultural unit who identify themselves as a culturally and historically distinct entity, separate from the rest of that culture.

Ethnicity, the characteristic cultural, linguistic, and religious traditions that a given group of people use to establish their distinct social identity—usually within a larger social unit.

Ethnocentrism, preference toward one's own way of life versus all others, and judgment of other groups' life-styles (usually negatively) in terms of the value system of one's own life-style.

Ethnography, the exploration and description of the social and cultural systems of one particular group.

Ethnology, the comparative study and description of the forms of social organization and cultural systems of human groups.

Ethnomusicology, the study of music in specific contexts.

Ethnoscience, the study of the classification systems used by societies.

Ethnosemantics, the study of the ranges of meaning attached to specific terms and classes of terms by members of groups.

Etics, the cognitive categories, logical constructs, and ideology used by an outside analyst attempting to understand a group's culture (the "analytical perspective").

Evolution, the process of change that biological and social forms undergo as a consequence of their adaptations to their environments. In narrow genetic terms, evolution is the change in gene and allele frequencies within a breeding population over generations.

Evolutionary change, the transgenerational change that comes about when social or biological forms adapt to their environments.

Evolutionary progress (sometimes called general evolution), the process by which a social or biological form can respond to the demands of the environment by becoming more adaptable and flexible. In order to achieve this, the form must develop to a new stage of organization that makes it more versatile in coping with problems of survival posed by the environment.

Evolutionism, doctrines concerning the evolution of anything—the universe, chemical forms, biological forms, and society and culture.

Exchange marriage, usually describes the situation in which two men marry each other's sister. The term is sometimes used for more complicated patterns in which groups exchange women to provide wives for the men.

Exogamy, the custom by which members of a group regularly marry outside the group.

Extended family, a linking together of two or more nuclear families: horizontally, through a sibling link; vertically, through the parent-child link.

External controls, the set of mechanisms that induce individual conformity to group expectations by means of sanctions, or the responses a social group makes as a consequence of an individual's behavior.

False consciousness, a subjective group consciousness that does not accord with the group's objective situation.

Family, a married couple or other group of adult kinsfolk and their immature offspring, all or most of whom share a common dwelling and who cooperate economically.

Family of orientation, nuclear or elementary family (consisting of husband, wife, and offspring) into which the individual is born and reared, and in which he or she is considered a child in relation to the parents.

Family of procreation, nuclear or elementary family (consisting of husband, wife, and offspring) formed by the marriage of the individual, in which he or she is a parent.

Fatalism, the view that one's destiny is foreordained and immutable.

Female husband, a form of gender role alteration found in some African societies in which a woman assumes the social role of a husband within a socially recognized marriage.

Femininity, the culturally prescribed set of characteristics designated to be proper for females in a given society.

Feudalism, the sociopolitical system characterizing medieval Europe in which all land was owned by a ruling aristocracy that extracted money, goods, and labor (often forced) from the peasant class in return for letting the peasants till the soil.

Fictive kin, extension of the affect and social behavior usually shown toward genealogically related kin to particular persons with whom one has special relationships—godparents, blood brothers, and so on.

Field study, the principal methods by which anthropologists gather information, using either the participant observation technique to investigate social behavior, excavation techniques to retrieve archaeological data, or recording techniques to study languages.

Flake tool, a tool made by preparing a flint core, then striking it to knock off a flake, which then could be further worked to produce the particular tool needed.

Fluorine dating, a technique for the dating of fossils that relies on the principle that bones and teeth buried in soil gradually absorb fluorine from the groundwater in the earth. Fluorine intake varies with soil conditions, so fluorine dating is useful only to determine whether a fossil has been in the soil as long as other remains found in the same site.

Folklore, refers to a series of genres or types of cultural standardized stories transmitted from person to person (usually orally or by example).

Folk taxonomy, the cognitive categories and their hierarchical relations characteristic of a particular culture by which a specific group classifies all the objects of the universe it recognizes.

Foraging society, a society with an economy based solely on the collection of wild plant foods, the hunting of animals, and/or fishing.

Foramen magnum, the "large opening" in the cranium of vertebrates through which the spinal cord passes.

Forced labor, deprivation of an individual's or group's freedom for a specified period, during which time they are compelled to perform specific tasks.

Formalism, a school of thought maintaining that the principles of economics are general enough to be applied to all societies.

Formal negative sanction, deliberately organized, social punishment of individuals' behavior that usually takes the form of legal punishment.

Formal positive sanction, deliberately organized, social response to individuals' behavior that takes the form of a ceremony conveying social approval.

Formal sanction, socially organized (positive or negative) response to individuals' behavior that is applied in a very visible, patterned manner under the direct or indirect leadership of authority figures.

Fossils, remains of plant and animal forms that lived in the past and that have been preserved through a process by which they either leave impressions in stone or become stonelike themselves.

Free morpheme, a unit of meaning (represented by a sound sequence) that can stand alone.

Functionalism, a mode of analysis, used particularly in the social sciences, which attempts to explain social and cultural phenomena in terms of the contributions they make to the maintenance of sociocultural systems.

Functionalist anthropology, a perspective of anthropology associated with Bronislaw Malinowski and A. R. Radcliffe-Brown. The former emphasized the meeting of biological and psychological "needs," the latter social "needs."

Gametes, the sex cells which, as sperm in males and eggs in females, combine to form a new human being as a fetus in a mother's womb.

Gender identity, the attachment of significance to a self-identification as a member of a sexually defined group, and the adopting of behavior culturally appropriate to that group.

Gender role dimorphism, the maintenance of significant, culturally specified distinctions between female and male role behavior by a society.

Gender roles, socially learned behaviors that are typically manifested by persons of one sex and rarely by persons of the opposite sex in a particular culture.

Genealogy, the list of all living and deceased kinfolk to which a particular individual perceives himself or herself to be connected through consanguineal and affinal links.

Gene flow, the movement of genes from one breeding population to another as a result of interbreeding in cases where previous intergroup contact had been impossible or avoided due to geographical, social, cultural, or political barriers.

Gene pool, the sum total of all individuals' genotypes included within a given breeding population.

Generalized exchange (reciprocity), the giving of gifts without expecting a direct return, but in expectation of an "evening out" of gifts in the long run.

Generative grammar, a theory about a specific language that accounts in a formal manner for all the possible (permitted) strings of elements of that language, and also for the structural relationships among the elements constituting such strings.

Genes, the physical structures found along chromosomes that determine or set the potential for one or more biological or behavioral characteristics of the organism, and that are inherited as units.

Genetic drift, the shift of gene frequencies as a consequence of genetic sampling errors that come from the migration of small subpopulations away from the parent group, or natural disasters that wipe out a large part of a population.

Genitor, the male parent believed to be the biological father of a child.

Genotype, the genetic component that each individual inherits from his or her parents.

Gestalt theory of learning, the theory that understanding occurs when a whole idea or pattern is suddenly comprehended; the whole (the new insight) is considered to be greater than the mere sum ot its parts.

Gift exchange, the giving of a gift from one group or individual to another, with the expectation that the gift will be returned in similar form and quantity at the time or at a later date.

Glottochronology, a statistical method for dating language change (also known as lexicostatistics).

Gonadal sex, refers to the form, structure, and position of the hormone-producing gonads (ovaries located within the pelvic cavity in females and testes located in the scrotum in males).

Gorilla, the largest of the anthropoid (great) apes and of the living primates; found exclusively in Africa.

Government, the administrative apparatus of the political organization in a state-level society.

Gracile australopithecines, one of two lines of australopithecine development, first appearing about 3.5 million years ago; usually refers to the fossil forms *Australopithecus africanus* and *Australopithecus habilis,* which are widely thought to be directly ancestral to humans.

Grammar, according to Leonard Bloomfield, "the meaningful arrangements of forms in a language."

Great tradition, the formal, literate tradition of a civilization, which is maintained by the elite of the society and which is most important in the urban areas.

Grid system, method of retrieving and recording the positions of data from an archaeological "dig."

Hand ax, an unspecialized flint bifacial core tool, primarily characteristic of the Lower and Middle Paleolithic, made by chipping flakes off a flint nodule and using the remaining core as the tool; produced by *Homo erectus,* later by *Homo sapiens neanderthalensis.*

Hand ax tradition, a technological tradition developed out of the pebble tool tradition, occurring from about 600,000 to about 60,000 years ago during the Lower and Middle Paleolithic; primarily associated with *Homo erectus.* Also called chelloid tradition.

Haploid number, number of chromosomes normally occurring in the nucleus of a gamete (sex cell). For humans the number is 23 (one-half the diploid number).

Hardy-Weinberg law, the principle that in large breeding populations, under conditions of random mating and where natural selection is not operating, the frequencies of genes or alleles will remain constant from one generation to the next.

Hemoglobin, complex protein molecule that carries iron through the bloodstream, giving blood its red color.

Heredity (genetic), the innate capacity of an individual to develop characteristics possessed by its parents and other lineal ancestors.

Heritability, the proportion of the measurable variation in a given trait in a specified population estimated to result from hereditary rather than environmental factors.

Heterozygote, the new cell formed when the sperm and egg contain different alleles of the same gene.

Heterozygous chromosomes, chromosome pairs containing two different alleles of the same gene.

Historical linguistics, the study of the how, where, and when the languages of the world originated, the characteristics of extinct languages, and the phylogenetic relationships of contemporary languages to one another.

Historical particularist school, a school of anthropology, fathered by Franz Boas, which rejected the evolutionist schemes of the nineteenth century and argued that every culture should be studied as a unique whole with its own history and that the discovery of general processes of social development is difficult or impossible. *See also* Cultural relativism; Historicism.

Historicism, a school of theory that dominated American anthropology through the 1930s, emphasizing first-hand field research and knowledge of the specifics of cultural things and events. *See also* Historical particularist school.

Holistic approach, refers to the inclusive nature of anthropology's study of humanity, including biological, social, cultural, psychological, economic, political, ecological, and other factors.

Homeostasis, the process by which a system maintains its equilibrium using feedback mechanisms to accommodate inputs from its environment.

Hominid, the common name for those primates referred to in the taxonomic family *Hominidae* (modern humans and their nearest evolutionary predecessors).

Hominidae, human beings, one of families of *Hominoidea,* along with the great apes. *See also* Hominid.

Hominoidea, one of two superfamilies of *Catarrhini,* consisting of apes and human beings.

Homo erectus, a grade in human evolution occurring between approximately 1,000,000 and 300,000 years ago.

Homo habilis, see *Australopithecus habilis.*

Homo sapiens neanderthalensis, the first subspecies of *Homo sapiens* appearing some 300,000 years ago and becoming extinct about 35,000 B.P. *See also* Neanderthal man.

Homo sapiens sapiens, the second subspecies of *Homo sapiens,* including all contemporary humans, appearing about 60,000 years ago. The first human subspecies was the now extinct *Homo sapiens neanderthalensis.*

Homozygote, the new cell formed when the sperm and egg contain the same allele of a particular gene.

Homozygous chromosomes, chromosome pairs containing the same allele of a particular gene.

Horizontal extended family, a household and cooperating unit of two siblings and their respective spouses and children.

Hormonal sex, the type of hormone mix (estrogens or androgens) produced by the gonads.

Horticulture, the preparation of land for planting and the tending of crops using only the hoe or digging stick; especially the absence of use of the plow.

Hunting and gathering society, a society that subsists on the collection of plants and animals existing in the natural environment.

Hwame•, women among the Mohave Indians of the American Southwest who gained social and legal status very much like that of men.

Hybrid vigor, the phenomenon that occurs when a new generation, whose parent groups were from previously separated breeding populations, is generally healthier and larger than either of the parent populations.

Hylobatidae, the so-called lesser apes (gibbon and siamang); along with the great apes (chimpanzee, gorilla, orangutan), and humans, they make up the *Hominoidea.*

Hypothesis, a tentative assumption, that must be tested, about the relationship(s) between specific events or phenomena.

Ideology, a belief system linked to and legitimating the political and economic interests of the group that subscribes to it.

Imperialism, the expansionist policy of nation-states by which one state assumes political and economic control over another.

Incest, usually refers to mating between father and daughter, mother and son, or brother and sister. In some societies the definition is extended to include larger numbers of consanguineal relatives, especially if the society is organized along the principle of lineages and clans.

Incest taboo, the nearly universal prohibition against sexual intercourse between family members, with the limits of incest varying from culture to culture on the basis of the society's kinship system and forms of social organization.

Independent invention, the process whereby two or more cultures develop similar elements without the benefit of cultural exchange or even contact.

Indigenous peoples, persons who are born, reared in, and inhabit a specific country, in contradistinction to immigrants and temporary visitors.

Industrialism, form of production characterizing postagricultural societies in which goods are produced by mechanical means using machines and labor organized into narrowly defined task groups that engage in repetitive, physically simplified, and highly segmented work.

Industrialization, the process involving the growth of manufacturing industries in hitherto predominantly agrarian, pastoral, or hunting and gathering societies.

Industrial society, a society with a high degree of economic development that largely utilizes mechanization and highly segmented labor specialization for the production of its goods and services.

Infanticide, the killing of a baby soon after birth.

Informal sanction, a social response to an individual's behavior which is enacted individually by group members, with minimal organization by social authority.

Informant, a member of a society in which a social scientist is engaged in research and who establishes a working relationship with the fieldworker, providing him or her with information regarding that society.

Instrumental belief system, an organized set of ideas about phenomena necessary for survival and the enacting of day-to-day (functional) tasks.

Integration, cultural, the condition of harmonious pattern maintenance potentially characterizing cultural systems.

Intelligence, the ability of human beings and other animals to learn from experience and to solve problems presented by a changing environment.

Internalized controls, the individual's beliefs and values that mirror the beliefs and values of the group culture, and which induce the individual to behave in ways appropriate to that culture.

Invention, the development of new ideas, techniques, resources, aptitudes, or applications that are adopted by a society and become part of its cultural repertoire.

Involution (sometimes called specific evolution), evolution through which a biological or social form adapts to its environment by becoming more and more specialized and efficient in exploiting the resources of that environment.

Irrigation, the artificial use of water for agriculture by means of human technology when naturally available water (rainfall or seasonal flooding) is insufficient or potentially too destructive to sustain desired crop production.

Kibbutz, a collective settlement in Israel with strong emphasis on communal life and values; one of the forms of cooperative agricultural villages in Israel that is collective in the organization of work, ownership of all resources, child rearing, and living arrangements to a greater or lesser degree.

Kin category, a terminologically distinguished aggregate of persons with whom one might or might not have frequent interaction, but who are conceived to stand in a clearly understood genealogical relationship to the user of the term.

Kindred, egocentric network of relatives linked genealogically to ego in a culturally specified manner. Each such network is different for each ego, with the exception of siblings.

Kinesics, the study of body movement as a mode of communication.

Kin group, terminologically distinguished aggregate of persons with whom one stands in specified genealogical relationships and with whom one interacts frequently in terms of these relationships.

Kinship, the social phenomenon whereby people establish connections with each other on the basis of genealogical linkages in culturally specified ways.

Kinship terminology, the set of contrasting terms that designate the culturally significant genealogical linkages between people and the egocentric social networks these perceived relationships generate.

Kulturkreis, a "culture circle" consisting of a cluster of associated traits representing one stratum in the diffusion of culture complexes.

Latifundia, any large agrarian holding organized as a productive system with some form of managerial hierarchy and a separate labor supply that might consist of slaves, rural proletarians, or various forms of bound labor.

Leadership, a process of interaction between (1) the person who occupies a position in the social structure at the focal point of group decision making and (2) other members of that group.

Legal sanction, a formal, unpleasant, socially enacted response to an individual's or group's noncompliance with the law, or a legal decision meant to compel that compliance.

Legitimacy, a central notion in political anthropology describing the acceptance of established political power by the general population as morally right.

Leveling mechanism, a cultural device that results in a reduction of wealth differentials between individuals, such as the sponsoring of expensive religious celebrations by rich peasants.

Levirate, the practice by which a man is expected to marry the wife or wives of a deceased brother.

Lexicostatistics, a method for investigating the historical relationship between languages, making use of statistical analyses of linguistic similarities and differences.

Lineage, a unilineal consanguineal kin group tracing descent from a known ancestor and found in two forms: patrilineage, where the relationship is traced through males; and matrilineage, where the relationship is traced through females.

Linguistic anthropology, a subfield of anthropology entailing the study of language across space and time and its relation to culture and social behavior.

Linguistics, the study of language, consisting of two large subcategories: (1) historical linguistics, which is concerned with the evolution of languages and language groups through time, and with reconstructing extinct protolanguages from which historically known languages differentiated; and (2) descriptive linguistics, which focuses on recording, transcribing, and analyzing the structures of languages distributed across the world today.

Little tradition, the localized cultures of rural villagers living in the broader cultural and social contexts of mass, industrial society, with its "great tradition." Currently the term is not used much because it is very ethnocentric.

Lower Paleolithic, the earliest subdivision of the Paleolithic prehistoric age, dating roughly from about 3 million to 200,000 years ago, and characterized by early pebble tools and hand axes.

Magic, the usually ritualized behavior that is intended to control, or at least to significantly influence, the basic processes of the universe without recourse to perceptibly instrumental acts.

Mana, a diffuse force or energylike entity that suffuses through various objects, places, and even people; recognized in various parts of the world, but especially well known in Polynesia and Melanesia.

Market economy, a system in which goods and services are exchanged and their relative values established in market places, generally via the use of money as a standard of value.

Market exchange, the process of distribution of goods and services and the establishing of their relative value (frequently in terms of money) at centers of activity known as markets.

Marriage, a difficult term to define, given enormous cross-cultural variety. However, all societies recognize (publicly) connections between two or more persons that confer social legitimacy to children—which is the basic minimum of marriage.

Masculinity, the set of culturally prescribed personal characteristics deemed proper for males in a society.

Matriarchy, a form of family organization characterized by the domination of domestic life or society as a whole by women.

Matricentric family, a family that is headed by a woman, often serially married to a number of men.

Matriclans, clans based on matrilineal descent.

Matrilateral prescriptive cross-cousin marriage, the rule by which a man must choose his spouse from among his mother's brother's daughters or their social equivalents.

Matrilineage, a kinship group made up of people all of whom trace relationships to one another through female links and are descended from a known female ancestor.

Matrilineal descent, the principle by which lineal kin links are traced exclusively through females—that is, a child is descended from his or her mother, mother's mother, and so on.

Matrilocal residence, the practice by which a newlywed couple moves into residence with, or in the locale of, the bride's mother's kin group.

Mazeway, a term coined by Anthony F. C. Wallace to designate each person's perception of his or her own cognitive system and its relationships to the cognitive system that the individual perceives to be shared by other members of his or her group.

Meiosis, the formation of new sex cells by the division of a cell into four new cells, with each new cell containing half the number of chromosomes of the original cell.

Melanin, the brown, granular substance found in the skin, hair, and some internal organs (for example, the liver and kidneys) that gives a brownish tint or color to the areas in which it is found.

Mesolithic, a term of convenience used by archaeologists to designate immediately preagricultural societies in the Old World; a frequently used diagnostic characteristic is the presence of microliths, small blades often set into bone or wood handles to make sickles for the harvesting of wild grains. In Europe it also featured the invention of the bow and arrow as a response to the emergence of forests with the shift from Pleistocene to Holocene climate.

Messianic movement, a revitalization movement based on the belief that a person or god will arrive to cure the evils of the world.

Mestizo, a term originally used to designate the offspring of a Spaniard and an Indian. The meaning has expanded to include all persons of mixed Spanish (or Portuguese) and Amerindian ancestry. In Latin America the term is also often used to designate rural villagers who are adopting urban cultural traits that are differentiating them from traditionalist Indians.

Metallurgy, the techniques of separating metals from their ores and working them into finished products.

Microlith, a small stone tool made from bladelettes or fragments of blades, associated with the Mesolithic period, approximately 13,000 to 6,000 B.C.

Middle Paleolithic, the age of *Homo sapiens neanderthalensis* and Mousteroid culture, occurring between approximately 300,000 and 35,000 years ago.

Migration, a permanent or semipermanent change of residence by a group, usually involving movement over large distances.

Millenarianism, revivalistic movement reacting to the perceived disparity between ideal and real social conditions, with the belief that this gap is about to close, usually with disastrous consequences for nonbelievers.

Milpa, technique of slash-and-burn horticulture as used by Maya Indians to make gardens in forested areas.

Minifundia, the tiny, often fragmented agrarian production units held under various tenure contracts.

Minority, a group that is distinguished from the larger society of which it is a part by particular traits such as language, national origin, religion, values, or customs. May also be used to refer to groups that, though a plurality in numbers, are nevertheless discriminated against socially, politically, and/or economically by the society's dominant patterns (e.g., women in the U.S.).

Mitosis, a form of somatic cell division by which a parent cell produces new cells with exactly the same number of chromosome pairs as the original parent cell.

Modernization, the process whereby traditional social units (such as tribes or villagers) are integrated into larger, overarching units (such as nation-states), while at the same time being split into units of production (such as factories) and consumption (such as nuclear families) that are characteristic of industrial societies.

Moiety, the name used to refer to a group that is one of two units of a larger group (for example, each clan of a society composed of two clans is a moiety). Both groups are usually, but not always, based on unilineal descent, and exogamous.

Money, a medium of exchange characteristic of market economies that is easily replaceable and/or exchangeable for another of like kind, portable, divisible into combinable units, and accepted by all participants in the market system in which it is used.

Mongoloid spot, a purplish-blue spot at the base of the spine that appears on some infants at birth; a trait common among peoples of Asia and also Native Americans.

Monogamy, the marriage rule that permits both the man and the woman only one spouse at a time.

Mores, important norms of a society, they have compelling social and emotional commitment and are deeply rooted in its belief system.

Morpheme, the smallest unit of meaning in a language.

Morphological sex, the physical appearance of a person's genitals and secondary sex characteristics.

Mousterian culture, a group of European Middle Paleolithic assemblages characterized by prepared-core flake tools, dating from somewhat more than 80,000 to less than 40,000 years ago.

Multilinear evolution, the study of cultural evolution recognizing regional variation and divergent evolutionary sequences.

Mutation, any change in the molecular composition of a gene or allele that expresses itself in the phenotype and is passed on to the next generation.

Myths, sacred tales or narratives that usually deal with the issue of origins (of nature, society, humans) and/or transformations.

National character, personality characteristics shared by the inhabitants of a nation.

Nativism, a revitalization movement initiated by members of a society to eliminate foreign persons, customs, and objects in order to improve their own way of life.

Natural selection, the process by which those organisms or groups of organisms that have the ability to survive and procreate in a given environment do so at the expense of those that lack the ability, with the result that the special qualities that allow some forms to survive and procreate would, over the generations, become outstanding characteristics of the entire group.

Neanderthal man (*Homo sapiens neanderthalensis*), a sub-species of *Homo sapiens* living from approximately 300,000 years ago to approximately 35,000 years ago, and thought to have descended from an earlier hominid called *Homo erectus. See also Homo sapiens neanderthalensis.*

Negative reciprocity, a form of gift exchange in which the giver attempts to get the better of the exchange.

Negative sanction, a punitive social response to individual behavior that does not meet with group approval.

Neighborhood association, a unit of social organization consisting of a group of households in a designated area that is part of a larger entity (for instance, a city) that share a number of mutual rights and obligations.

Neoclassicists, a new school of geneticists who propose that most of the molecular variations in natural populations are selectively neutral.

Neoevolutionism, an anthropological school of thought that proposes a return to the search for universal laws of culture change.

Neolithic, the stage in cultural evolution generally marked by the appearance of ground stone tools and frequently by the domestication of plants and animals, starting some 10,000 years ago.

Neolocal residence, the practice by which a newlywed couple is expected to establish its own independent residence, living with neither the husband's nor the wife's parents or relatives.

Neontology, a division of physical anthropology that concerns itself with the comparative biology of living primates, including population genetics, ecological pressures, body shapes (morphology), and the extent to which behavior is biologically programed.

Network study, the analysis of interpersonal relations, usually focused on a particular individual (ego), which examines the character of interactions between ego and other individuals.

Neutral mutations, a commonly occurring category of mutations that have no effect on the phenotype of the organism.

Nomadism, a characteristic trait associated with a number of ecologically adaptive systems in which continuing residential mobility is necessary for the subsistence of the group, with a resulting lack of permanent abode.

Nonverbal communication, the transmission of communication between organisms without the use of speech. Modes of communication include gesturing (with voice and body) and the manipulation of space between the communicating organisms.

Norm, a standard shared by members of a social group to which members are expected to conform.

Nuclear family, a small social unit consisting of a husband and wife and their children, typical of a monogamous marriage with neolocal residence; also forms a functioning subunit of extended and otherwise composite families.

Obligatio, one of four features of a legal decision identified by Leopold Pospisil, conferring rights on one party of a dispute and obligation on the other.

Oldowan culture, oldest recognized Lower Paleolithic assemblage, whose type site is Olduvai Gorge (Tanzania), dating from about 2,200,000 to 1,000,000 years ago and comprising unifacial core (pebble) tools and crude flakes.

Omaha kinship terminology, a system of classifying kinspeople most often associated with patrilineal descent organization.

Open system, a stratification system in which an individual may legitimately hope to change his or her status through personal efforts.

Orangutan, an Asian anthropoid ape, intermediate in size between the chimpanzee and gorilla.

Ovaries, the female gonads, located within the pelvic cavity.

Paleolithic (old Stone Age), the period of time (about 2.5 million to 10,000 B.C.) during which chipped stone tools, but not ground stone tools, were made.

Paleontology, the study of the fossil evidence of primate (including human) evolution.

Palynology, the study of fossilized pollen, used by archaeologists for dating and reconstructing paleoenvironments.

Paradigm, represents the underlying structure of a discipline—expressed in basic theories, laws, and generalizations, methods of research and evaluation, and instruments used for measuring and observing, which serves to define the problems of the discipline, the appropriate research methods, the nature of the data that are gathered, and the kind of explanations that are finally produced.

Parallel cousins, cousins linked by ascending generation relatives (often parental siblings) of the same generation and sex—for example, mother's sister's or father's brother's children.

Parallel evolution, the development of similar cultural traits among peoples with no (known) contact and between whom there has been no (known) cultural diffusion.

Parapithecus, one of several primate fossil populations found in the Fayum disposits in Egypt; thought to be ancestral to modern monkeys.

Participant observation, an ethnographic field research method wherein the ethnographer is immersed in and takes part in the day-to-day activities of the community being studied.

Pastoralism, a type of ecological adaptation found in geographically marginal areas of Europe, Asia, and Africa where natural resources cannot support agriculture, and hence the people are partially or entirely devoted to the care and herding of animals.

Patriarchy, a form of family organization in which power and authority are vested in the males, and in which descent is usually in the male line, with the children being members of the father's lineage, clan, or tribe.

Patrilateral parallel cousin marriage, marriage between brothers' children.

Patrilineage, an exogamous descent group based on genealogical links between males that are traceable back to a known male ancestor.

Patrilineal descent, the principle by which lineal kin links are traced through males—that is, a child is descended from his or her father, father's father, and so forth.

Patrilocal residence, a postmarital residence rule by which a newlywed couple takes up permanent residence with or near the groom's father's extended kin group.

Peasants, rural, agricultural members of civilizations who maintain a very traditional life-style (often rejecting urban values) while tied into the wider economic system of the whole society through markets where they sell their produce and purchase goods.

Pebble tool, the first manufactured stone tools consisting of somewhat larger than fist-sized pieces of flint that have had some six or seven flakes knocked off them; unifacial core tools; associated with *Australopithecus habilis* in Africa and also *Homo erectus* in East Asia.

Peonage, the state of indebtedness in which a tenant family's debts and the obligations bound to them are passed on from generation to generation.

Phenotype, all of a person's observable and measurable characteristics, such as eye color, hair color, body shape, behavior, physiological qualities, and biochemical processes.

Phonemes, indivisible, but in themselves meaningless, units of sound that are arranged in sequences to make up larger units, such as morphemes and words.

Phones, the sounds occurring in a speech utterance.

Phonetic features of sounds, phones described in terms of the physical processes by which they are produced, usually in terms of the points and organs of articulation.

Phonetic laws, patterns of change in the sounds used by languages as they evolved, expressed as rules or principles of change.

Phonological system, the articulatory phonetics and the phonemic system of a language.

Phonology, the combined study of phonetics and phonemics.

Phratry, a unilineal descent group composed of at least two clans claiming to be related by kinship. When there are only two such clans, each is called a moiety.

Phylogeny, the tracing of the history of the evolutionary development of a life form.

Physical anthropology, the study of human beings as biological organisms across space and time. Physical anthropology is divided into two areas: (1) paleontology, which is the study of the fossil evidence of primate evolution, and (2) neontology, which is the comparative biology of living primates.

Platyrrhini, one of two infraorders of the primate suborder *Anthropoidea,* consisting of all the New World monkeys (such as the spider monkey); characterized by vertical nostrils and often prehensile tails.

Pleistocene, earlier of two epochs (Pleistocene, Holocene) which together compose the Quaternary period; from perhaps 3,500,000 to 10,000 years ago.

Pliopithecus, a fossil ape appearing in Europe, Asia, and Africa from about 26 to 12 million years ago.

Plow, an agricultural tool generally requiring animal power, used to loosen, aerate, and invert the soil so as to cover weeds, expose a large area of soil to weathering, and prepare a seed bed. Its presence differentiates agriculture from horticulture (limited to digging sticks and hoes).

Pluralism, a characteristic of many complex societies, marked by the presence of several or numerous subgroups that coexist within a common political and economic system.

Political anthropology, the field of cultural anthropology that deals with that aspect of social behavior known as political organization, and concerns itself specifically with the organization and management of the public affairs of a society, especially pertaining to the sources and uses of power.

Political economy, the interpretation of the economy and the system of power and authority in a society, most frequently studied from a conflict theory perspective.

Political organization, that subsystem of social organization that specifically relates to the individuals or groups responsible for managing the affairs of public policy, or who control the appointment or action of those individuals or groups.

Polyandrous family, a family in which a woman has more than one husband at the same time.

Polyandry, a relatively rare form of multiple marriage in which a woman has more than one husband at the same time.

Polygamy, any form of marriage in which more than two persons are married.

Polygynous family, a family in which a man has more than one wife at the same time.

Polygyny, the most common form of multiple marriage, allowing one man to have more than one wife at the same time.

Polytypic species, a species with a widespread geographic location and an uneven distribution of its genetic variants among its local breeding populations.

Pongid, a common term for the members of the *Pongidae* family, including the three great apes; the orangutan, the gorilla, and the chimpanzee.

Positive sanctions, a social response to individual behavior that comes in some form of reward.

Positivism, an approach to knowledge embodying the scientific method, with its built-in tests for truth.

Possession, a trance state based on the culturally supported belief that curative or malevolent spirits may displace people's personalities and use their bodies as vehicles for temporary residence.

Potassium-argon (KA) method of dating, a method of physical-chemical dating that employs the decay of radioactive potassium (with a half-life of 1.3 billion $\pm$ 40 million years) to inert argon, allowing the approximate absolute dating of volcanic rocks and ash falling in the time range of 10,000 to more than 4 billion years ago.

Potlatch, ceremonial feasting accompanied by the giving of gifts to guests according to rank that was practiced by the Indians of the northwest coast area of the United States and Canada; a form of economic redistribution.

Power, political, the ability of leaders to compel compliance with their orders.

Pragmatics, the relationship(s) between signs and their users. The study of pragmatics is the study of how communication affects people.

Premarital sex, sexual intercourse between persons, one or both of whom has never been married.

Primates, the order of mammals that includes humans, the apes, Old and New World monkeys, and prosimians.

Primatologist, one who studies primates.

Private identity, the subjective sense of one's own personal continuity through time and some perception of one's own characteristics.

Profane, all that which is ordinary, or not sacred.

Projective instrument, a personality test that allows the subject to project his or her unconscious hopes, fears, or fantasies onto some carefully controlled stimulus.

Proletariat, the broad mass of people without access to the means of production and distribution and little voice in the political decisions of industrial, capitalist societies.

Prosimii (prosimian), the most primitive suborder ot the order of primates, including lemurs, lorises, tarsiers, and similar creatures.

Protestant Ethic, a set of values, originally associated with the rise and spread of Protestantism in Europe, which celebrates the virtues of self-discipline, hard work, initiative, acquisitiveness, and thrift.

Proxemics, the study of the manipulation and meaning of space.

Psychological sex, the self-image that a person holds about his or her own sexual identity.

Race, a folk category of the English language that refers to discrete groups of human beings who are categorically separated from one another on the basis of arbitrarily selected phenotypic traits.

Racial minorities, groups that are categorically separated from the majority members of the larger society on the basis of arbitrarily selected phenotypic traits.

Radioactive carbon dating, physical-chemical dating method that makes use of radioactive carbon present in all plants; good for dating remains from 50,000 to 5,000 years old.

Ramapithecus, a late Miocene hominid living some 10 to 14 million years ago in open woodland areas from Africa to India; regarded by many scientists as the earliest known hominid.

Random (genetic) drift, shift in gene and allele frequencies in a population due to sampling "error." When a small breeding population splits off from a larger one, its collection of genes may not adequately represent the frequencies of the larger population. These differences compound over succeeding generations, until the two populations are quite distinct. Along with mutation, gene flow, and natural selection, random drift is one of the mechanisms of organic evolution.

Rank society, a society in which there is equality of access to land and other economic resources, but unequal access to positions of prestige.

Recessive allele, version of a gene that is not able to influence an organism's phenotype when it is homologous with another version of the gene. *See also* Dominant allele.

Reciprocity, the giving and receiving of gifts, usually consisting of material items, favors, or specific forms of labor.

Redistribution, the enforced giving of surplus goods to a centralized authority, who then distributes them back to members of the society according to social conventions and his own predilections.

Reference group, the aggregate of people that an individual uses for comparison when assessing or evaluating their own and others' behavior.

Relative age, an element of some kin terminological systems that distinguishes kinspersons by their order of birth.

Relative dating, methods of archaeological analysis designed to determine sequences of deposition of cultural remains. There are two forms: seriation and stratigraphy.

Religious beliefs, the sets of convictions held by members of a society with regard to the supernatural, transcendental, and fundamental issues, such as life's meaning.

Revitalization movements, religious movements of a reformative nature that arise among exploited or disorganized groups (often after socioeconomic or political traumas) and that attempt to reinject culturally salient meaning into people's lives—often through a radical assault on existing conditions and/or institutions.

Revivalistic movement, a revitalization movement espousing the reintroduction of previous religious (or political) forms.

Rites of passage, rituals marking changes in status or social position undergone as a person passes through the culturally recognized life phases of his or her society.

Rites of solidarity, various rituals, usually but not necessarily religious, which in addition to their intended purposes also develop and maintain feelings of group solidarity among participants.

Rituals, culturally prescribed, consistently repeated, patterned sequences of (group) behavior.

Robust australopithecines, one of two lines of australopithecines, appearing some 3.5 million years ago and surviving until approximately 1 million years ago or even later; thought to have embodied two successive species: *Australopithecus robustus* and *Australopithecus boisei.*

Role conflict, the emotional stress experienced by a person whose socially expected behaviors are irreconcilable. This happens when a person occupies diverse social positions (statuses) yet in a given situation must act in terms of two or more (for instance, a lawyer who is also a mother asked by the court to defend a person accused of rape).

Roles, the expected (normative) behaviors that every society associates with each of its statuses.

Rorschach test, a projective test consisting of a series of inkblots, sometimes with quite elaborate shapes, that the subject is asked to identify. The subject's responses often reveal his or her underlying concerns and anxieties, and perhaps also basic personality configurations.

Sacred, a category of things, actions, and so on set apart as holy and entitled to reverence.

Sanctions, the responses a social group makes as a consequence of an individual's behavior.

Scapulimancy, a form of divination involving the forecasting of future events by a shaman's "reading" of the cracks in the burnt scapula (shoulder bone) of an animal.

Scientific racism, research strategies based on the assumption that groups' biological features underlie significant social and cultural differences. Not surprisingly, this kind of research always manages to find "significant" differences between "races."

Secondary sex characteristics, physiological changes developing at and after puberty, such as body hair, breasts, and voice changes.

Self-concept, a person's perceptions and evaluative feelings about his or her continuity, boundaries, and qualities.

Semantics, the relationship between signs and what they represent; the study of semantics is essentially the study of meaning.

Semantic universality, a concept used to describe a nonexistent phenomenon: the existence of a specific unit of meaning in all known cultures in the world.

Semiotic, the study of signs and sign-using behavior in general.

Serfdom, a system of peonage, operating through the mechanism of land residency, whereby serfs owe their landlords work simply because they live on lands to which the landlord holds legal title.

Serfs, members of feudal society who owed their labor and a portion of their produce to the landowner on whose property they lived and on whom they relied for protection.

Serial marriage, the process by which a man or woman marries and divorces a series of partners in succession.

Sexual dimorphism, differences in bodily features and size according to sex.

Sexual identity, the expectations about male and female behavior, established in children by the age of six, which affect the individual's learning ability, choice of work, and feelings about herself or himself.

Shamanism, the process by which certain gifted persons establish (usually with the aid of a trance or an ecstatic state of excitement) direct communication with the supernatural for the benefit of their social group.

Sickle-cell anemia, a genetically inherited disease showing a high level of balanced polymorphism found among populations whose ancestors came from regions of the world infested by malaria, especially Africa and the Arabian peninsula. When heterozygous with a normal hemoglobin allele, the trait produces a somewhat sickly person who has great resistance to malaria, however. When a person is homozygous for the sickle-cell allele, he or she may easily die at a young age due to extreme anemia.

Sign, an object, gesture, or sound that represents something else.

Silent trade, a form of exchange with no face-to-face interaction between the parties involved, often practiced where potential for conflict between groups exists. Traded items are simply left at agreed-upon places by both parties.

Site, a confined geographical area of interest to archaeologists in which are concentrated remains of past human activity. Some sites, of course, contain remains that do not deal with humans but are still interesting to scientists—dinosaur deposits, for instance.

Slash-and-burn agriculture, shifting cultivation, with recurrent clearing and burning of forests and planting of domesticates in the burnt fields; also called swidden farming.

Slavery, an extreme form of coerced work organization wherein the rights to people and their labor are owned by others, and both subordinate and superordinate positions are inherited.

Social class, a stratum in a social hierarchy based on differential group access to the means of production and control over distribution; usually but not necessarily endogamous, with little—but some—openness.

Social control, practices that induce members of a society to conform to the expected behavior patterns of their culture; also, mechanisms through which a society's rulers ensure the masses' conformity with the rules of the social order.

Social density, one measure of urban density that includes the number of culturally differentiated roles and the number of relationships each person has with other individuals.

Social identity, the socially recognized characteristics of a person that indicate his or her social position(s).

Socialism, a social form characterized by public ownership of all strategic resources and major distribution mechanisms. It features centralized economic and social planning, and is conceived by some Marxists to be a transitional stage to communism, when centralized bureaucracies will "wither away."

Social mobility, the upward or downward movement of individuals or groups of individuals in a society consisting of social hierarchies and unequal distribution of such social resources as occupations, education, power, and wealth.

Social organization, the ordering of social relations within social groups whereby individuals' choices and decisions are visibly patterned.

Social stratification, an arrangement of statuses or groups within a society into a pattern of socially superior and inferior ranks or groups that are open to a greater or lesser degree.

Social structure, the total pattern of ego-centered relationships (such as kinship systems and friendship networks) that occur within a society.

Societal structure, the total aggregate of discrete, bounded subgroups that compose a society.

Society, a socially bounded, spatially contiguous aggregation of people who participate in a number of overarching institutions and share to some degree an identifiable culture, and that contains within its boundaries some means of production and units of consumption—with relative stability across generations.

Sociolinguistics, the study of the societal correlates to variations in the patterning of linguistic behavior.

Somatic cells, the cells that make up all the bodily parts and that are constantly dying and being replaced; does not include central nervous system cells or sex cells.

Sorcery, a negatively shaded term to refer to magic—the use of supernatural agencies—to further the practicioner's goals.

Sororal polygyny, a marriage involving two or more sisters as wives of the same man at one time.

Sororate, the practice by which women are expected to marry the husband of a deceased sister.

Spacing mechanisms, the behaviors between neighboring groups of animals that help to maintain them at some distance from each other.

Species, an aggregate of organisms or populations capable of interbreeding and producing fertile offspring but not able to achieve this with members of other such aggregates.

Speech community, an aggregate of persons who share a set of conventions about how verbal communication is to take place.

State, a set of institutions in a stratified society that operates to maintain the status quo by: (1) organizing the provision of needed services, (2) planning the production and use of needed resources, (3) quelling internal discontent by buying off or subduing rebellious minorities or subordinate classes, and (4) organizing, administering, and financing the protection of the society against hostile external forces.

Statuses, the interrelated positions in a social structure or hierarchy, with each position carrying certain expectations of behavior (roles) with respect to those persons occupying the same and/or interrelated positions.

Stereoscopic vision, overlapping fields of vision resulting when the eyes are located toward the front of the skull, producing depth perception.

Stereotype, the attribution of certain presumed invariable personality or behavioral characteristics to all members of a particular group, most notably those groups defined by religion, sex, nationality, or ethnicity.

Stimulus diffusion, the spread of cultural traits beyond the groups with which the originating culture had direct contact.

Strategic resources, the category of resources vital to a group's survival.

Stratified society, a society in which there is structured inequality of access among groups not only to power and prestige, but also to the strategic resources that sustain life.

Stratigraphy, the arrangement of geological or archaeological deposits in superimposed layers or strata.

Structural-functionalism, an anthropological school of thought most prominently associated with its founder, A. R. Radcliffe-Brown; it emphasized the mutual interdependence of all parts and subgroups of a society, interpreting relationships between such groupings as contributing to the ongoing pattern maintenance of the society.

Structuralism, an analytical approach based on the assumption that observed phenomena are specific instances of the underlying, generalized principles of relationship or structure. Most prominently promoted by Claude Lévi-Strauss, the famous French ethnologist.

Structural linguistics, the study of the basic elements and rules for their combination that characterize the languages of the world today. Usually conceived to consist of phonology, syntactics, morphology, and semantics.

Subculture, culture of a subgroup of a society that shares its fundamental values, but which also has its own distinctive folkways, mores, values, and world view.

Subsistence farmers, those farmers whose efforts, regardless of their aspirations, yield only enough food to sustain their household units without significant capital gains.

Subsistence strategies, technological skills, tools, and behavior that a society uses to meet its subsistence needs.

Substantivists, a group of economic anthropologists who deny that economic models derived from developed market economies can be universally applied to all economic systems.

Supernatural, all things that are believed to exist but are beyond verifiability through the human senses.

Supernatural beliefs, organized systems of thoughts, ideas, and concerns regarding entities whose existence is not verifiable through the human senses.

Supernatural practices, that realm of human behavior deriving its meaning or significance from the relationship(s) that participants or onlookers believe to exist between the behavior and elements that are believed to exist but are beyond verification through the human senses.

Supraorbital ridge, the torus or bony bar surmounting orbital cavities which is large and continuous in apes and quite small and divided in *Homo sapiens.*

Surplus farmers, farmers whose subsistence techniques allow them to produce more than they can consume, and who are thus able to barter away or sell their surplus for goods—or to reinvest in their expending enterprise.

Swidden farming, shifting cultivation, with recurrent clearing and burning of vegetation and planting in the burnt fields. Fallow periods for each plot last many times longer than the periods of cultivation.

Symbiotic relationship, a relationship in which two dissimilar social or biological entities live together in a mutually beneficial way.

Symbol, a sign that represents some other (complex) thing with which it has no intrinsic connection.

Synchronics, the systematic comparison of ethnographic materials across a wide range of cultures at one arbitrarily selected point in time.

Syncretism, the combination into one system of belief and practice cultural elements from previously diverse sources.

Syntax, the relationships between signs. The study of syntax is the study of the rules of sequence and combination of signs.

Taboo (tabu), the belief in negative supernatural consequences that attach to the performance of certain acts or the violation of certain objects or places.

Technology, a society's use of knowledge, skills, implements, and sources of power in order to exploit and partially control the natural environment, and to engage in production and reproduction of its goods and services.

Tell, a large mound artificially created by successive levels of occupation, resulting in a highly stratified site.

Tenancy, a form of forced agricultural labor under which farmers plant their crops in the landowner's fields but owe the landowner a certain proportion of the crops they harvest.

Testes, the male gonads, suspended outside the body cavity in the scrotum.

Thalassemia, like sickle-cell anemia, a blood anemia carried by populations that are or have been in malaria-infested areas of the world—expecially around the Mediterranean, Asia Minor, and southern Asia. Also represents an example of balanced polymorphism, like sickle-cell anemia.

Thematic Apperception Test, a projective technique consisting of a series of drawings of people, usually in situations of interpersonal interaction. The subject is asked to make up stories about the various pictures, and the themes of these stories give the analyst clues to the subject's basic personality traits.

Third World, originally referred to non-Western peoples of the colonized societies of Asia, Africa, and Latin America. More recently, the term has also been associated with national minorities within the United States and Canada, such as Chicanos, blacks, Native Americans, Puerto Ricans, and Asian-Americans.

Totemism, the symbolic association of plants, animals, and objects with groups of people, especially the association of exogamous clans with animal species as their emblems and/or mythological ancestors.

Trade, the exchange of goods between people.

Traditionalism, the organizing of behavior in terms of standards derived from the past.

Transcendental belief system, a belief system providing people with organized ideas regarding states of existence inherently beyond the capacities of their senses to register, and about things that it is impossible for them to learn from their personal experience.

Transhumance, the seasonal migration of domesticated livestock and their herders for the purpose of grazing different pastures at different times of the year, usually rotation between highlands and lowlands.

Tribalism, the orientation toward tribal membership—rather than toward citizenship in nation-states—as the criterion of political allegiance and behavior.

Tribe, a relatively small group of people (small society) that share a culture, speak a common language or dialect, and share a perception of their common history and uniqueness. Often a term used to refer to unstratified social groups with a minimum of or no centralized political authority at all.

Typology, a method of classifying objects according to hierarchically arranged sets of diagnostic criteria.

Underdevelopment, the condition of state-level societies that have been exploited by the industrialization of the European, American, and Japanese nations, and have failed to benefit from industrialization themselves.

Undifferentiated system, a social system in which the ascriptive qualities of sex, age, or kinship determine social relations in most domains of society.

Uniformitarianism, originally (1785) called the Huttonian theory, which proposed that the key to the past geological history of the earth could be found by examining the existing forces at work. Principally, associated with the 19th century geologist Charles Lyell.

Unilineal descent, the reckoning of kinship connections through either exclusively female (matrilineal descent) or male (patrilineal descent) links.

Unilineal evolution, the theory that all human societies evolve through specific stages that are usually defined in terms of the occurrence of increasingly complex social and cultural elements.

Upper Paleolithic culture, the culture produced by modern *Homo sapiens sapiens,* beginning about 35,000 B.C. It is characterized by pervasive blade tool production, an "explosion" of artistic endeavors (cave painting), highly organized large-game hunting, and the efficient exploitation of previously uninhabited ecological niches—including the population of the New World, perhaps beginning as early as 20,000 years ago.

Urban anthropology, the application of anthropological research techniques and methods of analysis to the study of people living in cities.

Urbanism, an ill-defined term designating those qualities of life that presumably characterize all urban life-styles.

Urbanization, the worldwide process of urban growth at the expense of rural populations.

Uterine kin, kin related to one through female links.

Uxorilocal residence, the practice by which a newlywed couple takes up residence near the bride's mother's family but does not become a subordinate group contained within a larger extended family.

Values, the ideals of a culture that are concerned with correct goals and behavior.

Verbal communication, the uniquely human use of language to communicate.

Vertical extended family, a family in which parents, their married children, and their grandchildren share a residence and constitute a functioning social unit.

Virilocal residence, the practice by which a newlywed couple moves near the residence of the groom's father but does not become a subordinate group contained within a larger extended family.

Voluntary association, a group of persons who join together for a common objective or on the basis of a mutual interest.

Wernicke's area, the brain site where verbal comprehension takes place, located in the temporal lobe of the dominant hemisphere.

Westernization, the transplanting of Western European—American institutions to developing countries.

Witchcraft, the use of magic to control the behavior of another person or persons.

World view (*Weltanshauung*), the corpus of beliefs about the world shared by the members of a society, and represented in their myths, lore, ceremonies, social conduct, general values, and so on.

Yeomanry, in feudal societies, those who were granted special privileges in land and produce in exchange for military service in the militia of the lord.

Zinjanthropus, 1.75-million-year-old australopithecine fossil found in Kenya by Mary Leakey and thought to be a form of *Australopithecus robustus.*

About the Authors

David E. Hunter served as Academic Editor and Graphics Conceptualizer for *The Study of Anthropology.* He is the author of Chapter 2, "Human Biological and Cultural Evolution," Chapter 7, "Communication: Verbal and Nonverbal," Chapter 10, "Subsistence and Trade: Economic Anthropology," Chapter 12, "Behavior Control: Formal and Informal Sanctions," Chapter 13, "Belief Systems: The Sacred and the Profane," and Chapter 20, "Fieldwork I: Participant Observation in a Swiss Peasant Community," and is the co-author of Chapter 1, "The Study of Anthropology," and Chapter 17, "Peace and Conflict." Mr. Hunter received the B.A. degree *magna cum laude* in anthropology from the University of Arizona in 1965, and both his graduate degrees in cultural anthropology at Yale University: the M.Phil. in 1967 and the Ph.D. in 1970. His anthropological fieldwork consists of two periods of research among mountain peasants in Central Switzerland. An Associate Professor at Southern Connecticut State College, he is the author of a number of theoretical and ethnographic articles, has co-edited *Anthropology: Contemporary Perspectives* (1975) and *Encyclopedia of Anthropology* (1976), and co-authored *Doing Anthropology: A Student-Centered Approach to Cultural Anthropology* (1976), and devoted himself to the teaching of anthropology as a perspective on life and living—rather than "merely" as an academic discipline. He is currently living alone after four years of communal life. His principal form of recreation is Shotokan Karate-do, which he studies and teaches several times a week, and he currently is writing a novel.

Phillip Whitten served as Editor of *The Study of Anthropology,* and is co-author of Chapter 1, "The Study of Anthropology," and Chapter 17, "Peace and Conflict." Mr. Whitten earned his doctorate from Harvard University and has also received masters degrees from Harvard and from San Jose State University. For four years he worked as an editor and publisher with two publishing houses. He is the author or co-author of over forty articles and books, including *Anthropology: Contem-*

porary Perspectives (1975), *Encyclopedia of Anthropology* (1976), *Race and Politics in South Africa* (1976), and several children's books. He has also produced two educational films, one of which, "Learning," won the 1972 Merit Award of the American Psychological Association for "best educational film of the year." Currently he is serving as Series Editor for Harper and Row's "Contemporary Perspectives" reader series. A former All-America swimmer, Mr. Whitten continues to train regularly and competes in Masters Swimming ("for old folks"). He lives in Marblehead, Massachusetts with his wife, Gayle Johnson, an editor; and his son, Russell.

Contributors

James A. Clifton, author of Chapter 14, "Culture, Identity and the Individual: Psychological Anthropology," and Chapter 25, "Fieldwork II: Applied Anthropology among Wisconsin's Native Americans," is Professor of Humanism and Cultural Change and former director of the Action Program at the University of Wisconsin, Green Bay. Mr. Clifton received his Ph.D. from the University of Oregon in 1960. His major professional interests are ethnohistory, Native Americans, and applied anthropology. He is the author of numerous articles, books and monographs, most recently *A Place of Refuge for All Time* (1975), a study of migration and adaptation, and *The Prairie People* (1976).

Nancy Geilhufe, author of Chapter 18, "Urban Life," received her doctorate from Stanford University in 1972, focusing on ethnic relations and urban anthropology. She has done research on Mexican American family life, Chicanos and the police, and administration of justice and minority groups. She currently is involved in a study of complaint channels within government agencies, Ms. Geilhufe is Assistant Professor at San Jose State University, where she teaches courses in urban anthropology, anthropological theory, symbolic anthropology, and peoples of the southwestern United States.

Stewart E. Guthrie, author of Chapter 23, "Takatoya: A Japanese Peasant Community," teaches anthropology at the University of Rhode Island. He did his graduate work at the University of Tubingen, Brown, and Yale, where he wrote his Ph.D. dissertation on members of a new sect of Buddhism in the village of Takatoya. Mr. Guthrie has traveled extensively in Europe and Asia.

Helen Kreider Henderson, author of Chapter 16, "Modernization in the Third World," was educated at Syracuse University and the University of California at Berkeley, receiving her Ph.D. in 1969. She has done fieldwork in Onitsha, Nigeria and taught anthropology at Wellesley College, Pima Community College and, at present, Arizona State University. Her major areas of interest are religion and social change in West Africa. Her publications include *An Outline of Traditional Onitsha Ibo Socialization* (1966) with R.N. Henderson, and "Onitsha Ibo Funerary Ritual" in Ikenna Nzimiro (ed.), *Readings in Igbo Sociology.*

Richard N. Henderson, author of Chapter 24, "Onitsha, Nigeria: An African Urban Community," is Professor of Anthropology at the University of Arizona. Mr. Henderson received his doctorate at the University of California at Berkeley in 1963, taught for several years at Yale University, and did his primary fieldwork in Nigeria before coming to Arizona. His major areas of interest include social change, urbanism and religion. He is the author of the prize-winning ethnography, *The King in Every Man* (1972).

Anthony S. Kroch, author of Chapter 11, "Power in Society: Political Anthropology," and Chapter 19, "Social Research and Ethics," received his B.A. in anthropology from Harvard University in 1967 and his Ph.D. in Linguistics from the Massachusetts Institute of Technology in 1974. His field experience consists of two trips to eastern Senegal in 1966 and 1968, and a brief trip to the Brazilian state of Para in 1967. His major theoretical interests lie in linguistic and anthropological approaches to the study of ideology and communication. Mr. Kroch is presently Visiting Assistant Professor in Anthropology at Temple University after teaching for four years at the University of Connecticut.

Richard Borshay Lee, author of Chapter 21, "The !Kung San: A Hunting and Gathering Community," is a Canadian and a graduate of the University of Toronto (B.A. 1959; M.A. 1961). He received his Ph.D. in Anthropology in 1965 from the University of California at Berkeley where he studied with Sherwood L. Washburn. Starting from an early interest in biological and social evolution, Mr. Lee studied non-human primate behavior in East Africa and then in 1963 began a series of field studies of the society and ecology of the !Kung Bushman, a hunting and gathering people in Botswana. He has taught at Harvard and Rutgers Universities and since 1972 has been Associate Professor of Anthropology at the University of Toronto. Mr. Lee is the author of over 30 scientific papers and his books include co-editorship of *Man the Hunter* (1968), *The New Native Resistance* (1973), and *Kalahari Hunter-Gatherers* (1976).

M. Kay Martin, author of Chapter 3, "The Evolution of Social Forms," received her B.A. in psychology and Ph.D. in anthropology at the State University of New York at Buffalo. She is the author of *Foraging Societies: Uniformity or Diversity?* (1974) and co-author of *Female of the Species* (1975). Her primary research interests are hunting and gathering societies, kinship, and human sex roles. She is currently Assistant Professor of Anthropology at the University of California at Santa Barbara.

Malcolm McFee, author of Chapter 8, "Social Organization I: Marriage and the Family," and Chapter 9, "Social Organization II: Kinship," is Associate Professor of Anthropology at the University of Oregon, where he has taught the introductory courses for several years as well as classes on North American Indian Ethnology and Education, Cultural Transmission, and the History of Anthropology. He earned his doctorate at Stanford University in 1962 and taught at the University of Arizona prior to coming to Oregon. His major field research has been

on the Blackfeet Indian Reservation, and covers the last seventeen years. A part of this research was reported in his book, *Modern Blackfeet: Montanans on a Reservation* (1972). Mr. McFee has revived an interest in the peoples of Oceania and contemplates fieldwork concerning the effects of modern mass tourism on island local populations.

Alison F. Richard, author of Chapter 4, "Primatology and Human Nature," and Chapter 5, "Human Adaptation: Biological and Cultural," was born and educated in England, receiving a First Class Honors Degree in Archaeology and Anthropology from Cambridge University in 1969, and a Ph.D. from London University in 1973. Since 1972 she has been teaching anthropology at Yale University. Her primary interest is primate behavior and ecology, and she has spent a total of over two years studying the behavior and ecology of free-ranging prosimians in Madagascar. Other countries in which she has studied primates in the wild include Panama, Zaire and Pakistan.

Ian Robertson, author of Chapter 15, "Social Stratification," did his undergraduate work at the University of Natal in South Africa, where he was placed under restriction by order of the Prime Minister for his opposition to the racial policies of the regime. He subsequently took his doctorate at Harvard University and also did graduate work at Oxford and at Cambridge, where he currently teaches social sciences. Mr. Robertson is the author and co-author of numerous articles and several books, most recently *Social Problems* (1975) and *Race and Politics in South Africa* (1976).

Federico S. Vidal, author of Chapter 22, "Mutayr: A Tribe of Saudi Arabian Pastoral Nomads," was born and educated in Spain. After graduation he entered the Tribal Administration Service in Morocco, where for nearly seven years he was Administrator of the Tribe of Bani Itteft in the Western Riff (a post roughly equivalent to that of superintendant in an American Indian reservation). During his last two years in Morocco he was Assistant Director in the newly created Native Administration Academy, and taught Introductory Arabic and Ethnography of Northern Morocco. In 1947 he came to the United States to do graduate work at Harvard University, where he received his doctorate. He then joined the staff of the Arabian American Oil Company (ARAMCO) and spent nearly twenty-one years in Arabia as a research analyst and as an ARAMCO division head. Since 1971, Mr. Vidal has been Associate Professor of Anthropology at Southern Methodist University in Dallas, where he lives with his wife Charlotte and their two children. He is the author of a book on the Oasis of al-Hasa, and a number of articles in the *Encyclopedia of Islam* and the *Middle East Journal.*

Barbara Voorhies, author of Chapter 6, "Human Sex: Biological Bases and Cultural Frameworks" received her B.S. in geology from Tufts University in 1961 and her Ph.D. in anthropology from Yale in 1969. Her special field of interest is the archaeology of Mesoamerica. Ms. Voorhies has done fieldwork in Mexico and Guatemala, and she currently teaches anthropology at the University of California at Santa Barbara. She is co-author of *Female of the Species* (1975).

Index

Tell us what you think...

We are committed to making *The Study of Anthropology* a valuable tool for the teaching and learning of anthropology. Because we want to be sure that *The Study of Anthropology* continues to meet the needs and concerns of instructors and students, we would like your opinion of this edition. We invite you to tell us what you like about the text—as well as where you think improvements can be made. Your opinions will be taken into consideration in the preparation of future editions. Thank you for your help.

Please indicate whether you are ☐ an instructor; ☐ a student

Your name _____

School _____ City and State _____

Course Title _____

How does this text compare with texts you are using in other courses?

☐ Excellent ☐ Good ☐ Fair ☐ Poor ☐ Very Poor

Please circle the chapters that were required in the course.

Part I.   Chapters 1   2   3   Part IV. Chapters 15 16 17 18 19
Part II. Chapters 4   5   6   Part V.   Chapters 19 20 21 22 23 24 25
Part III. Chapters 7 8 9 10 11 12 13 14

What chapters did you read that were not assigned by your instructor? (Give chapter numbers.) _____

Please tell us your overall impression of the text.	Excellent	Good	Adequate	Poor	Very Poor
1. Did you find the text to be logically organized?	____	____	____	____	____
2. Was it written in a clear and understandable style?	____	____	____	____	____
3. Did the graphics enhance readability and understanding of topics?	____	____	____	____	____
4. Did the captions contribute to a further understanding of the material?	____	____	____	____	____
5. Were difficult concepts well explained?	____	____	____	____	____

Can you cite examples that illustrate any of your above comments? _____
_____

Which chapters did you particularly like and why? (Give chapter numbers.) _____
_____

Which chapters did you dislike and why? _____
_____

After taking this course, are you now interested in taking more courses in this field? ☐ Yes ☐ No
Do you feel that this text had any influence on your decision? ☐ Yes ☐ No

General Comments _____
_____

What topics did the instructor discuss that were not covered in the text? _____
_____

Did you use the Study Guide? ☐ Yes ☐ No   Comments _____

LANGUAGE FAMILIES OF THE WORLD

NORTH AMERICA

1. Eskimo-Aleut
   - A. Aleutian
   - B. Eskimoan
2. Nadéné
   - A. Eyak, Tlingit, Haida
   - B. Athabascan (Athapaskan)
3. Algonquian
   - A. Wakashan (incl. Nootka, Kwakiutl, Bella Bella, etc.)
   - B. Salishan (incl. Flathead, Bella Coola, etc.)
   - C. Algonquian
   - D. California Algonquian (Yurok and Wiyot)
4. Aztec-Tanoan
   - A. Uto-Aztecan
   - B. Tanoan
   - C. Zunian
   - D. Kiowan
5. Hokan-Siouan
   - A. Siouan (incl. Winnebago, Catawba-Tutelo, etc.)
   - B. Caddoan (incl. Arikara and Pawnee)
   - C. Muskogean
   - D. Iroquoian (incl. Tuscarora)
   - E. Yuman
   - F. Californian (incl. Shasta, Yana, Yuki, Pomo, Salinan, Chumash, etc.)
   - G. Keresan
6. Penutian (Classification questionable)
   - A. Sahaptan (incl. Klamath-Modoc, Takelma, Chinook, etc.)
   - B. Californian (incl. Wintu, Maidu, Yokuts, Costanoan, Miwok, etc. They may be unaffiliated.)
   - C. Tsimshian
7. Coahuiltecan
8. Mayan

SOUTH AMERICAN

9. Chibchan-Paezan
   - A. Chibchan
   - B. Paezan
10. Andean-Equatorial
    - A. Andean (incl. Araucanian, Ona-Yahgan, etc.)
    - B. Huelche
    - C. Quechua-Aymará
    - D. Jivaro
    - E. Tucano
    - F. Arawakan

11. Gê-Pano-Cariban
    - A. Gê
    - B. Bororó
    - C. Carajá
    - D. Pano
    - E. Huarpe
    - F. Nambicuara
    - G. Cariban

AFRICA

12. Hamito-Semitic (Afro-Asiatic)
    - A. Hamitic
    - B. Semitic
    - C. Chad (Chado-Hamitic)
13. Niger-Congo
    - A. Nigritic
    - B. Bantu

14. Central Saharan
15. Eastern Sudanic
16. Central Sudanic
17. Songhai (Songhaic)
18. Bushman-Hottentot (Khoisan or Click Languages)

EURASIA

19. Indo-European
    - A. Indo-Iranian
    - B. Slavic
    - C. Hellenic
    - D. Romance